D0026136

Quantum Communication, Computing, and Measurement

Quantum Communication, Computing, and Measurement

Edited by

O. Hirota
Tamagawa University
Machida, Tokyo, Japan

A. S. Holevo
Steklov Mathematical Institute
Moscow, Russia

and

C. M. Caves
University of New Mexico
Albuquerque, New Mexico

Plenum Press • New York and London

Library of Congress Cataloging-in-Publication Data

International Conference on Quantum Communication and Measurement (3rd
: 1996 : Shizuoka-shi, Japan)
    Quantum communication, computing, and measurement / edited by O.
Hirota, A.S. Holevo, and C.M. Caves.
        p.   cm.
    "Proceedings of the Third International Conference on Quantum
Communication and Measurement, held September 25-30, 1996, in
Shizuoka, Japan"--T.p. verso.
    Includes bibliographical references and index.
    ISBN 0-306-45685-0
    1. Optical communications--Congresses. 2. Quantum optics-
-Congresses. 3. Quantum electronics--Congresses.   I. Hirota, O.
(Osamu), 1948-   . II. Kholevo, A. S. (Aleksandr Semenovich)
III. Caves, C. M.   IV. Title.
TK5103.59.I55   1996
621.38--dc21   97-17030
                                                           CIP

Proceedings of the Third International Conference on Quantum Communication and Measurement,
held September 25–30, 1996, in Shizuoka, Japan

ISBN 0-306-45685-0

© 1997 Plenum Press, New York
A Division of Plenum Publishing Corporation
233 Spring Street, New York, N. Y. 10013

http://www.plenum.com

10 9 8 7 6 5 4 3 2 1

Printed in the United States of America

ORGANIZING COMMITTEE

O. Hirota	(Tamagawa University)
A. S. Holevo	(Steklov Mathematical Institute)
C. M. Caves	(University of New Mexico)
H. P. Yuen	(Northwestern University)
L. Accardi	(University of Rome II)

COMMITTEE MEMBERS

M. Ban	(Hitachi Ltd)
S. Barnett	(University of Strathclyde)
V. P. Belavkin	(Nottingham University)
K. Bergman	(Princeton University)
C. Fabre	(Ecole Normale)
K. Kasai	(CRL Ministry of P & Telecommun.)
Y. S. Kim	(Maryland University)
P. Kumar	(Northwestern University)
G. Milburn	(Queensland University)
M. Ohya	(Science University of Tokyo)
N. Obata	(Nagoya University)
I. Ojima	(Kyoto University)
M. Ozawa	(Nagoya University)
S. J. D. Phoenix	(British Telecom)
M. Sasaki	(CRL Ministry of P & Telecommun.)
C. Savage	(Australian National University)
S. Schiller	(Konstanz University)
P. Staszewski	(N. Copernicus University)
P. Tombesi	(University of Camerino)
A. Vourdas	(Liverpool University)
C. Xie	(Shanxi University)

LOCAL COMMITTEE

M. Osaki	(Tamagawa University)
K. Yamazaki	(Tamagawa University)
N. Watanabe	(Science University of Tokyo)

EDITORIAL MANAGEMENT

M. Osaki	(Tamagawa University)

PREFACE

This volume contains the proceedings of the Third International Conference on Quantum Communication and Measurement. The series of international conferences on quantum communication and measurement was established to encourage scientists working in the interdisciplinary research fields of quantum communication science and technology. The first such conference, organized by C. Benjaballah and O. Hirota under the title "Quantum Aspects of Optical Communication," assembled approximately 80 researchers in Paris in 1990. The second conference, held in Nottingham in 1994, was organized by V. P. Belavkin, R. L. Hudson, and O. Hirota and attracted about 130 participants from 22 countries. The present conference, organized by O. Hirota, A. S. Holevo, C. M. Caves, H. P. Yuen, and L. Accardi, was held September 25–30, 1996, in Fuji-Hakone Land, Japan, and involved about 120 researchers from 15 countries.

The topics at this third conference included the foundations of quantum communication and information theory, quantum measurement theory, quantum cryptography and quantum computation, quantum devices and high-precision measurements, generation of nonclassical light, and atom optics. Special emphasis was placed on bringing together research workers in experimental and engineering fields of quantum communication and quantum computing and theoreticians working in quantum measurement and information theory. Nineteen plenary and parallel sessions and one poster session were organized, at which a total of 82 papers were presented. Interesting and stimulating scientific discussions took place between and after sessions as well as in the evenings. The social program included a reception to welcome participants upon arrival and an excursion to Hakone Lake, which was followed by a party at Tamagawa University, where the participants were treated to a marvelous demonstration of traditional Japanese style dancing by students of Tamagawa University. The closing conference banquet culminated in the presentation of the first Quantum Communication Award, established by the International Committee for Quantum Communication and Measurement with the sponsorship of Tamagawa University.

The editors of this volume thank the conference participants for stimulating presentations and discussions at the meeting and for their contributions to this volume. We especially thank Dr. M. Osaki, Dr. K. Yamazaki, and the conference secretaries for their always patient assistance. We owe a special debt of gratitude to Dr. Osaki, who managed the laborious job of preparing this volume for publication within the Plenum format. In the name of all the participants, we express particular thanks to our sponsors: The Support Center for Advanced Telecommunication Technology Research, NTT, NEC, Mitsubishi Electric Corporation, Matsushita Electric Group, Toyota Motor, Nissan Motor, Tokyo Electric Power, and 55 other Japanese companies. Last but certainly not least, we thank the President of Tamagawa University, Professor Y. Obara, for his interest and generous support.

O. Hirota
A. S. Holevo
C. M. Caves

1996 International
Quantum Communication Award

The first quantum communication award was awarded to :

C. H.	Bennett	(IBM)
C. W.	Helstrom	(University of California)
A. S.	Holevo	(Steklov Mathematical Institute)
H. P.	Yuen	(Northwestern University)

The Quantum Communication Award was established in 1996 by the foundation of Tamagawa University to acknowledge the researchers who contributed in a major way to the development of quantum communication.

A half million Japanese yen has been given to each award recipient.

CONTENTS

Part II. Quantum Computing

Part III. Quantum Measurement Theory and Statistical Physics

SPEECHES OF ORGANIZERS

A. S. Holevo   (Reception 25 Sept.)

Dear colleagues! Ladies and gentlemen! Mina san(everybody)!

It is a great pleasure to open the 3rd International Conference on Quantum Communication and measurement here in the beautiful surrounding of the Fuji-Hakone Land. It rains but rain means good start. This Conference and to great extent the two previous Conferences were made possible due to the enormous enthusiasm and energy of our Japanese hosts, especially Professor Hirota and his collaborators, and to the generosity of the Japanese sponsors: the Tamagawa University Research Institute, Support Center for Advanced Telecommunication Technology Research, Nippon Telegraph and Telephone Corporation and 60 other Companies. Let me express our cordial thanks to all of them for making this meeting possible.

The QCM Conferences provide a unique opportunity of joining together experimental, theoretical and mathematical physicists interested in the new exiting development in quantum communication, information and measurement. Such interaction between specialists with different and often complementary visions of the same subject is of vital importance for the heath and success of future development.

Quantum Communication was born some thirty years ago and now achieves the age of maturity. However it is still a young and growing field as one sees from the Programs of the QCM Conferences. At the previous Conference quantum cryptography was introduced, and at the present Conference there will be a new section on quantum computing. Generally speaking, computing is a very peculiar way of information processing, and we hope very much that both quantum computing and quantum communication will gain from putting them is closer contact.

It is not easy to predict the future achievements, but it appears that the problematics of our Conferences on its frontal directions approaches some very deep and subtle issues of the Nature. Let me just remember that great Niels Bohr introduced quantum complementarity basing on remarkable analogies from biological behavior, in particular, from thinking process. And who knows, may be in human brain there is a personal quantum computer given us by God!

Of course, we have also many other important topics to discuss. Let me wish success to all participants of the Conference, and a big common success to our meeting! Goseichou arigato gozaimasita(Thank you for your attention)!

C. M. Caves   (Welcome party 27 Sept.)

I don't like giving speeches, but in this case I have been assigned an easy, indeed pleasant task—that is, expressing thanks for a job well done.

What makes for a successful international scientific meeting? An outstanding scientific program and smooth organization in all its aspects. This Third International Conference on Quantum Communications and Measurement is exemplary on both counts. The Conference has assembled an outstanding group of participants from around the world. The formal scientific presentations have been of uniformly high quality, and the discussions outside the scientific presentations have been most productive. The Conference is organized so smoothly that it deserves the ultimate compliment that the administration is invisible because nothing ever goes wrong. On top of all this and as an added benefit, the Conference site in Fuji-Hakone Land is magnificent, providing a spectacular view of Mount Fuji, its summit clothed in the first snow of the season.

All these good things do not happen by accident, and it is not hard to find those to whom we, as participants, can direct our thanks. On behalf of all the participants, I want to thank Tamagawa University and its president for the University's sponsorship and support, without which the Conference could not have happened. Again on behalf of all the participants, I want especially to thank Dr. Osamu Hirota and his staff at the Research Center for Quantum Communication. None of the good things I have mentioned would have happened without the tireless efforts of Dr. Hirota and his hard-working staff.

H. P. Yuen   (Banquet 29 Sept.)

On behalf of the organizing committee, I would like to thank you all for attending this conference. As you would probably agree, the quality of a conference is directly proportional to the quality of its attendees. And I believe we have had a great meeting that reflects very well on us.

Although this is officially the third International Conference on Quantum Communication and Measurement, there was actually a zeroth one I attended which was also organized by Professor Hirota here in Japan, almost exactly nine years ago. You can tell that a really great job has been done in arranging all the details of this conference, as in all the previous ones of this series. I don't know about the other organizing committee members, but the only thing I did was to attend a meeting Thursday evening. I think we should thank Professor Hirota and his able assistants for their effort and dedication. Also, Professor Hirota was so able to impress President Obara of Tamagawa University on the importance of this conference that he allotted fourteen million yen for its support, which made it possible for many overseas scientists to come. We should also thank President Obara for his generosity.

I have been to Japan many times before. The last time I was here for more than a few days was ten years ago when I was a visiting professor at NTT, spending six weeks in the Tokyo area. I must say I was somewhat bored. I wished I could speak Japanese. I didn't have a social life. I could not get any girl to dance with me in the clubs. This time the situation is better, although I still wish I could speak Japanese. As I see it, many things have improved in Japan. Hirota's group has made impressive progress, the food tastes better, the girls look prettier, more alluring. I am sure this trend would continue. So please come back to Japan, and please come to our next meeting whenever and wherever it will be. Thank you.

L. Accardi (Banquet 29 Sept.)

Scientists believe in empirical evidence and it is so evident that the present conference was a success on all fronts that it is almost superfluous to underline with words what is under the eyes of everybody.

The gratitude that we feel for Professor Hirota, for the organization of the present conference, should not induce us to forget that Professor Hirota is much more than the organizer of the present conference but also the person who has initiated the whole tradition of the series of conferences on QCM. With his energy and broad vision he has supported this enterprise in several parts of the world and with his broad vision he has accompanied the growth of the subject from a narrow specialistic discipline to a broad interdisciplinary field of research where physics, mathematics, advanced engineering, computer and information science undergo a fruitful process of cross–fertilization. Nowadays everybody speaks of interdisciplinarity because it is true that the most advanced problems, both in pure science and in advanced technology, require the creative merging of different cultures. Such a goal however requires an intense dialogue and confrontation of different points of view and this is not so easy both for objective and subjective reasons: because often there is a language (not to say *jargon*) gap to fill which requires time and continual efforts; because the intuitions in different fields are different and they play an important role in communication; because even the feeling of what might be important or simply interesting might vary depending on personal tastes and culture; because not everybody is open to such confrontations and sometimes some groups seem to tend towards an implosive closure into themselves directly refusing or contrasting any attempt to create a communication among different cultures.

The selection of the Scientific Committee of the present Meeting, by Professor Hirota, with representatives from physics, both theoretical and experimental, advanced engineering, quantum probability and quantum statistics, is a tangible testimony of his awareness of the problem and of his determination to overcome it. This was a courageous and successful choice and I believe that one of the essential ingredients of the particular success of the present meeting has been precisely this extremely well balanced mixture of different competences. In a very short time I could receive a good impression of what is going on in several fields of high interest and actuality and some of the talks even inspired and stimulated my own research in topics such as quantum computer, on which I knew very little before attending this conference. It would have been unconceivable to achieve these results by isolated reading in a lapse of time comparable to the duration of the present conference.

For all these reasons I believe that the best wish one could do, not only to Professor Hirota, but to all those who are interested in this beautiful and actively developing field of research, is that the future QCM meetings shall keep the present standard, and most of all the strategic vision that have characterized the present one.

Part I.
Quantum Communication and Information Theory

INFORMATION THEORETIC INTERPRETATIONS OF VON NEUMANN ENTROPY

Richard Jozsa[*]

School of Mathematics and Statistics
University of Plymouth
Plymouth, Devon PL4 8AA, England
Email: rjozsa@plymouth.ac.uk

We describe two information theoretic interpretations of von Neumann entropy, in terms of the communication of classical information and quantum information respectively.

Consider a situation in which Alice generates states $|a_i\rangle$ (called "letter" states) with *a priori* probabilities p_i. Let $\rho = \sum p_i |a_i\rangle\langle a_i|$ be the associated density matrix and let $H = -\text{Tr}\,\rho\log_2\rho$ be its von Neumann entropy.

Suppose that Alice sends the letter states to Bob through a noiseless channel in order to communicate classical information. If Bob is restricted to making separate measurements on the received letter states then the Kholevo theorem implies that the amount of information transmitted cannot exceed H bits/letter. In fact it will generally be significantly less than H. We show, however, that if Alice uses a block coding scheme consisting of a choice of codewords which respects the *a priori* probabilities of the letter states and Bob distinguishes whole words rather than individual letters, then the information transmitted per letter can always be made arbitrarily close to H and never exceeds H.

In a different scenario suppose that Alice wishes to send the letter states to Bob using the least possible number of Hilbert space dimensions per letter for the transmission. Thus Alice wishes to compress sequences of letter states by suitable quantum coding, into the smallest possible number of Hilbert space dimensions. On reception, Bob – applying a decoding procedure – must be able to regain the sequence of letter states with arbitrarily high fidelity. We show that Alice may (asymptotically) compress the sequence to H qubits/letter (i.e. 2^H Hilbert space dimensions per letter) and no further. This provides an interpretation of von Neumann entropy as the limit for compressibility of quantum information, analogous to the characterisation of Shannon entropy given by Shannon's source coding theorem.

---

[*]The results reported here were obtained in various collaborations [9, 16, 21] with B. Schumacher, W. Wootters, H. Barnum, C. Fuchs, P.Hausladen and M. Westmoreland. In particular B. Schumacher and W. Wootters contributed many of the fundamental ideas.

Quantum Communication, Computing, and Measurement
Edited by Hirota *et al.*, Plenum Press, New York, 1997

1. INTRODUCTION

The concepts of entropy and information are closely related in classical statistical physics. Boltzmann's famous formula $S = k \log W$ for thermodynamic entropy has a direct interpretation as the Shannon information of a uniform distribution of microstates. The essential role of information in thermodynamic considerations was highlighted by Szilard's analysis of the Maxwell demon "paradox" [1]. Subsequently the relationship between information theory and statistical physics was extensively developed by Brillouin [2], Jaynes [4] and more recently in the work of Bennett [3], Caves [6] and Zurek [5].

Entropy was defined for quantum states by von Neumann [7] in 1932. The definition was motivated by thermodynamic considerations and he used the concept to establish the irreversibility of the quantum measurement process. However the relationship between entropy and information for von Neumann's quantum entropy has been far less clear than in the classical case. This can be attributed to curious properties of quantum states when viewed as information carriers, properties which have no classical analogues. Indeed in a quantum context one may distinguish two different natural notions of information – classical information and quantum information.

Suppose that a sender, Alice, wishes to transmit classical information to a receiver, Bob, using quantum states as signals (which we assume are transmitted perfectly, without distortion). Messages a_i are sent as quantum states ρ_i which are generally non-orthogonal and message a_i is sent with *a priori* probability p_i. Bob will recover the messages by subjecting the received states to a measurement. If the signal states are non-orthogonal then Bob will be unable to distinguish them perfectly, and of all possible measurements, he should choose to perform the one that maximises the amount of information gained about the sent signal i.e. which maximises the mutual information. The probabilistic relation between inputs and outputs is superficially similar to a classical noisy channel – in both cases the analysis is based on the conditional probability $p_{j|i}$ that Bob records message a_j given that Alice sent message a_i. However there are fundamental differences. In the classical noisy channel the conditional probabilities are fixed, being characteristic of the noise in the channel whereas in our quantum situation the probabilities depend on a choice for Bob's measurement and the channel itself is assumed to be noiseless. Thus the quantum situation involves an extra (difficult) optimisation problem, over the choice of measurement [11, 13], which has no analogue in the classical case.

Suppose that the signal states are *pure* states and let $H(\rho)$ be the von Neumann entropy of the signal ensemble. We will see (as formulated precisely in §2 below) that if Alice is required only to send the signal states with their given *a priori* probabilities but can otherwise use the states as she wishes, then she is always able to communicate an amount of classical information per signal state equal to $H(\rho)$ and no more. This will provide a precise interpretation of von Neumann entropy in terms of the communication of classical information.

In a different scenario Alice may wish to convey to Bob the signal states themselves i.e. Alice has a quantum system in a state ρ_i with *a priori* probability p_i and wants Bob to end up with a similar system in the same state. In this situation we say that Alice wishes to communicate *quantum information* to Bob. For example the signal state may be the state of a quantum computer halfway through the process of some quantum computation. On receiving the state Bob will swap it into his quantum computer and complete the computation. Clearly Bob requires the quantum state *intact* and any attempt to identify the state will irreparably destroy coherences which are vital for the correct continuation of the computation.

In order to convey the state to Bob, Alice may simply send the state itself, but is she able to communicate the state in a more efficient manner? We will see in §3 that she is indeed able to communicate quantum information more efficiently than just sending the states themselves. She does this by "compressing" the information before transmission and the minimal resources for faithful transmission (i.e. the maximal amount of compression possible) is quantified by the von Neumann entropy of the signal ensemble.

Thus we will describe two information theoretic characterisations of von Neumann entropy. Both characterisations refer to optimal use of physical resources in a communication problem.

2. VON NEUMANN ENTROPY AND CLASSICAL INFORMATION

Consider an ensemble of states ρ_i with given *a priori* probabilities p_i. The states ρ_i are called *letter states*. Suppose that Alice wishes to communicate classical information to Bob and that *she is constrained to use the letter states with their given a priori probabilities*. (This is not to say that she must use the individual letter states themselves as separate messages! – c.f. below).

We quantify the amount of information received by Bob by the mutual information which for two random variables X and Y is given by [18]

$$I(X:Y) = H(X) - H(X|Y). \tag{1}$$

According to a theorem of Kholevo [11] (also stated by Levitin [10]) the amount of information accessible to Bob, by any measurement on Alice's sent signal messages, is bounded above by the entropy of the ensemble of signal states. More precisely suppose that Alice uses letter state ρ_i to represent messages a_i. Then for any choice of measurement by Bob, the mutual information $I(A:B)$ between Alice's input A and Bob's measurement outcome B is bounded by

$$I(A:B) \leq H(\rho) - \sum_i p_i H(\rho_i) \tag{2}$$

where $\rho = \sum p_i \rho_i$ is the average density matrix of the signal ensemble and for any density matrix ρ, $H(\rho) = -\operatorname{Tr} \rho \log_2 \rho$ is its von Neumann entropy. Note that we always use logarithms to base 2. We will restrict consideration to the case in which the letter states are *pure* states so that eq. (2) reduces to

$$I(A:B) \leq H(\rho). \tag{3}$$

According to standard (classical) information theory [18] Alice can use this scheme to send Bob up to, but no more than, $I(A:B)$ bits per letter with arbitrarily low probability of error. If the letter states ρ_i are all mutually orthogonal then an information rate at the upper bound $H(\rho)$ can be achieved by judicious choice of Bob's measurement. However if the letter states are not all orthogonal then no choice of Bob's measurement can yield an information rate approaching $H(\rho)$: Kholevo's theorem (3) provides an upper bound but this upper bound is generally not very strong [12–14]. For this reason we do not view Kholevo's theorem as providing an information theoretic interpretation of von Neumann entropy for a general ensemble of pure states.

To motivate our next development consider the following example. The ensemble of letter states consists of three states $|a\rangle$, $|b\rangle$ and $|c\rangle$ which are polarisation states of a photon each separated by 120° from the others and the letter states have equal *a priori* probabilities of 1/3. This letter ensemble has von Neumann entropy $H(\rho)$ of 1 bit whereas Bob's optimal measurement [12,15] yields a mutual information $I(A : B)$ of 0.585 bits. Suppose however that Alice does not use individual letter states as signals but instead sends *two* photons per signal using only the three states $|aa\rangle$, $|bb\rangle$ and $|cc\rangle$ with equal *a priori* probability. Note that in doing this she is still using the *individual* letter states with their correct *a priori* probabilities, as she is required to do. The signal ensemble now has entropy $H(\rho)$ of 1.5 bits but Bob's optimal measurement [15] now yields a mutual information of 1.369 bits i.e. 0.685 bits per letter state. This is higher than the original scheme (which yielded only 0.585 bits per letter).

Remark. Suppose that Alice uses two photons per signal and all nine possible signal states $|aa\rangle$, $|ab\rangle$ ... $|bc\rangle$, $|cc\rangle$ with equal *a priori* probabilities (rather than the restricted set of three signal states above). Then she will still respect the correct *a priori* letter probabilities but in this case the optimal mutual information available to Bob is again 0.585 bits per letter, providing no improvement over the original scheme. □

This example shows that it is sometimes possible to increase the amount of mutual information per letter – while respecting the original letter probabilities – by using a class of "codewords" composed of sequences of elementary letter states. We generally do not use all possible codewords but the overall use of the restricted class (with their *a priori* probabilities) is required to use up the letter states with their specified *a priori* probabilities.

The main result of this section states that in this we may always attain a mutual information apprpoaching the Kholevo bound $H(\rho)$ as closely as desired, and this bound cannot be exceeded. Note that Bob's optimal measurement will generally not be realisable as a sequence of measurements on individual letters so that the communication embodies a non-trivial *block coding* scheme.

We now give a precise formulation of the main result. Suppose we are given an ensemble $\mathcal{E}$ of letter states $|a_i\rangle$ of an elementary quantum system with *a priori* probabilities p_i. The letter ensemble has a density matrix

$$\rho = \sum_i p_i \, |a_i\rangle \langle a_i| \tag{4}$$

and von Neumann entropy $H(\rho) = -\operatorname{Tr} \rho \log_2 \rho$.

A *code* ("(N, l)-code") consists of N codewords $\{|c_k\rangle : k = 1, \ldots, N\}$ where each codeword is a sequence (i.e. product) of l letter states, but not all such sequences of letter states are codewords. Also each codeword is assigned an *a priori* probability p_{c_k}. The *tolerance* τ of the code is defined by:

$$\tau = \max_i |f_i - p_i| \tag{5}$$

where

$$f_i = \frac{1}{l} \sum_{k=1}^{N} p_{c_k} \left(\text{ number of occurrences of letter } |a_i\rangle \text{ in codeword } |c_k\rangle \right). \tag{6}$$

Thus f_i is the overall frequency of occurrence of the letter $|a_i\rangle$ among the Nl letters of all the codewords, taking into account the *a priori* probabilities of the codewords. A low tolerance code will use up the letters approximately with their given *a priori* probabilities p_i in the construction of the codewords.

Then we may consider the information transmissible using the ensemble of codeword states. The information per letter is just the mutual information of the codeword ensemble divided by l. We shall show:

Theorem 1: Let I_δ be the least upper bound on the information per letter transmissible with any code having tolerance $\leq \delta$. Then

$$\lim_{\delta \to 0} I_\delta = H(\rho) \qquad \qquad \square$$

This Theorem gives a precise information–theoretic interpretation of von Neumann entropy in quantum mechanics.

The full details of the proof of this theorem will be given in [16] and we outline here only the essential ingredients.

The Typical Subspace Λ:

This is a quantum analogue of typical sequences of classical information theory [18]. It is a fundamental ingredient for all quantum block coding considerations. Consider our ensemble of letter states $| a_i \rangle$ in a Hilbert space $\mathcal{H}$ of dimension d. Words $| a_1 \ldots a_l \rangle = | a_{i_1} \rangle \otimes \ldots \otimes | a_{i_l} \rangle$ of length l are contained in the lth order tensor power $\mathcal{H}_{[l]} = \mathcal{H} \otimes \cdots \otimes \mathcal{H}$ of $\mathcal{H}$ and are assigned *a priori* probabilities $p_{i_1} \ldots p_{i_l}$. The density matrix for the ensemble of all words of length l is $\rho_{[l]} = \rho \otimes \cdots \otimes \rho$. The eigenvalues of ρ, denoted $\lambda_1, \ldots, \lambda_d$ form a probability distribution $\mathcal{P}$ whose Shannon entropy is the von Neumann entropy $H(\rho)$. The eigenvalues of $\rho_{[l]}$ are all products $\lambda_{i_1} \ldots \lambda_{i_l}$ of length l. We may apply the classical theory of typical sequences [18] to $\mathcal{P}$ and define [8,9] the typical subspace $\Lambda \subseteq \mathcal{H}_{[l]}$ to be the span of all eigenvectors of $\rho_{[l]}$ belonging to eigenvalues $\lambda_{i_1} \ldots \lambda_{i_l}$ where $\lambda_{i_1}, \ldots, \lambda_{i_l}$ is a typical sequence for l independent trials of $\mathcal{P}$.

Then the following properties of Λ are direct consequences of standard properties of typical sequences. For any given $\epsilon, \delta > 0$ and for all sufficiently large l:

(i) Almost all of the weight of the ensemble of words of length l lies within Λ:

$$\text{Tr} \, \Pi_\Lambda \rho_{[l]} \Pi_\Lambda > 1 - \epsilon \qquad (7)$$

(Here Π_Λ is the projection onto Λ.)

(ii) The dimension of Λ is bounded by

$$(1 - \epsilon) 2^{l(H(\rho) - \delta)} \leq \dim \Lambda \leq 2^{l(H(\rho) + \delta)} \qquad (8)$$

(iii) The eigenvalues μ of $\rho_{[l]}$ corresponding to eigenstates spanning Λ fall within a narrow range

$$2^{-l(H(\rho) + \delta)} \leq \mu \leq 2^{-l(H(\rho) - \delta)} \qquad (9)$$

Thus Λ of dimension (approximately) $2^{lH(\rho)}$ is generally an *exponentially small* subspace inside $\mathcal{H}_{[l]}$ of dimension $2^{l \log_2 d}$ and yet it supports arbitrarily much of the entire weight of the word ensemble. The fact that the size of Λ is measured by $H(\rho)$ underlies both of our information theoretic interpretations of von Neumann entropy.

Bob's Measurement:

Suppose that Alice has chosen to use some set $| c_1 \rangle, \ldots, | c_N \rangle$ of N codeword states (with *a priori* probabilities $p_{c_1}, \ldots, p_{c_N}$). Given this ensemble there is no known way of specifying the measurement which results in the greatest mutual information. However the following prescription will suffice for theorem 1. First project the codeword states into the typical subspace to obtain $| \gamma_i \rangle = \Pi_\Lambda | c_i \rangle$ for $i = 1, \ldots, N$.

Remark. Alice will, in fact, choose her codewords by l independent samplings from the letter ensemble (c.f. next section). Thus by the properties of the typical subspace discussed above, the projection will have negligible effect on the states, yet we will be able to restrict our analysis to an exponentially smaller subspace. This greatly facilitates the analysis of the

probability of error in Bob's measurement and the size of the mutual information. $\square$
Consider the operator

$$\Phi = \sum_{i=1}^{N} |\gamma_i\rangle \langle \gamma_i|. \tag{10}$$

This is a positive operator whose support $supp(\Phi)$ is the subspace of Λ spanned by the $|\gamma_i\rangle$'s. On $supp(\Phi)$, $\sqrt{\Phi}$ exists and is invertible so we can form the states [17]

$$|\xi_i\rangle = \Phi^{-\frac{1}{2}} |\gamma_i\rangle \tag{11}$$

and the corresponding positive operators $|\xi_i\rangle \langle \xi_i|$. Then eqs. (10) and (11) immediately give that the collection $\{|\xi_i\rangle \langle \xi_i| : i = 1, \ldots, N\}$ is a resolution of the identity on $supp(\Phi)$

$$\sum_i |\xi_i\rangle \langle \xi_i| = 1_{supp(\Phi)}. \tag{12}$$

Hence if we supplement this collection with the projector onto $supp(\Phi)^\perp$ we obtain a positive operator valued measure (POVM). This is the measurement that Bob uses to distinguish among Alice's signal states.

Alice's Choice of Codewords:
Alice will choose N codewords $|c_1\rangle, \ldots, |c_N\rangle$ of length l for sufficiently large N and l, and use them with equal *a priori* probability. l will be chosen large enough so that Λ will have the properties stated above, for any chosen $\epsilon, \delta > 0$. Bob will apply the measurement described above. If Alice sends $|c_i\rangle$ then the probability that Bob obtains the outcome $|\xi_i\rangle$ of his POVM is

$$P(\xi_i|c_i) = |\langle \xi_i|c_i\rangle|^2 \tag{13}$$

so that the average probability of error P_E in Bob's outcome is given by

$$P_E = 1 - \frac{1}{N} \sum_{i=1}^{N} |\langle \xi_i|c_i\rangle|^2 \tag{14}$$

We will show that Alice may choose her codewords so that $\log N$ is approximately $lH(\rho)$ and P_E is as small as desired (i.e. the N codewords will be almost mutually orthogonal). This will achieve an information rate as close as desired to $H(\rho)$ bits per letter. Finally we may show that Alice's code can be chosen to have arbitrarily small tolerance in the sense of eq. (5) and that the information rate of $H(\rho)$ bits per letter cannot be exceeded in the limit of vanishing tolerance. The full derivation of these results will be given in [16] and here we will only broadly outline the arguments.

We will not specify Alice's precise choice of codewords but instead argue that almost any choice suffices! We use the method of random coding inspired by the success of this technique in the proof of Shannon's noisy coding theorem. Consider N codewords each of length l generated at random i.e. for each codeword we select a sequence of l letters independently from the letter ensemble, according to the *a priori* letter probabilities. The probability that the ith codeword is $|a_{i_1} a_{i_2} \ldots a_{i_l}\rangle$ is just $p_{i_1} \ldots p_{i_l}$. We may compute the average $\langle P_E\rangle$ of the error probability P_E over all such random codes (c.f. [16]) and a direct (somewhat lengthy) calculation gives

$$\langle P_E\rangle < 2\epsilon + N2^{-l(H(\rho)-3\delta)} \tag{15}$$

where ϵ and δ chosen arbitrarily at the outset, are the parameters in the definition of the typical subspace. Now if the average P_E is below the bound (15) then there must exist a particular code with P_E less than this bound. Hence for suitably large l Alice may take $N = 2^{l(H(\rho)-4\delta)}$ and still have $P_E < 3\epsilon$ i.e. Alice encodes $H(\rho) - 4\delta$ bits per letter with error probability less than 3ϵ (for any chosen $\epsilon, \delta > 0$). This demonstrates the existence of codes for the reliable communication of classical information at an asymptotic rate of $H(\rho)$ bits per letter.

Letter Frequencies in Alice's Codewords:
We now argue that the codewords above may be chosen to have, in addition, an arbitrarily small tolerance (in the sense of (5)). Our random choice of an (N, l) code amounts to choosing Nl letters independently according to their *a priori* distribution. Since the codewords are used equally, the letters are utilised with a frequency equal to their frequency of occurrence in the chosen list of Nl letters. We can apply the weak law of large numbers: for sufficiently large N and l the set of all such random codes can be divided up into two classes – a set of "typical" codes in which the letter frequencies approximate the *a priori* probabilities to within any fixed tolerance, and the remainder – a set of "atypical" codes with (arbitrarily) small total probability. Thus the atypical codes contribute very little to the overall average $\langle P_E \rangle$ in (15) so that $\langle P_E \rangle$ must remain small even if we restrict the average to typical codes only i.e. codes for which the letters are used with a frequency matching their *a priori* probabilities to within any specified tolerance.

To see that an information rate of $H(\rho)$ bits per letter cannot be exceeded consider any (N, l) code with (vanishingly) small tolerance. Let the code consist of words $| s_i \rangle$ with *a priori* probabilities p_{s_i} (not assumed to be equal). Let ρ_{code} and H_{code} denote the density matrix and von Neumann entropy of the codeword ensemble. Let ρ_k and H_k for $k = 1, \dots, l$ be the density matrix and entropy of the ensemble of letter states which appear as the kth letter in each codeword (taking into account the probabilities p_{s_i} of the codewords). Thus ρ_k is the reduced state of ρ_{code} obtained by partial trace over all letter positions except the kth. Subadditivity [19] of von Neumann entropy gives

$$H_{code} \leq H_1 + \cdots + H_l. \tag{16}$$

On the other hand, vanishingly small tolerance implies that the average density matrix of all Nl letters is ρ (to high accuracy):

$$\rho = \frac{1}{l}(\rho_1 + \cdots + \rho_l). \tag{17}$$

Concavity of von Neumann entropy [19] then gives

$$H(\rho) \geq \frac{1}{l}(H_1 + \cdots + H_l). \tag{18}$$

Combining eqs. (16) and (18) we see that $H_{code}/l \leq H(\rho)$. Finally Kholevo's theorem applied to the codeword ensemble, gives that the information rate is bounded by H_{code}. Thus the information per letter $\leq H_{code}/l \leq H(\rho)$ as required.

3. VON NEUMANN ENTROPY AND QUANTUM INFORMATION

Consider the ensemble of letter states $\mathcal{E}$ as above, lying in a Hilbert space of dimension d so that $0 \leq H(\rho) \leq \log_2 d$. It is convenient to measure the dimension of Hilbert spaces in terms of an equivalent number of two level systems or *qubits*. Thus a space of dimension d is viewed as equivalent to $\log_2 d$ qubits. Suppose that Alice wishes to communicate to Bob a long sequence of letter states drawn at random from the ensemble $\mathcal{E}$ and let us assume that the identity of each letter state is known to her.

She requires that Bob receives a (sufficiently) faithful representation of the sequence of letter states (as motivated in §1). She wishes to do this as efficiently as possible – using the least possible number of qubits per signal for the transmission. Clearly Alice may achieve her goal by using d qubits per letter (sending the letter states themselves) but this is not the optimal solution.

Recall first a classical analogue of the problem. If the letters are *classical* signals then according to Shannon's noiseless coding theorem [18] Alice may communicate them to Bob using Υ bits per signal where Υ is the Shannon entropy of the *a priori* probability distribution $\{p_i\}$ and this transmission rate is (asymptotically) optimal. Note that $\Upsilon \leq \log_2 n$ where n is the number of letters. The extra compression beyond $\log_2 n$ bits per signal (needed for the uncompressed transmission of n distinct signals) arises from a "redundancy" associated with the fact that the distribution $\{p_i\}$ is uneven.

Returning to the quantum scenario, since Alice knows the identity of the letter states, she may simply send Bob the classical information of their names a_i compressing the data to Υ bits per signal as in the classical case. On receiving this information Bob recreates the states in his laboratory. However this strategy is not optimal for two essential reasons. Firstly we may have a very large number of letter states in a very small (say 2 dimensional) Hilbert space. Thus Υ may be arbitrarily large even in a situation where only one qubit per letter is needed to transfer the states directly. Secondly, and most significantly, there is an extra non-classical "redundancy" associated with the fact that non-orthogonal quantum states can never be perfectly distinguished: if $\langle \alpha | \beta \rangle \neq 0$ then there is a non-zero amplitude for $| \alpha \rangle$ "to be " the state $| \beta \rangle$. Recall that for any ensemble of quantum states, the von Neumann entropy $H(\rho)$ is always less than or equal to the Shannon entropy of the *a priori* probability distribution Υ. A beautiful result, due to Schumacher [8] states that Alice may compress the quantum information of the stream of letter states to $H(\rho)$ qubits per letter and that this is optimal. The extra compression to $H(\rho)$ beyond the classical limit Υ arises from the "quantum redundancy". This is the content of the quantum noiseless coding theorem (theorem 2 below). [Note that in comparing classical and quantum results we regard 1 classical bit, within a quantum context, as being equivalent in terms of physical resources to 1 qubit since 1 classical bit requires two distinguishable (i.e. orthogonal) states for its physical realisation.]

To achieve the transmission of quantum information Alice will generally perform a "block coding" operation on the sequence of letter states and Bob will perform a decoding operation on the state received from Alice, to reconstitute the letter states. Since Alice knows the identity of the input sequence she may construct *any* (mixed) state whatever, of her choosing, to code the quantum information. Bob on the other hand, knows only the letter *ensemble* (and also the details of Alice's coding procedure). He will generally does not know the identities of the particular sequence of letter states. His decoding procedure is restricted to be any possible evolution allowed within the laws of quantum mechanics. The most general such process is a completely positive map [20] applied to the received state. Note that Alice's (more general) ability to construct an *arbitrary* state associated to the input letters, may be viewed as a completely positive map applied to the sequence of letter *names* stored as orthogonal states.

We will not require that Bob finishes up with a sequence of letter states which *perfectly* reproduces Alice's input sequence. It will suffice if the inputs and outputs are "sufficiently close" to each other (c.f. theorem 2 below for the precise statement). In general Bob will finish up with mixed states σ_i representing the letter states $| a_i \rangle$ and the closeness of input and output is measured by the *average fidelity*

$$\bar{F} = \sum p_i \langle a_i | \sigma_i | a_i \rangle. \tag{19}$$

Note that $\langle a_i \,|\, \sigma_i \,|\, a_i \rangle$ is the probability that σ_i will pass a test that checks its identity against $|\,a_i\rangle$. (In theorem 2 we will apply this fidelity measure to blocks of letters rather than individual letters).

We may now state the quantum noiseless coding theorem [8, 9, 21]. (Recall that we are requiring the letter states to be *pure* states.)

Theorem 2. (The Quantum Noiseless Coding Theorem).

For any $\epsilon, \delta > 0$

(a) If $H(\rho) + \delta$ qubits are available per letter state then for all sufficiently large K there exists a coding/decoding scheme which transmits blocks of K letter states with average block fidelity $> 1 - \epsilon$.

(b) If $H(\rho) - \delta$ qubits are available per letter state then for all sufficiently large K, for any coding/decoding scheme, the average fidelity of blocks of K letters satisfies $\bar{F} < \epsilon$.

□

We may describe an explicit coding/decoding scheme which achieves the condition in theorem 2(a). In fact it has already been given implicitly in the discussion in §2 of the typical subspace Λ. To code a block of K letters Alice projects their joint state into Λ of asymptotic size $KH(\rho)$ qubits. If the projection fails (i.e. the state projects to $\Lambda^{\perp}$) then she replaces the post-measurement state by any standard state in Λ. She then unitarily rotates Λ into a standard configuration of $KH(\rho)$ qubits and transmits them to Bob. On reception, Bob simply reverses the unitary rotation. It follows readily from properties of Λ in §2 that this prescription achieves the conditions of theorem 2(a). The full proof of the quantum noiseless theorem may be found in [8, 9, 21].

In our discussion above we have assumed from the outset that Alice has knowledge of the identity of the particular sequence of input letter states. One may consider a more general situation in which Alice does not know the identities of the input letters but only their *a priori* distribution. Since the states are generally non-orthogonal she is unable to identify them reliably. In this case her coding possibilities are more limited than before, now being restricted to completely positive maps on the input sequence of letter states themselves. However the optimal coding/decoding scheme described in the previous paragraph does not depend on Alice's knowledge of the input sequence. Indeed the typical subspace is defined entirely in terms of the input *ensemble*. Thus remarkably, we conclude that knowledge of the names of the input sequence of states does not lead to any further advantage in compressing the quantum information!

4. MIXED INPUT STATES?

It should be emphasised that theorems 1 and 2 both apply to a situation in which the input letter states are *pure* states. One may ask similar questions for the case of letter states being mixed states ρ_i. It appears plausible [16] that in theorem 1, $H(\rho)$ may be replaced by the mixed state Kholevo bound $H(\rho) - \sum p_i H(\rho_i)$ of eq. (2). For the issue of compression of quantum information, a study of examples indicates that knowledge of the identities of the input states *will* be of advantage in the case of mixed states, and that compression beyond $H(\rho)$ qubits per letter is generally possible (where $\rho = \sum p_i \rho_i$ is the average letter state). However the optimal limit of compression is unknown at present.

REFERENCES

[1] L. Szilard, *Z. Phys.* **53**, 840–856 (1929) (English translation reprinted in *Maxwell's Demon*, edited by H. Leff and A. Rex (Princeton University Press 1990).

[2] L. Brillouin, *Science and Information Theory*, second edition (Academic Press 1960).

[3] C. Bennett, *Int. J. Th. Phys.* **21** 305–340 (1982).

[4] E. Jaynes, *Papers on Probability, Statistics and Statistical Physics* edited by R. Rosenkrantz (Dordrecht, Holland: Reidel 1982).

[5] W. Zurek, *Nature* **341**, 119-124 (1989); *Phys. Rev. A***40**, 4731–4751 (1989).

[6] C. Caves, in *Complexity, Entropy and the Physics of Information* edited by W. Zurek, 91–115 (Addison-Wesley 1990).

[7] J. von Neumann, *Mathematical Foundations of Quantum Mechanics*, English translation by R. Beyer (Princeton University Press 1955).

[8] B. Schumacher, *Phys. Rev. A* **51**, 2738 (1995).

[9] R. Jozsa and B. Schumacher, *J. Modern Optics* **41**, 2343-2349 (1994).

[10] L. B. Levitin, in *Information Complexity and Control in Quantum Physics*, edited by A. Blaquieve, S. Diner, and G. Lochak (Springer, New York, 1987), pp. 15–47.

[11] A. S. Kholevo, Probl. Peredachi Inf. **9**, 3 (1973) [Probl. Inf. Transm. (USSR) **9**, 177 (1973)].

[12] A. S. Kholevo, Probl. Peredachi Inf. **9**, 110 (1973) [Probl. Inf. Transm. (USSR) **9** (2), 31 (1973)].

[13] C. Caves and C. Fuchs, *Phys. Rev. Lett.* **73**, 3047 (1994).

[14] R. Jozsa, D. Robb, and W. K. Wootters, *Phys. Rev. A* **49**, 668 (1994).

[15] A. Peres and W. K. Wootters, *Phys. Rev. Lett.* **66** 1119 (1991).

[16] P. Hausladen, R. Jozsa, B. Schumacher, M. Westmoreland and W. K. Wootters, *Phys. Rev. A* **54**, 1869–1876 (1996).

[17] L. P. Hughston, R. Jozsa, and W. K. Wootters, *Phys. Lett. A* **183**, 14 (1993).

[18] T. M. Cover and J. A. Thomas, *Elements of Information Theory*, (John Wiley and Sons, Inc. 1991).

[19] A. Wehrl, *Rev. Mod. Phys.* **50**, 221–260 (1978).

[20] K. Kraus, *States, Effects and Operations: Fundamental Notions of Quantum Theory* (Springer, Berlin 1983); K. Hellwig and K. Kraus, *Comm. Math. Phys.* **16**, 142–147 (1970).

[21] H. Barnum, C. Fuchs, R. Jozsa and B. Schumacher, *Phys. Rev. A* **54**, 4707–4710 (1996).

QUANTUM INFORMATION THEORY,
THE ENTROPY BOUND,
AND MATHEMATICAL RIGOR IN PHYSICS

Horace P. Yuen

Department of Electrical and Computer Engineering
Department of Physics and Astronomy
Northwestern University, Evanston, IL 60208

The fundamental role of the entropy bound, $I \leq S(\bar{\rho}) - \bar{S}(\rho)$, is illustrated through its use in determining the information capacities of quantum systems and the ultimate accuracy limits of precision quantum measurements, leading to a discussion on the relevance of mathematical rigor in the treatment of physics problems. The history of this bound is also reviewed.

1. THE ENTROPY BOUND AND QUANTUM INFORMATION THEORY

A basic concept of quantum information theory is the qubit, a two-dimensional quantum state space H_2. It is conventional wisdom that one can extract no more than one bit from one qubit [1]. While one may get one bit from one qubit simply by using a binary alphabet and two orthogonal states, to my knowledge there is no published proof that no more than one bit can be extracted from H_2. The problem is that one may choose a large alphabet Λ, modulate $\lambda \mapsto \rho_\lambda$ for density operators ρ_λ on H_2 and $\lambda \in \Lambda$, and get a noisy classical channel with any quantum measurement described by an arbitrary POM (positive operator-valued measure [2]) on H_2, which may perhaps yield more than one bit. For example, one may choose $\Lambda = [0, \pi), \rho_\lambda = |\lambda\rangle\langle\lambda|$ where $|\lambda\rangle$ is the unit vector in H_2 at an angle λ with respect to be a fixed coordinate axis, and measure the POM given by $X(\lambda) = \frac{1}{\pi}|\lambda\rangle\langle\lambda|, \int_0^\pi \frac{d\lambda}{\pi}|\lambda\rangle\langle\lambda| = 1$. With any probability density $p(\lambda)$, it is not a priori impossible that such a noisy channel has a mutual information larger than one bit per use because the alphabet size is much bigger than 2. A proof is required to rule out such possibilities.

The required proof is easily obtained from the entropy bound. In the general form [3], the entropy bound reads

$$I(\lambda; x) \leq S(\bar{\rho}) - \bar{S}(\rho_\lambda) \tag{1}$$

where $\lambda \in \Lambda \subseteq \Re^n$ varies over the alphabet $\Lambda, \lambda \mapsto \rho_\lambda$ is the state modulation on a Hilbert space $H, S(\rho) \equiv -Tr\rho\log\rho$ the Von Neumann entropy, $\bar{\rho} \equiv \int \rho_\lambda P(d\lambda)$ the average state with respect to the a priori distribution $P(d\lambda)$ on $\Lambda, \bar{S}(\rho_\lambda) \equiv \int S(\rho_\lambda)P(d\lambda), x$ the measurement outcome of an arbitrary POM $X(dx)$ on H, and I the mutual information between λ and x. For a purely continuous alphabet one can write $P(d\lambda) = p(\lambda)d\lambda$.

Also, the formal notation $X(dx) = X(x)dx$ renders the POM a direct generalization of the Dirac hermitean observable where $X(x) = |x\rangle\langle x|$ for orthogonal $|x\rangle$. An immediate consequence of (1) is

$$I(\lambda; x) \leq S(\bar{\rho}) \tag{2}$$

since $S(\rho_\lambda) \geq 0$. The special case of (1) for finite alphabet Λ and finite-dimensional state space H is often referred to as Holevo's Theorem [4]. To show that no more than one bit can be extracted from one qubit, we apply (2) to H_2 and arbitrary Λ and write $\bar{\rho} = p|1\rangle\langle 1| + (1-p)|2\rangle\langle 2|, \langle 1|2\rangle = 0, 1 \geq p \geq 0$. Thus $S(\bar{\rho}) = -p\log p - (1-p)\log(1-p)$ which is well known to have an upper bound of one bit achieved at $p = 1/2$.

2. HISTORY OF THE ENTROPY BOUND

That entropy provides a bound on information as indicated by (2) appeared natural to many people [5]-[6], but no proof was given. The stronger inequality (1) has a rather long and interesting history that perhaps only I can tell, but which may of course be still a partial history at that. The bound (1) was first stated with an incomplete (incorrect) proof by Forney [7] in 1963 in the case of infinite discrete alphabet Λ and infinite-dimensional H. Until ref. [4], the bound was always formulated only for measurements of hermitean observables, but the generalization to POM is actually trivial. As in the case of the quantum Cramer-Rao inequalities [8]-[9], one may just work on an extended state space and reduce the result back to the original space. Until the appearance of ref. [3], this bound was always discussed and treated for a discrete alphabet Λ, finite or infinite. However, the continuous case is conceptually important because it is not a priori known that the use of a continuous alphabet may not lead to higher capacity for the system.

In the published literature, (1) was first explicitly stated as a conjecture by Gordon [10] in 1964 which prompted Zador [11] to give a detailed unpublished treatment of the bound a year later. Zador gave a complete proof for the case of finite Λ and finite-dimensional H, and an incomplete sketch for the case of finite Λ and infinite-dimensional H. On the basis of this ref. [11], in 1967 Bowen [12] assumed it was already established that the capacity of the electromagnetic field is obtained by number states and photon counting. The entropy bound was stated as a theorem by Levitin [13], first in 1969 and also in many of his later papers. To my knowledge, he has never published a proof. In 1973 Holevo [4] published a correct proof for the POM case for finite Λ and finite-dimensional H.

I had always assumed that the bound was proved by Forney for infinite discrete Λ and infinite-dimensional H until 1982 when I tried to extend it to continuous alphabets using his approach to check a result that seemed to contradict the bound. (It actually does not, as described in ref. [3].) I discovered a serious gap in his proof and wrote to him about it, as I knew him as a most outstanding information and coding theorist. He replied that he could not close the gap either. In 1989-1990 I brought this issue to the attention of Ozawa, who showed that Uhlmann's inequality [14] can be used to give a straightforward proof of the bound in the general case. In 1991, I presented a conference paper [15] on the ultimate quantum limits on precision measurements which makes essential use of the entropy bound. In preparation for journal publication of this work (which is still not yet written!), ref. [3] was prepared including a treatment of the possibility of obtaining infinite capacity in a quantum system of finite energy.

3. THE ENTROPY BOUND AND QUANTUM CAPACITY

The quantum capacity of a physical system, or the maximum information transmission capacity of a quantum system, can be defined as the maximum (supremum) mutual information between λ and x by any choice of $\Lambda, p(\lambda), \rho_\lambda$ and $X(x)$ under the contstraints of the problem. If there is state transformation involved such as loss, one can introduce a completely positive map $\mathcal{T}$ on ρ_λ with constraints imposed on the input ρ_λ, and measurements on the output $\mathcal{T}\rho_\lambda$. The significance of this mutual information is provided, as in the usual classical case, by Shannon's coding theorem and its converse. Note that if feedback or other generalized processing are permitted, the truly ultimate quantum capacity has to be defined including such possible operations.

While the problem of determining the optimum quantum measurement $X(x)$ to maximize $I(\lambda; x)$ for fixed Λ and ρ_λ is difficult in general, it is easier to determine the free $(\mathcal{T} = 1)$ quantum capacity under a constraint on the average $\bar{\rho}$ which is often the more relevant problem. Assuming that the maximum exists, one merely needs to find a $\bar{\rho}$ to maximize $S(\bar{\rho})$ under the constraint, and expand the resulting $\bar{\rho}_0$ in its eigenstate expansion $\bar{\rho}_0 = \sum_i p_i |i\rangle\langle i|$ which always exists because density operator is trace class. The quantum capacity is then achieved by $\Lambda = \{i\}, \{p_i\}, i \mapsto |i\rangle\langle i|$, and $X(x) = |i\rangle\langle i|$. Incidentally, this also shows that if the constraint is only on $\bar{\rho}$ rather than on ρ_λ, the quantum capacity is always achieved by a discrete alphabet and hermitean observable measurement.

The above situation obtains in the case of an average energy constraint on a single boson field mode. Thus, for an average photon number N the single-mode quantum capacity is [3]

$$C(N) = (N+1)\log(N+1) - N \log N \tag{3}$$

which is achieved by number states and photon counting. The infinite bandwidth capacity with average power P constraint is $C = \pi\sqrt{\frac{2P}{3h}}$ [3], [12]. The quantum capacity of the linear loss channel is not known.

4. QUANTUM CAPACITY AND THE ULTIMATE LIMIT ON THE ACCURACY OF QUANTUM MEASUREMENTS

With the help of classical rate-distortion theory [16], one can determine lower bounds on the accuracy of quantum measurements via the quantum capacity as outlined in ref. [15]. For a single-mode field of average photon number N, the best root-mean-square error δr one may obtain for a real amplitude parameter r and $\delta\phi$ for a phase parameter ϕ vary as N^{-1},

$$\delta r \geq \frac{C_1}{N}, \quad \delta\phi \geq \frac{C_2}{N} \tag{4}$$

where the exact constants C_1 and C_2 depend on the a priori statistics of r and ϕ [15]. This N^{-1} dependence is known to be achievable, for example, through the use of TCS or squeezed states, for both the r case [17] and the ϕ case [18]. Note that the bound (4) on $\delta\phi$ cannot be obtained from the number phase uncertainty relation (which is not valid in general anyway)

$$\Delta N \Delta \Phi > \frac{1}{4} \tag{5}$$

because the estimation of ϕ need not be obtained from a phase measurement. Furthermore, the average N imposes no limit on the photon-number variance at all. If one considers a finite-dimensional state space with dimension N_m, then (5) leads to

$$\Delta \Phi \geq \frac{C_3}{N_m} \qquad (6)$$

This inequality (6) is not particularly useful since $\frac{C_3}{N_m} \to 0$ by merely considering an infinite-dimensional space. It is clear that one can spread any small amount of energy ϵ over an infinite number of dimensions, say by choosing $p_n > 0$, such that $\Sigma_n p_n = 1$, $\Sigma_n n p_n = \epsilon$, as in the case of the canonical distribution. If a peak energy constraint is to be imposed, it should be applied to the quantum average energy of a state, not to the dimension of the state space.

In the multimode case, the lower bounds are more complicated and decrease exponentially in N over a certain range of N and M, the total mode numbers. The only concrete system that is known to yield a better performance than N^{-1} is the TCS-homodyne frequency modulation scheme indicated in ref. [15], for which a root-mean-square error of the order $(MN)^{-1}$ can be obtained for sufficiently large N.

5. SIGNIFICANCE OF THE GENERAL ENTROPY BOUND

Does the general entropy bound have additional conceptual importance in applications as compared to Holevo's theorem? or is it merely a mathematical nicety? In other words, is it the case that a general result is readily established with just Holevo's theorem by taking limits on the dimension of H and the size of Λ? Caves and Drummond [19] suggest yes, at least for the boson capacity problem. In particular, they argue that the inevitable finite resolution in an experimental system renders the consideration of continuous alphabets unnecessary. However, finite-resolution is often the result of an additive noise in a model where both the variable and the noise are continuous quantities. It does not render the continuous variable or the problem discrete. More significantly, the correct continuous limit is needed to ascertain the fundamental limit when the practical finite resolution is made smaller and smaller. It is quite possible that the capacity is no longer bounded in such a situation, as for example in the case where the energy operator is given by P^2 for free fermions so that the capacity goes to infinite per use even under a finite energy constraint [3]. Indeed, I was led to consider the use of particle beams for communications because of this feature. Generally speaking, it is quite useful to exhibit the discrete nature of a result from its dependence on a practical parameter such as local oscillator power, although that may actually greatly complicate the problem. But surely one cannot omit such a parameter in the treatment and just claim that one can deal with the discrete case because such a parameter exists in reality; without the parameter the situation is continuous, at least in the sense that there is no general appropriate discrete representation similar to the case of space and time.

In general, the passing of limits to infinity has to be handled with care for mathematical correctness since there are many kinds of limits depending on the topology one employs. For the problems of optimality under discussion, mathematical rigor is indispensable for a meaningful conclusion if only because the result cannot be checked by an experiment. To proceed rigorously from the finite case, one has to first solve the finite problem with rigor and then show that the limit of the finite result yields the correct answer in the infinite case. The development in ref.[19] cannot be accepted as a proof of the fact that equ(3) is the quantum capacity because it only gives plausibility arguments and not a proof in the finite case, and it does not prove that the finite result gives the correct limit. For example, the use of "techniques drawn from quantum statistical physics" in maximizing the entropy is not generally correct because in such treatments the inequality constraints of the input probabilities $p_n \geq 0$ are ignored. In addition, the use of uncontrolled approximation without strict bounds does not establish the optimality of anything. Another point is that the use of fixed energy states or maximum energy constrainted states does not cut off the Hilbert space to a finite dimension, as is evident that a fixed energy coherent state has components in all $|n\rangle$. Neither does it lead to a maximum cut-off frequency for a similar reason. The use of finite-dimensional approximation in quantum mechanics is also tricky in this regard, say the canonical commutation rule has no finite-dimensional representation and so the quantum in such a space does not obey Bose-Einstein statistics. With the general entropy bound, one can establish general conclusions directly while a lot of additional arguments would be needed if Holevo's theorem is used instead. Indeed, there is not a single example for which such additional arguments have been successfully provided.

6. MATHEMATICAL RIGOR IN PHYSICS

It is quite legitimate to ask the following question. Since practically all the great successes in physics were obtained without mathematical rigor, why should it be different in the present case? One may further ask: Why is mathematical rigor generally practiced in computer science but not in physics? Is it necessary in the new area of quantum computation? The relation of mathematics to its applications in various different fields is a fascinating subject to many people, and is fascinating to me. Think about the indispensable Feynman path integral in high energy theories (except QED) and its complete lack of mathematical foundation. I hope to be able to delineate the full story at some future time, but right now I could only indicate brief and partial answers to the above questions.

When a certain mathematical system is applied to a situation which is an exact model of the system, or put it in the reverse way that the mathematical system is an exact model of the situation, with every basic mathematical entity meaningfully interpreted in the situation, mathematical rigor is required for logical consistency and correctness. This happens in the case of most computer science applications. It does not usually happen in physics, if only because the set of real numbers has no direct physical meaning. A general real number involves an infinite mathematical construction and has no direct empirical meaning. We do not measure anything with an infinite number of decimal places. On the other hand, we also do not know how to formulate most physical laws without using real numbers and other infinities such as infinite-dimensional spaces. (It is sometimes argued that no mathematical infinity is needed in actually predicting experimental outcomes in physics, but I have never seen a concrete demonstration on how that is going to be done in general. Numerical approximations to known laws for specific applications do not constitute such a demonstration, because the laws involving infinity are used in an indispensable way. For a successful demonstration, these laws have to be given a general finite representation. Thus, I would challenge anyone to show a theory without mathematical infinity that would predict the connection between spin and statistics, or the advance of Mercury's perihelion.) In the computation of physical quantities and the establishment of qualitative relations, which is largely what theoretical physics is about, one may proceed without mathematical rigor because validations finally come from experiments. However, there are interesting physical questions whose very nature is mathematical, or whose answers cannot be meaningfully confirmed by experiments, such as the question of which case allowed by the laws of physics is the best according to a given criterion. These questions are mathematical in that they can be meaningful posed only in a precise formulation and meaningfully answered only in a precise way. It is my contention that such problems can be regarded as solved only if they are solved rigorously.

I dream of a kind of future mathematics that is perfectly suited to physics, in which every fundamental entity or operation has an empirical interpretation. This mathematics would have many new uses I hope to be able to describe at some point, but at least there would be no question of abandoning rigor in the complete solution of a problem using this mathematics. In the meantime, we would still need to pursue rigor in addressing certain kinds of problems within the current mathematical formulation of physical laws, but this is not meant to undervalue the possible great importance of heuristics in any problem.

ACKNOWLEDGMENTS

I would like to acknowledge discussions with Masanao Ozawa and support from the Office of Naval Research.

REFERENCES

[1] C. H. Bennett, Physics Today, pp. 24-30, Oct. 1995.

[2] M. Ozawa, in *Squeezed States and Nonclassical Light*, ed. by P. Tombesi and E. R. Pike, Plenum, New York, 1989, p. 263.

[3] H. P. Yuen and M. Ozawa, Phys. Rev. Lett. 70, 363 (1993).

[4] A. S. Holevo, Probl. Inf. Transm. 9, 177 (1973).

[5] J. P. Gordon, Proc. IRE *50*, 1898 (1962).

[6] L. Brillouin, *Scientific Uncertainty and Information*, Academic Press, New York, 1964, Ch. 1 and Ch. 3.

[7] G. D. Forney, Jr., S. M. Thesis, MIT, 1963 (unpublished).

[8] H. P. Yuen and M. Lax, IEEE Trans. IT-19, 740 (1973).

[9] C. W. Helstrom and R. S. Kennedy, IEEE Trans. IT-20, 16 (1974).

[10] J. P. Gordon, in *Quantum Electronics and Coherent Light*, Fermi School of Physic Course XXXI, ed. by P. A. Miles, Academic Press, New York, 1964, p. 156.

[11] P. L. Zador, Bell Telephone Laboratories Technical Memorandum, MM65-1359-4, Murray-Hill, N.J., 1965.

[12] J. I. Bowen, IEEE Trans. IT-13, 203 (1967).

[13] L. B. Levitin, Proceedings of the Fourth All-Union Conference on Information and Coding Theory, Sec. II. (Tashkent, 1969), pp. 111-115.

[14] A. Uhlmann, Commun. Math. Phys. 54, 21 (1977).

[15] H. P. Yuen, in Proceedings of the Workshop on Squeezed State and Uncertainty Relations, NASA Conference Publication 3135, 1991, pp. 13-22.

[16] R. G. Gallager, *Information Theory and Reliable Communication*, Wiley, New York, 1968, Ch. 9.

[17] H. P. Yuen, Phys. Lett A *56*, 101 (1976).

[18] C. M. Caves, Phys. Rev. D *23*, 1693 (1981).

[19] C. M. Caves and P. D. Drummond, Rev. Mod. Phys. 66, 481 (1994).

CLASSICAL AND QUANTUM INFORMATION TRANSMISSION AND INTERACTIONS

Charles H. Bennett

IBM T.J. Watson Research Center
Yorktown Heights NY 10598, USA
email: bennetc@watson.ibm.com

Quantum information theory has recently been enlarged to include the use of quantum channels for the transmission not only of classical information but also of intact quantum states. We survey known upper and lower bounds on the capacity of quantum channels, alone or assisted by one- or two-way classical communication, to transmit intact quantum states, and relation of this capacity on the one hand to classical capacity and on the other to the quantitative theory of entanglement of pure and mixed states.

1. INTRODUCTION

The recent rapid progress in the theory of quantum information processing can be divided into two related parts: quantum computation, and quantum information theory. Although major practical questions remain concerning the physical realization of quntum computers, many of the most important theoretical questions in quantum computation have already been answered: quantum algorithms are known to provide an exponential speedup, compared to classical algorithms, for integer factoring and a few other problems, and quadratic speedup for much a broader range of problems. The discovery of quantum error-correcting codes and fault-tolerant gate arrays [1, 2] means that in principle finitely reliable components are sufficient to perform arbitrarily large reliable quantum computations, just as in the theory of classical computation.

Here I will concentrate on the second area: quantum information theory, where the classical notions of source, channel, code, and capacity have been generalized to encompass the optimal use of various channels, noiselss and noisy, for communicating not only classical information but also intact quantum states, and for sharing entanglement between separated observers. Although the fundamental physics and mathematics on which it is based is over fifty years old, the new theory has taken shape mostly over the last five years. Quantum data compression [3, 4], superdense coding [5], quantum teleportation [6], and entanglement concentration [7] exemplify nontrivial ways in which quantum channels can be used, alone or in combination with classical channels, to transmit quantum and classical information. More recently quantum error-correcting codes [8–19] and entanglement distillation protocols [19–22] have been discovered which allow noisy quantum channels, if not too noisy, to be substituted for noiseless ones in these applications. Important problems still open include finding exact expressions, rather than upper and lower bounds, for the classical and quantum capacities of noisy quantum channels.

Entanglement plays a central role in this enlarged information theory, complementary in several respects to the role of classical information. The entanglement between a pair of systems in a maximally-entangled Einstein-Podolsky-Rosen state is the purest form of quantum information: capable of connecting two observers separated by a space-like interval, it can neither be copied nor eavesdropped on without disturbance, nor can it be used by itself to send a classical message. Ordinary classical information, by contrast, can be read and copied at will, but can only propagate forward in time to a receiver in the sender's forward light cone.

A natural quantum analog of an information *source* is an ensemble $\mathcal{E}$ of pure or mixed states [23] $\rho_1, \rho_2, ... \rho_k$, emitted with known probabilities probabilities $p_1...p_k$. The quantum analog of a (discrete noiselss) channel is any quantum system capable of existing in an arbitrary state in some finite-dimensional Hilbert space, of being entangled with other similar quantum systems, and of remaining stably in this entangled or superposed state while enroute from sender to receiver. Just as a sequence of n bits, sent through a classical channel, can be used to transmit any of up to 2^n distinct classical messages, so a sequence of n elementary 2-state quantum systems or *qubits* can be used to transmit an arbitrary quantum state in a Hilbert space of up to 2^n dimensions. The quantum analog of a noisy channel is a quantum system that interacts unitarily with an outside environment while enroute from sender to receiver. Noisy channels (including noiseless ones as a special case) may equivalently be described as trace-preserving, completely positive linear maps on the space of density operators [24].

If the states ρ_i of a quantum source are all orthogonal, the source can be considered purely classical, because complete information about the source state can be extracted by a measurement at the sending end, transmitted classically to the receiving end, and used there to make arbitrarily many faithful replicas of the source state. On the other hand, if the source states are pure and non-orthogonal, then no classical measurement can extract complete information about the source state, and, whenever a source state is sent through a quantum channel, at most one faithful copy of the source state can be produced at the receiving end, and then only if no faithful copy remains behind at the sending end. An interesting intermediate situation occurs when the source states are non-orthogonal but commuting mixed states. Such a source can be "broadcast", ie, given an unknown one of the source states ρ_i, two systems A and B can be prepared in a joint state $\boldsymbol{\rho}_i(AB)$, which is not a clone of the source state (ie $\boldsymbol{\rho}_i(AB) \neq \rho_i(A) \otimes \rho_i(B)$), but whose partial trace over either subsystem agrees with the source state $\rho_i = \text{tr}_A(\boldsymbol{\rho}_i(AB)) = \text{tr}_B(\boldsymbol{\rho}_i(AB)) = \rho_i$. If the density matrices of the source states do not commute (this includes the case of pure non-orthogonal states), then the source can neither be cloned nor broadcast [23].

Because quantum information cannot be read or copied without disturbing it, whatever encoding apparatus is used at the sending end of a quantum channel must function rather blindly. If the channel is to transmit non-orthogonal pure states faithfully, it must operate on the states that pass through without knowing or learning anything about them. For the same reasons, assessment of the quality of quantum data transmission is a somewhat delicate matter. If the source states are pure, and a quantum channel produces output W_i (in general a mixed state) on input ψ_i, then the transmission's *fidelity* [3] is defined as

$$F = \sum_i p_i \langle \psi_i \, | \, W_i \, | \, \psi_i \rangle. \tag{1}$$

This is the expectation, averaged over channel inputs, that the output would pass a test for being the same as the input, conducted by someone who knew what the input was. When even the source states are mixed, fidelity must be defined [25] by a more complicated formula,

$$F = \sum_i p_i \left(\mathrm{tr} \sqrt{ \sqrt{\rho_i} \, W_i \sqrt{\rho_i} } \right)^2,$$ (2)

which represents the maximum of eq. 1 over "purifications" [25] of ρ_i, ie pure states ψ_i in a larger Hilbert space having ρ_i as their partial trace.

Here we summarize the known results on the channel resources needed for faithful transmission of classical information and quantum states, and the extent to which these resources can be substituted for one another. These substitutions can be expressed formally as reducibilities among information-transmission acts, the expression $A \leq B$ indicating that the resources neccessary to accomplish act B are sufficient to accomplish act A. A proper reducibility, in which $A \leq B$ but not $B \leq A$, is denoted $A < B$. An equivalence, in which $A \leq B$ and $B \leq A$, is denoted $A \equiv B$. As in classical information theory, some results are asymptotic in the limit of large n, depending for example on block codes in which n instances of act B suffice to perform m instances of act A.

Schumacher's quantum data compression [3, 4], an analog of Shannon's noiseless coding theorem, is typical of these asymptotic results. Classical coding allows information from a redundant source, eg a binary source emitting 0 and 1 with unequal probability, to be compressed without distortion into a bulk asymptotically approaching the source's Shannon entropy. Similarly, quantum data compression (cf. Fig. 1) allows signals from a redundant quantum source, eg one emitting horizontal ($\leftrightarrow$) and diagonal ($\nearrow$) photons with equal probability, to be compressed into a bulk approaching the source's von Neumann entropy, $H(\rho) = -\mathrm{tr}\rho \log_2 \rho$, where $\rho = \sum_i p_i \,|\, \psi_i \rangle\langle \psi_i \,|$, with fidelity approaching 1 in the limit of large n. Quantum data compression is performed essentially by projecting the state of a sequence of n source signals onto the subspace spanned by the $2^{n(H(\rho)+\epsilon)}$ most important eigenvectors of their joint density matrix (the n'th tensor power of ρ). For every positive ϵ and δ there exists an n such that for block size n or greater, the resulting projection has probability less that $\delta/2$ of failing (ie having the state not fall into the designated subspace), and fidelity greater than $1 - \delta/2$ if it does succeed. Thus the overall fidelity exceeds $1 - \delta$.

Though formally a close parallel to the classical noiseless coding theorem, quantum data compression is remarkable in that it can compress and re-expand each of 2^n distinct sequences of $\leftrightarrow$ and $\nearrow$ photons, with fidelity approaching 1 *for the entire sequence*, even though the sequences cannot be reliably distinguished from one another by any measurent.

Schumacher's theorem characterizes the amount of one of quantum resource—viz the number of 2-state quantum systems or *qubits* sent through the channel from sender to receiver—that are asymptotically necessary and sufficient for faithfully transmitting unknown pure states drawn from an arbitrary known source ensemble. Quantum superdense coding [5] and quantum teleportation [6] consume another quantum resource— namely entanglement, in the form of entangled pairs of particles previously shared between sender and receiver—and use it to assist, respectively, in the performance of faithful classical and quantum communication.

In quantum teleportation (cf. top of Fig. 2) the sender (sometimes called "Alice") takes particle 1, whose unknown state ξ_1 is to be teleported, and performs a joint measurement on it and particle 2, one member of the EPR pair. Particles 2 and 3 have been prepared beforehand in a maximally entangled EPR state, such as $\Phi_{23}^+ = \sqrt{\frac{1}{2}}(\leftrightarrow_2\leftrightarrow_3 + \updownarrow_2\updownarrow_3)$. The measurement on particles 1 and 2 projects them onto the

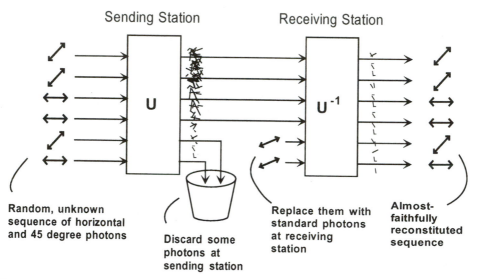

Sending Station

Receiving Station

U

U^{-1}

Random, unknown sequence of horizontal and 45 degree photons

Discard some photons at sending station

Replace them with standard photons at receiving station

Almost-faithfully reconstituted sequence

Figure 1. An example of quantum data compression. A random unknown sequence of horizontal and 45 degree diagonal photons is block-encoded by a unitary transformation U, designed to concentrate their quantum information into the upper photons in the block, then some of the lowermost photons are discarded. At the receiving end, the discarded photons are replaced by standard $22\frac{1}{2}$ degree photons and the unitary transformation is undone, resulting in a close approximation to the original state of the entire block. Shading indicates entanglement. In the limit of large block size, the entropy of the discarded photons approaches zero, and the fidelity of the final state relative to the initial state tends to unity.

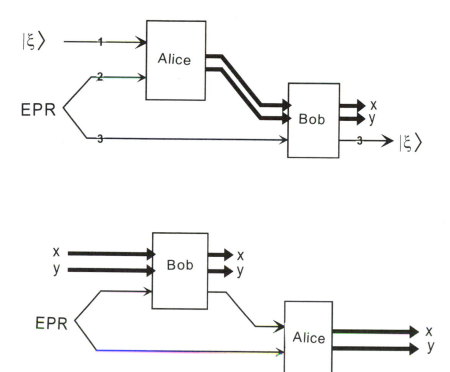

Figure 2. In quantum teleportation (top) prior sharing of an EPR pair, followed by transmission of a two-bit classical message (thick lines) from Alice to Bob, suffices to transmit an unknown quantum state $|\xi\rangle$, even when no direct quantum channel from Alice to Bob is available. The classical data (x,y) remains behind at the end, but is utterly uncorrelated with the state $|\xi\rangle$ it helped to teleport. In superdense coding (bottom) prior sharing of an EPR pair, and transmission of a *single* qubit from Bob to Alice, suffices to transmit an arbitrary two-bit classical message (x,y). In both teleportation and superdense coding, Alice performs a measurement in an orthonormal basis of maximally entangled states, while Bob performs a unitary transformation dependng on the classical data he has received.

so-called Bell basis, consisting of

$$\Phi_{12}^{\pm} = \sqrt{\tfrac{1}{2}}(\leftrightarrow_1 \leftrightarrow_2 \pm \updownarrow_1 \updownarrow_2) \quad \text{and} \quad \Psi_{12}^{\pm} = \sqrt{\tfrac{1}{2}}(\leftrightarrow_1 \updownarrow_2 \pm \updownarrow_1 \leftrightarrow_2), \tag{3}$$

four orthogonal maximally-entangled states. The Bell measurement generates two bits of classical data, and leaves particle 3, now held by the receiver ("Bob"), in a residual state which can be unitarily transformed into a replica ξ_3 of the original quantum state ξ_1 which has been destroyed. This transformation is effected by subjecting particle 3 to one of four unitary operations 1, σ_z, σ_x, or σ_y according to which of the four outcomes, Φ^+, Φ^-, Ψ^+, or Ψ^- was obtained in the Bell measurement conducted by Alice. Teleportation in effect splits the complete information in particle 1 into a classical part, carried by the two-bit message, and a purely quantum part, carried by the prior entanglement between particles 2 and 3. It avoids both cloning (the state ξ is destroyed in particle 1 before it is recreated in particle 3) and faster-than-light communication (the two-bit classical message must arrive at the receiver before the replica can be created).

A closely related effect is *superdense coding*, (cf. bottom of Fig. 2) a scheme due to Wiesner [5]. Here also Alice and Bob begin by sharing an EPR pair. The sender (whom we now call Bob because he performs the same actions as Bob in teleportation) then encodes a two-bit classical message by performing one of the four unitary operations mentioned above on his member of the pair, thereby placing the pair as a whole into a corresponding one of the four orthogonal Bell states. The treated particle is then sent to Alice, who by measuring the particles together can reliably recover both bits of the classical message. Thus the full classical information capacity of two particles is made available, even though only one is directly handled by the sender.

We adopt as our unit of entanglement, or *ebit*, the amount of entanglement in a maximally-entangled pair of qubits, e.g. a pair of spin-$\tfrac{1}{2}$ particles in the singlet state Ψ^-, or one of the other Bell states.

This definition of the unit of entanglement raises the question of how much entanglement should be attributed to other non-factorizable states, pure or mixed, of a general bipartite system, part of which is held by each of two observers. Various measures of entanglement have been proposed for various purposes, but for our purpose of quantifying information-transmission resources a natural choice, for pure states Ψ of a bipartite system, is the entropy of entanglement

$$E(A; B) = -\mathrm{tr}\rho_A \log_2 \rho_A = -\mathrm{tr}\rho_B \log_2 \rho_B, \tag{4}$$

defined as the apparent von Neumann entropy of either subsystem taken alone. Here $\rho_A = \mathrm{tr}_B |\Psi\rangle\langle\Psi|$ is Alice's partial density matrix obatained by tracing the pure state over Bob's degrees of freedom, and vice versa for ρ_B. Entropy of entanglement is a natural choice because it is extensive in particle number, and because on the one hand its expectation cannot be increased by local actions of Alice and Bob, even with the help of classical communication, while on the other hand pure bipartite states having the *same* entropy of entanglement can be transformed into one another by these means with efficiency approaching unity in the limit of large n [7]. For bipartite *mixed* states ρ, the situation is more complicated: the two subsystems' entropies may differ, and the mutual von Neumann information $I(A; B) = \mathrm{tr}\rho \log_2 \rho - \mathrm{tr}_A \rho \log_2 \rho - \mathrm{tr}_B \rho \log_2 \rho$, which for a pure state would be twice the entropy of entanglement, represents a combination of entanglement and classical correlation.

2. INFORMATION TRANSMISSION PRIMITIVES

We consider a number of elementary information-transmission acts involving two parties, Alice and Bob. First we have some acts involving noiseless classical and quantum communication. In the case of classical information, which can be copied, we distinguish between private transmission, with a definite sender and a receiver, and public communicaton, where one party publishes the information for everyone to read and the other party reads information that has perviously been made public.

- the transmission of a *qubit*, or two-state quantum system such as a spin-$\frac{1}{2}$ particle, from Alice to Bob. Note that this is a directed act, different from sending a qubit from Bob to Alice.

- the sharing of an *ebit*, or maximally-entangled pure state of two qubits, between sender and receiver. Notice that sharing an ebit is a symmetric act vis a vis Bob and Alice.

- the transmission of a one-bit secret message from Alice to Bob. Like the sending of a qubit this is a directed act, not equivalent to the transmission of a secret bit in the opposite diretion, from Bob to Alice.

- the sharing of a secret random bit, or cryptographic *keybit* between Alice and Bob. Like the sharing of an ebit, this is a symmetric act, but unlike sharing an ebit, it involves only classical information.

- the publication of a classical bit by one party, for example Alice (this is of course not equivalent to publication of a bit by Bob).

- the reading of a bit of public information by one party, eg Bob.

In addition to these noiseless communication primitives, we need to consider transmissions that are noisy and/or leaky. A leaky transmission is one which is deficient in privacy, because it leaks information to an eavesdropper ("Eve"). A noisy transmission is one in which the transmitted signal is stochastically altered enroute. These two notions are rather independent for classical information, where a channel can be noisy without being leaky, or vice versa, but if a *quantum* channel is leaky, it must also be noisy. In classical information theory, a leaky/noisy channel is described by a joint conditional probabity $P(B, E|A)$ where random variables B, E, and A represent respectively Bob's output, Eve's output, and Alice's input.

To see the intimate relation between noise and leakiness for quantum channels, note that, without loss of generality, a noisy quantum channel χ can be thought of as a unitary interaction U of the quantum information carrier, while enroute from Alice to Bob, with an environment (or, in cryptographic contexts, an eavesdropper) E initially in a standard state e_0. Rather than considering the effect of the channel on particular inputs, one can describe its effect on all inputs by noting its effect on one member (B) of a maximally entangled pair of systems (AB) in the appropriate-sized Hilbert space. In such a maximally-entangled state,

$$\Phi^+_{AB} = N^{-1/2} \sum_i |a_i\rangle \otimes |b_i\rangle, \tag{5}$$

where $|a_i\rangle$ and $|b_i\rangle$ are orthonormal bases for A and B, any ensemble $\mathcal{E}$ of states of B can be prepared by "filtering" [7, 22, 26] subsystem A, (ie performing a generalized measurement (POVM) on A and keeping or discarding B according to the result). Thus the effect of the channel on any input can be simulated by applying the same filtering operation to the A subsystem of the tripartite pure state Ξ_{ABE} of the ABE system obtained by having Alice prepare the AB system in entangled state Φ^+_{AB} then send subsystem B to Bob through the channel, where it interacts unitarily with the E system initially in state e_0.

The amount of information about A and B that leaks to the eavesdropper, and the amount of noise introduced into the AB subsystem by the act of eavesdropping, are equal, both being given by the entropy of entanglement of E with the AB subsystem in the tripartite state Ξ_{ABE}.

We therefore introduce two noisy primitives

- The transmission of a N-state quantum information carrier (represented by a vector in a N-dimensional Hilbert space) through a leaky/noisy channel χ from Alice to Bob.

- The sharing of a pair of N-state systems, in an entangled mixed state M_{AB}, between Alice and Bob (a mixed state is considered entangled if it is not expressible as a mixture of pure product states).

As was the case of the noiseless primitives, there is a close relation between noisy transmission of quantum information and sharing of noisy entanglement: a noisy quantum channel χ can be used to generate an entangled or unentangled mixed state $\hat{M}_{AB}(\chi)$ of the AB system, by transmitting the B half of a maximally entangled pair Φ^+_{AB} through the channel. Conversely a mixed bipartite state M_{AB} can be used to define a noisy channel $\hat{\chi}(M_{AB})$ by using M_{AB} in place of Φ^+_{AB} in a teleportation channel for d-dimensional information carriers.

The noisy primitives above are given for general d-state quantum systems rather than for qubits ($d=2$) because, in contrast to the noiseless case, a noisy d-state channel, or a noisy mixed state of two such systems, cannot in general be expressed as a product of noisy single-qubit channels, or noisy pairs of qubits.

3. REDUCTIONS AND EQUIVALENCES AMONG NOISELESS PRIMITIVES

The ability to transmit a qubit faithfully is a rather strong primitive that can be used to accomplish several other actions, for example sharing an ebit (this can be done by having Alice prepare an EPRB pair and send one member to Bob). Faithful transmission of a qubit can also be used to transmit a classical bit (this can be done by using two orthogonal states, agreed on beforehand by Bob and Alice, to encode the values 0 and 1). The classical bit so transmitted is secret, in the rather weak sense that if there were an eavesdropper listening to the channel, then the channel's fidelity for transmitting *other* quantum states, besides these two orthogonal ones, or for sharing an ebit, would be degraded (this is the basis of quantum cryptogrphy, in which tests for a quantum channel's fidelity are interspersed unpredictably with uses of the channel to transmit classical information). These reductions can be expressed

$$
\begin{array}{llll}
1 & \text{secret bit} & < & 1 \quad \text{qubit} \\
1 & \text{ebit} & < & 1 \quad \text{qubit.}
\end{array} \tag{6}
$$

These two uses to which a qubit can be put are mutually exclusive [27], in the sense that k qubits can be used simultaneously to share ℓ ebits between Alice and Bob *and* to transmit m classical bits from Alice to Bob if and only if $\ell + m \le k$.

Teleportation and superdense coding involve both entanglement and classical information transmission, as expressed respectively in the relations below

$$
\begin{array}{ccccccc}
1 & \text{qubit} & < & 1 & \text{ebit} & + & 2 & \text{public bits} \\
2 & \text{secret bits} & < & 1 & \text{ebit} & + & 1 & \text{qubit}
\end{array}
\tag{7}
$$

As noted previously, the sending of a public bit from Alice to Bob is a two-step process consisting of the publication of a bit by Alice and its reading by Bob. The two bits transmitted in supredense coding are secret in the weak sense noted earlier: eavesdropping would cause both the ebit and the qubit on the right to fail separate tests of fidelity. In each of these relations the two classical bits are transmitted in the same direction as the qubit. The reducibilities in equations 6 and 7 are all proper: in no case can the resoures on the left side be transformed into those on the right.

The relations considered so far can be considerably simplified if we make the idealization that classical public communication is free and unlimited. Then all the relations above can be summarized as

$$
1 \quad \text{secret bit} \quad \equiv \quad 1 \quad \text{key bit} \quad < \quad 1 \quad \text{ebit} \quad \equiv \quad 1 \quad \text{qubit}.
\tag{8}
$$

Here the equivalence between secret bits and key bits follows from the fact that, on the one hand, a secret one-bit message can be used to share a secret key bit, and on the other hand, a public message can be used to deliver a secret message bit, by XORing the message bit with a secret key bit known only by the sender and the receiver (this is the so-called Vernam cipher or one-time pad). Similarly, the equivalence between ebits and qubits follows from the fact that a qubit can be used to share an ebit, and, conversely, an ebit, plus public classical communication, can be used to teleport a qubit.

Besides simple equivalences we can have asymptotic equivalences, where n units of one resource can be simulated by m of another, and vice versa; with fidelity approaching 1 and the ratio m/n approaching a constant in the limit of large m and n. For example [7], local operations and classical communication allow Alice and Bob to interconvert, with asymptotically prefect fidelity and yield, in the limit of large block sizes, pure bipartite states having the same entropy of entanglement. This can be expressed by an asymptotic equivalence,

$$
1 \quad E\text{-entangled pure state} \quad \asymp \quad E \quad \text{ebits},
\tag{9}
$$

which holds in the presence of free classical communication. This equivalence represents the ability, on the one hand, to *concentrate* the entanglement of a supply of arbitrary partly-entangled pure states into a smaller number of maximally-entangled EPR pairs, and the ability on the other hand to *dilute* pure EPR pairs into a arbitrary partly-entangled pure states. The reciprocal actions of entanglement concentration and entanglement dilution differ in several respects: concentration requires no classical communication, and achieves perfect fidelity even for finite block sizes; while dilution appears to require at least one-way classical communication, and achieves perfect fidelity only in the limit of large block sizes. [7, 19].

4.   MIXED STATE ENTANGLEMENT

As noted earlier, entropy of entanglement is a natural measure of entanglement for pure states Ψ_{AB} because it represents both the asymptotic amount of pure entanglement (eg previously shared singlets) required to *prepare* the state and the asymptotic amount that can *be distilled* from it, by local actions and classical communication [7].

33

Furthermore, any pure state with nonzero entropy of entanglement violates some generalized Bell inequality [28]. The situation for mixed states is more complicated, and it is not clear that there is a single best generalization of the pure-state measure. Three natural entanglement measures for mixed states ρ_{AB}, each of which reduces to entropy of entanglement for pure states, are

- the two-way distillable entanglement $D_2(M_{AB})$, defined as the maximum asymptotic yield of pure singlets that can be produced from the given state by local operations and classical two-way communication.

- the one-way distillable entanglement $D_1(M_{AB})$, similar to the above, but allowing only one-way classical communication, from Alice to Bob, during the distillation process.

- the entanglement of formation $E(M_{AB})$, defined as least asymptotic amount of pure entanglement required to prepare an instance of mixed state M_{AB} by local operations and classical communication.

Although we will principally be interested in situations where at least one-way classical communication is possible, for completeness we should also define $D_0(M)$, the maximum asymptotic yield of pure ebits distillable from M without any classical communication. Clearly D_0 can never exceed D_1, and there are states for which D_0 is zero and D_1 positive. For example this is true if Alice holds qubits 1 and 2 and Bob holds qubits 3 and 4 of the mixed state

$$
\begin{aligned}
& |\,\Phi^+(13)\Phi^+(24)\rangle\langle\Phi^+(13)\Phi^+(24)\,| \\
+\ & |\,\Phi^+(13)\Phi^-(24)\rangle\langle\Phi^+(13)\Phi^-(24)\,| \\
+\ & |\,\Phi^-(13)\Psi^+(24)\rangle\langle\Phi^-(13)\Psi^+(24)\,| \\
+\ & |\,\Phi^-(13)\Psi^-(24)\rangle\langle\Phi^-(13)\Psi^-(24)\,|.
\end{aligned}
\tag{10}
$$

This may be described as a state in which Alice and Bob hold one of two Bell states of particles 1 and 3, but don't know which, and in addition hold a pair of random classical bits (embodied in particles 2 and 4) whose XOR, if they knew it, would tell them which Bell state particles 1 and 2 were in. More importantly, there are states for which D_1 is zero and D_2 is positive [19].

The distillable entanglements D_x for $x = 0, 1, 2$, and the entanglement of formation E for arbitrary bipartite mixed states M_{AB} obey the following asymptotic reducibilities:

$$
\begin{array}{llllll}
D_x(M_{AB}) & \text{pure ebits} & \preceq_x & 1 & \text{mixed state } M_{AB} & \preceq_0 \\
E(M_{AB}) & \text{pure ebits} & & & &
\end{array}
\tag{11}
$$

The sign $\preceq_x$ denotes an asymptotic reducibility without classical communication $(x=0)$, or with one- $(x=1)$ or two-way $(x=2)$ classical communication.

The distinction between D_1 and D_2 is important because one-way entanglement distillation protocols can be converted into quantum error-correcting codes [19], and can be used for reliable information storage in a noisy environment [19], an important consideration in design of quantum computers. On the other hand, two-way distillation protocols, although they cannot be used for information storage in a noisy environment, do allow allow reliable transmission of quantum states through channels too noisy to be overcome by any error-correcting code.

Exact expressions for $E(M)$ have been obtained for simple mixed states, but so far only upper and lower bounds are known for D_1 and D_2. Clearly $D_2 \le E$ (otherwise, E could be increased by local operations and classical communication); but no mixed state has been found for which the two measures are provably unequal. Horodecki, Horodecki, and Horodecki [22] recently showed that for bipartite states M of two qubits, $D_2(M) = 0$ iff $E(M) = 0$.

5. QUANTUM AND CLASSICAL CAPACITIES OF NOISY QUANTUM CHANNELS

A major achievement of classical information theory is the ability, using error-correcting codes, to send classical information with arbitrarily high reliably through noisy channels. Recently it has been found that analogously reliable transmission of intact quantum states through noisy channels is possible using quantum error-correcting codes [8–19] or entanglement purification (distillation) protocols [19, 20, 22]. As explained earlier, these two techniques are closely related: given a noisy channel χ, entanglement purification on the mixed state $\hat{M}_{AB}(\chi)$, obtained by sharing pure entanglement through χ, can be used to achieve reliable transmission of quantum states via teleportation; conversely, given a bipartite mixed state M_{AB} from which some entanglement can be distilled, a corresponding quantum error-correcting code can be found for the noisy teleportation channel $\hat{\chi}(M_{AB})$ [19].

In terms of reducibilities, we have

$$
\begin{array}{llll}
\text{1 bipartite state} & \hat{M}(\chi) & \leq_0 & \text{1 transmission via } \chi \\
\text{1 transmission via} & \hat{\chi}(M) & \leq_1 & \text{1 bipartite state } M.
\end{array}
\tag{12}
$$

The first of these reductions is complete in itself, requiring no classical communication; the second requires one-way (forward) classical communication to do the teleportation.

Paralleling the definition of capacity for classical channels, we define the quantum capacity $Q(\chi)$ of a channel χ in an asymptotic fashion, as the greatest number Q such that for any $R < Q$ and any $\delta > 0$, there exists a block size n such that any state of n qubits can be transmitted with fidelity at least δ by fewer than n/R forward uses of the quantum channel, unassisted by any classical communication. As with entanglement distillation from mixed states, we can define Q_1 and Q_2 as the asymptotic quantum capacities of a quantum channel assisted, respectively, by forward and two-way classical communication. Here, however, it can be shown [19] that forward communication alone does not increase the quantum capacity for any channel: $Q_0(\chi) = Q_1(\chi)$ for all χ. Hence Q_0 and Q_1 can safely be denoted by a single symbol Q. By contrast Q_2, the capacity of a quantum channel assisted by two-way classical communication, can be greater than Q, and can be positive for channels for which $Q = 0$.

The classical capacity C as usual is defined as the maximum asymptotic rate at which classical bits can be sent through the quantum channel. By definition, $Q \leq Q_2$, and, by using orthogonal quantum states to transmit classical bits (cf eq. 6), it follows that $Q \leq C$.

The main features of quantum error-correction are illustrated by two simple channels, analogous respectively to the classical binary symmetric and binary erasure channels:

- the *depolarizing channel* which with probability ϵ replaces the incoming qubit by a random qubit, without telling the receiver on which qubits this randomization has been performed; and

- the *quantum erasure channel* [29], which with probability ϵ replaces the incoming qubit by a state orthogonal to both $|0\rangle$ and $|1\rangle$, thereby both erasing the qubit and telling the receiver that it has been erased.

The depolarizing channel exhibits multiple thresholds as a function of noise intensity:

- for $\epsilon < 0.254$, all three capacities Q, Q_2, and C are positive [19, 30].

- for $\frac{1}{3} < \epsilon < \frac{2}{3}$, the one-way quantum capacity Q vanishes but Q_2 and C remain positive [13, 17, 19, 20].

- for $\frac{2}{3} \leq \epsilon < 1$, both quantum capacities vanish but the classical capacity remains positive [19].

- at $\epsilon = 1$ (completely depolarizing channel) all capacities vanish.

Unfortunately, exact expressions are not known for the quantum capacities of the depolarizing channel, as a function of ϵ, only upper and lower bounds [13, 17, 19, 20]. In particular it is not known where the threshold for vanishing of Q lies between 0.2454 and $\frac{1}{3}$. The capacities of the erasure channel, by contrast, are well understood, being given [31] by

$$Q = \max\{0, \ 1 - 2\epsilon\}$$
$$Q_2 = C = 1 - \epsilon. \tag{13}$$

The derivations of eq. 13 will be given in more detail elswehere [31] but are sketched here. The erasure channel's one-way capacity Q must vanish for $\epsilon \geq \frac{1}{2}$ because if it didn't, Alice could clone quantum information faithfully by dividing it among two or more receivers (cf. [19], section 4), each of whom would think he was seeing the source through an erasure channel. Linear interpolation between the 50% erasure channel and the noiseless channel (cf. [19] section 5.2) yields an upper bound $Q(\epsilon) \leq 1 - 2\epsilon$, which coincides with the lower bound obtained by using one-way hashing (cf. [19] section 3.2.3) to enable Bob to correct all the erased qubits. The erasure channel's two-way quantum capacity must be at least $1 - \epsilon$ by a straightforward construction in which Alice uses the erasure channel, in conjunction with classical communication, to share $1 - \epsilon$ good EPR pairs with Bob per channel use. These can then be used to teleport quantum information to Bob at the same rate $1 - \epsilon$. The classical capacity C can be no greater than this because of Holevo's upper bound [32] on the classical capacity of the $1 - \epsilon$ non-erased qubits. Of course $1 - \epsilon$ is also the capacity of a *classical* erasure channel.

When a quantum channel is used to transmit classical information, the question arises of whether the performance of the channel can be improved by using inputs that are entangled among two or more uses of the channel. In [33], for example, it is shown that many noisy single-qubit channels χ have the property that the error probability for transmitting a *single* bit through *two* uses of the channel can be made less if the two input states are allowed to be entangled than if they are required to be product states. A related question, to which the answer is not known, is whether there exist quantum channels χ for which the classical capacity is non-additive, in the sense that, by using entangled input states, more classical information can be sent through n uses of the channel than n times the amount that can be sent through one use of the channel. Kholevo's recent result [34] on attainability of his earlier entropy bound [32] on classical capacity suggests a negative answer.

6. CONCLUSION

Entanglement plays a central quantitative role in the theory of quantum information transmission in many ways complementary to the role of classical information. Quantum data compression and quantum error-correction are nontrivial extensions of classical information theory describing the ability of quantum channels to transmit intact quantum states, as well as classical information. Among the important open questions in quantum information theory are the establishment of exact expresssions, rather than upper and lower bounds, for the one- and two-way quantum capacities of noisy channels, and the development of a general theory of reducibilities among bipartite and mutipartite entangled states, both pure and mixed, with and without the help of classical communication.

ACKNOWLEDGMENTS

The work reviewed here reflects years of fruitful collaboration with Herb Bernstein, Gilles Brassard, Claude Crépeau, David DiVincenzo, Christopher Fuchs, Richard Jozsa, Ueli Maurer, Tal Mor, Asher Peres, Sandu Popescu, Ben Schumacher, John Smolin, Stephen Wiesner, and Bill Wootters; and discussions with David Deutsch, Artur Ekert, Chiara Macchiavello, Raymond Laflamme, Rolf Landauer, and Peter Shor, among others.

REFERENCES

[1] P. Shor, "Fault-tolerant Quantum Computation", Report No. quant-ph/9605011, May 1996.

[2] A. Kitaev, this conference; E. Knill, R. Laflamme, W. Zurek, "Threshold Accuracy for Quantum Computation", Report No. quant-ph/9610011; Aharonov and M. Ben-Or, "Fault Tolerant Quantum Computation with Constant Error", Report No. quant-ph/9611025.

[3] R. Jozsa and B. Schumacher, *J. Modern Optics* **41**, 2343-2349, (1994).

[4] H. Barnum, C.A. Fuchs, R. Jozsa, and B. Schumacher, "A General Fidelity Limit for Quantum Channels," Report No. quant-ph/9603014, March 1996.

[5] C. H. Bennett and S. J. Wiesner, *Phys. Rev. Lett.* **69**, 2881 (1992).

[6] C. H. Bennett, G. Brassard, C. Crépeau, R. Jozsa, A. Peres, and W. K. Wootters, *Phys. Rev. Lett.* **70**, 1895 (1993).

[7] C. H. Bennett, H. J. Bernstein, S. Popescu, and B. Schumacher, "Concentrating Partial Entanglement by Local Operations", Phys. Rev. A **53**, 2046 (1996).

[8] P. W. Shor, "Scheme for reducing decoherence in quantum memory", Phys. Rev. A **52**, 2493 (1995).

[9] I.L. Chuang and R. Laflamme, "Quantum Error Correction by Coding," Report No. quant-ph/9511003.

[10] A.R. Calderbank and P.W. Shor, "Good quantum error-correcting codes exist", Report No. quant-ph/9512032, December 1995.

[11] A. Steane, "Multiple Particle Interference and Quantum Error Correction," submitted to Proc. Roy. Soc. Lond. A Report No. quant-ph/9601029, January 1996.

[12] R. Laflamme, C. Miquel, J.-P. Paz, and W. H. Zurek, "Perfect quantum error correction code", Phys. Rev. Lett. **77**, 198 (1996), and Report No. quant-ph/9602019.

[13] A. Ekert and C. Machiavello, "Quantum error correction for communication", Report No. quant-ph/9602022.

[14] S. L. Braunstein, "Quantum error correction of dephasing in 3 qubits", Report No. quant-ph/9603024.

[15] M. B. Plenio, V. Vedral and P. L. Knight, "Optimal Realistic Quantum Error Correction Code", Report No. quant-ph/9603022.

[16] L. Vaidman, L. Goldenberg and S. Wiesner, "Error Prevention Scheme with Four Particles", Report No. quant-ph/9603031.

[17] E. Knill and R. Laflamme, "A general theory of quantum error correction codes," Report No. quant-ph/9604034.

[18] D. Gottesman, "A class of quantum error-correcting codes saturating the Hamming bound," Report No. quant-ph/9604038.

[19] C.H. Bennett, D.P. DiVincenzo, J. Smolin, and W.K. Wootters, "Mixed State Entanglement and Quantum Error Correction" Phys. Rev A **54** 3824-3851 (1996) (preprint: quant-ph/9604024).

[20] C.H. Bennett, G. Brassard, B. Schumacher, S. Popescu, J. Smolin, and W.K. Wootters, *Phys. Rev. Lett.* (1996).

[21] M. Horodecki, P. Horodecki, and R. Horodecki, "Separability of Mixed States: Necessary and Sufficient Conditions" Report No. quant-ph/9605038, May 1996.

[22] M. Horodecki, P. Horodecki, and R. Horodecki, "Distillability of Inseparable Quantum Systems" Report No. quant-ph/9607009, July 1996.

[23] H. Barnum, C.M.Caves, C.A. Fuchs, R. Jozsa, and B. Schumacher, "Noncommuting Mixed States Cannot be Broadcast", Report No. quant-ph/9511010, November 1995.

[24] *States, Effects, and Operations: Fundamental Notions of Quantum Theory*(Springer, Berlin, 1983), see also B. Schumacher, "Sending Entanglement through Noisy Channels" Report No. quant-ph/9604023, April 1996.

[25] R. Jozsa, "Fidelity for mixed quantum states", J. Mod. Opt. **41**, 2315 (1994).

[26] N. Gisin, *Phys. Lett*A **210**, 151 (1996).

[27] C.H. Bennett, D.P. DiVincenzo, J. Smolin, and W.K. Wootters, "Mixed State Entanglement and Quantum Error Correction" Phys. Rev A **54** 3824-3851 (1996), footnote 48.

[28] N. Gisin, *Phys. Lett.* **A 154**, 201 (1991).

[29] M. Grassl, T. Beth, and T. Pellizzari "Codes for the Quantum Erasure Channel", Report No. quant-ph/9610042

[30] "Quantum Error-Correcting Codes Need not Completely Reveal the Error Syndrome" Report No. quant-ph/9604006, April 1996.

[31] C.H. Bennett and J.A. Smolin, "One- and Two-way Capacities of Quantum Erasure Channels" (in preparation 1996).

[32] A.S.Kholevo *Probl. Inf. Transm. (USSR)* **9**, 177 (1973).

[33] C.H. Bennett, C.A. Fuchs, and J.A. Smolin, "Entanglement-Enhanced Classical Communication on a Noisy Quantum Channel," Report No. quant-ph/9611006.

[34] A.S. Holevo, "The Capacity of Quantum Channel with General Signal States", Report No. quant-ph/9611023, November 1996.

BOUNDS OF THE ACCESSIBLE INFORMATION UNDER THE INFLUENCE OF THERMAL NOISE

Masashi Ban[1], Masao Osaki[2], and Osamu Hirota[2]

[1] Advanced Research Laboratory, Hitachi Ltd.
  Hatoyama, Saitama 350-03, Japan
[2] Research Center for Quantum Communications
  Tamagawa University, Machida, Tokyo 194, Japan

Upper bound of the accessible information obtained in quantum detection processes for Gaussian state signals under the influence of thermal noise is derived by means of the superoperator representation of quantum states. It is shown that the upper bound is obtained by replacing the parameters of the Gaussian quantum state with the renormalized parameters including the thermal noise effect in the accessible information in the absence of thermal noise. Let S and N be sets of the parameters characterizing the signal and thermal noise, and let $I(S, N)$ $[I_0(S) = I(S, 0)]$ be the accessible information in the presence [absence] of thermal noise. Then the inequality $I(S, N) \leq I_0(S_N)$ is derived, where S_N stands for a set of the renormalized parameters including the thermal noise effect. Of course, the inequality $I(S, N) \leq H(S, N)$ is satisfied, where $H(S, N)$ is the Holevo bound of the accessible information. Furthermore, let $I_e(S, N)$ be the mutual information obtained in the detection process that minimizes the average probability of error. Then the inequality $I_e(S, N) \leq I(S, N)$ is satisfied. Therefore the following inequality is obtained

$$I_e(S, N) \leq I(S, N) \leq \min\left[I_0(S_N), H(S, N)\right].$$

Furthermore the method used to derive the upper bound of the accessible information can be applied for obtaining the lower bound of the Bayes cost.

1. INTRODUCTION

In quantum communication systems, a transmitter of information sends a receiver one of n possible messages represented by density operators $\hat{\rho}_1, \hat{\rho}_2, \ldots, \hat{\rho}_n$ with prior probabilities $p_1, p_2, \ldots, p_n$ ($\sum_{j=1}^{n} p_j = 1$). The receiver, on the other hand, performs a generalized quantum measurement on the received signal to infer the quantum state $\hat{\rho}_j$ sent by the transmitter. A generalized quantum measurement is described by a positive operator-valued measure (abbreviated as POM) [1] which is a set of non-negative Hermitian operators, $\{\hat{\Pi}_\mu \mid \mu \in \mathcal{S}\}$, satisfying the relation $\sum_{\mu \in \mathcal{S}} \hat{\Pi}_\mu = \hat{I}$, where $\hat{I}$ stands for an identity operator and μ represents an index specifying the measurement outcome and $\mathcal{S}$ is a set of the indices of all the possible measurement outcomes. One of the most important problems in the quantum communication theory is to find an optimum

Quantum Communication, Computing, and Measurement
Edited by Hirota *et al.*, Plenum Press, New York, 1997

quantum measurement on the received signal such that the mutual information I is maximized [2–5] or such that the Bayes cost C_B is minimized [1]. The mutual information is the appropriate measure of information successfully sent from the transmitter to the receiver [2]. On the other hand, the Bayes cost stands for the average cost incurred when we infer which quantum state has been received [1]. The Bayes cost includes the average probability of error P_e in the signal detection process.

The mutual information and the Bayes cost are important quantities to evaluate a performance of a signal detection process. Our task is to obtain an optimum POM which satisfies the requirement that the mutual information I should be maximized or that the Bayes cost C_B should be minimized in a signal detection process. Obtaining such a POM is also important for quantum computation and quantum cryptography [6] since a signal detection process is indispensable for reading a result of computation and for obtaining a key distribution. The maximum value of the mutual information is called the accessible information and the minimum value of the Bayes cost (in particular, the average probability of error) is called the Helstrom bound. In this paper we denote the accessible information as $I_\mathrm{opt} = \max_{\{\hat{\Pi}_\mu\}} I$ and the Helstrom bound as $C_{\mathrm{B\,opt}} = \min_{\{\hat{\Pi}_\mu\}} C_\mathrm{B}$.

The upper bound of the accessible information I_opt was obtained by Holevo, Yuen and Ozawa [3]. The lower bound, on the other hand, was found by Jozsa, Robb and Wootters [4]. These upper and lower bounds are expressed in terms of the von Neumann entropy S and the subentropy Q. The accessible information I_opt satisfies the inequality,

$$Q(\hat{\rho}) - \sum_{k=1}^{n} p_k Q(\hat{\rho}_k) \leq I_\mathrm{opt} \leq S(\hat{\rho}) - \sum_{k=1}^{n} p_k S(\hat{\rho}_k). \tag{1}$$

Here $\hat{\rho} = \sum_{k=1}^{n} p_k \hat{\rho}_k$ is a density operator of statistical mixture of the quantum states of the signal and the von Neumann entropy $S(\hat{\sigma})$ and the subentropy $Q(\hat{\sigma})$ are given by

$$S(\hat{\sigma}) = -\sum_{\nu} \lambda_\nu \ln \lambda_\nu, \quad Q(\hat{\sigma}) = -\sum_{\nu} \left[\prod_{\mu \neq \nu} \left(\frac{\lambda_\nu}{\lambda_\nu - \lambda_\mu} \right) \right] \lambda_\nu \ln \lambda_\nu, \tag{2}$$

where λ_ν is an eigenvalue of the statistical operator $\hat{\sigma}$ ($\hat{\sigma} = \hat{\rho}$ or $\hat{\sigma} = \hat{\rho}_k$). The upper bound of the accessible information is called the Holevo bound. Since the entropic upper and lower bounds does not depend on any quantum measurement carried out on the received signal, these bounds are general but may be fairly loose. Fuchs and Caves have recently found the more tight bounds of the accessible information that strongly depend on the structure of the quantum states of the signal [5]. But their bounds are much complicated in comparison with the entropic bounds.

The Bayes cost C_B is another quantity used to evaluate a performance of a quantum signal detection process. We can calculate, in principle, the minimum value of the Bayes cost by means of the quantum detection theory [1,7,8]. To obtain the minimum value and the optimum POM, we have to solve the operator equations for the POM,

$$\hat{\Pi}_j \left(\hat{W}_j - \hat{W}_k \right) \hat{\Pi}_k = 0, \quad \hat{W}_j - \sum_{k=1}^{n} \hat{\Pi}_k \hat{W}_k \geq 0, \tag{3}$$

where $\hat{W}_j = \sum_{k=1}^{n} C_{jk} \hat{\rho}_k p_k$ is the risk operator and C_{jk} is the cost incurred when we infer that the received quantum state is given by the density operator $\hat{\rho}_j$ even though the quantum state $\hat{\rho}_k$ has been actually received. In this case the set of indices becomes $\mathcal{S} = \{1, 2, \ldots, n\}$. The minimum value of the Bayes cost is calculated as $C_{\mathrm{B\,opt}} = \sum_{k=1}^{n} \mathrm{Tr}\left(\hat{\Pi}_k \hat{W}_k \right)$, where $\hat{\Pi}_1, \hat{\Pi}_2, \ldots, \hat{\Pi}_n$ are the solutions of Eq. (3). But it is too difficult to solve Eq. (3) except for simple signals. In particular, we cannot obtain an analytical expression of the minimum value of the Bayes cost in the presence of thermal noise unless $[\hat{\rho}_j, \hat{\rho}_k] = 0$. Thus obtaining the lower bound of the Bayes cost is important for evaluating quantum communication systems.

In this paper, we consider the upper bound of the accessible information and the lower bound of the Bayes cost in quantum detection processes for Gaussian state signals [7,9] under the influence of thermal noise. It will be shown that the upper bound of the accessible information I_{opt} and the lower bound of the Bayes cost $C_{\text{B opt}}$ are given by replacing the parameters characterizing the quantum states of the signal with the renormalized parameters including the thermal noise effects in the accessible information $I_{\text{opt}}^{(0)}$ and the minimum value of the Bayes cost $C_{\text{B opt}}^{(0)}$ obtained in the signal detection process without thermal noise. The thermal noise effects on signal detection processes are inevitable in practical communication systems, and obtaining $I_{\text{opt}}^{(0)}$ and $C_{\text{B opt}}^{(0)}$ is easier than obtaining I_{opt} and $C_{\text{B opt}}$. Therefore it is important in the quantum communication theory to obtain such upper and lower bounds. To derive the upper of the accessible information and lower bound of the Bayes cost, we use the superoperator representation [10] of quantum states, or equivalently thermofield dynamics [11], which enables us to treat mixed quantum states just like pure quantum states.

2. SUPEROPERATOR REPRESENTATION OF QUANTUM STATES

Quantum states of a signal that we consider in this paper belong to the class of Gaussian states [7,9]. Let $\hat{\rho}_j$ be a density operator which represents the jth quantum state of the signal in the presence of the thermal noise and let $\hat{\rho}_j^{(0)}$ be the corresponding density operator in the absence of the thermal noise. The density operators $\hat{\rho}_j$ and $\hat{\rho}_j^{(0)}$ are expressed as

$$\hat{\rho}_j = \frac{\hat{V}_j \hat{\rho}_{\text{th}} \hat{V}_j^{\dagger}}{\text{Tr}\left(\hat{V}_j \hat{\rho}_{\text{th}} \hat{V}_j^{\dagger}\right)}, \quad \hat{\rho}_j^{(0)} = \frac{\hat{V}_j |0\rangle\langle 0| \hat{V}_j^{\dagger}}{\langle 0| \hat{V}_j^{\dagger} \hat{V}_j |0\rangle} \equiv |\psi_j^{(0)}\rangle\langle\psi_j^{(0)}|, \tag{4}$$

where $\hat{\rho}_{\text{th}} = (1 + \bar{n})^{-1} \sum_{k=0}^{\infty} [\bar{n}/(1 + \bar{n})]^k |k\rangle\langle k|$ is the density operator of the thermal state and $\bar{n}$ is the average value of the photon number of the thermal noise and $|0\rangle$ is the vacuum state and we set $|\psi_j^{(0)}\rangle = \hat{V}_j |0\rangle / \sqrt{\langle 0| \hat{V}_j^{\dagger} \hat{V}_j |0\rangle}$. In Eq. (4), we assume that the operator $\hat{V}_j$ is given by

$$\hat{V}_j = \exp\left[\gamma_j \hat{a}^2 - \gamma_j^* \hat{a}^{\dagger 2} + i\phi_j \hat{a}^{\dagger} \hat{a} + \mu_j^* \hat{a} + \nu_j \hat{a}^{\dagger}\right], \tag{5}$$

where γ_j, μ_j, and ν_j are complex parameters and ϕ_j is a real parameter and $\hat{a}$ and $\hat{a}^{\dagger}$ are bosonic annihilation and creation operators. The operator $\hat{V}_j$ need not be unitary. It is easy to see that the signal quantum state represented by the density operator $\hat{\rho}_j$ includes thermal coherent state [12] and thermal squeezed state [13] which seem to be the most important states in quantum communication systems.

To obtain the superoperator representation of the quantum states given by Eqs. (4) and (5), we introduce three superoperators $\hat{\mathcal{K}}_{\pm}$ and $\hat{\mathcal{K}}_0$ by the relations [14],

$$\hat{\mathcal{K}}_+ \hat{A} = \hat{a}^{\dagger} \hat{A} \hat{a}, \quad \hat{\mathcal{K}}_- \hat{A} = \hat{a} \hat{A} \hat{a}^{\dagger}, \quad \hat{\mathcal{K}}_0 \hat{A} = \frac{1}{2}(\hat{a}^{\dagger} \hat{a} \hat{A} + \hat{A} \hat{a}^{\dagger} \hat{a} + \hat{A}), \tag{6}$$

where $\hat{A}$ stands for an arbitrary operator. Here a superoperator means an operator acting on operators [10,11]. It is easy to see that the superoperators $\hat{\mathcal{K}}_{\pm}$ and $\hat{\mathcal{K}}_0$ satisfy the SU(1,1) Lie commutation relations, $[\hat{\mathcal{K}}_-, \hat{\mathcal{K}}_+] = 2\hat{\mathcal{K}}_0$ and $[\hat{\mathcal{K}}_0, \hat{\mathcal{K}}_\pm] = \pm\hat{\mathcal{K}}_\pm$. Thus we obtain the useful decomposition formula for the SU(1,1) generators [15],

$$\exp\left[a_+\hat{\mathcal{K}}_+ + a_0\hat{\mathcal{K}}_0 + a_-\hat{\mathcal{K}}_-\right] = \exp\left[A_+\hat{\mathcal{K}}_+\right] \exp\left[(\ln A_0)\hat{\mathcal{K}}_0\right] \exp\left[A_-\hat{\mathcal{K}}_-\right], \quad (7)$$

where the parameters $A_\pm$ and A_0 are given by

$$A_\pm = \frac{(a_\pm/\phi)\sinh\phi}{\cosh\phi - (a_0/2\phi)\sinh\phi}, \quad A_0 = [\cosh\phi - (a_0/2\phi)\sinh\phi]^{-2}, \quad (8)$$

with $\phi = \sqrt{(a_0/2)^2 - a_+a_-}$.

It is important to note that the density operator of the thermal state is expressed in terms of the superoperators as

$$\hat{\rho}_{th} = \frac{1}{1+\bar{n}} \sum_{k=0}^{\infty} \frac{1}{k!} \left(\frac{\bar{n}}{1+\bar{n}}\right)^k (\hat{a}^\dagger)^k|0\rangle\langle0|\hat{a}^k$$

$$= \frac{1}{1+\bar{n}} \sum_{k=0}^{\infty} \frac{1}{k!} \left(\frac{\bar{n}}{1+\bar{n}}\right)^k \hat{\mathcal{K}}_+^k (|0\rangle\langle0|)$$

$$= \frac{1}{1+\bar{n}} \exp\left(\frac{\bar{n}}{1+\bar{n}}\hat{\mathcal{K}}_+\right)|0\rangle\langle0|. \quad (9)$$

When we use the SU(1,1) decomposition formula and the relations $\hat{\mathcal{K}}_-(|0\rangle\langle0|) = 0$ and $\hat{\mathcal{K}}_0(|0\rangle\langle0|) = \frac{1}{2}|0\rangle\langle0|$, we can express the density operator of the thermal state in the following form:

$$\hat{\rho}_{th} = \hat{\mathcal{L}}(|0\rangle\langle0|), \quad \hat{\mathcal{L}} = \exp[\theta(\hat{\mathcal{K}}_+ - \hat{\mathcal{K}}_- - 1)], \quad (10)$$

where we have introduced the parameter $\theta = \frac{1}{2}\ln(1 + 2\bar{n})$. Therefore we find from Eqs. (4)–(6) and (10) that the density operator $\hat{\rho}_j$ of the signal quantum state can be expressed as

$$\hat{\rho}_j = \frac{\hat{V}_j\hat{\mathcal{L}}(|0\rangle\langle0|)\hat{V}_j^\dagger}{\text{Tr}\left[\hat{V}_j\hat{\mathcal{L}}(|0\rangle\langle0|)\hat{V}_j^\dagger\right]} = \hat{\mathcal{L}}(|\psi_j\rangle\langle\psi_j|). \quad (11)$$

Here we set $|\psi_j\rangle = \hat{U}_j|0\rangle/\sqrt{\langle0|\hat{U}_j^\dagger\hat{U}_j|0\rangle}$ and the operator $\hat{U}_j$ is given by

$$\hat{U}_j = \exp\left[\gamma_j\hat{a}^2 - \gamma_j^*\hat{a}^{\dagger2} + i\phi_j\hat{a}^\dagger\hat{a} + \tilde{\mu}_j^*\hat{a} + \tilde{\nu}_j\hat{a}^\dagger\right], \quad (12)$$

where the renormalized parameters $\tilde{\mu}_j$ and $\tilde{\nu}_j$ which include the thermal noise effects are given by

$$\tilde{\mu}_j = \frac{(1+\bar{n})\mu_j + \bar{n}\nu_j}{\sqrt{1+2\bar{n}}}, \quad \tilde{\nu}_j = \frac{(1+\bar{n})\nu_j + \bar{n}\mu_j}{\sqrt{1+2\bar{n}}}. \quad (13)$$

It should be noted that the parameters γ_j and ϕ_j remain unchanged. The expression given by Eq. (11) is used to derive the upper and lower bounds.

3. UPPER BOUND OF THE ACCESSIBLE INFORMATION

In this section, we consider the upper bound of the accessible information I_{opt} in the quantum detection process for the signal whose quantum state is given by the density operator $\hat{\rho}_j$ in Eqs. (4) and (5). The mutual information I is calculated in terms of the POMs $\hat{\Pi}_\mu$'s, density operators $\hat{\rho}_j$'s, and prior probabilities p_j's [2],

$$I = \sum_{j=1}^{n} \sum_{\mu\in\mathcal{S}} P(\mu|j)p_j \ln\left[\frac{P(\mu|j)}{\sum_{k=1}^{n} P(\mu|k)p_k}\right], \quad (14)$$

where we set the unit of information as nats and $P(\mu|j) = \text{Tr}[\hat{\Pi}_\mu \hat{\rho}_j]$ is the conditional probability that the measurement outcome is indexed by parameter μ when the quantum state of the received signal is given by the density operator $\hat{\rho}_j$. Using the expression given by Eq. (11) and the relation $\text{Tr}[A(\hat{\mathcal{K}}_\pm B)] = \text{Tr}[(\hat{\mathcal{K}}_\mp A)B]$ for any operators $\hat{A}$ and $\hat{B}$, we can calculate the conditional probability $P(\mu|j)$ as

$$
\begin{aligned}
P(\mu|j) &= \text{Tr}\left[\hat{\Pi}_\mu \hat{\rho}_j\right] \\
&= \text{Tr}\left[\hat{\Pi}_\mu \hat{\mathcal{L}}(|\psi_j\rangle\langle\psi_j|)\right] \\
&= \text{Tr}\left[\hat{\mathcal{L}}^\dagger(\hat{\Pi}_\mu)|\psi_j\rangle\langle\psi_j|\right],
\end{aligned}
\tag{15}
$$

where the superoperator $\hat{\mathcal{L}}^\dagger = \exp[-\theta(\hat{\mathcal{K}}_+ - \hat{\mathcal{K}}_- + 1)]$ is the Hermitian conjugate of the superoperator $\hat{\mathcal{L}}$. Since the mutual information is considered a function of the conditional probabilities, we formally write it as $I\left(\text{Tr}[\hat{\Pi}_\mu\hat{\rho}_j]\right)$.

To perform the optimization, let us now introduce a set $\mathcal{U}$ of all possible POMs,

$$
\mathcal{U} = \{\hat{\Pi} = (\hat{\Pi}_1,\ldots,\hat{\Pi}_\mu,\ldots)\,|\,\hat{\Pi}_\mu \geq 0,\ \textstyle\sum_{\mu\in S}\hat{\Pi}_\mu = \hat{I}\}.
\tag{16}
$$

Thus our task is to find an element $\hat{\Pi}$ of the set $\mathcal{U}$ such that the mutual information should be maximized. The optimum POM $\hat{\Pi}$ is determined by the requirement that $\max_{\hat{\Pi}\in\mathcal{U}} I\left(\text{Tr}\left[\hat{\Pi}_\mu\hat{\rho}_j\right]\right)$. Then we can calculate the accessible information I_{opt} as follows:

$$
\begin{aligned}
I_{\text{opt}} &= \max_{\hat{\Pi}\in\mathcal{U}} I\left(\text{Tr}\left[\hat{\Pi}_\mu\hat{\rho}_j\right]\right) \\
&= \max_{\hat{\Pi}\in\mathcal{U}} I\left(\text{Tr}\left[\hat{\Pi}_\mu\hat{\mathcal{L}}(|\psi_j\rangle\langle\psi_j|)\right]\right) \\
&= \max_{\hat{\Pi}\in\mathcal{U}} I\left(\text{Tr}\left[\hat{\mathcal{L}}^\dagger(\hat{\Pi}_\mu)|\psi_j\rangle\langle\psi_j|\right]\right) \\
&= \max_{\hat{\Pi}'\in\tilde{\mathcal{U}}} I\left(\text{Tr}\left[\hat{\Pi}'_\mu|\psi_j\rangle\langle\psi_j|\right]\right),
\end{aligned}
\tag{17}
$$

where we have introduced the set $\tilde{\mathcal{U}} = \{\hat{\Pi}' = \hat{\mathcal{L}}^\dagger(\hat{\Pi})\,|\,\hat{\Pi}\in\mathcal{U}\}$ which is the range of the superoperator $\hat{\mathcal{L}}^\dagger$ when the domain is restricted to the set $\mathcal{U}$.

Let $\hat{\Pi}' = (\hat{\Pi}'_1,\ldots,\hat{\Pi}'_\mu,\ldots)$ be an arbitrary element of the set $\tilde{\mathcal{U}}$. Then there is some element $\hat{\Pi} = (\hat{\Pi}_1,\ldots,\hat{\Pi}_\mu,\ldots)$ of the set $\mathcal{U}$ such that $\hat{\Pi}'_\mu = \hat{\mathcal{L}}^\dagger(\hat{\Pi}_\mu)$ for all $\mu\in\mathcal{S}$. Using the relations $\sum_{\mu\in\mathcal{S}}\hat{\Pi}_\mu = \hat{I}$ and $\hat{\mathcal{L}}^\dagger(\hat{I}) = \hat{I}$, we can show that the relation $\sum_{\mu\in\mathcal{S}}\hat{\Pi}'_\mu = \hat{I}$ is satisfied. Furthermore, using the decomposition formula for the SU(1,1) generators, we can also show from the inequality $\hat{\Pi}_\mu \geq 0$ that the operator $\hat{\Pi}'_\mu$ is non-negative definite; that is, $\hat{\Pi}'_\mu \geq 0$ for all $\mu\in\mathcal{S}$. Thus $\hat{\Pi}'$ becomes a POM and belongs to the set $\mathcal{U}$. Therefore we have proved that $\hat{\Pi}'\in\tilde{\mathcal{U}} \rightarrow \hat{\Pi}'\in\mathcal{U}$. This means that $\tilde{\mathcal{U}}$ is a subset of $\mathcal{U}$; namely, $\tilde{\mathcal{U}} \subseteq \mathcal{U}$. This result provides the following inequality:

$$
\max_{\hat{\Pi}'\in\tilde{\mathcal{U}}} I\left(\text{Tr}\left[\hat{\Pi}'_\mu|\psi_j\rangle\langle\psi_j|\right]\right) \leq \max_{\hat{\Pi}'\in\mathcal{U}} I\left(\text{Tr}\left[\hat{\Pi}'_\mu|\psi_j\rangle\langle\psi_j|\right]\right).
\tag{18}
$$

Here the equality holds if and only if the optimum POM $\hat{\Pi}'_{\text{opt}}$ chosen among the elements of $\mathcal{U}$ belongs to the subset $\tilde{\mathcal{U}}$; that is, $\hat{\Pi}_{\text{opt}} \in \tilde{\mathcal{U}} \subseteq \mathcal{U}$. It is important to note that the quantity on the right-hand side in the inequality (18) is equal to the accessible information calculated in the quantum detection process, where the quantum states of the received signal are given by the pure states $|\psi_1\rangle, |\psi_2\rangle, \ldots, |\psi_n\rangle$.

We denote the accessible information for the signal given by Eqs. (4) and (5) in the presence of the thermal noise as $I_{\text{opt}}(\gamma, \phi, \mu, \nu)$ and the accessible information for the same signal in the absence of the thermal noise as $I_{\text{opt}}^{(0)}(\gamma, \phi, \mu, \nu)$. Then we obtain the inequality $I_{\text{opt}}(\gamma, \phi, \mu, \nu) \leq I_{\text{opt}}^{(0)}(\gamma, \phi, \tilde{\mu}, \tilde{\nu})$ from Eqs. (17) and (18). The renormalized parameters $\tilde{\mu}_j$ and $\tilde{\nu}_j$ which include the thermal noise effects are related to the original parameters μ_j and ν_j by Eq. (13). The inequality indicates that the upper bound of the accessible information for the signal in the presence of the thermal noise is obtained by replacing the signal parameters with the renormalized parameters including the thermal noise effects in the accessible information obtained for the same signal in the absence of the thermal noise. Furthermore let us denote the Holevo bound for the Gaussian state signal as $H(\gamma, \phi, \mu, \nu)$ and the mutual information as $I_e(\gamma, \phi, \mu, \nu)$ which is obtained in the detection process minimizing the average probability of error. It is clear that the mutual information $I_e(\gamma, \phi, \mu, \nu)$ is smaller than the accessible information $I_{\text{opt}}(\gamma, \phi, \mu, \nu)$. Therefore we finally obtain the following inequality [16],

$$I_e(\gamma, \phi, \mu, \nu) \leq I_{\text{opt}}(\gamma, \phi, \mu, \nu) \leq \min\left[I_{\text{opt}}^{(0)}(\gamma, \phi, \tilde{\mu}, \tilde{\nu}), H(\gamma, \phi, \mu, \nu)\right], \qquad (19)$$

where $\min[x, y] = x$ for $x \leq y$ and $\min[x, y] = y$ for $x > y$. This inequality is the main result of this contribution.

We now consider a binary signal detection to obtain an analytic expression of the upper bound of the accessible information, $I_{\text{opt}}^{(0)}(\gamma, \phi, \tilde{\mu}, \tilde{\nu})$, under the influence of the thermal noise. To this end, we have to obtain the accessible information $I_{\text{opt}}^{(0)}(\gamma, \phi, \mu, \nu)$ in the absence of the thermal noise. We first investigate a detection process for quantum states whose density operators are given by $\hat{\rho}_1$ and $\hat{\rho}_2$. To simplify the discussion, we confine ourselves to the case of $S = \{1, 2\}$. Thus the binary detection process we consider is described by POMs $\hat{\Pi}_1$ and $\hat{\Pi}_2$ which satisfy the relations $\hat{\Pi}_1 + \hat{\Pi}_2 = \hat{I}$ and $\hat{\Pi}_j \geq 0$. Suppose that the signal detection process described by $\hat{\Pi}_1$ and $\hat{\Pi}_2$ maximizes the mutual information. Then the POMs $\hat{\Pi}_1$ and $\hat{\Pi}_2$ satisfy the condition derived by Holevo [7],

$$\left(\hat{F}_j - \hat{\Gamma}\right)\hat{\Pi}_j = 0 \ (j = 1, 2), \quad \hat{\Gamma} = \sum_{j=1,2} \hat{\Pi}_j \hat{F}_j = \sum_{j=1,2} \hat{F}_j \hat{\Pi}_j, \qquad (20)$$

where $\hat{\Gamma}$ is called the Lagrange operator and $\hat{F}_j$ is given by

$$\hat{F}_j = \sum_{k=1,2} \hat{\rho}_k p_k \ln\left[\frac{P(j|k)}{\sum_{m=1,2} P(j|m) p_m}\right]. \qquad (21)$$

Then, if the operator $\hat{F}_1 - \hat{F}_2$ does not have zero eigenvalue, we can derive the following relations [16],

$$\hat{\Pi}_1 \hat{\Pi}_2 = \hat{\Pi}_2 \hat{\Pi}_1 = 0, \quad \hat{\Pi}_j^2 = \hat{\Pi}_j \ (j = 1, 2). \qquad (22)$$

This result indicates that the accessible information in the binary signal detection is obtained by a quantum measurement described by projection operators. It should be noted that Eq. (22) is valid for any density operators $\hat{\rho}_1$ and $\hat{\rho}_2$ as long as the operator $\hat{F}_1 - \hat{F}_2$ does not have zero eigenvalue.

Suppose that the signal quantum states in the absence of the thermal noise are given by $|\psi_1^{(0)}\rangle$ and $|\psi_2^{(0)}\rangle$, where $|\psi_j^{(0)}\rangle$ is given in Eqs. (4) and (5). In this case, we find from Eq. (22) that $\hat{\Pi}_1$ and $\hat{\Pi}_2$ become one-dimensional projection operators. Thus after some calculation, we obtain the accessible information [5, 17],

$$\begin{aligned}
I_{\text{opt}}^{(0)}(\gamma, \phi, \mu, \nu) = I_0 &+ \frac{1}{2}\left(1 + \sqrt{1 - 4p_1 p_2 \kappa^2}\right) \ln\left(1 + \sqrt{1 - 4p_1 p_2 \kappa^2}\right) \\
&+ \frac{1}{2}\left(1 - \sqrt{1 - 4p_1 p_2 \kappa^2}\right) \ln\left(1 - \sqrt{1 - 4p_1 p_2 \kappa^2}\right),
\end{aligned} \qquad (23)$$

where we set $\kappa = |\langle\psi_1^{(0)}|\psi_2^{(0)}\rangle|$ and $I_0 = -\ln 2 - p_1 \ln p_1 - p_2 \ln p_2$.

Using Eq. (23), we can obtain the analytic expression of the upper bound of the accessible information in the presence of the thermal noise. When the density operators of the signal quantum states are given by the density operators $\hat{\rho}_1 = \hat{V}_1 \hat{\rho}_{th} \hat{V}_1^\dagger / \text{Tr}\left(\hat{V}_1 \hat{\rho}_{th} \hat{V}_1^\dagger\right)$ and $\hat{\rho}_2 = \hat{V}_2 \hat{\rho}_{th} \hat{V}_2^\dagger / \text{Tr}\left(\hat{V}_2 \hat{\rho}_{th} \hat{V}_2^\dagger\right)$, the upper bound of the accessible information is obtained by substituting $\kappa = |\langle\psi_1|\psi_2\rangle|$ into Eq. (23), where $|\psi_j\rangle = \hat{U}_j|0\rangle/\sqrt{\langle 0|\hat{U}_j^\dagger \hat{U}_j|0\rangle}$ and the operator $\hat{U}_j$ is given by Eq. (12). In particular, when we consider the binary detection process for thermal coherent states, $\hat{\rho}_1 = \hat{D}(\alpha)\hat{\rho}_{th}\hat{D}^\dagger(\alpha)$ and $\hat{\rho}_2 = \hat{D}(\beta)\hat{\rho}_{th}\hat{D}^\dagger(\beta)$, where $\hat{D}(\alpha) = \exp[\alpha\hat{a}^\dagger - \alpha^*\hat{a}]$ is the displacement operator, we can obtain the inequality,

$$I_{opt} \leq I_0 + \frac{1}{2}\left[1 + \sqrt{1 - 4p_1p_2\exp\left(-\frac{|\alpha-\beta|^2}{1+2\bar{n}}\right)}\right]\ln\left[1 + \sqrt{1 - 4p_1p_2\exp\left(-\frac{|\alpha-\beta|^2}{1+2\bar{n}}\right)}\right]$$

$$+ \frac{1}{2}\left[1 - \sqrt{1 - 4p_1p_2\exp\left(-\frac{|\alpha-\beta|^2}{1+2\bar{n}}\right)}\right]\ln\left[1 - \sqrt{1 - 4p_1p_2\exp\left(-\frac{|\alpha-\beta|^2}{1+2\bar{n}}\right)}\right]. \quad (24)$$

In optical communication systems where $\bar{n} \ll 1$ is satisfied, the right-hand side of this inequality becomes a much more tight bound of the accessible information than the Holevo bound.

Before closing this section, we evaluate the inequality (19) for the binary phase-shift keyed coherent state signal with the equal prior probabilities, where the statistical operators of the signal are given by $\hat{\rho}_1 = \hat{D}(\alpha)\hat{\rho}_{th}\hat{D}^\dagger(\alpha)$ and $\hat{\rho}_2 = \hat{D}(-\alpha)\hat{\rho}_{th}\hat{D}^\dagger(-\alpha)$. The our upper bound is obtained from Eq. (24) by substituting $\beta = -\alpha$ and $p_1 = p_2 = \frac{1}{2}$. The mutual information I_e in the detection process minimizing the average probability of error can be calculated from Eq. (3) by numerical calculation. The Holevo bound H is also obtained numerically. The results are plotted as function of the photon number of the signal $n_s = |\alpha|^2$ for the several values of the photon number of the thermal noise in Fig. 3. We see from the figure as follows. When the average value of the photon number of the thermal noise is not so large, our bound of the accessible information is superior to the Holevo bound. On the other hand, if the average value of the photon number of the thermal noise is large, the Holevo bound becomes more tight than ours for $n_s > 1$ while our bound is still smaller for $n_s \ll 1$.

4. LOWER BOUND OF THE BAYES COST

In this section, we consider the lower bound of the Bayes cost C_B [1, 7, 8] in the quantum detection process for the Gaussian state signal under the influence of the thermal noise. In this case the number of the indices μ's is equal to the number of the quantum states of the signal, that is, $S = \{1, 2, \ldots, n\}$. The Bayes cost C_B to be minimized is given by

$$C_B = \sum_{j=1}^{n}\sum_{k=1}^{n} p_k C_{jk} \text{Tr}\left[\hat{\Pi}_j\hat{\rho}_k\right], \quad (25)$$

where the quantity C_{jk} is the cost incurred when we infer that the received quantum state is described by the density operator $\hat{\rho}_j$ even though the quantum state $\hat{\rho}_k$ has actually been received [1]. Since the cost is reduced by the correct detection, the inequality $C_{jj} < C_{jk}$ is satisfied. In the following, we denote the Bayes cost as $C_B(\text{Tr}[\hat{\Pi}_j\hat{\rho}_k])$. The necessary and sufficient condition for the POM $\hat{\Pi}$ to minimize the Bayes cost is given by Eq. (3). But it is difficult to obtain the optimum POM from Eq. (3).

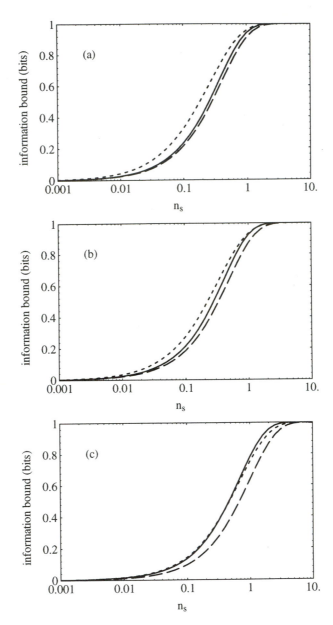

Figure 1. Plots of the bounds for the accessible information in the detection process for the binary phase-shift keyed coherent state signal, where (a) $\bar{n} = 0.05$, (b) $\bar{n} = 0.1$, and (c) $\bar{n} = 0.5$. In the figures, the solid line stands for our bound, the dotted line for the Holevo bound, and the dashed line for the mutual information in the detection process minimizing the average probability of error.

From the same argument used for deriving the upper bound of the accessible information, we find the following relation:

$$
\begin{aligned}
C_{\mathrm{B\,opt}} &= \min_{\hat{\Pi} \in \mathcal{U}} C_{\mathrm{B}} \left(\mathrm{Tr} \left[\hat{\Pi}_j \hat{\mathcal{L}}(|\psi_k\rangle\langle\psi_k|) \right] \right) \\
&= \min_{\hat{\Pi} \in \mathcal{U}} C_{\mathrm{B}} \left(\mathrm{Tr} \left[\hat{\mathcal{L}}^\dagger(\hat{\Pi}_j)|\psi_k\rangle\langle\psi_k| \right] \right) \\
&= \min_{\hat{\Pi}' \in \tilde{\mathcal{U}}} C_{\mathrm{B}} \left(\mathrm{Tr} \left[\hat{\Pi}'_j |\psi_k\rangle\langle\psi_k| \right] \right) \\
&\geq \min_{\hat{\Pi}' \in \mathcal{U}} C_{\mathrm{B}} \left(\mathrm{Tr} \left[\hat{\Pi}'_j |\psi_k\rangle\langle\psi_k| \right] \right).
\end{aligned}
\tag{26}
$$

In the last inequality we have used the fact that $\tilde{\mathcal{U}}$ is a subset of $\mathcal{U}$, and the equality holds if and only if the optimum POM $\hat{\Pi}_{\mathrm{opt}}$ chosen among the elements of the set $\mathcal{U}$ such that the Bayes cost in the detection process for the quantum states $(|\psi_1\rangle, |\psi_2\rangle, \ldots, |\psi_n\rangle)$ should be minimized belongs to the subset $\tilde{\mathcal{U}}$; namely, $\hat{\Pi}_{\mathrm{opt}} \in \tilde{\mathcal{U}} \subseteq \mathcal{U}$. Let $C_{\mathrm{B\,opt}}(\gamma, \phi, \mu, \nu)$ be the minimum value of the Bayes cost in the quantum detection process for the signal $(\hat{\rho}_1, \hat{\rho}_2, \ldots, \hat{\rho}_n)$ and let $C_{\mathrm{B\,opt}}^{(0)}(\gamma, \phi, \mu, \nu)$ be the minimum value of the Bayes cost in the detection process for the signal $(|\psi_1^{(0)}\rangle, |\psi_2^{(0)}\rangle, \ldots, |\psi_n^{(0)}\rangle)$, where $\hat{\rho}_j$ and $|\psi_j^{(0)}\rangle$ are given in Eqs. (4) and (5). Then from Eq. (26), we can obtain the following inequality:

$$
C_{\mathrm{B\,opt}}(\gamma, \phi, \mu, \nu) \geq C_{\mathrm{B\,opt}}^{(0)}(\gamma, \phi, \tilde{\mu}, \tilde{\nu}),
\tag{27}
$$

where the renormalized parameters $\tilde{\mu}_j$ and $\tilde{\nu}_j$ including the thermal noise effects are given by Eq. (13). Thus the lower bound of the Bayes cost $C_{\mathrm{B\,opt}}$ is obtained from $C_{\mathrm{B\,opt}}^{(0)}$ by substituting the renormalized parameters.

The average probability of error P_{e} which is one of the most important quantities to evaluate a performance of a quantum communication system is obtained as $P_{\mathrm{e}} = 1 + C_{\mathrm{B}}$ by substituting $C_{jk} = -\delta_{jk}$ into Eq. (25). Let us denote as $P_{\mathrm{opt}}(\gamma, \phi, \mu, \nu)$ and $P_{\mathrm{opt}}^{(0)}(\gamma, \phi, \mu, \nu)$ the minimum values of the average probability of error in the signal detection processes in the presence and absence of the thermal noise. Then from the inequality (27), we obtain $P_{\mathrm{opt}}(\gamma, \phi, \mu, \nu) \geq P_{\mathrm{opt}}^{(0)}(\gamma, \phi, \tilde{\mu}, \tilde{\nu})$. In the absence of the thermal noise, the quantum states of the signal considered here become pure and linearly independent. Thus we can apply Kennedy's lemma [1] to obtain the minimum value of the average probability of error and the optimum POM. The lemma ensures that the minimum value of the average probability of error for a linearly independent pure quantum state signal is attained by a quantum measurement described by a set of one-dimensional projection operators. This lemma greatly simplifies calculation of the minimum values of the average probability of error $P_{\mathrm{opt}}^{(0)}(\gamma, \phi, \mu, \nu)$. The analytic expressions of $P_{\mathrm{opt}}^{(0)}(\gamma, \phi, \mu, \nu)$ have been obtained for the several coherent state signals [1, 18]. Thus we can obtain the lower bound $P_{\mathrm{opt}}^{(0)}(\gamma, \phi, \tilde{\mu}, \tilde{\nu})$ under the influence of the thermal noise.

We now consider a binary signal detection process which is very important in practical digital communication systems. The signal takes quantum states $\hat{\rho}_1$ and $\hat{\rho}_2$ with prior probabilities p_1 and p_2, where the density operator $\hat{\rho}_j$ ($j = 1, 2$) is given in Eqs. (4) and (5). In the absence of the thermal noise, since the quantum state of the signal becomes pure, the minimum value of the average probability of error is obtained [1, 18] as

$$
P_{\mathrm{opt}}^{(0)} = \frac{1}{2} \left[1 - \sqrt{1 - \Gamma_{12}(\gamma, \phi, \mu, \nu)} \right],
\tag{28}
$$

where $\Gamma_{12}(\gamma, \phi, \mu, \nu) = |\langle\psi_1^{(0)}|\psi_2^{(0)}\rangle|^2$ and $|\psi_j^{(0)}\rangle = \hat{V}_j|0\rangle/\sqrt{\langle 0|\hat{V}_j^\dagger \hat{V}_j|0\rangle}$. Then the minimum value of the average probability of error P_{opt} in the binary signal detection process under the influence of the thermal noise satisfy the inequality,

$$P_{\text{opt}} \geq \frac{1}{2}\left[1 - \sqrt{1 - \Gamma_{12}(\gamma, \phi, \tilde{\mu}, \tilde{\nu})}\right],\tag{29}$$

where $\Gamma_{12}(\gamma, \phi, \tilde{\mu}, \tilde{\nu}) = |\langle\psi_1|\psi_2\rangle|^2$ and $|\psi_j\rangle = \hat{U}_j|0\rangle/\sqrt{\langle 0|\hat{U}_j^\dagger\hat{U}_j|0\rangle}$ and the operator $\hat{U}_j$ is given by Eq. (12).

Let us consider, for instance, the binary phase-shift keyed coherent state signal under the influence of the thermal noise, where $\hat{\rho}_1 = \hat{D}(\alpha)\hat{\rho}_{\text{th}}\hat{D}^\dagger(\alpha)$ and $\hat{\rho}_2 = \hat{D}(-\alpha)$ $\hat{\rho}_{\text{th}}\hat{D}^\dagger(-\alpha)$. For simplicity, we assume the equal prior probabilities, $p_1 = p_2 = \frac{1}{2}$. Since $\hat{V}_1 = \hat{D}(\alpha)$ and $\hat{V}_2 = \hat{D}(-\alpha)$, we obtain $\hat{U}_1 = \hat{D}(\alpha/\sqrt{1+2\bar{n}})$ and $\hat{U}_2 = \hat{D}(-\alpha/\sqrt{1+2\bar{n}})$. Thus the lower bound of the average probability of error is obtained by substituting $\Gamma_{12}(\gamma, \phi, \tilde{\mu}, \tilde{\nu}) = \exp\left[-4n_s/(1+2\bar{n})\right]$ into Eq. (29), where $n_s = |\alpha|^2$ is the average value of the photon number in each bit of the signal. Among the conventional optical measurements, the lower average probability of error for the binary phase-shift keyed coherent state signal is attained by the homodyne detection and it is given by $P_{\text{hom}} = \frac{1}{2}\left[1 - \text{erf}\left(\sqrt{2n_s/(1+2\bar{n})}\right)\right]$, where $\text{erf}(x) = \frac{2}{\sqrt{\pi}}\int_0^x dt\, e^{-t^2}$ is the error function. Since the minimum value of the average probability of error obtained by the quantum detection theory is smaller than the average probability of error in any conventional optical measurement, we can obtain the inequality,

$$\frac{1}{2}\left[1 - \text{erf}\left(\frac{D}{\sqrt{2}}\right)\right] \geq P_{\text{opt}} \geq \frac{1}{2}\left[1 - \sqrt{1 - \exp(-D^2)}\right],\tag{30}$$

where $D = \sqrt{4n_s/(1+2\bar{n})}$ represents the equivalent signal-to-noise ratio [1]. For an M-ary coherent state signal, where the quantum states are given by the density operators $\hat{\rho}_1, \hat{\rho}_2, \ldots, \hat{\rho}_M$ with $\hat{\rho}_j = \hat{D}(\alpha_j)\hat{\rho}_{\text{th}}\hat{D}^\dagger(\alpha_j)$, the lower bound of the average probability of error can be obtained by replacing the complex amplitude α_j with $\tilde{\alpha}_j = \alpha_j/\sqrt{1+2\bar{n}}$ in the minimum value of the average probability of error $P_{\text{opt}}^{(0)}(\alpha_1, \alpha_2, \ldots, \alpha_M)$ for the thermal noise-free M-ary coherent state signal whose quantum states are given by pure coherent states $|\alpha_1\rangle, |\alpha_2\rangle, \ldots, |\alpha_M\rangle$; that is, the lower bound of the average probability of error is given by $P_{\text{opt}}^{(0)}(\tilde{\alpha}_1, \tilde{\alpha}_2, \ldots, \tilde{\alpha}_M)$. In the absence of the thermal noise, since the analytic expressions of the minimum value of the average probability of error for the several coherent state signals have been obtained by the present authors [18], we can use the results to obtain the lower bounds of the average probability of error in the presence of the thermal noise.

5. SUMMARY

In this contribution, by means of the superoperator representation of quantum states, we have obtained the upper bound of the accessible information and the lower bound of the Bayes cost in the quantum detection processes for the Gaussian state signals under the influence of the thermal noise. The analytic expressions expressions of the upper and lower bounds for the binary quantum state signals have been given. The method we applied in this paper can be used for evaluating any quantity that is a function of the conditional probabilities, $P(\mu|j) = \text{Tr}[\hat{\Pi}_\mu\hat{\rho}_j]$. Let $\mathcal{F}(x)$ be an analytic function of x. Then for the Gaussian quantum state given in Eqs. (4) and (5), we can obtain the inequalities,

$$\max_{\hat{\Pi}\in\mathcal{U}}\mathcal{F}\left(\text{Tr}\left[\hat{\Pi}_\mu\hat{\rho}_j\right]\right) \leq \max_{\hat{\Pi}\in\mathcal{U}}\mathcal{F}\left(\text{Tr}\left[\hat{\Pi}_\mu|\psi_j\rangle\langle\psi_j|\right]\right),\tag{31}$$

$$\min_{\hat{\Pi}\in\mathcal{U}}\mathcal{F}\left(\text{Tr}\left[\hat{\Pi}_\mu\hat{\rho}_j\right]\right) \geq \min_{\hat{\Pi}\in\mathcal{U}}\mathcal{F}\left(\text{Tr}\left[\hat{\Pi}_\mu|\psi_j\rangle\langle\psi_j|\right]\right),\tag{32}$$

where the set $\mathcal{U}$ is given by Eq. (16). The superoperator representation of quantum states that we have used here seems to be very useful for investigating quantum communication and information systems under the influence of the thermal noise.

ACKNOWLEDGMENTS

One of the authors (M.B.) would like to thank Dr. M. Hirokawa of Tokyo Gakugei University for his useful comments on operator algebra. He is also grateful to the members of the quantum communication group of Tamagawa University for their hospitality.

REFERENCES

[1] C. W. Helstrom, *Quantum Detection and Estimation Theory* (Academic Press, New York, 1976).

[2] C. M. Caves and P. D. Drummond, Rev. Mod. Phys. **66**, 481 (1994).

[3] A. S. Holevo, Prob. Inf. Transm. **9**, 177 (1973); H. P. Yuen and M. Ozawa, Phys. Rev. Lett. **70**, 363 (1993).

[4] R. Jozsa, D. Robb and W. K. Wootters, Phys. Rev. A **49**, 668 (1994).

[5] C. A. Fuchs and C. M. Caves, Phys. Rev. Lett. **73**, 3047 (1994).

[6] C. H. Bennett, Physics Today **48** (No.10), 24 (1995); D. P. DiVincenzo, Science **270**, 255 (1995).

[7] A. S. Holevo, J. Multivar. Anal. **3**, 337 (1973).

[8] H. P. Yuen, R. S. Kennedy and M. Lax, IEEE Trans. Inform. Theory **IT-21**, 125 (1975); V. P. Belavkin, Statistics **1**, 315 (1975).

[9] B. L. Schumaker, Phys. Rep. **135**, 317 (1986).

[10] U. Fano, Rev. Mod. Phys. **26**, 74 (1957); J. A. Crawford, Nuovo Cimento **10**, 698 (1958); I. Prigogine, C. George, F. Henin and L. Rosenfeld, Chem. Scr. **4**, 5 (1973).

[11] H. Umezawa, *Advanced Field Theory* (American Institute of Physics, New York, 1993), and references therein.

[12] G. Lachs, Phys. Rev. **138**, B1012 (1965).

[13] M. S. Kim, F. A. M. de Oliveira and P. L. Knight, Phys. Rev. A **40**, 2494 (1989).

[14] M. Ban, J. Math. Phys. **33**, 3213 (1992); M. Ban, Phys. Rev. A **47**, 5093 (1993).

[15] R. M. Wilcox, J. Math. Phys. **8**, 962 (1967); M. Ban, J. Opt. Soc. Am. B **10**, 1347 (1993).

[16] M. Ban, M. Osaki ans O. Hirota, Phys. Rev. A **54**, 2718 (1996).

[17] L. B. Levitin, in *Quantum Communications and Measurement* (Plenum, New York, 1995) p.439; M. Ban, M. Osaki and O. Hirota, J. Mod. Opt. **43**, 2337 (1996).

[18] M. Osaki and O. Hirota, in *Quantum Communications and Measurement* (Plenum, New York, 1995) p.401; M. Osaki, M. Ban and O. Hirota, Phys. Rev. A **54**, 1691 (1996).

TECHNIQUES FOR BOUNDING QUANTUM CORRELATIONS

Michael J. W. Hall

Theoretical Physics, IAS, Australian National University
Canberra, ACT 0200, Australia

1. INTRODUCTION

This paper is concerned with the limits imposed by quantum mechanics on correlations between statistical sources. Typical examples are the correlations between the transmitter and receiver of a quantum communication channel, and between the measurement results of two detectors that make simultaneous measurements.

In the following section *mutual information* is identified as a natural figure of merit for the degree of correlation between two sources. While mutual information bounds are therefore emphasised in the paper, it should be noted that a number of the methods used to obtain these bounds are in fact applicable to all measures of correlation. In particular, some corresponding results for *coincidence rates* are given in sections 3–6.

In section 3, two basic types of quantum correlation are defined, corresponding to communication and joint-measurement contexts. The non-classical nature of such correlations with respect to mutual information is briefly discussed, via Bell-type inequalities in the joint-measurement context, and a semi-classical "quantum chessboard" example in the communication context.

In section 4, mappings between the communication and joint-measurement contexts are noted which allow results in one context to be obtained from results in the other context. In this way, for example, Holevo's bound for information transfer in the communication context [1,2] may be obtained from a joint-measurement inequality.

In section 5, a symmetry of quantum correlation in the communication context, between signal states and measurement results, is used to obtain measurement dependent correlation bounds from measurement independent bounds, and to estimate optimal bounds. As an example, a dual bound to Holevo's bound is found which depends upon the measurement made at the receiver.

Finally, in section 6 an information exclusion principle for complementary observables is described, which is typically stronger than Holevo's bound and allows derivation of the optimal signal states for optical communication based on homodyne and heterodyne detection.

2. MEASURES OF CORRELATION

Consider two statistical sources X and Y, which together generate joint pairs of outputs (for example, the transmitter and receiver of a communication channel, or two detectors making joint measurements). The pairwise correlation between X and Y is then characterised by a joint probability distribution, P_{XY}, where $P_{XY}(x, y)$ is the joint probability that source X generates output x and source Y generates output y.

It is useful to quantify the degree of correlation between X and Y by some measure $M[P_{XY}]$ (so that, e.g., different communication channels can be compared). There are some obvious properties that such a measure should satisfy: (i) the correlation of a source with another source cannot be greater than the correlation of the source with itself; (ii) the degree of correlation between two sources is symmetric with respect to the labelling of the sources; and (iii) the degree of correlation between two sources is not less than that of two uncorrelated sources with the same marginal probability distributions. These properties can be summarised respectively as

$$M[P_{XX}], M[P_{YY}] \geq M[P_{XY}] = M[P_{YX}] \geq M[P_X P_Y], \tag{1}$$

where $P_X(x)$, $P_Y(y)$ denote the marginal probability distributions for sources X and Y respectively.

A correlation measure satisfying (1) is the Shannon mutual information [3], defined by

$$I[P_{XY}] = \sum_{x,y} P_{XY}(x, y) \log_2 \frac{P_{XY}(x, y)}{P_X(x) P_Y(y)}. \tag{2}$$

This measure is moreover invariant under reparametrisations of both discrete and continuous outputs, and has a simple physical interpretation: it is the amount of data gained per output of a long sequence of outputs of one source, about the corresponding sequence of outputs of the other source (as measured by the number of bits required to represent the data) [3,4]. Note for discrete outputs that $I[P_{XX}]$ is just the entropy of source X.

Another common measure of correlation is the *coincidence rate*, with

$$C[P_{XY}] = \sum_x P_{XY}(x, x). \tag{3}$$

In a communication context $P_e = 1 - C[P_{XY}]$ is the average error probability of the channel. Note however that $C[P_{XY}]$ is only well-defined when there is an identification of the output ranges of X and Y, is not invariant under reparametrisations of continuous outputs, and does not in general satisfy the last inequality in (1).

3. CLASSICAL AND SEMI-CLASSICAL BOUNDS

Two formal types of quantum correlation may be defined according to their operator structure and generic physical context. The first is the *joint-measurement* context, where X and Y are two detectors which simultaneously measure observables M and N respectively for some input state ρ. If $\{M_i\}$ and $\{N_j\}$ are the commuting probability operator measures (POMs) for M and N respectively, the corresponding joint probability distribution is given by

$$P_{XY}(i, j) = tr[\rho M_i N_j]. \tag{4}$$

The second is the *communication* context, where X and Y are the transmitter and receiver respectively of a communication channel. If signal state ρ_i is transmitted with prior probability p_i, and an observable A with POM $\{A_j\}$ is measured at the receiver, then the corresponding joint probability distribution is

$$P_{XY}(i, j) = p_i tr[\rho_i A_j]. \tag{5}$$

The non-classical nature of quantum correlations in the joint-measurement context is perhaps best demonstrated by their violation of Bell-type inequalities. For example, if four experimentally testable propositions a, a', b, b' are assumed to have some joint probability distribution and either of a, a' may be jointly tested with either of b, b', with neither test influencing the statistics of the other (local realism), then the measured joint probabilities must satisfy the classical Bell inequality [5]

$$p(a, b) + p(a, b') + p(a', b) - p(a', b') \leq p(a) + p(b), \tag{6}$$

which is well known to be violated by some quantum systems. Analogously, if four observables A, A', B, B' have some joint probability distribution, and either of A, A' may be jointly measured with either of B, B', with neither measurement influencing the statistics of the other, one may derive a classical *information* Bell inequality [6]

$$I[P_{AB}] + I[P_{AB'}] + I[P_{A'B}] - I[P_{A'B'}] \leq I[P_{AA}] + I[P_{BB}], \tag{7}$$

which again is violated by some quantum systems.

Note that the formal similarity of (6) and (7) is not accidental: classical probabilities and entropies may both be defined as additive measures on Boolean algebras (see pp. 106-108 of [3]), and (6) and (7) represent a particular identity for certain such measures. Indeed, the same underlying identity leads to the *coincidence rate* Bell inequality

$$C[P_{AB}] + C[P_{AB'}] + C[P_{A'B}] - C[P_{A'B'}] \leq 2 \tag{8}$$

(which also follows directly from (6) above), for the case where A, A', B, B' have identical ranges of measurement outcomes.

In the communication context, the non-classical nature of quantum correlations may easily be seen by considering a semi-classical "quantum chessboard". Suppose in particular that signals correspond to placing a quantum system at random in one of a number of "squares" of a two-dimensional phase space, and are distinguished without error at the receiver. If the squares occupy a total area A of phase space, then the maximum number of distinct signals is at most $A/2\hbar$ from the uncertainty principle (since the system, and hence each "square", must occupy an area of at least $2\hbar$). Thus the number of binary digits required to represent the data gained per signal, i.e., the degree of correlation between the transmitter and receiver as measured by the mutual information, has the semi-classical upper bound

$$I_{max} \leq \log_2 A/(2\hbar). \tag{9}$$

This bound has a rigorous counterpart known as Holevo's bound (see next section), and is clearly quantum in origin. In particular, classical signals may occupy arbitrarily small phase space areas and hence have no analogous upper bound.

4. CONTEXT MAPPINGS

Mappings from one correlation context to the other provide a means to generate new bounds from old. The trick is to find mappings under which the joint probability distributions (4) and (5), and hence the corresponding measures of correlation, are invariant.

For example, in the joint-measurement context suppose that M and N are observables of two subsystems 1 and 2 respectively, where the composite system is described by state ρ. The mutual information calculated from (2) and (4), $I(M, N \mid \rho)$ say, then satisfies the inequality [7]

$$I(M, N \mid \rho) \leq S(\rho_1) + S(\rho_2) - S(\rho), \qquad (10)$$

ere $S(\sigma)$ denotes the quantum entropy $-tr[\sigma \log_2 \sigma]$ of state σ, and ρ_1, ρ_2 are the uced density operators for subsystems 1 and 2.

To translate (10) into the communication context, let $\mathcal{E}$ denote a signal ensemble $\{\rho_i; p_i\}$ with a countable number of signal states, and A a corresponding receiver measurement, with associated mutual information $I(A \mid \mathcal{E})$ calculated from (2) and (5). If $\{\mid \psi_i\rangle\}$ is a complete orthonormal basis in an ancillary Hilbert space, then define the *context mapping*

$$M_i = \mid \psi_i\rangle\langle\psi_i \mid, N_j = A_j, \rho = \sum_i p_i \mid \psi_i\rangle\langle\psi_i \mid \otimes \rho_i. \qquad (11)$$

The joint probability distributions calculated from (4) and (5) are then identical, and substitution of (11) into (10) yields the result

$$I(A \mid \mathcal{E}) \leq S(\sum_i p_i \rho_i) - \sum_i p_i S(\rho_i) \qquad (12)$$

in the communication context.

The derived inequality (12) may be recognised as Holevo's communication bound [1,2]. Note that in the semi-classical limit up to $A/2\hbar$ mutually orthogonal states can be assigned within an area A of a 2-dimensional phase space, and that the entropy of a mixture of N such states is bounded by $\log_2 N$. The Holevo bound (12) thus implies the "chessboard" bound (9) in the semi-classical limit.

As a second example of exploiting context mappings, consider a binary communication channel where two states ρ_0, ρ_1 are transmitted with probabilities p_0, p_1 respectively, and a two-valued measurement with POM $\{A_0, A_1\}$ is made at the receiver. The corresponding coincidence rate calculated from (3) and (5) then satisfies the tight upper bound [8]

$$C(A \mid \mathcal{E}) \leq p_0 + p_1 F(\rho_1 - (p_0/p_1)\rho_0), \qquad (13)$$

where $F(\eta)$ denotes the sum of the positive eigenvalues of operator η.

To obtain a matching result in the joint-measurement context, let M and N be (two-valued) observables for subsystems 1 and 2 respectively of a composite system described by some state ρ, with corresponding coincidence rate $C(M, N \mid \rho)$ calculated from (3) and (4), and define the context mapping

$$p_i = tr[\rho M_i], \rho_i = tr_1[\rho M_i]/tr[\rho M_i], A_j = N_j. \qquad (14)$$

The corresponding probability distributions calculated from (4) and (5) are then identical (even for *arbitrary* M and N), and substitution of (14) into (13) yields the tight upper bound

$$C(M, N \mid \rho) \leq tr[\rho M_0] + F(tr_1[\rho(M_1 - M_0)]) \qquad (15)$$

in the joint-measurement context (and a similar result with observables M, N and subsystems 1, 2 reversed).

In general, substitution of context mapping (11) into context mapping (14) yields an identity, but not vice versa, i.e., they are one-sided inverses. Thus while applying (11) to inequality (15) simply reproduces the original inequality (13), applying (14) to the Holevo bound (12) yields the new result

$$I(M, N \mid \rho) \leq S(\rho_2) - \sum_i tr[\rho M_i] S(tr_1[\rho M_i]/tr[\rho M_i]) \qquad (16)$$

(and a similar result with observables M, N and subsystems 1, 2 reversed).

Finally, note for the communication context that if the signal states ρ_i are *pure*, i.e., $\rho_i \equiv |\ s_i\rangle\langle s_i\ |$, then one may define an alternative context mapping by replacing ρ in (11) by the pure state $|\ \Psi\rangle\langle\Psi\ |$, where $|\ \Psi\rangle = \sum_i \sqrt{p_i}\ |\ \psi_i\rangle\otimes\ |\ s_i\rangle$. However, substitution of this mapping into, for example, the joint-measurement inequality (16), yields only $I(A\ |\ \mathcal{E}) \leq S(\sum_i p_i\ |\ s_i\rangle\langle s_i\ |)$, which is equivalent to the Holevo bound (12) for pure signal states.

5. SOURCE DUALITY

The central equality in (1) reflects the property that a measure of correlation should be symmetric with respect to the labelling of sources X and Y, which is indeed the case for both mutual information and coincidence rate. In fact, noting by definition that $P_{XY}(x, y) = P_{YX}(y, x)$, this property further holds for figures of merit of the general form

$$M = \sum_{x,y} P_{XY}(x, y)m(x, y) \qquad (17)$$

where m is any function satisfying $m(x, y) = m(y, x)$ (for example, the minimum variance measure with $m(x, y) = -(x - y)^2$).

The roles of sources X and Y do not change under relabelling in the joint-measurement context: both sources remain measurement detectors. This invariance is reflected by the formal symmetry of (4) with respect to the detector observables M and N. However, there is no such apparent symmetry reflected in (5) for the communication context: it is not immediately clear whether relabelling a transmitter as a receiver and vice versa can be formally modelled by mapping signal states to measurement outcomes and vice versa.

The structure of P_{XY} in (5) implies that a formal swapping of roles in the communication context would involve mapping the set of operators $\{p_i\rho_i\}$ to a POM $\{A'_i\}$, and mapping the POM $\{A_j\}$ to a set of operators $\{p'_j\rho'_j\}$, such that

$$p_i tr[\rho_i A_j] = p'_j tr[\rho'_j A'_i], \qquad (18)$$

and where $\mathcal{E}' = \{\rho'_j; p'_j\}$ is a signal ensemble. The communication channel $(\mathcal{E}, A)$ with transmitter X and receiver Y would then be formally equivalent to the communication channel $(\mathcal{E}', A')$ with transmitter Y and receiver X, where output pair (i, j) of $(\mathcal{E}, A)$ is identified with output pair (j, i) of $(\mathcal{E}', A')$.

The product form of (18) and the cyclic property of the trace operation immediately suggest looking for mappings of the form

$$p'_j\rho'_j = KA_jL, A'_i = L^{-1}p_i\rho_i K^{-1} \qquad (19)$$

for suitable operators K and L, so that (18) is satisfied identically. To determine K and L, note first that swapping the roles of transmitter and receiver *twice* should yield the original communication channel, implying from (19) that $K = L$. Summing over i in (19) then yields $1 = K^{-1}\sum_i p_i\rho_i K^{-1}$, and hence one has

$$K = L = (\sum p_i\rho_i)^{1/2}. \qquad (20)$$

Relation (18) (taking (19) and (20) as definitions), reflects a symmetry between the roles of sources X and Y in the communication context, and may therefore be called *source duality*. This symmetry was first noted in [9], in connection with mutual information for communication channels with discrete signal ensembles and POMs on finite Hilbert spaces. It is seen here that source duality is a fundamental symmetry in the communication context, and that *all* figures of merit satisfying the central equality in (1) (such as those in (17)) are invariant under this symmetry. This invariance under source duality allows results in the communication context to be mapped to "dual" results, and in particular for new bounds to be obtained from old ones.

For example, from (2), (5) and (18)-(20) one has $I(A \mid \mathcal{E}) = I(A' \mid \mathcal{E}')$, and hence from the Holevo bound (12) one may derive the *dual* bound

$$I(A \mid \mathcal{E}) \leq S(\sum_i p_i \rho_i) - \sum_j tr[KA_jK]S(KA_jK/tr[KA_jK]), \tag{21}$$

where K is defined in (20) above. An interesting feature of the dual Holevo bound (21) is that it is *measurement dependent.* Unfortunately, for the case of complete measurements ($A_j \equiv \mid a_j \rangle \langle a_j \mid$), the second term in (21) vanishes, and the dual bound becomes no stronger than the original bound (12). Hence the usefulness of the bound is primarily in the case of degenerate or incomplete measurements.

As a second example, from the coincidence rate bound (13) one can use source duality to obtain the (tight) dual bound

$$C(A \mid \mathcal{E}) = C(A' \mid \mathcal{E}') \leq tr[KA_0K] + F(KA_1K - KA_0K) \tag{22}$$

for binary communication, which again is measurement-dependent. For the case where the average signal state is proportional to the unit operator on a two-dimensional Hilbert space, i.e., $p_0\rho_0 + p_1\rho_1 = \frac{1}{2}\mathbf{1}$, this can be simplified to give

$$C(A \mid \mathcal{E}) \leq \frac{1}{2}(1 + tr[\| A_1 - A_0 \|]). \tag{23}$$

Further discussion of source duality, including the use of mappings (19) and (20) to estimate optimal bounds, will be given elsewhere [4].

6.   INFORMATION EXCLUSION

Attention is primarily restricted in this section to mutual information in the communication context, with generalisations to other figures of merit and to the joint-measurement context being discussed at the end.

From the complementarity of quantum observables, one expects that the better some observable A is at extracting information from a signal ensemble $\mathcal{E}$, the worse a complementary observable B will perform with respect to $\mathcal{E}$. This expectation may be given heuristic support by returning to the semi-classical "quantum chessboard" considered in section 3.

In particular, for a two-dimensional phase space with position and momentum coordinates X and P, consider a rectangular grid ("chessboard") on the phase space, with N_X columns parallel to the P-axis and N_P rows parallel to the X-axis. If signals are generated by placing a quantum system at random into one of the grid "squares", then a measurement of position will yield $\log_2 N_X$ bits of information, while a measurement of the complementary momentum observable will yield $\log_2 N_P$ bits of information. Moreover, since each signal must occupy an area of at least $2\hbar$, the total number of "squares" available, $N_X N_P$, is bounded by $(4\Delta X \Delta P)/(2\hbar)$, where ΔX and ΔP are the position and momentum half-widths of the "chessboard". Hence one has the semi-classical bound

$$I(X \mid \mathcal{E}) + I(P \mid \mathcal{E}) = \log_2 N_X + \log_2 N_P \leq \log_2 2\Delta X \Delta P/\hbar. \tag{24}$$

It is clear that (24) is a stronger result than the corresponding semi-classical bound (9) - not only are *each* of the position and momentum gains bounded by the logarithm of the number of non-overlapping states available, but so is their sum. Geometrically, the bound (9) states that the number of "squares" in a quantum chessboard is constrained by the phase space area available, while the bound (24) states further that for a given chessboard area one can only increase the number of rows at the expense of the number of columns, and vice versa.

Inequality (24) is an example of an *information exclusion relation* [10]. Such relations quantify the notion that the information which can be gained from measurement of a given observable, under some constraint, can be increased only at the expense of the information which can be gained from measurement of a complementary observable. Another example is the exclusion relation

$$I(\sigma_1 \mid \mathcal{E}) + I(\sigma_2 \mid \mathcal{E}) + I(\sigma_3 \mid \mathcal{E}) \leq \log_2 2 \tag{25}$$

for the information gains corresponding to orthogonal spin components of a spin-$\frac{1}{2}$ particle [10].

Remarkably, inequality (24) can in fact be *rigorously* derived [10], providing that if $\mathcal{E}$ denotes the signal ensemble $\{\rho_i; p_i\}$, then ΔX and ΔP are taken to be the root-mean-square deviations of position and momentum for the ensemble density operator $\rho_{\mathcal{E}} = \sum_i p_i \rho_i$. Moreover, as will be seen, it provides a stronger bound than both the Holevo bound (12) and the dual bound (21), and allows the optimal signal states to be derived for an optical communication channel based on either homodyne or balanced homodyne detection.

In particular, consider a harmonic oscillator (e.g., a single-mode optical field) with annihilation operator a, and define the quadrature observables X_1, X_2 by

$$X_1 = \frac{1}{2}(a + a^\dagger), X_2 = \frac{1}{2i}(a - a^\dagger). \tag{26}$$

The position and momentum observables are then proportional to X_1 and X_2 respectively. But, as may be verified from (2) with summation replaced by integration, mutual information is invariant under the rescaling of continuous outputs, and hence from (24) one finds

$$I(X_1 \mid \mathcal{E}) + I(X_2 \mid \mathcal{E}) \leq \log_2 4\Delta X_1 \Delta X_2. \tag{27}$$

Noting that the geometric mean is no greater than the arithmetic mean, one has

$$2\Delta X_1 \Delta X_2 \leq Var(X_1) + Var(X_2) \leq \langle X_1^2 + X_2^2 \rangle = \langle a^\dagger a + \frac{1}{2} \rangle, \tag{28}$$

and hence from (27) one has the information exclusion relation

$$I(X_1 \mid \mathcal{E}) + I(X_2 \mid \mathcal{E}) \leq \log_2[2n_s + 1] \tag{29}$$

for an ensemble of oscillators with average (photon) number $n_s = tr[\rho_{\mathcal{E}} a^\dagger a]$ per signal. This is rather stronger than the corresponding Holevo bound

$$I(X_1 \mid \mathcal{E}), I(X_2 \mid \mathcal{E}) \leq \log_2[n_s + 1] + n_s \log_2[1 + 1/n_s] \tag{30}$$

following from either of (12) or (21).

Ideal homodyne detection measures a quadrature observable of the field [2], and hence (29) restricts the amount of information which may be obtained via homodyne detection to be no greater than $\log_2[2n_s + 1]$. But this upper bound is known to be achievable via transmission of a Gaussian ensemble of squeezed-coherent states [2], and hence this is the *optimal* signal ensemble for single-mode optical communication based on homodyne detection. Note the optimal ensemble cannot be derived from the Holevo bound (30). Note also from (29) that the upper bound can only be achieved for quadrature X_1 if the information carried by the complementary quadrature X_2 is zero, and vice versa.

Ideal *heterodyne* detection (or equivalently balanced-homodyne detection) corresponds to a (non-ideal) *joint* measurement of quadratures X_1 and X_2. In particular, one measures the commuting observables $X_1 + Y_1$, $X_2 - Y_2$, where Y_1, Y_2 are orthogonal quadratures of a second "image-band" field [2]. Since two oscillators are involved, one must consider a *four*-dimensional quantum chessboard to obtain a relevant information exclusion relation.

In particular, for a four-dimensional phase space with position and momentum observables X, X', P, P', one may, either by heuristically counting hypercubes on a 4-dimensional chessboard or by rigorous calculation [10], obtain the exclusion relation

$$I(X, X' \mid \mathcal{E}) + I(P, P' \mid \mathcal{E}) \leq \log_2 16 \Delta X \Delta X' \Delta P \Delta P'/(2\hbar)^2, \tag{31}$$

in analogy to (24). Choosing X, X', P, P' to be proportional to the observables $X_1 + Y_1$, $X_2 - Y_2$, $X_2 + Y_2$, $X_1 - Y_1$ respectively, and assuming that the second oscillator is in its ground state, this reduces to

$$I(X_1 + Y_1, X_2 - Y_2 \mid \mathcal{E}) + I(X_2 + Y_2, X_1 - Y_1 \mid \mathcal{E}) \leq \log_2[4Var(X_1 + \frac{1}{4})Var(X_2 + \frac{1}{4})]$$
$$\leq 2\log_2[n_s + 1], \tag{32}$$

where the second line follows using a similar relation to (28).

Now, the first term in (32) is by definition the information gain corresponding to ideal heterodyne detection, $I(Het \mid \mathcal{E})$ say. Moreover, the second term is the information gained by ideal heterodyne detection in the case that the annihilation operator b of the second oscillator is replaced by $-b$ (i.e., Y_1 and Y_2 are replaced by $-Y_1$ and $-Y_2$ respectively). But such a replacement is equivalent to instead replacing the vacuum state of the second oscillator (defined by $b \mid 0\rangle = 0$), by the state defined by $-b \mid 0\rangle = 0$, which is of course the same state. Thus the second term is also equal to $I(Het \mid \mathcal{E})$, and (32) simplifies to

$$I(Het \mid \mathcal{E}) \leq \log_2[n_s + 1]. \tag{33}$$

The upper bound (33) is again stronger than the corresponding Holevo upper bound in (30) above. Moreover, the bound in (33) may be achieved via transmission of a Gaussian ensemble of Glauber coherent states [2], and hence this is the *optimal* signal ensemble for single-mode optical communication based on ideal heterodyne detection.

In practice, homodyne and heterodyne measurements will not be ideal, and the exclusion relations (29) and (33) must be generalised to take account of noise. For the case of *Gaussian* noise (e.g., arising from thermal noise, linear amplification/attenuation, and/or detector inefficiencies), the exclusion relations (29) and (33) have been generalised in [10] and [4] respectively, with

$$I(X_1 \mid \mathcal{E}, n_\gamma) + I(X_2 \mid \mathcal{E}, n_\gamma) \leq \log_2[1 + n_s/(n_\gamma + 1/2)], \tag{34}$$

$$I(Het \mid \mathcal{E}, n_\gamma) \leq \log_2[1 + n_s/(n_\gamma + 1)], \tag{35}$$

where n_γ denotes the noise variance. The optimal signal ensemble for homodyne detection in the absence of noise does not achieve the upper bound in (34) (*cf.* Eq. (40)

of [11]), and hence it is not known whether it remains optimal in the presence of noise. However, for heterodyne detection the upper bound in (35) is again achievable via transmission of a Gaussian ensemble of coherent states, for *any* value of n_γ (*cf.* Eq. (30) of [11]), and hence this signal ensemble remains optimal in the presence of noise.

Context mappings and source duality (sections 4 and 5) may be applied to information exclusion relations to obtain new results. For example, the relation

$$I(M, \sigma_1 \mid \rho) + I(M, \sigma_2 \mid \rho) + I(M, \sigma_3 \mid \rho) \leq \log_2 2 \tag{36}$$

follows immediately from (25) and the context mapping (15), where M is any observable of some quantum system, and $\sigma_1, \sigma_2, \sigma_3$ are orthogonal spin components of a spin-$\frac{1}{2}$ particle. Thus M can be strongly correlated with a given spin component only at the expense of being weakly correlated with the complementary spin components.

Finally, one may search for analogous exclusion relations for other measures of correlation, such as coincidence rate. For example, it is not difficult to show that

$$C(A \mid \mathcal{E}) + C(B \mid \mathcal{E}) \leq 1 + \max_{a,b} \mid \langle a \mid b \rangle \mid \tag{37}$$

for Hermitian observables A, B with normalised eigenstates $\{\mid a \rangle\}$, $\{\mid b \rangle\}$ respectively. The usefulness of such a bound is not clear however, as the upper bound is "weak" in the sense that it cannot generally be attained when one of $C(A \mid \mathcal{E})$, $C(B \mid \mathcal{E})$ has a value corresponding to random correlation (i.e., $1/N$ for the case of N possible measurement outcomes). This is a consequence of the violation in general of the last inequality in (1) for coincidence rates.

REFERENCES

[1] A S Holevo *Probl. Inf. Trans.* **9** (1973) 177; H P Yuen and M Ozawa *Phys. Rev. Lett.* **70** (1993) 363.

[2] C M Caves and P D Drummond *Rev. Mod. Phys.* **66** (1994) 481.

[3] F M Reza *An Introduction to Information Theory* (McGraw-Hill, New York, 1961).

[4] M J W Hall *Phys. Rev. A* **55** (1997) 100.

[5] A Fine *Phys. Rev. Lett.* **48** (1982) 291.

[6] S L Braunstein and C M Caves *Ann. Phys. (N.Y.)* (1990) 22, Eq. (6.5); N J Cerf and C Adami (unpublished), Eq. (21).

[7] G Lindblad *Commun. Math. Phys.* **33** (1973) 305; S M Barnett and S J D Phoenix *Phys. Rev. A* **44** (1991) 535.

[8] C W Helstrom *Quantum Detection and Estimation Theory* (Academic, New York, 1976), section IV.2(a).

[9] L P Hughston, R Josza, and W K Wootters *Phys. Lett. A* **183** (1993) 14.

[10] M J W Hall *Phys. Rev. Lett.* **74** (1995) 3307.

[11] M J W Hall *Phys. Rev. A* **50** (1994) 3295.

RELATION BETWEEN CHANNEL CAPACITY AND QUANTUM MINIMAX DECISION IN QUANTUM INFORMATION THEORY

Kentaro Kato[1], Masao Osaki[1], Tomohiro Suzuki[1], Masashi Ban[2], and Osamu Hirota[1]

[1] Research Center for Quantum Communications,
 Tamagawa University, Machida, Tokyo, Japan
[2] Advanced Research Laboratory, Hitachi, Ltd.
 Akanuma 2520, Hatoyama, Saitama 350-03, Japan

1. INTRODUCTION

Derivation of the optimum detection operators for the mutual information is one of the most important topics to establish the quantum information theory. For information-optimum detection, Holevo has shown a necessary condition of the information-optimum detection operators [1]. However, the explicit representation of the information-optimum detection operators has not been given except for a few cases [2–4]. So far there were researches about the upper or lower bound of the accessible information which is the optimum (maximum) mutual information for given signal quantum states with coding theory. In the general case, the upper bound is given by Holevo, called "Holevo's bound" [5] and the lower bound is the "subentropy" defined by Jozsa [6]. In some cases of specified signal quantum states and detection process, Ban and Schumacher showed tighter upper bounds, respectively [7,8].

On the other hand, we have shown analytical representations of the optimum detection operators that minimize the error probability for some signal quantum states [9,10]. It was based on the fundamental researches of the optimum detections for the error probability [1,11–14]. In the derivation process, it was revealed that the quantum minimax formula can give more solutions than the quantum Bayes formula.

In this paper, we would like to show the explicit representation of the information-optimum detection operators for some signal quantum states. This means, we show that the solutions of the quantum minimax formula satisfy the necessary condition of the information-optimum detection for binary, ternary, and quadrature phase shift keyed signals with coherent states.

2. OPTIMUM CONDITIONS FOR MUTUAL INFORMATION AND ERROR PROBABILITY

The mutual information, defined as follows, is one of the parameters to evaluate a detection system.

$$I = \sum_i \xi_i \sum_j P(j|i) \log \left[\frac{P(j|i)}{\sum_k \xi_k P(j|k)} \right],$$ (1)

where ξ_i is *a priori* probability of the signal i and $P(j|i)$ is a conditional probability that the signal j is chosen when the signal i is true. A detection of some signal quantum states is also characterized by this conditional probability that is described by a density operator of a signal $\hat{\rho}_i$ and a detection operator $\hat{\Pi}_j$ as follows:

$$P(j|i) = \text{Tr}\hat{\rho}_i \hat{\Pi}_j = \text{Tr}\hat{\Pi}_j \hat{\rho}_i.$$ (2)

The detection operator is a simultaneous representation of a measurement and a decision processes. In general, it is a probability operator-valued measure (POM) satisfying the following conditions.

$$\sum_i \hat{\Pi}_i = \hat{I}, \quad \hat{\Pi}_i \geq 0, \forall i.$$ (3)

2.1. INFORMATION-OPTIMUM DETECTION

The information-optimum detection is a detection maximizing the mutual information with respect to the detection operators. Therefore the optimum mutual information is defined as follows:

$$\max_{\hat{\Pi}} I = \max_{\hat{\Pi}} \left(\sum_i \xi_i \sum_j \text{Tr}\hat{\Pi}_j \hat{\rho}_i \log \left[\frac{\text{Tr}\hat{\Pi}_j \hat{\rho}_i}{\sum_k \xi_k \text{Tr}\hat{\Pi}_j \hat{\rho}_k} \right] \right).$$ (4)

Based on this concept, Holevo gave the necessary condition to the detection operators maximizing the mutual information as follows [1]:

$$\hat{\Pi}_i \left(\hat{F}_i - \hat{F}_j \right) \hat{\Pi}_j = 0, \forall i, j,$$ (5)

where

$$\hat{F}_j = \sum_l \xi_l \log \left[\frac{P(j|l)}{\sum_k \xi_k P(j|k)} \right] \hat{\rho}_l.$$ (6)

In general, this necessary condition is too difficult to be solved.

2.2. QUANTUM MINIMAX FORMULA

The alternative parameter to evaluate the detection performance is the error probability defined as follows:

$$P_e = 1 - \sum_i \xi_i P(i|i),$$ (7)

and the optimization formulae are known as the quantum Bayes, Neyman-Pearson, and minimax formulae [1, 11–14]. Especially the quantum minimax formula can give more solutions than others. The necessary and sufficient condition of the quantum minimax formula is as follows:

$$\begin{aligned} \text{Tr}\hat{\Pi}_i \hat{\rho}_i &= \text{Tr}\hat{\Pi}_j \hat{\rho}_j, \quad \forall i, j, \\ \hat{\Pi}_i \left[\xi_i \hat{\rho}_i - \xi_j \hat{\rho}_j \right] \hat{\Pi}_j &= 0, \quad \forall i, j, \\ \hat{\Gamma} - \xi_i \hat{\rho}_i &\geq 0, \quad \forall i, \end{aligned}$$ (8)

where $\hat{\Gamma}$ is called a "Lagrange operator" defined by

$$\hat{\Gamma} = \sum_{i=1}^{M} \xi_i \hat{\rho}_i \hat{\Pi}_i. \tag{9}$$

3. INFORMATION-OPTIMUM DETECTION PROCESS

Let us show that the optimum detection operators by the quantum minimax formula satisfy the necessary condition of the information-optimum detection. In the proofs, the signal quantum states are assumed to be binary, ternary, and quaternary phase shift keyed signals with coherent states.

3.1. BINARY PHASE SHIFT KEYED SIGNAL

In the case of the binary phase shift keyed signal with coherent states $|\alpha\rangle, |-\alpha\rangle$, the solution of the quantum minimax formula in Eq. (8) satisfies the following conditions.

$$\begin{aligned}
P(1|1) &= P(2|2), \\
P(2|1) &= P(1|2), \\
\xi_1 &= \xi_2 = \tfrac{1}{2}.
\end{aligned} \tag{10}$$

where we used

$$P(2|1) = 1 - P(1|1), P(1|2) = 1 - P(2|2). \tag{11}$$

Since $\xi_1 = \xi_2 = \tfrac{1}{2}$, Eq. (8) also supplies the condition as follows:

$$\hat{\Pi}_1 \left[\hat{\rho}_1 - \hat{\rho}_2 \right] \hat{\Pi}_2 = 0. \tag{12}$$

For binary signals, there is possibility to treat general signal quantum states. If *a priori* probabilities of signals resulting from the quantum minimax formula are equal, namely, $\xi_1 = \xi_2 = \tfrac{1}{2}$, the signal quantum states can be selected arbitrary. For examples, in the case of all the pure states or some mixed states.

Then, $\hat{F}_1$ and $\hat{F}_2$ in Eq. (6) can be written down with Eq. (10) as follows:

$$\begin{aligned}
\hat{F}_1 &= \tfrac{1}{2} \log \left[\frac{P(1|1)}{\frac{1}{2}P(1|1) + \frac{1}{2}P(1|2)} \right] \hat{\rho}_1 + \tfrac{1}{2} \log \left[\frac{P(1|2)}{\frac{1}{2}P(1|1) + \frac{1}{2}P(1|2)} \right] \hat{\rho}_2 \\
&= \tfrac{1}{2} \log \left[2P(1|1) \right] \hat{\rho}_1 + \tfrac{1}{2} \log \left[2P(1|2) \right] \hat{\rho}_2 \\
&\equiv A\hat{\rho}_1 + B\hat{\rho}_2, \\
\hat{F}_2 &= \tfrac{1}{2} \log \left[\frac{P(2|1)}{\frac{1}{2}P(2|1) + \frac{1}{2}P(2|2)} \right] \hat{\rho}_1 + \tfrac{1}{2} \log \left[\frac{P(2|2)}{\frac{1}{2}P(2|1) + \frac{1}{2}P(2|2)} \right] \hat{\rho}_2 \\
&= \tfrac{1}{2} \log \left[2P(2|1) \right] \hat{\rho}_1 + \tfrac{1}{2} \log \left[2P(2|2) \right] \hat{\rho}_2 \\
&\equiv B\hat{\rho}_1 + A\hat{\rho}_2,
\end{aligned} \tag{13}$$

where we define A and B as follows:

$$\begin{aligned}
A &\equiv \tfrac{1}{2} \log \left[2P(1|1) \right] = \tfrac{1}{2} \log \left[2P(2|2) \right], \\
B &\equiv \tfrac{1}{2} \log \left[2P(2|1) \right] = \tfrac{1}{2} \log \left[2P(1|2) \right].
\end{aligned} \tag{14}$$

Evidently, subtraction of $\hat{F}_1$ and $\hat{F}_2$ is as follows:

$$\begin{aligned}
\hat{F}_1 - \hat{F}_2 &= A\hat{\rho}_1 + B\hat{\rho}_2 - B\hat{\rho}_1 - A\hat{\rho}_2 \\
&= (A - B)(\hat{\rho}_1 - \hat{\rho}_2).
\end{aligned} \tag{15}$$

The necessary condition in Eq. (5) is satisfied with Eq. (12),

$$\hat{\Pi}_1 (\hat{F}_1 - \hat{F}_2) \hat{\Pi}_2 = (A - B) \cdot \hat{\Pi}_1 (\hat{\rho}_1 - \hat{\rho}_2) \hat{\Pi}_2 = 0, \tag{16}$$

since $(A-B)$ is not equal to zero except for $P(1|1) = P(2|1)$ (in this case, no information can be obtained).

Therefore it is proved that the optimum detection operators by the quantum minimax formula satisfy the necessary condition of the information-optimum detection.

3.2. TERNARY PHASE SHIFT KEYED SIGNAL

Let us assume the signal quantum states as follows:

$$|\alpha\rangle, |\alpha e^{i\frac{2\pi}{3}}\rangle, |\alpha e^{-i\frac{2\pi}{3}}\rangle. \tag{17}$$

Then the solution of the quantum minimax formula satisfy the next conditions.

$$
\begin{aligned}
&P(1|1) = P(2|2) = P(3|3), \\
&P(2|1) = P(3|1) = P(1|2) = P(3|2) = P(1|3) = P(2|3), \\
&\xi_1 = \xi_2 = \xi_3 = \tfrac{1}{3}.
\end{aligned}
\tag{18}
$$

Furthermore, the optimum detection operators by the quantum minimax formula in Eq. (8) hold the next conditions.

$$\hat{\Pi}_1(\hat{\rho}_1 - \hat{\rho}_2)\hat{\Pi}_2 = \hat{\Pi}_2(\hat{\rho}_2 - \hat{\rho}_3)\hat{\Pi}_3 = \hat{\Pi}_3(\hat{\rho}_3 - \hat{\rho}_1)\hat{\Pi}_1 = 0. \tag{19}$$

With the conditions by Eq. (18), the representations of $\hat{F}_j, j = 1, 2, 3$ in Eq. (6) are simplified as follows:

$$
\begin{aligned}
\hat{F}_1 &= \tfrac{1}{3}\left\{\log\left[3P(1|1)\right]\hat{\rho}_1 + \log\left[3P(1|2)\right]\hat{\rho}_2 + \log\left[3P(1|3)\right]\hat{\rho}_3\right\} \\
&\equiv A'\hat{\rho}_1 + B'\hat{\rho}_2 + B'\hat{\rho}_3, \\
\hat{F}_2 &= \tfrac{1}{3}\left\{\log\left[3P(2|1)\right]\hat{\rho}_1 + \log\left[3P(2|2)\right]\hat{\rho}_2 + \log\left[3P(2|3)\right]\hat{\rho}_3\right\} \\
&\equiv B'\hat{\rho}_1 + A'\hat{\rho}_2 + B'\hat{\rho}_3, \\
\hat{F}_3 &= \tfrac{1}{3}\left\{\log\left[3P(3|1)\right]\hat{\rho}_1 + \log\left[3P(3|2)\right]\hat{\rho}_2 + \log\left[3P(3|3)\right]\hat{\rho}_3\right\} \\
&\equiv B'\hat{\rho}_1 + B'\hat{\rho}_2 + A'\hat{\rho}_3,
\end{aligned}
\tag{20}
$$

where we defined the parameters as follows:

$$
\begin{aligned}
A' &\equiv \tfrac{1}{3}\log\left[3P(i|i)\right], \forall i, \\
B' &\equiv \tfrac{1}{3}\log\left[3P(i|j)\right], \forall i, j(i \neq j).
\end{aligned}
\tag{21}
$$

Then, it is easy to find the following relations of $\hat{F}_j$'s.

$$
\begin{aligned}
\hat{F}_1 - \hat{F}_2 &= (A' - B')(\hat{\rho}_1 - \hat{\rho}_2), \\
\hat{F}_2 - \hat{F}_3 &= (A' - B')(\hat{\rho}_2 - \hat{\rho}_3), \\
\hat{F}_3 - \hat{F}_1 &= (A' - B')(\hat{\rho}_3 - \hat{\rho}_1).
\end{aligned}
\tag{22}
$$

Finally, the necessary condition in Eq. (5) is satisfied with the conditions in Eq. (19)

$$\hat{\Pi}_i(\hat{F}_i - \hat{F}_j)\hat{\Pi}_j = (A' - B') \cdot \hat{\Pi}_i(\hat{\rho}_i - \hat{\rho}_j)\hat{\Pi}_j = 0, \forall i, j. \tag{23}$$

3.3. QUADRATURE PHASE SHIFT KEYED SIGNAL

The quadrature phase shift keyed signal with coherent states are given as follows:

$$|\alpha\rangle, |i\alpha\rangle, |-\alpha\rangle, |-i\alpha\rangle. \tag{24}$$

The solution of the quantum minimax formula satisfy the next conditions.

$$P(1|1) = P(2|2) = P(3|3) = P(4|4),$$
$$P(2|1) = P(4|1) = P(1|2) = P(3|2) = P(2|3) = P(4|3) = P(1|4) = P(3|4),$$
$$P(3|1) = P(4|2) = P(1|3) = P(2|4),$$
$$\xi_1 = \xi_2 = \xi_3 = \xi_4 = \tfrac{1}{4},$$

(25)

and

$$\hat{\Pi}_i(\hat{\rho}_i - \hat{\rho}_j)\hat{\Pi}_j = 0, \forall i, j.$$

(26)

While the proof of this case becomes a little complex compared with the others, it can be proved with the same manner of the previous cases and the fundamental properties of the optimum detection operators by the quantum minimax formula. Detailed discussion will be given in subsequent papers.

4. NUMERICAL ANALYSES OF THE OPTIMUM MUTUAL INFORMATION

As shown in the previous section, it is proved that the necessary condition of the information-optimum detection is satisfied by the solutions of the quantum minimax formula. Then, we give the following conjecture.

Conjecture *the mutual information attained by the optimum detection operators of the quantum minimax formula is the optimum mutual information for set of states with certain symmetry.*

To evaluate the optimum mutual information, it is compared with Holevo's bound (upper bound), the subentropy (lower bound), and the mutual information achieved by a conventional detector, such as a homodyne or a heterodyne detector.

Holevo's bound for pure signal quantum states is given by the von Neumann entropy defined as follows:

$$S = -\text{Tr}\hat{\rho}_{\text{total}} \log \hat{\rho}_{\text{total}},$$

(27)

where $\hat{\rho}_{\text{total}} = \sum_i \xi_i \hat{\rho}_i$. With the eigenvalues of the density operator $\hat{\rho}_{\text{total}}$, denoting λ_j, Eq. (27) can be rewritten as follows:

$$S = -\sum_j \lambda_j \log \lambda_j.$$

(28)

The subentropy, proposed by Jozsa [6], is defined with the eigenvalues of the density operator as follows:

$$Q = -\sum_{k=1}^{n} \left(\prod_{l \neq k} \frac{\lambda_k}{\lambda_k - \lambda_l} \right) \lambda_k \log \lambda_k.$$

(29)

The mutual information achieved by the homodyne or the heterodyne detector is given in appendix A.

4.1. BINARY PHASE SHIFT KEYED (BPSK) SIGNAL

To compare the each information, the absolute value of the inner product of signal quantum states is used as a common parameter. For the binary phase shift keyed signal with coherent states, it becomes as follows:

$$k \equiv \langle \alpha | - \alpha \rangle = \exp[-2|\alpha|^2].$$

(30)

Each mutual information is depicted in Fig. 1.

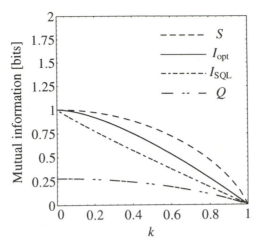

Figure 1. Mutual information for BPSK signal. S: Holevo bound, I_{opt}: the optimum mutual information, I_{SQL}: mutual information by homodyne, and Q: subentropy.

4.2. TERNARY PHASE SHIFT KEYED (3PSK) SIGNAL

For the ternary phase shift keyed signal, the absolute value of the inner product that is used as a common parameter is as follows:

$$k \equiv |\kappa| = \left|\langle\alpha|\alpha e^{i\frac{2\pi}{3}}\rangle\right| = \left|\langle\alpha|\alpha e^{-i\frac{2\pi}{3}}\rangle\right| = \exp[-\frac{3}{2}|\alpha|^2]. \tag{31}$$

In Fig. 2, the results are given.

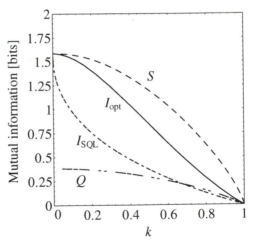

Figure 2. Mutual information for 3PSK signal. S: Holevo bound, I_{opt}: the optimum mutual information, I_{SQL}: mutual information by heterodyne, and Q: subentropy.

4.3. QUADRATURE PHASE SHIFT KEYED (QPSK) SIGNAL

For the quadrature phase shift keyed signal, the common parameter is the absolute value of one of the inner products defined as follows:

$$k \equiv |\kappa| = |\langle\alpha|i\alpha\rangle| = \exp[-|\alpha|^2]. \tag{32}$$

Each mutual information is compared in Fig. 3.

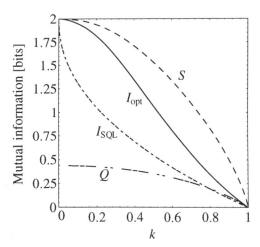

Figure 3. Mutual information for QPSK signal. S: Holevo bound, I_{opt}: the optimum mutual information, I_{SQL}: mutual information by heterodyne, and Q: subentropy.

5. CONCLUSION

In this paper, we have shown that the necessary condition of the information-optimum detection is satisfied by the optimum detection operators derived from the quantum minimax formula for the coherent state signals of binary, ternary and quadrature phase shift keyed. It is true that the condition is just only necessary condition, so that the information-optimum detection operators may be different from those by the quantum minimax formula. From the comparison by the numerical results, however, the mutual information obtained by these detection operators is much superior to those by conventional detectors and exists between Holevo's bound and the subentropy. Hence we make a conjecture that the mutual information attained by the optimum detection operators of the quantum minimax formula is the optimum mutual information for set of states with certain symmetry. In other words, the optimum detection operators by the quantum minimax formula describe the information-optimum detection processes for set of states with certain symmetry.

Furthermore, the minimax condition is satisfied when all *a priori* probabilities of signals are equal each other for these signal quantum states. This situation corresponds to the maximization of the original information, namely, our obtained optimum mutual information will be the channel capacity for the code length one.

A. CONVENTIONAL DETECTIONS

Homodyne and heterodyne detections are the measurements of the quadrature amplitudes defined as follows:

$$\hat{x}_c = \frac{\hat{a} + \hat{a}^\dagger}{2}, \hat{x}_s = \frac{\hat{a} - \hat{a}^\dagger}{2i},$$ (33)

where $\hat{a}$ and $\hat{a}^\dagger$ are the photon annihilation and creation operators, respectively. That is, the homodyne measures one of the quadrature amplitudes and the heterodyne measures both of them simultaneously.

A.1. HOMODYNE DETECTION OF THE BINARY PHASE SHIFT KEYED SIGNAL

Since the signal quantum states are assumed to be the coherent states, probability density functions by a homodyne receiver are represented as follows:

$$
\begin{aligned}
p(x_c|1) &= \sqrt{\tfrac{2}{\pi}} \exp\left[-2(x_c - \alpha)^2\right], \\
p(x_c|2) &= \sqrt{\tfrac{2}{\pi}} \exp\left[-2(x_c + \alpha)^2\right].
\end{aligned}
\tag{34}
$$

Then, the conditional probabilities used in Eq. (1) are given as follows:

$$
\begin{cases}
P(1|1) = \displaystyle\int_0^\infty p(x_c|1)\mathrm{d}x_c, & P(2|1) = \displaystyle\int_{-\infty}^0 p(x_c|1)\mathrm{d}x_c, \\
P(1|2) = \displaystyle\int_0^\infty p(x_c|2)\mathrm{d}x_c, & P(2|2) = \displaystyle\int_{-\infty}^0 p(x_c|2)\mathrm{d}x_c.
\end{cases}
\tag{35}
$$

A.2. HETERODYNE DETECTION OF THE TERNARY PHASE SHIFT KEYED SIGNAL

For the ternary phase shift keyed signal, heterodyne detection is a conventional detection scheme. The probability density functions by a heterodyne receiver are given as follows:

$$
\begin{aligned}
p(x_c, x_s|1) &= \tfrac{1}{\pi} \exp\left[-(x_c - \alpha)^2 - x_s^2\right], \\
p(x_c, x_s|2) &= \tfrac{1}{\pi} \exp\left[-(x_c + \tfrac{\alpha}{2})^2 - (x_s - \tfrac{\sqrt{3}\alpha}{2})^2\right], \\
p(x_c, x_s|3) &= \tfrac{1}{\pi} \exp\left[-(x_c + \tfrac{\alpha}{2})^2 - (x_s + \tfrac{\sqrt{3}\alpha}{2})^2\right].
\end{aligned}
\tag{36}
$$

Conditional probabilities are presented as follows:

$$
P(j|i) = \iint_{D_j} p(x_c, x_s|i)\mathrm{d}x_c\mathrm{d}x_s,
\tag{37}
$$

where

$$
\begin{aligned}
D_1 &= \left\{(x_c, x_s)|x_c \geq 0, -\sqrt{3}x_c \leq x_s < \sqrt{3}x_c\right\}, \\
D_2 &= \left\{(x_c, x_s)|x_c \geq 0, x_s \geq \sqrt{3}x_c\right\} \cup \left\{(x_c, x_s)|x_c < 0, x_s > 0\right\}, \\
D_3 &= \left\{(x_c, x_s)|x_c \geq 0, x_s < -\sqrt{3}x_c\right\} \cup \left\{(x_c, x_s)|x_c < 0, x_s \leq 0\right\}.
\end{aligned}
\tag{38}
$$

A.3. HETERODYNE DETECTION OF THE QUADRATURE PHASE SHIFT KEYED SIGNAL

Probability density functions are defined as follows:

$$
\begin{aligned}
p(x_c, x_s|1) &= \tfrac{1}{\pi} \exp\left[-(x_c - \alpha)^2 - x_s^2\right], \\
p(x_c, x_s|2) &= \tfrac{1}{\pi} \exp\left[-x_c^2 - (x_s - \alpha)^2\right], \\
p(x_c, x_s|3) &= \tfrac{1}{\pi} \exp\left[-(x_c + \alpha)^2 - x_s^2\right], \\
p(x_c, x_s|4) &= \tfrac{1}{\pi} \exp\left[-x_c^2 - (x_s + \alpha)^2\right].
\end{aligned}
\tag{39}
$$

Conditional probabilities are presented as follows:

$$
P(j|i) = \iint_{D_j} p(x_c, x_s|i)\mathrm{d}x_c\mathrm{d}x_s,
\tag{40}
$$

where

$$
\begin{aligned}
D_1 &= \left\{(x_c, x_s)|x_c \geq 0, -x_c \leq x_s < x_c\right\}, \\
D_2 &= \left\{(x_c, x_s)| - x_s < x_c \leq x_s, x_s \geq 0\right\}, \\
D_3 &= \left\{(x_c, x_s)|x_c < 0, x_c < x_s \leq -x_c\right\}, \\
D_4 &= \left\{(x_c, x_s)|x_s \leq x_c < -x_s, x_s < 0\right\}.
\end{aligned}
\tag{41}
$$

REFERENCES

[1] A. S. Holevo, J. Multivar. Anal., **3**, 337, (1973).

[2] E. B. Davies, IEEE Trans. Inform. Theory, **IT24**, 596, (1978).

[3] L. B. Levitin, in *Information, Complexity, and Control in Quantum Physics*, edited by A. Blaquière, S. Diner, and G. Lochak (Springer, Vienna, 1987).

[4] M. Ban, M. Osaki, and O. Hirota, J. Mod. Opt., **43**, 2337 (1996).

[5] A. S. Holevo, Probl. Inf. Transm. (USSR) **9**, 177, (1973) [Probl. Peredachi Inf. **9** (3), (1973)].

[6] R. Jozsa, D. Robb, and W. K. Wootters Phys. Rev. A, **49**, 668, (1994).

[7] B. Schumacher, M. Westmoreland, and W. K. Wootters, Phys. Rev. Lett. **76**, 3452, (1996).

[8] M. Ban, M. Osaki, and O. Hirota, Phys. Rev. A, **54**, 2718 (1996).

[9] M. Osaki, and O. Hirota, in *Quantum Communications and Measurement*, edited by V. P. Belavkin, O. Hirota, and R. L. Hudson (Plenum Publishing, NY, 1995), p.401.

[10] M. Osaki, M. Ban, and O. Hirota, Phys. Rev. A, **54**, 1691, (1996).

[11] C. W. Helstrom, *Quantum Detection and Estimation Theory.* (Academic Press, NY, 1976).

[12] H. P. Yuen, R. S. Kennedy, and M. Lax, IEEE Trans. Inform. Theory, **IT-21**, 125, (1975).

[13] A. S. Holevo, *Proceedings of the Steklov Institute of Mathematics,* **124**, (1976). AMS Transl. Issue3, (1978).

[14] O. Hirota and S. Ikehara, The Trans. the IECE Japan, **E65**, 627, (1982).

OPTIMUM BINARY SIGNAL DETECTIONS
FOR ERROR PROBABILITY AND MUTUAL INFORMATION

Masao Osaki[1], Masashi Ban[2], and Osamu Hirota[1]

[1] Research Center for Quantum Communications, Tamagawa University
Tamagawa-gakuen, Machida, Tokyo 194, Japan
[2] Advanced Research Laboratory, Hitachi, Ltd.
Akanuma 2520, Hatoyama, Saitama 350-03, Japan

1. INTRODUCTION

Optimizing a signal detection process to minimize the error probability or to maximize the mutual information is one of the most interesting subject to implement super-reliable communication systems, quantum computers, etc [1–6]. The optimum detection operators which are the mathematical description of the optimum signal detection process have been derived for some signal quantum states in the case of the error probability [7,8]. However, in the case of the maximum mutual information, the derivation of the optimum detection operators have been much difficult [9,10].

Recently, one of authors proposed new algorithm to derive the optimum detection operators for both cases [6], where it is revealed for the binary pure state signal that both the optimum detection operators are identical while the conditions to be optimum are different. In this paper, we extend the investigation to the binary mixed state signals. It will be shown that both the optimum detection processes for the error probability and the mutual information are different except for some cases.

2. ERROR PROBABILITY AND MUTUAL INFORMATION

Both the error probability and the mutual information are the most important parameters to evaluate a system performance. For a binary signal, error probability P_e and mutual information I can be represented as follows:

$$
\begin{aligned}
P_e &= \xi_1 P(2|1) + \xi_2 P(1|2) = 1 - \{\xi_1 P(1|1) + \xi_2 P(2|2)\}, \\
I &= \xi_1 P(1|1) \log \left[\frac{P(1|1)}{\xi_1 P(1|1) + \xi_2 P(1|2)}\right] + \xi_2 P(1|2) \log \left[\frac{P(1|2)}{\xi_1 P(1|1) + \xi_2 P(1|2)}\right] \\
&\quad + \xi_1 P(2|1) \log \left[\frac{P(2|1)}{\xi_1 P(2|1) + \xi_2 P(2|2)}\right] + \xi_2 P(2|2) \log \left[\frac{P(2|2)}{\xi_1 P(2|1) + \xi_2 P(2|2)}\right],
\end{aligned}
\tag{1}
$$

where ξ_i is *a priori* probability of signal i, namely,

$$
\xi_1 + \xi_2 = 1,
\tag{2}
$$

Quantum Communication, Computing, and Measurement
Edited by Hirota *et al.*, Plenum Press, New York, 1997

and $P(j|i)$ is a conditional probability indicating the probability that j is chosen when signal i is true. In the quantum detection theory, the conditional probability is represented as follows:

$$P(j|i) = \mathrm{Tr}\hat{\Pi}_j \hat{\rho}_i = \mathrm{Tr}\hat{\rho}_i \hat{\Pi}_j, \tag{3}$$

where $\hat{\rho}_i$ is a density operator for signal i, $\hat{\Pi}_j$ is a detection operator for signal j, and 'Tr' denotes a trace of operator. The detection operator must be a probability operator valued measure, so that it satisfies the next condition.

$$\sum_{j=1}^{M} \hat{\Pi}_j = \hat{I}, \quad \hat{\Pi}_j \geq 0, \forall j. \tag{4}$$

3. CONDITIONS TO BE THE OPTIMUM DETECTIONS

Based on the quantum Bayes criterion, the necessary and sufficient condition for detection operators to minimize the error probability is as follows [1–3]:

$$\hat{\Pi}_1 \left[\xi_1 \hat{\rho}_1 - \xi_2 \hat{\rho}_2\right] \hat{\Pi}_2 = 0, \\ \hat{\Gamma} - \xi_i \hat{\rho}_i \geq 0, \forall i, \tag{5}$$

where $\hat{\Gamma}$ is called Lagrange operator defined as follows:

$$\hat{\Gamma} = \xi_1 \hat{\rho}_1 \hat{\Pi}_1 + \xi_2 \hat{\rho}_2 \hat{\Pi}_2. \tag{6}$$

On the other hand, the necessary condition for detection operators to maximize the mutual information is as follows [3]:

$$\hat{\Pi}_1 \left[\hat{F}_1 - \hat{F}_2\right] \hat{\Pi}_2 = 0, \tag{7}$$

where $\hat{F}_j$ is defined by

$$\hat{F}_j = \sum_{\ell=1}^{2} \xi_\ell \hat{\rho}_\ell \log \left[\frac{P(j|\ell)}{\sum_{k=1}^{2} \xi_k P(j|k)}\right]. \tag{8}$$

4. THE OPTIMUM DETECTION OPERATOR FOR BINARY SIGNALS

For binary signal detection, there are useful lemmas.

Lemma 1. *The optimum detection operator for any binary signal must be an orthonormal resolution of identity, namely, it is a projection valued measure.*

This lemma is given by Helstrom for the case of the minimum error probability and by Ban for the case of the maximum mutual information [1, 6]. Hence, we have

$$\hat{\Pi}_1 + \hat{\Pi}_2 = \hat{I}_s, \\ \hat{\Pi}_j \equiv |\omega_j\rangle\langle\omega_j|, \tag{9}$$

where $\hat{I}_s$ is the identity operator of a signal space spanned by signal quantum states and $|\omega_j\rangle$ is called a measurement state satisfying the next relation.

$$\langle\omega_i|\omega_j\rangle = \delta_{ij}. \tag{10}$$

With the assumption that signal space is a two dimensional space, a useful lemma is given by one of authors [6].

Lemma 2. *When the optimum detection operators are assumed to be projectors, the optimum detection operators can be represented by an appropriate rotation of any orthonormal bases on the signal space.*

For two dimensional signal space H_s with its element $|\psi\rangle$,

$$
\begin{aligned}
|\psi\rangle &\in H_s, \\
|\psi\rangle &= c_1|e_1\rangle + c_2|e_2\rangle,
\end{aligned} \tag{11}
$$

where c_1, c_2 are complex numbers and $|e_1\rangle, |e_2\rangle$ are the orthonormal bases of H_s, namely, $\langle e_i|e_j\rangle = \delta_{ij}$, the measurement states for a binary signal can be represented as follows [6]:

$$
\begin{bmatrix} |\omega_1\rangle \\ |\omega_2\rangle \end{bmatrix} = \begin{bmatrix} \cos\phi & \sin\phi \\ -\sin\phi & \cos\phi \end{bmatrix} \begin{bmatrix} |e_1\rangle \\ |e_2\rangle \end{bmatrix}, \tag{12}
$$

where ϕ indicates the rotation phase. Hence the error probability and the mutual information are the functions of the rotation phase such as, $P_e(\phi), I(\phi)$.

The concept of the optimization of the detection processes are given as follows:

$$
\begin{aligned}
P_{e,\text{opt}} &= \min_\phi P_e(\phi), \\
I_{\text{opt}} &= \max_\phi I(\phi).
\end{aligned} \tag{13}
$$

Here we define the optimum detection phases which give the minimum error probability and the maximum mutual information by $\phi_{\text{opt},P_e}, \phi_{\text{opt},I}$, respectively.

It has been proved that both the optimum detection phases are equal each other for any binary pure state signal [6].

Then we are interested in the investigation of the cases of mixed state signals.

5. OPTIMUM DETECTIONS OF SPIN 1/2 STATES WITH THERMAL NOISE

Let us treat the binary signal which consists of the spin $1/2$ states with thermal noise. Signal quantum states are assumed as follows:

$$
\begin{aligned}
\hat{\rho}_1 &= \begin{bmatrix} 1 - f_1 & 0 \\ 0 & f_1 \end{bmatrix}, \\
\hat{\rho}_2 &= \begin{bmatrix} \frac{1}{2} + \left(\frac{1}{2} - f_2\right)\cos\theta & \left(\frac{1}{2} - f_2\right)\sin\theta \\ \left(\frac{1}{2} - f_2\right)\sin\theta & \frac{1}{2} - \left(\frac{1}{2} - f_2\right)\cos\theta \end{bmatrix},
\end{aligned} \tag{14}
$$

where θ indicates the degree of the overlap of each state and f_i is a thermal noise with its value $0 \leq f_i \leq \frac{1}{2}$.

With the representation of the measurement states in Eq. (12) we have

$$
\begin{bmatrix} |\omega_1\rangle \\ |\omega_2\rangle \end{bmatrix} = \begin{bmatrix} \cos\phi & \sin\phi \\ -\sin\phi & \cos\phi \end{bmatrix} \begin{bmatrix} |\uparrow\rangle \\ |\downarrow\rangle \end{bmatrix}. \tag{15}
$$

As a result, the conditional probabilities can be calculated as follows:

$$
\begin{aligned}
P(1|1) &= \text{Tr}\hat{\Pi}_1\hat{\rho}_1 = \tfrac{1}{2}\left[1 + (1 - 2f_1)\cos 2\phi\right], \\
P(2|1) &= 1 - P(1|1), \\
P(2|2) &= \text{Tr}\hat{\Pi}_2\hat{\rho}_2 = \tfrac{1}{2}\left[1 - (1 - 2f_2)\cos(2\phi - \theta)\right], \\
P(1|2) &= 1 - P(2|2).
\end{aligned} \tag{16}
$$

5.1. NUMERICAL ANALYSES OF THE OPTIMUM DETECTIONS

Let us show the numerical results of the optimum detections for the error probability and the mutual information. As an example, let us compare the optimum mutual information (I_{opt}) and the mutual information attained by the optimum detection phase for the error probability (I by ϕ_{opt,P_e}).

Assume that the degree of the overlap of each state θ is equal to 90° and the case of pure states signal, namely, $f_1 = f_2 = 0$. The optimum mutual information and the mutual information by error probability optimum detection are shown in Fig. 1. It is apparent that both the optimum detections are equal for all *a priori* probabilities.

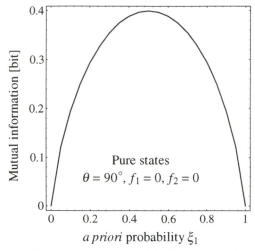

Figure 1. Comparison of the optimum mutual information (I_{opt} : solid line) and the mutual information by the error probability optimum detection (I by ϕ_{opt,P_e} : dashed line) for pure states signal.

Next, let us assume that signal quantum states are mixed states with equal thermal noise, namely, $f_1 = f_2$. Each mutual information is compared in Fig. 2. It is revealed that each optimum detection is different except for $\xi_1 = \xi_2 = \frac{1}{2}$.

Finally, the case of the mixed signal quantum states with different thermal noise is considered in Fig. 3. In this case, both the optimum detection processes are completely different.

6. CONCLUSION

In this paper, we have tried to compare the optimum detections for the error probability and the mutual information for binary signals. In detail, we assumed the spin $\frac{1}{2}$ states with thermal noise to treat the signal space as a two dimensional Hilbert space. With the comparison of the optimum mutual information and the mutual information obtained by the optimum detection for the error probability, it is revealed that the optimum detection processes are essentially different except for some special conditions, such as pure signal quantum states or mixed state signals with equal thermal noise and equal *a priori* probabilities. The result of the numerical analyses is summarized in table 1.

The maximization of the optimum mutual information with respect to *a priori* probabilities gives a channel capacity with code length one. This channel capacity will play an important roles to evaluate the effect of the quantum coding.

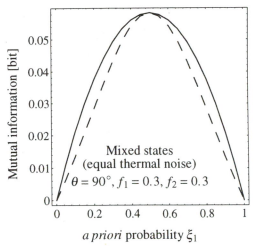

Figure 2. Comparison of the optimum mutual information (I_{opt} : solid line) and the mutual information by the error probability optimum detection (I by ϕ_{opt,P_e} : dashed line) for mixed states with equal thermal noise.

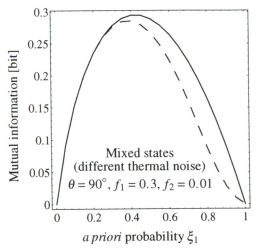

Figure 3. Comparison of the optimum mutual information (I_{opt} : solid line) and the mutual information by the error probability optimum detection (I by ϕ_{opt,P_e} : dashed line) for mixed states with different thermal noise.

Table 1. Relation between the optimum detections for the error probability and the mutual information.

Signal quantum states	Pure states	Mixed state: equal thermal noise	Mixed state: different thermal noise
The optimum detections	Equal for all *a priori* probabilities	Different except for $\xi_1 = \xi_2 = 1/2$	Completely different

REFERENCES

[1] C. W. Helstrom, *Quantum Detection and Estimation Theory.* (Academic Press, NY, 1976).

[2] H. P. Yuen, R. S. Kennedy, and M. Lax, IEEE Trans. Inform. Theory, **IT-21**, 125, (1975).

[3] A. S. Holevo, J. Multivar. Anal., **3**, 337, (1973).

[4] A. S. Holevo, Probl. Inf. Transm. (USSR) **9**, 177, (1973) [Probl. Peredachi Inf. **9** (3), (1973)].

[5] R. Jozsa, D. Robb, and W. K. Wootters Phys. Rev. A, **49**, 668, (1994).

[6] M. Ban, M. Osaki, and O. Hirota, J. Mod. Opt., **43**, 2337 (1996).

[7] M. Osaki, and O. Hirota, in *Quantum Communications and Measurement*, edited by V. P. Belavkin, O. Hirota, and R. L. Hudson (Plenum Publishing, NY, 1995), p.401.

[8] M. Osaki, M. Ban, and O. Hirota, Phys. Rev. A, **54**, 1691, (1996).

[9] E. B. Davies, IEEE Trans. Inform. Theory, **IT24**, 596, (1978).

[10] L. B. Levitin, in *Information, Complexity, and Control in Quantum Physics*, edited by A. Blaquière, S. Diner, and G. Lochak (Springer, Vienna, 1987).

ENTANGLEMENT-ENHANCED CLASSICAL COMMUNICATION ON A NOISY QUANTUM CHANNEL

Charles H. Bennett[1], Christopher A. Fuchs[2,3], and John A. Smolin[1]

[1] IBM Research Division, Yorktown Heights, NY 10598

[2] Département IRO, Université de Montréal, C. P. 6128,
Succursale centre-ville, Montréal, Canada H3C 3J7

[3] Present address: Norman Bridge Laboratory of Physics 12-33, California
Institute of Technology, Pasadena, CA 91125

We consider the problem of sending a single classical bit through a noisy quantum channel, when two uses of the channel are available as a resource. For a quantum channel, the possibility exists of entangling the channel inputs, which of course cannot be done with a classical channel. We show that, for certain noisy quantum channels, such entangled transmissions increase the receiver's probability of a correct inference, above what can be achieved by product state transmissions.

1. INTRODUCTION

Much of the growing field of quantum information theory is founded upon the asking of a single question: for a given task, can it help to use an entangled pair of particles as a resource? In this contribution, we ask just this question again, but in the context of a simple classical communication problem. The task is to use a noisy quantum channel as effectively as possible for the communication of a *single* bit, 0 or 1, given that only two transmissions through the channel are allowed.* Alice, the transmitter, may use any means allowed by the laws of quantum mechanics for encoding the bit in the two transmissions; Bob, the receiver, may use any means allowed by quantum mechanics for measuring the output of the channel in an attempt to infer the actual bit. The question is, can the use of an encoding that takes advantage of entanglement between the transmissions increase Bob's capability of inference?

As an example, the channel in question could be a somewhat depolarizing fiber optic cable. The two transmissions would then be represented by two separate photons being sent through the cable. In this case, the bit is to be encoded somehow in the polarization degrees of freedom of the photons, each represented by a two-dimensional Hilbert space $\mathcal{H}_2$. For this, our question boils down to whether the optimal encoding

---

*Information theoretically, this means that Alice sends each message with equal probability. The methods described here apply, with slight modification, to the case of unequal probabilities as well. We focus on the case of a full bit because the significant quantum behavior reported herein can be illustrated without such complications.

for such a channel will be in terms of product states—say by some $|\psi_0\rangle|\psi_0\rangle$ and $|\psi_1\rangle|\psi_1\rangle$ for 0 and 1 respectively—or rather by some *entangled* states $|\Psi_0\rangle$ and $|\Psi_1\rangle$ on $\mathcal{H}_2 \otimes \mathcal{H}_2$.

Extensive numerical work shows that there are noise models for which entangled transmissions are more reliable for carrying the bit from sender to receiver than product-state transmissions. In fact, such noise models seem to be the rule rather than the exception.

This paper is devoted to demonstrating the existence of this effect—i.e., entanglement-enhanced classical communication—for a particularly simple noisy quantum channel, the "two-Pauli channel." In Section 2 below, we develop the formalism required to give the general problem a precise statement. In Section 3, we introduce the two-Pauli channel and analyze what can be done with it upon one transmission and, alternatively, upon two transmissions but with product-state inputs. In Section 4, we find the optimal (entangled) encoding for two transmissions through the channel. We close the paper in Section 5 with a brief discussion of another channel of interest. Also we pose the deeper information-theoretic question of whether entanglement can be used to increase the classical information carrying capacity of a noisy quantum channel.

2. NOISY CHANNEL PRELIMINARIES

The general description of the problem is the following. The action of a noisy channel on the physical system transmitted through it is described by a mapping ϕ from input density operators to output density operators on that system. In all cases, the mapping is assumed to come about via an interaction between the system of interest and an independently prepared environment, to which neither Alice nor Bob has access. Thus a noisy channel is captured formally by a mapping of the form

$$\rho \longrightarrow \phi(\rho) = \mathrm{tr}_\mathrm{E}\left(U(\rho \otimes \sigma)U^\dagger\right) , \qquad (1)$$

where σ is the initial state of the environment, U is the unitary interaction between the system and environment, and tr_E denotes a partial trace over the environment's Hilbert space. For specificity, we assume ρ is a density operator on a d-dimensional Hilbert space $\mathcal{H}_d$.

A convenient means of representing all possible noise models is given by the Kraus representation theorem [1,2]. This states that Eq. (1) can be written in the form

$$\phi(\rho) = \sum_i A_i \rho A_i^\dagger , \qquad (2)$$

where the A_i satisfy the completeness relation

$$\sum_i A_i^\dagger A_i = I . \qquad (3)$$

Conversely, any set of operators A_i satisfying Eq. (3) can be used in Eq. (2) to give rise to a valid noisy channel in the sense of Eq. (1).

In the language of the Kraus theorem, the situation of two transmissions through the channel is described by the mapping

$$R \longrightarrow \Phi(R) = \sum_{i,j}(A_i \otimes A_j)R(A_i \otimes A_j)^\dagger , \qquad (4)$$

where R denotes a density operator on the d^2-dimensional Hilbert space $\mathcal{H}_d \otimes \mathcal{H}_d$.

In our particular problem, Alice encodes the bit she wishes to transmit to Bob by preparing a quantum system in one of two states R_0 or R_1 on $\mathcal{H}_d \otimes \mathcal{H}_d$. The action of the channel via Eq. (4) leads to one of two possible output density operators for Bob at the receiving end, say either $\tilde{R}_0$ or $\tilde{R}_1$ respectively.

For the problem of distinguishing the two density operators $\tilde{R}_0$ and $\tilde{R}_1$, we imagine Bob performing a general quantum mechanical measurement, or positive operator-valued measure (POVM) $\{E_b\}$, and then using the acquired data to venture a guess about the identity of the density operator. Depending upon which bit s Alice has sent, the probability of Bob's measurement outcomes will be given by $\mathrm{tr}(\tilde{R}_s E_b)$. Clearly the best strategy for Bob in identifying the bit—upon finding an outcome b—is to guess the value of s for which $\mathrm{tr}(\tilde{R}_s E_b)$ is the largest. Since each input is equally likely, this gives rise to an average probability of error given by

$$P_e(\{E_b\}) = \frac{1}{2}\sum_b \min\left\{\mathrm{tr}(\tilde{R}_0 E_b), \mathrm{tr}(\tilde{R}_1 E_b)\right\}. \tag{5}$$

This makes it clear that the best measurement on Bob's part is to choose the one that minimizes this expression. It turns out that this measurement can be described by a standard von Neumann measurement of the Hermitian operator $\Gamma = \tilde{R}_1 - \tilde{R}_0$ [3]. Moreover, with this measurement, Eq. (5) reduces to [4]

$$P_e = \frac{1}{2} - \frac{1}{4}\mathrm{tr}\left|\tilde{R}_1 - \tilde{R}_0\right|. \tag{6}$$

Here $\mathrm{tr}|A|$, for any Hermitian operator A, should be interpreted as the sum of the absolute value of A's eigenvalues.

The question we ask in this paper can now be stated in a precise manner. For any two orthogonal pure state inputs $|0\rangle$ and $|1\rangle$ on $\mathcal{H}_d \otimes \mathcal{H}_d$, what is the smallest possible value that

$$P_e = \frac{1}{2} - \frac{1}{4}\mathrm{tr}\left|\Phi(|1\rangle\langle 1|) - \Phi(|0\rangle\langle 0|)\right|$$
$$= \frac{1}{2} - \frac{1}{4}\mathrm{tr}\left|\Phi\left(|1\rangle\langle 1| - |0\rangle\langle 0|\right)\right| \tag{7}$$

can take? And, more importantly, is it ever the case that the smallest value can be achieved only by entangled states?[†]

3. THE TWO-PAULI CHANNEL

The *two-Pauli channel* is a noisy quantum channel on a single qubit, $\mathcal{H}_2$, described by three Kraussian A_i operators:

$$A_1 = \sqrt{x}\,I, \qquad A_2 = \sqrt{\tfrac{1}{2}(1-x)}\,\sigma_1, \qquad A_3 = -i\sqrt{\tfrac{1}{2}(1-x)}\,\sigma_2, \tag{8}$$

where I is the identity operator and σ_1, σ_2, and σ_3 are the standard Pauli matrices, i.e.,

$$\sigma_1 = \begin{pmatrix} 0 & 1 \\ 1 & 0 \end{pmatrix}, \qquad \sigma_2 = \begin{pmatrix} 0 & -i \\ i & 0 \end{pmatrix}, \qquad \sigma_3 = \begin{pmatrix} 1 & 0 \\ 0 & -1 \end{pmatrix}. \tag{9}$$

This channel has a simple interpretation: with probability x, it leaves the qubit alone; with probability $1 - x$ it randomly applies one of the two Pauli rotations to the qubit.

[†]Of course, in principle, one must consider the possibility that the optimal inputs might be nonorthogonal or even mixed states. A proof that such possibilities are less than optimal is given in the Appendix. This is in accord with the intuition that inputs with less than maximal distinguishability cannot help for this problem.

Note that, because there is no A_i in Eq. (8) corresponding to the Pauli matrix σ_3, the two-Pauli channel cannot be thought of as a simple depolarizing channel. Nor can it be thought of as a simple dephasing channel, where only one Pauli rotation σ_j acts on the qubit. A classical bit can be sent perfectly through a dephasing channel by choosing $|0\rangle$ and $|1\rangle$ to be eigenstates of σ_j. Moreover, numerical work demonstrates that there is no benefit from using entangled transmissions for the depolarizing channel. It turns out that the asymmetry of the two-Pauli channel is just right for seeing the entanglement enhancement effect in a particularly clean way.

Let us gain some intuition about the two-Pauli channel by first considering only one transmission through it. Suppose we consider two possible (commuting) inputs, ρ_+ and ρ_-, given in Bloch sphere representation by

$$\rho_{\pm} = \frac{1}{2}\left(I \pm \vec{a} \cdot \vec{\sigma}\right) . \tag{10}$$

Here, $\vec{a} = (a_1, a_2, a_3)$ is any real vector of length 1 or less, and $\vec{\sigma}$ is the vector of Pauli matrices.

One can easily verify that the action of the channel on these two density operators is:

$$\rho_{\pm} \longrightarrow \phi(\rho_{\pm}) = \frac{1}{2}\left(I \pm \vec{b} \cdot \vec{\sigma}\right) , \tag{11}$$

where

$$\vec{b} = \left(a_1 x, \, a_2 x, \, a_3(2x - 1)\right) . \tag{12}$$

Note that one transmission through the channel takes commuting density operators to commuting density operators. We shall see that this feature is not necessarily true for two transmissions.

If we now specifically consider the channel for communication purposes, we should make the final states as distinguishable as possible. This means we should pick the vector $\vec{a}$ so that $\phi(\rho_+)$ and $\phi(\rho_-)$ are as pure as possible. How to do this will depend upon the value of the parameter x, since the eigenvalues of both ρ_+ and ρ_- are

$$\frac{1}{2} \pm \frac{1}{2}\sqrt{(a_1^2 + a_2^2)x^2 + a_3^2(2x - 1)^2} . \tag{13}$$

If $x \geq \frac{1}{3}$, then $|x| \geq |2x - 1|$. Hence, clearly, the optimal inputs will be pure states with $a_3 = 0$. If, on the other hand, $x \leq \frac{1}{3}$, then $|x| \leq |2x - 1|$. The optimal inputs in this case will again be pure states but with $a_1 = a_2 = 0$.

The probability of error in guessing the identity of the states works out easily enough. It is just

$$P_e = \begin{cases} x & \text{if} \quad x \leq \frac{1}{3} \\ \frac{1}{2} - \frac{1}{2}x & \text{if} \quad x \geq \frac{1}{3} \end{cases} . \tag{14}$$

With this much of an introduction to the two-Pauli channel, let us now briefly consider two transmissions through the channel, but with those transmissions restricted to be product states. There is not much to be said here. If we assume two inputs of the form

$$R_0 = \rho_0 \otimes \rho_0 \quad \text{and} \quad R_1 = \rho_1 \otimes \rho_1 , \tag{15}$$

then the error probability remains the same as above. This is verified easily. Since $\tilde{R}_0$ and $\tilde{R}_1$ themselves commute when the inputs are orthogonal and pure, working out Eq. (6) in this case is hardly more difficult than for the single transmission case. The best possible error probability remains that listed in Eq. (14).

This perhaps surprising fact, that two (unentangled) uses of the channel yield no better distinguishability between two equiprobable messages than a single use, also holds for 0/1-symmetric classical channels such as the binary symmetric channel. In such a symmetric situation, majority voting only works for three or more uses of the channel.

4. ENTANGLED TRANSMISSIONS

In this Section, we turn to the problem of sending entangled transmissions through the channel. A convenient basis with which to write the input states for two transmissions through the two-Pauli channel is the Bell operator basis, where the four orthonormal basis vectors are

$$|\Phi^\pm\rangle = \frac{1}{\sqrt{2}}\left(|\uparrow\rangle|\uparrow\rangle \pm |\downarrow\rangle|\downarrow\rangle\right) \quad \text{and} \quad |\Psi^\pm\rangle = \frac{1}{\sqrt{2}}\left(|\uparrow\rangle|\downarrow\rangle \pm |\downarrow\rangle|\uparrow\rangle\right). \quad (16)$$

We use the usual notation that

$$|\uparrow\rangle = \begin{pmatrix} 1 \\ 0 \end{pmatrix} \quad \text{and} \quad |\downarrow\rangle = \begin{pmatrix} 0 \\ 1 \end{pmatrix} \quad (17)$$

for the eigenvectors of σ_3. With respect to this basis, an arbitrary set of two input states can be written as

$$|0\rangle = a_0|\Phi^+\rangle + b_0|\Phi^-\rangle + c_0|\Psi^+\rangle + d_0|\Psi^-\rangle \quad (18)$$

and

$$|1\rangle = a_1|\Phi^+\rangle + b_1|\Phi^-\rangle + c_1|\Psi^+\rangle + d_1|\Psi^-\rangle. \quad (19)$$

Making the effort to work through Eq. (4), we find that the output density operator

$$\tilde{R}_0 = \Phi(|0\rangle\langle0|) \quad (20)$$

expressed in the basis of Eq. (17) is

$$\begin{bmatrix} ea_0^2 + fb_0^2 + gc_0^2 + gd_0^2 & ha_0b_0 & xa_0c_0 & ka_0d_0 \\ ha_0b_0 & fa_0^2 + eb_0^2 + gc_0^2 + gd_0^2 & kb_0c_0 & xb_0d_0 \\ xa_0c_0 & kb_0c_0 & ga_0^2 + gb_0^2 + ec_0^2 + fd_0^2 & hc_0d_0 \\ ka_0d_0 & xb_0d_0 & hc_0d_0 & ga_0^2 + gb_0^2 + fc_0^2 + ed_0^2 \end{bmatrix}$$

where

$$e = \frac{1}{2}(1 - 2x + 3x^2) \quad (21)$$

$$f = \frac{1}{2}(1 - x)^2 \quad (22)$$

$$g = x(1 - x) \quad (23)$$

$$h = 2x - 1 \quad (24)$$

$$k = x(2x - 1) \quad (25)$$

A similar expression holds for $\Phi(|1\rangle\langle1|)$ but with 1 exchanged for 0 everywhere.

Before tackling the problem at hand, it is worthwhile exploring a few features of this noise model. For instance, it would be convenient if it worked out that, as with

83

the product state, whenever $|0\rangle$ and $|1\rangle$ are orthogonal, $\Phi(|0\rangle\langle 0|)$ and $\Phi(|1\rangle\langle 1|)$ were assured to commute. This, unfortunately, is not the case. A simple counterexample suffices to show this. Simply take

$$|0\rangle = \begin{pmatrix} -0.459506 \\ -0.870791 \\ 0.127295 \\ 0.119889 \end{pmatrix} \quad \text{and} \quad |1\rangle = \begin{pmatrix} -0.578111 \\ 0.163069 \\ -0.770549 \\ -0.213192 \end{pmatrix} . \tag{26}$$

Then $\langle 0|1\rangle = 0$, but

$$\left[\Phi(|1\rangle\langle 1|),\ \Phi(|0\rangle\langle 0|) \right] \neq 0 . \tag{27}$$

Interestingly enough, however, there are special cases where the commutativity of the two outputs is assured. For instance, take

$$|0\rangle = \cos\alpha\,|B_1\rangle + \sin\alpha\,|B_2\rangle \tag{28}$$

$$|1\rangle = -\sin\alpha\,|B_1\rangle + \cos\alpha\,|B_2\rangle , \tag{29}$$

where $|B_1\rangle$ and $|B_2\rangle$ are any two Bell states. Then it is easily checked that $\Phi(|0\rangle\langle 0|)$ and $\Phi(|1\rangle\langle 1|)$ do indeed commute in this case.

As an alternate example, let $|0\rangle$ be any non-Bell state vector in the plane spanned by $|\Phi^+\rangle$ and $|\Psi^+\rangle$, and let $|1\rangle$ be any non-Bell state vector in the plane spanned by $|\Phi^-\rangle$ and $|\Psi^-\rangle$. It turns out that the outputs of the two-Pauli channel due to these inputs never commute *except* in the case that the channel parameter x equals either 0, 1, or 1/3.

These examples give some hint that the two-Pauli channel is channel fairly rich in structure. So, with this, let us return to the question of the optimal input states for two transmissions. Numerical work demonstrates that for channel parameter values $x \leq 1/3$, the optimal inputs are product states of the form given by Eq. (15). However, for channel parameters $1/3 < x < 1$, entangled inputs give the minimal error probabilities. Moreover, within the latter regime, though there appear to be many equivalent optimal entangled signals, two inputs can always be taken to be of the form

$$|0\rangle = \cos\alpha\,|\Phi^+\rangle + \sin\alpha\,|\Psi^+\rangle, \tag{30}$$

and

$$|1\rangle = -\sin\alpha\,|\Phi^+\rangle + \cos\alpha\,|\Psi^+\rangle \tag{31}$$

without any loss of performance.

The remainder of this Section is devoted to fleshing out the consequences of taking Eqs. (30) and (31) as an ansatz in our problem. The best probability of error in Bob's inference of the signal, in accordance with Eq. (7), follows after some algebra:

$$P_e(\alpha) = \frac{1}{2} - \frac{1}{2} \left[\left\{ \frac{1}{4}\left(1 - 4x + 5x^2\right)^2 \cos^2 2\alpha + x^2 \sin^2 2\alpha \right\}^{1/2} \right.$$
$$\left. + \frac{1}{2}(1 - x)\left|(1 - 3x)\cos 2\alpha\right| \right]. \tag{32}$$

If we define

$$F = \frac{1}{4}(1 - x)(1 - 5x)(1 - 2x + 5x^2) \tag{33}$$

$$G = \frac{1}{2}(1 - x)(1 - 3x) \tag{34}$$

$$Z = \cos 2\alpha , \tag{35}$$

the error probability as a function of the ansatz can be written more compactly as

$$P_e(Z) = \frac{1}{2} - \frac{1}{2}\left(\sqrt{FZ^2 + x^2} + |GZ|\right) . \tag{36}$$

Our task now reduces to optimizing the ansatz in order to find the two inputs that lead to the most distinguishable outputs. This is done by extremizing Eq. (36):

$$\frac{\partial P_e(Z)}{\partial Z} = 0 . \tag{37}$$

This variational equation will have a solution for an optimal Z as long as x is such that Z^2 remains within the range set by Eq. (35), i.e., between 0 and 1. This occurs for

$$0 \le \frac{G^2 x^2}{F(F - G)} \le 1 , \tag{38}$$

which, in turn, requires that

$$x \ge \frac{4}{15} - \frac{41}{30}\left(15\sqrt{330} - 73\right)^{-1/3} + \frac{1}{30}\left(15\sqrt{330} - 73\right)^{1/3} \approx 0.227539 \tag{39}$$

Since we only need solutions for $x \ge 1/3$, this implies that our ansatz at least remains valid within the range of interest.

For a given x, the optimal Z^2 works out to be given by

$$Z^2 = \frac{(1 - 3x)^2}{4x(5x - 1)(1 - 2x + 5x^2)}. \tag{40}$$

Hence the optimal version of Eq. (32) reduces to

$$P_e = \frac{1}{2} - 2\sqrt{\frac{x^5}{(5x - 1)(1 - 2x + 5x^2)}} . \tag{41}$$

This demonstrates our point: as long as $1/3 < x < 1$, entangled transmissions through the two-Pauli channel are more effective at disabling noise than product state transmissions. To convey a feeling for the effectiveness of entangled transmissions, we tabulate a few representative points below:

x	P_e (product states)	P_e (entangled states)
.50	0.250000	0.241801
.60	0.200000	0.188231
.70	0.150000	0.137817
.80	0.100000	0.090072
.90	0.050000	0.044319
.95	0.025000	0.022009

5. DISCUSSION

This paper has been largely devoted to developing a formal framework for tackling the question of entanglement-enhanced classical communication and demonstrating the existence of this effect for a particular noisy channel, the two-Pauli channel. However, computer simulations further corroborate that this example is not in any way isolated: it may be a property of most noisy channels. For instance, another example where entangled transmissions are effective is a "amplitude damping channel," where the qubit arises from either one or no photons in a mode. The noise in this channel is due to the possibility of a photon being lost. The Kraussian A_i operators for this channel [5] are

$$A_1 = \begin{pmatrix} \sqrt{x} & 0 \\ 0 & 1 \end{pmatrix} \quad \text{and} \quad A_2 = \begin{pmatrix} 0 & 0 \\ \sqrt{1-x} & 0 \end{pmatrix} . \tag{42}$$

and an analysis similar to the preceding one for the two-Pauli channel can be carried out in like manner.

Finally, let us emphasize that what we have shown here is that, by increasing our resources from one to two transmissions and allowing those transmissions to be entangled, we can make a classical bit more resilient to noise. This has no analog in classical information theory. A deeper question arises from comparing the increase in resources to the overall information transmittable by those resources. This is the question of whether the classical information capacity of a noisy quantum channel can be increased by entangling transmissions [7]. Let us close the paper by making this question precise.

If n possible inputs to a channel—used with prior probabilities $\pi_1, \pi_2, \ldots, \pi_n$—lead to n distinct density operators $\rho_1, \rho_2, \ldots, \rho_n$ at the output (with like prior probabilities), then for a fixed POVM $\{E_b\}$, the mutual information recoverable about the identity of the input is

$$I\big(\{\pi_i\}, \{E_b\}\big) = -\sum_b \text{tr}(\rho E_b) \log \text{tr}(\rho E_b) + \sum_{i=1}^{n} \pi_i \sum_b \text{tr}(\rho_i E_b) \log \text{tr}(\rho_i E_b) , \tag{43}$$

where

$$\rho = \sum_{i=1}^{n} \pi_i \rho_i . \tag{44}$$

This is the Shannon information of the output symbols minus the average Shannon information of the output symbols conditioned on the input. The channel capacity for the given set of inputs is found by optimizing the prior probabilities of the inputs and optimizing the quantum measurement used at the output:

$$C(\rho_1, \rho_2, \ldots, \rho_n) = \max_{\{\pi_i\}} \max_{\{E_b\}} I\big(\{\pi_i\}, \{E_b\}\big) . \tag{45}$$

This defines the ultimate information carrying capacity for a single transmission through the channel as a function of the particular input quantum states.

What we are in search of is a comparison of the best possible capacity (as a function of the inputs) for one transmission versus the same for two transmissions. That is to say, under completely general uses of the channel, what is the best possible channel capacity

$$C\big(\Phi(|1\rangle\langle 1|), \Phi(|2\rangle\langle 2|), \ldots, \Phi(|n\rangle\langle n|)\big) , \tag{46}$$

where an optimization must also encompass the number of inputs n? Moreover, how does this number compare to a similarly defined capacity C_1 for a single transmission through the channel? If Eq. (46) turns out to be more than twice C_1, then we would have that classical information capacities are "super-additive" with respect to multiple uses of the same channel. The existence of this phenomenon would be yet another surprising quantum effect indeed.

6. APPENDIX: WHY ORTHOGONAL SIGNAL STATES?

Suppose we have any quantum channel whatsoever and that its action on density operators is given (in standard form) by a trace-preserving completely positive map

$$\rho \longrightarrow \mathcal{E}(\rho) = \sum_i B_i \rho B_i^\dagger , \tag{47}$$

where

$$\sum_i B_i^\dagger B_i = I . \tag{48}$$

For the problem of finding the two inputs that lead to two maximally distinguishable outputs (as in these notes), how do we know that the optimal inputs should pure states rather than mixed? Given that the inputs are pure states, how do we know that the optimal ones must be orthogonal?

If we grant two standard facts from linear algebra [6], then we can answer both these questions quite readily. The first fact is that, for any operator A,

$$\max_U \text{ Re tr}(UA) = \text{tr}|A| \tag{49}$$

where the maximum is taken over all unitary operators U. The second fact is that, for any two $n \times n$ Hermitian operators A and B,

$$\sum_{i=1}^n \lambda_{n-i+1}(A)\lambda_i(B) \leq \text{tr}(AB) \leq \sum_{i=1}^n \lambda_i(A)\lambda_i(B) , \tag{50}$$

where $\lambda_i(X)$ denotes the i'th eigenvalue of X when enumerated in nonincreasing order.

Now, in order to minimize the probability of error in carrying one bit across the given channel, we must find two states ρ_1 and ρ_0 such that

$$\text{tr}\big|\mathcal{E}(\rho_1) - \mathcal{E}(\rho_0)\big| \tag{51}$$

is maximized. Therefore, let us focus on this expression. Define the "conjugate" mapping $\mathcal{E}^*$ to $\mathcal{E}$ by the action

$$X \longrightarrow \mathcal{E}^*(X) = \sum_i B_i^\dagger X B_i . \tag{52}$$

Then

$$
\begin{aligned}
\text{tr}\big|\mathcal{E}(\rho_1) - \mathcal{E}(\rho_0)\big| &= \text{tr}\big|\mathcal{E}(\rho_1 - \rho_0)\big| \\
&= \max_U \text{ Re tr}\Big(U\mathcal{E}(\rho_1 - \rho_0)\Big) \\
&= \max_U \frac{1}{2}\text{tr}\Big((U + U^\dagger)\mathcal{E}(\rho_1 - \rho_0)\Big) \\
&= \max_U \frac{1}{2}\text{tr}\Big((\rho_1 - \rho_0)\mathcal{E}^*(U + U^\dagger)\Big) \\
&= \max_U \frac{1}{2}\Big[\text{tr}\Big(\rho_1\mathcal{E}^*(U + U^\dagger)\Big) - \text{tr}\Big(\rho_0\mathcal{E}^*(U + U^\dagger)\Big)\Big] . \tag{53}
\end{aligned}
$$

(For the second to last step in this, we used the cyclic property of the trace.) Note that, because $U + U^\dagger$ is an Hermitian operator, the operator $\mathcal{E}^*(U + U^\dagger)$ is also Hermitian.

Let us focus, for the moment, on any particular unitary operator U in the maximization procedure above. Using Eq. (50), we have

$$\text{tr}\Big(\rho_1\mathcal{E}^*(U + U^\dagger)\Big) \leq \sum_{i=1}^n \lambda_i(\rho_1)\lambda_i\Big(\mathcal{E}^*(U + U^\dagger)\Big) \leq \lambda_1\Big(\mathcal{E}^*(U + U^\dagger)\Big) \tag{54}$$

and

$$- \operatorname{tr}\left(\rho_0 \mathcal{E}^*(U + U^\dagger)\right) \leq -\sum_{i=1}^{n} \lambda_i(\rho_0)\lambda_{n-i+1}\left(\mathcal{E}^*(U + U^\dagger)\right) \leq -\lambda_n\left(\mathcal{E}^*(U + U^\dagger)\right). \quad (55)$$

However, if ρ_1 and ρ_0 are chosen to be the eigenprojectors of $\mathcal{E}^*(U + U^\dagger)$, then equality will be achieved throughout these equations. Thus for any particular U,

$$\max_{\rho_0,\rho_1} \operatorname{tr}\left((\rho_1 - \rho_0)\mathcal{E}^*(U + U^\dagger)\right) = \lambda_1\left(\mathcal{E}^*(U + U^\dagger)\right) - \lambda_n\left(\mathcal{E}^*(U + U^\dagger)\right) \quad (56)$$

and ρ_1 and ρ_0 must be orthogonal pure states to achieve this.

Therefore, it follows that the input states optimal for leading to the maximal distinguishability of the associated outputs will be orthogonal pure states.

7. ACKNOWLEDGMENTS

We would like to thank David DiVincenzo, Hideo Mabuchi, and Bill Wootters for helpful discussions, and the Institute for Theoretical Physics, UCSB under NSF grant PHY94-07194 for their hospitality. C.A.F. was supported by NSERC. C.H.B. and J.A.S. were supported in part by the US Army Research Office.

REFERENCES

[1] K. Kraus, *States, Effects, and Operations: Fundamental Notions of Quantum Theory.* Lecture Notes in Physics, vol. 190, Berlin: Springer-Verlag, 1983.

[2] M.-D. Choi, "Completely positive linear maps on complex matrices," *Linear Algebra and Its Applications*, vol. 10, pp. 285–290, 1975.

[3] C. W. Helstrom, *Quantum Detection and Estimation Theory.* Mathematics in Science and Engineering, vol. 123, New York: Academic Press, 1976.

[4] C. A. Fuchs, "Information Gain vs. State Disturbance in Quantum Theory," submitted to *Physica D* special issue for PhysComp96. Also in LANL quantum physics archive quant-ph/9611010.

[5] I. L. Chuang and Y. Yamamoto, "The Persistent Qubit," to appear in *Physical Review A*, January 1997.

[6] A. W. Marshall and I. Olkin, *Inequalities: Theory of Majorization and Its Applications.* Mathematics in Science and Engineering, vol. 143, New York: Academic Press, 1979.

[7] C. H. Bennett, D. P. DiVincenzo, J. A. Smolin, and W. K. Wootters, "Mixed State Entanglement and Quantum Error Correction," *Physical Review A* **54** 3824-3851 (1996). Also in LANL quantum physics archive quant-ph/9604024.

SECURITY AGAINST EAVESDROPPING IN QUANTUM CRYPTOGRAPHY

Norbert Lütkenhaus and Stephen M. Barnett

University of Strathclyde, Glasgow G4 0NG, Scotland
EMail: {norbert, steve}@phys.strath.ac.uk

1. INTRODUCTION TO QUANTUM CRYPTOGRAPHY

Quantum cryptography is a method for providing two parties who want to communicate securely with a secret key to be used in established protocols of classical cryptography. For more reviews of this topic see [1–3]. Bennett and Brassard showed that it is possible, at least ideally, to create a secret key, shared by sender and receiver, without both parties sharing any secret beforehand. We refer to this protocol as the *BB84* protocol [4]. To achieve this goal, sender and receiver are linked by two channels. The first channel is a public channel. The information distributed on it is available to both parties *and* to a potential eavesdropper. To demonstrate the principle of quantum cryptography we assume that the signals on this channel can not be changed by third parties. The second channel is a channel with strong quantum features. An eavesdropper can interact with the signal in an effort to extract information about the signals. The signal states are chosen in such a way that there is always, on average, a back reaction onto the signal states. We assume the quantum channel to be noiseless and perfect so that the back reaction of the eavesdropper's activity manifests itself as an induced error rate in the signal transmission.

The BB84 protocol uses the polarisation states of single photons as signal states. The signal states are, for example, linear vertical or horizontal polarised photons or right or left circular polarised photons. The sender sends a sequence of single photons with a polarisation chosen randomly from the four given ones. The receiver uses randomly one out of two given polarisation analysers for each signal photon. One of the analysers distinguishes between the two linear polarisations, the other between the circular polarisations. Therefore the sequence of signals contains two types of transmissions. In the first type the photon is prepared in a polarisation state which the polarisation analyser, chosen by the receiver, is able to distinguish unambiguously. An example is that a horizontal polarised photon is sent and the receiver chooses to use the linear polarisation analyser. Signals of this type will be refered to as deterministic signals since, the outcome of the polarisation measurement is fully determined by the state of the signal photon. The remaining signals are non-deterministic signals. An example for this is a horizontal linear polarised photon which triggers with equal probability the outcome "right circular" and "left circular" in the polarisation analyser distinguishing in the circular polarisation basis. Sender and receiver can distinguish between deterministic and non-deterministic signals using the public channel without giving away any information about the specific signal. They just compare the polarisation basis of the signal and the measuring polarisation analyser, both of which can be "linear" or "circular". The signal sequence of the deterministic bits can then be transformed into a binary key by assigning "0" for linear horizontal or right circular polarised photons and "1" for the remaining linear vertical or left circular polarised photons.

In this idealisation the security of quantum cryptography is given by the fact that the four polarisation states are not four orthogonal states and so there exists no quantum non-demolition measurement which could distinguish between them. Even more importantly, each attempt to distinguish between any of the states will change, in average, the states of the signals. This state-change destroys the perfect correlation between the signal and the measurement outcomes for the deterministic signals. A test checking this correlation will reveal any attempt at eavesdropping. If the test shows that the correlation is still perfect then sender and receiver can be sure that there was no eavesdropping attack and their shared binary key is perfectly secret.

In the practical realisation of quantum cryptography we face two specific problems. The public channel needs to be implemented in such a way that sender and receiver can ensure that the messages being received are really coming from each other. This is the problem of *authentication* for which various techniques are in use. In general, however, there will be the need for the two parties to share a limited amount of secret knowledge, for example in form of a secret key, before the authentication can take place. Quantum cryptography then generates a large secret key from a small secret key.

The work presented here deals with the second problem arising from the fact that all realistic quantum channels are noisy. Therefore the correlation between the signals and the measurement outcomes for the deterministic signals will not be perfect. Noise has the same effect on the signals as the activity of an eavesdropper. It is therefore necessary to think of all state change of the signals to be due to eavesdropping activity. It is intuitively clear that an eavesdropper can only have gained a small amount of information on the key if the correlation tested by sender and receiver are still strong, that is, if there are only a few transmission errors for the deterministic signals. One can hope to give a bound on the eavesdropper's Shannon information as a function of the error rate in the deterministic signals. Such bounds have been obtained assuming that the eavesdropper is restricted to von Neumann measurements only [5] or to a restricted class of more general measurements [6]. Here we present a sharp bound [7, 8] on the Shannon information of an eavesdropper which is valid for all eavesdropping attacks which access each signal photon independently of each other. It therefore does not include coherent attacks in which the product state of all signal photons is attacked. The sharp bound does not take into account that an eavesdropper can make use of the later acquired knowledge about the polarisation basis of the signal photons to *change* the measurement of the signal. However, we are able to give a rough upper bound for this situation. The reason that this is possible is that the eavesdropper has to decide how to interact with the signal states before he acquires the additional knowledge about the polarisation basis.

2. GENERALISED MEASUREMENTS

The key input to derive the bounds given in this paper is the most general description of a measurement on a given system. Any measurement can be described by a set of operators A_l defined on the Hilbert space $\mathcal{H}$ of the system the measurement is performed on. The only restriction on the operators is that

$$\sum_{l \in K} A_l^\dagger A_l = \mathbb{1}_{\mathcal{H}} .$$ (1)

where K is some finite or countable infinite index set. The link between these operators and a measurement is given by the following formulas which describe the probabilities that a particular outcome of a measurement is triggered, and which give the final state of the measured system after that outcome was registered. For the sake of simplicity we assume the set of outcomes to be discrete. The probability that the outcome k is triggered by an input state with density matrix ρ is given by

$$p_k = \text{Tr}_{\mathcal{H}} \left(\rho \sum_{l \in K_k} A_l^\dagger A_l \right)$$ (2)

where the K_k are disjunct subsets of K with $K = \bigcup_k K_k$. The final density matrix $\tilde{\rho}^{(k)}$ of the selected states belonging to this outcome is given by

$$\tilde{\rho}^{(k)} = \frac{\sum_{l \in K_k} A_l \rho A_l^\dagger}{\text{Tr}_{\mathcal{H}} \left(\rho \sum_{l \in K_k} A_l^\dagger A_l \right)} .$$ (3)

The density matrix of the final state, which does not select any states, but describes the whole ensemble for all outcomes is given by

$$\tilde{\rho} = \sum_k p_k \tilde{\rho}^{(k)} = \sum_{l \in K} A_l \rho A_l^\dagger .$$ (4)

It is important to choose the correct Hilbert space $\mathcal{H}$ to describe the measurement. To describe a spin measurement of an electron and the back reaction onto that spin we will choose $\mathcal{H}$ to be the Hilbert space of the spin of electron. If we are interested in the position or momentum of the electron as well we have to add the Hilbert space of spatial modes. It is a bit less obvious in quantum optics. If $\mathcal{H}$ is the one-photon polarisation Hilbert space then we implicitly assume that precisely one photon remains after the measurement. An eavesdropper may absorb the photon and so the final state is the vacuum. Therefore the adequate Hilbert space is the full Hilbert space of a light mode plus the polarisation degree of freedom. It turns out that we can derive the bounds presented here by restricting the Hilbert space to that of a single photon and later generalise it to the full Hilbert space.

3.   ESTIMATE OF THE SHANNON INFORMATION

The relevant expression for the Shannon information per signal is given with the help of the function $h(x) = -x \log x$, where $\log$ refers to basis 2, as

$$I = \sum_{\Psi=0,1} h\left[p(\Psi)\right] + \sum_{\substack{\alpha=\circ,+ \\ k}} h\left[p(k_\alpha)\right] - \sum_{\substack{\Psi=0,1 \\ k,\alpha}} h\left[p(\Psi, k_\alpha)\right] .$$ (5)

An eavesdropper gains this Shannon information on the binary key whose signals are given by $\Psi = 0, 1$ when he learns, from communication on the public channel, the polarisation basis $\alpha = \circ, +$ (linear or circular) used for each signal, and registers the outcome k on the measurement apparatus triggered by each signal. The probabilities that a "0" or a "1" is sent are denoted by $p(\Psi)$, the probability that outcome k is triggered by a photon prepared as basis state of the linear or circular polarisation basis is written as $p(k_\alpha)$, and the joint probability distribution for both events is $p(\Psi, k_\alpha)$.

We would like to give an upper bound on this Shannon information as a function of the *measured* disturbance of the quantum channel given as the error rate in the deterministic signals. This error rate is basically the fidelity measure D_{fid} of the channel, given by

$$D_{\text{fid}} = 1 - \frac{1}{4} \sum_{j=1}^{4} \text{Tr}_{\mathcal{H}} (\rho_i \tilde{\rho}_i). \tag{6}$$

The definition of D_{fid} assumes here the use of the one photon polarisation Hilbert space. The expression $\text{Tr}_{\mathcal{H}} (\rho_i \tilde{\rho}_i)$ is the overlap between the input state ρ_i, which is one of the four signal states, and the final state $\tilde{\rho}_i$ of the eavesdropper's measurement performed on this input state ρ_i. This can be interpreted as the probability that the final state is still recognised as the initial state in apparatus of the receiver. Then D_{fid} is the error rate averaged over the four signal states.

It can be shown [8] that the optimal eavesdropping strategy can be given by operators A_k which can be described by real matrices in a representation for which the signal states are real density matrices. Each operator A_k, which can always be expressed in the form

$$A_k = \sqrt{a_k} O_k + \left(\sqrt{b_k} - \sqrt{a_k} \right) O_k P_k \tag{7}$$

with real, positive numbers a_k and b_k, $(b_k \geq a_k)$, projection operators P_k and orthogonal operators O_k. The optimal strategy satisfies the symmetry that for each such operator the set of operators A_k contains as well the operator

$$\tilde{A}_k = \sqrt{a_k} O_k + \left(\sqrt{b_k} - \sqrt{a_k} \right) O_k \overline{P}_k \tag{8}$$

which employs the orthogonal complement $\overline{P}_k = \mathbb{1}_{\mathcal{H}} - P_k$. The optimal eavesdropping strategy associates a measurement outcome with each of the operators A_k separately so that we do not need to employ any partitions $K^{(k)}$. For such an eavesdropping strategy the measured disturbance D_{fid} is given by

$$D_{\text{fid}} = \sum_i \left[\frac{1}{4} \text{Tr}_{\mathcal{H}} (\rho_i E_i) - \sum_{k \in K} \left(\frac{1}{4} \sqrt{a_k b_k} \text{Tr}_{\mathcal{H}} \left(O_k \rho_i O_k^{\text{T}} E_i \right) \right. \right.$$
$$\left. \left. + \frac{1}{4} \frac{\left(\sqrt{b_k} - \sqrt{a_k} \right)^2}{2} \left(\text{Tr}_{\mathcal{H}} \left(O_k P_k \rho_i P_k O_k^{\text{T}} E_i \right) + \text{Tr}_{\mathcal{H}} \left(O_k \overline{P}_k \rho_i \overline{P}_k O_k^{\text{T}} E_i \right) \right) \right) \right].$$

Here E_i is the projection operator describing the effect of the polarisation analyser. For the one photon space we have $E_i = \rho_i$. The Shannon information is given by the expression

$$I = \sum_k \frac{a_k + b_k}{2} \left[1 - \log(1 + \eta_k^2) + \right.$$
$$\frac{1}{2(1 + \eta_k^2)} \left\{ (\eta_k^2 + c_k - \eta_k^2 c_k) \log(\eta_k^2 + c_k - \eta_k^2 c_k) \right.$$
$$+ (1 - c_k + \eta_k^2 c_k) \log(1 - c_k + \eta_k^2 c_k)$$
$$+ (\eta_k^2 + d_k - \eta_k^2 d_k) \log(\eta_k^2 + d_k - \eta_k^2 d_k)$$
$$\left. \left. + (1 - d_k + \eta_k^2 d_k) \log(1 - d_k + \eta_k^2 d_k) \right\} \right]. \tag{9}$$

In this expression we used the definitions of the overlaps $c_k = \text{Tr}_{\mathcal{H}} (\rho_1 P_k)$ and $d_k = \text{Tr}_{\mathcal{H}} (\rho_3 P_k)$ and of the characteristic parameters $\eta_k = \sqrt{\frac{a_k}{b_k}}$ with $\eta \in [0, 1]$. For $\eta_k = 1$ an operator A_k takes the characteristics of the identity operator, which corresponds to non-interference of the eavesdropper, and for $\eta_k = 0$ the eavesdropping strategy tends to a von Neumann projection measurement. The overlaps are restricted by the inequality

$$(d_k - \frac{1}{2})^2 + (c_k - \frac{1}{2})^2 \leq \frac{1}{4} . \tag{10}$$

We can find the optimal choice of orthogonal operators O_k and P_k. The optimal choices are given in a later section. As a result we find now the inequality for the disturbance

$$D_{\text{fid}} \geq \sum_{k \in K} \frac{a_k + b_k}{2} \frac{1}{4} \frac{(1 - \eta_k)^2}{1 + \eta_k^2} . \tag{11}$$

Note that the condition (1) implies that

$$\sum_k \frac{a_k + b_k}{2} = 1 \tag{12}$$

so that the expressions $\frac{a_k + b_k}{2}$ have the property of a probability. The Shannon information can be estimated by

$$I \leq \sum_k \frac{a_k + b_k}{2} \frac{1}{2} \left(1 - \log(1 + \eta_k^2) + \frac{\eta_k^2}{1 + \eta_k^2} \log \eta_k^2 \right) . \tag{13}$$

It can be shown that the optimal choice of the characteristic parameters η_k is for them to take the same value $\tilde{\eta}$. The proof uses variation methods. Then we find the inequalities

$$D_{fid} \geq \frac{1}{4} \frac{(1 - \tilde{\eta})^2}{1 + \tilde{\eta}^2} , \tag{14}$$

$$I \leq \frac{1}{2} \left(1 - \log(1 + \tilde{\eta}^2) + \frac{\tilde{\eta}^2}{1 + \tilde{\eta}^2} \log \tilde{\eta}^2 \right) . \tag{15}$$

If we actually measure the average error rate D_{fid} and find the value D_m we can bound the value of $\tilde{\eta}$ by

$$\tilde{\eta} \geq \bar{\eta} := \begin{cases} \frac{1 - 2\sqrt{2}\sqrt{(1 - 2D_m)D_m}}{1 - 4D_m} , & D_m \leq \frac{1}{4} \\ 0 , & D_m \geq \frac{1}{4} \end{cases} \tag{16}$$

which leads to the bound of the eavesdropper's Shannon information [7,8] as

$$I_S \leq \frac{1}{2} \left(1 - \log(1 + \bar{\eta}^2) + \frac{\bar{\eta}^2}{1 + \bar{\eta}^2} \log \bar{\eta}^2 \right) . \tag{17}$$

It can be shown that this bound can be further estimated by the linear bound

$$I \leq \frac{2}{\ln 2} D_m \tag{18}$$

where $\ln 2$ is the natural logarithm of 2. For small D_m this bound is nearly as good as the bound (17) which will later be shown to be sharp. The sharp bound and the linear approximation are plotted in figure 1 as a function of the measured fidelity disturbance. Typical values for experimental realisations using the BB84 protocol achieve an error rate of 4 % for 30 km or 1.5 % for 10 km distance between sender and receiver.

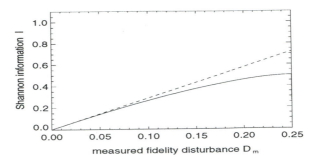

Figure 1. The bound on the Shannon information in the sharp (continuous line) and the linear bound (dashed line) as a function of the measured disturbance D_m.

4. PRIVACY AMPLIFICATION

For the purpose of secret communication the amount of Shannon information possibly leaked to an eavesdropper according to the previous estimate is far too high. However, making use of the technique of *privacy amplification* [9] it is possible to reduce Eve's total amount of Shannon information on the remaining key. For that the key has to be shortened using *hash functions*. The characteristic quantity for the fraction by which the key has to be shortened is the parameter τ_1. If we shorten the key by the fraction τ_1 then the eavesdropper is left at most with a Shannon information of 1 bit on the *whole* key. Each bit by which the key is is shortened additionally decreases this remaining Shannon information exponentially. The parameter τ_1 can be expressed with the help of the *collision probability* $\langle p_c(y) \rangle_y$ as

$$\tau_1 = 1 + \log \langle p_c(y) \rangle_y^{\frac{1}{N}} \ . \tag{19}$$

The collision probability $\langle p_c(y) \rangle_y = \sum_x p(x|y)^2$ refers to the probability distribution $p(x|y)$ over all possible signal string x, conditioned on the event that the eavesdropper measured a particular string of measurement results y.

Before they can apply the technique of privacy amplification, the sender and the receiver have to perform some type of error correction on their shared key. We assume that this process can be done without the eavesdropper gaining any additional knowledge and without the creation of any correlations between the signals. A possible realisation would be to use block parity comparison where the compared parity bit is encoded using some short shared secret key from the same source which gives the key used in the authentication of the public channel. In this case the collision probability is given by

$$\langle p_c(y) \rangle^{\frac{1}{n}} = \sum_{k,\alpha,\psi} \frac{p^{(c)}(\psi, k_\alpha)^2}{p^{(c)}(k_\alpha)} \ , \tag{20}$$

where the probabilities $p^{(c)}(\psi, k_\alpha)$ and $p^{(c)}(k_\alpha)$ now refer to the corrected key, and it takes only those signal transmissions which were correctly received into account. The joint probability distribution $p^{(c)}(\psi, k_\alpha)$ is given, with a normalisation constant C, by

$$p^{(c)}(\psi, k_\alpha) = \frac{1}{C} \mathrm{Tr}_\mathcal{H} \left(A_k \rho_{\psi_\alpha} A_k^\dagger \rho_{\psi_\alpha} \right) \ . \tag{21}$$

It is again possible to show general properties of the A_k which lead to an optimal information gain by the eavesdropper, along with minimal disturbance of the signal transmission. The optimal A_k can be shown to be real (in the real representation of the signal states) and to consist of symmetric or anti-symmetric matrices. The symmetric matrices can have eigenvalues of different or of the same sign so that they can be written as

$$A_k^{(\pm)} = \sqrt{a_k}\mathbb{1}_\mathcal{H} - \left(\sqrt{a_k} \pm \sqrt{b_k}\right) P_k \tag{22}$$

with the a_k and b_k satisfying, as before, $b_k \geq a_k \geq 0$ and P_k is a projection operator. To each such operator the set of operators A_k contains an operator

$$\tilde{A}_k^{(\pm)} = \sqrt{a_k}\mathbb{1}_\mathcal{H} - \left(\sqrt{a_k} \pm \sqrt{b_k}\right) \overline{P_k} \tag{23}$$

using the orthonormal complement $\overline{P_k} = \mathbb{1}_\mathcal{H} - P_k$. I refrain from giving the expressions for the collision probability and the disturbance D_fid in the general form and give instead the forms optimised with respect to the choice of projection operators P_k. At this stage they are given with the help of the characteristic parameter η_k which satisfies $\eta_k^2 = \frac{a_k}{b_k}$ and takes values in the range $\eta_k \in [-1, 1]$ which is in contrast to the calculations leading to the bound on the Shannon information. The disturbance satisfies the inequality

$$D_\mathrm{fid} \geq \sum_{k \in K^{(\pm)}} \frac{a_k + b_k}{2} \frac{1}{4} \frac{(\eta_k - 1)^2}{\eta_k^2 + 1} + \sum_{k \in K^{(a)}} \frac{a_k + b_k}{2} \frac{1}{4}, \tag{24}$$

where $K^{(\pm)}$ is the index set of the symmetric operators and $K^{(a)}$ the index set of the anti-symmetric operators. The collision probability is bound by

$$\left\langle p_c^{(c)}(y)\right\rangle^{\frac{1}{n}} \leq \frac{\sum_k \frac{a_k + b_k}{2} \frac{1}{2} \frac{1}{1 + \eta_k^2} \frac{17 + 12\eta_k + 6\eta_k^2 + 12\eta_k^3 + 17\eta_k^4}{3 + 2\eta_k + 3\eta_k^2}}{\sum_k \frac{a_k + b_k}{2} \frac{3 + 2\eta_k + 3\eta_k^2}{1 + \eta_k^2}}. \tag{25}$$

We use again a variation method to show that the optimal eavesdropping strategy employs characteristic parameters η_k with the same value $\tilde{\eta}$. Also it is clear that it is of disadvantage to the eavesdropper to use anti-symmetric operators A_k. This leads to the estimates

$$D_\mathrm{fid} \geq \frac{1}{4} \sum_{k \in K} \frac{(\tilde{\eta} - 1)^2}{\tilde{\eta}^2 + 1} \tag{26}$$

and

$$\left\langle p_c^{(c)}(y)\right\rangle^{\frac{1}{N}} \leq \frac{1}{2} \frac{17 + 12\tilde{\eta} + 6\tilde{\eta}^2 + 12\tilde{\eta}^3 + 17\tilde{\eta}^4}{(3 + 2\tilde{\eta} + 3\tilde{\eta}^2)^2}. \tag{27}$$

The measured disturbance D_m leads to a bound on $\tilde{\eta}$ given by

$$\tilde{\eta} \geq \overline{\eta} := \begin{cases} \frac{1 - 2\sqrt{2}\sqrt{(1-2D_m)D_m}}{1 - 4D_m} & D_m \leq \frac{1}{2} \\ -1 & D_m \geq \frac{1}{2} \end{cases}. \tag{28}$$

This finally allows us to bound the parameter τ_1 (19) by the inequality [8]

$$\tau_1 \leq \begin{cases} \log\left(\frac{17 + 12\overline{\eta} + 6\overline{\eta}^2 + 12\overline{\eta}^3 + 17\overline{\eta}^4}{(3 + 2\overline{\eta} + 3\overline{\eta}^2)^2}\right) & D_m \leq \frac{1}{3} \\ 1 & \frac{1}{3} \leq D_m \leq 1 \end{cases} \tag{29}$$

This bound is shown in figure 2. Typical error rates in the BT experiment are $e \in [0.01, 0.05]$ which corresponds to $\tau_1 \in [0.05, 0.26]$.

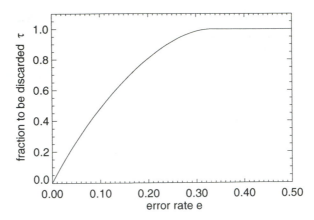

Figure 2. The parameter τ_1 as a function of the error rate. The error rate e is equal to the disturbance measure D_{fid}.

5. VALIDITY OF THE BOUNDS

The derivation of the bounds presented above assumes that the eavesdropper interacts with the signal photons but does not absorb them. In the experimental realisation, however, an absorption of about 90 % is observed. The validity of the bounds can be extended to accommodate the possibility of absorption by re-defining the average error rate as refering only to those signals where the polarisation analyser successfully measured a signal. It can be shown that the eavesdropper cannot increase the trade-off between information and induced error rate by forwarding signal states to the receiver which contain more than one photon. The basic tool for this extension of the validity of the bounds is that one can show that each eavesdropper strategy is equivalent to an eavesdropper strategy which results in final states which are Fock states of fixed photon number.

6. DELAYED MEASUREMENTS

The description of a delayed measurement needed here is that the eavesdropper has effectively two eavesdropping strategies at hand: one for each signal set of linear or circular polarisation. They are given by the A-operators $\{A_k\}_{k \in K}$ and $\{B_l\}_{l \in L}$ with two index sets K and L which are not necessarily of the same size. The strategies cannot be chosen independently of each other since they must be alternative descriptions of the quantum channel viewed as a non-selective measurement. This means that the equality

$$\sum_{k \in K} A_k \rho A_k^{\dagger} = \sum_{l \in L} B_l \rho B_l^{\dagger} \tag{30}$$

must hold for all density matrices ρ. An example of relations between the sets $\{A_k\}_{k \in K}$ and $\{B_l\}_{l \in L}$ satisfying this equality is the choice $B_l = \sum_k c_{lk} A_k$ with $\sum_k c_{lk} \bar{c}_{kn} = \delta_{ln}$. One can give a crude estimate of the Shannon information and of the collision probability because the disturbance is independent of the overlaps c_k and d_k. To give the bounds let the eavesdropper choose the projection operators P_k of the set of operators

A_k and B_k independently. Quantum mechanics will put some restrictions on that relation so that the resulting bounds are no longer sharp. Thus the eavesdropper's Shannon information may increase by a factor 2. The collision probability is bounded by

$$\left\langle p_c^{(c)}(y)\right\rangle^{\frac{1}{n}} \le \frac{1+\tilde{\eta}^4}{(1+\tilde{\eta}^2)^2}, \tag{31}$$

where $\tilde{\eta}$ is bounded by the measured disturbance D_{fid} as given in (28). The resulting bound for the fraction τ_1 of bits to be discarded during privacy amplification is plotted in figure 3. In this estimate we can prove security against eavesdropping as long as the error rate is less than 25 %. This result is likely to remain valid if we allow n-photon operations as in the previous chapter. Formal proof, however, should be postponed until a sharp bound for delayed choice eavesdropping strategies can be given. Clearer understanding of the restrictions imposed by (30) is essential for the derivation of the sharp bound.

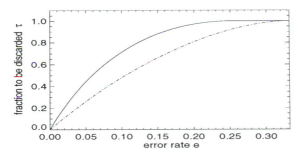

Figure 3. The crude bound of the fraction τ_1 of bits to be discarded during privacy amplification allowing for delayed measurements (solid line). This is compared to the sharp bound for non-delayed measurements (dashed line).

REFERENCES

[1] R. J. Hughes, D. M. Alde, P. Dyer, G. G. Luther, G. L. Morgan, and M. Schauer, "Quantum cryptography," Contemp. Phys. **36**, 149–163 (1995).

[2] S. J. D. Phoenix and P. D. Townsend, "Quantum cryptography and secure optical communications," BT Technol. J. **11**, 65–75 (1993).

[3] S. J. D. Phoenix and P. D. Townsend, "Quantum cryptography - how to beat the code breakers using quantum mechanics," Contemp. Phys. **36**, 165–195 (1995).

[4] C. H. Bennett and G. Brassard, "Quantum cryptography: Public key distribution and coin tossing.," In *Proceedings of IEEE International Conference on Computers, Systems, and Signal Processing, Bangalore, India*, (IEEE, New York, 1984) pp. 175–179.

[5] B. Huttner and A. K. Ekert, "Information gain in quantum eavesdropping," J. Mod. Opt. **41**, 2455–2466 (1994).

[6] A. K. Ekert and B. Huttner and G. M. N. Palma and A. Peres, "Eavesdropping on quantum-cryptographical systems," Phys. Rev. A **50**, 1047–1056 (1994).

[7] N. Lütkenhaus, "Security against eavesdropping in quantum cryptography," Phys. Rev. A **54**, 97 (1996).

[8] N. Lütkenhaus, Ph.D. thesis, University of Strathclyde, 1996.

[9] C. H. Bennett, G. Brassard, C. Crépeau, and U. M. Maurer, "Generalized privacy amplification," IEEE Trans. Inf. Theo. **41**, 1915 (1995).

A LINEAR PROGRAMMING APPROACH
TO ATTAINABLE CRAMÉR-RAO TYPE BOUNDS

Masahito Hayashi

Department of Mathematics, Kyoto University, Kyoto 606-01, Japan
e-mail adress: masahito@kusm.kyoto-u.ac.jp

The author studies the relation between the attainable Cramér-Rao type bound and the duality theorem in the infinite dimensional linear programming. By this approach, the attainable Cramér-Rao type bound for a 3-parameter spin 1/2 model is explicitly derived.

1. INTRODUCTION

It is well-known that the lower bound of quantum Cramér-Rao inequality $V_\rho(M) \geq J_\rho^S$ cannot be attained unless all the SLDs commute, where we denote by $V_\rho(M)$ a covariance matrix for a state ρ by a measurement M, the SLD Fisher information matrix for a state ρ by J_ρ^S. We therefore often treat an optimization problem for $\operatorname{tr} GV_\rho(M)$ to be minimized, where G is an arbitrary real positive symmetric matrix. If there is a function C_ρ (possibly depending on G) such that $\operatorname{tr} GV_\rho \geq C_\rho$ holds for all M, C_ρ is called a Cramér-Rao type bound, or simply a CR bound. Our purpose is to find the most informative (i.e. attainable) CR bound under locally unbiasedness conditions. To author's knowledge, there has been known only two models for which this optimization problem was explicitly solved in mixed state models. One is the estimation of complex amplitudes of coherent signals in Gaussian noise solved by Yuen and Lax [2], and Holevo [1]. Another one is the estimation of a 2-parameter spin 1/2 model solved by Nagaoka [3]. In pure state case, see Fujiwara and Nagaoka [4].

In this paper, a completely different approach to the optimization problem is given based on an infinite dimensional linear programming technique [5]. In addition, the most informative CR bound for a 3-parameter spin 1/2 model is explicitly derived by this approach.

2. SLD INNER PRODUCT AND LOCALLY UNBIASEDNESS CONDITIONS

Definition 2.1   For a subset $\Theta \subset \mathbf{R}^n$ the map $f : \Theta \to \mathcal{T}_{sa}(\mathcal{H})$ is called a C^k-map, if the k-th derivative of f is well defined on the interior of Θ, where $\mathcal{T}_{sa}(\mathcal{H})$ is the set of selfadjoint trace class operators on $\mathcal{H}$.

By $\mathcal{T}_{sa}^{+,1}(\mathcal{H})$ we denote the set $\{\rho \in \mathcal{T}_{sa}(\mathcal{H}) | \rho \geq 0, \ \operatorname{tr}_\mathcal{H} \rho = 1\}$.

Quantum Communication, Computing, and Measurement
Edited by Hirota *et al.*, Plenum Press, New York, 1997

Definition 2.2 We call $P \subset \mathcal{T}_{sa}^{+,1}(\mathcal{H})$ an n-dimensional C^k-*state manifold*, if P is an n-dimensional C^k-manifold which satisfies the condition: there exists a family $\{U_\lambda\}_{\lambda \in \Lambda}$ of open sets of P such that for any $\lambda \in \Lambda$ there exist $\Theta_\lambda \subset \mathbf{R}^n$ and C^k map $\phi_\lambda : \Theta_\lambda \to U_\lambda$.

We assume that we are given a family of density operators P which is a state manifold. The space $\mathcal{L}_{sa}^2(\rho)$ is defined as follows.

Definition 2.3 For $\rho \in \mathcal{T}_{sa}(\mathcal{H})$, $\mathcal{L}_{sa}^2(\rho)$ consists of selfadjoint operators X on $\mathcal{H}$ satisfying the following conditions:

$$1) \; \phi_j \in \mathcal{D}(X) \text{ with respect to } j \text{ such that } s_j \neq 0 \tag{2.1}$$
$$2) \; \langle X|X\rangle_\rho^{sa} := \sum_j s_j \langle X\phi_j|X\phi_j\rangle < \infty, \tag{2.2}$$

where $\rho = \sum_j s_j|\phi_j\rangle\langle\phi_j|$ is the spectral decomposition of ρ.

Definition 2.4 We call a state ρ *faithful*, if it satisfies the following condition:

$$X \in \mathcal{L}_{sa}^2(\rho) \text{ and } \langle X|X\rangle_\rho^{sa} = 0 \implies X = 0 \tag{2.3}$$

We assume that all of the given family of density operators are faithful. For $X, Y \in L_{sa}^2(\rho)$, define

$$\langle X|Y\rangle_\rho^{sa} := \frac{1}{4}\left(\langle X + Y|X + Y\rangle_\rho^{sa} - \langle X - Y|X - Y\rangle_\rho^{sa}\right). \tag{2.4}$$

We denote the norm with respect to this inner product by $\| \; \|_\rho^S$. We call the inner product the SLD inner product.

Theorem 2.1 *If $\mathcal{H}$ is separable, $\mathcal{L}_{sa}^2(\rho)$ is a real Hilbert space with respect to the SLD inner product.*

For a proof see Holevo [6].

We define $\rho \circ X := \frac{1}{2}(\rho \cdot X + X \cdot \rho) \in \mathcal{T}_{sa}(\mathcal{H})$ for $X \in \mathcal{L}_{sa}^2(\rho)$. We denote the inner product of the real Hilbert space $\mathcal{L}_{sa}^2(\rho)$ by J_ρ^S. We identify the dual of $\mathcal{L}_{sa}^2(\rho)$ with $\mathcal{L}_{sa}^{2,*}(\rho) := \{\rho \circ X | X \in \mathcal{L}_{sa}^2(\rho)\}$ as follows.

$$
\begin{array}{ccc}
\mathcal{L}_{sa}^{2,*}(\rho) \times \mathcal{L}_{sa}^2(\rho) & \to & \mathbf{R} \\
\cup\!| & & \cup\!| \\
(x, X) & \mapsto & \mathrm{tr}_{\mathcal{H}} \, xX.
\end{array}
\tag{2.5}
$$

We may regard J_ρ^S as an element of $\mathrm{Hom}_{sa}(\mathcal{L}_{sa}^2(\rho), \mathcal{L}_{sa}^{2,*}(\rho))$ by

$$
\begin{array}{ccc}
J_\rho^S : \mathcal{L}_{sa}^2(\rho) & \to & \mathcal{L}_{sa}^{2,*}(\rho) \\
\cup\!| & & \cup\!| \\
X & \mapsto & \rho \circ X.
\end{array}
\tag{2.6}
$$

We identify $\frac{\partial}{\partial\theta^i} \in T_\rho P$ with $\frac{\partial\rho}{\partial\theta^i} \in \mathcal{T}_{sa}(\mathcal{H})$, and we assume that $T_\rho P \subset \mathcal{L}_{sa}^{2,*}(\rho)$. We denote $J_S^\rho|_{T_\rho^* P}$ by $J_{S,T}^\rho$. We identify $T_\rho^* P$ with $J_{S,T}^{\rho,-1}(T_\rho P)$. We call the inner product $J_{S,T}^{\rho,-1}$ on $T_\rho P$ the *SLD inner product. By $\| \; \|_S$ we denote the norm of *SLD inner product $J_{S,T}^{\rho,-1}$. By $\mathcal{M}(\Omega, \mathcal{H})$ we denote the set of generalized measurements on $\mathcal{H}$ whose measurable space is Ω.

Definition 2.5   We define an affine map E from $\mathcal{M}(T_\rho P, \mathcal{H})$ to $\mathrm{Hom}(\mathcal{T}_{sa}(\mathcal{H}), T_\rho P)$ by

$$E(M)(\tau) := \int_{T_\rho P} x \, \mathrm{tr}_{\mathcal{H}}\big(M(\,dx)\tau\big), \ \forall \tau \in \mathcal{T}_{sa}(\mathcal{H}). \tag{2.7}$$

Let us define the locally unbiasedness condition.

Definition 2.6   We call $M \in \mathcal{M}(T_\rho P, \mathcal{H})$ *locally unbiased* on $\rho \in P$, if the map $E(M) : \mathcal{T}_{sa}(\mathcal{H}) \to T_\rho P$ satisfies the following condition:

$$E(M)(\rho) = 0 \tag{2.8}$$
$$E(M)|_{T_\rho P} = \mathrm{Id}_{T_\rho P}. \tag{2.9}$$

We denote the set of locally unbiased measurements on $\rho \in P$ by $\mathcal{U}(T_\rho P)$.

Lemma 2.1   *For $M \in \mathcal{M}(T_\rho P, \mathcal{H})$, the condition (2.9) is equivalent to the following equation:*

$$\int_{T_\rho P} \mathrm{tr}_{\mathcal{H}} \, a(x) M(\,dx) = \mathrm{tr}_{T_\rho P} \, a, \ \forall a \in \mathrm{End}(T_\rho P). \tag{2.10}$$

By taking basis, it is easy to verify this.

Let g be a nonnegative inner product on $T_\rho P$, then we call $\inf_{M \in \mathcal{U}(T_\rho P)} \mathrm{tr}_{T_\rho P} V_\rho(M) g$ the attainable Cramér-Rao bound.

3.   LINEAR PROGRAMMING APPROACH

We introduce a new approach to the attainable Cramér-Rao type bound. In this approach, we apply the duality theorem of the infinite dimensional linear programming [5]. But, we don't have to know the duality theorem for this section. In the noncommutative case, there is no infimum of covariance matrices under the locally unbiasedness conditions. Therefore, we minimize the following value $\mathcal{D}_g^\rho$ under the locally unbiasedness conditons. Let g be a nonnegative inner product on $T_\rho P$.

Definition 3.1   We define the *deviation* $\mathcal{D}_g^\rho$ for a measurement $M \in \mathcal{M}(T_\rho P, \mathcal{H})$ as follow:

$$\mathcal{D}_g^\rho(M) := \mathrm{tr}_{T_\rho^* P} \, g V_\rho(M) = \int_{T_\rho P} g(x, x) \, \mathrm{tr}_{\mathcal{H}} \, M(\,dx)\rho.$$

We introduce the useful theorem to minimize the deviation $\mathcal{D}_g^\rho(M)$ under the locally unbiasedness conditions.

Theorem 3.1   *We have the inequality*

$$\inf_{M \in \mathcal{U}(T_\rho P)} \mathcal{D}_g^\rho(M) \geq \sup_{(a,S) \in \mathcal{U}^*(g)} (\mathrm{tr}_{T_\rho P} \, a + \mathrm{tr}_{\mathcal{H}} \, S), \tag{3.1}$$

where

$$\mathcal{U}^*(g) := \{(a, S) \in \mathrm{End}(T_\rho P) \times \mathcal{T}_{sa}(\mathcal{H}) | g(x, x) \cdot \rho - S - a(x) \in \mathcal{T}_{sa}^+(\mathcal{H}), \ \forall x \in T_\rho P\}.$$

Notice that $T_\rho P$ is a subset $\mathcal{T}_{sa}(\mathcal{H})$.

We call the calculation of $\sup_{(a,S) \in \mathcal{U}^*(g)} (\mathrm{tr}_{T_\rho P} \, a + \mathrm{tr}_{\mathcal{H}} \, S)$ the dual problem.

Corollary 3.1　*If there exist a sequence of locally unbiased measurements $\{M_k\}$ and an element (a', S') of $\mathcal{U}^*(g)$ satisfying the condition*

$$\mathcal{R}_g^\rho(a', S'; M_k) \to 0 \ (as \ k \to 0), \tag{3.2}$$

then

$$\lim_{k\to\infty} \mathcal{D}_g^\rho(M_k) = \mathrm{tr}_{T_\rho P}\, a' + \mathrm{tr}_{\mathcal{H}}\, S' = \inf_{M\in\mathcal{U}(T_\rho P)} \mathcal{D}_g^\rho(M) = \sup_{(a,S)\in\mathcal{U}^*(g)} (\mathrm{tr}_{T_\rho P}\, a + \mathrm{tr}_{\mathcal{H}}\, S) \tag{3.3}$$

where $\mathcal{R}_g^\rho$ is defined as

$$\mathcal{R}_g^\rho(a, S; M) := \mathrm{tr}_{\mathcal{H}} \int_{T_\rho P} R_g^\rho(a, S; x) M(\,dx) \tag{3.4}$$

$$R_g^\rho(a, S; x) := g(x, x) \cdot \rho - S - a(x). \tag{3.5}$$

We call $(a, S) \in \mathcal{U}^*(g)$ the Lagrange multiplier.

Proof of Theorem 3.1 and Corollary 3.1　For $M \in \mathcal{U}(T_\rho P)$ and $(a, S) \in \mathcal{U}^*(g)$, we have

$$\mathcal{R}_g^\rho(a, S; M)$$
$$= \mathrm{tr}_{\mathcal{H}} \int_{T_\rho P} g(x, x) \cdot \rho M(\,dx) - \mathrm{tr}_{\mathcal{H}} \int_{T_\rho P} SM(\,dx) - \mathrm{tr}_{\mathcal{H}} \int_{T_\rho P} a(x)M(\,dx)$$
$$= \mathcal{D}_g^\rho(M) - \mathrm{tr}_{T_\rho P}\, a - \mathrm{tr}_{\mathcal{H}}\, S. \tag{3.6}$$

Since we have $R_g^\rho(a, S; x) \geq 0$ for any $x \in T_\rho P$, we obtain $\mathcal{R}_g^\rho(a, S; M) \geq 0$. By (3.6), the proof is complete. $\quad\square$

When $\dim \mathcal{H} < \infty$, we have the equality in (3.1). See Hayashi [7][8].

4.　MAXIMUM

In this section, we consider the dual problem. Let us define a linear functional on $\mathrm{End}(T_\rho P) \times \mathcal{T}_{sa}(\mathcal{H})$, denoted by Tr, in the following way, where in this section, we regard $T_\rho P$ as a real Hilbert space with respect to $J_{S,T}^{\rho,-1}$.

Definition 4.1　The functional Tr is defined by

$$\mathrm{Tr} : \mathrm{End}(T_\rho P) \times \mathcal{T}_{sa}(\mathcal{H}) \to \qquad \mathbf{R}$$
$$\Downarrow \qquad\qquad\qquad\qquad \Downarrow$$
$$(a, S) \qquad\qquad \mapsto \mathrm{tr}_{T_\rho P}\, a + \mathrm{tr}_{\mathcal{H}}\, S.$$

Lemma 4.1　*If the dimension of $\mathcal{H}$ is finite, then the set $\mathcal{U}^*(g) \cap \mathrm{Tr}^{-1}([0, \infty))$ is compact.*

We assume that the norm of $\mathrm{End}(T_\rho P)$ is the operator norm $\|\ \|_o$, and the norm of $\mathcal{T}_{sa}(\mathcal{H})$ is the trace norm $\|\ \|_t$. We define the norm $\|\ \|_{o,t}$ of $\mathrm{End}(T_\rho P) \times \mathcal{T}_{sa}(\mathcal{H})$ as follows:

$$\|(a, S)\|_{o,t} := \|a\|_o + \|S\|_t, \ \forall(a, S) \in \mathrm{End}(T_\rho P) \times \mathcal{T}_{sa}(\mathcal{H}).$$

Proof　We have

$$\mathcal{U}^*(g) = \cap_{x\in T_\rho P}\{(a, S)|g(x, x) \cdot \rho - S - a(x) \in \mathcal{T}_{sa}^+(\mathcal{H})\}.$$

Moreover, $\{(a, S)|g(x, x) \cdot \rho - S - a(x) \in \mathcal{T}^+_{sa}(\mathcal{H})\}$ is closed. Thus, $\mathcal{U}^*(g)$ is closed. Because $\mathrm{Tr}^{-1}([0, \infty))$ is closed, $\mathcal{U}^*(g) \cap \mathrm{Tr}^{-1}([0, \infty))$ is closed. Therefore, it is sufficient to show that it is bounded with respect to the norm $\|\ \|_{o,t}$. Denote $n := \dim T_\rho P$. For $(a, S) \in \mathcal{U}^*(g) \cap \mathrm{Tr}^{-1}([0, \infty))$, we have $\mathrm{tr}_{T_\rho P}\, a \leq n\|a\|_o$. Choose $z \in T_\rho P$ such that $\|z\|_S = 1$, $\|a(z)\|_S = \|a\|_o$. For $r > 0$, we have

$$g(r \cdot z, r \cdot z)\rho - a(r \cdot z) - S \geq 0. \tag{4.1}$$

Substitute $r = 0$, then $-S \geq 0$. Let us calculate the left hand side of (4.1).

$$g(r \cdot z, r \cdot z)\rho - a(r \cdot z) - S = r^2 \cdot g(z, z)\rho - r \cdot J^{\rho,-1}_{S,T}(a(z)) \circ \rho - S$$

$$= \left(\sqrt{g(z, z)}r - \frac{1}{2\sqrt{g(z, z)}}J^{\rho,-1}_{S,T}(a(z))\right) \cdot \rho \cdot \left(\sqrt{g(z, z)}r - \frac{1}{2\sqrt{g(z, z)}}J^{\rho,-1}_{S,T}(a(z))\right)$$

$$- \frac{1}{4g(z, z)}J^{\rho,-1}_{S,T}(a(z)) \cdot \rho \cdot J^{\rho,-1}_{S,T}(a(z)) - S. \tag{4.2}$$

Let $\{e_i\}$ be a complete orthonormal system of $\mathcal{H}$ which consists of eigenvectors of $J^{\rho,-1}_{S,T}(a(z))$. Substitute r for the eigenvalue α_i of $\frac{1}{2g(z,z)}J^{\rho,-1}_{S,T}(a(z))$ corresponding to the eigenvector e_i, then we have

$$\left\langle e_i \middle| \left(\sqrt{g(z, z)}\alpha_i - \frac{1}{2\sqrt{g(z, z)}}J^{\rho,-1}_{S,T}(a(z))\right) \cdot \rho \cdot \left(\sqrt{g(z, z)}\alpha_i - \frac{1}{2\sqrt{g(z, z)}}J^{\rho,-1}_{S,T}(a(z))\right) \middle| e_i \right\rangle = 0.$$

By (4.1), we have

$$\left\langle e_i \middle| -\frac{1}{4g(z, z)}J^{\rho,-1}_{S,T}(a(z)) \cdot \rho \cdot J^{\rho,-1}_{S,T}(a(z)) - S \middle| e_i \right\rangle \geq 0.$$

Therefore, we have

$$\mathrm{tr}_{\mathcal{H}}\left(-\frac{1}{4g(z, z)}J^{\rho,-1}_{S,T}(a(z)) \cdot \rho \cdot J^{\rho,-1}_{S,T}(a(z)) - S\right) \geq 0.$$

Thus, we get

$$\mathrm{tr}_{\mathcal{H}}\, S \leq -\frac{1}{4g(z, z)}\langle a(z)|a(z)\rangle^\rho_S = -\frac{\|a\|^2_o}{4g(z, z)},$$

$$\mathrm{tr}_{\mathcal{H}}\, S \leq -\frac{\|a\|^2_o}{4\|g\|_o}.$$

Therefore, we obtain

$$0 \leq \mathrm{Tr}(a, S) \leq n\|a\|_o - \frac{\|a\|^2_o}{4\|g\|_o}.$$

Hence, $0 \leq \|a\|_o(n - \frac{\|a\|_o}{4\|g\|_o})$. Thus, $0 \leq \|a\|_o \leq 4n\|g\|_o$. As $-S \geq 0$, we have $\|S\| = -\mathrm{tr}_{\mathcal{H}}\, S$. Therefore, we obtain the following inequalities:

$$0 \leq \|S\| \leq \mathrm{tr}\, a \leq n\|a\|_o \leq 4\|g\|_o n^2.$$

Thus, $\mathcal{U}^*(g) \cap \mathrm{Tr}^{-1}([0, \infty))$ is bounded, hence compact. $\qquad\square$
We have the following corollary.

Corollary 4.1   *There exists the maximum of the right hand side of (3.1).*

Assume that $\rho \in P_1 \subset P_2$ and $T_\rho P_1 \subset T_\rho P_2$, $T_\rho P_1 \neq T_\rho P_2$. From the imbedding map $i : P_1 \hookrightarrow P_2$, we have $di_\rho : T_\rho P_1 \hookrightarrow T_\rho P_2$ and $di_\rho^* : T_\rho^* P_2 \to T_\rho^* P_1$. By identifying the dual $T_\rho^* P_i$ with $T_\rho P_i$ ($i = 1, 2$), we may regard di_ρ^* as $di_\rho^* : T_\rho P_2 \to T_\rho P_1$. Let g be a nonnegative inner product on $T_\rho P_1$, then $di_\rho g\, di_\rho^*$ is a nonnegative inner product on $T_\rho P_2$.

Lemma 4.2   *We have the inequality*

$$\max_{(a,S) \in \mathcal{U}^*(g)} \left(\mathrm{tr}_{T_\rho P_1}\, a + \mathrm{tr}_\mathcal{H}\, S \right) \leq \max_{(a',S) \in \mathcal{U}^*(\, di_\rho g\, di_\rho^*)} \left(\mathrm{tr}_{T_\rho P_2}\, a' + \mathrm{tr}_\mathcal{H}\, S \right). \tag{4.3}$$

Moreover the equality holds, if and only if there exists $(a', S) \in \mathcal{U}^*(\, di_\rho g\, di_\rho^*)$ such that $a'(T_\rho P_1) \subset T_\rho P_1$, and the maximum of the right hand side is attained by (a', S).

Proof   We have $(\, di_\rho a\, di_\rho^*, S) \in \mathcal{U}^*(\, di_\rho g\, di_\rho^*)$ for $(a, S) \in \mathcal{U}^*(g)$.

$$F : \mathcal{U}^*(g) \to \mathcal{U}^*(\, di_\rho g\, di_\rho^*)$$
$$\Downarrow \qquad\qquad \Downarrow \tag{4.4}$$
$$(a, S) \mapsto (\, di_\rho a\, di_\rho^*, S).$$

Then, we have $\mathrm{Tr}(a, S) = \mathrm{Tr}(F(a, S))$. In (4.3) the equality holds, if and only if

$$\max_{(a',S) \in \mathcal{U}^*(\, di_\rho g\, di_\rho^*)} \mathrm{Tr}(a', S) = \max_{(a',S) \in \mathrm{Im}\, F} \mathrm{Tr}(a', S). \tag{4.5}$$

By the definition of $\mathcal{U}^*(\, di_\rho g\, di_\rho^*)$, as $di_\rho g\, di_\rho^*(\mathrm{Ker}\, di_\rho^*) = 0$, we have $a'(\mathrm{Ker}\, di_\rho^*) = 0$ for $(a', S) \in \mathcal{U}^*(\, di_\rho g\, di_\rho^*)$. Thus, $(a', S) \in \mathrm{Im}\, F$ for $(a', S) \in \mathcal{U}^*(\, di_\rho g\, di_\rho^*)$, if and only if $a'(T_\rho P_1) \subset T_\rho P_1$. Thus, the proof is complete.   □

5.   3-PARAMETER SPIN 1/2 MODEL

In this section, we consider a 3-parameter spin $1/2$ model. Let us define the Pauli matrices $\sigma_1, \sigma_2, \sigma_3$ in the usual way:

$$\sigma_1 = \begin{pmatrix} 0 & 1 \\ 1 & 0 \end{pmatrix}, \quad \sigma_2 = \begin{pmatrix} 0 & -i \\ i & 0 \end{pmatrix}, \quad \sigma_3 = \begin{pmatrix} 1 & 0 \\ 0 & -1 \end{pmatrix}.$$

Assume that $\dim \mathcal{H} = 2$, $\dim T_\rho P = 3$, and that $\rho \in T_{sa}^{+,1}(\mathcal{H})$ is not a pure state. We may assume that $\rho = \frac{1}{2}(Id + \alpha\sigma_3)$. By $S(T_\rho P)$ we denote the unit sphere in $T_\rho P$ with respect to the *SLD inner product. We assume that g is a quadratic form on $T_\rho P$. We denote $J_{S,T}^\ell$ by J. In this section, we assume $T_\rho P$ to be a real Hilbert space with respect to the *SLD inner product $J_{S,T}^\ell$. $f^3 = \frac{\sqrt{1-\alpha^2}}{2}\sigma_3$, $f^i = \frac{\sigma_i}{2}$, $(i = 1, 2)$ is an orthonormal base on $T_\rho P$. The dual base of f^i is $f_3 = \frac{-\alpha}{\sqrt{1-\alpha^2}}\, Id + \frac{1}{\sqrt{1-\alpha^2}}\sigma_3$, $f_i = \sigma_i$ ($i = 1, 2$) . We need some lemmas.

Lemma 5.1   *For $y \in T_\rho P$, we have*

$$\det(r\, \mathrm{Id}_\mathcal{H} - J^{-1}(y))$$
$$= \left(r + \frac{\alpha y^3}{\sqrt{1-\alpha^2}} + \sqrt{\frac{\alpha^2(y^3)^2}{(1-\alpha^2)} + 1} \right) \left(r + \frac{\alpha y^3}{\sqrt{1-\alpha^2}} - \sqrt{\frac{\alpha^2(y^3)^2}{(1-\alpha^2)} + 1} \right).$$

Proof We have

$$J^{-1}(y) = y^3 \frac{1}{1-\alpha^2}(-\alpha \operatorname{Id}_{\mathcal{H}} + \sigma_3) + \sum_{i=2}^{3} y^i \sigma_i. \tag{5.1}$$

Since there exists $t \in \mathbf{R}$ such that $\exp(\sqrt{-1}t\sigma_3)(y^1\sigma_1 + y^2\sigma_2)\exp(-\sqrt{-1}t\sigma_3) = \sqrt{(y^1)^2 + (y^2)^2}\sigma_1$, we may assume that $y^2 = 0$. We have

$$J^{-1}(y) = \begin{pmatrix} \frac{-\alpha+1}{\sqrt{1-\alpha^2}}y^3 & y^1 \\ y^1 & \frac{-\alpha-1}{\sqrt{1-\alpha^2}}y^3 \end{pmatrix}.$$

Therefore,

$$\det(r\operatorname{Id}_{\mathcal{H}} - J^{-1}(y))$$
$$= r^2 + \frac{\alpha y^3}{\sqrt{1-\alpha^2}}r - (y^1)^2 - (y^3)^2$$
$$= \left(r + \frac{\alpha y^3}{\sqrt{1-\alpha^2}} + \sqrt{\frac{\alpha^2(y^3)^2}{(1-\alpha^2)} + 1}\right)\left(r + \frac{\alpha y^3}{\sqrt{1-\alpha^2}} - \sqrt{\frac{\alpha^2(y^3)^2}{(1-\alpha^2)} + 1}\right).$$

$\square$

Lemma 5.2 For $z \in S(T_pP)$, we have

$$J^{-1}(z) \cdot \rho \cdot J^{-1}(z) = (\operatorname{Id}_{\mathcal{H}} - \rho). \tag{5.2}$$

Proof In the same way as above, we may assume that $z^3 = 0$. Then we have

$$J^{-1}(z) \cdot \rho \cdot J^{-1}(z) = \begin{pmatrix} \frac{-\alpha+1}{\sqrt{1-\alpha^2}}z^3 & z^1 \\ z^1 & \frac{-\alpha-1}{\sqrt{1-\alpha^2}}z^3 \end{pmatrix}\begin{pmatrix} \frac{1+\alpha}{2} & 0 \\ 0 & \frac{1-\alpha}{2} \end{pmatrix}\begin{pmatrix} \frac{-\alpha+1}{\sqrt{1-\alpha^2}}z^3 & z^1 \\ z^1 & \frac{-\alpha-1}{\sqrt{1-\alpha^2}}z^3 \end{pmatrix}$$
$$= \begin{pmatrix} \frac{1-\alpha}{2} & 0 \\ 0 & \frac{1+\alpha}{2} \end{pmatrix} = \operatorname{Id}_{\mathcal{H}} - \rho.$$

$\square$

For $x \in T_pP$, we denote the spectral measure of $J^{-1}x$ by $M_{J^{-1}x} \in \mathcal{M}_s(\mathbf{R}, \mathcal{H})$. For $y \in T_pP$ we define the map (y) in the following way:

$$\begin{array}{ccc} (y) : \mathbf{R} & \to & T_pP \\ \Cup & & \Cup \\ c & \mapsto & c \cdot y. \end{array} \tag{5.3}$$

Put $M^y_{J^{-1}x} := (y)_* M_{J^{-1}x} \in \mathcal{M}(T_pP, \mathcal{H})$. This is important to establish the optimal measurement.

Lemma 5.3 We have the following equation with respect to $E(M^y_{J^{-1}x}) \in \operatorname{Hom}(\mathcal{L}^{2,*}_{sa}(\rho), T_pP) \subset \operatorname{Hom}(\mathcal{L}^{2,*}_{sa}(\rho), \mathcal{L}^2_{sa}(\rho))$.

$$E(M^y_{J^{-1}x}) = y \otimes J^{-1}x = |y\rangle\langle x|. \tag{5.4}$$

Proof For $\tau \in \mathcal{L}^{2,*}_{sa}(\rho) = T_{sa}(\mathcal{H})$, we have

$$E(M^y_{J^{-1}x})(\tau) = \int_{T_pP} x_1 \operatorname{tr}_{\mathcal{H}} M^y_{J^{-1}x}(dx_1)\tau = y \operatorname{tr}_{\mathcal{H}} \tau J^{-1}x. \tag{5.5}$$

$\square$

By Theorem 3.1 and Corollary 3.1 we obtain the following theorem about the attainable Cramér-Rao type bound.

Theorem 5.1   *Let g be a nonnegative inner product on $T_\rho P$, then*

$$\inf_{M \in \mathcal{U}(T_\rho P)} \mathcal{D}_g^\rho(M) = (\mathrm{tr}_{T_\rho P} \sqrt{Jg})^2. \tag{5.6}$$

Moreover, the optimal measurement is given by a random measurement (i.e. a convex combination of simple measurements).

Proof   Take the Lagrange multipliers in the following way:

$$a(x) := 2\beta \cdot \sqrt{Jg}x, \quad S := -\frac{\beta^2}{2}(Id - \alpha\sigma_3) = -\beta^2(Id_{\mathcal{H}} - \rho),$$

where we put $\beta := \mathrm{tr}_{T_\rho P} \sqrt{Jg}$. Then, we have

$$
\begin{aligned}
R_g^\rho(a, S; x) &= g(x, x) \cdot \rho - a(x) - S \\
&= J^{-1}(\sqrt{Jg}x, \sqrt{Jg}x) \cdot \rho - 2\beta \cdot \sqrt{Jg}x + \beta^2(Id_{\mathcal{H}} - \rho) \\
&= J^{-1}(y, y) \cdot \rho - 2\beta \cdot y + \beta^2(Id_{\mathcal{H}} - \rho) \\
&= r^2\rho - 2\beta rz + \beta^2(Id_{\mathcal{H}} - \rho) \\
&= r^2\rho - 2\beta r\rho \circ J^{-1}(z) + \beta^2(Id_{\mathcal{H}} - \rho) \\
&= \left(r - \beta J^{-1}(z)\right)\rho\left(r - \beta J^{-1}(z)\right) + \beta^2\left((Id_{\mathcal{H}} - \rho) - J^{-1}(z) \cdot \rho \cdot J^{-1}(z)\right) \\
&= \left(r - \beta J^{-1}(z)\right)\rho\left(r - \beta J^{-1}(z)\right),
\end{aligned}
$$

where $z \in S_{J^{-1}}(T_\rho P)$, $r > 0$, $y = r \cdot z$, $y = \sqrt{Jg}(x)$. We derive the last equation from Lemma 5.2. Therefore, $(a, S) \in \mathcal{U}^*(g)$. Thus, $\mathrm{tr}_{T_\rho P} a + \mathrm{tr}_{\mathcal{H}} S = \left(\mathrm{tr}_{T_\rho P} \sqrt{Jg}\right)^2$ is a Cramér-Rao type bound.

First let us consider the case in which g is nondegenerate. By Lemma 5.1, one of eigenvalues of $\beta J^{-1}z$ is positive and another is negative. We denote the positive one by $r(z)^+$, another by $r(z)^-$. We denote their eigenvectors by $v(z)^+$, $v(z)^-$, respectively. As we have $r(-z)^+ = -r(z)^-$, $r(-z)^- = -r(z)^+$, $v(-z)^+ = v(z)^-$, $v(-z)^- = v(z)^+$, we have

$$
\begin{aligned}
R_g^\rho(a, S; M_{\beta J^{-1}z}^{\sqrt{Jg}^{-1}z}) &= \left\langle v(z)^+ \middle| \left(r(z)^+ - \beta J^{-1}(z)\right)\rho\left(r(z)^+ - \beta J^{-1}(z)\right) \middle| v(z)^+ \right\rangle \\
&\quad + \left\langle v(-z)^+ \middle| \left(r(-z)^+ - \beta J^{-1}(z)\right)\rho\left(r(-z)^+ - \beta J^{-1}(z)\right) \middle| v(-z)^+ \right\rangle \\
&= 0. \tag{5.7}
\end{aligned}
$$

Diagonalize $\sqrt{Jg}$ in the following way:

$$\sqrt{Jg} = \sum_{i=1}^{3} W_i e_i \otimes J^{-1}e_i = \sum_{i=1}^{3} W_i |e_i\rangle\langle e_i|, \quad e_i \in S(T_\rho P). \tag{5.8}$$

Put $M := \sum_{i=1}^{3} \frac{W_i}{\beta} M_{\beta J^{-1}e_i}^{\sqrt{Jg}^{-1}e_i} \in \mathcal{M}(T_\rho P, \mathcal{H})$. Then, we have $R_g^\rho(a, S; M) = 0$. By (2.7) and Lemma 5.3, we have

$$
\begin{aligned}
E(M) &= \sum_{i=1}^{3} \frac{W_i}{\beta} E(M_{\beta J^{-1}e_i}^{\sqrt{Jg}^{-1}e_i}) = \sum_{i=1}^{3} \frac{W_i}{\beta} \left|\sqrt{Jg}^{-1}e_i\right\rangle\left\langle \beta e_i\right| \\
&= \sum_{i=1}^{3} \frac{W_i}{\beta} |W_i^{-1}e_i\rangle\langle \beta e_i| = \sum_{i=1}^{3} |e_i\rangle\langle e_i|.
\end{aligned}
$$

Thus, the measurement $M \in \mathcal{M}(T_\rho P, \mathcal{H})$ satisfies the locally unbiasedness conditions. As it satisfies the conditions of Corollary 3.1, the random measurement $M \in \mathcal{M}(T_\rho P, \mathcal{H})$ attains a Cramér-Rao type bound$(\mathrm{tr}_{T_\rho P} \sqrt{Jg})^2$. Thus, $(\mathrm{tr}_{T_\rho P} \sqrt{Jg})^2$ is the attainable Cramér-Rao type bound.

Next let us consider the case in which g is degenerate. Let $\{A_n\}$ be a sequence of positive valued 3×3 symmetric matrices with $\lim_{n \to \infty} A_n = Jg$, where every A_n and $\sqrt{Jg}$ commute with each other, and $\mathrm{tr}_{\mathcal{H}} A_n = \sqrt{Jg} = \beta$. Let us take complete orthonormal system e_1, e_2, e_3 of the eigenvectors of A_n, Jg. Let W_i^n, $i = 1, 2, 3$ be the eigenvalues of $\sqrt{A_n}$. We define $M_n \in \mathcal{M}(T_\rho P, \mathcal{H})$ in the following way:

$$M_n := \sum_{i=1}^{3} \frac{W_i^n}{\beta_n} M_{\beta J^{-1} e_i}^{A_n^{-1} e_i}. \tag{5.9}$$

We can show $M_n \in \mathcal{U}(T_\rho P)$ in the same way as the case in which g is nondegenerate. Then, we have

$$\lim_{n \to \infty} \mathcal{R}_g^\rho(a, S; M_n) = \sum_{i=1}^{3} \lim_{n \to \infty} \frac{W_i^n}{\beta} \mathcal{R}_g^\rho(M_{\beta J^{-1} e_i}^{A_n^{-1} e_i}) = 0.$$

The proof is complete. $\qquad\qquad\qquad\qquad\qquad\qquad\qquad\qquad\qquad\qquad\qquad\quad\square$

Finally let us consider a 2-parameter case. Put $P_1 := T_{sa}^{+,1}(\mathbf{C}^2)$ and assume that $P_2 \subset P_1$, $\dim P_2 = 2$. Let $g := \sum_{i=1}^{2}(W_i)^2 e_i \otimes e_i$ be a quadratic form on $T_\rho P_2$, where e_1, e_2 is complete orthonormal system of $T_\rho^* P_2$. The maximum of the duality problem is given the following Lagrange multiplier,

$$a(x) := 2\beta \cdot (\sqrt{Jg})(x), \; S := -\beta^2(Id - \rho), \; \beta = \mathrm{tr} \sqrt{Jg},$$

(a,S) satisfies the conditions of the equality of Lemma 4.2. The optimal measurement is given by the random measurement which is the limit of the optimal measurement sequence given in the case of degenerate g in Theorem 5.1.

ACKNOWLEDGMENT

I wish to thank Dr. A. Fujiwara for introducing me into this subject, and Prof. K. Ueno for useful commnets about this paper.

REFERENCES

[1] A. S. Holevo, *Probabilistic and Statistical Aspects of Quantum Theory* (North-Holland, Amsterdam, 1982).

[2] H. P. Yuen and M. Lax, "Multiple-parameter quantum estimation and measurement of nonselfadjoint observables," *IEEE trans. Inform. Theory*, IT-19, pp740-750 (1973).

[3] H. Nagaoka, "A generalization of the simultaneous diagonalization of hermitian matrices and its relation to quantum estimation theory," *Trans. Jap. Soci. Ind. App. Math.*, vol.1, No.4, pp.305-318 (1991)(in Japanese).

[4] A. Fujiwara and H. Nagaoka, "Coherency in view of quantum estimation theory," in *Quantum coherence and decoherence*, edited by K. Fujikawa and Y. A. Ono, (Elsevier, Amsterdam, 1996), pp.303-306.

[5] R. M. Van Style and R. J. B. Wets, "A duality theory for abstract mathematical programs with applications to optimal control theory," *Journal of mathematical analysis and application,* vol.22, pp.679-706,(1968).

[6] A. S. Holevo, "Commutation superoperator of a state and its application to the noncommutative statistics," *Reports on mathematical physics,* vol.12, pp.251-271,(1977).

[7] M. Hayashi, "The minimization of deviation under locally unbiased conditions," *Master's Thesis, Depertment of Mathematics, Kyoto University,* (1996)(in Japanese).

[8] M. Hayashi, "A Linear Programming Approach to Attainable Cramér-Rao type Bounds and Randomness Condition," *to appear.*

NON-COMMUTATIVE EXTENSION OF
INFORMATION GEOMETRY II

Hiroshi Hasegawa[1] and Dénes Petz[2]

[1] Research Center for Quantum Communications, Tamagawa University
Tamagawa-gakuen, Machida, Tokyo 194, Japan
[2] Department of Mathematical Analysis, Technical University of Budapest
H-1521 Budapest XI. Sztoczek u.2, Hungary

The Fisher information provides a canonical Riemannian metric in the geometric approach to classical statistics. It seems that the quantum analogue of the Fisher information is not uniquely defined, and it is necessary to study the possible candidates and to compare them on physical grounds. Description of monotone metrics under coarse graining has been given by Petz and this class of metrics fixes many candidates. Here we show that the skew information $I_p(\rho, K) \equiv -\frac{1}{2}\mathrm{Tr}[\rho^p, K][\rho^{1-p}, K]$ first introduced by Wigner, Yanase and Dyson (WYD) many years ago yields a monotone metric for all values of p; $-1 \leq p \leq 2$ (for $p = 0,1$ under a proper limiting procedure and beyond the limits with a change of the sign of I_p). Furthermore, we argue that the symmetry between I_p and I_{1-p} is identical to the quantum version of Amari's duality concept for smooth statistical manifolds.

1. INTRODUCTION

This presentation is a summary of our collaboration on the extension of *information geometry* in classical statistics to the quantum mechanical setting since the last QCM workshop held in 1994. We deal with the construction of a Riemannian geometry on a manifold of finite dimensional density matrices parametrized by $\theta = (\theta^1, \theta^2, \ldots, \theta^r) \in \Theta$ in a matrix algebra $\mathcal{M}_n$. References on this topic from a general point of view are [1] and [2]. In the present workshop, we revisit the old notion of *skew information* [3] from the newly developed quantum geometric standpoint.

In 1963, Wigner and Yanase [4] investigated a trace quantity of matrices in $\mathcal{M}_n$,

$$-\mathrm{Tr}[\rho^{1/2}, k]^2 \qquad ([\ ,\ ] \text{ represents a commutator}), \qquad (1.1)$$

where ρ and k are self-adjoint elements in $\mathcal{M}_n$, in particular, ρ is positive definite and $\mathrm{Tr}\rho = 1$,i.e. a density matrix, while k is supposed to represent a conserved quantity of the quantum system under consideration: they proved that the above quantity is convex with respect to ρ like $\mathrm{Tr}\rho\log\rho$ and represents a kind of information content. They further supplemented to this work in [5], saying that the amount of this information depends on the non-commutativity of ρ and k that is needed for a measurement of non-commuting observables with k by means of external apparatus; hence the origin

Quantum Communication, Computing, and Measurement
Edited by Hirota *et al.*, Plenum Press, New York, 1997

of the naming "information content relative to k". It is important to note that Dyson [4] was said to propose a generalizing idea to expression (1.1) of Wigner and Yanase in regard to retaining the nature of information i.e.

$$I_p(\rho, k) = -\text{Tr}[\rho^p, k][\rho^{1-p}, k], \qquad 0 < p < 1, \tag{1.2}$$

guessing that it would be possible to prove the convexity of this expression with respect to ρ: this is the so-called Wigner-Yanase-Dyson conjecture whose correctness was verified later fully by Lieb [6] in a more general context. (For various modifications of (1.2), see [3]).

Being motivated by the classical information geometry discussed by Amari in his Lecture Notes [7], Hasegawa [8] proposed to define the quantum mechanical α-divergence $D_\alpha(\rho, \sigma)$ for two density matrices ρ and σ:

$$D_\alpha(\rho, \sigma) = \frac{4}{1-\alpha^2}\text{Tr}(\rho - \sigma^{\frac{1+\alpha}{2}}\rho^{\frac{1-\alpha}{2}}), \qquad \alpha \in \mathbf{R} = (-\infty, \infty), \tag{1.3}$$

$$\text{Tr}\rho = \text{Tr}\sigma = 1, \tag{1.4}$$

which is a natural generalization of the α-divergence $D_\alpha(p, q)$ for classical probability density functions $p(x)$ and $q(x)$ in Amari's formulation. It is well-known that $D_\alpha(p, q)$ is a globaly defined distance function between the two probabilities p and q but lacking the symmetry between them, i.e. $D_\alpha(p, q) \neq D_\alpha(q, p)$. What is significant about this function for the geometry of the statistical manifold is, when the two density functions are infinitesimally distant from each other, the Riemannian metric structure arises in such a way that

$$D_\alpha(p + dp, p) = D(p, p + dp) = \frac{1}{2}E_p(d\log p, d\log p)$$

$$= \frac{1}{2}E_p(\frac{\partial \log p}{\partial \theta^i}\frac{\partial \log p}{\partial \theta^j})d\theta^i d\theta^j \qquad \text{up to } O(d\theta)^2, \tag{1.5}$$

$$\text{for the expansion} \qquad dp = \frac{\partial p}{\partial \theta^i}d\theta^i, \quad \text{where} \tag{1.6}$$

$$E_p(\frac{\partial \log p}{\partial \theta^i}\frac{\partial \log p}{\partial \theta^j}) = \int p(x)\frac{\partial \log p}{\partial \theta^i}\frac{\partial \log p}{\partial \theta^j}d\mu(x) \equiv g_{ij}^F(\theta) \tag{1.7}$$

represents the Fisher information metric tensor expressed as a scalar product of the tangent vector

$$\partial_i: \quad \partial_i \log p = \frac{\partial}{\partial \theta_i}\log p. \tag{1.8}$$

The success of the definition of the quantum α-divergence (1.3) and (1.4) can be seen in the full parallelism of its Riemannian metric structure compared to the classical formulation above for the two infinitesimally distant density matrices ρ and $\rho + d\rho$. Here, $d\rho$ consists of a commutative part $d^c\rho$ with ρ and a non-commutative part such that

$$d\rho = d^c\rho + [\rho, \Delta] \qquad (\Delta \text{ is an anti-selfadjoint}) \tag{1.9}$$

$$= (\frac{\partial \rho}{\partial \theta_i} + [\rho, \Delta_i])d\theta^i, \qquad d^c\rho = \frac{\partial \rho}{\partial \theta_i}d\theta_i \quad \text{and} \quad \Delta = \Delta_i d\theta^i \tag{1.10}$$

in terms of which

$$D_\alpha(\rho + d\rho, \rho) = D_\alpha(\rho, \rho + d\rho)$$

$$= \frac{1}{2}\text{Tr}\rho(d^c \log \rho \, d^c \log \rho) + \frac{2}{1-\alpha^2}\text{Tr}[\rho^{\frac{1-\alpha}{2}}, \Delta][\rho^{\frac{1+\alpha}{2}}, \Delta]$$

$$= \frac{1}{2}(\text{Tr}\rho\frac{\partial \log \rho}{\partial \theta^i}\frac{\partial \log \rho}{\partial \theta^j} + \frac{4}{1-\alpha^2}\text{Tr}[\rho^{\frac{1-\alpha}{2}}, \Delta_i][\rho^{\frac{1+\alpha}{2}}, \Delta_j])d\theta^i d\theta^j$$

$$\equiv \frac{1}{2}g_{ij}^{(\alpha)}d\theta^i d\theta^j \tag{1.11}$$

up to $O(d\theta)^2$ and $\alpha \neq \pm 1$. The limit $\alpha \to \pm 1$ yields the familiar Kubo-Mori metric, which should be rendered to a full treatment separately (see [9] and [10]).

We can observe that the non-commutative part of $d\rho$ with ρ gives rise to an additional Riemannian metric in the form

$$\frac{1}{2p(1-p)}\text{Tr}[\rho^p, \Delta][\rho^{1-p}, \Delta], \qquad p = \frac{1-\alpha}{2}, \tag{1.12}$$

which, apart from the factor $1/p(1-p)$, is just equal to the WYD skew information $I_p(\rho, i\Delta)$.

From this observation, we see that the Riemannian metric tensor for quantum information geometry is of such a structure that it consists of two parts; the first part arising from the commutative $d\rho$ and the second from the non-commutative $d\rho$ with ρ, the first part being identified precisely with the classical Fisher form but the second part depending on the starting definition of the inner product on matrix spaces that induces the metric. We need, therefore, some axiomatic specification of inner products on $\mathcal{M}_n$ for a Riemannian metric to be well-defined as a quantum information metric. The *theory of monotone metrics on matrix spaces* by Petz [11] meets this need, which we will discuss in the next two sections. In Sec.4 we will discuss a problem of characterizing the WYD metric in terms of Amari's notion of *duality* in the information geometry.

2. MONOTONE RIEMANNIAN METRICS FOR QUANTUM STATISTICS [11]

We consider $\mathcal{M}_n(C)$ which can be regarded as a vector space whose elements are denoted by $A, B, \ldots$ and their adjoint by $A^*, B^*, \ldots$. An inner product of two elements A, B can be defined by a sesquilinear form $K(B, A)$ (linear in A and anti-linear in B), which may be written in terms of a linear superoperator K on $\mathcal{M}_n(C)$, $A \mapsto K(A) \in \mathcal{M}_n(C)$, and the standard Hilbert-Schmidt inner product as

$$K(B, A) = \langle B, K(A) \rangle = \text{Tr}B^*K(A). \tag{2.1}$$

In case that the linear superoperator K is positive definite and self-adjoint on $\mathcal{M}_n(C)$ (in the Hilbert-Schmidt sense), a positive quantity $K(A, A)$ induces a length of A which is called here a metric of A. We suppose further that the superoperator K depends on a density matrix $\rho \in \mathcal{M}_n^{++}$ (all positive definite self-adjoint elements in $\mathcal{M}_n$) and $\text{Tr}\rho = 1$, which is denoted by K_ρ; also the corresponding positive form K by K_ρ. We then impose a physical condition on the metric defined by K_ρ and A that by any stochastic mapping T of elements ρ and A (i.e. a completely positive map of ρ and A) the resulting metric does not exceed the original one: it means that a coarse-graining of a (quantum) state may reduce but may not increase the metric. All these requirements are now listed as follows.

(a) $(A, B) \mapsto K_\rho(A, B)$ is sesquilinear,

(b) $K_\rho(A, A) \geq 0$ and the equality holds if and only if $A = 0$,

(c) $\rho \mapsto K_\rho(A, A)$ is continuous on $\mathcal{M}_n^{++}$ for every fixed A,

(d) monotonicity condition: $K_{T(\rho)}(T(A), T(A)) \leq K_\rho(A, A)$ for every stochastic mapping $T : \quad \mathcal{M}_n(C) \mapsto \mathcal{M}_m(C)$,

The metric $K_\rho(A, A)$ which satisfies (a)–(d) will be called a *monotone metric*. In
condition (d) the stochastic mapping T may be taken to be any unitary conjugation
$U^* \cdot U$ for which the inequality must be replaced by the equality, implying the unitary
covariance

(d') $K_{U\rho U}(U^*AU, U^*AU) = K_\rho(A, A)$,

It implies the fact that the density matrix ρ of K_ρ may be understood to be represented
always as diagonal.

For the purpose of application to geometry, it is sufficient to restrict the metric
tensor to be real i.e. $g_{ji} = g_{ij} = $ real. For this to be the case, it is more convenient
to restrict the vectors $A, B, \cdots$ always to be self-adjoint: then expression (2.1) may be
replaced by

$$K'(B, A) = \frac{1}{2}(K(B, A) + K(A, B))$$
$$= K'(A, B), \qquad A^* = A, \quad B^* = B, \qquad (2.2)$$

which is a symmetric, bilinear form of any pair of self-adjoint elements in $\mathcal{M}_n(C)$, and

$$K'_\rho(A, A) = \sum_{i=1}^{n} c(\lambda_i)A_{ii}^2 + 2\sum_{i<j} c(\lambda_i, \lambda_j)|A_{ij}|^2, \qquad (2.3)$$

$$\rho = \sum_{i=1}^{n} \lambda_i e_{ii} \quad (0 < \lambda_i < 1).$$

The two-variable function $c(\lambda, \mu) = c(\mu, \lambda)$ is called "Morozova-Chentsov function"
after the names of Russian mathematicians who obtained the expression for the first
time [12]. Conditions (b),(c) and (d) are shown to restrict the possible form of the two
functions $c(\lambda)$ and $c(\lambda, \mu)$ in (2.3), reducing their degree of freedom to one. Namely,

Theorem 1 *Suppose that (b),(c) and (d) hold for a real, bilinear form $K'_\rho(A, B)$ on
self-adjoint element in $\mathcal{M}_n$. Then, the two functions $c(\lambda)$ and $c(\lambda, \mu)$ on $R^+ \times R^+$ in
the ρ-diagonalized representation of the metric $K'_\rho(A, A)$ satisfy the following:*

(i) $c(\lambda), c(\lambda, \mu)(= c(\mu, \lambda))$ *are continuous, positive functions,*

(ii) $\lim_{\mu \to \lambda} c(\lambda, \mu) = c(\lambda) = c\lambda^{-1}$, *with a positive constant $c = 1$ hereafter.*

(iii) $c(\lambda, \mu)$ *is homogeneous of order -1 in λ and μ, implying*
$c(x\lambda, x\mu) = \frac{1}{x}c(\lambda, \mu)$ *for any $x > 0$.*

Different from the approach in [12], Petz has given a proof of **Theorem 1** by means
of *operator monotone function* initiated by Löwner in 1932. We do not go into detail,
but in order to show the power of this notion for the present problem we summarize
a result which clarifies the Morozova-Chentsov (M-C) function $c(\lambda, \mu)$ by means of the
operator monotonicity in **Theorem 2** after giving its definition:

Definition 1 *A real non-negative function $f : R^+ \to R^+$ is operator monotone, if, for any x and $y \in M_n^{++}$ and for every $n \in N$, $x \le y$ implies $f(x) \le f(y)$. (See for example [13],[15].)*

Theorem 2 *There exists a one-to-one correspondence (apart from normalization) between the M-C function $c(\lambda, \mu)$ for a symmetric monotone metric $K_\rho'(A, A)$ and an operator monotone function f as follows*

$$\textbf{i)} \quad f(x) = \frac{1}{c(x, 1)}, \qquad \textbf{ii)} \quad c(\lambda, \mu) = \frac{1}{\mu f(\lambda/\mu)}, \qquad (2.4)$$

$$\textit{where by virtue of symmetry} \quad c(\lambda, \mu) = c(\mu, \lambda), \ x f(1/x) = f(x). \qquad (2.5)$$

*That is, for a given M-C function $c(\lambda, \mu)$, $f(x)$ defined by **i)** is operator monotone and, conversely, for a given operator monotone function f the function $c(\lambda, \mu)$ defined by **ii)** yields an M-C function.*

Previously, three important monotone metrics have been given together with many other examples [11]:

Symmetric logarithmic-derivative metric K^{Sl}

$$c(\lambda, \mu) = \frac{2}{\lambda + \mu} \quad \text{for which} \quad f(x) = \frac{1}{2}(x + 1); \qquad (2.6)$$

Kubo-Mori metric K^{KM}

$$c(\lambda, \mu) = \frac{\log \lambda - \log \mu}{\lambda - \mu} \quad \text{for which} \quad f(x) = \frac{x - 1}{\log x}; \qquad (2.7)$$

Right logarithmic-derivative metric K^{Rl}

$$c(\lambda, \mu) = \frac{1}{2}\left(\frac{1}{\lambda} + \frac{1}{\mu}\right) \quad \text{for which} \quad f(x) = \frac{2x}{x + 1}. \qquad (2.8)$$

From a viewpoint of *operator mean*, Kubo and Ando [13] obtained a remarkable result that any normalized operator monotone function f lies between the maximum $f_{\max}(x) = \frac{1}{2}(x + 1)$ (arithmetic mean) and the minimum $f_{\min}(x) = \frac{2x}{x+1}$ (harmonic mean). Correspondingly, for every monotone metric $K_\rho(A, A)$ with a fixed A the following inequalities hold

$$K_\rho^{Sl} \le K_\rho \le K_\rho^{Rl}. \qquad (2.9)$$

Therefore, our present interest is whether the WYD metrics are monotone metrics or not and, if they are, in what ranges they lie in the inequalities (2.9). The full answer will be seen in the next section.

3. WIGNER-YANASE-DYSON METRICS WITH MONOTONICITY

We begin by determining the M-C function $c(\lambda, \mu)$ for the WYD metric (1.12) and the corresponding f-function. If this function can be proved to be operator monotone, then we can say that the WYD metric is surely a monotone metric by virtue of Theorem 2. The determination can be easily done by taking the ρ-diagonal representation of the matrix under the trace in (1.12), showing that

$$c(\lambda_j, \lambda_k)|A_{jk}|^2 = \frac{1}{p(1 - p)}(\lambda_j^p - \lambda_k^p)(\lambda_j^{1-p} - \lambda_k^{1-p})|\Delta_{jk}|^2, \qquad j \ne k.$$

But since $A_{jk} = (\lambda_j - \lambda_k)\Delta_{jk}$ and $\Delta_{jk}^* = -\Delta_{kj}$, we get

$$c(\lambda, \mu) = \frac{1}{p(1-p)} \frac{(\lambda^p - \mu^p)(\lambda^{1-p} - \mu^{1-p})}{(\lambda - \mu)^2}, \tag{3.1}$$

for which properties i), ii) and iii) in **Theorem 1** can be checked. Hence

$$f(x) = p(1-p)\frac{(x-1)^2}{(x^p - 1)(x^{1-p} - 1)} \equiv f_p(x), \tag{3.2}$$

and changing the parameter p to α, $p = \frac{1-\alpha}{2}$

$$f_\alpha(x) = \frac{1-\alpha^2}{4} \frac{(x-1)^2}{(x^{\frac{1-\alpha}{2}} - 1)(x^{\frac{1+\alpha}{2}} - 1)}. \tag{3.2'}$$

Let us ask now whether this function is operator monotone. An affirmative answer has been obtained for the case $0 < p < 1$ [14]. Here we outline the full answer both for $0 < p < 1$ and for $-1 < p < 0$ on an equal footing. (Case for $1 < p < 2$ reduces to the latter case.) The keyword of the proof is an integral representation of the inverse of $f_p(x)$ in (3.2), which can be given by

$$\frac{1}{f_p(x)} = \frac{\sin p\pi}{\pi} \int_0^\infty d\lambda \lambda^{p-1} \int_0^1 ds \int_0^1 dt \frac{1}{x((1-t)\lambda + (1-s)) + (t\lambda + s)}, \quad 0 < p < 1, \tag{3.3}$$

$$= \frac{\sin p\pi}{p\pi} \int_0^\infty d\lambda \lambda^{-|p|} \int_0^1 ds \int_0^1 dt \frac{x(1-t)+t}{[x((1-t)\lambda + (1-s)) + (t\lambda + s)]^2}, \quad -1 < p < 0. \tag{3.3'}$$

This is based on the integral representation of a fractional power of a positive quantity, namely

$$z^{p-1} = \frac{\sin p\pi}{\pi} \int_0^\infty \frac{\lambda^{p-1}}{\lambda + z} d\lambda, \quad 0 < p < 1, \tag{3.4}$$

$$= \frac{\sin p\pi}{p\pi} \int_0^\infty \frac{\lambda^{-|p|}}{(\lambda + z)^2} d\lambda, \quad -1 < p < 0. \tag{3.4'}$$

(The latter is obtainable from the former by replacing $p \to 1 - p$ and a differentiation). Accordingly, we perform the λ-integration first in (3.3) and (3.3') and then the rest double integrations which can be made elementarily to obtain the desired expressions.

In order to assure the operator monotonicity of $f_p(x)$ in both cases, let us set up another definition in comparison with **Definition 1**.

Definition 2 *We say, a real non-negative function $f : R^+ \to R^+$ is operator monotone-decreasing, if, for any x and $y \in M_n^{++}$ and for every $n \in N$, $x \le y$ implies $f(x) \ge f(y)$.*

Evidently, by Definitions 1 and 2, the inverse of an operator monotone function is operator monotone-decreasing and *vice versa* . Then, it is easy to see that $f_p(x)$ given in (3.3) is operator monotone, because the integrand is operator monotone-decreasing(a linear function $ax + b$, $a > 0, b \ge 0$, is operator monotone and so $(ax + b)^{-1}$ is operator monotone-decreasing). Since the triple integration there is made always with positive coefficients, the result $\frac{1}{f_p(x)}$ is operator monotone-decreasing, and hence $f_p(x)$ is operator monotone. Thus, the same reasoning also applies to the expression (3.3'), if its integrand is shown to be operator monotone-decreasing, and this is indeed the case: a function of the form $(cx + d)/(ax + b)^2, a, c > 0$ and $b, d \geq 0$, is operator monotone-decreasing [15].

We thus establish the operator monotonicity of the f-functions associated with the WYD metrics given by (3.2) or (3.2') for all cases. Strictly speaking, the above proof may lose the validity for some special parameter values because of a divergence of the integration (3.3) or (3.3'); the case $p = \pm 1$, and 0 listed as

$$
\begin{array}{cccc}
p = & -1 & 0 & +1 \\
\alpha = & 3 & 1 & -1 \\
& (\text{ Right log.derivative} & \text{Kubo-Mori} & \text{Kubo-Mori })
\end{array}
$$

The operator monotonicity for these situations has been verified by other means [11]. It is remarkable to see the absence of f_{max} in the above list (symmetric logarithmic-derivative metric): there exists $maximum$ f_{max} of all the WYD f-functions which satisfies

$$
f_{max}^{WYD}(x) = \frac{1}{4}(x^{1/2} + 1)^2 < f_{max}(x) = \frac{x+1}{2}
$$

This corresponds to the original Wigner-Yanase metric (1.1). There exists a gap between these two maxima which can not be filled by any WYD f-function. The feature can be seen in Fig.1: This figure illustrates how the functions $f_\alpha(x)$ behave on the real line $[0, 1]$ with α from 0 to 3, showing that $f_\alpha; \alpha > 3$ is forbidden.

4. CHARACTERIZATION OF THE WYD METRICS BY DUALITY

Let ρ be a density matrix and T_ρ be the tangent space at ρ in the quantum statistical manifold. It was seen above that the monotone metric is uniquely determined in the subspace

$$
T_\rho^c = \{X \in T_\rho : \rho X - X\rho = 0\}, \tag{4.1}
$$

and therefore, it is worthwhile to decompose the tangent space as $T_\rho = T_\rho^c \oplus T_\rho^X$, where $T_\rho^X = \{i[\rho, X] \in T_\rho : X = X^*\}$. Using the superoperator $\mathcal{L}_\rho$: $X \mapsto i[\rho, X]$, we may put this decomposition in the form $Ker\mathcal{L}_\rho \oplus Rng\mathcal{L}_\rho$.

It is a useful observation that the kernel and the range of $\mathcal{L}_\rho$ remain unchanged when ρ is replaced by $g(\rho)$ and g is a monotone function, $\mathbf{R}^+ \to \mathbf{R}$. We say that a symmetric metric K_ρ admits dual affine connections if, for a pair of such monotone functions g and g^*,

$$
K_\rho(\mathcal{L}_\rho(X), \mathcal{L}_\rho(Y)) = \langle \mathcal{L}_{g(\rho)}(X), \mathcal{L}_{g^*(\rho)}(Y)\rangle. \tag{4.2}
$$

Note that (4.2) is equivalently written as

$$
K_\rho(A, B) = \frac{\partial^2}{\partial t \partial s} \text{Trg}(\rho + tA)g^*(\rho + sB)|_{t=s=0}, \quad A = i[\rho, X], B = i[\rho, Y].
$$

It follows that

$$
\partial_C K_\rho(A, B) = \langle \delta_C \delta_A g(\rho), \delta_B g^*(\rho)\rangle + \langle \delta_A g(\rho), \delta_C \delta_B g^*(\rho)\rangle, \tag{4.3}
$$

which stands for the quantum version of Amari's duality concept in affine connections. Namely, the first term of the right-hand side of (4.3) represents an affine connection as regards three directions A, B and C and then the second term its dual connection as regards B, A and C, both adding up to yield a derivative of the metric in the direction C[7]. The WYD skew information is seen to have this form, where both g and g^* are the power function, and we want to show that this is the unique possibility for the metrics with this dual structure.

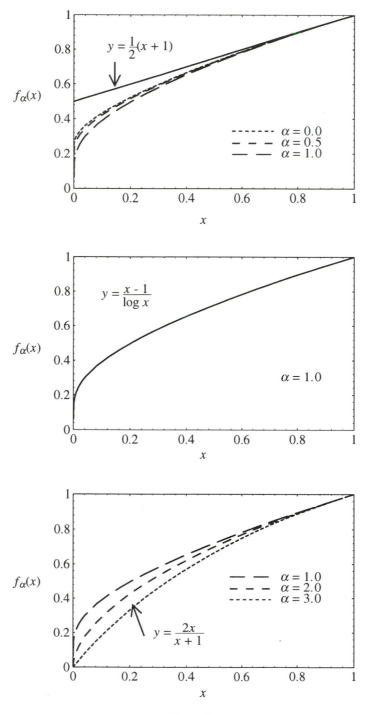

Figure 1

Theorem 3 *In the class of symmetric monotone metrics, the Wigner-Yanase-Dyson skew information is characterized by the property that it admits dual affine connections.*

In the sketch of the proof of this theorem we assume that the functions g and g^* appearing in definition (4.2) are continuous and smooth on $\mathbf{R}^+$. It is an analogous task to the derivation of expression (3.1) to compute the Morozova-Chentsov function for the metric (4.2), and we get

$$c(\lambda, \mu) = \frac{(g(\lambda) - g(\mu))(g^*(\lambda) - g^*(\mu))}{(\lambda - \mu)^2} \tag{4.4}$$

From the property $c(t\lambda, t\mu) = t^{-1}c(\lambda, \mu)$ we deduce that, under the condition $g(0)g^*(0) = 0$, $g(t\lambda)g^*(t\lambda) = tg(\lambda)g^*(\lambda)$ must hold. This implies that

$$g(x)g^*(x) = cx \qquad (x \in \mathbf{R}^+). \tag{4.5}$$

Another necessary condition comes from the property that $lim_{\lambda \to \mu}c(\lambda, \mu) = \mu^{-1}$. In this way, we arrive at the condition

$$g'(x)g^{*\prime}(x) = x^{-1} \qquad (x > 0). \tag{4.6}$$

(4.5) and (4.6) together have the solution $g(x) = ax^p$ and $g^*(x) = bx^{1-p}$, $ab = c = \frac{1}{p(1-p)}$, and the possible limit $lim_{p \to 0, or 1}$ allowing x and $\log x$.

Note that the operator-monotonicity condition fixes the set of the possible values of p as $-1 \leq p \leq 2$ (or, $|\alpha| \leq 3$). From the present standpoint, we can say that the reason of the absence of the metric for the *symmetric logarithmic-derivative* and other those lying in the gap in Fig.1 as a WYD type is because the above duality is lacking in these metrics. In a later publication we shall give a more detailed account of this dual structure.

REFERENCES

[1] H.Hasegawa, Non-commutative extension of the information geometry, in Proc. Intern. Workshop on Quantum Communications and Measurement, Nottingham 1994, eds. V.P. Belavkin, O. Hirota and R.L. Hudson, Plenum, 1995.

[2] D.Petz and Cs. Sudár, Geometry of quantum states, J. Math. Phys. **37**(1996),2662–2673.

[3] M.Ohya and D.Petz, Quantum Entroppy and Its Use, Springer-Verlag, Heidelberg, 1993.

[4] E.P.Wigner and M.M.Yanase, Information content of distributions, Proc. Nat. Acad. Sci. USA **49**(1963), 910-918.

[5] E.P.Wigner and M.M.Yanase, On the positive semidefinite nature of a certain matrix expression, Canad. J. Math. **16**(1964), 397-406.

[6] E.H.Lieb, Convex trace functions and the Wigner-Yanase-Dyson conjecture, Advances in Math. **11**(1973), 267-288.

[7] S.Amari, Differential-Geometrical Methods in Statistics, Lecture Notes in Statistics **28**(1985).

[8] H.Hasegawa, α-divergence of the non-commutative information geometry, Rep. Math. Phys. **33**(1933), 87-93.

[9] D.Petz, Geometry of canonical corretation on the state space of a quantum system, J. Math. Phys. **35**(1994), 780-795.

[10] H.Hasegawa, Exponential and mixture families in quantum statistics, Rep. Math. Phys. **39**(1997), 49-68.

[11] D.Petz, Monotone metrices on matrix spaces, Linear Algebra Appl. **244**(1996), 81-96.

[12] E.A.Morozova and N.N.Chentsov, Markov invariant geometry on state manifold (in Russia), Itogi Naukini Tekhniki **36**(1990), 69-102.

[13] F.Kubo and T.Ando, Means of positive linear operators, Math Ann. **246**(1980) 205– 224.

[14] D.Petz and H.Hasegawa, On the Riemannian metric of α-entropies of density matrices, Lett. Math. Phys. **38**(1996),221-255.

[15] F.Hansen and G.K.Pedersen, Jensen's inequality for operators and Löwner's theorem, Math. Ann.**258**(1982), 229-241.

WAVELETS AND INFORMATION-PRESERVING TRANSFORMATIONS

Y. S. Kim

Department of Physics, University of Maryland
College Park, Maryland 20742, U.S.A.

The underlying mathematics of the wavelet formalism is a representation of the inhomogeneous Lorentz group or the affine group. Within the framework of wavelets, it is possible to define the "window" which allows us to introduce a Lorentz-covariant cut-off procedure. The window plays the central role in tackling the problem of photon localization. It is possible to make a transition from light waves to photons through the window. On the other hand, the windowed wave function loses analyticity. This loss of analyticity can be measured in terms of entropy difference. It is shown that this entropy difference can be defined in a Lorentz-invariant manner within the framework of the wavelet formalism.

1. INTRODUCTION

One of the still-unsolved problems in quantum mechanics is the transition from classical light waves to photons. Light waves are classical objects, and their quantum counterparts are photons. Then, are photons light waves? From the traditional theoretical point of view, the answer is NO [1]. However, this negative answer does not prevent us from examining how close photons are to waves by employing a new mathematical device called wavelet. The word "wavelet" is relatively new in physics [2,3], but its concept was formulated in the 1960s [4]. The wavelet combines the traditional Fourier transformation with dilation or "squeeze" and translational symmetries. Since the squeezes and translations are the basic symmetries in the Poincaré group, and since the Fourier transformation is the standard language for the superposition principle, the wavelet formulation of light waves gives a covariant description of the superposition principle applicable to light waves.

Photons are relativistic particles requiring a covariant theoretical description. Wave functions in classical optics satisfy the superposition principle and can be localized, but they are not covariant under Lorentz transformations. The wavelet formalism makes light waves covariant, and this makes light waves closer to photons. Furthermore, the formalism allows us to make a quantitative analysis of the difference between these two clearly defined physical concepts. In this way, we can assert that photons are waves with a proper qualification [5].

In order to carry out this program, we need another important property of wavelets: translation symmetry. This symmetry allows us to introduce the concept of "window" [6–9]. The window allows us to keep a function defined within a specified interval and let it vanish outside the interval or the window. This finite interval requires the concept of translation. From the mathematical point of view, this translational symmetry is very cumbersome and is often misunderstood by physicists. For instance, the translation does not commute with the Lorentz boost.

However, it is possible to define the order of transformations to preserve the information contained in the window [5]. The windowing process is a cut-off process, which leads to a loss of information. This information loss can be formulated in terms of the entropy change. It is shown that this entropy change can be formulated in a covariant manner. In this report, we give a brief review of the earlier work on this subject. Sections 2, 3, 4 consist of review of the recent paper by Han, Kim, and Noz [5]. We report a new result in Sec. 5. This section deals with entropy.

2. LIGHT WAVES AND WAVELETS

For light waves, we start with the usual expression

$$F(z,t) = \frac{1}{\sqrt{2\pi}} \int g(k)e^{iku}dk , \tag{1}$$

where $u = (z-t)$. Even though light waves do not satisfy the Schrödinger equation, the very concept of the superposition principle was derived from the behavior of light waves. Furthermore, it was reconfirmed recently that light waves satisfy the superposition principle [10]. It is not difficult to carry out a spectral analysis on Eq.(1) and give a probability interpretation.

Before getting into the wavelet formalism, let us consider the expression

$$A(z,t) = \int \frac{1}{\sqrt{2\pi\omega}}a(k)e^{iku}dk . \tag{2}$$

This is the basic form we use in quantum electrodynamics, and is thus very familiar to us. We regard this as a classical quantity, with an understanding that it will become the photon field after second quantization. This is a covariant expression in the sense that the norm

$$\int \frac{|a(k)|^2}{2\pi\omega}dk . \tag{3}$$

is invariant under Lorentz transformations, because the integral measure $(1/\omega)dk$ is Lorentz-invariant. It is possible to give a particle interpretation to Eq.(2) after second quantization. However, $A(z,t)$ cannot be used for the localization of photons. On the other hand, it is possible to give a localized probability interpretation to $F(z,t)$ of Eq.(1), while it does not accept the particle interpretation of quantum field theory.

Under the Lorentz boost:

$$z' = (\cosh \eta)z + (\sinh \eta)t , \qquad t' = (\sinh \eta)z + (\cosh \eta)t , \tag{4}$$

the variables u and k become $e^{-\eta}u$ and $e^{\eta}k$ respectively. Thus, the Lorentz boost is a squeeze transformation in the phase space of u and k [11]. The expression given in Eq.(1) is not covariant if $g(k)$ is a scalar function, because the measure dk is not invariant. If $g(k)$ is not a scalar function, what is its transformation property? It was shown by Han, Kim, and Noz [12] that we can solve this covariance problem by replacing $F(u)$ and $g(k)$ by $F'(u)$ and $g'(k)$ respectively defined as

$$F'(u) = \sqrt{\frac{p}{\sigma}}F(u) , \qquad g'(k) = \sqrt{\frac{\sigma}{p}}g(k) , \tag{5}$$

where p is the average value of the momentum:

$$p = \frac{\int k|g(k)|^2 dk}{\int |g(k)|^2 dk} \ , \tag{6}$$

which becomes $p = e^\eta$ under the Lorentz boost. Then the functions of Eq.(5) will satisfy Parseval's equation:

$$\int |F'(u)|^2 du = \int |g'(k)|^2 dk \tag{7}$$

in every Lorentz frame without the burden of carrying the multipliers as given in Eq. (5). We can simplify the above cumbersome procedure by introducing the form

$$G(u) = \frac{1}{\sqrt{2\pi p}} \int g(k) e^{iku} dk \ . \tag{8}$$

where the procedure for the Lorentz boost is to replace p by $e^\eta p$, and k in $g(k)$ by $e^{-\eta}$. As is shown in Ref. [12], this is a squeeze transformation. This is precisely the wavelet form for the localized light wave, and this definition is consistent with the form given in earlier papers on wavelets [2, 4].

We are quite familiar with the expression of Eq.(1) for wave optics, and with that of Eq.(2) for quantum electrodynamics. The above expression satisfies the same superposition principle as Eq.(1), and has the same covariance property as Eq.(2). It is quite similar to both Eq.(1) and Eq.(2), but they are not the same. The difference between $F(u)$ of Eq.(1) and the wavelet $G(u)$ is insignificant. Other than the factor $\sqrt{\sigma}$ where σ has the dimension of the energy, the wavelet $G(u)$ has the same property as $F(u)$ in every Lorentz frame [12].

However, there is a still a significant difference between $G(u)$ of Eq.(8) and $A(u)$ of Eq.(2). In Eq.(2), the factor $1/\sqrt{\omega}$ is inside the integral and is a variable. Thus the superposition principle is not applicable to $A(u)$ with $a(k)$ as a spectral function. On the other hand, in Eq.(8), the factor $1/\sqrt{p}$ is constant. Thus, the superposition principle is applicable to $G(u)$ with $g(u)$ as a spectral function.

This difference disappears if the spectral functions $g(k)$ and $a(k)$ are delta functions. The difference becomes non-trivial as the widths of these functions increase. If the widths can be controlled, the difference can also be controlled. In so doing, it is essential that the spectral functions vanish for $k = 0$ and for infinite values of k. We can achieve this goal by using the concept of window.

3. WINDOWS

Here, the window means that the spectral function is non-zero within a finite interval, and vanishes everywhere else. There is a tendency to regard this type of cut-off procedure as an approximation. On the other hand, we have to keep in mind that physics is an experimental science. When we measure in laboratories, we do not measure functions, but we take data points from which functions are constructed. It is well known that functions so constructed can never be unique. This is the limitation of accuracy in physics.

Thus, when we deal with a localized distribution, the window is a very useful mathematical device. Because of the inherent gap between a function and a collection of data points, we do have the freedom of choosing a windowed function for a localized distribution. The problem here is the question of covariance. Let us choose a window in one Lorentz frame. How would this window look in a different Lorentz frame? Is this window going to preserve all the information given in the initial frame.

In order to answer these questions, we have to examine the translation symmetry of wavelets, particularly the translation combined with squeeze transformations. The problem here is that this affiance symmetry can sometimes lead to information preserving windows and sometimes non-preserving windows. Let us look at this problem closely.

The problem is caused by the fact that squeeze transformations do not commute with translations. In the present case, the squeeze corresponds to a multiplication of the variable k by a real constant, while the translation is achieved by an addition of a real number. To a given number, we can add another number, and we can also multiply it by another real number. This combined mathematical operation is called the affine transformation [13]. Since the multiplication does not commute with addition, affine transformations can only be achieved by matrices. We can write the addition of b to x as

$$\begin{pmatrix} x' \\ 1 \end{pmatrix} = \begin{pmatrix} 1 & b \\ 0 & 1 \end{pmatrix} \begin{pmatrix} x \\ 1 \end{pmatrix} . \tag{9}$$

This results in $x' = x + b$. This is a translation. We can represent the multiplication of x by e^η as

$$\begin{pmatrix} x' \\ 1 \end{pmatrix} = \begin{pmatrix} e^\eta & 0 \\ 0 & 1 \end{pmatrix} \begin{pmatrix} x \\ 1 \end{pmatrix} , \tag{10}$$

which leads to $x' = e^\eta x$. This is a squeeze transformation.

We are interested in combined transformations. The translation does not commute with the squeeze. If the squeeze precedes the translation, we shall call this the affine transformation of the first kind, and the transformation takes the form

$$x' = e^\eta x + b . \tag{11}$$

If the translation is made first, we shall call this the affine transformation of the second kind, and the transformation takes the form

$$x' = e^\eta(x + b) . \tag{12}$$

The distinction between the first and second kinds is not mathematically precise, because the translation subgroup of the affine group is an invariant subgroup. We make this distinction purely for convenience. Whether we choose the first kind or second kind depends on the physical problem under consideration. For a covariant description of light waves, the affine transformation of the second kind is more appropriate, and the inverse of Eq.(12) is

$$x = e^{-\eta}x' - b = e^{-\eta}(x' - e^\eta b) . \tag{13}$$

Therefore, the transformation of a function $f(x)$ corresponding to the vector transformation of Eq.(12) is

$$f\left(e^{-\eta}x - b\right) = f\left(e^{-\eta}(x - e^\eta b)\right) . \tag{14}$$

Next, does this translation lead to a problem in normalization as the squeeze did? The normalization integral does not depend on the translation parameter b, but it does depend on the multiplication parameter η. Indeed,

$$\int |f(e^{-\eta}x - b)|^2 dx = e^\eta \int |f(x - b)|^2 dx . \tag{15}$$

In order to preserve the normalization under the affine transformation, we can introduce the form [2]

$$e^{-\eta/2} f(e^{-\eta}x - b) . \tag{16}$$

This is the wavelet form of the function $f(e^{-\eta}x - b)$. This is of course the wavelet form of the second kind. The wavelet of the first kind will be

$$e^{-\eta/2} f\left(e^{-\eta}(x - b)\right) . \tag{17}$$

Both the first and second kinds of wavelet forms are implicitly discussed in the literature [2]. Here, we are using this concept in constructing an information-preserving window under Lorentz boosts.

With this preparation, we can allow the function to be nonzero within the interval

$$a \leq x \leq a + w , \tag{18}$$

while demanding that the function vanish everywhere else. The parameter w determines the size of the window. The window can be translated or expanded/contracted according to the operation of the affine group. We can now define the window of the first kind and the window of the second kind. Both windows can be translated according to the transformation given in Eq.(18). The window of the first kind is not affected by the scale transformation. However, the size and location of the window of the second kind becomes affected by the scale transformation according to Eq.(12). We can choose either of these two windows depending on our need. The window of the first kind is useful when we describe an observer with a fixed scope.

On the other hand, the window of the second kind is covariant and defines the information-preserving boundary conditions [5]. The width of this window is proportional to the average momentum, and the ratio w/p is a Lorentz-invariant quantity, where w is the width of the window. Indeed, this information-preserving window will play an important role in the photon localization problem.

4.   PHOTON LOCALIZATION PROBLEM

Let us go back to Eq.(2). $A(u)$ is a classical amplitude, and it becomes a photon field after second quantization. If it is to be localized, $a(k)$ must have a non-zero distribution, and $A(u)$ is therefore a polychromatic [14–16]. $A(u)$ of Eq.(2) and $G(u)$ of Eq.(8) are numerically equal if

$$a(k) = \sqrt{\frac{k}{p}} g(k) , \tag{19}$$

where the window is defined over a finite interval of k which does not include the point $k = 0$. It is thus possible to jump from the wavelet $G(u)$ to the photon field $A(u)$ using the above equation. Furthermore, since k and p have the same Lorentz-transformation property, this relation is Lorentz-invariant. Both $a(k)$ and $g(k)$ can be regarded as distribution functions which can be constructed from experimental data.

However, the above equality does not say that $a(k)$ is equal to $g(k)$. The intensity distribution of the localized light wave is not directly translated into the photon-number distribution. This is the quantitative difference between wavelets and photons. As we stated before, this difference becomes insignificant when the window becomes narrow. However, as the window becomes narrower, the wavelet becomes more wide-spread. The wavelet then becomes non-localizable. This is why we are saying that photons are not localizable.

However, there are no rules saying that $a(k)$ and $g(k)$ should be the same. As long as we can transform from one expression to other as in Eq.(19, the transition from wavelets to photons can be carried out within the window. This point needs further investigation in the future.

5. ENTROPY FORMULATION OF THE INFORMATION LOSS

We now introduce the concept of entropy to deal with the information loss due the windowing process. We use in this report the standard form for the entropy:

$$S = -\int \rho(k)\ln[\rho(k)]dk, \qquad (20)$$

where $\rho(k)$ is the probability distribution function, with the normalization condition

$$\int \rho(k)dk = 1. \qquad (21)$$

If the Lorentz boost transforms k into $e^{\eta}k$, the distribution becomes widespread for positive values of η. The normalization integral becomes

$$\int e^{-\eta}\rho(e^{-\eta}k)dk = 1. \qquad (22)$$

This normalization condition is form-invariant and is valid for all normalizable probability distribution functions. The Lorentz-boosted entropy takes the form

$$S' = -\int e^{-\eta}\rho(e^{-\eta}k)\ln[e^{-\eta}\rho(e^{-\eta}k)]dk, \qquad (23)$$

which becomes

$$S' = -\int \rho(k)\ln[\rho(k)]dk + \eta, \qquad (24)$$

The effect of the Lorentz boost is very simple. The boost simply add the parameter η to the original expression:

$$S' - S = \eta. \qquad (25)$$

The entropy difference between the analytic and windowed distribution functions is

$$\Delta S = -\int \{\rho_A(k)\ln[\rho_A(k)] - \rho_W(k)\ln[\rho_W(k)]\}\,dk, \qquad (26)$$

where $\rho_A(k)$ and $\rho_W(k)$ are the probability distributions in the analytic and windowed forms respectively. The integration of this expression will produce a number. The question then is whether this is a Lorentz-invariant quantity. Let us go back to Eq.(25). The Lorentz-transformed entropy of the analytic form will produce η, and so will the windowed form. They will cancel each other. Thus the expression for the entropy difference given in Eq.(26) is a Lorentz-invariant expression.

It is shown in Ref. [5] that an information-preserving window can be defined. In this report, we have shown that the information loss due to the windowing process can also be defined in terms of a the Lorentz invariance of the entropy difference.

REFERENCES

[1] T. D. Newton and E. P. Wigner, Rev. Mod. Phys. **21**, 400 (1949).

[2] I. Daubechies, *Ten Lectures on Wavelets* (Society for Industrial and Applied Mathematics, Philadelphia, PA, 1992).

[3] G. Kaiser, *A Friendly Guide to Wavelets* (Birkhauser, Boston, 1994).

[4] E. W. Aslaksen and J. R. Klauder, J. Math. Phys. **9**, 206 (1968) and **10**, 2267 (1969).

[5] D. Han, Y. S. Kim, and M. E. Noz, Phys. Lett. A **206**, 299 (1996).

[6] B. DeFacio, in *Workshop on Squeezed States and Uncertainty Relations*, Proceedings, D. Han, Y. S. Kim, and W. W. Zachary, eds. (NASA Conference Publications No. 3135, 1992).

[7] H. H. Szu and H. J. Caulfield, Optical Engineering **31**, 1823 (1992).

[8] G. Kaiser, in *Progress in Wavelets and Applications*, Proc., Y. Meyer and S. Roques, eds. (Editions Frontieres, Paris, 1993), and the references contained in this paper.

[9] D. Han, Y. S. Kim, and M. E. Noz, in *Second International Workshop on Squeezed States and Uncertainty Relations*, D. Han, Y. S. Kim, V. I. Man'ko, eds. (NASA Conference Publications No. 3219, 1993).

[10] A. Aspect, P. Grangier, and G. Roger, J. Optics (Paris) **20**, 119 (1989).

[11] Y. S. Kim and E. P. Wigner, Phys. Rev. A **36**, 1293 (1987).

[12] D. Han, Y. S. Kim, and M. E. Noz, Phys. Rev. A **35**, 1682 (1987).

[13] R. Gilmore, *Lie Groups, Lie Algebras, and Some of Their Applications* (John Wiley and Sons, New York, 1974).

[14] U. M. Titulaer and R. J. Glauber, Phys. Rev. **145**, 1041 (1966).

[15] H. Fearn and R. Loudon, J. Opt. Soc. Am. B **6**, 917 (1989).

[16] R. A. Campos, B. E. A. Saleh, and M. C. Teich, Phys. Rev. A **42** 4127 (1990).

ON THE REALIZATION
OF RECEIVED QUANTUM STATE CONTROL
BY UNITARY TRANSFORMATION

Tsuyoshi Sasaki-Usuda and Masayasu Hata

Nagoya Institute of Technology
Gokiso-cho, Showa-ku, Nagoya, 466, Japan
usuda@ics.nitech.ac.jp

Necessary and sufficient conditions of an optimum pair of signals for given decision operators are given. These conditions show what kind of signals are desired for the output of the unitary transformation in a received quantum state control system by unitary process in order to achieve the Helstrom's bound. We show pictures of optimum signals which the conditions imply. Then we consider as examples two of received quantum state control systems by unitary process.

1. INTRODUCTION

The purpose of the quantum communication theory [1,2] is to overcome the standard quantum limit (SQL) which is the theoretical limitation predicted by the classical communication theory.

It was Helstrom who first gave a method to overcome the SQL. He showed the theory of the optimum quantum receiver which is the optimization of quantum measurement and decision processes and also showed the new limitation of a quantum system [1]. We call this limitation Helstrom's bound. However, it is not clear by his theory what physical process corresponds to the optimum quantum receiver and this gave rise to a realization problem.

As another method to overcome the SQL, Hirota proposed a concept of a received quantum state control [3,4] which has been studied in a research field of the quantum state control [5,6]. It says we can overcome the SQL by merely inserting a received quantum state controller before a quantum measurement process in a conventional system. Furthermore, it has potential to break the Helstrom's bound.

Our purpose is to construct the design theory of such systems. So far some systems have been proposed as physical realizations and shown that the SQL can be overcome [7-10]. Since we proposed in QCM94 a system with an optical Kerr medium as a received quantum state controller [10], studies to apply a unitary transformation have been progressed [11] although systems are limited by the Helstrom's bound for this type of the realization. Such a study has been developed as a study of a realization strategy for the optimum decision process because a realization of a unitary-type received quantum state control gives a manner for a realization of the optimum quantum receiver [12-14], that is, they have the same goal in a certain sense.

A realization of the optimum quantum receiver was first found by Dolinar [15], in which an example of a realization for binary coherent signals was given. It was M. Sasaki who proposed an algorithm of a realization for the case of arbitrary linearly independent and binary signals [14]. So it was proved that a physical realization of the optimum quantum receiver exists in such case. We think the study of the realization problem of the optimum quantum receiver got over a difficulty.

However, although his algorithm gives a realization, realization methods are not unique. So his realization is not necessarily the best of a great number of realizations. If so, what realization should we select ? In some cases, an easily experimentable unitary transformation may be desired, in the other cases, less effect of classical noise takes precedence. Or a system with lower cost might be desired in some cases. After all, for constructing the design theory which we aim for, realization methods which are met various kinds of needs should be shown. That is, we should go on a study in order to find out all kinds of realizations.

In this paper, we would like to consider a suitable pair of signals for given standard decision operators since the quantum measurement process is represented by them in a received quantum state control system. This is to clarify what kind of signals are desired as an output of the unitary transformer in a unitary-type received quantum state control system. Needless to say, we must consider a unitary transformer by which such signals can be generated. We will show conditions of the optimum signals for given decision operators and also show pictures of desired signals. The 'optimum condition' in the quantum theory will be also discussed. As examples, we will consider two of unitary-type received quantum state control systems which were proposed up to this time.

2. RECEIVED QUANTUM STATE CONTROL

2.1. CONCEPT OF RECEIVED QUANTUM STATE CONTROL

A quantum communication system is called a received quantum state control system if it contains at the receiver part a quantum state controller by which the SQL is overcome. The term 'SQL' is used in various ways in literature. We takes the following definition [16,17] since our main interest is to construct a digital communication system with a lower error probability.

Definition 1. *The standard quantum limit (SQL) is defined as the minimum error probability achieved by the quantum measurement based on the orthonormal spectrum measure of the signal observable.*

The general model of the received quantum state control system for a digital communication system is given in Fig.1. This shows that it is almost the same as a conventional communication system but the only difference is the existence of the received quantum state controller. That is, in a received quantum state control system, a transmitter, a channel, and a received signal are the same as that in a conventional system. The received signal is however transformed by a received quantum state controller and the transformed signal is detected by a conventional quantum measurement. This quantum measurement is the same as the receiver in the conventional system and is represented by standard decision operators [16-18] which will be explained in the next section.

There are two types of a received quantum state control. One is the received quantum state control which is constructed by a unitary device. The other is a non-unitary-type. However, we here consider a realization by a unitary-type.

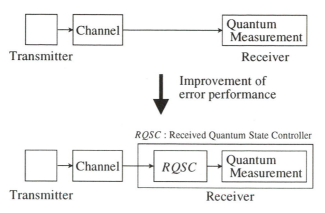

Figure 1. Concept of received quantum state control.

2.2. RECEIVED QUANTUM STATE CONTROL BY UNITARY PROCESS

An error probability of a received quantum state control by unitary process is

$$P_{\mathrm{e}} = 1 - \sum_i \xi_i \mathrm{Tr} \hat{U} \hat{\rho}_i \hat{U}^\dagger \hat{\Pi}_i, \tag{1}$$

where $\hat{\rho}_i$ and ξ_i are the quantum state and its prior probability of the received signal, which correspond to a message i, respectively, $\hat{U}$ is a unitary operator representing the received quantum state controller, and $\hat{\Pi}_i$ is a standard decision operator representing the quantum measurement after the quantum state control. Clearly, this system is limited by the Helstrom's bound since the inner product for different signal states is kept by a unitary transformation. Mathematically, what we do by this system is replacing the quantum measurement process for the signal $\hat{\rho}_i$ from $\hat{\Pi}_i$ to $\hat{U}^\dagger \hat{\Pi}_i \hat{U}$. If we select the best unitary transformation, it is expected to achieve the Helstrom's bound, so that what we are going to do is equivalent to solve the realization problem of the optimum quantum receiver. That is, a received quantum state control system by unitary process gives one realization of the optimum quantum receiver. Hence, we can use results of studies of a realization of the optimum quantum receiver and we would like to concentrate in this paper to achieve the Helstrom's bound.

3. OPTIMUM PAIR OF SIGNALS FOR STANDARD DECISION OPERATORS

In this section, we would like to consider what signal is desired at the output of the unitary transformer in a received quantum state control by unitary process. Because the quantum measurement process is represented by standard decision operators in a received quantum state control system, it is sufficient to consider a suitable pair of signals for standard decision operators, i.e., a pair of signals for which the standard decision operators are optimum. This is what we mean by the title of this section.

3.1. STANDARD DECISION OPERATOR

Definition 2. *If the decision operator consists of the projection-valued measure (PVM) of the signal observable such as*

$$\hat{\Pi}_{i(SD)} = \int f(x)|x\rangle\langle x|dx, \tag{2}$$

$$\sum_i \hat{\Pi}_{i(SD)} = \hat{I} \quad and \quad \hat{\Pi}_{i(SD)} \geq 0, \tag{3}$$

where $f(x)$ is Wald's decision function. Then it is called the standard decision operator.

A quantum measurement process which is characterized by standard decision operators is called a standard quantum measurement process [18]. Although the above definition is rigorous, we relax the strictness in this paper and regard a decision operator which has the form of Eqs.(2) and (3) as a standard decision operator. That is, we allow not only a decision operator based on a measurement of a signal observable but also that based on a measurement of another well-known observable.

3.2. A NECESSARY AND SUFFICIENT CONDITION OF AN OPTIMUM PAIR OF SIGNALS FOR GIVEN STANDARD DECISION OPERATORS

Here we will show conditions of an optimum pair of signals for given decision operators. In the following, we consider the case of linearly independent and binary signals. Here for simplicity, the prior probabilities of the signals are assumed to be equal. The conditions are as follows:

Condition 1. *A pair of signals $\{|\psi_0\rangle, |\psi_1\rangle\}$ is optimum for given decision operators $\{\hat{\Pi}_0, \hat{\Pi}_1\}$ if and only if the following two conditions are satisfied.*

(1) $\{\hat{\Pi}_0, \hat{\Pi}_1\}$ are orthogonal on a space $\mathcal{H}_S$ spanned by $\{|\psi_0\rangle, |\psi_1\rangle\}$.

(2) Let the representations of $\{\hat{\Pi}_0, \hat{\Pi}_1\}$ on the space $\mathcal{H}_S$ be $|\omega_0\rangle\langle\omega_0|$, $|\omega_1\rangle\langle\omega_1|$ ($|\omega_0\rangle$, $|\omega_1\rangle \in \mathcal{H}_S$) when the condition (1) is satisfied. Then $\{|\psi_0\rangle, |\psi_1\rangle\}$ are represented as

$$|\psi_0\rangle = \sqrt{1-\varepsilon}|\omega_0\rangle + e^{i\Psi_0}\sqrt{\varepsilon}|\omega_1\rangle, \tag{4}$$

$$|\psi_1\rangle = \sqrt{\varepsilon}|\omega_0\rangle + e^{i\Psi_1}\sqrt{1-\varepsilon}|\omega_1\rangle, \tag{5}$$

where $0 < \varepsilon < \frac{1}{2}, 0 \leq \Psi_0, \Psi_1 \leq 2\pi$.

The above condition directly comes from the necessary and sufficient condition by Helstrom [1] of the optimum decision operator for a given pair of signals. We only rewrote his condition for our purpose. Furthermore, if we specify the above condition to the case of using standard decision operators, we obtain the following condition:

Condition 2. *Let $\{\hat{\Pi}_0, \hat{\Pi}_1\}$ be standard decision operators defined by Eqs.(2) and (3).*
A pair of signals $\{|\psi_0\rangle, |\psi_1\rangle\}$ is optimum for $\{\hat{\Pi}_0, \hat{\Pi}_1\}$ if and only if for any x,

$$\frac{\langle x|\psi_0\rangle}{\langle x|\psi_1\rangle} = \begin{cases} C & f(x) = 0, \\ (C^*)^{-1} & f(x) = 1, \end{cases} \tag{6}$$

where C is a constant independent of x, satisfying $|C| < 1$ and $\arg C = -\arg\langle\psi_0|\psi_1\rangle$.

This is a necessary and sufficient condition of the optimum pair of signals for given standard decision operators. The proof of this condition will be given in the appendix. The constant C is related to the error probability ε and the inner product $\kappa \equiv \langle \psi_0 | \psi_1 \rangle$ as

$$|C| = \sqrt{\frac{\varepsilon}{1 - \varepsilon}} = \frac{1}{|\kappa|}\left(1 - \sqrt{1 - |\kappa|^2}\right). \qquad (7)$$

The above condition gives a picture of the signals. Actually, Eq.(6) implies that the wave function for the message 1 is proportional to that for the message 0 in the same region of the signal decision and the constant ratio of the wave functions in one region is the inverse of the complex conjugate of that in the other region. We show this picture in Fig.2 in which the squares of the absolute values of the wave functions, in short the probability distributions, are drawn. Eigenvalues of the observable are discrete in Fig.2(a) and continuous in Fig.2(b). It may be difficult to generate such signals in the continuous case compared with in the discrete case because the wave functions must be discontinuous at the boundary of the regions, which is at $x = 0$ in Fig.2(b), in order to satisfy Eq.(6). But the case that the wave functions for both messages 0 and 1 vanish at $x = 0$ is an exception. Therefore, it may be better to find the signals in which the wave functions vanish at the boundary as shown in Fig.3. Anyhow, the signals characterized in Figs.2 or 3 are desired by a unitary transformation. However if we fix the signals before the unitary transformer, the value of C is determined by Eq.(7). So the desired unitary transformer is much restricted. We should determine the value of $f(x)$ to meet the needs.

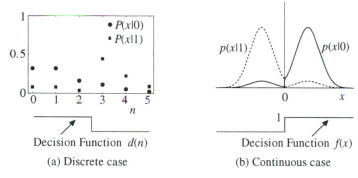

(a) Discrete case · · · · · (b) Continuous case

Figure 2. Probability distributions of optimum signals for given standard decision operators; Pictures of optimum signals (1).

Now we consider the 'optimum condition'. From Figs.2 and 3, the decision function is also optimum in a classical sense. What is the difference of optima in the quantum and the classical theories ? In the classical theory, an optimization is only concerned with the likelihood ratio. So the decision as shown in Fig.4 is also optimum. In the quantum theory, however, it is not optimum. In order to be optimum in the quantum theory, the ratio of the probability distributions for messages 0 and 1 must be constant in the same region of a signal decision. This means optimization is necessary not only for the *likelihood ratio* but also for the *signals*, strictly speaking, the forms of probability distributions. Furthermore this is achieved by 'quantum interference' based on a quantum state transformation [11,17]. In the classical theory, however, the error probability which is once optimized by the likelihood ratio can not be improved how we transform the probability distributions. If the result of the measurement of the signal observable satisfies the above condition 2, the SQL is the same as the Helstrom's bound. In this case, a quantum interference by a unitary transformation only degrades the system performance.

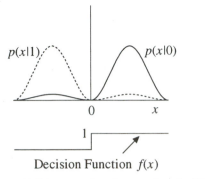

Decision Function $f(x)$

Figure 3. Picture of optimum signals (2).

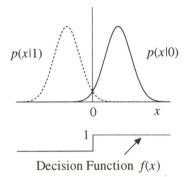

Decision Function $f(x)$

Figure 4. Gaussian distributions; Picture of optimum signals in the classical theory.

3.3. EXAMPLES

Here we will consider as examples two of received quantum state control systems by unitary processes with the above pictures (Figs.2 and 3).

(A) SYSTEM 1 [10]

First, we consider the system proposed in QCM94. In this system, the received signal states are coherent states $\{|\alpha\rangle, |-\alpha\rangle\}$, the received quantum state controller is an optical Kerr medium, and the quantum measurement is a homodyne detector which realizes a measurement of a quadrature-phase amplitude operator. This system overcomes the SQL but does not achieve the Helstrom's bound. The signal quantum states after the unitary transformation by the optical Kerr medium are

$$|\psi_0\rangle = \hat{U}_k|\alpha\rangle, \quad |\psi_1\rangle = \hat{U}_k|-\alpha\rangle, \tag{8}$$

where $\hat{U}_k = \exp[\frac{i}{2}\gamma\hat{n}(\hat{n}-1)]$ is the unitary operator describing the unitary evolution through the Kerr medium, $\hat{n} = \hat{a}^\dagger\hat{a}$, and γ is a nonlinear parameter and is proportional to the third-order nonlinear susceptibility $\chi^{(3)}$ of the Kerr medium. The standard decision operators are based on the measurement of the quadrature-phase amplitude operator $\hat{X}_\phi \equiv \frac{1}{2}(\hat{a}e^{-i\phi} + \hat{a}^\dagger e^{i\phi})$ and represented as

$$\hat{\Pi}_0 = \int_0^\infty |x_\phi\rangle\langle x_\phi| \mathrm{d}x_\phi, \quad \hat{\Pi}_1 = \int_{-\infty}^0 |x_\phi\rangle\langle x_\phi| \mathrm{d}x_\phi, \tag{9}$$

where $\hat{X}_\phi|x_\phi\rangle = x_\phi|x_\phi\rangle$ and ϕ is a detection phase.

The wave functions of the signals in the X_ϕ-representation are

$$\langle x_\phi|\psi_0\rangle = \sum_n \frac{\alpha^n}{\sqrt{n!}} \exp\left[-\frac{1}{2}|\alpha|^2\right] \cdot \exp\left[\frac{i}{2}\gamma n(n-1)\right] \cdot \langle x_\phi|n\rangle, \tag{10}$$

$$\langle x_\phi|\psi_1\rangle = \sum_n \frac{(-\alpha)^n}{\sqrt{n!}} \exp\left[-\frac{1}{2}|\alpha|^2\right] \cdot \exp\left[\frac{i}{2}\gamma n(n-1)\right] \cdot \langle x_\phi|n\rangle, \tag{11}$$

$$\langle x_\phi|n\rangle = \left(\frac{1}{2^n n!}\sqrt{\frac{2}{\pi}}\right)^{1/2} H_n\left[\sqrt{2}x_\phi\right] \cdot e^{-x_\phi^2} \cdot e^{-in\phi} \cdot e^{i\theta_0}, \tag{12}$$

where θ_0 is an arbitrary phase factor.

Fig.5 shows that the probability distributions of the signals at the output of the Kerr medium with $\alpha = 1$, $\gamma = 0.30$, and $\phi = -0.19$, which are the squares of the absolute values of the wave functions in Eqs.(10) and (11). We can see from Fig.5 that the probability distribution of the message 0 has a small peak in $x < 0$, so that, it seems to be closer to the distributions in Figs.2(b) and 3 than the probability distribution for a coherent state which gives the SQL. The probability distribution of the message 1 is symmetric with respect to $x = 0$. Therefore, although the system with the optical Kerr medium does not satisfy the condition in Eq.(6), it has a close characteristic to that implied by the condition of Eq.(6).

(B) SYSTEM 2 [14]

Now we consider the system proposed by M.Sasaki. This system is a physical realization of the optimum quantum receiver, which is derived by Sasaki's algorithm. It is also a unitary-type received quantum state control. In this system, the signals are $\{|0\rangle, |\alpha\rangle\}$, the received quantum state controller is a unitary transformer described by $\hat{U}_s = \exp[\gamma(|\eta_1\rangle\langle\eta_0| - |\eta_0\rangle\langle\eta_1|)]$, and the quantum measurement is a photon counting. Where $|\eta_0\rangle = |0\rangle, |\eta_1\rangle = (|\alpha\rangle - \kappa|0\rangle)/\sqrt{1-\kappa^2}$, $\kappa = \langle 0|\alpha\rangle$, and $\gamma = \frac{1}{2}\sin^{-1}\kappa$. The unitary transformation is defined on the space spanned by signals $|0\rangle$ and $|\alpha\rangle$. However, Sasaki still showed the extension of the unitary operator to an operator on the whole space and represented it by annhilation and creation operators $\hat{a}, \hat{a}^\dagger$ [14]. The signals after the unitary transformation are

$$|\psi_0\rangle = \hat{U}_s|0\rangle = \sqrt{1-\varepsilon}|0\rangle - \sqrt{\varepsilon}|\eta_1\rangle, \quad |\psi_1\rangle = \hat{U}_s|\alpha\rangle = \sqrt{\varepsilon}|0\rangle - \sqrt{1-\varepsilon}|\eta_1\rangle, \qquad (13)$$

where $\varepsilon = \frac{1}{2}\left(1 - \sqrt{1-\kappa^2}\right)$. The standard decision operators are

$$\hat{\Pi}_0 = |0\rangle\langle 0|, \quad \hat{\Pi}_1 = \sum_{n=1}^{\infty} |n\rangle\langle n| = \hat{I} - |0\rangle\langle 0|, \qquad (14)$$

where $\hat{n}|n\rangle = n|n\rangle$. The wave functions of signals in the n-representation are

$$\langle n|\psi_0\rangle = \begin{cases} \sqrt{1-\varepsilon} & n = 0, \\ -\sqrt{\varepsilon} \cdot \langle n|\eta_1\rangle & n \neq 0, \end{cases} \qquad (15)$$

$$\langle n|\psi_1\rangle = \begin{cases} \sqrt{\varepsilon} & n = 0, \\ -\sqrt{1-\varepsilon} \cdot \langle n|\eta_1\rangle & n \neq 0. \end{cases} \qquad (16)$$

Therefore, we obtain

$$\frac{\langle n|\psi_0\rangle}{\langle n|\psi_1\rangle} = \begin{cases} \sqrt{(1-\varepsilon)/\varepsilon} & n = 0, \\ \sqrt{\varepsilon/(1-\varepsilon)} & n \neq 0. \end{cases} \qquad (17)$$

We see from the above equation that the signals (13) satisfy the condition 2 for the standard decision operators (14).

We show in Fig.6 the probability distributions of the signals at the output of the unitary transformer with $\alpha = 1.5$. We can easily see from Fig.6 that the distribution for the message 0 is proportional to that for the message 1 in a same region of the signal decision.

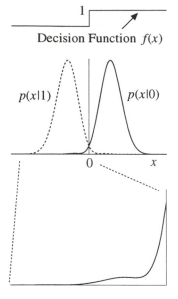

Figure 5. Probability distributions of signals in system 1.

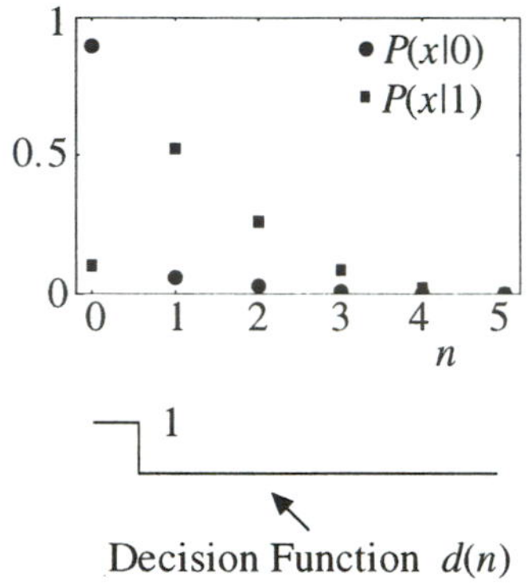

Figure 6. Probability distributions of signals in system 2.

The characteristics in Fig.6 are more natural than those in the case of continuous eigenvalues in Fig.2(b). If eigenvalues of the observable are discrete, probabilities are different in the front and the rear of the boundary in almost all cases, so that it seems to be comparatively easy to satisfy the optimum condition.

4. CONCLUSION

We have shown that what kind of signals are desired for the output of the unitary transformer in a received quantum state control system. We gave necessary and sufficient conditions for such signals, in particular in the case that the quantum measurement is represented by standard decision operators. We see from these conditions that the wave function must be discontinuous at the boundary of the signal decision when eigenvalues of the observable are continuous. So it is difficult to achieve the Helstrom's bound in such case. Contrary it is relatively easy to achieve the Helstrom's bound when eigenvalues of the observable are discrete. In fact, all physical realizations of the optimum quantum receiver shown by Sasaki, et.al. [12-14] are the discrete case. The next problem is to clarify desired quantum states corresponding to the pictures which was shown here and to find a unitary transformation in order to generate such states.

Acknowledgments

The authors would like to thank Prof. O. Hirota (Tamagawa Univ.) and Dr. M. Sasaki (CRL Ministry of P & Telecommun).
This work was supported by Grants of Ministry of Education, Japan.

REFERENCES

[1] C. W. Helstrom, *Quantum detection and estimation theory*, (Academic Press, New York, 1976).

[2] A. S. Holevo, *Probabilistic and statistical aspect of quantum theory*, (North-Holland, Amsterdam, 1982).

[3] O. Hirota, et. al., Trans. IEICE of Japan, **E70**, 801, 1987.

[4] O. Hirota, in LNP-378 (Springer-Verlag, Berlin, 1991), pp.223-230.

[5] H. P. Yuen, Phys. Rev. **A13**, 2226, 1976.

[6] O. Hirota and S. Ikehara, Trans. IECE of Japan, **E61**, 273, 1978.

[7] S. Bun, et. al., Trans. IEICE of Japan, **E73**, 1647, 1990.

[8] H. Koyano, et. al., in LNP-378 (Springer-Verlag, Berlin, 1991), pp.249-258.

[9] T. Sasaki and O. Hirota, Trans. IEICE of Japan, **E75-B**, 514, 1992.

[10] T. S. Usuda and O. Hirota, *Quantum communications and measurement*, edited by V. P. Belavkin, O. Hirota, and R. L. Hudson (Plenum Press, 1995), pp.419-427.

[11] M. Sasaki, T. S. Usuda, and O. Hirota, Phys. Rev. **A51**, 1702, 1995.

[12] M. Sasaki and O. Hirota, Phys. Lett. **A210**, 21, 1996.

[13] M. Sasaki, T. S. Usuda, O. Hirota, and A. S. Holevo, Phys. Rev. **A53**, 1273, 1996.

[14] M. Sasaki and O. Hirota, Phys. Rev. **A54**, 2728, 1996.

[15] S. J. Dolinar, Quarterly Progress Report No.111, Research Laboratory of Electronics, M.I.T., 115, 1973.

[16] O. Hirota, *Annals of New York Academy of Sciences*, **755**, 863, 1995.

[17] R. Momose, M. Osaki, M. Ban, M. Sasaki, and O. Hirota, Proc. of FICSSUR, 307, 1996.

[18] R. Momose and O. Hirota, Tech. Group Rep. in IEICE of Japan, **95**, No.457, pp.31-36, 1996.

[19] O. Hirota, Phys. Lett. **A155**, 343, 1991.

[20] R. S. Kennedy, Quarterly Progress Report No.110, Research Laboratory of Electronics, M.I.T., 142, 1973.

[21] R. S. Kennedy, Quarterly Progress Report No.113, Research Laboratory of Electronics, M.I.T., 129, 1974.

[22] M. Osaki and O. Hirota, *Quantum communications and measurement*, edited by V. P. Belavkin, O. Hirota, and R. L. Hudson (Plenum Press, 1995), pp.401-409.

APPENDIX   PROOF OF CONDITION 2.

In order to prove the sufficiency, assume Eq.(6).

$$\langle\psi_0|\psi_0\rangle = C\int\{1-f(x)\}\langle\psi_0|x\rangle\langle x|\psi_1\rangle dx + C^{-1}\int f(x)\langle\psi_1|x\rangle\langle x|\psi_0\rangle dx = 1, \quad (A1)$$

$$\langle\psi_1|\psi_1\rangle = C^{-1}\int\{1-f(x)\}\langle\psi_1|x\rangle\langle x|\psi_0\rangle dx + C\int f(x)\langle\psi_0|x\rangle\langle x|\psi_1\rangle dx = 1. \quad (A2)$$

Adding Eq.(A1) by (A2),

$$2 = C\kappa + C^{-1}\kappa^*, \quad (A3)$$

where $\kappa \equiv \langle\psi_0|\psi_1\rangle$. From Eq.(A3) and the condition $|C| < 1$,

$$C = \frac{1}{\kappa}\left(1 - \sqrt{1-|\kappa|^2}\right). \quad (A4)$$

Since

$$\kappa = \langle\psi_0|\psi_1\rangle = C^{-1}\int\{1-f(x)\}\langle\psi_0|x\rangle\langle x|\psi_0\rangle dx + C^*\int f(x)\langle\psi_0|x\rangle\langle x|\psi_0\rangle dx$$

$$= C^{-1} + (C^* - C^{-1})\int f(x)|\langle x|\psi_0\rangle|^2 dx, \quad (A5)$$

$$\int f(x)|\langle x|\psi_0\rangle|^2 dx = \frac{\kappa - C^{-1}}{C^* - C^{-1}} = \frac{\kappa C - 1}{|C|^2 - 1}. \quad (A6)$$

The error probability ε becomes from the above equations,

$$\varepsilon = \frac{1}{2}(\langle\psi_0|\hat{\Pi}_1|\psi_0\rangle + \langle\psi_1|\hat{\Pi}_0|\psi_1\rangle)$$

$$= \frac{1}{2}\left[1 - \int f(x)|\langle x|\psi_0\rangle|^2 dx + |C|^2\int f(x)|\langle x|\psi_0\rangle|^2 dx\right]$$

$$= \frac{1}{2}\left\{1 - (1-|C|^2)\cdot\frac{\kappa C - 1}{|C|^2 - 1}\right\} = \frac{1}{2}\kappa C = \frac{1}{2}\left(1 - \sqrt{1-|\kappa|^2}\right). \quad (A7)$$

This shows the optimum error probability for the signals $\{|\psi_0\rangle, |\psi_1\rangle\}$. Thus, $\{\hat{\Pi}_0, \hat{\Pi}_1\}$ are the optimum decision operators for the signals $\{|\psi_0\rangle, |\psi_1\rangle\}$.

Next, we will prove the necessity. Assume that $\{\hat{\Pi}_0, \hat{\Pi}_1\}$ are the optimum decision operators for the signals $\{|\psi_0\rangle, |\psi_1\rangle\}$ and ε is the optimum error probability. Then a relation $|\kappa| = 2\sqrt{\varepsilon(1-\varepsilon)}$ is held. From the quantum detection theory, $\langle\psi_0|\hat{\Pi}_1|\psi_0\rangle = \langle\psi_1|\hat{\Pi}_0|\psi_1\rangle = \varepsilon$ if the prior probabilities of signals are equal. Introduce complex-valued functions $g_0(x)$ and $g_1(x)$ which are defined as follows.

$$g_0(x) \stackrel{\text{def}}{=} \begin{cases} \langle x|\psi_0\rangle/\sqrt{\varepsilon} & f(x) = 0, \\ \langle x|\psi_0\rangle/\sqrt{1-\varepsilon} & f(x) = 1, \end{cases} \quad (A8)$$

$$g_1(x) \stackrel{\text{def}}{=} \begin{cases} \langle x|\psi_1\rangle/\sqrt{1-\varepsilon} & f(x) = 0, \\ \langle x|\psi_1\rangle/\sqrt{\varepsilon} & f(x) = 1. \end{cases} \quad (A9)$$

Since $\langle\psi_0|\hat{\Pi}_1|\psi_0\rangle = \int\{1-f(x)\}|\langle x|\psi_0\rangle|^2 dx = \int\{1-f(x)\}\varepsilon|g_0(x)|^2 dx = \varepsilon$,

$$\int\{1-f(x)\}|g_0(x)|^2 dx = 1.$$

We also obtain $\int f(x)|g_0(x)|^2 dx = \int\{1-f(x)\}|g_1(x)|^2 dx = \int f(x)|g_1(x)|^2 dx = 1$. Thus,

$$\int|g_0(x)|^2 dx = \int|g_1(x)|^2 dx = 2. \quad (A10)$$

Since

$$|\kappa| = \left|\int \{1 - f(x)\}\sqrt{\varepsilon(1-\varepsilon)}g_0{}^*(x)g_1(x)\mathrm{d}x + \int f(x)\sqrt{\varepsilon(1-\varepsilon)}g_0{}^*(x)g_1(x)\mathrm{d}x\right|$$

$$= \sqrt{\varepsilon(1-\varepsilon)}\left|\int g_0{}^*(x)g_1(x)\mathrm{d}x\right| = 2\sqrt{\varepsilon(1-\varepsilon)},$$

$$\left|\int g_0{}^*(x)g_1(x)\mathrm{d}x\right| = 2. \tag{A11}$$

For absolutely square integrable complex-valued functions $g_0(x)$ and $g_1(x)$,

$$\int (|g_0(x)| - |g_1(x)|)^2 \mathrm{d}x \geq 0, \tag{A12}$$

$$\int |g_0(x)|^2\mathrm{d}x + \int |g_1(x)|^2\mathrm{d}x \geq 2\int |g_0(x)|\,|g_1(x)|\,\mathrm{d}x \geq 2\left|\int g_0{}^*(x)g_1(x)\mathrm{d}x\right|. \tag{A13}$$

From Eqs.(A10) and (A11), the signs of equality are attained in Eqs.(A12) and (A13). Thus,

$$|g_0(x)| = |g_1(x)|, \quad \forall x, \tag{A14}$$

$$\int |g_0(x)|\,|g_1(x)|\,\mathrm{d}x = \left|\int g_0{}^*(x)g_1(x)\mathrm{d}x\right|, \tag{A15}$$

The above Eq.(A15) is held when $\arg(g_0{}^*(x)g_1(x))$ is constant of x, so that

$$\arg(g_0{}^*(x)g_1(x)) = \arg\kappa, \quad \forall x. \tag{A16}$$

From Eqs.(A14) and (A16),

$$\frac{\langle x|\psi_0\rangle}{\langle x|\psi_1\rangle} = \begin{cases} \frac{\sqrt{\varepsilon}g_0(x)}{\sqrt{1-\varepsilon}g_1(x)} = C & f(x) = 0, \\ \frac{\sqrt{1-\varepsilon}g_0(x)}{\sqrt{\varepsilon}g_1(x)} = (C^*)^{-1} & f(x) = 1, \end{cases} \tag{A17}$$

where we determined $C = \sqrt{\varepsilon/(1-\varepsilon)}\exp(-\mathrm{i}\cdot\arg\kappa)$. Hence, the expansion coefficients of $\{|\psi_0\rangle, |\psi_1\rangle\}$ have the relation (6).

PROPERTIES OF QUANTUM CRYPTOGRAPHY BASED ON ORTHOGONAL STATES: GOLDENBERG AND VAIDMAN SCHEME

Kouichi Yamazaki, Takashi Matsui, and Osamu Hirota

Tamagawa University, Japan

Properties of quantum key distribution scheme based on orthogonal quantum states proposed by Goldenberg and Vaidman (GV scheme) are theoretically clarified. First, it is shown that multiple-particle sources can be applied to the GV scheme instead of single-particle ones. Then, probabilities that an eavesdropper is detected is given for an eavesdropping method which is a simple modification of that used to show the security of the scheme. Finally, the security of the GV scheme against the eavesdropping method is discussed based on information theory.

1. INTRODUCTION

The security of a cryptosystem depends on how secretly a key for encryption and decryption can be kept. It is one-time pad cryptosystem that seems to be the most secure. In this scheme, a key is a random sequence and each key is used only once for encryption and decryption. Then, the system requires the two legitimate users, a transmitter Alice and a receiver Bob, to share random sequences secretly. In this case, how to distribute a random sequence secretly is the most important problem. The quantum cryptography provides such a secret key distribution scheme. In order to establish a pair of secrete random sequences between separated users, several types of quantum key distribution schemes using nonorthogonal states as information carriers have been proposed[1]. Security of these schemes rely on the back reaction onto the system by a measurement and the impossibility of cloning nonorthogonal quantum states[2]. Furthermore, effects of eavesdropping on quantum cryptosystem based on nonorthogonal states were investigated[3,4].

Recently, a new method of quantum key distribution scheme was proposed by L. Goldenberg and L. Vaidman[5]. (We call this the GV scheme hereafter.) In the scheme, orthogonal states are used for secret key distribution. Since the back reaction and the noncloning theorem can not be used to guarantee the security of the scheme using orthogonal states, it uses causality instead. As well as the case using nonorthogonal sates, a part of transmitted data are used to check the security of the channel. However, because of the orthogonality, all transmitted data except for them can be used to make a key. Therefore, it can be used to send not only random sequences but also data sequences.

In this paper, we clarify properties of the GV scheme from the viewpoint of engineering. First, we analyze the applicability of multiple particle sources instead of single particle ones to the GV scheme. Second, we analyze the effects of an eavesdropping on the security of the GV scheme, where we restrict ourselves to considering an eavesdropping method which is the simple modification of the method used in [5] to prove its security. In [3], Ekert et al. discussed the quantum key distribution systems in the presence of an eavesdropping. They showed that even if an eavesdropper is present, secret key distribution can be made by an error correction coding technique with proper information rate if mutual information of the channel between the legitimate users is more than that of the transmitter-eavesdropper (T-E) channel. Then, we give the mutual information of channel between legitimate users and the T-E channel for the eavesdropping method, and maximization for the T-E channel is discussed based on Ban's method[6]. Finally, using the mutual information as a criterion, we compare the GV schemes with single particle sources and that with multiple particle sources.

2. PRELIMINARIES

We explain the quantum cryptosystem based on the orthogonal quantum states proposed by Goldenberg and Vaidman, briefly. After that, a modification of the system is considered.

2.1. GV SCHEME

The GV scheme uses orthogonal quantum states as information carriers. Then, it can not use the back reaction onto the system by a measurement and the impossibility of cloning nonorthogonal quantum states to prove the security of the system. The GV scheme has the following two properties to make the system secure. First, two transmitted orthogonal states $|\Psi_0\rangle$, $|\Psi_1\rangle$ of information carriers are superpositions of two wave packets, $|a\rangle$ and $|b\rangle$.

$$\left\{ |\Psi_0\rangle = \frac{1}{\sqrt{2}} (|a\rangle + |b\rangle), \, |\Psi_1\rangle = \frac{1}{\sqrt{2}} (|a\rangle - |b\rangle) \right\} \tag{1}$$

These wave packets are not transmitted simultaneously. Namely, one of these two component, $|b\rangle$, for example, is delayed during period τ at the transmitter side before being transmitted into the channel. On the other hand, $|a\rangle$ is transmitted without delay, and it is delayed during τ at the receiver side so as to be detected with $|b\rangle$ simultaneously. The second is that the time when the signal is transmitted is not announced.

Let us consider that someone, Eve, intends to eavesdrop on the system by his probe $|\Phi\rangle$ interacting with the signal. If we assume that the eavesdropping is not detected, then the state evolution should be given as follows:

$$\begin{cases} |\Psi_0 : t_1\rangle |\Phi : t_1\rangle \to |\Psi_0 : t_2\rangle |\Phi_0 : t_2\rangle \\ |\Psi_1 : t_1\rangle |\Phi : t_1\rangle \to |\Psi_1 : t_2\rangle |\Phi_1 : t_2\rangle \end{cases} \tag{2}$$

where, t_1 is when a signal is transmitted, and t_2 is when it is received. This evolution with respect to the signal is the same as the case without an eavesdropper. Because if the interaction changes the state evolution, the legitimate users can find the eavesdropper. In order to show the impossibility of eavesdropping without being detected, let us study the evolution of each component of the information carriers, separately. From eqs.(1)

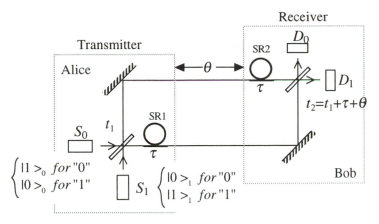

Figure 1. Block diagram of GV scheme.

and (2), they are given by

$$\begin{cases} |a:t_1\rangle|\varPhi:t_1\rangle \\ \quad \to \dfrac{1}{2}\{|a:t_2\rangle(|\varPhi_0:t_2\rangle + |\varPhi_1:t_2\rangle) + |b:t_2\rangle(|\varPhi_0:t_2\rangle - |\varPhi_1:t_2\rangle)\} \\ |b:t_1\rangle|\varPhi:t_1\rangle \\ \quad \to \dfrac{1}{2}\{|a:t_2\rangle(|\varPhi_0:t_2\rangle - |\varPhi_1:t_2\rangle) + |b:t_2\rangle(|\varPhi_0:t_2\rangle + |\varPhi_1:t_2\rangle)\} \end{cases} \quad (3)$$

This shows that $|b:t_1\rangle$ yields $|a:t_2\rangle$ as well as $|b:t_2\rangle$ through the interaction by Eve, if we assume that $|\varPhi_0:t_2\rangle \neq |\varPhi_1:t_2\rangle$ that is required for Eve to extract some amount of information. However, this evolution is impossible because of the delay as will be shown in the following with a concrete system.

The GV scheme can be realized by a system which consists of Mach-Zehnder interferometer with two sources S_0 and S_1, and two detectors D_0 and D_1 (Fig.1). There are delay lines with delay time τ at the transmitter (SR1) in the lower path, and at the receiver (SR2) in the upper path, respectively. Eve can try to eavesdrop only on the transmission line. In order to transmit binary data, one particle is sent from the source S_0 for symbol "0" , and from the source S_1 for "1". If a particle is transmitted at t_1 from S_0 (S_1), it should be received at $t_2 (= t_1 + \tau + \theta)$ in $D_0(D_1)$. Here, θ is a traveling time from the transmitter and the receiver. The two transmitted states are given as follows:

$$\left\{ |\varPsi_0\rangle = \frac{1}{\sqrt{2}}(|1\rangle_u|0\rangle_l + |0\rangle_u|1\rangle_l), \ |\varPsi_1\rangle = \frac{1}{\sqrt{2}}(|1\rangle_u|0\rangle_l - |0\rangle_u|1\rangle_l) \right\} \quad (4)$$

Two components $|a\rangle$ and $|b\rangle$ in eq.(1) correspond to $|1\rangle_u|0\rangle_l$ and $|0\rangle_u|1\rangle_l$, respectively. Here $|a\rangle$ and $|b\rangle$ represent particles passing through the upper and lower paths, respectively. In this case, a component $|b\rangle$ evolves through the interaction as follows:

$$\begin{aligned} |0\rangle_u|1:t_1\rangle_l|\varPhi:t_1\rangle \\ \to \frac{1}{2}\{|1:t_2\rangle_u|0\rangle_l(|\varPhi_0:t_2\rangle - |\varPhi_1:t_2\rangle) + |0\rangle_u|1:t_2\rangle_l(|\varPhi_0:t_2\rangle + |\varPhi_1:t_2\rangle)\} \end{aligned} \quad (5)$$

This shows that $|b:t_1\rangle$ generates $|a:t_2\rangle$ representing a particle passing through the upper path, but the generated particle can not be detected at t_2, but at $t_2 + \tau$. Because,

141

the interaction is to start after the delay at the transmitter, and the generated particle is to be delayed again at the receiver. This is why, an interaction given by eq.(5) is impossible, and then, anyone can not eavesdrop on the system without being detected. In this scheme, by informing a fraction of Bob's measurement results and the measurement time to Alice publicly after transmitting a sequence of data, they can check whether there exists an eavesdropper or not. This is the GV quantum key distribution scheme.

2.2. MULTIPLE-PARTICLE SOURCES

In this section, we consider the applicability of multiple-particle sources to the GV scheme instead of one-particle sources. When n-particle sources are used, the two transmitted states are given by,

$$
\begin{cases}
|\Psi_0\rangle = \dfrac{1}{\sqrt{2^n}} \displaystyle\sum_{k=0}^{n} \dfrac{\sqrt{n!}}{\sqrt{k! \cdot (n-k)!}} |n-k\rangle_u |k\rangle_l \\[4mm]
|\Psi_1\rangle = \dfrac{1}{\sqrt{2^n}} \displaystyle\sum_{k=0}^{n} (-1)^k \dfrac{\sqrt{n!}}{\sqrt{k! \cdot (n-k)!}} |n-k\rangle_u |k\rangle_l
\end{cases}
\tag{6}
$$

According to the notation used in the previous section, we can express these by two components, $|a\rangle$ and $|b\rangle$, as follows:

$$
\begin{cases}
|a\rangle = \dfrac{1}{\sqrt{2^{n-1}}} \displaystyle\sum_{k=0}^{\lfloor \frac{n}{2} \rfloor} \dfrac{\sqrt{n!}}{\sqrt{2k! \cdot (n-2k)!}} |n-2k\rangle_u |2k\rangle_l \\[4mm]
|b\rangle = \dfrac{1}{\sqrt{2^{n-1}}} \displaystyle\sum_{k=0}^{\lfloor \frac{n-1}{2} \rfloor} \dfrac{\sqrt{n!}}{\sqrt{(2k+1)! \cdot (n-2k-1)!}} |n-2k-1\rangle_u |2k+1\rangle_l)
\end{cases}
\tag{7}
$$

Here, $\lfloor \cdot \rfloor$ means its integer part. In order to show the applicability we will consider the evolution of a component which includes a state whose all n particles pass through the lower path. If we assume n to be odd number, for example, such a state is included in $|b\rangle$. In the evolution of $|b\rangle$ in this case, the probability that all n particles pass though the lower path before the interaction is given by

$$
\Pr(|0\rangle_u |n{:}\ t_1\rangle_l) = \frac{1}{2^{n-1}}
\tag{8}
$$

while after the interaction it becomes

$$
\Pr(|0\rangle_u |n{:}\ t_2\rangle_l) = \frac{1}{2^{n-1}} \cdot \frac{1 + \mathrm{Re}\langle \Phi_0 {:}\ t_2 | \Phi_1 {:}\ t_2 \rangle}{2}
\tag{9}
$$

Clearly, $\Pr(|0\rangle_u |n{:}\ t_2\rangle_l)$ is smaller than $\Pr(|0\rangle_u |n{:}\ t_1\rangle_l)$ if $|\Phi_0 {:}\ t_2\rangle \neq |\Phi_1 {:}\ t_2\rangle$. This shows that the interaction yields states $|k{:}\ t_2\rangle_u |n-k{:}\ t_2\rangle_l (k \neq 0)$ in which one or more particles pass through the upper path from $|0\rangle_u |n{:}\ t_1\rangle_l$. However, these particles through the upper path can not be received at the correct time t_2 but at $t_2 + \tau$. Therefore the eavesdropping without being detected is also impossible in the system using n-particle sources.

3. EAVESDROPPING

Next, let us consider the effect of eavesdropping on the GV scheme. As shown previously, no one can eavesdrop on the system without being detected. That is, if someone eavesdrops on the system, he is detected with a certain probability. Let us compare these probabilities between one-particle source system and multiple-particle source system. We may consider several kinds of eavesdropping method. Here, we restrict ourselves to considering a particular eavesdropping method represented by the interaction which is slight modification of that expressed by eq.(2), which was used to prove the security of the GV scheme.

In the case of single-particle sources, though state-evolution given by eq.(5) must hold in order not to be detected for Eve, it is impossible because $|1 : t_2\rangle_u|0\rangle_\ell$ violates the casuality. However, if it is transformed into $|1 : t_2 + \tau\rangle_u|0\rangle_\ell$, that is,

$$|0\rangle_u|1 : t_1\rangle_l|\Phi : t_1\rangle \rightarrow \frac{1}{2}(|1 : t_2 + \tau\rangle_u|0\rangle_l(|\Phi_0 : t_2\rangle - |\Phi_1 : t_2\rangle) \\ + |0\rangle_u|1 : t_2\rangle_l(|\Phi_0 : t_2\rangle + |\Phi_1 : t_2\rangle))$$

(10)

the eavesdropping is possible in principle. In this modification, a condition $\langle\Phi_0|\Phi_1\rangle = 0$ is required in order to make the interaction unitary. We will consider the eavesdropping method expressed by this interaction. In this case, state-evaluations from t_1 to t_2, are given as follows:

$$\begin{cases} |\Psi_0 : t_1\rangle|\Phi : t_1\rangle \rightarrow |\Psi_0 : t_2\rangle|\Phi_0 : t_2\rangle \\ \quad + \frac{1}{2\sqrt{2}}(|1 : t_2 + \tau\rangle_u|0\rangle_1 - |1 : t_2\rangle_u|0\rangle_1)(|\Phi_0 : t_2\rangle - |\Phi_1 : t_2\rangle) \\ |\Psi_1 : t_1\rangle|\Phi : t_1\rangle \rightarrow |\Psi_1 : t_2\rangle|\Phi_1 : t_2\rangle \\ \quad - \frac{1}{2\sqrt{2}}(|1 : t_2 + \tau\rangle_u|0\rangle_1 - |1 : t_2\rangle_u|0\rangle_1)(|\Phi_0 : t_2\rangle - |\Phi_1 : t_2\rangle) \end{cases}$$

(11)

Because of the modification, the second terms in the right hand sides are added, and then, a particle is not always detected at the correct time in the correct detector. The probability that Eve is detected by one received signal is

$$\begin{aligned} \mathrm{Pr}^{single-particle}(\text{detection}) &= 1 - \mathrm{Pr}(1, t_2, D_0; 0, D_1|\Psi_0, t_1) \\ &= 1 - \mathrm{Pr}(0, D_0; 1, t_2, D_1|\Psi_1, t_1) \\ &= \frac{3}{8} \end{aligned}$$

(12)

Next, let us go on multiple-particle source system. If we assume the interaction represented by eq.(2), only the results caused by $|0\rangle_u|n : t_1\rangle_l$ violates the causality. However, if we transform it into the following, it does not violate the casuality and then, it is possible in principle.

$$|0\rangle_u|n : t_1\rangle_l|\Phi : t_1\rangle \rightarrow \frac{1}{2}\{|n : t_2 + \tau\rangle_u|0\rangle_l(|\Phi_0 : t_2\rangle - |\Phi_1 : t_2\rangle) \\ + |0\rangle_u|n : t_2\rangle_l(|\Phi_0 : t_2\rangle + |\Phi_1 : t_2\rangle)\}$$

(13)

Because of the above modification in order not to violate causality, each transmitted quantum state develops as follows:

$$\begin{cases} |\Psi_0 : t_1\rangle|\Phi : t_1\rangle \rightarrow |\Psi_0 : t_2\rangle|\Phi_0 : t_2\rangle \\ \quad + \frac{1}{2\sqrt{2}}(|n : t_2 + \tau\rangle_u|0\rangle_l - |n : t_2\rangle_u|0\rangle_l)(|\Phi_0 : t_2\rangle - |\Phi_1 : t_2\rangle) \\ |\Psi_1 : t_1\rangle|\Phi : t_1\rangle \rightarrow |\Psi_1 : t_2\rangle|\Phi_1 : t_2\rangle \\ \quad - \frac{1}{2\sqrt{2}}(|n : t_2 + \tau\rangle_u|0\rangle_l - |n : t_2\rangle_u|0\rangle_l)(|\Phi_0 : t_2\rangle - |\Phi_1 : t_2\rangle) \end{cases}$$

(14)

In this case, the probability to detect Eve is given by

$$\begin{aligned}
\mathrm{Pr}^{n-\mathrm{particle}}(\text{detection}) &= 1 - \mathrm{Pr}(n, t_2, D_0; 0, D_1|\Psi_0, t_1) \\
&= 1 - \mathrm{Pr}(0, D_0; n, t_2, D_1|\Psi_1, t_1) \\
&= \frac{2^{n+1} - 1}{2^{2n+1}}
\end{aligned} \tag{15}$$

Comparing eqs.(12) and (15), it is found that the probability becomes smaller as the number of particle increases. Because probability that all n particles pass through the lower pass decreases as the number of particle increases.

Finally, we consider effect of an eavesdropping on the GV scheme based on information theory. If the mutual information of the channel between Alice and Bob is more than that between Alice and Eve, the secure communication can be realized by a proper channel coding technique. We will clarify the system by means of such a criterion.

In order to obtain mutual information of the channel between Alice and Eve, transition probabilities should be given. Density operators of total system after the interaction are easily obtained from eq.(14). By taking the partial trace of the density operator with respect to the signal mode, the density operators ρ_i^{eve} ($i=0, 1$) representing Eve's probe are given as follows:

$$\begin{cases}
\rho_0^{\mathrm{eve}} = (1 - \dfrac{1}{2^{n+1}})|\Phi_0\rangle\langle\Phi_0| + \dfrac{1}{2^{n+1}}|\Phi_1\rangle\langle\Phi_1| \\
\rho_1^{\mathrm{eve}} = \dfrac{1}{2^{n+1}}|\Phi_0\rangle\langle\Phi_0| + (1 - \dfrac{1}{2^{n+1}})|\Phi_1\rangle\langle\Phi_1|
\end{cases} \tag{16}$$

Eve, of course, tries to extract as much information as possible from them. According to Ban's optimization method[6], the optimum detection operators for this purpose are $\{\Pi_0 = |\Phi_0\rangle\langle\Phi_0|, \ \Pi_1 = |\Phi_1\rangle\langle\Phi_1|\}$. This results in transition probabilities given by

$$\mathrm{Pr}^{\mathrm{eve}}("j"|\rho_i^{\mathrm{eve}}) = \begin{cases}
1 - \dfrac{1}{2^{n+1}} & for \ i = j \\
\dfrac{1}{2^{n+1}} & for \ i \neq j
\end{cases} \tag{17}$$

Then, if Alice transmits two symbols with equally *a priori* probabilities, mutual information of the channel between Alice and Eve is

$$I_{A-E} = 1 + (1 - \frac{1}{2^{n+1}})\log_2(1 - \frac{1}{2^{n+1}}) + \frac{1}{2^{n+1}}\log_2\frac{1}{2^{n+1}} \quad (\text{bit}) \tag{18}$$

On the other hand, in the channel between Alice and Bob, Bob never changes the detection scheme depending on the presence or the absence of Eve. Because he can notice that after measurement. Probabilities $\mathrm{Pr}(k, t_a, D_0; n - k, t_b, D_1|\cdot)$ that k particles are detected at t_a in the detector D_0, and $n - k$ particle is detected at t_b in detector D_1 are given as follows:

$$\begin{cases}
\mathrm{Pr}(n, t_2, D_0; 0, D_1|"0") = \mathrm{Pr}(0, D_0; n, t_2 + \tau, D_1|"1") = 1 - \dfrac{2^{n+1} - 1}{2^{2n+1}} \\
\mathrm{Pr}(k, \cdot, D_o; n - k, \cdot, D_1|\cdot) = \dfrac{1}{2^{2n+1}}\binom{n}{k} \quad (\text{except for the avobe two cases})
\end{cases} \tag{19}$$

Then, mutual information under equally *a priori* probabilities condition is given by using these probabilities as follows:

$$\begin{aligned}
I_{A-B} = &- \left(1 - \frac{2^{n+1} - 2}{2^{2n+1}}\right)\log\frac{1}{2}\left(1 - \frac{2^{n+1} - 2}{2^{2n+1}}\right) \\
&+ \left(1 - \frac{2^{n+1} - 1}{2^{2n+1}}\right)\log\left(1 - \frac{2^{n+1} - 1}{2^{2n+1}}\right) + \frac{1}{2^{2n+1}}\log\left(\frac{1}{2^{2n+1}}\right) \quad (\text{bit})
\end{aligned} \tag{20}$$

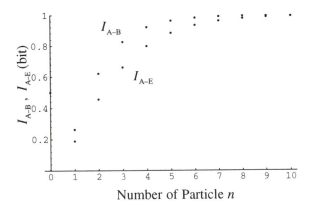

Figure 2. Mutual information of A-B channel and A-E channel.

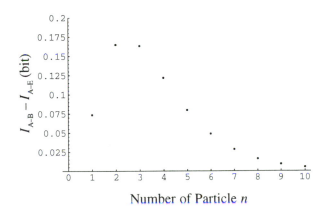

Figure 3. Difference of mutual information of two channels.

We plot I_{A-B} and I_{A-E} as a function of the number of particle in fig.2. It is found that mutual information I_{A-B} is always bigger than I_{A-E} for any number of particles. Therefore, Alice and Bob can communicate secretly by using a proper error control coding scheme. The more the difference between the two mutual informations is, the better it is for the legitimate users. Then, we plot the difference $I_{A-B} - I_{A-E}$ in fig.3. Fig.3 shows that two-particle sources are the best for the GV scheme on the base of this criterion.

4. CONCLUSION

We clarified the quantum cryptosystem based on orthogonal quantum states. First, we showed that multiple-particle sources can be applied instead of single-particle ones to the GV scheme. Next, we investigated effects of a particular eavesdropping on the GV scheme based on information theory. As a result, it was shown that two-particle sources are the most suitable for the GV scheme against the considered eavesdropping method.

ACKNOWLEDGEMENT

This work was partially supported by Grant-in-Aid for Encouragement of Young Scientists of the Ministry of Education.

REFERENCES

[1] *For example*, C. H. Bennett and G. Brassard, in *Proc. of the IEEE Int. Conf. on Computers, Systems, and Signal Processing, Bangalore, India* (IEEE, New York, 1984), pp.175-179. *and* A. K. Ekert, Phys. Rev. Lett. **67**, 661 (1991).

[2] W. K. Wootters and W. H. Zurek, Nature **299**, 802 (1982).

[3] A. K. Ekert, B. Huttner, G. M. Palma and A. Peres, Phys. Rev. A **50**, 1047 (1994).

[4] N. Lütkenhaus, Phys. Rev. A **54**, 97 (1996).

[5] L. Goldenberg and L. Vaidman, Phys. Rev. Lett. **75**, 1239 (1995).

[6] M. Ban, M. Osaki and O. Hirota, J. Mod. Opt. **43**, 2337 (1996).

COMPUTATION OF MUTUAL ENTROPY
IN QUANTUM AMPLIFIER PROCESSES

Shigeru Furuichi, Masanori Ohya, and Hiroki Suyari

Department of Information Sciences
Science University of Tokyo
Email:suyari@is.noda.sut.ac.jp

The mathematical concept "lifting" which stems from "compound state" and "transition expectation" could have been applied to optical communication processes and quantum Markov chains. In the latest study of lifting for the optical communication processes it was succesful to rigorously derive the error probability and SNR for quantum amplifier processes.

In this paper the mutual entropy for quantum amplifier processes which is one of the most important efficiencies concerning the channel capacity is rigorously derived from the concept of "lifting" and its computational results of the mutual entropy are discussed.

1. INTRODUCTION

Quantum mutual entropy is one of the important complexities for not only a channel capacity of optical communication processes but also mamy dynamical changes in quantum physics [7, 12]. In this paper the quantum mutual entropy is derived from a lifting expression for quantum amplifier processes. In section 2, mathematical concepts, "quantum channel, lifting, quatum mutual entropy" in quantum information theory are briefly reviewd. In section 3, the lifting expression for quantum amplifier processes is shown [14]. In section 4, the P representation for the output state of quantum amplifier processes is derived from the lifting expression through its characteristic function. Then, by using this P representation, the quantum mutual entropy for the quantum amplifier processes is derived. Finally, the computational results of the mutual entropy are presented and discussed.

2. QUANTUM CHANNEL, LIFTING, QUANTUM MUTUAL ENTROPY

A quantum channel represents a state change from an input system to an output one, corresponding to a channel in classical Shannon theory. Then, in order to construct a quantum channel, two Hilbert spaces $\mathcal{H}_1$ and $\mathcal{H}_2$ are prepared for input and output sysytem, respectively. Let $B(\mathcal{H}_k)$ $(k = 1, 2)$ be the set of all bounded linear operators on $\mathcal{H}_k$, and $\mathfrak{S}(\mathcal{H}_k)$ be the set of all states (density operators) on the Hilbert spaces $\mathcal{H}_k$. Then a quantum channel is defined as follows :

Quantum Communication, Computing, and Measurement
Edited by Hirota *et al.*, Plenum Press, New York, 1997

Definition 2.1 *[9, 11] : A mapping $\Lambda^* : \mathfrak{S}(\mathcal{H}_1) \longrightarrow \mathfrak{S}(\mathcal{H}_2)$ is called a completely positive channel (channel for short) if the dual map $\Lambda : B(\mathcal{H}_2) \longrightarrow B(\mathcal{H}_1)$ satisfies the completely positivity.*

The concept of "channel" is deeply related to that of "lifting" introduced in [2].

Definition 2.2 *: Let $\mathfrak{S}_0, \mathfrak{S}_1$ be the set of all states on $\mathcal{H}_0, \mathcal{H}_1$ respectively. A lifting from $\mathfrak{S}_0$ to $\mathfrak{S}_0 \otimes \mathfrak{S}_1$ is a continuous map*

$$\mathcal{E}^* : \mathfrak{S}_0 \to \mathfrak{S}_0 \otimes \mathfrak{S}_1. \tag{2.1}$$

The concept "lifting" is a common sense in mathematical physics, such as open system, reduction theory and so on. However a lifting should be treated as one of the mathematical methods to obtain a quantum mechanical channel [9,11], which plyas an important role in quantum information theory, quantum dynamical change of state and so on. That is, once we can obtain the lifting expression, we can get a channel in the following way :

$$\Lambda^* \rho = tr_{\mathcal{K}} \mathcal{E}^* \rho \tag{2.2}$$

Such a treatment of lifting has the following two different backgrounds. The first one is that a lifting stems from the mathematical unification of "Accardi's transition expectation [1]" and "Ohya's compound state [9, 10]". This mathematical unification can make it possible to express many kinds of state change in quantum Markov chains [3] and quantum information theory [14], such as a nonlinear lifting and nondemolition state change. The other one is that a lifting enables us to get a quautum channel easier, because most of expressions for dynamical change involves some mutual interactions between two physical systems in each mathematical formulation, and the lifting can directly derive each state change from each mathematical expression such as attenuation processes and amplifier processes.

Next, based on the above quantum channel, quantum mutual entropy is reviewed in the following manner.

Let the Schatten decomposition of $\rho \in \mathfrak{S}(\mathcal{H})$ be

$$\rho = \sum_k \lambda_k E_k, \quad \lambda_1 \geq \lambda_2 \geq \cdots \geq \lambda_n \geq \cdots, \quad E_i \perp E_j \quad (i \neq j) \tag{2.3}$$

where λ_k is an eigenvalue of ρ and E_k is the associated one dimensional projection. The Schatten decomposition is not unique unless every λ_k is nondegenerated.

In order to formulate the quamtum mutual entropy, the joint probability in quantum system should be introducd. However, in general the joint probability does not exist in quantum system [6]. Then a compound state was introduced in stead of the joint probability in quantum system [9,10].

If we can obtain the above Schatten decomposition, the compound state σ_E can be formulated as

$$\sigma_E \equiv \sum_k \lambda_k E_k \otimes \Lambda^* E_k. \tag{2.4}$$

Then the defnition of the mutual entropy $I(\rho; \Lambda^*)$ is given by following :

Definition 2.3 *[9, 11] : The quantum mutual entropy $I(\rho; \Lambda^*)$ is defined by*

$$I(\rho; \Lambda^*) \equiv \sup_E \{S(\sigma_E, \sigma_0) ; E = \{E_k\}\} \tag{2.5}$$

where $\sigma_0 \equiv \rho \otimes \Lambda^* \rho$ and $S(\sigma_E, \sigma_0)$ is the relative entropy defined by

$$S(\sigma_E, \sigma_0) \equiv tr\sigma_E (\log \sigma_E - \log \sigma_0). \tag{2.6}$$

In the above definition of quantum mutual entropy, we have to take "sup" over all Sahtten decompositions when some eigenvalues are degenerated.

Then we have the following fundamental inequality of Shannon's type.

Theorem 2.4 *[9,11] : For an input state ρ and a channel Λ^*, the following inequalities hold.*

$$0 \leq I(\rho; \Lambda^*) \leq \min\{S(\rho), S(\Lambda^*\rho)\} \tag{2.7}$$

This theorem means that the information correctly transmitted through a channel Λ^* is always less than the initial information $S(\rho)$. In other words, the mutual entropy is useful as an efficiency of communication processes from the information theoretical points of view. This relation implies the next inequality :

$$0 \leq \text{MER} \equiv \frac{I(\rho : \Lambda^*)}{S(\rho)} \leq 1 \tag{2.8}$$

Then the quantity $\frac{I(\rho:\Lambda^*)}{S(\rho)}$, which is called MER (Mutual entropy - Entropy - Ratio), expresses an efficiency of information transmission [18].

3. LIFTING EXPRESSION FOR QUANTUM AMPLIFIER PROCESSES

In this section, one of the procedures to get a lifting expression for an optical communication process is briefly discussed. As one of such examples, we take a quantum amplifier process.

In many references on quantum optics, the expression on quantum amplifier process is given by a change of operator as follows :

$$c = \sqrt{G}a + \sqrt{G-1}b^+ \tag{3.1}$$

where a is an annihilation operator on Hilbert space $\mathcal{H}$ and b^+ is a creation operator on another Hilbert space $\mathcal{K}$. G is gain of this amplifier. More precisely, we can write down an annihilation operator c on tensor product Hilbert space $\mathcal{H} \otimes \mathcal{K}$ by

$$c = \mu a \otimes 1 + \nu 1 \otimes b^+ \tag{3.2}$$

where $\mu = \sqrt{G}, \nu = \sqrt{G-1}$.

In order to get a state change from the above change of operator, we have to solve the following eigen equation :

$$c|\gamma\rangle = \gamma|\gamma\rangle \tag{3.3}$$

where $|\gamma\rangle$ is an eigenvector of c on a tensor Hilbert space $\mathcal{H} \otimes \mathcal{K}$. From this eigen equation we obtain the inner product $\langle \alpha \otimes \beta \mid \gamma \rangle$:

$$\langle \alpha \otimes \beta \mid \gamma \rangle = \frac{1}{\mu} \exp\left[-\frac{|\alpha|^2}{2} - \frac{|\beta|^2}{2} - \frac{|\gamma|^2}{2} - \frac{\nu}{\mu}\alpha^*\beta^* + \frac{1}{\mu}\alpha^*\gamma\right] \tag{3.4}$$

where $|\alpha\rangle$ and $|\beta\rangle$ are coherent state vectors in $\mathcal{H}$ and $\mathcal{K}$, respectively.

During the procedure to obtain the above inner product, we apply some formulas such as

$$\frac{1}{\pi}\int d^2w \exp\{-\mid w \mid^2 + aw + bw^* + cw^2 + dw^{*2}\} = \frac{1}{\sqrt{1-4cd}} \exp\left\{\frac{a^2d + ab + b^2c}{1-4cd}\right\}. \tag{3.5}$$

For the details to derive (3.4), see [14].

Then a quantum expression for a linear amplifier can be written as :

$$V_G |\alpha\rangle = |\gamma\rangle \tag{3.6}$$

Therefore, the lifting $\mathcal{E}^*$ and the quantum mechanical channel Λ^* are given by the followings :

$$\mathcal{E}^* \rho = V_G \rho V_G^* \tag{3.7}$$

$$\Lambda^* \rho \equiv tr_K \mathcal{E}^* \rho = tr_K V_G \rho V_G^* \tag{3.8}$$

This expression can be applied to the rigorous derivation of some efficiencies such as error probability and SNR [14]. In this paper we applied this lifting expression to the derivation of quantum mutual entropy in the next section.

4. DERIVATION OF QUANTUM MUTUAL ENTROPY FOR QUANTUM AMPLIFIER PROCESSES

For the computation of the quantum mutual entropy shown in section 2, the following lemma is useful :

Lemma 4.1 *[9, 11]* :

$$S(\sigma_E, \sigma_0) = \sum_k \lambda_k S(\Lambda^* E_k, \Lambda^* \rho) \tag{4.1}$$

If an initial state ρ has the nondegenerate Shatten decomposition, the mutual entropy $I(\rho; \Lambda^*)$ is equal to $S(\sigma_E, \sigma_0)$:

$$I(\rho; \Lambda^*) = S(\sigma_E, \sigma_0) = \sum_k \lambda_k S(\Lambda^* E_k, \Lambda^* \rho)$$

$$= \sum_k \sum_{m,n} \lambda_k \langle m| \Lambda^* E_k |n\rangle \left(\langle n| \log \Lambda^* E_k |m\rangle - \langle n| \log \Lambda^* \rho |m\rangle \right)$$

$$= \sum_{k,m,n} \lambda_k \langle m| \Lambda^* E_k |n\rangle$$

$$\times \left(\sum_{s=1}^{\infty} \sum_{t=0}^{s} \frac{(-1)^{-(t+1)}}{t! (s-t)!} \langle n| (\Lambda^* E_k)^t |m\rangle - \sum_{u=1}^{\infty} \sum_{v=0}^{u} \frac{(-1)^{-(v+1)}}{v! (u-v)!} \langle n| (\Lambda^* \rho)^v |m\rangle \right) \tag{4.2}$$

where

$$\langle n| (\Lambda^* \rho)^t |m\rangle = \sum_{\phi_1, \cdots, \phi_{t-1}} \langle n| \Lambda^* \rho |\phi_1\rangle \langle \phi_1| \Lambda^* \rho |\phi_2\rangle \cdots \langle \phi_{t-1}| \Lambda^* \rho |m\rangle$$

and $\{\phi_i\}$ can be chosen as any CONS of the Hilbert space $\mathcal{H}_2$.

Therefore we have to compute $\langle m| \Lambda^* \rho |n\rangle$ and $\langle m| \Lambda^* E_k |n\rangle$.

Here we consider the modulation "OOK (On-Off Keying)" . Other modulation can be almost similarly discussed as OOK.

In case of OOK, we suppose the initial state ρ given by

$$\rho = (1 - \lambda) |0\rangle \langle 0| + \lambda |\theta\rangle \langle \theta| \tag{4.3}$$

where $|0\rangle \langle 0|$ is a vacuume state and $|\theta\rangle \langle \theta|$ is a coherent state.

In general, if an initial state ρ is given by a superposition of $|x_0\rangle \langle x_0|$ and $|x_1\rangle \langle x_1|$ such that $\rho = (1 - \lambda) |x_0\rangle \langle x_0| + \lambda |x_1\rangle \langle x_1|$, it is known that ρ has an unique nondegenerate Shatten decomposition [13]. From the lemma in the paper [13], $\rho = (1 - \lambda) |0\rangle \langle 0| + \lambda |\theta\rangle \langle \theta|$ has the following unique Shatten decomposition :

$$\rho = \lambda_0 E_0 + \lambda_1 E_1 = \lambda_0 |\varphi_0\rangle \langle \varphi_0| + \lambda_1 |\varphi_1\rangle \langle \varphi_1| \tag{4.4}$$

where the eigenvalues μ_0 and μ_1 can be computed as

$$\lambda_i = \frac{1}{2}\left\{1 - (-1)^{(i+1)}\sqrt{1 - 4\lambda(1-\lambda)\left(1 - \exp\left(-|\theta|^2\right)\right)}\right\} \quad (i = 0, 1) \qquad (4.5)$$

Moreover each eigenvector $|\varphi_0\rangle$ and $|\varphi_1\rangle$ must be written by a superposition of $|0\rangle$ and $|\theta\rangle$. When each eigenvector is given by the following :

$$|\varphi_0\rangle = a\,|0\rangle + b\,|\theta\rangle\,, \quad |\varphi_1\rangle = c\,|0\rangle + d\,|\theta\rangle\,, \qquad (4.6)$$

the relations among $a, b, c, d \in C$ can be computed by

$$|a|^2 = \frac{\tau_1^2}{\kappa_1}, \ |b|^2 = \frac{1}{\kappa_1}, \ |c|^2 = \frac{\tau_2^2}{\kappa_2}, \ |d|^2 = \frac{1}{\kappa_2} \ ab^* = a^*b = \frac{\tau_1}{\kappa_1}, \ cd^* = c^*d = \frac{\tau_2}{\kappa_2},$$

$$\tau_i \equiv \frac{-(1-2\lambda) - (-1)^i\sqrt{1 - 4\lambda(1-\lambda)(1 - \exp(-|\theta|^2))}}{2(1-\lambda)\exp(-\frac{1}{2}|\theta|^2)} \quad (i = 1, 2)$$

$$\kappa_i \equiv \tau_i^2 + 2\exp\left(-\frac{1}{2}|\theta|^2\right)\tau_i + 1 \quad (i = 1, 2)$$

Then, in order to compute $\langle m|\,\Lambda^* E_k\,|n\rangle$ and $\langle m|\,\Lambda^*\rho\,|n\rangle$, we apply the normally ordered characteristic function [4, 17] $\chi_N(\eta)$ and P representation [5, 16] of $\Lambda^* E_k$ and $\Lambda^*\rho$, respectively.

A normally ordered characteristic function $\chi_N(\eta)$ w.r.t. the output state $\Lambda^*\rho$ of an amplifier process can be computed by the lifting expression (3.8) :

$$\chi_N(\eta) = tr\Lambda^*\rho e^{\eta a^+}e^{-\eta^* a} \qquad (4.7)$$

$$= \exp\left[-|\nu|^2\,|\eta|^2 + \mu\gamma\eta - \mu\gamma\eta^*\right] \qquad (4.8)$$

In the above calculation, (3.5) is used. If a density operator $\Lambda^*\rho$ has a P representation, then $\chi_N(\eta)$ is given by

$$\chi_N(\eta) = \int e^{\eta\alpha^* - \eta^*\alpha}P(\alpha)\,d^2\alpha. \qquad (4.9)$$

P representation $P(\alpha)$ exists if $\chi_N(\eta)$ has its Fourier transform. Then P representation $P(\alpha)$ is expressed by the inverse Fourier transform of $\chi_N(\eta)$:

$$P(\alpha) = \frac{1}{\pi^2}\int e^{\alpha\eta^* - \alpha^*\eta}\chi_N(\eta)\,d^2\eta. \qquad (4.10)$$

For the output state $\Lambda^*\rho$ of an amplifier process, P representation $P(\alpha)$ can be computed by (4.8) and (4.10)

$$P(\alpha) = \frac{1}{\pi\,|\nu|^2}\exp\left[-\left|\frac{\mu}{\nu}\right|^2|\gamma|^2 - \frac{1}{|\nu|^2}|\alpha|^2 + \frac{\mu\gamma^*}{|\nu|^2}\alpha + \frac{\mu\gamma}{|\nu|^2}\alpha^*\right] \qquad (4.11)$$

Therefore, by using this P representation $P(\alpha)$, we can write down $\Lambda^*\rho$ by the following :

$$\Lambda^*\rho = \int P(\alpha)\,|\alpha\rangle\,\langle\alpha|d^2\alpha \qquad (4.12)$$

This implies

$$\langle m|\,\Lambda^*\rho\,|n\rangle = \int P(\alpha)\,\langle m\mid\alpha\rangle\,\langle\alpha\mid n\rangle d^2\alpha$$

$$= \frac{\exp\left[-\left|\frac{\mu\gamma}{\nu}\right|^2\right]}{|\mu|^2\sqrt{m!n!}}\sum_{k,l}\frac{\left(\frac{\mu\gamma^*}{|\nu|^2}\right)^k\left(\frac{\mu\gamma}{|\nu|^2}\right)^l}{k!\ l!}\left|\frac{\nu}{\mu}\right|^{2(l+n)}\sqrt{(k+m)!\,(l+n)!}\delta_{k+m,l+n} \qquad (4.13)$$

In the above calculation, we applied (3.5) and the next identity :

$$\frac{1}{\pi\sqrt{i!j!}} \int \exp\left[-C|\alpha|^2\right] \alpha^i (\alpha^*)^j d^2\alpha = \delta_{ij} C^{-(i+1)}. \quad (C > 0) \tag{4.14}$$

$\langle m|\Lambda^* E_k |n\rangle$ can be computed as similar as $\langle m|\Lambda^*\rho|n\rangle$.

Then if we substitute these results $\langle m|\Lambda^*\rho|n\rangle$ and $\langle m|\Lambda^* E_k |n\rangle$ into (4.2), then we can rigorously compute the quantum mutual entropy for amplifier processes.

5. COMPUTER EXPERIMENTS

The derivation of the mutual entropy in the previous section is very complicated for the actual numerical computation. However, the diagonal elements $\langle n|\Lambda^*\rho|n\rangle$ dominates the other offdiagonal elements, which was checked by some numerical compuation. That is, if the input state of the amplifier is given by a coherent state, we can say that

$$\langle m|\Lambda^*\rho|n\rangle \cong \langle n|\Lambda^*\rho|n\rangle \delta_{mn}. \tag{5.1}$$

Then (4.13) implies the following :

$$\langle n|\Lambda^*\rho|n\rangle = \frac{1}{|\mu|^2 n!} \exp\left[-\left|\frac{\mu\gamma}{\nu}\right|^2\right]\left|\frac{\nu}{\mu}\right|^{2n} \sum_{k=0}^{\infty}\left|\frac{\gamma}{\nu}\right|^{2k}\frac{(n+k)!}{(k!)^2}$$

As similar as the compuation of $\langle n|\Lambda^*\rho|n\rangle$, $\langle n|\Lambda^* E_0 |n\rangle$ and $\langle n|\Lambda^* E_1 |n\rangle$ can be computed by

$$\langle n|\Lambda^* E_0 |n\rangle = \frac{|a|^2}{|\mu|^2}\left|\frac{\nu}{\mu}\right|^{2n} + \frac{ab^*}{|\mu|^2}\left|\frac{\nu}{\mu}\right|^{2n}\exp\left[-\frac{|\gamma|^2}{2}\right] + \frac{a^*b}{|\mu|^2}\left|\frac{\nu}{\mu}\right|^{2n}\exp\left[-\frac{|\gamma|^2}{2}\right]$$
$$+\frac{|b|^2}{|\mu|^2 n!}\exp\left[-\left|\frac{\mu\gamma}{\nu}\right|^2\right]\left|\frac{\nu}{\mu}\right|^{2n}\sum_{k=0}^{\infty}\left|\frac{\gamma}{\nu}\right|^{2k}\frac{(n+k)!}{(k!)^2}$$

$$\langle n|\Lambda^* E_1 |n\rangle = \frac{|c|^2}{|\mu|^2}\left|\frac{\nu}{\mu}\right|^{2n} + \frac{cd^*}{|\mu|^2}\left|\frac{\nu}{\mu}\right|^{2n}\exp\left[-\frac{|\gamma|^2}{2}\right] + \frac{c^*d}{|\mu|^2}\left|\frac{\nu}{\mu}\right|^{2n}\exp\left[-\frac{|\gamma|^2}{2}\right]$$
$$+\frac{|d|^2}{|\mu|^2 n!}\exp\left[-\left|\frac{\mu\gamma}{\nu}\right|^2\right]\left|\frac{\nu}{\mu}\right|^{2n}\sum_{k=0}^{\infty}\left|\frac{\gamma}{\nu}\right|^{2k}\frac{(n+k)!}{(k!)^2}$$

Therefore if we apply (5.1) then the mutual entropy $I(\rho\,;\,\Lambda^*)$ can be computed as follows :

$$I(\rho\,;\,\Lambda^*) = S(\sigma_E, \sigma_0) = \sum_{k=0}^{1}\lambda_k S(\Lambda^* E_k, \Lambda^*\rho)$$
$$= S(\Lambda^*\rho) - \lambda_0 S(\Lambda^* E_0) - \lambda_1 S(\Lambda^* E_1)$$
$$\cong -\sum_n \langle n|\Lambda^*\rho|n\rangle \log\langle n|\Lambda^*\rho|n\rangle + \sum_{k=0}^{1}\lambda_k \sum_n \langle n|\Lambda^* E_k |n\rangle \log\langle n|\Lambda^* E_k |n\rangle$$

Fig.1 and Fig.2 are the computational results on mutual entropy and MER w.r.t $\rho = (1-\lambda)|0\rangle\langle 0| + \lambda|\theta\rangle\langle\theta|$ and the gain G of the amplifier processes, respectively.

From these graphs we find that the mutual entropy and MER are decresing w.r.t. gain G for any parameter λ expressing initial superposition. On the other hand, both of them have the minimum value at $\lambda = 0.5$, because the initial entropy $S(\rho)$ has the maximum value at this point. Some of these results can be also read from the error probability and SNR. The total discussions with error probability, SNR and mutual entropy will be done in our forthcoming paper.

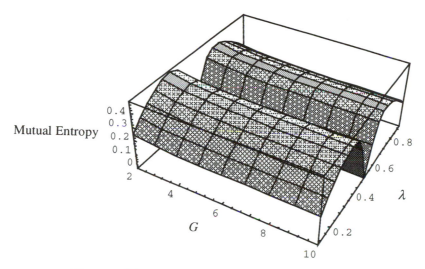

Figure 1. Mutual Entropy for Quantum Amplifier

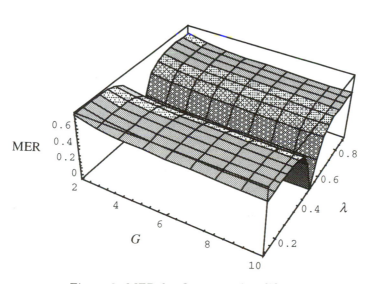

Figure 2. MER for Quantum Amplifier

6. CONCLUSION

In this paper the exact computation of the mutual entropy for the amplifier processes is given from the lifting expression. Also in another paper [14] we have already deriven error probability and SNR from the lifting expression. It means that, once we can get the lifting expression of optical communication process, we can derive the most important efficiencies "Error Probability, SNR and Mutual Entropy" altogether.

Now we study the application of a squeezed state to the optical communication processes by "lifting" [15]. Also the technique of lifting in our papers is now applied to other physical models to expain the irreversible processes in quantum systems. These results will be reported in other paper.

REFERENCES

[1] Accardi L. ; Noncommutative Markov chains. In : internatinal School of Mathematical Physics, Camerino, 268-295, 1974.

[2] Accardi L. and Ohya M. ; Compoud channels, transition expectations and liftings, to appear in J. Multivariate Analysis.

[3] Accardi L., Ohya M. and Suyari H. ; Computation of mutual entropy in quantum Markov chains, Open Systems and Information Dynamics, 2, 337-354, 1994.

[4] Gardiner, C.W. ; Quantum Noise, Springer-Verlag, 1991.

[5] Glauber, R.J. ; Coherent and incoherent states of the radiation field, Phys. Rev. Vol.131, pp.2766-2788 (1963).

[6] Ingarden R.S.and Urbanik K. ; Quantum information thermodynamics", Acta Phys. Polon. 21, 281-304, 1962.

[7] Ingarden R.S., Kossakowski A. and Ohya M. ; Open Systems and Information Dynamics, Kluwer, in press.

[8] Louisell, W.H. ; Quantum Statistical Properties of Radiation, John Wiley and Sons, New York, 1973.

[9] Ohya M.; On compound state and mutual information in quantum information theory. IEEE Transactions of Information Theory IT-29, 770-774, 1983.

[10] Ohya M. ; Note on quantum probability. Letter al Nuovo Cimento 38, 402-404, 1983.

[11] Ohya M. ; Some aspects of quantum information theory and their applications to irreversible processes, Reports on Mathematical Physics, 27, 19-47, 1989.

[12] Ohya M. and Petz D. ; Quantum Entropy and its Use, Springer-Verlag, 1993.

[13] Ohya M. and Petz D. and Watanabe N. ; On capacities of quantum channels, preprint.

[14] Ohya M. and Suyari H. ; An application of lifting theory to optical communication processes, Rep. on Math. Phys., 36, 403-420, 1995.

[15] Ohya M. and Suyari H. and Furuichi S. ; An application of squeezed vacuum state to optical communication processes, preprint.

[16] Sudarschan E.C.G. ; Equivalence of semiclassical and quantum mechanical descriptions of statistical light beams, Phys. Rev. Lett., 10, 277-279, 1963.

[17] Walls D.F. and Milburn G.J. ; Quantum Optics, Springer-Verlag, 1994.

[18] Watanabe N. ; Effciency of optical modulations for photon number states, Quantum Probability and related Topics 6, 489-498, 1991.

Part II.
Quantum Computing

QUANTUM COMPUTING AND DECOHERENCE
IN QUANTUM OPTICAL SYSTEMS

J. I. Cirac[1], T. Pellizzari[2], J. F. Poyatos[1], and P. Zoller[2]

[1] Departamento de Fisica, Universidad de Castilla–La Mancha,
13071 Ciudad Real, Spain
[2] Institut für Theoretische Physik, Universiät Innsbruck,
Technikerstrasse 25, A–6020 Innsbruck, Austria

We present recent theoretical results in the context of quantum computing and error correction. In particular, a short review of the ion trap quantum computer is given. Moreover, we present a novel scheme for quantum gate error correction in the ion trap model system. Finally, a method for a tomographic characterization of quantum gates is presented.

1. INTRODUCTION

The prospect of speeding up certain classes of computations by taking advantage of the quantum mechanical superposition principle and the physics of quantum entanglement has received a great deal of attention lately. The potentially useful quantum algorithms so far include factorisation of large numbers [1], database search [2] and simulation of quantum mechanical systems [3]. Recent theoretical and experimental progress in atomic physics and quantum optics has shown that small–scale quantum computing is feasible [4–7].

Computational speed–up is not the only motivation to do research into quantum computing. In particular, a quantum computer may be viewed as a generic *quantum state synthesizer* and can be used to prepare multi–particle entangled states. The simplest example is a system of two spin-$\frac{1}{2}$ particles which provide the basis for tests of bell inequalities [8], quantum teleportation [9] and quantum cryptography [10]. Entangled states of three spin-$\frac{1}{2}$ particles (GHZ states) predict violation of locality without any need of inequalities [11]. In fact, these applications of quantum computing will very likely come sooner than any computational useful device because much smaller quantum systems are sufficient. Finally, the possibility to entangle atoms promises a novel type of atomic spectroscopy below the standard quantum limit [12,13]. We find it convenient to discuss these applications in the language of quantum computing.

One of the most promising candidates for realizing a first prototype is the *ion trap quantum computer*, which is based on quantum bits represented by ions stored in a linear Paul trap [4]. Quantum gates between any arbitrary pair of quantum bits are performed by temporarily exciting a collective mode of motion in which all the ions participate. This phonon mode provides the *quantum bus* for transferring quantum coherence between the ions. Experimental progress towards the realization of this proposal has been

Quantum Communication, Computing, and Measurement
Edited by Hirota *et al.*, Plenum Press, New York, 1997

made recently. The main idea of the proposal has been demonstrated in an experiment with a single ion at the NIST Boulder facility [6]. At present five experimental groups are pursuing experiments to realizing an ion trap quantum computer.

However, building a quantum computer is an extremely difficult task. The major obstacle is the coupling of the quantum computer to the environment, which destroys quantum mechanical superpositions very rapidly. This effect is usually referred to as *decoherence* [14]. It is thus of crucial importance to finding schemes to actively suppress and *undo* the effects of decoherence.

The errors which can take place in a quantum computer can be roughly classified as *memory errors* and *gate errors*. The former take place in a quantum register while no quantum computations are performed. The latter destroy quantum mechanical coherences by the application of erroneous quantum gates. Schemes to protect a static quantum state against decoherence (memory errors) were first discovered independently by Peter Shor [15] and Andrew Steane [16]. Their proposals gave rise to a large number of subsequent publications (see, e.g., [17–19]). Thus the theory of *quantum error correcting codes* is increasingly well understood. However, these schemes require the application of flawless quantum gates in order to perform the necessary steps for quantum error correction.

The problem of gate errors, i.e errors that are induced during quantum gates, has been addressed only recently. Two different approaches have been proposed, one of which is discussed in this paper. Firstly, an error correction scheme for the ion trap quantum computer was proposed by Cirac *et al.* [20]. This scheme is capable to correct for errors due to decays in the phonon mode during quantum gate operations. This is a specific but important source of errors in the ion trap proposal. The computational overhead in the number of elementary quantum gates is moderate and the number of required ions is the same as for the uncorrected case. Secondly, Peter Shor has proposed an ingenious scheme to correct for the most general error which can take place during quantum gates [21]. However, Shors scheme requires a large computational overhead both in memory and time which seem to prevent a proof–of–principle demonstration in the near future.

The present paper is organized as follows. In Section 2 we establish the notation and formulate general physical requirements for building a quantum computer. The ion trap quantum computer [4] is shortly reviewed in Section 3. Decoherence, error correction and in particular the aforementioned scheme for correcting errors during quantum gates [20] in the the ion trap quantum computer is discussed in Section 4. Finally, in Section 5 we present a scheme to fully characterize the performance of a quantum gate by means of a tomographic measurement [22]. We wish to characterize the input–output characteristics of this two-bit quantum gate to evaluate implementations of quantum gates in the laboratory, as well as a theoretical tool to compare the expected performance of specific quantum computer model systems.

2. BASIC PRINCIPLES AND PHYSICAL REQUIREMENTS

For more detailed reviews on quantum computing and quantum algorithms (in particular Shor's factorization algorithm [1]) we refer the reader to [23, 24]. A quantum computer can be thought of as N spin-1/2 systems with levels $|0\rangle$ and $|1\rangle$, representing the quantum bits or qubits. The most general state of the qc is an entangled state

$$|\psi\rangle = \sum_{x=0}^{2^N-1} c_x |x\rangle \equiv \sum_{\underline{x}=\{0,1\}^N} c_{\underline{x}} |\underline{x}\rangle$$

of quantum registers $|x\rangle = |x_{N-1}\rangle_{N-1} \dots |x_0\rangle_0 \in \mathcal{H}(N-1)_2 \otimes \dots \otimes \mathcal{H}(0)_2$ with $x = \sum_{n=0}^{N-1} x_n 2^n$ the binary decomposition of x. Quantum computations correspond to processes $|\psi_{in}\rangle \rightarrow |\psi_{out}\rangle = \hat{U}|\psi_{in}\rangle$ where a given input state is mapped onto an output state by a unitary transformation $\hat{U}$. This can be carried out as a sequence of elementary steps (quantum gates) involving operations on a few qubits. In particular, a two-bit gate operation corresponds to conditional dynamics [25] represented by the unitary operator,

$$\hat{U} = |0\rangle_{11}\langle 0| \otimes 1_2 + |1\rangle_{11}\langle 1| \otimes \hat{U}_2$$

where we apply the unitary operation $\hat{U}_2$ to the target bit if the control bit is in state $|1\rangle$. It has been shown [25,27–30] that any operation can be decomposed into universal two-bit gates, for example into a controlled–NOT gates between two qubits (and rotations on a single qubit). A controlled–NOT is defined by $\hat{C}_{12} : |\epsilon_1\rangle|\epsilon_2\rangle \rightarrow |\epsilon_1\rangle|\epsilon_1 \oplus \epsilon_2\rangle$ with $\epsilon_{1,2} = 0, 1$, and $\oplus$ denotes addition modulo 2. The question is, therefore, how to implement two-bit entanglement operations on systems of atoms and photons in the laboratory.

We shall now formulate general requirements that any physical system used for quantum computing must fulfill:

1. We need to identify a physical mechanism to entangle the quantum bits in order to perform two-bit quantum gates, and to combine these operations into a quantum network.

2. The system must provide stable storage for the quantum bits. In particular, if no error correction is performed the the quantum mechanical superpositions must prevail for the time required to complete the computation. If error correction is performed this condition can be weakened. Moreover, the errors introduced by quantum gates must be small. Again, for error–corrected quantum networks this requirement is less stringent.

3. A means is needed to performing reliable measurements of the state of the quantum bits. This is needed for resetting the computer before the computation, for reading out the final result and for intermediate error correction steps.

3. THE ION TRAP QUANTUM COMPUTER

At present the most realistic proposal for a quantum computer model is based on a string of cold ions interacting with laser light and moving in a linear Paul trap [4]. The basic elements of the computer (i.e. the qubits) are the ions themselves. The two states of the n–th qubit are identified with two of the internal states of the corresponding ion. In this system independent manipulation of each individual qubit is accomplished by directing different laser beams to each of the ions. A two-bit quantum gate can be implemented by exciting the collective quantized motion of the ions with lasers. The coupling of the motion of the ions is provided by the Coulomb repulsion which is much stronger than any other interaction for typical separations between the ions of a few optical wavelengths. The confinement of the motion along X, Y and Z directions can be described by an (anisotropic) harmonic potential of frequencies $\nu_x \ll \nu_y, \nu_z$. The ions have been previously laser cooled so that they undergo very small oscillations around the equilibrium position. In this case, the motion of the ions is described in terms of normal modes. Moreover, it is assumed that sideband cooling has left all the normal modes in their corresponding (quantum) ground states. For this to be possible, one

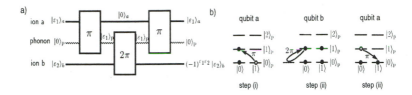

Figure 1. Implementation of the universal two-bit gate C_{ab} : $|\varepsilon_1\rangle_a|\varepsilon_2\rangle_b \rightarrow (-1)^{\varepsilon_1\varepsilon_2}|\varepsilon_1\rangle_a|\varepsilon_2\rangle_b$ in an ion trap quantum computer: (a) schematic diagram, (b) ion operations steps (i) to (iii) according to Eq. (1).

has to assume that the Lamb–Dicke limit holds for all the modes, i.e. the oscillation amplitudes are much smaller than the laser wavelength [31].

Single qubit gates can be performed by acting with a resonant laser beam on the corresponding ion. Two–bit quantum gates are implemented by entangling two ions through exchange of a phonon with a laser tuned to the lower motional sideband. The scheme is outlined in Fig. 1. A universal two–bit quantum gate between ions a and b can be carried out in three steps [4]: (i) A π laser pulse swaps the qubit of the ion a to the center-of-mass mode; (ii) a conditional sign change is introduced through an auxiliary state $|e'\rangle$ with the help of a 2π pulse on ion b. (iii) The qubit of ion a is restored by inverting step (i). This corresponds to the sequence

$$C_{ab} : |\varepsilon_1\rangle_a|\varepsilon_2\rangle_b|0\rangle_p \xrightarrow{(i)} |0\rangle_a|\varepsilon_2\rangle_b|\varepsilon_1\rangle_p$$
$$\xrightarrow{(ii)} (-1)^{\varepsilon_1\varepsilon_2}|0\rangle_a|\varepsilon_2\rangle_b|\varepsilon_1\rangle_p \qquad (1)$$
$$\xrightarrow{(iii)} (-1)^{\varepsilon_1\varepsilon_2}|\varepsilon_1\rangle_a|\varepsilon_2\rangle_b|0\rangle_p$$

where $|\varepsilon_{1,2} = 0, 1\rangle_{a,b}$ represent the state of the ion and $|n\rangle_p$ refers to phonons in the center-of-mass motion. In a remarkable experiment a two-bit quantum gate based on a single trapped ion has been demonstrated at NIST Boulder [6].

Decoherence [14] in an ion trap is due to spontaneous decay of the internal atomic states, and damping and heating of the motion of the ion. Application of stored ions in ultrahigh precision spectroscopy [12,31] shows that the decoherence times can be quite long, longer than the time required to perform many operations. Spontaneous emission is suppressed using metastable or Raman transitions [6]. Collisions with background atoms can be avoided at sufficiently low pressures for very long times, and other couplings that affect the moving charges can be made sufficiently small [12]. Moreover, the final readout of the quantum register (state measurement of the individual qubits) at the end of the computation can be accomplished using the quantum jumps technique with essentially unit efficiency [6].

It should be noted, however, that the number of gate operations required to perform even simple computational tasks is significant [32–34], and we should not expect that the present model systems can be scaled up to useful computing machines in the near future [33, 35].

4. DECOHERENCE AND ERROR CORRECTION

The central difficulty of entangling a large number of particles is decoherence [14]. Quantum computing involves manipulating quantum states that are in coherent superpositions. Due to coupling to an environment these superpositions tend to be fragile and decay easily: this decay is called decoherence and corresponds to errors during the computation. There are two kinds of errors. A static superposition state in a quantum register will typically decay even when no quantum computations are performed. This effect will give rise to memory errors. A second kind or error occurs during gate operations, for example when the system is coupled to auxiliary degrees of freedom which undergo damping. These are referred to as computational errors.

4.1. ERROR CORRECTING CODES

During the last year various ingenious error correction codes have been developed to protect quantum superposition and entanglement (memory errors) [17]. Shor [15] and Steane [16] have independently proposed schemes based on classical error correcting codes. The central idea is to store single qubits redundantly in several quantum bits which undergo independent decoherence. These schemes allow to correct any error which takes place in any one of the "physical" qubits. Steane [16], and Calderbank and Shor [18] have outlined schemes which uses only seven bits. Finally, Knill and Laflamme [17] have pointed out that the smallest quantum code distributes the quantum information of a single logical qubit over five physical qubits [19]. Note that error correcting codes that restrict the possible errors can be shorter. For example, if only dephasing is considered the smallest code has length three [36]. Finally, Grassl et al. have shown that if the position of the erroneous quantum bit is known the smallest error correcting code has length four [37]. All error correction schemes have to be complemented with an appropriate encoding circuit which takes the initial superposition and the extra qubits in $|0\rangle$ to the encoded state. In addition one needs a decoding circuit, and by reading out the extra qubits at the decoder's output one learns which one of the possible alternatives (no error plus all possible 1-bit errors) was realized. The original unknown superposition state can then be restored by an appropriate unitary transformation. These schemes are based on the assumption of a perfect physical implementation of quantum circuits. As a sideremark we note that very recently an extension of the above described schemes has been proposed by Shor that allows for quantum error correction during computations with erroneous quantum circuits [21].

In quantum optical systems the coupling to an environment is typically described as Markovian dynamics, and decay and quantum noise modeled as quantum jumps of a system wave function [38]. Mabuchi and Zoller [39] have discussed the possibility of *inverting quantum jumps*, assuming that they are observed by continuously monitoring the system decay channels. This can be used to conserve an unknown superposition state.

4.2. ERROR CORRECTION IN THE ION TRAP QUANTUM COMPUTER

The error correction schemes discussed above have focused on preserving a given entangled state. Cirac et al. have proposed a method to correct for effects of decoherence in the dynamical process of preparation and modification of entangled states (gate errors) [20]. The proposed scheme is a first-order error correction that allows to effectively square the number of gate operations relative to the uncorrected case. The motivation is that in quantum optical systems entanglement is achieved by coupling qubits to another degree of freedom. This auxiliary quantum system undergoes decoherence by coupling to a heat bath. For example, in the ion trap quantum computer [4] the qubits can be stored in long–lived atomic ground states [6] with decoherence time $\simeq 1000$s [12]. Two bit quantum gates are implemented by coupling the ions to the collective center-of-mass motion in the trap which decoheres in a time $\simeq 1$ms [6]. Thus, at least in present experiments, gate errors predominate.

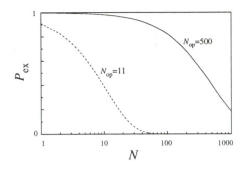

Figure 2. Probability of measuring the correct result P_{ex} after the application of N 2–bit quantum gates $C_{ab}^L: |\varepsilon_1\rangle_a^L |\varepsilon_2\rangle_b^L \to (-1)^{\varepsilon_1 \varepsilon_2} |\varepsilon_1\rangle_a^L |\varepsilon_2\rangle_b^L$ to the initial state $\propto |0\rangle_a^L |0\rangle_b^L + |1\rangle_a^L |1\rangle_b^L$. Dashed line: quantum gate without error correction. Solid line: present error correcting scheme. The parameters have been chosen such that the probability for an error within a single gate C_{ab}^L without error correction is $p = 0.09$.

Here we summarize some of the key ideas of the scheme and illustrate how the correction scheme can be implemented in an ion trap quantum computer. We assume that the phonons of the center-of-mass mode are coupled to a zero temperature reservoir. The essential results are summarized in Fig. 2, where we plot the fidelity for successful operation as a function of the number of applied two bit gates. Note that the number of reliable gates N_{op} is effectively squared.

The error-corrected quantum gate is based on the following three elements [see Fig. 3]:

1. *Redundant encoding in logical qubits:* At the beginning of the gate operation between the ions a and b, we encode each of the logical qubits in two physical qubits $a_{1,2}$ and $b_{1,2}$, respectively,

$$|\varepsilon\rangle_x \overset{\mathcal{U}}{\to} |\varepsilon\rangle_x^L \propto |\varepsilon\rangle_{x_1} |0\rangle_{x_2} + |1-\varepsilon\rangle_{x_1} |1\rangle_{x_2} \qquad (2)$$

with $\varepsilon = 0, 1$ and $x = a, b$. After the gate we decode. These *two physical qubits* are stored in a *single four–level ion* $|0\rangle_x \equiv |0\rangle_{x_1} |0\rangle_{x_2} \cdots$ [see Fig. 3b]. The unitary transformation $\mathcal{U}$ thus requires only a *single–ion* operation. In addition, these qubits can be manipulated independently with *single–ion* operations (laser pulses). Allowed computational inputs are states of the form

$$|\Psi(0)\rangle = \sum_{\varepsilon_1, \varepsilon_2 = 0,1} |\varepsilon_1\rangle_a^L |\varepsilon_2\rangle_b^L |0\rangle_{\text{p}} \chi_{\varepsilon_1, \varepsilon_2} \qquad (3)$$

where the χ's denote coefficients in the superposition.

2. *Gate operation for logical qubits:* Our aim is to perform the universal gate C_{ab}^L : $|\varepsilon_1\rangle_a^L |\varepsilon_2\rangle_b^L \to (-1)^{\varepsilon_1 \varepsilon_2} |\varepsilon_1\rangle_a^L |\varepsilon_2\rangle_b^L$ between the logical qubits a and b stored in the physical qubits $a_{1,2}$ and $b_{1,2}$, respectively. Using Eq. (2) we decompose [see Fig. 3]:

$$C_{a,b}^L = C_{a_2,b_1} C_{a_1,b_2} C_{a_2,b_2} C_{a_1,b_1} \qquad (4)$$

Each of these four subgates are now performed in essentially the same way as in the uncorrected case Eq. (1).

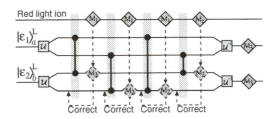

Red light ion

$|\varepsilon_1\rangle_a^L$

$|\varepsilon_2\rangle_b^L$

Correct Correct Correct Correct

Figure 3. Logical two–qubit gate with error correction (see text).

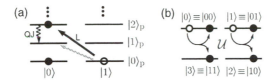

(a)

QJ

$|2\rangle_p$

$|1\rangle_p$

$|0\rangle_p$

$|0\rangle$ $|1\rangle$

(b) $|0\rangle \equiv |00\rangle$ $|1\rangle \equiv |01\rangle$

$\mathcal{U}$

$|3\rangle \equiv |11\rangle$ $|2\rangle \equiv |10\rangle$

Figure 4. (a) Step (i) of Eq. (1) that is tune the laser (L) to the first (dim arrow) or second (black arrow) motional sideband. Occurrence of a quantum jump is indicated by QJ. (b) Redundant encoding in a 4–level ion as in Eq. (2).

Each of the four subgates C_{a_i,b_j} acts only on two physical qubits at a time. As an example we consider the operation C_{a_1,b_1}. The state of the quantum computer Eq. (3) before the subgate can be rearranged as

$$|\Psi(0)\rangle = \sum_{\varepsilon_1,\varepsilon_2=0,1} |\varepsilon_1\rangle_{a_1}|\varepsilon_2\rangle_{b_1}|0\rangle_p|R_{\varepsilon_1,\varepsilon_2}\rangle, \qquad (5)$$

with

$$|R_{\varepsilon_1,\varepsilon_2}\rangle = |0\rangle_{a_2}|0\rangle_{b_2}\chi_{\varepsilon_1,\varepsilon_2} + |0\rangle_{a_2}|1\rangle_{b_2}\chi_{\varepsilon_1,1-\varepsilon_2} \qquad (6)$$
$$+|1\rangle_{a_2}|0\rangle_{b_2}\chi_{1-\varepsilon_1,\varepsilon_2} + |1\rangle_{a_2}|1\rangle_{b_2}\chi_{1-\varepsilon_1,1-\varepsilon_2}.$$

The subgate C_{a_1,b_1} operates on the first three kets of Eq. (5) only. If something goes wrong we have a "backup" in $|R_{\varepsilon_1,\varepsilon_2}\rangle$.

3. We perform the elementary quantum gates (1) via the *second motional sideband involving two phonons*. Presence of one phonon after the gate operation indicates that there was an error, i.e. a decay $|2\rangle_p \rightarrow |1\rangle_p$ happened some time during the gate operation. Thus, after each subgate a measurement is performed to detect the presence or absence of phonons. This measurement requires an extra ion (the *right light ion* in Fig. 3).

Thus the scheme consists of the following elements [compare Fig. 4]: Firstly, a phonon decay during one of the subgates will transform the state of the QC into a state with one phonon $|1\rangle_p$. The state of the quantum computer after the jump will remain unaffected until the end of the subgate (independent of the jump time). Thus the occurrence of a jump can be detected, for example with an extra ion. Secondly, if a jump was detected after one of the subgates, we wish to recover the state before this particular operation. This information can be "restored from the backup" (6). This involves single ion operations together with measurements on one of the physical qubits.

A remarkable feature of the scheme is that error testing measurements are performed *after* the gate operation to correct errors which accumulated *during* the computation. The overhead required by the scheme is a rather moderate: each logical qubit is encoded into two qubits that are stored in the same (four–level) ion. This has the advantage that one-qubit gates (for which decoherence is assumed to be negligible) are the same with or without the redundant encoding. On the other hand, implementation of the two–qubit gate requires an overhead of four two–qubit subgates. A proof-of-principle experiment to demonstrate the possibility of correcting effects of decoherence in dissipative quantum dynamics could be performed with three trapped ions which seems to be attainable with present technology [6].

5. TOMOGRAPHY OF A QUANTUM GATE

Both from an experimental and theoretical point of view it is essential to characterize the input–output (transfer–)characteristics of a quantum gate in the sense of a "black box" [7] (for general references on quantum *state* tomography see [40–43]). In general, a given quantum dynamics $\mathcal{E}$ transforms input states ρ_{in} into output states ρ_{out}, i.e. $\rho_{\text{in}} \longrightarrow \rho_{\text{out}} = \mathcal{E}[\rho_{\text{in}}]$ with $\mathcal{E}$ a linear mapping. The aim is to characterize the process $\mathcal{E}$ by a sequence of measurements. In particular, we outline a procedure for characterizing a two–qubit gate [22]. This can be implemented using only (i) product states as inputs, and (ii) single qubit measurements on the outputs. This avoids utilizing any interaction (entanglement) between the qubits which would be required to prepare Bell state inputs and perform Bell measurements. Otherwise the decoherence and errors induced by the measurement itself would distort the characterization of $\mathcal{E}$.

A general scheme to characterize quantum dynamics has been developed [22]. Let us assume that the system is initially prepared in the pure state $|\Psi_{\text{in}}\rangle = \sum_{i=0}^{N} c_i |i\rangle$. By $|E\rangle$ we denote the initial state of the environment (extension to mixed initial states is straightforward). Thus, the initial state of the system–plus–environment is transformed according to $|i\rangle|E\rangle \xrightarrow{\mathcal{E}} \sum_{j=0}^{M} |j\rangle|E_j^i\rangle$ where the states $|E_j^i\rangle$ are unnormalized states of the environment. Tracing over the environment degrees of freedom we obtain the reduced system density operator,

$$\hat{\rho}_{\text{out}} = \sum_{i,i'=0}^{N} c_i \, [c_{i'}]^* \, \hat{R}_{i'i} \equiv \sum_{i,i'=0}^{N} c_i \, [c_{i'}]^* \left[\sum_{j,j'=0}^{M} (E_{j'}^{i'}|E_j^i) \, |j\rangle\langle j'| \right].$$

Knowledge of the "process operators" $\hat{R}_{i'i}$ (which are independent of the inputs) is sufficient to predict the final density operator for any input state. The problem of fully characterizing the physical process $\mathcal{E}$ is reduced to finding the $\hat{R}_{i'i}$'s. We now prepare the system intially in $(N+1)^2$ different initial (pure) input states, and in each of these cases we obtain a corresponding output density matrix ρ_{out} (which can be measured by standard tomographic techniques). This gives a set of linear equations relating the $\hat{R}_{i'i}$'s to the ρ_{out}'s. It can be shown that with an appropriate choice of input states this set equations can always be inverted.

In the case of a universal two–qubit gate the system is composed of two two–level subsystems 1 and 2 with levels $|0\rangle_{1,2}$ and $|1\rangle_{1,2}$ each. A basis for the initial states is given by $|i\rangle = |i_1\rangle_1 |i_2\rangle_1$ (with $i = 2i_1 + i_2$, and $i_1, i_2 = 0, 1$). The quantum tomography of the output states can be carried out along the lines proposed by Wootters [44]. One writes the output operators as $\hat{\rho}_{\text{out}} = \sum \lambda_{q_1 q_2} \hat{\sigma}_{q_1}^1 \otimes \hat{\sigma}_{q_2}^2$, where $\hat{\sigma}_k^{1,2}$ denote the spin Pauli matrices (and the idetity operator). By measuring the observables $\hat{\sigma}_{q_1}^1 \otimes \hat{\sigma}_{q_2}^2$ one can determine the coefficients λ_{q_1,q_2}. An example of the 16 possible product input states are states of the form $|\psi_a\rangle_1 |\psi_b\rangle_2$ ($a, b = 1, \ldots, 4$) with $|\psi_1\rangle = |0\rangle$, $|\psi_2\rangle \propto |0\rangle + |1\rangle$, $|\psi_3\rangle = |1\rangle$, $|\psi_4\rangle \propto |0\rangle + i|1\rangle$. On the basis of this tomographic measurement of the gate three global parameters are introduced in Ref. [22] to characterize the performance of the quantum gate: (i) the "Gate Fidelity" ($\mathcal{F}$) that expresses how close the experimental gate is to the ideal one; (ii) the "Gate Purity" ($\mathcal{P}$) that reflects to what extent the gate experiences decoherence; and (iii) the "Quantum Degree of the Gate" ($\mathcal{Q}$), a measure of the possibility to produce (quantum) entangled states out of initial product states. For details and numerical results we refer the reader to Ref. [22].

6. CONCLUSIONS

It can not be overemphasized that the concepts and schemes presented in this paper are only a starting point to acquire first experience in the field of quantum computing. Even though ion trap technology will presumably lead to the first prototype implementation, it is very unlikely that it will remain the most attractive architecture for all future times. There is cleary an upper limit on the maximum number of ions one can store, cool and manipulate in a trap.

At present nobody can predict what and if any technology will lead to computationally useful quantum computers. For example, a solid state realization of a quantum computer is certainly desirable, yet it seems unrealistic with current technology due to very short decoherence times.

From a mathematical point of view, more algorithms need to be found to justify the effort of building quantum computers. Yet even in the absence of many computationally useful algorithms a quantum computer might still be useful, for example as a simulator of quantum dynamics [3] or for improved high precision spectroscopy [12,13].

It should be stated clearly that the development of a quantum computer is not just a technological problem. Instead, a lot of new physics will be necessary to make quantum computing feasible. On the other hand, in the not too distant future the realization of small prototype systems with a few qubits is likely. In any case the next few years should be interesting ones for the quantum computer.

ACKNOWLEDGEMENTS

This work was supported in part by the Austrian Science Foundation, the "Acciones Integradas" between Austria and Spain, and the European TMR network under contract ERB4061PL95–1412.

REFERENCES

[1] P.W. Shor, in *Proceedings of the 35th Annual Symposium on the Foundations of Computer Science*, S. Goldwassser ed. (IEEE Computer Society Press, Los Alamitos, Ca, 1994), p. 124.

[2] L. K. Grover, preprint quant-ph/9605043 on http://xxx.lanl.gov (1996).

[3] S. Lloyd, preprint (1996).

[4] J.I. Cirac and P. Zoller, Phys. Rev. Lett. **74**, 4091 (1995).

[5] T. Pellizzari, S. A. Gardiner, J. I. Cirac, and P. Zoller, Phys. Rev. Lett. **75**, 3788 (1995).

[6] C. Monroe, D.M. Meekhof, B.E. King, W.M. Itano, and D.J. Wineland Phys. Rev. Lett. **75**, 4714 (1995).

[7] Q. A. Turchette *et al.*, Phys. Rev. Lett. **75**, 4710 (1995).

[8] J. S. Bell, Physics **1**, 195 (1964).

[9] C.H. Bennett, G. Brassard, C. Crepeau, R. Josza, A. Peres, and W. K. Wootters, Phys. Rev. Lett. **70**, 1895 (1993).

[10] C. H. Bennet and G. Brassard, Lecture Notes in Computer Science, p. 809 (Springer, 1985).

[11] D. M. Greenberger *et al.*, Am J. Phys. **58**, 1131 (1990).

[12] D.J. Wineland, J.J. Bollinger, W.M. Itano, F.L. Moore, and D. Heinzen, Phys. Rev. A **46**, R6797 (1992).

[13] D. J. Wineland, J.J. Bollinger, W. M. Itano, and D.J. Heinzen, Phys. Rev. A **50**, 67 (1994) project.

[14] R. Landauer, Philos. Trans. R. Soc. London A **353**,367 (1995); W. G. Unruh, Phys. Rev. A **51**, 992 (1995).

[15] P.W. Shor, Phys. Rev. A **52**, R2493 (1995).

[16] A. Steane, Proc. Roy. Soc. London A, in press.

[17] E. Knill and R. Laflamme, preprint quant-ph/9600034 on http://xxx.lanl.gov.

[18] A. R. Calderbank and P. W. Shor, preprint quant-ph/9512032 on http://xxx.lanl.gov.

[19] R. Laflamme, C. Miquel, J. P. Paz, and W. H. Zurek, preprint quant-ph/9602019 on http://xxx.lanl.gov (1996).

[20] J. I. Cirac, T. Pellizzari, and P. Zoller, Science **273** 5279 (1996).

[21] Shor P. W., preprint quant-ph/9605011 on http://xxx.lanl.gov (1996).

[22] J. F. Poyatos, J. I. Cirac and P. Zoller, Phys. Rev. Lett., in press.

[23] D. P. DiVincenzo, Science **270**, 255 (1995).

[24] A. Ekert and R. Josza, Rev. of Mod. Phys. **68**, 733 (1996).

[25] A. Barenco, D. Deutsch, A. Ekert and R. Josza, Phys. Rev. Lett. **74**, 4083 (1995).

[26] A. Barenco, Proc. R. Soc. London A **449**, 679 (1995).

[27] D. Deutsch, A. Barenco, and A. Ekert, Proc. R. Soc. London A **449**, 669 (1995).

[28] D. P. DiVincenzo, Phys. Rev. A **51**, 1015 (1995).

[29] T. Sleator and H. Weinfurter, Phys. Rev. Lett. **74**, 4087 (1995).

[30] S. Lloyd, Phys. Rev. Lett. bf 75, 346 (1995).

[31] R. Blatt, Proc. 14th ICAP, ed. D. Wineland *et al.* (AIP Press, 1995), p. 219.

[32] V. Vedral, A. Barenco, and A. Ekert, Phys. Rev. A **54**, 147 (1996).

[33] R. J. Hughes, D.F.V. James, E.H. Knill, R. Laflamme and A.G. Petschek, preprint quant-ph/9604026, available on http://xxx.lanl.gov (1996).

[34] D. Beckman *et al.* , preprint quant-ph/9602016, available on http://xxx.lanl.gov (1996).

[35] M. Plenio and P. Knight, Phys. Rev. A **53**, 2986 (1996).

[36] S. L. Braunstein, preprint quant-ph/9603024, available on http://xxx.lanl.gov (1996).

[37] M. Grassl, Th. Beth, and T. Pellizzari, preprint (1996).

[38] H. J. Carmichael, in *An Open Systems Approach to Quantum Optics*, Lecture Notes in Physics, m18 (Springer, Berlin, 1993); J. Dalibard *et al.*, Phys. Rev. Lett. **68**, 580 (1992); C. W. Gardiner, A. S. Parkins, and P. Zoller, Phys. Rev. A **46**, 4363 (1992).

[39] H. Mabuchi and P. Zoller, Phys. Rev. Lett. **76**, 3108 (1996).

[40] S. Wallentowitz and W. Vogel, Phys. Rev. Lett. **75**, 2932 (1995).

[41] P. J. Bardroff, E. Mayr, and W. P. Schleich, Phys. Rev. A, **51** 4963 (1995).

[42] C.D'Helon and G.J. Milburn, preprint.

[43] J. F. Poyatos, R. Walser, J. I. Cirac, P. Zoller, Phys. Rev. A, **53**, R1966 (1996).

[44] W.K. Wootters, Ann. Phys. (N.Y.) **176**, 1 (1987).

UNITARY DYNAMICS FOR QUANTUM CODEWORDS

Asher Peres

Institute for Theoretical Physics
University of California
Santa Barbara, CA 93106
Permanent address: Technion—Israel Institute of Technology,
32 000 Haifa, Israel

A quantum codeword is a redundant representation of a logical qubit by means of several physical qubits. It is constructed in such a way that if one of the physical qubits is perturbed, for example if it gets entangled with an unknown environment, there still is enough information encoded in the other physical qubits to restore the logical qubit, and disentangle it from the environment. The recovery procedure may consist of the detection of an error syndrome, followed by the correction of the error, as in the classical case. However, it can also be performed by means of unitary operations, without having to know the error syndrome.

Since quantum codewords span only a restricted subspace of the complete physical Hilbert space, the unitary operations that generate quantum dynamics (that is, the computational process) are subject to considerable arbitrariness, similar to the gauge freedom in quantum field theory. Quantum codewords can thus serve as a toy model for investigating the quantization of constrained dynamical systems.

1.   INTRODUCTION

In *classical* communication and computing systems, logical bits, having values 0 or 1, are implemented in a highly redundant way by bistable elements, such as magnetic domains. The bistability is enforced by coupling the bit carriers to a dissipative environment. Errors may then occur, because of thermal fluctuations and other hardware imperfections. To take care of these errors, various correction methods have been developed [1], involving the use of redundant bits (that are implemented by additional bistable elements).

In *quantum* communication and computing, the situation is more complicated: in spite of their name, the logical "qubits" (quantum binary digits) are not restricted to the discrete values 0 and 1. Their value can be represented by any point on the surface of a Poincaré sphere. Moreover, any set of qubits can be in an *entangled* state: none of the individual qubits has a pure quantum state, it is only the state of all the qubits together that is pure [2].

The qubits of a quantum computer are materialized by single quanta, such as trapped ions [3]. Their coupling to a dissipative environment (which was the standard stabilizing mechanism for classical bits) is now to be avoided as much as possible, because it readily leads to decoherence, namely to the loss of phase relationships. Yet, disturbances due to the environment cannot be completely eliminated: e.g., even if there are no residual gas molecules in the vacuum of an ion trap, there still are the vacuum fluctuations of the quantized electromagnetic field, which induce spontaneous transitions between the energy levels of the ions. Therefore, error control is an essential part of any quantum communication or computing system.

This goal is much more difficult to achieve than classical error correction, because qubits cannot be read, or copied, or duplicated, without altering their quantum state in an unpredictable way [4]. The feasibility of quantum error correction, which for some time had been in doubt, was first demonstrated by Shor [5]. As in the classical case, *redundancy* is an essential element, but this cannot be a simple repetitive redundancy, where each bit has several identical replicas and a majority vote is taken to establish the truth. This is because qubits, contrary to ordinary classical bits, can be *entangled*, and usually they are. As a trivial example, in the singlet state of two spin-$\frac{1}{2}$ particles, each particle, taken separately, is in a completely random state. Therefore, comparing the states of spin-$\frac{1}{2}$ particles that belong to different (redundant) singlets would give no information whatsoever.

All quantum error correction methods [5–9] use several physical qubits for representing one logical qubit. These physical qubits are prepared in a carefully chosen, highly entangled state. None of these qubits, taken alone, carries any information. However, a large enough subset of them may contain a sufficient amount of information, encoded in relative phases, for determining and exactly restoring the state of the logical qubit, including its entanglement with the other logical qubits in the quantum computer.

In this article, I review the quantum mechanical principles that make error correction possible. (I shall not discuss how to actually design new codewords; the most efficient techniques involve a combination of classical coding theory and of the theory of finite groups.) Since quantum codewords span only a restricted subspace of the complete physical Hilbert space, the unitary operations that generate the quantum dynamical evolution (that is, the computational process) are subject to considerable arbitrariness. The latter is similar to the gauge freedom in quantum field theory. Quantum codewords can thus serve as a simple toy model for investigating the quantization of constrained dynamical systems, such as field theories with gauge groups.

2.   ENCODING AND DECODING

In the following, I shall usually consider codewords that represent a single logical qubit. It is also possible, and perhaps it may be more efficient, to encode several qubits into larger codewords. However, no new physical principles are involved in this, and the simple case of a single qubit is sufficient for illustrating these principles.

The quantum state of a single logical qubit will be denoted as

$$\psi = \alpha \, |0\rangle + \beta \, |1\rangle, \tag{1}$$

where the coefficients α and β are complex numbers. The symbols $|0\rangle$ and $|1\rangle$ represent any two orthogonal quantum states, such as "up" and "down" for a spin, or the ground state and an excited state of a trapped ion.

In a quantum computer, there are many logical qubits, typically in a collective, highly entangled state, and any particular qubit has no definite state. I shall still use the same symbol ψ for representing the state of the entire computer, and Eq. (1) could now be written as

$$\psi = |\alpha\rangle \otimes |0\rangle + |\beta\rangle \otimes |1\rangle, \tag{2}$$

where one particular qubit has been singled out for the discussion, and the symbols $|\alpha\rangle$ and $|\beta\rangle$ represent the collective states of all the other qubits, that are correlated with $|0\rangle$ and $|1\rangle$, respectively. However, to simplify the notation and improve readability, I shall still write the computer state as in Eq. (1). In the following, Dirac's ket notation will in general *not* be used for generic state vectors (such as ψ, α, β) and the $\otimes$ sign will sometimes be omitted, when the meaning is clear. Kets will be used only for denoting basis vectors such as $|0\rangle$ and $|1\rangle$, and their direct products. The latter will be labelled by binary numbers, such as

$$|9\rangle \equiv |01001\rangle \equiv |0\rangle \otimes |1\rangle \otimes |0\rangle \otimes |0\rangle \otimes |1\rangle. \tag{3}$$

In order to encode the qubit ψ in Eq. (1), we intoduce an auxiliary system, called *ancilla,*[*] initially in a state $|000\ldots\rangle$. The ancilla is made of n qubits, and we can use the mutually orthogonal vectors $|a\rangle$, with $a = 0, 1, \ldots, 2^n - 1$ (the number a being written in binary notation) as a basis for its quantum states. These labels are called *syndromes*, because, as we shall see, the presence of an ancilla state with $a \neq 0$ may serve to identify an error in the encoded state that represents ψ.

Encoding is a unitary transformation, E, performed on a physical qubit and its ancilla together:

$$|z\rangle \otimes |a = 0\rangle \to E\left(|z\rangle \otimes |a = 0\rangle\right) \equiv |Z_0\rangle, \tag{4}$$

where $|z\rangle$ means either $|0\rangle$ or $|1\rangle$. This unitary transformation is executed by a quantum circuit (an array of quantum gates). However, from the theorist's point of view, it is also convenient to consider $|z\rangle \otimes |a = 0\rangle$ and $|Z_0\rangle$ as two different representations of the same qubit $|z\rangle$: its logical representation, and its physical representation. The first one is convenient for discussing matters of principle, such as quantum algorithms, while the physical representation is the one where qubits are actually materialized by distinct physical systems (and the latter are the ones that may be subject to independent errors).[†]

3. ERROR CORRECTION

If there are 2^n syndromes (including the null syndrome for no error), it is possible to identify and correct up to $2^n - 1$ different errors that affect the physical qubits, with the help of a suitable decoding method, as explained below. Let $|Z_a\rangle$, with $a = 0, \ldots, 2^n - 1$, be a complete set of orthonormal vectors describing the physical qubits of which the codewords are made: $|0_0\rangle$ and $|1_0\rangle$ are the two error free states that represent $|0\rangle$ and $|1\rangle$, and all the other $|0_a\rangle$ and $|1_a\rangle$ are the results of errors (affecting one physical qubit in the codeword, or several ones, this does not matter at this stage). These $|Z_a\rangle$ are defined in such a way that $|0_a\rangle$ and $|1_a\rangle$ result from the *same* errors in the physical qubits of $|0_0\rangle$ and $|1_0\rangle$ (for example, the third qubit is flipped). We thus have two complete orthonormal bases, $|z\rangle \otimes |a\rangle$ and $|Z_a\rangle$. These two bases uniquely define a unitary transformation E, such that

---

[*]This is the Latin word for housemaid.

[†]These two different representations are analogous to the use of normal modes vs. local coordinates for describing the small oscillations of a mechanical system [10]. One description is mathematically simple, the other one is related to directly accessible quantities.

$$E\left(|z\rangle \otimes |a\rangle\right) = |Z_a\rangle, \qquad (5)$$

and

$$E^\dagger |Z_a\rangle = |z\rangle \otimes |a\rangle, \qquad (6)$$

where a runs from 0 to $2^n - 1$. Thus, E is the encoding matrix, and $E^\dagger$ is the decoding matrix. If the original and corrupted codewords are chosen in such a way that E is a real orthogonal matrix (not a complex unitary one), then $E^\dagger$ is the transposed matrix, and therefore E and $E^\dagger$ are implemented by the *same* quantum circuit, executed in two opposite directions. (If E is complex, the encoding and decoding circuits must also have opposite phase shifts.)

The $2^n - 1$ "standard errors" $|Z_0\rangle \to |Z_a\rangle$ are not the only ones that can be corrected by the $E^\dagger$ decoding. Any error of type

$$|Z_0\rangle \to U|Z_0\rangle = \sum_a c_a |Z_a\rangle, \qquad (7)$$

is also corrected, since

$$E^\dagger \sum_a c_a |Z_a\rangle = |z\rangle \otimes \sum_a c_a |a\rangle, \qquad (8)$$

is a direct product of $|z\rangle$ with the ancilla in some irrelevant corrupted state. Note that *no knowledge of the syndrome is needed* in order to correct the error [11]. Error correction is a logical operation that can be performed automatically, without having to execute quantum measurements. We know that the error is corrected, even if we don't know the nature of that error.

It is essential that the result on the right hand side of (8) be a direct product. Only if the new ancilla state is the same for $|z\rangle = |0\rangle$ and $|z\rangle = |1\rangle$, and therefore also for the complete computer state in Eq. (2), is it possible to coherently detach the ancilla from the rest of the computer, and replace it by a fresh ancilla (or restore it to its original state $|a = 0\rangle$ by a dissipative process involving still another, extraneous, physical system).[†] This means, in the graphical formalism of quantum circuits, that the "wires" corresponding to the old ancilla stop, and new "wires" enter into the circuit, with a standard quantum state for the new ancilla.

There are many plausible scenarios for the emergence of coherent superpositions of corrupted states, as in (8). For example, in an ion trap, a residual gas molecule, whose wave function is spread over a domain much larger than the inter-ion spacing, can be scattered by all the ions, as by a diffraction grating, and then all the ions are left in a collective recoil state (namely, a coherent superposition of states where one of the ions recoiled and the other ones did not). Furthermore, *mixtures* of errors of type (8) are also corrigible. Indeed, if

$$\rho = \sum_j p_j \sum_{ab} c_{ja} |Z_a\rangle \langle Z_b| c_{jb}^*, \qquad (9)$$

with $p_j > 0$ and $\sum p_j = 1$, then

$$E^\dagger \rho\, E = |z\rangle \langle z| \otimes \sum_j p_j \sum_{ab} c_{ja} |a\rangle \langle b| c_{jb}^*, \qquad (10)$$

[†]The introduction of a dissipative process in the quantum computer, which essentially is an analog device with a continuous evolution, brings it a step closer to a conventional digital computer!

174

again is a direct product of the logical qubit and the corrupted ancilla.

These mixtures include the case where a physical qubit in the codeword gets entangled with an unknown environment, which is the typical source of error. Let η be the initial, unknown state of the environment, and let its interaction with a physical qubit cause the following unitary evolution:

$$
\begin{aligned}
|0\rangle \otimes \eta &\rightarrow |0\rangle \otimes \mu + |1\rangle \otimes \nu, \\
|1\rangle \otimes \eta &\rightarrow |0\rangle \otimes \sigma + |1\rangle \otimes \tau,
\end{aligned}
\tag{11}
$$

where the new environment states μ, ν, σ, and τ, are also unknown, except for unitarity constraints. Now assume that the physical qubit, that has become entangled with the environment in such a way, was originally part of a codeword,

$$
|Z_0\rangle = |X_{z0}\rangle \otimes |0\rangle + |X_{z1}\rangle \otimes |1\rangle.
\tag{12}
$$

That codeword, together with its environment, thus evolve as

$$
Z_0 \otimes \eta \rightarrow Z' = X_{z0} \otimes \left(|0\rangle \otimes \mu + |1\rangle \otimes \nu\right) + X_{z1} \otimes \left(|0\rangle \otimes \sigma + |1\rangle \otimes \tau\right),
\tag{13}
$$

where I have omitted most of the ket signs, for brevity. This can be written as

$$
\begin{aligned}
Z' = &\left[X_{z0} \otimes |0\rangle + X_{z1} \otimes |1\rangle\right] \frac{\mu + \tau}{2} + \left[X_{z0} \otimes |0\rangle - X_{z1} \otimes |1\rangle\right] \frac{\mu - \tau}{2} + \\
&\left[X_{z0} \otimes |1\rangle + X_{z1} \otimes |0\rangle\right] \frac{\nu + \sigma}{2} + \left[X_{z0} \otimes |1\rangle - X_{z1} \otimes |0\rangle\right] \frac{\nu - \sigma}{2}.
\end{aligned}
\tag{14}
$$

On the right hand side, the vectors

$$
\begin{aligned}
Z_0 &= X_{z0} \otimes |0\rangle + X_{z1} \otimes |1\rangle, \\
Z_r &= X_{z0} \otimes |0\rangle - X_{z1} \otimes |1\rangle, \\
Z_s &= X_{z0} \otimes |1\rangle + X_{z1} \otimes |0\rangle, \\
Z_t &= X_{z0} \otimes |1\rangle - X_{z1} \otimes |0\rangle,
\end{aligned}
\tag{15}
$$

correspond, respectively, to a correct codeword, to a phase error ($|1\rangle \rightarrow -|1\rangle$), a bit error ($|0\rangle \leftrightarrow |1\rangle$), which is the only classical type of error, and to a combined phase and bit error. If these three types of errors can be corrected, we can also correct any type of entanglement with the environment, as we shall soon see.

For this to be possible, it is sufficient that the eight vectors in Eq. (15) be mutually orthogonal (recall that the index z means 0 or 1).[§] The simplest way of achieving this is to construct the codewords $|0_0\rangle$ and $|1_0\rangle$ in such a way that the following scalar products hold:

$$
\langle X_{zy}, X_{z'y'}\rangle = \tfrac{1}{2} \delta_{zz'} \delta_{yy'}.
\tag{16}
$$

(There are 10 such scalar products, since each index in this equation may take the values 0 and 1.) If these conditions are satified, the decoding of Z' by $E^\dagger$ gives, by virtue of Eq. (6),

$$
E^\dagger Z' = |z\rangle \otimes \left(|a = 0\rangle \otimes \frac{\mu + \tau}{2} + |r\rangle \otimes \frac{\mu - \tau}{2} + |s\rangle \otimes \frac{\nu + \sigma}{2} + |t\rangle \otimes \frac{\nu - \sigma}{2}\right).
\tag{17}
$$

[§]There is a slight risk of confusion here, because the same symbol 0 refers to the bit-value 0, and to the error free state of a codeword. I see no way of circumventing this difficulty without causing further confusion.

The expression in parentheses is an entangled state of the ancilla and the unknown environment. We cannot know it explicitly, but this is not necessary: it is sufficient to know that it is the same state for $|z\rangle = |0\rangle$ or $|z\rangle = |1\rangle$, or any linear combination thereof, as in Eq. (1). We merely have to discard the old ancilla and bring in a new one.

How to construct codewords that actually satisfy Eq. (16), when *any* one of their physical qubits is singled out, is a difficult problem, best handled by a combination of classical codeword theory [1] and finite group theory. I shall not enter into this subject here. I only mention that in order to correct an arbitrary error in any one of its qubits, a codeword must have at least five qubits: each one contributes three distinct vectors, like Z_r, Z_s, and Z_t in Eq. (15), and these, together with the error free vector Z_0, make 16 vectors for each logical qubit value, and therefore $32 = 2^5$ in the total. Longer codewords can correct more than one erroneous qubit. For example, Steane's linear code [7], with 7 qubits, can correct not only any error in a single physical qubit, but also a phase error, $|1\rangle \rightarrow -|1\rangle$, in one of them, and a bit error, $|0\rangle \leftrightarrow |1\rangle$, in another one (check! $1 + 7 \times 3 + 7 \times 6 = 2^{7-1}$). A well designed codeword is one where the orthogonal basis $|Z_a\rangle$ corresponds to the most plausible physical sources of errors.

The error correction method proposed above, in Eq. (6), is conceptually simple, but it has the disadvantage of leaving the logical qubit $|z\rangle$ in a "bare" state, vulnerable to new errors that would be not be detected. It is therefore necessary to re-encode that qubit immediately, with another ancilla (or with the same ancilla, reset to $|a = 0\rangle$ by interaction with still another system). A more complicated but safer method is to bring in a second ancilla, in a standard state $|b = 0\rangle$, and have it interact with the complete codeword in such a way that

$$|Z_a\rangle \otimes |b = 0\rangle \rightarrow |Z_0\rangle \otimes |b = a\rangle. \tag{18}$$

This is also a unitary transformation, which can be implemented by a quantum circuit. Note that now the unitary matrix that performs that error recovery is of order 2^{2n+1}, instead of 2^{n+1}.

Naturally, errors can also occur in the encoding and decoding process. More sophisticated methods can however be designed, that allow fault tolerant computation. An adaptive strategy is used, with several alternative paths for error correction. Most paths fail, because new errors are created; however, these errors can be detected, and there is a high probability that one of the paths will eventually lead to the correct result. As a consequence, the error correction circuits are able to correct old errors faster than they introduce new ones. There is then a high probability for keeping the number of errors small enough, so that the correction machinery can successfully deal with them [12].

4.   CONSTRAINED DYNAMICS

A quantum codeword is a redundant representation of a logical qubit by means of several physical qubits. Since quantum codewords span only a restricted subspace of the complete physical Hilbert space, the unitary operations that generate quantum dynamics (that is, the computational process) are subject to considerable arbitrariness. This is most easily seen with the logical representation, $|z\rangle \otimes |a = 0\rangle$. A unitary transformation, $\mathbb{1} \otimes g$, where g acts solely on the ancilla's states, generates

$$(\mathbb{1} \otimes g)\left(|z\rangle \otimes |a = 0\rangle\right) = |z\rangle \otimes \sum_a c_a |a\rangle. \tag{19}$$

This is a corrupted, but corrigible codeword. In the physical representation, this harmless unitary transformation becomes

$$G = E\left(\mathbb{1} \otimes g\right) E^{\dagger}. \tag{20}$$

The unitary matrices G are a representation (usually a reducible one) of the Un group. Consecutive applications of various transformations of this type merely convert one corrigible error into another corrigible error. These transformations do not mix the two complementary subspaces that represent the logical 0 and 1.

On the other hand, a genuine unitary transformation (one that is actually needed for the computation) is, in the logical representation, $\psi \to \psi' = (u \otimes \mathbb{1})\psi$. It is encoded into

$$U = E\left(u \otimes \mathbb{1}\right) E^{\dagger}, \tag{21}$$

for the physical representation. Thus, in summary, all the "legal" unitary transformations are of type $E\left(u \otimes g\right) E^{\dagger}$, for codewords that represent a single logical qubit.

For unitary transformations involving two logical qubits, the encoded representation, including the possibility of corrigible errors, is likewise

$$U_{12} = (E_1 \otimes E_2)\left[u_{12} \otimes (g_1 \otimes g_2)\right](E_1^{\dagger} \otimes E_2^{\dagger}), \tag{22}$$

where u_{12} acts on the two logical qubits, and g_1 and g_2 act on their respective ancillas. (I am assuming here that each logical qubit is encoded separately, and that block coding is not used.) It is obvious that in unitary transformations of that type, the logical steps are not affected by the occurrence or evolution of corrigible errors.

Among these unitary transformations, there is a subgroup leaving the zero-syndrome ancilla invariant (such a subgroup is called the *little group* of the invariant state):

$$g \left|a = 0\right\rangle = \left|a = 0\right\rangle. \tag{23}$$

Let us now focus our attention on these transformations, that do not induce errors in correct codewords. They only modify corrupted codewords, while keeping them corrigible. We may imagine, if we wish, that error free codewords are stabilized by erecting around them a high potential barrier: conceptually, we add to the Hamiltonian a potential term, equal to zero for the legal codeword states, and to a large positive number for erroneous states. This artifice is similar to, but much simpler than, the use of the quantum Zeno effect, that was proposed by several authors as a way of reducing errors. It is actually not difficult to devise quantum circuits that act like a potential barrier (the only serious difficulty is that such a circuit must activate high frequency interactions with extraneous qubits, and the latter may themselves be subject to errors, and induce new ones).

In the logical basis, a "legal" (error free) state, $\left|z\right\rangle \otimes \left|a = 0\right\rangle$, which is invariant under the little group of $\left|a = 0\right\rangle$, is recognized as being orthogonal to all $\left|z'\right\rangle \otimes \left|a \neq 0\right\rangle$. This can be written as an orthogonality relation

$$\langle C_{\alpha}, \psi \rangle = 0, \tag{24}$$

where C_{α} is any linear combination of the various $\left|z'\right\rangle \otimes \left|a\right\rangle$ with $a \neq 0$. There are $2(2^n - 1)$ linearly independent C_{α}, that span the "illegal" subspace (including incorrigible errors). Let us normalize them by $\langle C_{\alpha}, C_{\beta} \rangle = \delta_{\alpha\beta}$. After a legal unitary evolution, $U\psi$ still is a legal state, and therefore

$$\langle C_\alpha , U\psi \rangle = 0. \tag{25}$$

It follows that

$$U\,C_\alpha = \sum_\beta A_{\alpha\beta}(U)\,C_\beta, \tag{26}$$

where the matrices $A_{\alpha\beta}(U)$ are a unitary representation of U. (If all legal U are considered, that representation will not, in general, be irreducible.)

It is also possible to construct Hermitian *operators* that express the same constraints. Recall that the codewords are defined in a Hilbert space with 2^{n+1} dimensions. Now consider

$$M = \sum_{\alpha\beta} |C_\alpha\rangle\, M_{\alpha\beta}\, \langle C_\beta|, \tag{27}$$

where $M_{\alpha\beta}$ is any matrix of order $2(2^n - 1)$. Any legal state obeys $M\psi = 0$. Another constraint (for the same codeword) could be $N\psi = 0$, where

$$N = \sum_{\alpha\beta} |C_\alpha\rangle\, N_{\alpha\beta}\, \langle C_\beta|, \tag{28}$$

and $N_{\alpha\beta}$ is any other Hermitian matrix. It is easily shown that

$$[M, N] = iP, \tag{29}$$

where P is still another Hermitian operator of the same type, and satisfies $P\psi = 0$ for all legal states. Finally, we note that if there are many logical qubits in the quantum computer, its state obeys the nonlocal "spacelike" constraint equation

$$M_1 \otimes N_2 \otimes \cdots \psi = 0, \tag{30}$$

where the various operators refer to different codewords.

These equations are not completely trivial. They are like those appearing in a quantum field theory with a gauge group. For example, the canonical momenta of the free electromagnetic field are $\pi^k = E^k$, where $\mathbf{E}$ is the electric field vector. They satisfy the constraint $\partial_k \pi^k = 0$. This cannot hold as an operator equation, because $\partial_k \pi^k$ does not commute with some other field operators. However, a legal state vector (one without "longitudinal photons") obeys the constraint $\partial_k \pi^k \psi = 0$. The situation becomes more complicated for theories with non-Abelian gauge groups, such as general relativity: singular Schwinger terms appear, and the factor ordering problem cannot be discussed without regularization.¶

An important problem in quantum field theory (or, in general, in quantum mechanics with constrained dynamical variables) is to properly define a Hermitian scalar product. Should we include in it the spurious particles that are generated by the gauge freedom, such as longitudinal photons? When we consider codewords, the situation becomes simple and clear, as we shall now see.

Consider indeed two different logical states of a quantum codeword, say

$$\Phi = E\left(\phi \otimes \sum_a c_a\, |a\rangle\right), \tag{31}$$

¶For a recent review, see ref. [13].

and

$$\Psi = E\left(\psi \otimes \sum_a c_a |a\rangle\right). \tag{32}$$

On the left hand side, there is the physical representation of the codeword, and, in the parenthesis on the right hand side, its logical representation. Note that, irrespective of the logical state (ϕ or ψ), the ancilla has the same state $\sum c_a |a\rangle$, because that state represents the syndrome of the error, and the latter, caused by an interaction with the environment, is independent of the logical state of the qubit, as may be seen in Eq. (15). It then readily follows from the unitarity of E that the scalar products,

$$\langle \Phi, \Psi \rangle = \langle \phi, \psi \rangle, \tag{33}$$

are the same for any two non-orthogonal states of a logical qubit, and for their representation by codewords, even by corrupted ones. Further work is in progress, in order to exploit the analogies of quantum codeword dynamics with gauge field theory.

ACKNOWLEDGMENTS

I am grateful to Peter Shor and Andrew Steane for clarifying remarks. This research was supported in part by the National Science Foundation under Grant No. PHY94-07194.

REFERENCES

[1] D. Welsh, *Codes and Cryptography*, Oxford University Press (1989), Chapt. 4.

[2] A. Peres, *Quantum Theory: Concepts and Methods*, Kluwer, Dordrecht (1993), Chapt. 5.

[3] J. I. Cirac and P. Zoller, Phys. Rev. Lett. 74 (1995) 4091.

[4] W. K. Wootters and W. H. Zurek, Nature 299 (1982) 802.

[5] P. W. Shor, Phys. Rev. A 52 (1995) 2493.

[6] R. Laflamme, C. Miquel, J. P. Paz, and W. H. Zurek, Phys. Rev. Lett. 77 (1996) 198.

[7] A. M. Steane, Phys. Rev. Lett. 77 (1996) 793; Proc. Roy. Soc. (London) A 452 (1996) 2551.

[8] C. H. Bennett, D. P. DiVincenzo, J. A. Smolin, and W. K. Wootters, Phys. Rev. A 54 (1996) 3824.

[9] E. Knill and R. Laflamme, "A theory of quantum error-correcting codes" (Los Alamos report LA-UR-96-1300).

[10] H. Goldstein, *Classical Mechanics*, Addison-Wesley, Reading (1980), Chapt. 6.

[11] A. Peres, Phys. Rev. A 32 (1985) 3266.

[12] P. W. Shor, "Fault tolerant quantum computation" in *Proc. 37th Symposium on Foundations of Computer Science* (1996) in press.

[13] N. C. Tsamis and R. P. Woodard, Phys. Rev. D 36 (1987) 3641.

QUANTUM ERROR CORRECTION WITH IMPERFECT GATES

A. Yu. Kitaev

L.D.Landau Institute for Theoretical Physics
117940, Kosygina St. 2
Moscow 117940, Russia
e-mail: kitaevitp.ac.ru

Quantum error correction can be performed fault-tolerantly. This allows to store a quantum state intact (with arbitrary small error probability) for arbitrary long time at a constant decoherence rate.

A quantum computer is capable to solve some computational problems (e.g. factoring of integers and the discrete logarithm [1]) which are exponentially hard for an ordinary computer. Howevere, physical implementation of a quantum computer still remains a big problem. Besides physical and technological difficulties, an essential theoretical issue is whether quantum computation can be performed fault-tolerantly. Error-correcting quantum codes [2–8] give only partial solution to this problem. Generally, use of error correcting codes requires some ideal device to recover a codeword (or its quantum analogue) from error. In this report I show how to recover from error despite new errors that may come during the process. This fault-tolerant recovery procedure allows to store a quantum state intact for an arbitrary long time under constant (but low enough) error rate. Note: the error rate is the decoherence probability per a codebit per unit time whereas the stored quantum state belongs to some low-dimensional *information subspace* of the 2^n-dimensional state space of n qubits.

This work was done before I learned about Shor's paper [9] where fault-tolerant quantum computing was suggested. This latter result goes far beyond simple storage of quantum states. However, Shor's method requires the error rate to be as low as $(\log t)^{-c}$ where t is the storage/computation time. Thus, combining both methods makes it possible to perform arbitrary long quantum computation at constant error rate [11].

1.   ERROR-CORRECTING CODES

Codes can be most naturally introduced in connection with the information transmission problem. (We will use codes for another purpose, however). A classical communication channel receives binary words of length n which may be distored while being transmitted. This process is described by transition probabilities $P(x \mapsto y)$ between an input word x and an output word y. In the simplest model, $P(x \mapsto y) = p^{d(x,y)}(1 - p)^{n-d(x,y)}$, where $d(x, y)$ is the Hamming distance between x and y (p is the error probability per bit). To simplify this description, we may divide all transitions into likely and unlikely ones, by saying that a transition is unlikely if its probability is smaller than a given number. Equivalently, a transition $x \mapsto y$ is unlikely if $d(x,y) > k$, where k is a given number. Denote by $N = \mathbf{B}^n = \{0,1\}^n$ the set of all binary words, $E \subseteq N \times N$ the set of likely transitions. Error correction is possible if input words belong to a subset $M \subseteq N$ such that any two distinct words $x_1, x_2 \in M$ are not glued by E (i.e. there is no such y that $(x_1, y) \in E$ and $(x_2, y) \in E$). The subset $M \subseteq \mathbf{B}^n$ is called a *classical code*. To be more exact, a classical code is an injection $C : M \to \mathbf{B}^n$, where M is a given set of messages to be encoded.

An input of a quantum channel is a quantum state of n qubits, $|\xi\rangle \in \mathcal{N} = \mathcal{B}^{\otimes n}$ (where $\mathcal{B} = \mathbf{C}^2$ is the state space of a single qubit). A quantum channel is described by a superoperator (i.e. operator acting on density operators). In this report I will stay with a naive approach, assuming that errors occur to each qubit with probability p. See [11] for rigorous consideration. * We can also define a (likely) error space $\mathcal{E} \subseteq \mathbf{L}(\mathcal{N})$, where $\mathbf{L}(\mathcal{N})$ is the space of linear operators $\mathcal{N} \to \mathcal{N}$. More specifically, $\mathcal{E}$ is the linear span of all operators acting on arbitrary k qubits. A quantum code is a linear subspace $\mathcal{M} \subseteq \mathcal{B}^{\otimes n}$, or an isometric injection $\mathcal{M} \to \mathcal{B}^{\otimes n}$. Errors can be recovered if any two orthogonal vectors $|\xi\rangle, |\eta\rangle \in \mathcal{M}$ remain orthogonal, meaning that $\langle \xi Y^\dagger | X \eta \rangle = 0$ for any $X, Y \in \mathcal{E}$.

The simplest classical code is based on repetition: 0 is represented by $(0, \ldots, 0)$, 1 by $(1, \ldots, 1)$. Does this construction extend to the quantum case? Of course, one can define a mapping $\mathcal{B} \to \mathcal{B}^{\otimes n}$ by the formulas $|0\rangle \mapsto |0, \ldots, 0\rangle$, $|1\rangle \mapsto |1, \ldots, 1\rangle$. However, such a code does not protect even from one error. Indeed, the corresponding error space $\mathcal{E}$ is the linear span of the identity operator (no errors) and the Pauli operators $\sigma_\gamma[j]$, $(\gamma = x, y, z, \; j = 1, \ldots, n)$. (This notation means the the Pauli operator σ_γ acts on the j-th qubit). Let us take two orthogonal vectors from the information subspace,

$$|\xi\rangle = 2^{-1/2}\big(|0, \ldots, 0\rangle + |1, \ldots, 1\rangle\big) \qquad |\eta\rangle = 2^{-1/2}\big(|0, \ldots, 0\rangle - |1, \ldots, 1\rangle\big)$$

and check the above error correction criterion. Consider two operators from the error space, $X = 1$ and $Y = \sigma_z[j]$. The operator Y preserves the vector $|0, \ldots, 0\rangle$ whereas the vector $|1, \ldots, 1\rangle$ is multiplied by factor -1 (such operators are called *phase errors*). Clearly, $Y|\xi\rangle = X|\eta\rangle = |\eta\rangle$, so orthogonal vectors do not remain orthogonal! Thus, repetition is not sutable for quantum coding. The simplest quantum error-correcting code maps 1 qubit into 5, see below.

More general and widely used classical codes are linear codes [10]. A linear code can be described by a collection of linear forms (check sums) which vanish on the codewords. A quantum analogue of a check sum is an operator of the form $\sigma(\gamma_1, \ldots, \gamma_n) = \sigma_{\gamma_1}[1] \ldots \sigma_{\gamma_n}[n]$ $(\gamma_j \in \{0, x, y, z\})$, where $\sigma_0 = 1$. Consider several operators of this form, $X_k = \sigma(f_k)$ $(k = 1, \ldots, s)$ which commute with each other. (This condition can be repesented in terms of f_k, see below). Let us define the information subspace as follows

$$\mathcal{M} = \big\{ |\xi\rangle \in \mathcal{B}^{\otimes n} : X_j|\xi\rangle = |\xi\rangle \; (j = 1, \ldots, s) \big\}. \tag{1}$$

To check whether a given quatum state belongs to $\mathcal{M}$, one should measure the eigenvalues of $X_1, \ldots, X_s$ — all the eigenvalues must be equal to 1. (Hence the operators $X_1, \ldots, X_s$ are called *check operators*). This wide class of quantum codes was first described in ref. [8]. We will call such codes *symplectic* because of an intrinsic symplectic structure which underlie their properties.

---

* The naive approach may be misleading in estimating the probability of a specific event because quantum mechanics involves addition of amplitudes rather than probabilities. As a heuristic rule, one may take the square root of the naive probability to be an upper bound for the true one.

In study of symplectic codes commutation relations between the Pauli matrices play an important role. These relations become mathematically clear if we change the notations: $\sigma_0 = \sigma_{00} = 1$, $\sigma_x = \sigma_{10}$, $\sigma_y = \sigma_{11}$, $\sigma_z = \sigma_{01}$. The index set $G = \{0, x, y, z\} = \{00, 10, 11, 11\}$ can be identified with the group $\mathbf{Z}_2 \times \mathbf{Z}_2$. Then

$$\sigma_{\alpha\beta}\sigma_{\alpha'\beta'} = (-\mathrm{i})^{\alpha\beta'-\beta\alpha'}\sigma_{\alpha+\alpha',\beta+\beta'} = (-1)^{\alpha\beta'-\beta\alpha'}\sigma_{\alpha',\beta'}\sigma_{\alpha,\beta}$$

$$\sigma(f)\sigma(g) = (-1)^{\omega(f,g)}\sigma(g)\sigma(f) \tag{2}$$

where ω is the canonical skew-symmetric bilinear form on the group G^n

$$\omega\big((\alpha_1\beta_1,\ldots,\alpha_n\beta_n), (\alpha'_1\beta'_1,\ldots,\alpha'_n\beta'_n)\big) = \sum_{j=1}^{n}\alpha_j\beta'_j - \beta_j\alpha'_j \quad (\mathrm{mod}\ 2). \tag{3}$$

Hence the operators $X_j = \sigma(f_j)$ commute with each other iff $\omega(f_j, f_m) = 0$ for every j and m. It follows that the form ω vanishes on the linear subspace (subgroup) $F \subseteq G^n$ generated by $f_1, \ldots, f_s$. It is called a *characteristic subspace* of a symplectic code. (Beware that it is a subspace over the residui field modulo 2, not over complex numbers!) The information subspace $\mathcal{M}$ depends on F rather than the check vectors $f_1, \ldots, f_s$. From now on, s stands for the dimensionality of F, i.e. linearly dependent check vectors are excluded. The dimensionality of $\mathcal{M}$ equals 2^{n-s}, which is sufficient to encode a state of $n - s$ qubits.

Let us turn to the error-correcting properties of symplectic codes. The error space $\mathcal{E} = \mathcal{E}(n, k)$ is generated by the operators $\sigma(g) : g \in E(n, k)$, where

$$E(n, k) = \big\{g \in G^n : |\operatorname{Supp}(g)| \leq k\big\},$$
$$\operatorname{Supp}(\alpha_1\beta_1,\ldots,\alpha_n\beta_n) = \big\{j : \alpha_j \neq 0 \text{ or } \beta_j \neq 0\big\}.$$

By abuse of language, vectors $g \in E(n, k)$ will be called called "errors". (Thus, "correcting errors from $E(n, k)$" and "correcting k errors" is the same). Two errors, g' and g'' are called *equivalent* if the corresponding operators $\sigma(g')$ and $\sigma(g'')$ coincide on the information subspace $\mathcal{M}$. This condition can be written as $g' - g'' \in F$. Errors equivalent to 0 may be neglected because they do not affect quantum states from the information subspace.

Suppose that a quantum state $|\xi\rangle \in \mathcal{M}$ undergoes an error g. The resulting state $\sigma(g)|\xi\rangle$ is an eigenvector of all the check operators X_j. The corresponding eigenvalues are equal to $(-1)^{\mu_j(g)}$, where $\mu_j(g) = \omega(f_j, g)$. The binary vector $\mu(g) = (\mu_1(g),\ldots,\mu_s(g))$ is called the error *syndrom*. Obviously, equivalent errors have the same syndrom but the coinverse is not always true.

Theorem 1 *A symplectic code corrects k errors iff any two errors $g', g'' \in E(n, k)$ with equal syndroms are equivalent.*

Proof.
Let $|\xi\rangle, |\eta\rangle \in \mathcal{M}$ be arbitrary orthogonal vectors. The condition $\langle\xi\sigma(g')^\dagger|\sigma(g'')\eta\rangle = 0$ is guaranteed, for every $|\xi\rangle$ and $|\eta\rangle$, in the following two cases:

1. The errors g' and g'' are equivalent. (Make use of the fact that the operator $\sigma(g')$ is unitary).

2. The errors g' and g'' have different syndroms. Then $\sigma(g')|\xi\rangle$ and $\sigma(g'')|\eta\rangle$ belong to different eigenspaces of some check operator.

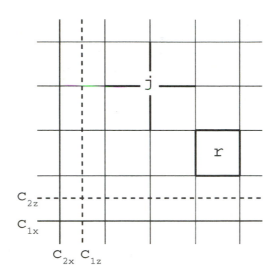

Figure 1. The toric code TOR(5).

Q.E.D.

This proof is based on the general error correction criterion. It is also possible to describe a correction procedure explicitly. First, the eigenvalues of the check operators are measured, yielding the error syndrom $\mu(g)$. The corresponding error g can be determined uniquely, up to equivalence. (This step may be computationally difficult). Finally, the operator $\sigma(g)$ is applied, which cancels the error.

Let $F_+ = \{g \in G^k : \mu(g) = 0\}$. Obviously, $F_+ \supseteq F$. Theorem 1 can be formulated as follows: *A symplectic code corrects k errors iff $E(n, 2k) \cap F_+ \subseteq F$.*

Example of a symplectic code which maps 1 qubit into 5 and corrects 1 error (see [6, 7]). The check vectors $f_1, \ldots, f_4$ are given by the rows of the following table:

1	0	1	0	0	1	0	1	0	0
1	0	0	1	1	0	0	0	0	1
0	1	0	0	0	1	1	0	0	1
0	1	0	1	0	0	0	1	1	0

Any two pairs of columns are linearly independent, hence $E(4, 2) \cap F_+ = \{0\}$.

2. TORIC CODES

Now I am going to describe an infinite sequence of symplectic codes $\text{TOR}(k) : k = 1, 2, \ldots$ which map 2 qubits into $n = 2k^2$. These codes are not optimal in any sense but they have the following nice properties:

1. Each check operators involves bounded number of qubits (at most 4).

2. Each qubit is involved in a bounded number of check operators (at most 4).

3. The number of corrected errors is unlimited. (More specifically, the code $\text{TOR}(k)$ corrects $\left\lfloor \frac{k-1}{2} \right\rfloor$ errors).

Such codes are called *local check codes*.

Consider a $k \times k$ square lattice on the torus (see fig. 1). Let A_0 be the set of vertices of this lattice, A_1 the set of edges, A_2 the set of faces (i.e. square cells). We associate a qubit with each edge. (So there are $n = 2k^2$ qubits). Check operators are associated with each face $r \in A_2$ and each vertex $j \in A_0$,

$$X_r = \prod_{l \in \text{ border}(r)} \sigma_x[l], \qquad X_j = \prod_{l \in \text{ star}(j)} \sigma_z[l]. \qquad (4)$$

It is easy to verify that these operators commute with each other. The key observation is that a border and a star either have 2 common edges or do not overlap at all.

There are two relations between the check operators: $\prod_{r \in A_2} X_r = 1$ and $\prod_{j \in A_0} X_j = 1$. It follows that $s = 2k^2 - 2$, hence the dimensionality of the information subspace equals $2^{n-s} = 4$.

Let us define *information operators* $Y_{x1}, Y_{x2}, Y_{z1}, Y_{z2}$ to be the products of $\sigma_x[l]$ or $\sigma_z[l]$ over all edges along the cycles c_{x1}, c_{x2} or cocycles (cuts) c_{z1}, c_{z2} (see fig. 1). The information operators commute with the check ones but do not commute with each other. The commutation relations between $Y_{x1}, Y_{x2}, Y_{z1}, Y_{z2}$ are as follows

$$Y_{xk}Y_{xl} = Y_{xl}Y_{xk}, \qquad Y_{zk}Y_{zl} = Y_{zl}Y_{zk}, \qquad Y_{xk}Y_{zl} = (-1)^{\delta_{kl}}Y_{zl}Y_{xk}, \qquad Y_{\gamma k}^2 = 1.$$

One can show that $Y_{x1}, Y_{x2}, Y_{z1}, Y_{z2}$ act on the information subspace $\mathcal{M}$ exactly the same way as the Pauli matrices $\sigma_x[1], \sigma_x[2], \sigma_z[1], \sigma_z[2]$ on two qubits. Hence $\mathcal{M}$ can be canonically identified with $\mathcal{B}^{\otimes 2}$. For practical applications, it is enough to use 1 of the 2 information qubits corresponding to $\mathcal{M}$.

Error-correcting properties of the toric codes are related to homology of the torus. Let us decompose each vector $g = (\alpha_1\beta_1, \ldots, \alpha_n\beta_n) \in G^n$ into an *x-component* $g_x = (\alpha_1 0, \ldots, \alpha_n 0)$ and a *z-component* $g_z = (0\beta_1, \ldots, 0\beta_n)$. (The corresponding operators $\sigma(g_x)$ and $\sigma(g_z)$ consist of $\sigma_x[j]$ and $\sigma_z[j]$, respectively). Each x-error corresponds to a 1-chain, the syndrom being represented by its boundary. An x-error g is equivalent to 0 iff the operator $\sigma(g)$ can be constructed from the check operators. This is the case iff g is a boundary of some 2-chain. Hence, two nonequivalent errors with equal syndroms must differ by a nontrivial cycle. Such a cycle includes $\geq k$ edges. It follows that the code $\text{TOR}(k)$ corrects $\lfloor \frac{k-1}{2} \rfloor$ x-errors. (z-errors are treated similarly, but cycles are replaced with cocycles).

3. FAULT-TOLERANT PROCEDURES FOR ERROR CORRECTION

The usual error correction procedure was described after the proof of Theorem 1. It can be realize by a quantum circuit. Unfortunately, absolutely reliable quantum gates do not exist, so new errors may occur during error correction. Real quantum gates (to be constructed one day) should suffer from noise and decoherence. We will assume that the error rate (error probability per gate) p is arbitrarily small but constant. The problem is how to decrease an effective error probability for encoded qubits. To begin with, let us make the correction procedure stable to a fixed number (say, 2) errors during its execution.

Recall that the correction procedure consists of 3 steps. The second step is a classical computation, so it is safe. (However, the computation should not last too long, otherwise the qubits will decohere because of interaction with their environment). The third step is also rather safe because one error spoils one qubit. The most dangerous is the first step, the measurement. First of all, a single error in the syndrom can make impossible to determine the error in the qubits. What is even worse, one error during a

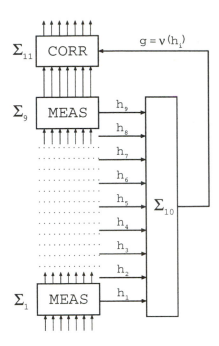

Figure 2. An error correction procedure which is stable to 2 new errors.

measurement can spoil *all the qubits involved in this measurement.* [†] That is why local check codes are especially useful for fault-tolerant error correction. For a local check code, all the measurements can be organized into a quantum circuit of bounded depth. Therefore, one error will spoil a bounded number of qubits. We just have to satisfy the inequality

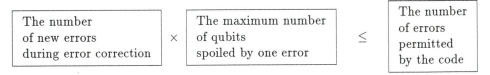

| The number of new errors during error correction | $\times$ | The maximum number of qubits spoiled by one error | $\leq$ | The number of errors permitted by the code |

The right hand side is not limited, so "the number of new errors" can be arbitrary large. For this, the code parameter k should be large enough.

In the above consideration we didn't worry about errors in the syndrom. To ensure that the syndrom is correct, all the measurements must be repeated several time. For example, assume that up to 2 errors may happen during error correction. Then we have to measure the whole syndrom 9 times. The corresponding circuit is schematically drawn in fig. 2. It consists of 11 blocks (subcircuits). The blocks $\Sigma_1, \ldots, \Sigma_9$ perform syndrom measurements. The block Σ_{10} selects 3 identical measurement results $h_i = h_{i+1} = h_{i+2}$, coming one by one, and compute the corresponding error $g : \mu(g) = h_i$. Such results must exist (because at least 7 of 9 measurements are correct) but possibly are not unique. In any case, at least 1 of 3 selected results was correct for the time of measurement (no matter which, because they are identical). Subsequent wrong measurements may disturb some of the qubits, but not too many. Therefore, the computed value of g is nearly correct after all the measurements are done. Actual corrections are made to the qubits by the block Σ_{11}.

[†] P. Shor [9] suggested a special procedure which prevents errors from being so destructive. I do not use this result.

Note that this procedure works with a *constant* number of qubits n and takes a constant time t. [‡] It allows to reduce the effective error probability to $O(p^3)$, because 3 errors can still spoil the encoded quantum state. However, we must remember that quantum probability is a subtle thing, see footnote on page 182. A reliable upper bound for the effective error probability is $p_1 = O(p^{3/2})$, see ref. [11]. It is not also too bad.

The above result can be improved by the use of *cascade codes*. We have already encoded 1 qubit into n. Let us encode each of these n qubits again. Thus we reduce the effective error probability down to $p_2 = O\left((p^{3/2})^{3/2}\right)$. Now we need n^2 code qubits. Proceeding this way, we find that effective error probability ϵ is attained with $\sim (log(1/\epsilon))^\alpha$ qubits, where $\alpha = log_{3/2} n$.

One problem is still remaining: how to perform error correction for a cascade code? For simplicity, consider the 2-level code, $\text{TOR}(k)$ substituted into $\text{TOR}(k)$. The top level correcting circuit must work with qubits represented in the code $\text{TOR}(k)$. So, we must be able to manipulate with encoded qubits. Moreover, such manipulation must be fault-tolerant. Thus we have arrived to a harder problem than the original one: we must not only store a quantum state but also make some quantum computations fault-tolerantly. Fortunately, these are rather simple computations, just syndrom measurements. Such a measurement can be performed by a circuit with gates of two types:

$$ S = \frac{1}{\sqrt{2}} \begin{pmatrix} 1 & 1 \\ 1 & -1 \end{pmatrix}, \qquad \hat{\oplus} : |a, b\rangle \mapsto |a, a \oplus b\rangle, \tag{5} $$

where $\oplus$ stands for addition modulo 2. So, we should realize these gates on qubits represented in the code $\text{TOR}(k)$. Such a realization must be a quantum circuit constructed from the same gates. It must be stable to 2 errors.

I will describe these realizations very briefly. To perform the operation S on an encoded information qubit, one should apply the operator S to each code qubit separately. After that, the code qubits should be permuted as follows. The square lattice on the torus (fig. 1) is flipped around the diagonal and shifted by $1/2$ of its period in both directions. This operation transforms the vertex operators X_j into the face operators X_r and conversely. Clearly, the information subspace is invariant under this transformation. The information operators Y_{xk} and Y_{zk} are exchanged. Now recall that Y_{xk} and Y_{zk} represent the action of σ_x and σ_z on the information qubits. Therefore, each of the 2 information qubits undergoes the transformation $\sigma_x \leftrightarrow \sigma_z$. It is exactly what we need, because $S\sigma_x S^\dagger = \sigma_z$, $S\sigma_z S^\dagger = \sigma_x$.

The operator $\hat{\oplus}$ is realized by bitwise action of $\hat{\oplus}$ on the code qubits.

ACKNOWLEDGMENTS

This work was supported by the Russian Foundation for Fundamental Research, grant No 96-01-01113.

REFERENCES

[1] P. W. Shor, "Algorithms for quantum computation: discrete log and factoring", *Proceedings of the 35th Annual Symposium on the Foundations of Computer Science* (IEEE Computer Society Press, Los Alamitos, CA, 1994), p. 124.

[‡] I didn't try to calculate the actual value of the code parameter k which is necessary for the procedure to work. Probably, it is about 20 which corresponds to $n \sim 1000$ qubits. It is somewhat expensive. However, my purpose is to propose a method rather than a practically usable algorithm; optimization is a separate task.

[2] P. W. Shor, "Scheme for reducing decoherence in quantum memory," *Phys. Rev. A* **52**, 2493–2496 (1995).

[3] A. M. Steane, "Multiple particle interference and quantum error correction", LANL e-print quant-ph/9601029, http://xxx.lanl.gov (submitted to *Proc. Roy. Soc. London A*).

[4] C. H. Bennett, G. Brassard, S. Popescu, B. Schumacher, J. A. Smolin, and W. K. Wootters, "Purification of noisy entanglement and faithful teleportation via noisy channels," *Phys. Rev. Lett.* **76**, 722 (1996).

[5] A. R. Calderbank and P. W. Shor, "Good quantum error-correcting codes exist", LANL e-print quant-ph/9512032, http://xxx.lanl.gov (to appear in *Phys. Rev. A*).

[6] R. Laflamme, C. Miquel, J. P. Paz,and W. H. Zurek, "Perfect quantum error correction code," LANL e-print quant-ph/9602019, http://xxx.lanl.gov

[7] C. H. Bennett, D. P. DiVincenzo, J. A. Smolin, W. K. Wootters, "Mixed state entanglement and quantum error-correcting codes", LANL e-print quant-ph/9604024, http://xxx.lanl.gov

[8] A. R. Calderbank, E. M. Rains, P. W. Shor, and N. J. A. Sloane, "Quantum error correction and orthogonal geometry", LANL e-print quant-ph/9605005, http://xxx.lanl.gov

[9] P. W. Shor, "Fault-tolerant quantum computation", LANL e-print quant-ph/9605011, http://xxx.lanl.gov

[10] F. J. MacWilliams and N. J. A. Sloane, "The Theory of Error-Correcting Codes", North-Holland, Amsterdam (1977).

[11] A. Yu. Kitaev, "Quantum computing: algorithms and error correction", *Russian Mathematical Surveys*, to appear.

ELIMINATING THE EFFECTS OF SPONTANEOUS EMISSION IN QUANTUM COMPUTATIONS WITH COLD TRAPPED IONS

C. D'Helon and G. J. Milburn

Department of Physics
University of Queensland, St. Lucia 4072 Australia
email: dhelon@wilson.physics.uq.oz.au

We propose two quantum error correction schemes which increase the maximum storage time for qubits in a system of cold trapped ions. Both schemes consider only the errors introduced by the decoherence due to spontaneous emission from the upper levels of the ions. A "watchdog" approach is adopted in conjunction with selective coherent feedback to eliminate these errors immediately following spontaneous emission events.

Our physical system consists of N ions confined in a linear rf trap, as proposed by Cirac and Zoller [1] for the implementation of a quantum computer. Each of the ions is laser-cooled into the Lamb-Dicke limit, and experiences harmonic motion at the trapping frequency ν. Qubits are represented by two-level electronic transitions $|0\rangle \leftrightarrow |1\rangle$ consisting of hyperfine levels in order to minimise the atomic recoil from spontaneous emission events.

Assuming that we are able to distinguish between the spontaneous emission from different ions, our error correction schemes rely on continuously monitoring quantum jumps from the excited level $|1\rangle$ into the ground level $|0\rangle$. Whenever a quantum jump corresponding to a spontaneous emission event is detected, selective coherent feedback is applied to the system to recover the initial state. As shown by Mabuchi and Zoller [2], quantum jumps can be inverted in this manner given that qubits are encoded redundantly in a Hilbert space spanning logical and error states.

The first section of this article outlines an error correction scheme based on entangling two ions for each qubit, which requires the use of an alternative logical basis consisting of Fourier-transformed states. In the second section a different error correction scheme is presented which relies on encoding qubits redundantly using complementary electronic number states.

USING FOURIER-TRANSFORMED STATES

For the purposes of quantum computation, an alternative logical basis $\tilde{L}$ can be used instead of the logical basis L comprising the electronic levels $|0\rangle, |1\rangle$. The basis $\tilde{L}$ has the advantage that both amplitude coefficients of an arbitrary qubit can be preserved when there is a spontaneous emission from the excited level $|1\rangle$, enabling us to restore the initial qubit.

The alternative set of Fourier-transformed states $|\tilde{0}\rangle, |\tilde{1}\rangle$ making up $\tilde{L}$, can be obtained by applying a laser pulse $V_i^{\pi/2}(-\pi/2)$ which rotates the electronic levels of the i-th ion, as given by

$$|\tilde{0}\rangle_i = V_i^{\pi/2}(-\pi/2)|0\rangle_i = \frac{1}{\sqrt{2}}(|0\rangle_i + |1\rangle_i) \tag{1}$$

$$|\tilde{1}\rangle_i = V_i^{\pi/2}(-\pi/2)|1\rangle_i = \frac{1}{\sqrt{2}}(|0\rangle_i - |1\rangle_i) \ . \tag{2}$$

The unitary transformation [1]

$$V_i^k(\phi) = \exp[-ik/2(|1\rangle_i\langle 0|e^{-i\phi} + |0\rangle_i\langle 1|e^{i\phi})] \tag{3}$$

is obtained by applying a standing wave k-pulse (with laser phase ϕ) on resonance with the electronic transition $|0\rangle_i \leftrightarrow |1\rangle_i$ of the i-th ion. The equilibrium position of the ion is placed at an antinode of the standing wave for the duration of the pulse.

Cirac and Zoller [1] have shown how a controlled-not gate U_{cn} can be implemented for two ions i, j, by employing a common vibrational mode to give a net effect

$$U_{cn}|0\rangle_i|0\rangle_j = |0\rangle_i|0\rangle_j \tag{4}$$

$$U_{cn}|0\rangle_i|1\rangle_j = |0\rangle_i|1\rangle_j \tag{5}$$

$$U_{cn}|1\rangle_i|0\rangle_j = |1\rangle_i|1\rangle_j \tag{6}$$

$$U_{cn}|1\rangle_i|1\rangle_j = |1\rangle_i|0\rangle_j \ , \tag{7}$$

using a series of sideband laser pulses with the equilibrium positions of the ions at the nodes of the respective standing waves. An experimental realisation of this quantum gate has been demonstrated recently by Monroe et al. [3]. If the same quantum transformation U_{cn} is applied to the logical states of $\tilde{L}$, we find that this transformation remains a controlled-not gate

$$U_{cn}|\tilde{0}\rangle_i|\tilde{0}\rangle_j = |\tilde{0}\rangle_i|\tilde{0}\rangle_j \tag{8}$$

$$U_{cn}|\tilde{0}\rangle_i|\tilde{1}\rangle_j = |\tilde{1}\rangle_i|\tilde{1}\rangle_j \tag{9}$$

$$U_{cn}|\tilde{1}\rangle_i|\tilde{0}\rangle_j = |\tilde{1}\rangle_i|\tilde{0}\rangle_j \tag{10}$$

$$U_{cn}|\tilde{1}\rangle_i|\tilde{1}\rangle_j = |\tilde{0}\rangle_i|\tilde{1}\rangle_j \ , \tag{11}$$

except that the order of the control and target qubits is swapped around. We also note that the same laser pulse $V^k(\phi)$ which rotates the electronic levels can be used to implement rotations in $\tilde{L}$, and therefore any arbitrary quantum computation can be implemented in the logical basis $\tilde{L}$.

Given an arbitrary state $|\psi\rangle_a = c_0|0\rangle_a + c_1|1\rangle_a$ for ion a, the corresponding qubit $|\tilde{\psi}\rangle_a$ in the $\tilde{L}$ basis,

$$|\tilde{\psi}_a\rangle = c_0|\tilde{0}\rangle_a + c_1|\tilde{1}\rangle_a \ , \tag{12}$$

can be prepared by applying a $V_a^{\pi/2}(-\pi/2)$ laser pulse to that ion.

Our error correction scheme is implemented by entangling this arbitrary qubit with the state of a different qubit b. We assume that the ion b is in the ground state $|0\rangle_b$ initially, and apply a $V_b^{\pi/2}(-\pi/2)$ laser pulse to prepare it in the logical state $|\tilde{0}\rangle_b$. Following this, a controlled-not gate U_{cn} is applied to the two ion system, using qubit a as the control qubit, to obtain the desired entangled state,

$$|\tilde{\psi}\rangle_{ab} = c_0|\tilde{0}\rangle_a \otimes |\tilde{0}\rangle_b + c_1|\tilde{1}\rangle_a \otimes |\tilde{1}\rangle_b \ . \tag{13}$$

The amplitude coefficients of the qubit $|\tilde{\psi}\rangle_a$ are encoded in the entangled state $|\tilde{\psi}\rangle_{ab}$, which therefore represents the same qubit with its information content spread over both ions. Hence, if spontaneous emission occurs from the excited level of ion a, reducing its state to the ground level $|0\rangle_a$, the amplitude coefficients of the original qubit will be preserved,

$$(|0\rangle_a\langle 1|)|\tilde{\psi}\rangle_{ab} = c_0|0\rangle_a \otimes |\tilde{0}\rangle_b - c_1|0\rangle_a \otimes |\tilde{1}\rangle_b \ , \tag{14}$$

and it becomes possible to restore the entangled state $|\tilde{\psi}\rangle_{ab}$ via a coherent feedback process.

First a $V_a^{\pi/2}(\pi/2)$ laser pulse is applied to rotate the state of ion a into a logical state, ie. $|0\rangle_a \to |\tilde{1}\rangle_a$, so that the state of the two ion system becomes

$$c_0|\tilde{1}\rangle_a \otimes |\tilde{0}\rangle_b - c_1|\tilde{1}\rangle_a \otimes |\tilde{1}\rangle_b \ , \tag{15}$$

and then a controlled-not gate U_{cn} is applied, using qubit b as the control qubit, in order to entangle the ions

$$c_0|\tilde{1}\rangle_a \otimes |\tilde{0}\rangle_b - c_1|\tilde{0}\rangle_a \otimes |\tilde{1}\rangle_b \ . \tag{16}$$

Finally, a resonant π-pulse $V_a^\pi(-\pi/2)$ is applied to rotate the logical states,

$$V_a^\pi(-\pi/2)|\tilde{0}\rangle_a = -|\tilde{1}\rangle_a \tag{17}$$
$$V_a^\pi(-\pi/2)|\tilde{1}\rangle_a = |\tilde{0}\rangle_a \ , \tag{18}$$

and restore the initial state $|\tilde{\psi}\rangle_{ab}$.

We have assumed that we can tell accurately which ion has emitted spontaneously, so that we can apply this feedback process selectively to the appropriate ions. For example, if spontaneous emission occurs from the excited level of ion b, the same process as above, with the ions a, b interchanged, would enable us to recover the initial state $|\tilde{\psi}\rangle_{ab}$.

In general this quantum error correction scheme can be extended in a straightforward manner to store N/2 independent qubits, using a string of N trapped ions.

USING ELECTRONIC NUMBER STATES

A system of N trapped ions can be used to store information much more efficiently, by encoding it in the amplitude coefficients of the corresponding electronic number states. The electronic number states $|k\rangle_e$ form a logical basis, and are defined by the product of the individual electronic levels of the ions arranged in some definite order,

$$|k\rangle_e = |S_N\rangle_N \otimes |S_{N-1}\rangle_{N-1} \otimes ... \otimes |S_1\rangle_1 \ , \tag{19}$$

where $S_i = 0, 1$ represents a ground or excited state respectively. For an N-ion system, there are 2^N electronic number states labeled by the integer k,

$$k = S_N \times 2^{N-1} + S_{N-1} \times 2^{N-2} + ... + S_1 \times 2^0 \ , \tag{20}$$

representing the binary string $S_N S_{N-1}...S_1$, ($0 \le k \le 2^N - 1$), hence there are $2^N - 1$ independent amplitude coefficients available for encoding.

Spontaneous emission from the excited level $|1\rangle_j$ of the j-th ion to its ground level will eliminate those amplitude coefficients of the number states $|q\rangle$ which include the ground state $|0\rangle_j$, ie. containing $S_j = 0$. However the amplitude coefficients of the complementary number states $|\bar{q}\rangle$, where $\bar{q}$ is the complement of q (modulo 2^N), will be preserved.

Therefore if the initial state $|\psi\rangle$ is prepared so that the amplitude coefficients of the electronic number states $|q\rangle$ and $|\bar{q}\rangle$ are equal for all q, we are able to restore $|\psi\rangle$ after each spontaneous emission from any of the ions. The desired N-ion state

$$|\psi\rangle = \sum_{q=0}^{2^{N-1}-1} c_q(|q\rangle + |\bar{q}\rangle) , \qquad (21)$$

can be obtained by first generating an arbitrary (N-1)-ion state using a series of one-bit and two-bit operations to entangle the ions as reported by Cirac and Zoller [1]. This state is then coupled to the ground or excited state of an additional ion and each electronic number state is complemented ie. $|q\rangle \rightarrow \frac{1}{\sqrt{2}}(|q\rangle + |\bar{q}\rangle)$. This last transformation is also used to recreate the initial state after each spontaneous emission event and its implementation is presented below in detail.

To demonstrate how our error correction scheme works, we consider a three ion system (N=3). An arbitrary 2-ion state is given by

$$c_0|0\rangle + c_1|1\rangle + c_2|2\rangle + c_3|3\rangle , \qquad (22)$$

which for the purposes of our scheme would be transformed into the required 3-ion state $|\psi\rangle$ by coupling it to a third ion and applying a complementing procedure,

$$|\psi\rangle = A|0\rangle + B|1\rangle + C|2\rangle + D|3\rangle + D|4\rangle + C|5\rangle + B|6\rangle + A|7\rangle , \qquad (23)$$

where the electronic number states $|k\rangle_e = |S_a\rangle_a \otimes |S_b\rangle_b \otimes |S_c\rangle_c$ for the ions a, b, c, are labeled by $k = 4S_a + 2S_b + S_c$.

Hence, if spontaneous emission occurs from the excited level of ion a, this state is reduced to

$$(|0\rangle_a\langle 1|)|\psi\rangle = \sqrt{2}(D|0\rangle + C|1\rangle + B|2\rangle + A|3\rangle) , \qquad (24)$$

but still contains the original amplitude coefficients.

The coherent feedback process necessary to recreate the initial state $|\psi\rangle$ consists of two steps. First a resonant π-pulse $V_a^\pi(-\pi/2)$ is applied to ion a

$$V_a^\pi(-\pi/2)|0\rangle_a = |1\rangle_a \qquad (25)$$
$$V_a^\pi(-\pi/2)|1\rangle_a = -|0\rangle_a , \qquad (26)$$

to match the amplitude coefficients with their initial electronic number states, resulting in a state

$$\sqrt{2}(D|4\rangle + C|5\rangle + B|6\rangle + A|7\rangle) . \qquad (27)$$

Following this, the initial state $|\psi\rangle$ is obtained by complementing each electronic number state ie. $|q\rangle \rightarrow \frac{1}{\sqrt{2}}(|q\rangle + |\bar{q}\rangle)$. The complementing procedure is basically an extension of the controlled-not gate U_{cn} to N ions, and its implementation requires a vibrational mode common to all the ions.

We start by applying a $V^{\pi/2}(-\pi/2)$ laser pulse to each of the ions to rotate the electronic levels,

$$V_i^{\pi/2}(-\pi/2)|S_i\rangle_i = |\tilde{S}_i\rangle_i , \qquad (28)$$

which transforms an arbitrary electronic number state $|k\rangle_e$ coupled to the vibrational state $|n\rangle_{vib}$ into

$$|n\rangle_{vib} \otimes (|\tilde{S_N}\rangle_N \otimes |\tilde{S_{N-1}}\rangle_{N-1} \otimes ... \otimes |\tilde{S_1}\rangle_1) . \qquad (29)$$

Then a unitary transformation U,

$$U = \exp\left(i\pi a^\dagger a \sum_{j=1}^{N}(\sigma_z^{(j)} + 1/2)\right) \quad , \tag{30}$$

is applied to the N-ion system, where a, $a^\dagger$ are the annihilation and creation operators of the vibrational mode, and $\sigma_z^{(j)}$ is the population inversion of the j-th ion transition. This transformation is generated by a Hamiltonian $H = \hbar a^\dagger a \sum_{j=1}^{N} \chi_j(\sigma_z^{(j)} + 1/2)$ which can be obtained by applying far-detuned standing wave pulses to the ion transitions, as shown by the authors [4], with the equilibrium position of each ion placed at a node of the corresponding standing wave. The parameters $\chi_j = \eta_j^2 \Omega_j^2/(N\Delta)$ depend on the Lamb-Dicke parameters η_j, and the Rabi frequencies Ω_j of the ions, as well as the detuning Δ, $(|\Delta| \gg \nu)$ of the laser pulses from the ion transitions. For a single ion, U is equivalent to the controlled-not gate U_{cn} discussed in the previous section.

If the vibrational state coupled to the ions is $|0\rangle_{vib}$, the Fourier-transformed states $|\tilde{S}_i\rangle_i$ remain unchanged by U, whereas if it is $|1\rangle_{vib}$, these states are complemented, ie. $|\tilde{S}_i\rangle_i \rightarrow |\tilde{\bar{S}}_i\rangle_i$, where $\bar{S}_i$ is the complement of S_i (modulo 2).

Hence if the vibrational state is prepared in a superposition $\frac{1}{\sqrt{2}}(|0\rangle_{vib} + |1\rangle_{vib})$, the transformation U entangles the vibrational and electronic modes of the N-ion system:

$$\frac{1}{\sqrt{2}}[|0\rangle_{vib} \otimes (|\tilde{S}_N\rangle_N ... |\tilde{S}_1\rangle_1) + |1\rangle_{vib} \otimes (|\tilde{\bar{S}}_N\rangle_N ... |\tilde{\bar{S}}_1\rangle_1)] \quad . \tag{31}$$

Another $V^{\pi/2}(\pi/2)$ laser pulse is applied to each of the ions, to rotate the Fourier-transformed states, and the resultant state of the system is given by

$$\frac{1}{\sqrt{2}}[|0\rangle_{vib} \otimes (|S_N\rangle_N ... |S_1\rangle_1) + |1\rangle_{vib} \otimes (|\bar{S}_N\rangle_N ... |\bar{S}_1\rangle_1)] \quad . \tag{32}$$

Finally, to obtain the required transformation for complementing electronic number states, $|q\rangle \rightarrow \frac{1}{\sqrt{2}}(|q\rangle + |\bar{q}\rangle)$, a controlled-not gate U_{cn} is applied to the vibrational state and one of the ions, which acts as a control qubit, in order to disentangle the vibrational and electronic modes:

$$\frac{1}{\sqrt{2}}|n\rangle_{vib} \otimes (|S_N\rangle_N ... |S_1\rangle_1 + |\bar{S}_N\rangle_N ... |\bar{S}_1\rangle_1) \quad , \tag{33}$$

where $n = 0, 1$ for the vibrational state.

Once again, we have assumed that we know accurately which ion has emitted spontaneously, so that this coherent feedback process can be applied selectively. If spontaneous emission occurs from one of the other ions, the same process as above, with the resonant π-pulse $V^\pi(-\pi/2)$ applied to the respective ion, can be used to reconstruct the initial state $|\psi\rangle$.

We note that the error correction scheme presented in this section allows an N-ion system to encode the equivalent of $(2^{N-1} - 1)$ qubits in the amplitude coefficients of its electronic number states.

In conclusion, we have proposed two quantum error correction schemes which rely on continuous monitoring of spontaneous emission and selective coherent feedback to eliminate errors as soon as they are detected.

REFERENCES

[1] J.I.Cirac and P.Zoller, Phys. Rev. Lett. **74**, 4091 (1995).

[2] H.Mabuchi and P.Zoller, Phys. Rev. Lett. **76**, 3108 (1996).

[3] C.Monroe, D.M.Meekhoff, B.E.King, W.M.Itano and D.J.Wineland, Phys. Rev. Lett. **75**, 4714 (1995).

[4] C.D'Helon and G.J.Milburn, to be published in Phys. Rev. A.

INTEGRABILITY AND COMPUTABILITY IN SIMULATING QUANTUM SYSTEMS

K. Umeno

Laboratory for Information Representation, Frontier Research Program
The Institute of Physical and Chemical Research (RIKEN)
2-1 Hirosawa, Wako, Saitama 351-01, Japan
E-mail: chaosken@giraffe.riken.go.jp

An impossibility theorem on approximately simulating quantum non-integrable Hamiltonian systems is presented here. This result shows that there is a trade-off between the unitary property and the energy expectation conservation law in time-discretization of quantum non-integrable systems, whose classical counterpart is Ge-Marsden's impossibility result about simulating classically non-integrable Hamiltonian systems using integration schemes preserving symplectic (Lie-Poisson) property.

1. INTRODUCTION

Recently, much attention is directed to investigate the interrelation between physics and computation. To connect physics with computation, we can classify the problems into the the following classes:

class (1): Connection between classical physics and classical computation,
class (2): Connection between quantum physics and classical computation,
class (3): Connection between classical physics and quantum computation, and
class (4): Connection between quantum physics and quantum computation.

Concerning the class (4), *simulating* quantum behavior such as quantum chaos using classical computers is known to be a notoriously difficult computational problem [4]. One of the main difficulties is that one must discretize a continuous time parameter of equations of motion in order to simulate on computers. Thus, it is an important question to ask whether we can always have a suitable time-discretization scheme for the Schrödinger equation.

In this paper, I will give a somewhat negative answer to this question: In the case of *quantum non-integrable* systems with an explicit time-independent Hamiltonian operator, no *explicit* time-discretization algorithm preserving unitary property can simulate quantum non-integrable behavior without violating the conservation law of energy expectation. Since the original quantum nature must have these two properties, namely, the conservation law of energy expectation and the unitary property of time evolution, this means that there is a fundamental limit in simulating quantum non-integrable behavior using unitary maps like quantum computers. This negative result can be regarded as a quantum analogue of Ge-Marsden's theorem [7]: No symplectic integrator can simulate non-integrable behavior in a class of autonomous Hamiltonian systems without violating, the energy conservation. These fundamental limits, whether quantum or classical, suggest the importance of the notion of integrability in simulating physical behavior. In Section 2, we give a brief explanation of time-discretization preserving unitary property. In Section 3, we give a theorem about the impossibility of simulating quantum non-integrable systems. In Section 4, we discuss various aspects about our results.

2. SIMULATION TECHNOLOGY PRESERVING UNITARY PROPERTY

Time-evolution of quantum computation can be seen as a class of successive iterations of unitary transformations [1, 2, 5]. The time-evolution operator has the form of

$$U(\Delta t) = \exp\left[-i\Delta t H/\hbar\right],\tag{1}$$

where H is a Hamiltonian operator with Hermitian property, Δt is the time duration of each computation process and an exponential operator $\exp[xA]$ is defined as

$$\exp[xA] = \sum_{n=0}^{\infty} \frac{(xA)^n}{n!}, \quad x = -i\Delta t/\hbar \tag{2}$$

Let A and B be Hermitian operators as the generators of two *different* elementary processes of unitary dynamics.

In general, A does not commute with B:

$$[A, B] = AB - BA \neq 0.\tag{3}$$

To track computational processes retaining unitary property, evaluating the following time-evolution operator

$$\exp[x(A + B)]\tag{4}$$

is relevant to various problems. In fact, there are infinitely many methods to get perturbation series of Eq.(4). The Feynman path-integral method [3]

$$\exp[x(A + B)] \approx \left[1 + \frac{x(A + B)}{n}\right]^n\tag{5}$$

discovered in his study of quantum electro-dynamics is a first-order method based on the identity

$$\exp[x(A + B)] = \lim_{n \to \infty} \left[1 + \frac{x(A + B)}{n}\right]^n.\tag{6}$$

However, the above approximation breaks unitary property in each elementary dynamical process $1 + \frac{x(A+B)}{n}$, as is easily checked. On the contrary, Trotter formula [14]

$$\exp[x(A + B)] = \left[\exp(\frac{xA}{n})\exp(\frac{xB}{n})\right]^n + O\left(\frac{x^2}{n}\right)\tag{7}$$

based on the identity

$$\exp[x(A + B)] = \lim_{n \to \infty} \left[\exp(\frac{xA}{n})\exp(\frac{xB}{n})\right]^n\tag{8}$$

preserves the unitary property in each elementary process $\exp(\frac{xA}{n})\exp(\frac{xB}{n})$, as is also easily checked. The second order formula called leap frog method has the form

$$\exp\left[x(A+B)\right] = \left[\exp(\frac{xA}{2n})\exp(\frac{xB}{n})\exp(\frac{xA}{2n})\right]^n + O\left(\frac{x^3}{n^2}\right). \tag{9}$$

Furthermore, many other higher-order formulas for exponential operators $\exp\left[x(A+B)\right]$ preserving the symmetry corresponding to the unitary propery were recently discovered independently both in the development of simulation technology called quantum Monte Carlo methods [10, 13] to simulate density matrices, or in the development of simulation technology called symplectic integrators [9,11–13,15,23] to simulate classical Hamiltonian dynamical systems. It is an easy task to extend these decomposition formulas of the exponential operators $\exp\left[x(A+B)\right]$ to more generalized exponential operators $\exp\left[x\sum_{j=1}^{l} A_j\right]$ of multi noncommutative operators $A_1, A_2, \cdots, A_l$. Thus, an application of these successive composition formulas of exponential operators to quantum computations of $\exp\left[x\sum_{j=1}^{l} A_j\right]$ can give us a unified view of this kind of simulations as follows: Let us consider the problem of approximately simulating $\exp\left[x\sum_{j=1}^{l} A_j\right]$ for $t \le t' \le t + \Delta t$ based on an explicit algorithm on quantum model of computation whose each elementary process is successively generated by explicitly time-dependent Hamiltonians $Q_j(t, \Delta t), 1 \le j \le m$. Then, each s-th order approximation formula has a form:

$$\exp\left[x\sum_{j=1}^{l} A_j\right] = \prod_{j=1}^{m} \exp\left[xQ_j(t, \Delta t)\right] + O(x^{s+1}). \tag{10}$$

The relation

$$\sum_{j=1}^{l} A_j = \sum_{j=1}^{m} Q_j(t, \Delta t) \tag{11}$$

must hold from the lowest order terms in x in Eq. (10).

3. THEOREM

Let us consider a time-independent Hamiltonian $H(q, p)$ in a certain class of the set of Hermitian operators $\tilde{G} = \{G(q, p)\}$, where q and p denotes the canonical conjugate operators in the standard sense of quantum mechanics.

We can define *quantum non-integrability* as follows:

Definition 1 *We call a quantum Hamiltonian system with a time-independent Hamiltonian operator H quantum non-integrable if the following relation holds:*

$$[\Phi, H] = 0 \Longrightarrow \Phi = F(H), \tag{12}$$

where $\Phi \in \tilde{G}$ and F is a some function of a variable.

Since H is a time-independent Hamiltonian operator, the expectation value of H must be preserved:

$$\frac{d}{dt} < H > = \frac{d}{dt} < \Psi|H|\Psi > = 0, \tag{13}$$

where $< \Psi|$ is the state vector.

Here, we prove the following theorem:

Theorem 1 *If an explicit algorithm preserving unitary property can simulate a quantum non-integrable system with a time-independent Hamiltonian H approximately, the conservation law of the expectation value of the Hamiltonian operator < H > must break down.*

Remark 1: This theorem does *not* depend on the order and types of approximate algorithms we choose.

Remark 2: A class of explicit algorithms preserving unitary property involves universal quantum Turing machines in the sense of Deutsch [2]. Thus, as is shown in Ref. [19, 20], this theorem means that there is no (discrete time) quantum computers to simulate quantum non-integrable systems without breaking the conservation law of the energy expectation. However, the present theorem says not only the limitation of quantum computers but also a more general statement that there is a universal trade-off between the unitary property and the conservation law of energy expectation in time-discretization of quantum non-integrable systems.

(Proof of Theorem 1)

By using the expression of quantum algorithms in Eq. (10), we can consider an s-th order algorithm of approximately simulating the quantum dynamics of H for the time duration Δt of a computational step as follows:

$$\exp[xH] = \prod_{j=1}^{m} \exp[xQ_j(t, \Delta t)] + \mathrm{O}(x^{s+1}), \tag{14}$$

where $x = -i\Delta t/\hbar$ and $1 \le s < \infty$. Each quantum algorithm $Q_j(t, \Delta t)$ has a corresponding *time-dependent* Hamiltonian $H_j(t)$ satisfying

$$Q_j(t, \Delta t) = T(\exp \int_{t}^{t+\Delta t} H_j(s)ds) = 1 + \sum_{n=1}^{\infty} (-\frac{i}{\hbar})^n \int_{0}^{t_1} dt_1 \cdots \int_{0}^{t_{n-1}} dt_n H_j(t_1) \cdots H_j(t_n), \tag{15}$$

where T denotes the time ordering. The resulting quantum algorithm has also a Hamiltonian $\tilde{H}(t, \Delta t)$ satisfying the relation

$$\prod_{j=1}^{m} \exp[xQ_j(\Delta t + t, t)] = \exp(x\tilde{H}(t, \Delta t)). \tag{16}$$

By successively applying the Baker-Campbell-Hausdorff formula,

$$\exp X \exp Y = \exp Z, \tag{17}$$

where

$$Z = X + Y + \frac{1}{2}[X, Y] + \frac{1}{12}([X, [X, Y]] + [Y, [Y, X]]) + \frac{1}{24}[X, [Y, [Y, X]]] + \cdots \tag{18}$$

to the system (16), we can compute the corresponding Hamiltonian $\tilde{H}$ in a form

$$\tilde{H}(q, p, t, \Delta t) = H + \sum_{n=s}^{\infty} (\Delta t)^s H_s(t) = H + \mathrm{O}(x^s), \tag{19}$$

where $H_s(t)$ is a correction term of order s. We assume that the energy expectation $< \tilde{H} >$ in the quantum simulation is also preserved:

$$< H > = < \tilde{H} > = \mathrm{Const.} \quad \mathrm{for} \quad t \le t' \le t + \Delta t. \tag{20}$$

Since we can choose Δt an arbitrary real number, the relation (20) means the following commutation relations hold:

$$\left[H, \tilde{H}\right] = 0 \quad \text{and} \quad [H, H_n] = 0 \quad \text{for} \quad n \geq s. \tag{21}$$

However, from the assumption of *quantum non-integrability* of H, it follows that that $\tilde{H} = F(H)$. This means that the quantum algorithm $\tilde{H}$ generates the *exact* quantum dynamics of H. This exactness ($s \to \infty$) contradicts the assumption that the underlying quantum algorithm gives an *approximate* tracking of the dynamics of H in the finite order s.

(End of Proof)

4. DISCUSSIONS

The key of the present analysis is in *quantum non-integrability*. How generic is the notion of quantum non-integrability in quantum mechanics? In classical mechanics, it is known that most dynamical systems are non-integrable since the famous Poincaré theorem in the last century. Furthermore, we have exact criteria of classical non-integrability for explicitly given Hamiltonian systems based on the singularity analysis [8, 16–18, 22, 24, 25].

On the contrary, in quantum mechanics, we do not have any theorem guaranteeing the generic character of quantum non-integrable systems corresponding to the Poincaré theorem in classical mechanics nor exact criteria of quantum non-integrability for explicitly given Hamiltonian operators. In other words, it is not a trivial thing to connect classical non-integrability with quantum non-integrability [6, 21]. Recently, the present author found that the quantum Hamiltonian system with a time-independent Hamiltonian operator $H = \frac{1}{2}(p_x^2 + p_y^2 + q_1^2 q_2^2)$ would be quantum-nonintegrable under the hypothesis of the Weyl rule for canonical variables p_i, q_i using the Moyal bracket, based on Ziglin's result of proof of its classical non-integrability [20]. For the classical system of this system, it was shown in Ref. [15] that we cannot avoid energy fluctuations for some specific initial conditions like $(q_1, q_2, p_1, p_2) = (1000, 0.002, 0, 0)$, because the higher-order correction terms H_s also become bigger as

$$|H_s| \approx AB^s, \tag{22}$$

where A and B are some positive real constants. It can be easily predicted that this divergence of the higher-order correction terms H_s can also occur in quantum non-integrable systems like a quantum version of the above system. This model can be a vivid example causing rather general phenomena of the breakdown of the conservation law of energy expectation for quantum non-integrable systems by using any finite-order time-discretization preserving unitary property, which Theorem 1 asserts. This result has an interesting implication concerning the usual energy-time uncertain relations. From the energy-time uncertain relations $\Delta t \cdot \Delta E \geq \hbar$, it follows that

$$\Delta t^s |H_s| \approx \Delta E \geq \frac{\hbar}{\Delta t}. \tag{23}$$

This inequality gives a lower-bound of Δt which depends only on the order s of time-discretization and the correction terms H_s for any order s. Thus, this analysis shows that our naive view that the continuous nature of time in quantum mechanics is naturally obtained as the continuous limit Δt is not universal, at least in quantum non-integrable systems. It will be an interesting and important open problems to consider time-discretization of quantum non-integrable systems in connection with the foundation of quantum mechanics.

ACKNOWLEDGEMENTS

This work was supported in part by the Special Researcher's Program to promote basic sciences at RIKEN and from the Frontier Research Program. I would like to thank Prof. Shun-ichi Amari for his continual encouragement.

REFERENCES

[1] BENIOFF, P., "Quantum mechanical Hamiltonian models of Turing machines," *J. Stat. Phys.* **29** (1982), 515-546.

[2] DEUTSCH, D., "Quantum theory, the Church-Turing principle and the universal quantum computer," *Proc. R. Soc. Lond.* **A400**(1985), 96-118.

[3] FEYNMAN, R. P., "An operator calculus having applications in quantum electro-dynamics," *Phys. Rev.* **84** (1951), 108-128.

[4] FEYNMAN, R. P., "Simulating physics with computers," *Int. J. of Theor. Phys.* **21** (1982), 467-488.

[5] FEYNMAN, R. P., "Quantum mechanical computers," *Foundations of Physics* **16** (1986), 507-531.

[6] HIETARINTA, J.,"Quantum integrability is not a trivial consequence of classical integrability," *Phys. Lett. A* **93** (1982), 55-57. i

[7] GE, Z. and J. E. MARSDEN, "Lie-Poisson Hamilton-Jacobi theory and Lie-Poisson integrators," *Phys. Lett. A* **133** (1988), 134–139.

[8] ITO, H., "Non-integrability of Hénon-Heiles system and a theorem of Ziglin," *Kodai Math. J.***8**(1985), 120-138.

[9] RUTH, R. D., "A canonical integration technique," *IEEE Trans. on Nuclear Sci.* **30**(1983), 2669-2671.

[10] SUZUKI, M.(Editor), *Quantum Monte Carlo Methods*, Springer-Verlag (1987).

[11] SUZUKI, M., "General theory of higher-order decomposition of exponential opera-tors and symplectic integrators," *Phys. Lett.* **A165**(1992), 387-395.

[12] SUZUKI, M., "General decomposition theory of ordered exponentials," *Proc. Japan. Acad.* **69 Ser.** B(1993), 161-166.

[13] SUZUKI, M. and K. UMENO, "Higher-Order decomposition theory of exponential operators and its applications to QMC and nonlinear dynamics." In *Computer Simulation Studies in Condensed-Matter Physics VI*, Springer-Verlag (1993), 74-86.

[14] TROTTER, H. F. *Proc. Am. Math. Phys.* **10** (1959)545.

[15] UMENO, K. and M. SUZUKI, "Symplectic and intermittent behaviour of Hamilto-nian flow,"*Phys. Lett.* **A181** (1993), 387-392.

[16] UMENO, K., "Non-integrable character of Hamiltonian systems with symmetric and global coupling," *Physica D***82** (1995), 11-35.

[17] UMENO, K., "Non-perturbative non-integrability of non-homogeneous nonlinear lattices induced by non-resonance hypothesis," *Physica D***94** (1996), 116-134.

[18] UMENO, K., "Variational symmetry in non-integrable Hamiltonian systems," *J. of Nonlinear Mathematical Physics* **4** (1996), (1996), 69-77.

[19] UMENO, K. "Simulating quantum non-integrable systems with quantum computers", Extended abstract accepted for Workshop of *PhysComp 96*(1996).

[20] UMENO, K. "Simulating quantum chaos with quantum computers", submitted to World Scientific(Singapore), *Proc. of APCTP(Asia Pacific Center for Theoretical Physics) Inauguration Conference* June 4-10(1996) Seoul, Korea.

[21] WEIGERT, S."The problem of quantum integrability"*Physica* **D 56**(1992)107-119.

[22] YOSHIDA, H., "A criterion for the non-existence of an additional integral in Hamiltonian systems with a homogeneous potential,"*Physica D***29** (1987),128-142.

[23] YOSHIDA, H. "Construction of higher order symplectic integrators," *Phys. Lett. A***150** (1990),262-268.

[24] ZIGLIN, S. L., "Branching of solutions and non-existence of first integrals in Hamiltonian mechanics. I." *Functional Anal. Appl.***16** (1983), 181-189.

[25] ZIGLIN, S. L., "Branchiing of solutions and non-existence of first integrals in Hamiltonian mechanics. II." *Functional Anal. Appl.***17** (1983), 6-17.

SLOWING DOWN THE DECOHERENCE OF QUANTUM BITS

P. Tombesi and D. Vitali

Dipartimento di Matematica e Fisica, Università di Camerino
via Madonna delle Carceri 62032 Camerino, Italy
FAX: +39-737/40042, E-mail: tombesi@camars.unicam.it

By means of a suitable feedback it is shown that a quantum superposition of number states, forming a qubit, can be preserved for a longer time with respect to the case without feedback.

1. INTRODUCTION

The introduction of quantum complexity theory [1, 2] leads to the question of whether complex problems can be solved with a classical computer or a computer based on fundamental quantum mechanical principles [3]. The algorithm recently introduced by Shor [4] for highly efficient factorization uses the linearity of the superposition principle among quantum states, and this enhanced the expectations for a quantum computer. One of the most interesting aspects of quantum computation relies indeed on the ability of evaluating exponentially many parallel inputs and to obtain an answer depending upon the interferences among various superposed results [5]. It seems that a new paradigm for computation is now emerging.

In a quantum computer information is stored in a quantum register composed of N two-level systems representing the quantum bits or qubits. What is then required to a quantum computer is to efficiently manipulate in its register superpositions of quantum states. It is then obvious that coherence and entanglement are essential ingredients of any device to be used as a quantum computational network which, in analogy to the situation for a classical computer, can be decomposed into the so called quantum logic gates [6]. The central obstacle, however, is the fragility of the entangled linear superpositions of N qubits with respect to decoherence by coupling to an environment. This loss of coherence should then be reduced as much as possible, because the decoherence time should be much larger than the calculation time, otherwise there is a strong limitation on the numbers one is able to factorize with Shor's algorithm. Most proposals for reducing decoherence in quantum computation are based on the so called quantum error correction codes (see for example Ref. [7]), which is a way to use *software* to preserve linear superposition states. Essentially in these approaches the entangled superposition state of N qubits is "encoded" in a larger number of qubits so that, assuming that only a fraction of qubits decoheres, it is possible to reconstruct the original state with a suitable decoding procedure.

We propose a different and essentially complementary scheme, which uses *hardware* to slow down decoherence. We consider the physical situation corresponding to the quantum phase gate experimentally demonstrated by Turchette *et al.* [8], in which the qubits are represented by different optical modes in a cavity ("flying qubits"). We propose to continuosly monitor each mode through homodyne measurements and to feed back the corresponding photocurrent in such a way as to stabilize the linear superposition state. In fact, by applying the quantum optical feedback theory of Wiseman and Milburn [9], the decoherence time can be significantly increased [10]. An idea, similar to that in spirit, was proposed in Ref. [11] in which continuous monitoring of the decay channels and an astute design of the gate are used to reduce decoherence.

2. THE FEEDBACK MODEL

Let us consider the linear superposition of photon's Fock states $\psi(0) = c_0|0\rangle + c_1|1\rangle$ considered by Turchette *et al.* [8] for an optical mode inside a cavity with damping constant γ_a, in presence of a homodyne measurement of the quadrature operator $\hat{x} = (a+a^\dagger)/2$. We do not address, however, to the quantum logic gate rather to the physical control of decoherence of that particular superposition. We assume that the measured output current is then fed back to the system by means of some electro-optical or all-optical device. To study the resulting system we follow the theory of quantum feedback as recently proposed by Wiseman and Milburn [9]. Following these authors the master equation for the reduced density matrix in presence of homodyne-mediated feedback can be written as

$$\dot{\rho} = \mathcal{L}_0\rho + \gamma_a\mathcal{K}(a\rho + \rho a^\dagger) + \frac{\gamma_a}{2\eta}\mathcal{K}^2\rho, \tag{1}$$

where $\mathcal{K}$ is a generic superoperator describing how the fed back current acts on the system and η is the efficiency of the homodyne detection. The second term in the r.h.s. represents the feedback effect while the third is a diffusion term due to the unavoidable back-action of the feedback process. The cavity mode is labeled by the boson operators $a, a^\dagger$. The standard Liouville super-operator $\mathcal{L}_0$ is given by

$$\mathcal{L}_0\rho = -\frac{i}{\hbar}[H_0, \rho] + \frac{\gamma_a}{2}(2a\rho a^\dagger - a^\dagger a\rho - \rho a^\dagger a). \tag{2}$$

To simplify our presentation we assume that there is no free evolution of the mode inside the cavity, by setting $H_0 = 0$. Then we choose the following super-operator $\mathcal{K}$

$$\mathcal{K}\rho = -ig[\hat{x}_\theta, \rho], \tag{3}$$

where g is a constant representing the gain of the feedback process, $\hat{x}_\theta = (ae^{i\theta} + a^\dagger e^{-i\theta})/2$ and θ is a phase parameter which can be controlled by the experimenter. This particular choice for $\mathcal{K}$ means that the feedback loop adds a driving term to the mode dynamics, which could be achieved, e.g., by using an electro-optic device with variable transmittivity driven by the homodyne photocurrent.It can be easily shown [10] that Eq. (1) becomes

$$\begin{aligned}\dot{\rho} = &\frac{\gamma}{2}(N+1)(2a\rho a^\dagger - a^\dagger a\rho - \rho a^\dagger a) + \frac{\gamma}{2}N(2a^\dagger\rho a - aa^\dagger\rho - \rho aa^\dagger) \\ &-\frac{\gamma}{2}M(2a^\dagger\rho a^\dagger - a^\dagger a^\dagger\rho - \rho a^\dagger a^\dagger) - \frac{\gamma}{2}M^*(2a\rho a - aa\rho - \rho aa) \\ &-i[(\delta a^\dagger a + \tilde{g}^* a^\dagger a^\dagger + \tilde{g}aa), \rho]\end{aligned} \tag{4}$$

where $\gamma = \gamma_a(1 + g\sin\theta)$, $N = \gamma_a g^2/(4\gamma\eta)$, $M = -\gamma_a g e^{-i\theta}(ge^{-i\theta}/2\eta - i)/(2\gamma)$, $\delta = (\gamma_a g\cos\theta)/2$ and $\tilde{g} = \gamma_a g e^{i\theta}/4$.

3. THE WIGNER FUNCTION

This master equation by standard techniques [12] can be converted into an evolution equation for the Wigner function. Assuming the initial state in a superposition of Fock states $c_0|0\rangle + c_1|1\rangle$, the Wigner function at initial time is

$$W(x_1, x_2; 0)$$
$$= \frac{2}{\pi}\left[1 + 4|c_1|^2(x_1^2 + x_2^2 - \tfrac{1}{2}) + 4x_1 Re(c_0 c_1^*) + 4x_2 Im(c_0^* c_1)\right] e^{-2(x_1^2 + x_2^2)} . \quad (5)$$

The Wigner function at time t is obtained through the Chapman-Kolmogorov equation [13]

$$W(\mathbf{x}; t) = \int dy_1\, dy_2\, P(\mathbf{x}; t|\mathbf{y}; 0)\, W(\mathbf{x}; 0), \quad (6)$$

where bold face letters means two dimensional vectors and the transition probability density $P(\mathbf{x}; t|\mathbf{y}; 0)$ is given by [13]

$$P(\mathbf{x}; t|\mathbf{y}; 0) = \frac{1}{2\pi\sqrt{Det\Sigma(t)}} \exp\left[-\frac{1}{2}\langle \mathbf{y} - G^{-1}(t)\mathbf{x}|G^T(t)\Sigma^{-1}(t)G(t)|\mathbf{y} - G^{-1}(t)\mathbf{x}\rangle\right], \quad (7)$$

with G^T the transpose of the 2×2 matrix G given by $G(t) = e^{-\Gamma t}$, while the matrix Σ is given by

$$\Sigma(t) = 2\int_0^t d\tau\, G(\tau)\, D\, G^T(\tau) \quad (8)$$

with

$$\Gamma = \frac{\gamma_a}{2}\begin{pmatrix} 1 + 2g\sin\theta & 0 \\ 2g\cos\theta & 1 \end{pmatrix}. \quad (9)$$

$$D = \frac{\gamma_a}{8}\begin{pmatrix} 1 + 2g\sin\theta + \frac{g^2\sin^2\theta}{\eta} & g\cos\theta(1 + \frac{g\sin\theta}{\eta}) \\ g\cos\theta(1 + \frac{g\sin\theta}{\eta}) & 1 + \frac{g^2\cos^2\theta}{\eta} \end{pmatrix} \quad (10)$$

The two matrices Γ and D are obtained from the master equation (4) by standard methods as for example in Ref. [13]. Following these methods one obtains that $G(t)$ becomes

$$G(t) = e^{-\frac{\gamma_a t}{2}}\begin{pmatrix} e^{-\gamma_a tg\sin\theta} & 0 \\ -\cot\theta(1 - e^{-\gamma_a tg\sin\theta}) & 1 \end{pmatrix} \quad (11)$$

and the matrix $\Sigma(t)$ is given by

$$\Sigma(t)_{11} = \frac{1}{4}\frac{1 + 2g\sin\theta + \frac{g^2\sin^2\theta}{\eta}}{1 + 2g\sin\theta}[1 - e^{-\gamma_a t(1 + 2g\sin\theta)}] \quad (12)$$

$$\Sigma(t)_{12} = \Sigma(t)_{21} = \cot\theta\Sigma(t)_{11} - \frac{1}{4}\cot\theta[1 - e^{-\gamma_a t(1 + g\sin\theta)}] \quad (13)$$

$$\Sigma(t)_{22} = \cot^2\theta\Sigma(t)_{11} - \frac{1}{2}\cot^2\theta[1 - e^{-\gamma_a t(1 + g\sin\theta)}] + \frac{1}{4}(1 + \cot^2\theta)[1 - e^{-\gamma_a t}] . \quad (14)$$

Performing the integration of (5) one gets the general expression for the time evolution of the Wigner function

$$W(x_1, x_2; t) = \frac{\sqrt{DetU(t)}}{2\pi} \exp\left[-\frac{1}{2}\left(U(t)_{11}x_1^2 + 2U(t)_{12}x_1 x_2 + U(t)_{22}x_2^2\right)\right] \quad (15)$$
$$\times \left[1 + |c_1|^2\left[Tr\{U(t)\Sigma(t)\} - 2 + v_1^2 + v_2^2\right] + 2v_1 Re(c_0 c_1^*) + 2v_2 Im(c_0^* c_1)\right]$$

where

$$U(t) = \left(\Sigma(t) + \frac{G(t)G^T(t)}{4} \right)^{-1}, \tag{16}$$

and

$$v_i = \frac{1}{2} \left(G^T(t) U(t) \right)_{ij} x_j . \tag{17}$$

The above equations give the complete analytical solution of the homodyne feedback model. Using these expressions is possible to see under which conditions it is possible to slow down the decoherence and therefore preserve as much as possible the initial superposition of number states against cavity losses.

4. THE MARGINAL DISTRIBUTION

In the present feedback model one performs a continuous homodyne measurement of the quadrature $\hat{x}$ and therefore an experimental characterization of decoherence can be obtained from the reconstruction of the time-evolved probability distribution $P(x;t)$

In the basis of the eigenstates of $\hat{x}$, the initial state $|\psi(0)\rangle = c_0|0\rangle + c_1|1\rangle$ is written as $\psi(x) = c_0\psi_0(x) + c_1\psi_1(x)$, so that the corresponding probability density is

$$P(x,0) = |\psi(x)|^2 = |c_0|^2|\psi_0(x)|^2 + |c_1|^2|\psi_1(x)|^2 \tag{18}$$
$$+2|c_0c_1\psi_0(x)\psi_1(x)|\cos(\varphi_0(x) - \varphi_1(x) + \delta_0 - \delta_1)$$

being $\psi_i(x) = |\psi_i(x)|e^{i\varphi_i(x)}$ and $c_i = |c_i|e^{i\delta_i}$. In absence of dissipation (i.e. $\gamma_a = 0$) we only have the unitary evolution and the probability density at time t can be easily written down. In presence of dissipation, however, the probability distribution can be written as

$$P(x,t) = |c_0|^2 P_0(x,t) + |c_1|^2 P_1(x,t) + 2|c_0c_1|\sqrt{P_0(x,t)P_1(x,t)}F(x,t) \tag{19}$$

with the obvious meaning of $P_i(x,t)$ and with $F(x,t)$ a decaying function describing decoherence and which can be called "fringe function".

The probability distribution $P(x;t)$ is the marginal distribution of the Wigner function (15), i.e.

$$P(x;t) = \int dx_2 \, W(x, x_2; t), \tag{20}$$

where we wrote $x = x_1$ for simplicity. Performing this integral and referring to the parametrization (19), we get

$$P_0(x,t) = \frac{1}{\sqrt{2\pi U^{-1}_{11}}} e^{-\frac{x^2}{2U^{-1}_{11}}} \tag{21}$$

$$P_1(x,t) = \frac{1}{\sqrt{2\pi U^{-1}_{11}}} e^{-\frac{x^2}{2U^{-1}_{11}}} \left[1 + \frac{G^2_{11} + G^2_{12}}{4U^{-1}_{11}} \left(\frac{x^2}{U^{-1}_{11}} - 1 \right) \right] \tag{22}$$

$$F(x,t) = \frac{\frac{x}{2U^{-1}_{11}} \left(G_{11}\cos(\delta_0 - \delta_1) - G_{12}\sin(\delta_0 - \delta_1) \right)}{\left[1 + \frac{G^2_{11}+G^2_{12}}{4U^{-1}_{11}} \left(\frac{x^2}{U^{-1}_{11}} - 1 \right) \right]^{\frac{1}{2}}}, \tag{23}$$

where G_{11} and G_{12} are given by (11) and

$$4U^{-1}_{11} = \frac{1 + 2g\sin\theta + g^2\sin^2\theta/\eta}{1 + 2g\sin\theta}[1 - e^{-\gamma_a t(1+2g\sin\theta)}] + e^{-\gamma_a t(1+2g\sin\theta)} . \tag{24}$$

Let us see the behavior of the fringe function. The case without feedback is obtained setting $g = 0$ and gives

$$F(x,t) = \frac{2xe^{-\gamma_a t/2}\cos(\delta_0 - \delta_1)}{[1 + e^{-\gamma_a t}(4x^2 - 1)]^{\frac{1}{2}}} , \qquad (25)$$

showing that decoherence is manifested by the decay $F(x,t) \simeq e^{-\gamma_a t/2}$ at large times, as it can be expected.

In the presence of feedback, the system is stable (i.e. it reaches a steady state) for $1 + 2g\sin\theta > 0$; from (23), it is possible to derive an expression for the long time behaviour of the fringe function which is valid both in the stable and the unstable case. One always has an exponential decay given by

$$F(x,t) \simeq \cos(\delta_0 - \delta_1)e^{-\frac{\gamma_a t}{2}|1 + 2g\sin\theta|} , \qquad (26)$$

except for the instability threshold case $1 + 2g\sin\theta = 0$ which is characterized by a power law decay $F(x,t) \simeq (\gamma_a t)^{-1}$. Comparing Eqs. (26) and (25), the study of the fringe function suggests therefore that decoherence is slowed down by homodyne feedback for all the initial superposition with $\cos(\delta_0 - \delta_1) \neq 0$, i.e. $\mathrm{Re}(c_0^* c_1) \neq 0$, provided that the feedback parameter satisfy the condition

$$-1 < g\sin\theta < 0 , \qquad (27)$$

whatever the value of the homodyne detection efficiency η is.

In the ideal case of unit efficiency, the particular parameter choice $g\sin\theta = -1$ shows a peculiar behavior which is worth considering. In fact it is possible to prove that in this case, the probability distribution $P(x,t)$ decreases exponentially according to

$$P(x,t) = e^{-\gamma_a t/2}P(xe^{-\gamma_a t/2}, 0) \qquad (28)$$

for all initial states and it can be seen from (19) that this implies a perfect preservation of the fringe function at any time, i.e.

$$F(x,t) = \cos(\delta_0 - \delta_1) . \qquad (29)$$

This means that the "interference pattern" of the initial state remains unchanged during the time evolution and one has "perfectly frozen decoherence". Actually, because of the instability, the initial probability distribution exponentially broadens and flattens so that from a practical point of view the interference pattern associated to the linear superposition vanishes al large times also in this case.

5. THE FIDELITY FUNCTION

The characterization of decoherence in terms of the homodyne-measured probability distribution $P(x,t)$ could be checked experimentally, but it only gives a partial description of the preservation properties of the feedback model, because all the informations are "projected" along the $\hat{x}$ quadrature. A consequence of this is the fact that, because $G_{12}(t) = 0$, the fringe function is not able to characterize the decoherence of the states with $\cos(\delta_0 - \delta_1) = 0$. A better description of how the present feedback model is able to preserve a generic initial state in the cavity is given by the fidelity $F(t)$

$$F(t) = \langle\psi(0)|\rho(t)|\psi(0)\rangle = \pi\int dx_1 dx_2 W(x_1, x_2; 0)W(x_1, x_2; t) , \qquad (30)$$

i.e. the probability of finding the initial state $|\psi(0)\rangle$ at time t.

In the vacuum bath case ($g = 0$), one has the general result

$$F(t)_{vac} = 1 - |c_1|^2(1 + e^{-\gamma_a t}) + 2|c_1|^4 e^{-\gamma_a t} + 2|c_0|^2|c_1|^2 e^{-\gamma_a t/2} . \tag{31}$$

This expression shows that in the standard case of a vacuum bath, the fidelity for a generic linear superposition of $|0\rangle$ and $|1\rangle$ decays exponentially as $e^{-\gamma_a t/2}$ and that this decay is "isotropic", that is, it depends only on the modulus of the linear coefficients c_0 and c_1, and not on their relative phase $\delta_0 - \delta_1$.

As suggested by the study of $P(x, t)$, the presence of feedback can improve the preservation of the initial superposition state. By this we mean that feedback allows to slow down significantly the decay of the fidelity. From the above analytical expressions it is straightforward to derive the general expression for the $F(t)$ in the general case, but this expression is very cumbersome. Anyway one can understand the main effects of the feedback model by considering the special case $\theta = -\pi/2$, which is considerably simpler. In fact, in this case, the dynamics of the two orthogonal quadratures $\hat{x}$ and $\hat{x}_\theta = \hat{y}$ are uncoupled and the feedback loop affects only the dynamics of the homodyne-measured quadrature $\hat{x}$, while the orthogonal quadrature follows the usual dynamics in presence of a vacuum bath (see the expression for $G(t)$ and $\Sigma(t)$). The fidelity in the case $\theta = -\pi/2$ is given by

$$F(t) = \sqrt{\frac{2U(t)_{11}}{4 + U(t)_{11}}} \tag{32}$$

$$\times \left\{ 1 + \left[A(t) + \frac{C(t)^2}{8} - \frac{3}{2} + \frac{4 + B(t)^2}{4 + U(t)_{11}} \right] |c_1|^2 \right.$$

$$+ \left[-\frac{3A(t)}{2} - \frac{C(t)^2}{16} + \frac{12B(t)^2}{(4 + U(t)_{11})^2} \right.$$

$$\left. + \frac{8A(t) - 3B(t)^2 + C(t)^2}{8 + 2U(t)_{11}} \right] |c_1|^4$$

$$\left. + \frac{8B(t)}{4 + U(t)_{11}}(\mathrm{Re}(c_0^* c_1))^2 + C(t)(\mathrm{Im}(c_0^* c_1))^2 \right\} ,$$

where

$$A(t) = \mathrm{Tr}\{U(t)\Sigma(t)\} - 2 = -e^{-\gamma_a t} - \frac{e^{-\gamma_a t(1-2g)}}{1 + \frac{g^2}{\eta(1-2g)}(1 - e^{-\gamma_a t(1-2g)})} \tag{33}$$

$$B(t) = \frac{1}{2}(G^T(t)U(t))_{11} = 2\frac{e^{-\gamma_a t(1/2-g)}}{1 + \frac{g^2}{\eta(1-2g)}(1 - e^{-\gamma_a t(1-2g)})} \tag{34}$$

$$C(t) = \frac{1}{2}(G^T(t)U(t))_{22} = 2e^{-\gamma_a t/2} . \tag{35}$$

Let us discuss the general properties of the fidelity in this case. First of all, differently from the vacuum case, in presence of feedback one has anisotropy, i.e., the decay of $F(t)$ depends on the relative phase of c_0 and c_1. This means that feedback can partially protect some states better than others. This is not a surprise since in the feedback model the measured quadrature $\hat{x}$ plays a privileged role. This is well shown by the last two terms in (32): the term proportional to $(\mathrm{Re}(c_0^* c_1))^2$ explicitly depends on the feedback gain g while the term proportional to $(\mathrm{Im}(c_0^* c_1))^2$ does not depend on the feedback gain and decays as $e^{-\gamma_a t/2}$, like the fidelity in the vacuum case. One has a decay for $F(t)$ slower than that of the vacuum case whenever the first term prevails over the second one. For a derivation of the conditions under which it is possible to slow down the decay of the fidelity, one has to distinguish the stable and the unstable cases. In the stable case the eigenvalues of the matrix Γ are both positive, i.e., $g < 1/2$. In this case $F(t)$ decays to the constant value $|c_0|^2$ and its asymptotic decay is given by $F(t) \sim e^{-\gamma_a t(1/2-g)}$ whenever $\text{Re}(c_0^* c_1) \neq 0$. This means that when $0 < g < 1/2$ states with a relative phase $\delta_0 - \delta_1$ between c_0 and c_1 close to zero are protected by our feedback model, while this feedback is less effective when this relative phase is close to $\pi/2$. In the unstable case $g \geq 1/2$, $F(t)$ always decays to zero as $F(t) \sim e^{-\gamma_a t(g-1/2)}$ because $U(t)_{11} \sim e^{-\gamma_a t(2g-1)}$. Therefore we can conclude that it is possible to improve the protection of the states (especially those with a relative phase $\delta_0 - \delta_1$ close to zero) with respect to the standard vacuum bath case, whenever $0 < g < 1/2$. The slowest decay of the fidelity, and therefore the best state protection, is obtained at the instability threshold $g = 1/2$, where one has the power law decay $F(t) \sim t^{-1/2}$. Note that these results coincide with those obtained by looking at the fringe function $F(x,t)$ under the condition considered here $\theta = -\pi/2$. A qualitative description of how the present homodyne feedback model is able to improve the protection of the initial superposition state with respect to the standard vacuum bath case is given by Figs. 1, 2 and 3. In Fig. 1 the Wigner function of the state $|\psi(0)\rangle = (|0\rangle - \sqrt{3}|1\rangle)/2$ is plotted. Fig. 2 shows the Wigner function evolved at time $\gamma_a t = 1$ in the presence of feedback (parameters are $g = 1/2$, $\theta = -\pi/2$, $\eta = 1$), while Fig. 3 shows the Wigner function at the same time $\gamma_a t = 1$ evolved without feedback. It can be clearly seen that in the presence of feedback, the state of the mode after a cavity decay time is much more similar to the initial state than the one evolved without feedback.

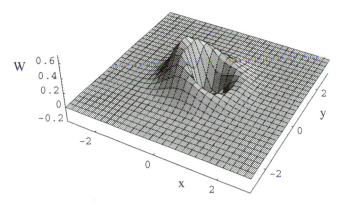

Figure 1. Wigner function of the initial superposition state referred in the text.

Using the above expression it can also be seen that protection worsens as the phase ϕ of the initial superposition approaches $\pi/2$. Moreover, as it can be easily expected, another crucial parameter is the detection efficiency η. In fact, the decay of the fidelity becomes faster and faster as η becomes smaller and smaller. Anyway, differently from the fringe function, the behavior of the fidelity in the "frozen decoherence" case $\eta = 1$ and $g \sin \theta = -1$ shows no peculiar aspect and, as suggested by the above asymptotic expressions, one has a decay similar to the no feedback case.

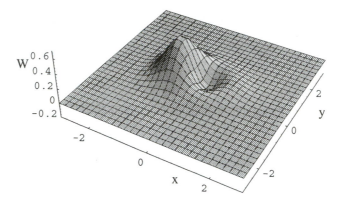

Figure 2. Wigner function of the state evolved after a time $\gamma_a t = 1$ in the presence of feedback. Parameter values are: $g = 1/2$, $\theta = -\pi/2$, $\eta = 1$.

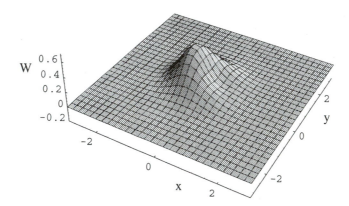

Figure 3. Wigner function of the state evolved after a time $\gamma_a t = 1$ in the absence of feedback.

6. CONCLUSIONS

In conclusion, these results show that it is possible, with an appropriate use of feedback, to preserve a linear superposition state of a qubit against decoherence within a given level of fidelity for a longer time with respect to the vacuum case. This means that feedback may increase the time a quantum computer has at disposition to perform a calculation. Due to the dependence of the feedback model on the relative phase of the coefficients of the initial state, this state preservation becomes more efficient when the states involved in the calculations belong to the restricted subensemble of superposition states characterized by a relative phase $\delta_0 - \delta_1$ close to zero.

REFERENCES

[1] D. Deutsch and R. Jozsa, Proc. R. Soc. London A **439**, 553 (1992).

[2] A. Berthiaume and G. Brassard, J. Mod Opt. **41**, 2521 (1994).

[3] R. Feynman, Int. J. Theor. Phys. **21**, 467 (1982).

[4] P.W. Shor, in *Proceedings of the 35th Annual Symposium on FOCS* edited by S. Goldwasser (IEEE Computer Society Press, New York 1994).

[5] A. Ekert, in *Proc. ICAP '94, Boulder*, edited by D. Wineland, C. Wieman and S. Smith, AIP Conf. Proc. 323 (AIP, New York 1995) and references therein.

[6] D. Deutsch, Proc. R. Soc. London A **425**, 73 (1989).

[7] P.W. Shor, Phys. Rev. A **52**, R2493 (1995); R. Laflamme, C. Miquel, J.P. Paz and W.H. Zurek, Phys. Rev. Lett. **77**, 198 (1996); A.M. Steane, Phys. Rev. Lett. **77**, 793 (1996); A. Ekert and C. Macchiavello, Phys. Rev. Lett. **77**, 2585 (1996).

[8] Q.A. Turchette, C.J. Hood, W. Lange, H. Mabuchi and H.J. Kimble, Phys. Rev. Lett. **75**, 4710 (1995).

[9] H.M. Wiseman, and G.J. Milburn, Phys. Rev. Lett. **70**, 548 (1993); Phys. Rev A **49**,1350 (1994); Phys. Rev. A **49**, 4110 (1994); H.M. Wiseman, Phys. Rev. A **49**, 2133 (1994).

[10] P. Tombesi and D. Vitali, Appl. Phys. B **60**, S69 (1995).

[11] T. Pellizzari, S.A. Gardiner, J.I. Cirac, and P. Zoller, Phys. Rev. Lett. **75**, 3788 (1995).

[12] W. H. Louisell,*Quantum Statistical Properties of Radiation* (Wiley, New York 1973).

[13] H. Risken, *The Fokker-Planck Equation* (Springer-Verlag, Berlin 1989).

QUANTUM CAPACITY OF NOISY QUANTUM CHANNEL

Masanori Ohya and Noboru Watanabe

Department of Information Sciences
Science University of Tokyo
Noda City, Chiba 278, Japan
E-mail watanabe@is.noda.sut.ac.jp

1. INTRODUCTION

In quantum communication theory, the quantum mutual entropy [4] is an important tool to analyse the efficiency of information transmission. It is the amount of information correctly transmitted from an input system to an output system through a quantum channel. The supremum of the quantum mutual entropy over a certain set of states with a fixed quantum channel is the quantum capacity of the channel. The capacity for quantum systems has been discussed in several papers, like [1,2,12]. In [8], we studied the quantum capacity for purely quantum channels.

In this paper, we briefly review quantum channels and quantum mutual entropy and we show a useful proposition to calculate the quantum mutual entropy in §2. In §3, we explain the capacity of quantum channels in [8]. In §4, we compute the quantum capacity of a noisy quantum channel with respect to a subset of the state space under a certain energy constraint.

2. QUANTUM CHANNELS AND QUANTUM MUTUAL ENTROPY

Let $(\mathbf{B}(\mathcal{H}_1), \mathfrak{S}(\mathcal{H}_1))$ and $(\mathbf{B}(\mathcal{H}_2), \mathfrak{S}(\mathcal{H}_2))$ be an input and an output systems, respectively, where $\mathbf{B}(\mathcal{H}_k)$ is the set of all bounded linear operators on a separable Hilbert space $\mathcal{H}_k$ and $\mathfrak{S}(\mathcal{H}_k)$ is the set of all density operators on $\mathcal{H}_k$ $(k = 1, 2)$. The quantum channel Λ^* is a mapping from $\mathfrak{S}(\mathcal{H}_1)$ to $\mathfrak{S}(\mathcal{H}_2)$. Λ^* is called a linear channel if Λ^* is affine (i.e., $\Lambda^*(\Sigma_n \lambda_n \rho_n) = \Sigma_n \lambda_n \Lambda^*(\rho_n)$, $\forall \lambda_n \geq 0$, $\Sigma_n \lambda_n = 1$, $\forall \rho_n \in \mathfrak{S}(\mathcal{H}_1)$). Λ^* is called a CP (complete positive) channel if its dual map Λ from $\mathbf{B}(\mathcal{H}_2)$ to $\mathbf{B}(\mathcal{H}_1)$ is completely positive (i.e., $\langle x, \sum_{i,j=1}^{n} A_i^* \Lambda(B_i^* B_j) A_j x \rangle \geq 0$ for any $n \in \mathbb{N}$, $A_i \in \mathbf{B}(\mathcal{H}_1)$, $B_j \in \mathbf{B}(\mathcal{H}_2)$ and any $x \in \mathcal{H}_1$), where the dual map Λ of Λ^* is defined by

$$tr\Lambda^*(\rho)B = tr\rho\Lambda(B), \quad \forall \rho \in \mathfrak{S}(\mathcal{H}_1), \ \forall B \in \mathbf{B}(\mathcal{H}_2).$$

Let $\mathcal{K}_1$ and $\mathcal{K}_2$ be two Hilbert spaces expressing noise and loss systems, respectively. The quantum channel with the influence of noise and loss was constructed in [4] as

$$\Lambda^*(\rho) = tr_{\mathcal{K}_2} \Pi^*(\rho \otimes \xi), \tag{2.1}$$

for any $\rho \in \mathfrak{S}(\mathcal{H}_1)$, where $\xi \in \mathfrak{S}(\mathcal{K}_1)$ is a noise state and Π^* is the CP channel from $\mathfrak{S}(\mathcal{H}_1 \otimes \mathcal{K}_1)$ to $\mathfrak{S}(\mathcal{H}_2 \otimes \mathcal{K}_2)$, which represents the physical property of the channel. The examples of channels are discussed in [4] as follows:

(1) Attenuation channel Λ_0^* was formulated in [4] such as

$$\Lambda_0^*(\rho) = tr_{\mathcal{K}_2} \Pi_0^* (\rho \otimes \xi_0) \tag{2.2}$$

$$= tr_{\mathcal{K}_2} V_0 (\rho \otimes |0\rangle \langle 0|) V_0^*, \tag{2.3}$$

where $|0\rangle \langle 0|$ is the vacuum state in $\mathfrak{S}(\mathcal{K}_1)$, V_0 is the mapping from $\mathcal{H}_1 \otimes \mathcal{K}_1$ to $\mathcal{H}_2 \otimes \mathcal{K}_2$ given by

$$V_0(|n_1\rangle \otimes |0\rangle) = \sum_j^{n_1} C_j^{n_1} |j\rangle \otimes |n_1 - j\rangle, \tag{2.4}$$

$$C_j^{n_1} = \sqrt{\frac{n_1!}{j!(n_1 - j)!}} \eta^j (1 - \eta)^{n_1 - j} \tag{2.5}$$

and η is a transmission rate.

(2) Quantum channel Λ^* with a noise $\xi = |m_1\rangle \langle m_1|$ is defined in [9] as

$$\Lambda^*(\rho) = tr_{\mathcal{K}_2} \Pi^* (\rho \otimes \xi), \tag{2.6}$$

$$= tr_{\mathcal{K}_2} V (\rho \otimes |m_1\rangle \langle m_1|) V^* \tag{2.7}$$

where $|m_1\rangle \langle m_1|$ is the m_1 photon number state in $\mathfrak{S}(\mathcal{K}_1)$, V is the mapping from $\mathcal{H}_1 \otimes \mathcal{K}_1$ to $\mathcal{H}_2 \otimes \mathcal{K}_2$ given by

$$V(|n_1\rangle \otimes |m_1\rangle) = \sum_j^{n_1 + m_1} C_j^{n_1, m_1} |j\rangle \otimes |n_1 + m_1 - j\rangle \tag{2.8}$$

$$C_j^{n_1, m_1} = \sum_{r=L}^{K} (-1)^{n_1 + j - r} \frac{\sqrt{n_1! m_1! j! (n_1 + m_1 - j)!}}{r!(n_1 - j)!(j - r)!(m_1 - j + r)!}$$

$$\times \sqrt{\eta^{m_1 - j + 2r}(1 - \eta)^{n_1 + j - 2r}} \tag{2.9}$$

and $K = \min\{n_1, j\}$, $L = \max\{m_1 - j, 0\}$. A quantum channel Λ^* with such a noise is called a noisy quantum channel.

The quantum entropy is formulated by von Neumann [3] such as

$$S(\rho) = -tr \rho \log \rho \tag{2.10}$$

for any input state $\rho \in \mathfrak{S}(\mathcal{H}_1)$.

Let us denote the von Neumann - Schatten decomposition [4,7] of ρ by

$$\rho = \sum_n \lambda_n E_n, \tag{2.11}$$

where λ_n is the eigenvalue of ρ and $E_n = |x_n> < x_n|$ is one dimensional orthogonal projection generated by the eigenvector $|x_n\rangle$ of λ_n. The von Neumann - Schatten decomposition is not unique generally. The compound state [4] expressing the correlation between ρ and $\Lambda^* \rho$ is defined by

$$\sigma_E = \sum_n \lambda_n E_n \otimes \Lambda^* E_n \tag{2.12}$$

for the von Neumann - Schatten decomposition $E = \{E_n\}$ of ρ and a quantum channel Λ^*.

The quantum mutual entropy introduced in [4] with respect to an input state ρ and a quantum channel Λ^* is given by

$$I(\rho; \Lambda^*) \equiv \sup\{S(\sigma_E, \sigma_0); E = \{E_n\}\} \tag{2.13}$$
$$= \sup\{\sum_n \lambda_n S(\Lambda^* E_n, \Lambda^* \rho); E = \{E_n\}\}, \tag{2.14}$$

where $\sigma_0 = \rho \otimes \Lambda^* \rho$ and $S(\sigma_E, \sigma_0)$ is the relative entropy [7] with respect to σ_E and σ_0 defined by

$$S(\sigma_E, \sigma_0) \equiv tr\sigma_E(\log \sigma_E - \log \sigma_0).$$

This mutual entropy satisfies the following fundamental inequality [4]:

$$0 \leq I(\rho; \Lambda^*) \leq \min\{S(\rho), S(\Lambda^* \rho)\}. \tag{2.15}$$

The above mutual entropy is one for a purely quantum channel and it contains other definitions of the mutual entropy for classical - quantum (c - q for short), q - c or c - c channels [6]. This quantum mutual entropy is generalrized to C*-systems [5].

The following proposition is useful to calculate the quantum mutual entropy numerically.

Proposition 2.1: For any state

$$\rho = \lambda|x\rangle\langle x| + (1 - \lambda)|y\rangle\langle y| \quad (\lambda \in [0, 1])$$

represenred by any nonorthogonal unit vectors $|x\rangle, |y\rangle \in \mathcal{H}$, the von Neumann - Schatten decompotion of ρ is uniquely written by

$$\rho = \|\rho\| |z_0^{x,y}\rangle \langle z_0^{x,y}| + (1 - \|\rho\|) |z_1^{x,y}\rangle \langle z_1^{x,y}|, \tag{2.16}$$

where

$$\|\rho\| = \frac{1 + \sqrt{1 - 4\lambda(1 - \lambda)(1 - |\langle x, \ y\rangle|^2)}}{2}$$
$$|z_0^{x,y}\rangle = a_{x,y} |x\rangle + b_{x,y} |y\rangle$$
$$|z_1^{x,y}\rangle = c_{x,y} |x\rangle + c_{x,y} |y\rangle,$$

$$|a_{x,y}|^2 = \frac{\tau_{x,y}^2}{\tau_{x,y}^2 + 2|\langle x, y\rangle|\tau_{x,y} + 1}$$

$$|b_{c,y}|^2 = \frac{1}{\tau_{x,y}^2 + 2|\langle x, y\rangle|\tau_{x,y} + 1}$$

$$\bar{a}_{x,y}b_{x,y} = a_{x,y}\bar{b}_{x,y} = \frac{\tau_{x,y}}{\tau_{x,y}^2 + 2|\langle x, y\rangle|\tau_{x,y} + 1}$$

$$\tau_{x,y} = \frac{-(1 - 2\lambda) + \sqrt{1 - 4\lambda(1 - \lambda)(1 - |\langle x, \ y\rangle|^2)}}{2(1 - \lambda)|\langle x, y\rangle|}$$

$$|c_{x,y}|^2 = \frac{t_{x,y}^2}{t_{x,y}^2 + 2|\langle x, y\rangle|t_{x,y} + 1}$$

$$|d_{x,y}|^2 = \frac{1}{t_{x,y}^2 + 2|\langle x, y \rangle| t_{x,y} + 1}$$

$$\bar{c}_{x,y} d_{x,y} = c_{x,y} \bar{d}_{x,y} = \frac{t_{x,y}}{t_{x,y}^2 + 2|\langle x, y \rangle| t_{x,y} + 1}$$

$$t_{x,y} = -\frac{1 + |\langle x, y \rangle| \tau_{x,y}}{\tau_{x,y} + |\langle x, y \rangle|}.$$

See the paper [11] for this proof.

3. CAPACITY OF QUANTUM CHANNELS

In this section, we briefly explain the quantum capacity studied in [8].

Let $\mathcal{H}_j^{(N)}$, $\mathbf{B}(\mathcal{H}_j^{(N)})$ and $\mathfrak{S}(\mathcal{H}_j^{(N)})$ be the N-fold tensor products of $\mathcal{H}_j$, $\mathbf{B}(\mathcal{H}_j)$ and $\mathfrak{S}(\mathcal{H}_j)$ given by

$$\mathcal{H}_j^{(N)} = \overset{N}{\underset{i=1}{\otimes}} \mathcal{H}_j, \ \mathbf{B}(\mathcal{H}_j^{(N)}) = \overset{N}{\underset{i=1}{\otimes}} \mathbf{B}(\mathcal{H}_j), \ \mathfrak{S}(\mathcal{H}_j^{(N)}) = \overset{N}{\underset{i=1}{\otimes}} \mathfrak{S}(\mathcal{H}_j) \quad (j = 1, 2).$$

The quantum channel Λ_N^* from $\mathfrak{S}(\mathcal{H}_1^{(N)})$ to $\mathfrak{S}(\mathcal{H}_2^{(N)})$ defined by

$$\Lambda_N^* = \Lambda^* \otimes \cdots \otimes \Lambda^* \tag{3.1}$$

is called a memoryless channel, where Λ^* is the quantum channel from $\mathfrak{S}(\mathcal{H}_1)$ to $\mathfrak{S}(\mathcal{H}_2)$. The quantum mutual entropy with respect to the input state $\rho^{(N)} \in \mathfrak{S}(\mathcal{H}_1^{(N)})$ and the channel Λ_N^* is decribed by

$$I(\rho^{(N)}; \ \Lambda_N^*) = \sup \left\{ \sum_j p_j^{(N)} S(\Lambda_N^* \rho_j^{(N)}, \Lambda_N^* \rho^{(N)}); \rho^{(N)} = \sum_j p_j^{(N)} \rho_j^{(N)} \right\}, \tag{3.2}$$

where the supremum is taken over all von Neumann - Schatten decompositions $\sum_j p_j^{(N)} \rho_j^{(N)}$ of $\rho^{(N)}$. The pair $((p_j^{(N)}), (\rho_j^{(N)}))$ of $(p_j^{(N)})$ and $(\rho_j^{(N)})$ is called a quantum code of order N if $(p_j^{(N)})$ is a priori probability vector and $(\rho_j^{(N)})$ is the orthogonal pure states in $\mathfrak{S}(\mathcal{H}_1^{(N)})$. Moreover $((p_j^{(N)}), (\rho_j^{(N)}))$ is called a pseudo-quantum code of order N if $(p_j^{(N)})$ is a priori probability vector and $(\rho_j^{(N)})$ is pure states in $\mathfrak{S}(\mathcal{H}_1^{(N)})$. We denote the set of all quantum codes (resp. pseudo-quantum codes) of order N by $\mathcal{C}_q^{(N)}$ (resp. $\mathcal{C}_{pq}^{(N)}$). The quantum mutual entropy with respect to the quantum codes (resp. pseudo-quantum codes) and the quantum channel Λ_N^* is defined by

$$I(((p_j^{(N)}), (\rho_j^{(N)})), \Lambda_N^*) = I(\rho^{(N)}; \ \Lambda_N^*) \tag{3.3}$$

where $\rho^{(N)} = \sum_j p_j^{(N)} \rho_j^{(N)}$. Based on the quantum mutual entropy, the quantum capacity and the pseudo quantum capacity for the quantum channel Λ_N^* are formulated as

$$C_q(\Lambda_N^*) = \sup \left\{ I(((p_j^{(N)}), (\rho_j^{(N)})), \Lambda_N^*); \ ((p_j^{(N)}), (\rho_j^{(N)})) \in \mathcal{C}_q^{(N)} \right\}, \tag{3.4}$$

$$C_{pq}(\Lambda_N^*) = \sup \left\{ I(((p_j^{(N)}), (\rho_j^{(N)})), \Lambda_N^*); \ ((p_j^{(N)}), (\rho_j^{(N)})) \in \mathcal{C}_{pq}^{(N)} \right\}. \tag{3.5}$$

From the above definitions, the inequality

$$C_q(\Lambda_N^*) \leq C_{pq}(\Lambda_N^*) \tag{3.6}$$

216

is held. Moreover the mean quantum capacity and the mean pseudo-quantum capacity per single use are given by

$$C_q^{(\infty)}(\Lambda^*) = \lim_{N \to \infty} \frac{1}{N} C_q(\Lambda_N^*) \tag{3.7}$$

$$C_{pq}^{(\infty)}(\Lambda^*) = \lim_{N \to \infty} \frac{1}{N} C_{pq}(\Lambda_N^*) \tag{3.8}$$

In order to estimate the quantum mutual entropy , the concept of divergence center is as follows:. Let $\{\rho_i : i \in I\}$ be a family of states and $R > 0$. The state ρ is called a divergence center for $\{\rho_i : i \in I\}$ with radius R if

$$S(\rho_i, \rho) \le R \qquad \text{for every } i \in I.$$

We obtained the following results in [8]. (1) Let $\Lambda^* : \mathfrak{S}(\mathcal{H}_1) \to \mathfrak{S}(\mathcal{H}_2)$ be a channel with finite dimensional $\mathcal{H}_2$. Then the pseudo quantum capacity $C_{pq}(\Lambda^*)$ equals to the divergence radius of the range of Λ^*. (2) The mean quantum capacity $C_q^{(\infty)}(\Lambda_0^*)$ and the mean pseudo-quantum capacity $C_{pq}^{(\infty)}(\Lambda_0^*)$ for the attenuation channel Λ_0^* are 0.

The capacity of a quantum channel Λ^* for a subset $\mathcal{S}$ of $\mathfrak{S}(\mathcal{H}_1)$ is defined by

$$C_q^{\mathcal{S}}(\Lambda^*) = \sup \{ I(\rho, \Lambda^*) : \ \rho \in \mathcal{S} \}. \tag{3.9}$$

We are interested in the capacity of a quantum channel subject to a certain energy constraint

$$C_q^{\mathcal{S}}(\Lambda^*)_e = \sup \{ I(\rho, \Lambda^*) : \ \rho \in \mathcal{S}, \ E(\rho) \le e \}, \tag{3.10}$$

where $E(\rho)$ is the averaged energy in ρ. The details of this section are discussed in [6,8].

4. CAPACITY OF NOISY QUANTUM CHANNEL

The exact value of the capacity for a physical channel is a very important to be found. In this section, we compute the exact capacity C_q for a noisy quantum channel Λ^* (2.6) under a certain energy constraint. Note that the pseudo-quantum capacity C_{pq} is difficult to compute.

Let $\mathcal{S}$ be the subset of $\mathfrak{S}(\mathcal{H}_1)$ given by

$$\mathcal{S} = \{ \rho = \lambda |0\rangle \langle 0| + (1 - \lambda) |\theta\rangle \langle \theta| ; \ \lambda \in [0, 1], \ \theta \in \mathbb{C} \},$$

where $|0\rangle \langle 0|$ is the vacuum state and $|\theta\rangle \langle \theta|$ is a coherent state on $\mathcal{H}_1$. From proposition 2.1, the von Neumann - Schatten decomposition of ρ is uniquely written as

$$\rho = \|\rho\| E_0^{0,\theta} + (1 - \|\rho\|) E_1^{0,\theta}, \tag{4.1}$$

where $E_j^{0,\theta} = \left| z_j^{0,\theta} \right\rangle \left\langle z_j^{0,\theta} \right|$ $(j = 0, 1)$. We assume that a noise state ξ of Λ^* is expressed as a chorerent state $\xi = |\gamma\rangle \langle \gamma|$. For the above input state $\rho \in \mathcal{S}$, the output state $\Lambda^* \rho$ is

$$\Lambda^*(\rho) = \lambda \left| \sqrt{1 - \eta \gamma} \right\rangle \left\langle \sqrt{1 - \eta \gamma} \right|$$
$$+ (1 - \lambda) \left| \sqrt{\eta}\theta + \sqrt{1 - \eta \gamma} \right\rangle \left\langle \sqrt{\eta}\theta + \sqrt{1 - \eta \gamma} \right|.$$

Let $\Lambda^* E_j^{0,\theta}$ be the decomposition denoted by

$$\Lambda^* E_j^{0,\theta} = \tilde{\lambda}_j \tilde{E}_{j0} + (1 - \tilde{\lambda}_j)\tilde{E}_{j1}, \tag{4.2}$$

where $\tilde{\lambda}_j$ $(j = 0, 1)$ are the constants such that

$$\tilde{\lambda}_0 = \frac{1}{2}(1 + \exp(-\frac{1}{2}(1 - \eta)|\theta|^2))$$
$$\times \frac{\tau_{0,\theta}^2 + 2\exp(-\frac{1}{2}|\theta_\eta|^2)\tau_{0,\theta} + 1}{\tau_{0,\theta}^2 + 2\exp(-\frac{1}{2}|\theta|^2)\tau_{0,\theta} + 1}$$

$$\tilde{\lambda}_1 = \frac{1}{2}(1 + \exp(-\frac{1}{2}(1 - \eta)|\theta|^2))$$
$$\times \frac{t_{0,\theta}^2 + 2\exp(-\frac{1}{2}|\theta_\eta|^2)t_{0,\theta} + 1}{t_{0,\theta}^2 + 2\exp(-\frac{1}{2}|\theta|^2)t_{0,\theta} + 1}.$$

When one dimemsional projection $\tilde{E}_{jk}$ is written as $\tilde{E}_{jk} = |\tilde{x}_{jk}\rangle\langle\tilde{x}_{jk}|$, the vectors $\tilde{x}_{jk}$ $(j, k = 0, 1)$ satisfy the following conditions:

$$\langle\tilde{x}_{00}, \tilde{x}_{01}\rangle = \frac{\tau^2 - 1}{\sqrt{(\tau^2 + 1)^2 - 4\exp(-|\theta_\eta|^2)\tau^2}} \neq 0,$$

$$\langle\tilde{x}_{10}, \tilde{x}_{11}\rangle = \frac{t^2 - 1}{\sqrt{(t^2 + 1)^2 - 4\exp(-|\theta_\eta|^2)t^2}} \neq 0.$$

From Proposition 2.1, the eigenvalues of $\Lambda^* E_j^{0,\theta}$ $(j = 0, 1)$ are

$$\tilde{\lambda}_{j0}^{\tilde{x}_{j0},\tilde{x}_{j1}} = \frac{1}{2}\left\{1 + \sqrt{1 - \tilde{\lambda}_j(1 - \tilde{\lambda}_j)(1 - |\langle\tilde{x}_{j0}, \tilde{x}_{j1}\rangle|^2)}\right\},$$

$$\tilde{\lambda}_{j1}^{\tilde{x}_{j0},\tilde{x}_{j1}} = \frac{1}{2}\left\{1 + \sqrt{1 - \tilde{\lambda}_j(1 - \tilde{\lambda}_j)(1 - |\langle\tilde{x}_{j0}, \tilde{x}_{j1}\rangle|^2)}\right\}.$$

The quantum mutual entropy (2.13) with respect to an input state $\rho \in \mathcal{S}$ and the noisy quantum channel Λ^* defined by (2.6) with the coherent noise ξ is determined by

$$I(\rho; \Lambda^*) = S(\Lambda^*\rho) - \|\rho\|S(\Lambda^* E_0^{0,\theta}) - (1 - \|\rho\|)S(\Lambda^* E_1^{0,\theta}) \tag{4.3}$$

where

$$S(\Lambda^*\rho) = -\sum_{j=0}^{1} \tilde{\lambda}_j^{\sqrt{1-\eta}\gamma, \sqrt{\eta}\theta + \sqrt{1-\eta}\gamma} \log \tilde{\lambda}_j^{\sqrt{1-\eta}\gamma, \sqrt{\eta}\theta + \sqrt{1-\eta}\gamma}$$

$$S(\Lambda^* E_j^{0,\theta}) = -\sum_{i=0}^{1} \tilde{\lambda}_{ji}^{\tilde{x}_{j0},\tilde{x}_{j1}} \log \tilde{\lambda}_{ji}^{\tilde{x}_{j0},\tilde{x}_{j1}}.$$

From the above results , we explicitly compute the quantum capacity

$$C_q^{(1)}(\Lambda^*)_e = \sup_{\lambda,\theta}\left\{I(\rho; \Lambda^*); |\theta|^2 \leq e\right\}, \tag{4.4}$$

$$C_q^{(2)}(\Lambda^*)_e = \sup_{\lambda,\theta}\left\{I(\rho; \Lambda^*); (1 - \lambda)|\theta|^2 \leq e\right\} \tag{4.5}$$

as shown below.

218

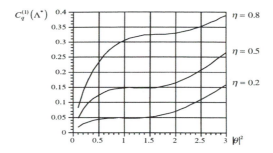

Figure 1. Quantum Capacity $C_q^{(1)}(\Lambda^*)$.

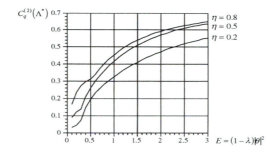

Figure 2. Quantum Capacity $C_q^{(2)}(\Lambda^*)$.

(1) For each $\eta \in \{0.2, 0.5, 0.8\}$, $\lambda \in [0, 1]$ and $|\theta|^2 \leq 3$, we have the quantum capacity of the noisy quantum channel Λ^* with the coherent noise ξ such as Fig.1:

(2) For each $\eta \in \{0.2, 0.5, 0.8\}$ and fix $E = (1 - \lambda)|\theta|^2 \leq 3$, we obtain the quantum capacity of the quantum mechanical channel Λ^* with the coherent noise ξ such as Fig.2:

Since the above quantum capacity is a quantity to measure the ability for information transmission of a quantum channel, it is important to investigate a logical gate for quantum computer. Fredkin - Toffoli - Milburn (FTM) gate is one of logical gates for quantum computer. This gate can be rigorously formulated as a quantum channel and the conservation of information through the FTM gate is shown by means of the quantum mutual entropy. These facts are presented in [10].

REFERENCES

[1] A. Fujiwara and H. Nagaoka, Capacity of memoryless quantum communication channels, Math. Eng. Tech. Rep. **94-22**, University of Tokyo,1994.

[2] A.S. Holevo, Capacity of a quantum communication channel, Problems Inform. Transmission, **15**, 247–253, 1979.

[3] von Neumann, *Die Mathematischen Grundlagen der Quantenmechanik*, Springer-Berlin, 1932.

[4] M. Ohya, On compound state and mutual information in quantum information theory, IEEE Trans. Information Theory, **29**, 770–777, 1983.

[5] M. Ohya, Some aspects of quantum information theory and their applications to irreversible processes, Rep. Math. Phys. **27**, 19–47, 1989.

[6] M. Ohya, Fundamentals of quantum mutual entropy and capacity, submitted.

[7] M. Ohya and D. Petz, *Quantum Entropy and Its Use*, Springer, 1993.

[8] M. Ohya, D. Petz and N. Watanabe, On capacities of quantum channels, to be published.

[9] M. Ohya and N. Watanabe, Construction and analysis of a mathematical model in quantum communication processes, Electronics and Communications in Japan, Part 1, **68**, No.2, 29-34 , 1985.

[10] M. Ohya and N. Watanabe, On mathematical treatment of Fredkin - Toffoli - Milburn gate, to appear.

[11] M. Ohya and N. Watanabe, SUT preprint.

[12] H.P. Yuen and M. Ozawa, Ultimate information carrying limit of quantum systems, Phys. Rev. Lett. **70**, pp. 363–366, 1993.

Part III.
Quantum Measurement Theory and Statistical Physics

ON COVARIANT INSTRUMENTS
IN QUANTUM MEASUREMENT THEORY

A. S. Holevo

Steklov Mathematical Institute,
Vavilova 42, 117966 Moscow, Russia
e-mail: HOLEVO@CLASS.MI.RAS.RU

A convenient representation for c.p. instruments on $B(\mathcal{H})$ is suggested, similar to the Stinespring-Kraus representation for c.p. maps, however involving possibly nonclosable unbounded operators. The structure of c.p. instruments, covariant with respect to one-dimensional rotations, describing angle (phase) measurements, is studied in detail.

1. Let $\mathcal{H}$ be a separable Hilbert space, describing observed quantum system. Consider a measurement process, which consists of the interaction of the system with the measurement apparatus, described by another Hilbert space $\mathcal{H}_0$, and subsequent measurement of certain observable in $\mathcal{H}_0$ with values in a measurable space $(\mathcal{X}, \mathcal{B})$. Let us denote by U the unitary operator in $\mathcal{H} \otimes \mathcal{H}_0$, describing the interaction, and by $E_0 : B \rightarrow E_0(B); B \in \mathcal{B}$ the spectral measure of the observable in $\mathcal{H}_0$, and let ψ, ψ_0 be, correspondingly, the vectors of initial states of the system and the apparatus. Then the measurement probability distribution can be written as

$$\mu_\psi(B) = \mathrm{Tr}U(S_\psi \otimes S_{\psi_0})U^*(I \otimes E_0(B)) = \mathrm{Tr}S_\psi \mathcal{M}(B)[I], \qquad (1.1)$$

where $S_\psi = |\psi)(\psi|$ and

$$\mathcal{M}(B)[X] = \mathrm{Tr}_{\mathcal{H}_0}(I \otimes S_{\psi_0})U^*(X \otimes E_0(B))U. \qquad (1.2)$$

Here $\mathcal{M}(B)$ is what is called *completely positive (c.p.) instrument with the value space* $(\mathcal{X}, \mathcal{B})$, that is a measure $B \rightarrow \mathcal{M}(B)[\cdot]$ on $(\mathcal{X}, \mathcal{B})$, whose values are bounded linear normal c.p. maps $X \rightarrow \mathcal{M}(B)[X]$ of the algebra $B(\mathcal{H})$ of all bounded operators in $\mathcal{H}$, such that for any state S and observable X, the scalar measure $B \rightarrow< S, \mathcal{M}(B)[X] >$ is σ-additive, and satisfying the normalization condition $\mathcal{M}(\mathcal{X})[I] = I$. This notion was studied by Ozawa [1], who introduced complete positivity into the definitions of Ludwig, and Davies and Lewis (see [2], [3]), and showed that *any* c.p. instrument can be obtained from a quantum measurement process as described above. Let us write (1.2) as

$$\mathcal{M}(B)[X] = V^*(X \otimes E_0(B))V \qquad (1.3)$$

with $V = U|\psi_0)$ being a linear isometry from $\mathcal{H}$ to $\mathcal{H} \otimes \mathcal{H}_0$. Given a c.p. instrument one can always find a representation (1.3), generalizing Stinespring representation for

Quantum Communication, Computing, and Measurement
Edited by Hirota *et al.*, Plenum Press, New York, 1997

a c.p. map, and from this one can restore (essentially non-unique) construction of the measurement process.

The importance of the concept of instrument lies in the fact that it gives a condensed linear description, in terms of the system alone, of the measurement statistics consisting of the probability distribution (1.1) and of *posterior states* of the system, i. e. the states $S_\psi(x)$ conditioned upon certain outcome x of the measurement, namely, for all ψ, B, X

$$(\psi|\mathcal{M}(B)[X]\psi) = \int_B \mathrm{Tr} S_\psi(x) X \, \mu_\psi(dx).$$

The purpose of this paper is to give further insight into the structure of c.p. instruments, by proving Radon-Nikodym type theorems giving densities of the instrument with respect to a scalar measure and allowing more explicit description of the measurement statistics.

Proposition 1*. *There exist a positive σ-finite measure μ on (X, B), dense domain $D \subset H$, and a countable family of functions $x \to A_k(x)$, defined for almost all x, such that $A_k(x)$ are linear operators from D to H, satisfying*

$$\int_X \sum_k \|A_k(x)\psi\|^2 \mu(dx) = \|\psi\|^2; \quad \psi \in D, \tag{1.4}$$

and

$$(\psi|\mathcal{M}(B)[X]\psi) = \int_B \sum_k (A_k(x)\psi|X A_k(x)\psi)\mu(dx); \quad \psi \in D. \tag{1.5}$$

Proof. According to von Neumann's spectral theorem, H_0 can be decomposed into the direct integral

$$H_0 = \int_X \oplus H(x)\mu(dx) \tag{1.6}$$

with respect to some positive σ-finite measure μ, diagonalizing the spectral measure E_0:

$$E_0(B)\phi = \int_B \oplus \phi(x)\mu(dx), \tag{1.7}$$

where $\phi(x) \in H(x)$ are the components of the vector $\phi \in H_0$ in the decomposition (1.6). In what follows we shall fix a measurable field of orthonormal bases $\{e_{k,x}\}$ in the direct integral (1.6) and denote $\phi_k(x) = (e_{k,x}|\phi(x))$, where the inner product is in $H(x)$ (note that $\phi_k(x)$ are defined μ-almost everywhere).

The tensor product $K = H \otimes H_0$ has the direct integral decomposition

$$H \otimes H_0 = \int_X \oplus (H \otimes H(x))\mu(dx).$$

Let $\psi \in H$. The decomposition of the vector $V\psi \in H \otimes H_0$ then reads

$$V\psi = \int_X \oplus \sum_k (V\psi)_k(x)e_{k,x}\mu(dx),$$

where $(V\psi)_k(x)$ are (equivalence classes of) μ-measurable functions with values in H satisfying

$$\int_X \sum_k \|(V\psi)_k(x)\psi\|^2 \mu(dx) = \|\psi\|^2; \quad \psi \in H, \tag{1.8}$$

since V is isometric. Since V is linear, we have for μ-almost all x

$$(V(\sum_j \lambda_j \psi_j))_k(x) = \sum_j \lambda_j (V\psi_j)_k(x), \tag{1.9}$$

---

*See [13] for related results.

where $\{\psi_j\} \subset \mathcal{H}$ is a fixed countable system of vectors, and λ_j are complex numbers, only finite number of which are non-zero.

Let us now fix an orthonormal basis $\{\psi_j\} \subset \mathcal{H}$ and let $\mathcal{D} = \lin\{\psi_j\}$ be its linear span. We define linear operators $A_k(x)$ on $\mathcal{D}$ by the relation

$$A_k(x)(\sum_j \lambda_j \psi_j) = \sum_j (V\psi_j)_k^0(x),$$

where $(V\psi_j)_k^0$ is a fixed representative of the equivalence class $(V\psi_j)_k$. Then by (1.9), for any fixed $\psi \in \mathcal{D}$ there is a subset $\mathcal{X}_\psi \subset \mathcal{X}$, such that $\mu(\mathcal{X} \setminus \mathcal{X}_\psi) = 0$ and

$$A_k(x)\psi = (V\psi)_k(x), \text{ for all } k, \text{ and all } x \in \mathcal{X}_\psi. \tag{1.10}$$

Combining (1.3), (1.7) and (1.10), we obtain (1.5). The normalization condition (1.4) follows from (1.7) and (1.10). □

The probability distribution of outcomes is

$$\mu_\psi(B) = (\psi|\mathcal{M}(B)[I]\psi) = \int_B \sum_k \|A_k(x)\psi\|^2 \mu(dx). \tag{1.11}$$

The posterior state corresponding to the outcome x is

$$S_\psi(x) = \frac{\sum_k |A_k(x)\psi)(A_k(x)\psi|}{\sum_k \|A_k(x)\psi\|^2}. \tag{1.12}$$

In the case where the multiplicity of E_0 is one, the range of k is singleton, and formulas (1.5), (1.11), (1.12) become

$$(\psi|\mathcal{M}(B)[X]\psi) = \int_B (A(x)\psi|XA(x)\psi)\mu(dx), \tag{1.13}$$

$$\mu_\psi(dx) = \|A(x)\psi\|^2 \mu(dx), \tag{1.14}$$

$$S_\psi(x) = \frac{|A(x)\psi)(A(x)\psi|}{\|A(x)\psi\|^2}, \tag{1.15}$$

where $A(x)$ is a family of operators from $\mathcal{D}$ to $\mathcal{H}$, satisfying

$$\int \|A(x)\psi\|^2 \mu(dx) = \|\psi\|^2, \quad \psi \in \mathcal{D}.$$

In this case pure initial state gives rize to pure posterior states, and the corresponding instrument may be called *pure* (see [4] for an information-theoretic characterization of pure instruments).

Note that if the measure μ is non-atomic, operators $A_k(x)$ in the representation (1.5) need not be bounded, nor even closable, as the following example shows.

Example 1. The idea of this example goes back to Gordon and Louisell [5] (see also [6]). Let $\mathcal{H} = L^2(\mathbf{R})$ and Q be the position observable in $\mathcal{H}$ given by the operator of multiplication by the independent variable $x \in \mathbf{R}$. Let $\Psi_x; x \in \mathbf{R}$ be a measurable family of unit vectors in $\mathcal{H}$. We take $\mathcal{D} = C_0(\mathbf{R})$ (subspace of continuous functions with compact support), and define

$$A(x)\psi = \Psi_x \cdot \psi(x), \quad \psi \in \mathcal{D}. \tag{1.16}$$

In Dirac's notations $A(x) = |\Psi_x)(x|$, where $|x)$ is the generalized eigenvector of Q, $Q|x) = x|x)$. The generalized eigenvector $|x)$ is an antilinear unbounded nonclosable form satisfying $\psi(x) = (x|\psi)$ for $\psi \in \mathcal{D}$. The relation (1.13) with $\mu(dx) = dx$ defines pure c.p. instrument, whose probability distribution is

$$\mu_\psi(dx) = \|\psi(x)\|^2 dx$$

and the posterior states are

$$S_x = |\Psi_x)(\Psi_x|.$$

This instrument thus corresponds to precise measurement of the position, accompanied with the preparation of the state Ψ_x, depending on the outcome x of the measurement.

2. Let G be a locally compact second countable group, and $g \to V_g$ a continuous unitary representation of G in $\mathcal{H}$, leaving invariant the algebra $B(\mathcal{H})$. An instrument $\mathcal{M}$ with the value space G is called *covariant* if

$$V_g \mathcal{M}(B)[V_g^* X V_g] V_g^* = \mathcal{M}(gB)[X] \tag{2.1}$$

for all $g \in G, X \in \mathcal{A}, B \in \mathcal{B}$, where $\mathcal{B}$ is the σ-algebra of Borel subsets of G. The definition (in a slightly more general form, allowing a transitive G-space as the value space of the instrument) was given by Davies [3], who studied covariant (not necessarily c.p.) instruments in the case of compact G and dim $\mathcal{H} < \infty$.

The importance of the condition of covariance lies in the fact that it provides a correspondence principle between classical kinematical variables and the quantum instruments. Let $g \in G$ be such a variable, then the transformation $x \to gx$, where $x \in G$, describes a motion in a classical space G. The representation V_g gives the corresponding transformation of quantum states $\psi \to \psi_g = V_g \psi$. Equation (2.1) is equivalent to the following properties of the measurement probability distribution and the posterior states:

$$\mu_{\psi_g}(B) = \mu_\psi(g^{-1}B),$$
$$S_{\psi_g}(x) = V_g S_\psi(g^{-1}x) V_g^*,$$

expressing the principle of correspondence.

As shown in [7], for covariant c.p. instrument one can find the representation (1.3) such that there is a unitary representation $g \to D_g$ in $\mathcal{H}_0$ satisfying

$$(V_g \otimes D_g)V = VV_g, \tag{2.2}$$

$$D_g E_0(B) D_g^* = E_0(g^{-1}B). \tag{2.3}$$

The last equation means that (D, E_0) is an *imprimitivity system* in $\mathcal{H}_0$ (see e.g. [8] - [10]). By the Mackey imprimitivity theorem, (D, E_0) is unitarily equivalent to the special system in the space $L_h^2(G)$ of square integrable functions $f(x); x \in G$, with values in a separable Hilbert space h, defined as

$$D_g f(x) = f(g^{-1}x), \quad E_0(B)f(x) = 1_B(x)f(x),$$

where 1_B is the indicator of a set $B \in \mathcal{B}$. Let us fix an orthonormal basis $\{e_k\}$ in h. Then $\mathcal{K} = \mathcal{H} \otimes L_h^2(G)$ is represented as the space of functions $\psi_k(x); k = 1, ...,$ dim $h; x \in G$, with values in $\mathcal{H}$, satisfying

$$\int_G \sum_k \|\psi_k(x)\|^2 d_l x < \infty,$$

where $d_l x$ is the left Haar measure on G. The *intertwining equation* (2.2) is then equivalent to

$$V_g(VV_g^* \psi)_k(x) = (V\psi)_k(gx) \tag{2.4}$$

for all g and almost all $x \in G$.

For "nice" groups G we were able to show that there exist a dense domain $\mathcal{D} \subset \mathcal{H}$, invariant under the representation, and such that the functions $x \to (V\psi)_k(x)$ are continuous for $\psi \in \mathcal{D}$, and therefore have unambiguously defined value for every $x \in G$. Then there is a sequence of linear operators A_k from $\mathcal{D}$ to $\mathcal{H}$, such that

$$A_k\psi = (V\psi)_k(e), \quad \psi \in \mathcal{D},$$

where e is the neutral element of G, and the equation (2.4) has the unique solution

$$(V\psi)_k(g) = V_g A_k V_g^* \psi.$$

If this is so, we have the representation of the type (1.5) with explicitly covariant $A_k(x) = V_x A_k V_x^*$, where $\mu(dx)$ is the Haar measure on G. The "nice" groups include Abelian locally compact groups, in particular, one-dimensional rotations and translations [12].

In what follows we give the proof for a particularly important and simple case, where G is the one-dimensional rotation group T .

3. In this Section we find the general form of c.p. instrument, covariant with respect to one-dimensional rotations. Let $G = [0, 2\pi)$ with the operation of addition modulo 2π, denoted as $\dotplus$, and let $\theta \to V_\theta$; $\theta \in [0, 2\pi)$, be a continuous unitary representation of G in $\mathcal{H}$. The intertwining equation (2.4) reads

$$V_\theta(V V_\theta^* \psi)_k(\phi) = (V\psi)_k(\phi \dotplus \theta); \quad \theta \in [0, 2\pi). \tag{3.1}$$

By Stone's theorem, $V_\theta = \exp(-i\theta L)$, where L is self-adjoint operator with purely point spectrum $\Lambda \subset \hat{G} = Z = \{..., -1, 0, 1, ...\}$. To simplify notations we assume that the multiplicity of the spectrum is one (this restriction can be easily relaxed). Then there is an orthonormal basis $\{|l\rangle; l \in \Lambda\}$ in $\mathcal{H}$, consisting of eigenvectors of L:

$$L|l\rangle = l|l\rangle; \quad l \in \Lambda.$$

Proposition 2. Let $\mathcal{D} = \text{lin}\{|l\rangle; l \in \Lambda\}$. Arbitrary c.p. instrument, covariant with respect to the representation $\theta \to V_\theta$, has the form

$$(\psi|\mathcal{M}(d\theta)[X]\psi) = \sum_k (A_k(\theta)\psi|X A_k(\theta)\psi)\frac{d\theta}{2\pi}; \quad \psi \in \mathcal{D}, \tag{3.2}$$

where $A_k(\theta) = V_\theta A_k V_\theta^*$ and A_k are linear operators from $\mathcal{D}$ to $\mathcal{H}$, satisfying

$$\sum_k \||A_k|l\rangle\|^2 = 1; \quad l \in \Lambda. \tag{3.3}$$

Proof. Apparently $\mathcal{D}$ is invariant under V_θ. Consider the function

$$c_{m,l,k}(\theta) = (m|(V|l\rangle)_k(\theta)) \tag{3.4}$$

The equation (3.1) implies

$$c_{m,l,k}(\phi \dotplus \theta) = e^{i\theta(l-m)}c_{m,l,k}(\phi) \tag{3.5}$$

for all $\theta \in [0, 2\pi)$ and almost all ϕ. The normalization condition (1.8) with $\mu(d\theta) = \frac{d\theta}{2\pi}$ implies

$$\int_0^{2\pi} \sum_k \sum_m |c_{m,l,k}(\theta)|^2 \frac{d\theta}{2\pi} = 1; \quad l \in \Lambda. \tag{3.6}$$

Denoting
$$c^\epsilon_{m,l,k}(\theta) = \epsilon^{-1} \int_0^\epsilon c_{m,l,k}(\phi \dot{+} \theta) d\phi,$$

we have that $c^\epsilon_{m,l,k}(\theta)$ is continuous for every $\epsilon > 0$. By integrating equation (3.5) we see that
$$c^\epsilon_{m,l,k}(\theta) = e^{i\theta(l-m)} c^\epsilon_{m,l,k}(0).$$

Since $c^\epsilon_{m,l,k}(\theta)$ converges to $c_{m,l,k}(\theta)$ in the mean as $\epsilon \to 0$, we have
$$|c^\epsilon_{m,l,k}(0) - c^{\epsilon'}_{m,l,k}(0)| \le \int_0^{2\pi} |c^\epsilon_{m,l,k}(\theta) - c^{\epsilon'}_{m,l,k}(\theta)| \frac{d\theta}{2\pi} \to 0$$

as $\epsilon, \epsilon' \to 0$. Thus there exist $c_{m,l,k} = \lim_{\epsilon \to 0} c^\epsilon_{m,l,k}(0)$. Therefore $c^\epsilon_{m,l,k}(\theta)$ converges pointwise to $e^{i(l-m)\theta} c_{m,l,k}$ and hence
$$c_{m,l,k}(\theta) = e^{i(l-m)\theta} c_{m,l,k}. \tag{3.7}$$

From (3.6)
$$\sum_k \sum_m |c_{m,l,k}|^2 = 1, \quad l \in \Lambda.$$

Defining
$$\psi_{l,k} = \sum_{m \in \Lambda} c_{m,l,k} |m\rangle,$$

we have
$$\sum_k \|\psi_{l,k}\|^2 = 1, \quad l \in \Lambda. \tag{3.8}$$

The operators
$$A_k = \sum_{l \in \Lambda} |\psi_{l,k})(l| \tag{3.9}$$

are then defined on $\mathcal{D}$ and satisfy (3.3). Moreover for $\psi \in \mathcal{D}$
$$A_k(\theta)\psi = V_\theta A_k V_\theta^* \psi = \sum_{m,l \in \Lambda} c_{m,l,k}(\theta) |m\rangle(l|\psi) = (V\psi)_k(\theta)$$

by (3.4). This proves (3.2). Note that the functions $A_k(\theta)\psi$ are continuous in θ for $\psi \in \mathcal{D}$.$\square$

The probability distribution of the instrument (3.2)
$$\mu_\psi(d\theta) = \sum_k \|A_k V_\theta \psi\|^2 \frac{d\theta}{2\pi}.$$

Let us look for the instruments minimizing the angular uncertainty [11]
$$\Delta_\psi(n) = n^{-2} \left[|\hat{\mu}_\psi(n)|^{-2} - 1 \right],$$

where
$$\hat{\mu}_\psi(n) = \int_0^{2\pi} e^{i\theta n} \mu_\psi(d\theta) = \sum_l \sum_k (\psi|l)(l+n|\psi)(\psi_{l,k}|\psi_{l+n,k}).$$

Assuming $(l|\psi) \ge 0$, which always can be achieved via a gauge transformation choosing appropriate phase factors for elements of the basis $|l\rangle$, the maximum under the condition (3.8) is attained if $\psi_{l,k} \equiv \Psi_k$, whence
$$A_k(\theta) = \sqrt{2\pi} V_\theta |\Psi_k)(\theta|,$$

where

$$|\theta) = \frac{1}{\sqrt{2\pi}} \sum_{l \in \Lambda} e^{-i\theta l} |l).$$

This is a kind of instrument considered in Example 1. Its probability distribution is

$$\mu_\psi(d\theta) = \left| \sum_{l \in \Lambda} e^{i\theta l} (l|\psi) \right|^2 \frac{d\theta}{2\pi} = |(\theta|\psi)|^2 d\theta = \mathrm{Tr} S_\psi M(d\theta),$$

where $M(d\theta) = |\theta)(\theta| d\theta$ is a positive operator valued measure (p.o.m.) representing canonical angle observable [11]. We have

$$(\theta|\theta') = \frac{1}{2\pi} \sum_{l \in \Lambda} e^{il(\theta-\theta')},$$

therefore this p.o.m. is usual spectral measure only if $\Lambda = \mathbb{Z}$, when this is a periodic delta-function.

We now develop another useful representation for the operators $A_k(\theta)$. For any $m \in \mathbb{Z}$ and $l \in \Lambda$ we define

$$a_{m,k}(l) = \begin{cases} (l - m|\psi_{l,k}), & \text{if } l - m \in \Lambda, \\ 0 & \text{otherwise.} \end{cases} \tag{3.10}$$

Then $\psi_{l,k} = \sum_m a_{m,k}(l)|l - m)$. Relation (3.8) implies

$$\sum_k \sum_m \|a_{m,k}(l)\|^2 = 1, \quad l \in \Lambda. \tag{3.11}$$

For any $m \in \mathbb{Z}$ we define the partial isometry

$$P_m = \int_0^{2\pi} e^{-i\theta m} M(d\theta) = \sum_{l:l \in \Lambda, l-m \in \Lambda} |l - m)(l|, \tag{3.12}$$

satisfying generalized canonical commutation relation

$$V_\theta P_m = e^{i\theta m} P_m V_\theta.$$

Then $\psi_{l,k} = \sum_m a_{m,k}(l)P_m|l)$ and

$$A_k(\theta) = \sum_m e^{i\theta m} P_m a_{m,k}(L), \tag{3.13}$$

where

$$a_{m,k}(L) = \sum_{l \in \Lambda} a_{m,k}(l)|l)(l|$$

is essentially normal operator on the domain $\mathcal{D}$. The relation (3.13) gives the desired alternative form of the operators $A_k(\theta)$.

Example 2. Assume $\Lambda = \mathbb{Z}$ (this is the case for measurements of angle of rotation with infinite spin, neglecting inessential complications due to possible degeneracy of spectrum). In this case isometries (3.12) form the unitary group

$$P_m = U^m, \quad m \in \mathbb{Z}, \tag{3.14}$$

where $U = \sum_l |l - 1)(l|$. By Stone's theorem,

$$U = \exp(-i\Theta), \tag{3.15}$$

229

where Θ is the self-adjoint operator

$$\Theta = \int_0^{2\pi} \theta E(d\theta), \tag{3.16}$$

with the spectral measure E, defined formally as

$$E(d\theta) = |\theta)(\theta|d\theta, \tag{3.17}$$

$|\theta); \theta \in [0, 2\pi)$, being the generalized eigenvectors of Θ, satisfying

$$(\theta|l) = \frac{1}{\sqrt{2\pi}} e^{i\theta l} \tag{3.18}$$

for all $l \in Z$. The functions $A_k(\theta)$ in the representation (3.2) of the covariant instrument take the form

$$A_k(\theta) = \sum_m e^{i\theta m} U^m a_{m,k}(L) = \sum_m e^{i(\theta - \Theta)m} a_{m,k}(L). \tag{3.19}$$

Let us consider particular case where $a_{m,k}(l)$ *do not depend on l:*

$$a_{m,k}(l) = a_{m,k}. \tag{3.20}$$

Then

$$A_k(\theta) = \tilde{a}_k(\theta - \Theta), \tag{3.21}$$

where

$$\tilde{a}_k(\theta) = \sum_m e^{i\theta m} a_{m,k} \tag{3.22}$$

are the functions, satisfying

$$\int_0^{2\pi} \sum_k |\tilde{a}_k(\theta)|^2 \frac{d\theta}{2\pi} = 1. \tag{3.23}$$

This structure of $A_k(\theta)$ is characteristic for approximate measurement of Θ, admitting von Neumann's type of realization described below (see [3], [6] for the case $\theta \in R$). Let $\mathcal{H}_0$ be a copy of the Hilbert space $\mathcal{H}$ spanned by the basis $\{|l)_0; l = 0, 1, ...\}$. In $\mathcal{H}_0$ we can define the operator L_0 and the spectral measure $E_0(d\theta) = |\theta)_0 \,_0(\theta|d\theta$ in the way similar to L and $E(d\theta)$. The space $\mathcal{H}_0$ will describe the measurement apparatus, the initial state of which is

$$S_0 = \sum_k |a_k)_0 \,_0(a_k|, \tag{3.24}$$

where

$$|a_k)_0 = \sum_m a_{m,k}|m)_0. \tag{3.25}$$

Interaction between the system and the apparatus is given by the unitary operator

$$\mathcal{U} = \exp(-i\Theta \otimes L_0) = \sum_m U^m \otimes |m)_0 \,_0(m|, \tag{3.26}$$

and the measured observable of the apparatus is

$$\Theta_0 = \int_0^{2\pi} \theta E(d\theta).$$

From (3.19), (3.18), (3.25) and (3.26) it follows that

$$A_k(\theta) = {}_0(\theta|\mathcal{U}|a_k)_0, \tag{3.27}$$

hence the described measurement process is a realization of the covariant instrument $\mathcal{M}(d\theta)$:

$$\sum_k (A_k(\theta)\psi|XA_k(\theta)\psi)\frac{d\theta}{2\pi} =$$

$$\sum_k (\psi| \otimes {}_0(a_k|\mathcal{U}^*(X \otimes E_0(d\theta))\mathcal{U}|a_k)_0 \otimes |\psi); \psi \in \mathcal{D}. \tag{3.28}$$

If we try to apply similar argument to measurement of phase of a harmonic oscillator, where $L = -N$ (N is the number operator) and $\Lambda = \{0, -1, ...\}$ we find that ansatz (3.20) is compatible with the condition $a_{m,k}(l) = 0$ for $l - m > 0$ only if $a_{m,k} = 0$ for $m < 0$. Assuming this, we can repeat the above construction with isometric (but non-unitary) U and p.o.m. $M_0(d\theta)$ which is not a spectral measure. If the spectrum Λ of L is bounded (e. g. in the case of measurement of angle of rotation for a system with finite spin), the ansatz (3.20) is not compatible with the requirement $a_{m,k}(l) = 0$ for $l - m \notin \Lambda$, and the construction of Example 2 cannot be directly transferred to this case.

ACKNOWLEDGEMENTS

The author is grateful to Prof. O. Hirota (Tamagawa University), Prof. M. Ozawa (Nagoya University) and Prof. L. Lanz (University of Milan) for their hospitality and stimulating discussions.

REFERENCES

[1] M. Ozawa, Quantum measuring processes of continuous observables, J. Math. Phys. **25**, 79-89 (1984).

[2] Foundations of Quantum Mechanics and Ordered Linear Spaces (eds. A. Hartkämper, H. Neumann), Lect. Notes Phys. **29** (Springer- Verlag, Berlin-Heidelberg- NY, 1974).

[3] E. B. Davies, Quantum Theory of Open Systems (Academic Press, London, 1976).

[4] M. Ozawa, On information gain by quantum measurements of continuous observables, J. Math. Phys. **27**, 759- 763 (1986).

[5] J.-P. Gordon, W. Louisell, in Physics of Quantum Electronics, p. 833-840 (eds. P.L.Kelley, B.Lax, P.E.Tannenwald, McGraw-Hill, NY, 1966).

[6] M. Ozawa, Realization of measurement and the standard quantum limit, in Squeezed and Nonclassical Light, p.263-286 (eds. P. Tombesi, E. R. Pike, Plenum Press, NY, 1989).

[7] L. V. Denisov, On the Stinespring- type theorem for covariant instruments in noncommutative probability theory, Preprint N 20, Steklov Mathematical Institute (1990).

[8] A. S. Holevo, Covariant measurements and imprimitivity systems, Lect. Notes Math. **1396**, 229- 255 (1989).

[9] A. S. Holevo, Generalized imprimitivity systems for Abelian groups, Soviet Math. (Iz. VUZ), **27**, (1983).

[10] A. S. Holevo, On generalization of canonical quantization, Math. USSR Izvestiya **28**, 175- 188 (1987).

[11] A. S. Holevo, Probabilistic and Statistical Aspects of Quantum Theory (North Holland, Amsterdam, 1982).

[12] A. S. Holevo, On covariant instruments in quantum measurement theory. Preprint. University of Milan. October 1995.

[13] M. Ozawa, Mathematical characterization of measurement statistics, in: Quantum Communication and Measurement, 109-117, (eds. V. P. Belavkin, O. Hirota and R. L. Hudson, Plenum Press, NY-London, 1995).

QUANTUM STATE REDUCTION
AND THE QUANTUM BAYES PRINCIPLE

Masanao Ozawa

School of Informatics and Sciences,
Nagoya University, Nagoya 464-01, Japan

This paper gives new foundations of quantum state reduction without appealing to the projection postulate for the probe measurement. For this purpose, the quantum Bayes principle is formulated as the most fundamental principle for determining the state of a quantum system, and the joint probability distribution for the outcomes of local successive measurements on a noninteracting entangled system is derived without assuming the projection postulate.

1. INTRODUCTION

In the discussion of new devices of measurement such as quantum nondemolition measurements and related proposals in the last two decades, the problem of the mathematical characterization of all the possible quantum measurements allowed in the standard formulation of quantum mechanics turned out to be of considerable potential importance in engineering and precision measurement experiments. When a new device of measurement is proposed, it is necessary, in general, to specify how the apparatus is prepared, how it interacts with the object, and how the outcome is obtained from it; these specifications will be called a model of measurement. On the other hand, a quantum measurement is specified from a statistical point of view by the outcome probability distribution and the state reduction, i.e., the state change from the state before measurement to the state after measurement conditional upon the outcome. If two measurements have the same outcome probability distribution and the same state reduction, they are statistically equivalent.

The conventional derivation of the state reduction from a given model of measurement is to compute the state of the object-apparatus composite system just after the measuring interaction and to apply the projection postulate to the subsequent measurement of the probe observable. This prescription is, however, not only controversial from the interpretational point of view but also even physically inconsistent. Some evidences of physical inconsistency can be pointed out as follows: (1) In some measuring apparatuses, the instrument for probe measurement such as a photon counter does not operate just as described by the projection postulate [IUO90]. (2) When the probe observable has continuous spectrum, the projection postulate to be applied cannot be formulated properly in the standard formulation of quantum mechanics [Oza84]. (3) State reduction should determine the state of the measured system at the instant just after the measuring interaction and just before the probe measurement, and hence the

Quantum Communication, Computing, and Measurement
Edited by Hirota *et al.*, Plenum Press, New York, 1997

application of the projection postulate to the probe measurement is irrelevant to the state reduction [Oza89b, Oza95b].

A mathematically rigorous and physically consistent derivation of the state reduction from any model of measurement without applying the projection postulate to the probe measurement has been established in [Oza83, Oza84, Oza85a]. Based on this derivation, the problem of the mathematical characterization of all the possible quantum measurements was solved as follows [Oza83, Oza84]: A measurement, with the outcome distribution $P(dx|\rho)$ and the state reduction $\rho \mapsto \rho_x$, is realizable in the standard formulation of quantum mechanics if and only if its statistics are representable by a normalized completely positive (CP) map valued measure $\mathbf{X}$ in such a way that $\mathbf{X}(dx)\rho = \rho_x P(dx|\rho)$, where the CP maps $\mathbf{X}(\Delta)$ are defined on the space of trace class operators for all Borel subsets Δ of the space of possible outcomes. The statistical equivalence classes of measurements are thus characterized as the normalized CP map valued measures.

In this paper, I will discuss further the foundations of quantum state reduction. The quantum Bayes principle will be formulated as the most fundamental principle for determining the state of a quantum system. The joint probability distribution will be also derived for the outcomes of local successive measurements on a noninteracting entangled system without assuming the projection postulate. This joint probability distribution and the quantum Bayes principle will naturally lead to the state reduction for an arbitrary model of measurement.

For simplicity we will be confined to measurements of *discrete observables*, but it will be easy for the reader to generalize the argument to continuous observables and to join the argument to the general theory developed in such papers as [Oza84, Oza85a, Oza85b, Oza86, Oza89a, Oza91, Oza93, Oza95a].

2. QUANTUM BAYES PRINCIPLE

Let X, Y be two (discrete) random variables. Suppose that we know the joint probability distribution $\Pr\{X = x, Y = y\}$. Then, the prior distribution of X is defined as the marginal distribution of X, i.e.,

$$\Pr\{X = x\} = \sum_y \Pr\{X = x, Y = y\}. \tag{1}$$

If one measures Y, the *information* $Y = y$ changes the probability distribution of X for any outcome y. The posterior distribution of X is defined as the conditional probability distribution of X given $Y = y$, i.e.,

$$\Pr\{X = x|Y = y\} = \frac{\Pr\{X = x, Y = y\}}{\sum_x \Pr\{X = x, Y = y\}}. \tag{2}$$

This method of changing the probability distribution from the prior distribution to the posterior distribution is called as the Bayes principle. The Bayes principle is one of the most fundamental principle in the statistical inference.

In quantum mechanics, the notion of probability distribution is related to the notion of state. Roughly speaking, "the state of the system" is equivalent to "the probability distributions of all the observables of the system". Thus the Bayes principle yields the state change of a quantum system if the probability distributions of all the observables of the system has changed by the Bayes principle. We formulate this principle of state changes as follows:

The Quantum Bayes Principle: If an information changes the probability distributions of *all* the observables of a quantum system according to the Bayes principle, then the information changes the *state* of the system according to the change of the probability distributions.

3. QUANTUM RULES

By the quantum rules we mean the following three basic principles in nonrelativistic quantum mechanics.

1. *Schrödinger Equation*: The time evolution of the system is given by

$$\psi \mapsto e^{-iH\tau/\hbar}\psi,$$

   where H is the Hamiltonian of the system.

2. *Statistical Formula*: The probability distribution of the outcome of the measurement of an observable A in the state ψ is given by

$$\Pr\{A = a\} = \|E^A(a)\psi\|^2$$

   where $E^A(a)$ denotes the projection operator with the range $\{\psi \in \mathcal{H}|\ A\psi = a\psi\}$— if a is an eigenvalue of A, it is the spectral projection corresponding to a; otherwise $E^A(a) = 0$.

3. *Projection Postulate* [Lud51]: The state change caused by the measurement of an observable A with the outcome a is given by

$$\psi \mapsto \frac{E^A(a)\psi}{\|E^A(a)\psi\|}.$$

From the above quantum rules, we can deduce

4. *Joint Probability Distributions of Successive Measurements* [Wig63]: If any sequence of observables $A_1, \ldots, A_n$ in a system originally in the state ψ are measured at the times $0 \le t_1 < \cdots < t_n$, then the joint probability distribution of the outcomes is given by

$$
\begin{aligned}
\Pr\{A_1(t_1) &= a_1, \ldots, A_n(t_n) = a_n\} \\
&= \|E^{A_n}(a_n)e^{-iH(t_n - t_{n-1})/\hbar} \cdots E^{A_1}(a_1)e^{-iHt_1/\hbar}\psi\|^2.
\end{aligned}
$$

By rule 4 with $0 = t_1 < \cdots < t_n \approx 0$, we obtain

5. *Simultaneous Measurability of Commuting Observables*: Mutually commuting observables $A_1, \ldots, A_n$ are simultaneously measurable. The joint probability distribution of the outcomes in the state ψ is given by

$$\Pr\{A_1 = a_1, \ldots, A_n = a_n\} = \|E^{A_1}(a_1) \cdots E^{A_n}(a_n)\psi\|^2.$$

4. DIFFICULTIES IN THE PROJECTION POSTULATE

As shown above, the projection postulate plays one of the most fundamental roles in foundations of quantum mechanics. The following difficulties in this postulate, however, have been pointed out among others:

1. There are measurements of an observable A which does not satisfy the projection postulate.

2. If A has a continuous spectrum, we have no projection postulate for the measurement of A [Oza84, Oza85a].

In order to illustrate the measurement of an observable which does not satisfy the projection postulate, consider a model of measurement in which the object interacts with the apparatus for a finite time interval. Let $A = \sum_n a_n |\phi_n\rangle\langle\phi_n|$ be the observable to be measured and $B = \sum_m b_m |\xi_m\rangle\langle\xi_m|$ the probe observable in the apparatus. Let ξ be the apparatus initial state and U the unitary evolution of the object-apparatus composite system under measuring interaction. The measuring interaction transduces the observable A to the probe observable B and the outcome of the measurement is obtained by amplifying B after the interaction, in the subsequent stage of the apparatus, to the directly sensible extent. Then we have:

1. The measurement *with* the projection postulate is described by

$$U : \phi_n \otimes \xi \mapsto \phi_n \otimes \xi_n.$$

2. The measurement *without* the projection postulate is described by

$$U : \phi_n \otimes \xi \mapsto \phi'_n \otimes \xi_n$$

where $\{\phi'_n\}$ is an *arbitrary* family of states.

By linearity, the unitary U in 2 satisfies

$$U : \left(\sum_n c_n \phi_n \right) \otimes \xi \mapsto \sum_n c_n \phi'_n \otimes \xi_n.$$

Hence, the outcome probability distribution of the measurement with process 2, which is obtained by the probability distribution of the probe observable, satisfies, in fact, the statistical formula for the observable A.

A typical example of measurement without the projection postulate is the photon counting. In this case, the measured observable is the number operator $A = \hat{n} = \sum_n n |n\rangle\langle n|$ and the time evolution of the composite system can be described by

$$U : |n\rangle \otimes \xi \mapsto |0\rangle \otimes \xi_n,$$

in the idealized model—for a more detailed model, see [IUO90].

5. LOCAL MEASUREMENT THEOREM

Let $\mathbf{S}_1$ be a quantum system with the free Hamiltonian H_1 and the Hilbert space $\mathcal{H}_1$ and let $\mathbf{S}_2$ a system with the free Hamiltonian H_2 and the Hilbert space $\mathcal{H}_2$. Let A be an observable of the system $\mathbf{S}_1$ and B an observable of the system $\mathbf{S}_2$. Suppose that the composite system $\mathbf{S}_{12} = \mathbf{S}_1 + \mathbf{S}_2$ is initially in the state (density operator) $\rho(0) = \rho$. Suppose that at the time t_1 the observable A is measured by an apparatus $\mathbf{A}$, at the time t_2 $(0 < t_1 < t_2)$ the observable B is measured by any apparatus measuring B, and that there is no interaction between $\mathbf{S}_1$ and $\mathbf{S}_2$—namely, the system $\mathbf{S}_{12}$ is a noninteracting entangled system. Denote the joint probability distribution of the outcomes of the A-measurement and the B-measurement by

$$\Pr\{A(t_1) = a, B(t_2) = b\|\rho\}.$$

According to rule 4, if the A-measurement satisfies the projection postulate, the joint probability distribution is given by

$$\Pr\{A(t_1) = a, B(t_2) = b\|\rho\} = \mathrm{Tr}\left[\left(e^{iH_1t_1/\hbar}E^A(a)e^{-iH_1t_1/\hbar} \otimes e^{iH_2t_2/\hbar}E^B(b)e^{-iH_2t_2/\hbar}\right)\rho\right].$$
(3)

In what follows we shall derive the above formula *without* assuming the projection postulate.

We note that this joint probability distribution should be affine in the state ρ. To show this, suppose that the state ρ is the mixture of states ρ_1 and ρ_2

$$\rho = \alpha\rho_1 + (1 - \alpha)\rho_2$$
(4)

where $0 < \alpha < 1$. This means that the measured system $\mathbf{S}_{12}$ is a random sample from the ensemble with the density operator ρ_1 with probability α and from the ensemble with the density operator ρ_2 with probability $1 - \alpha$. Hence we have

$$\begin{aligned}&\Pr\{A(t_1) = a, B(t_2) = b\|\rho\} \\ &= \alpha\Pr\{A(t_1) = a, B(t_2) = b\|\rho_1\} + (1 - \alpha)\Pr\{A(t_1) = a, B(t_2) = b\|\rho_2\}.\end{aligned}$$
(5)

Next, we introduce an important condition for the measuring apparatus which leads to the desired formula (3). We say that the measuring apparatus $\mathbf{A}$ is *local* at the system $\mathbf{S}_1$ if the measuring interaction occurs only in the apparatus and the system $\mathbf{S}_1$, or precisely, if the operator representing the measuring interaction commutes with every observable of $\mathbf{S}_2$. If this is the case, the total Hamiltonian of the composite system $\mathbf{A} + \mathbf{S}_1 + \mathbf{S}_2$ during the measuring interaction is represented by

$$H_{tot} = H_{\mathbf{A}} \otimes 1 \otimes 1 + 1 \otimes H_1 \otimes 1 + 1 \otimes 1 \otimes H_2 + KH_{int} \otimes 1$$
(6)

where $H_{\mathbf{A}}$ is the free Hamiltonian of the apparatus, H_{int} is the operator on $\mathcal{H}_{\mathbf{A}} \otimes \mathcal{H}_1$ representing the measuring interaction, where $\mathcal{H}_{\mathbf{A}}$ is the Hilbert space of the apparatus, and K is the coupling constant. Then, we can show that there is a unitary operator U on the Hilbert space $\mathcal{H}_{\mathbf{A}} \otimes \mathcal{H}_1$ such that the state of the system $\mathbf{S}_{12}$ at the time $t + \Delta t$, where t is the time of measurement and Δt is the duration of measuring interaction, is obtained by

$$\rho(t + \Delta t) = \mathrm{Tr}_{\mathbf{A}}\left[\left(U \otimes e^{-iH_2\Delta t/\hbar}\right)\left(\sigma \otimes \rho(t)\right)\left(U^\dagger \otimes e^{iH_2\Delta t/\hbar}\right)\right],$$
(7)

where σ is the prepared state of the apparatus at the time of measurement. In fact, U is given by

$$U = e^{-i(1\otimes H_1 + KH_{int})\Delta t/\hbar}.$$

Now, we shall prove the following theorem on the joint probability distribution of the outcomes of the A-measurement and the B-measurement.

Theorem 5.1 (Local Measurement Theorem) *If the measuring apparatus $\mathbf{A}$ measuring A is local at the system $\mathbf{S}_1$, the joint probability distribution of the outcomes of the A-measurement and the B-measurement is given by*

$$\Pr\{A(t_1) = a, B(t_2) = b\|\rho\} = \mathrm{Tr}\left[\left(e^{iH_1t_1/\hbar}E^A(a)e^{-iH_1t_1/\hbar} \otimes e^{iH_2t_2/\hbar}E^B(b)e^{-iH_2t_2/\hbar}\right)\rho\right].$$
(8)

Proof. For any real numbers a, b and any density operator ρ on $\mathcal{H}_1 \otimes \mathcal{H}_2$, let

$$P(a, b, \rho) = \Pr\{A(t_1) = a, B(t_2) = b\|\rho\}.$$

By (5), the function $\rho \mapsto P(a, b, \rho)$ is a positive affine function on the space of density operators on $\mathcal{H}_1 \otimes \mathcal{H}_2$. Since the convex set of density operators is a base of the base norm space of trace class operators, this affine function is extended uniquely to a positive linear functional on the space of trace class operators. By the Schatten-von Neumann duality theorem, the space of bounded operators is the dual space of the space of trace class operators, and hence there is a positive operator $F(a, b)$ on $\mathcal{H}_1 \otimes \mathcal{H}_2$ such that

$$P(a, b, \rho) = \text{Tr}[F(a, b)\rho].$$

For any ρ we have

$$\text{Tr}\left[\sum_b F(a, b)\rho\right] = \Pr\{A(t_1) = a\|\rho\} = \text{Tr}\left[\left(e^{iH_1 t_1/\hbar} E^A(a) e^{-iH_1 t_1/\hbar} \otimes 1\right)\rho\right],$$

and hence we have

$$\sum_b F(a, b) = e^{iH_1 t_1/\hbar} E^A(a) e^{-iH_1 t_1/\hbar} \otimes 1. \tag{9}$$

By the locality condition (7), for any ρ we have

$$\text{Tr}\left[\sum_a F(a, b)\rho\right]$$
$$= \Pr\{B(t_2) = b\|\rho\}$$
$$= \text{Tr}\left[\left(1 \otimes E^B(b)\right)\rho(t_2)\right]$$
$$= \text{Tr}\left[\left(1 \otimes e^{iH_2 \tau/\hbar} E^B(b) e^{-iH_2 \tau/\hbar}\right) \text{Tr}_A\left[\left(U \otimes e^{-iH_2 \Delta t/\hbar}\right)(\sigma \otimes \rho(t_1))\left(U^\dagger \otimes e^{iH_2 \Delta t/\hbar}\right)\right]\right]$$
$$= \text{Tr}\left[\left(1 \otimes e^{iH_2 t_2/\hbar} E^B(b) e^{-iH_2 t_2/\hbar}\right)\rho\right]$$

where $\tau = t_2 - t_1 - \Delta t$ and hence

$$\sum_a F(a, b) = 1 \otimes e^{iH_2 t_2/\hbar} E^B(b) e^{-iH_2 t_2/\hbar}. \tag{10}$$

Since every positive operator valued measure on a product space with projection valued marginal measures is the product of its marginal measures [Dav76, page 39], by (9) and (10) we have

$$F(a, b) = e^{iH_1 t_1/\hbar} E^A(a) e^{-iH_1 t_1/\hbar} \otimes e^{iH_2 t_2/\hbar} E^B(b) e^{-iH_2 t_2/\hbar}.$$

Therefore, (8) follows. $\square$

6. QUANTUM STATE REDUCTION

Consider a model of measurement on a system **S** at the time t. Let **A** be the apparatus with the probe observable A. The measurement is carried out by the interaction between **S** and **A** from the time t to the time $t + \Delta t$. The object **S** is free from the apparatus **A** after the time $t + \Delta t$. Suppose that at the time t the object **S** is in the state $\rho(t)$ and that the apparatus **A** is prepared in the state σ. Let U be the unitary operator representing the time evolution of the object-probe composite system **A** + **S** from the time t to $t + \Delta t$. Then the system **A** + **S** is in the state $U(\sigma \otimes \rho(t))U^\dagger$ at the time $t + \Delta t$. The outcome of this measurement is obtained by the measurement, local at the system $\mathbf{A}$, of the probe observable A at the time $t + \Delta t$. Hence, the probability distribution of the outcome $\mathbf{a}$ of this measurement is given by

$$\Pr\{\mathbf{a} = a\} = \Pr\{A(t + \Delta t) = a\} = \operatorname{Tr}\left[\left(E^A(a) \otimes 1\right) U(\sigma \otimes \rho(t))U^\dagger\right]. \quad (11)$$

In order to determine the state reduction caused by this measurement, suppose that the observer were to measure an arbitrary observable B of the object $\mathbf{S}$ at the time $t + \Delta t + \tau$ with $\tau \geq 0$. Then the joint probability distribution of the outcome $\mathbf{a}$ and the outcome $B(t + \Delta t + \tau)$ of the B-measurement at $t + \Delta t + \tau$ is identical with the joint probability distribution of the outcomes of the A-measurement at $t + \Delta t$ and the B-measurement at $t + \Delta t + \tau$, i.e.,

$$\Pr\{\mathbf{a} = a, B(t + \Delta t + \tau) = b\} = \Pr\{A(t + \Delta t) = a, B(t + \Delta t + \tau) = b\}. \quad (12)$$

By the local measurement theorem, we have

$$\begin{aligned}
&\Pr\{A(t + \Delta t) = a, B(t + \Delta t + \tau) = b\} \\
&\quad = \operatorname{Tr}\left[\left(E^A(a) \otimes e^{iH\tau/\hbar} E^B(b)e^{-iH\tau/\hbar}\right) U(\sigma \otimes \rho(t))U^\dagger\right]. \quad (13)
\end{aligned}$$

Thus, the prior probability distribution of $B(t + \Delta t + \tau)$ is the marginal distribution of $B(t + \Delta t + \tau)$, i.e.,

$$\begin{aligned}
\Pr\{B(t + \Delta t + \tau) = b\} &= \sum_a \Pr\{A(t + \Delta t) = a, B(t + \Delta t + \tau) = b\} \\
&= \operatorname{Tr}\left[\left(1 \otimes e^{iH\tau/\hbar} E^B(b)e^{-iH\tau/\hbar}\right) U(\sigma \otimes \rho(t)) U^\dagger\right] \\
&= \operatorname{Tr}\left[e^{iH\tau/\hbar} E^B(b)e^{-iH\tau/\hbar}\operatorname{Tr}_{\mathbf{A}}\left[U(\sigma \otimes \rho(t)) U^\dagger\right]\right] \quad (14)
\end{aligned}$$

where $\operatorname{Tr}_{\mathbf{A}}$ is the partial trace over the Hilbert space of the apparatus. Thus we can define the prior state of the system $\mathbf{S}$ at the time $t + \Delta t$ by

$$\rho(t + \Delta t) = \operatorname{Tr}_{\mathbf{A}}\left[U(\sigma \otimes \rho(t)) U^\dagger\right], \quad (15)$$

which describes the prior probability distributions of all observable B of the system $\mathbf{S}$ after the time $t + \Delta t$. Since this state change $\rho(t) \mapsto \rho(t + \Delta t)$ does not depend on the outcome of the measurement, this process is called the *nonselective measurement*.

If one reads out the outcome $\mathbf{a}$, or $A(t + \Delta t)$, of this measurement, the information $\mathbf{a} = a$ changes the probability distribution of $B(t + \Delta t + \tau)$ for any outcome a from the prior distribution to the posterior distribution according to the Bayes principle. The posterior distribution of $B(t + \Delta t + \tau)$ is defined as the conditional probability distribution of $B(t + \Delta t + \tau)$ given $\mathbf{a} = a$, i.e.,

$$\begin{aligned}
&\Pr\{B(t + \Delta t + \tau) = b|\mathbf{a} = a\} \\
&= \frac{\Pr\{\mathbf{a} = a, B(t + \Delta t + \tau) = b\}}{\Pr\{\mathbf{a} = a\}} \\
&= \frac{\operatorname{Tr}\left[\left(E^A(a) \otimes e^{iH\tau/\hbar} E^B(b)e^{-iH\tau/\hbar}\right) U(\sigma \otimes \rho(t))U^\dagger\right]}{\operatorname{Tr}\left[\left(E^A(a) \otimes 1\right) U(\sigma \otimes \rho(t)) U^\dagger\right]} \\
&= \frac{\operatorname{Tr}\left[e^{iH\tau/\hbar} E^B(b)e^{-iH\tau/\hbar}\operatorname{Tr}_{\mathbf{A}}[(E^A(a) \otimes 1)U(\sigma \otimes \rho(t))U^\dagger]\right]}{\operatorname{Tr}\left[(E^A(a) \otimes 1) U(\sigma \otimes \rho(t))U^\dagger\right]}. \quad (16)
\end{aligned}$$

Thus, letting

$$\rho(t + \Delta t|\mathbf{a} = a) = \frac{\operatorname{Tr}_{\mathbf{A}}\left[\left(E^A(a) \otimes 1\right) U(\sigma \otimes \rho(t)) U^\dagger\right]}{\operatorname{Tr}\left[(E^A(a) \otimes 1) U(\sigma \otimes \rho(t)) U^\dagger\right]}, \quad (17)$$

239

we have

$$\Pr\{B(t + \Delta t + \tau) = b | \mathbf{a} = a\} = \text{Tr}[e^{iH\tau/\hbar} E^B(b) e^{-iH\tau/\hbar} \rho(t + \Delta t | \mathbf{a} = a)]. \qquad (18)$$

This shows that the posterior distribution of the outcome of the measurement of *any* observable B of the object **S** after the time $t + \Delta t$ is described by the state $\rho(t + \Delta t | \mathbf{a} = a)$. Therefore, we can conclude that the information $\mathbf{a} = a$ changes the state of the system **S** at the time $t + \Delta t$ from the *prior state* $\rho(t + \Delta t)$ to the *posterior state* $\rho(t + \Delta t | \mathbf{a} = a)$ according to the quantum Bayes principle.

The state reduction $\rho(t) \mapsto \rho(t + \Delta t | \mathbf{a} = a)$ is thus obtained as the composition of the state change $\rho(t) \mapsto \rho(t + \Delta t)$ by the measuring interaction and the state change $\rho(t + \Delta t) \mapsto \rho(t + \Delta t | \mathbf{a} = a)$ by the information on the outcome of the measurement.

7. CONCLUSION

We have formulated the quantum Bayes principle and proved the local measurement theorem. These theoretical foundations lead to the following new derivation of state reduction. From the time t of measurement to the time $t + \Delta t$ just after measurement, the object **S** interacts with the apparatus **A**. Thus the state of the object changes dynamically

$$\rho(t) \mapsto \rho(t + \Delta t) = \text{Tr}_{\mathbf{A}} \left[U \left(\sigma \otimes \rho(t) \right) U^{\dagger} \right]. \qquad (19)$$

This process is the nonselective measurement, which does not depends on the outcome of the measurement. The state reduction is the state change of the object from the time t to the time $t + \Delta t$ depending upon the outcome $\mathbf{a}$. According to the quantum Bayes principle, the information $\mathbf{a} = a$ changes the state of the object at the time $t + \Delta t$ from the prior state $\rho(t + \Delta t)$ to the posterior state $\rho(t + \Delta t | \mathbf{a} = a)$, i.e.,

$$\rho(t + \Delta t) \mapsto \rho(t + \Delta t | \mathbf{a} = a) = \frac{\text{Tr}_{\mathbf{A}}[(E^A(a) \otimes 1)U(\sigma \otimes \rho(t))U^{\dagger}]}{\text{Tr}[(E^A(a) \otimes 1)U(\sigma \otimes \rho(t))U^{\dagger}]}. \qquad (20)$$

This change of state includes no dynamical element. Thus the state reduction is obtained as the composition of the dynamical change $\rho(t) \mapsto \rho(t + \Delta t)$ and the *informatical* change $\rho(t + \Delta t) \mapsto \rho(t + \Delta t | \mathbf{a} = a)$.

The above derivation does not assume the projection postulate for the probe measurement. Formula (20) shows that the state after measurement conditional upon the outcome of the measurement does not depend on whether the probe measurement satisfies the projection postulate or not. Thus, formula (20) applies to any measurements whose probe measurement may not satisfy the projection postulate such as photon counting.

REFERENCES

[Dav76] E. B. Davies, *Quantum Theory of Open Systems*, Academic Press, London, 1976.

[IUO90] N. Imoto, M. Ueda, and T. Ogawa, *Phys. Rev. A*, **41**, 4127–4130, (1990).

[Lud51] G. Lüders, *Ann. Physik (6)*, **8**, 322–328, (1951).

[Oza83] M. Ozawa, *Lecture Notes in Math.*, **1021**, pages 518–525, Springer, Berlin, (1983).

[Oza84] M. Ozawa, *J. Math. Phys.*, **25**, 79–87, (1984).

[Oza85a] M. Ozawa, *Publ. RIMS, Kyoto Univ.*, **21**, 279–295, (1985).

[Oza85b] M. Ozawa, *J. Math. Phys.*, **26**, 1948–1955, (1985).

[Oza86]   M. Ozawa, *J. Math. Phys.*, **27**, 759–763, (1986).

[Oza89a] M. Ozawa, in P. Tombesi and E. R. Pike, editors, *Squeezed and Nonclassical Light*, pages 263–286, Plenum, New York, 1989.

[Oza89b] M. Ozawa, *Annals of the Japan Association for Philosophy of Science*, **7**, 185–194, (1989).

[Oza91]   M. Ozawa, *Lecture Notes in Physics*, **378**, pages 3–17, Springer, Berlin, 1991.

[Oza93]   M. Ozawa, *J. Math. Phys.*, **34**, 5596–5624, (1993).

[Oza95a] M. Ozawa, in V. P. Belavkin, O. Hirota, and R. L. Hudson, editors, *Quantum Communications and Measurement*, pages 109–117, Plenum, New York, 1995.

[Oza95b] M. Ozawa, *Journal of the Japan Association for Philosophy of Science*, **23**, 15–21, (1995).

[Wig63]   E. P. Wigner, *Am. J. Phys.*, **31**, 6–15, (1963).

ON THE QUANTUM THEORY OF DIRECT DETECTION

A. Barchielli

Dipartimento di Matematica, Politecnico di Milano
Piazza Leonardo da Vinci 32, I-20133 Milano, Italy
and Istituto Nazionale di Fisica Nucleare, Sezione di Milano

By using the theory of measurements continuous in time in quantum mechanics [1]–[8], a photon detection theory has been formulated [9]–[12]; see Refs. [10]–[12] and [8] for detailed references. A quantum source as an atom, an ion or a more complicated system, eventually placed inside an optical cavity, is stimulated by lasers or by a thermal bath. The emitted light is detected by photon counters (direct detection), possibly after interference with a reference laser beam (heterodyne and homodyne detection). Just to illustrate detection theory, in this paper I shall present only counting processes [1], [3]–[12] (direct detection). Moreover, I shall consider only a concrete example: I shall take as a source a three–level atom in the so called Λ configuration; although simple, such a system shows, when suitably stimulated by lasers, an interesting behaviour: the so called electron–shelving effect (or quantum jumps) [9,13].

We denote by $|j\rangle$, $j = 0, 1, 2$, the three states; the free atomic Hamiltonian is

$$H_{\mathrm{A}} = -\hbar \sum_{j=1}^{2} \omega_j |j\rangle\langle j|, \qquad \omega_j > 0; \tag{1}$$

note that $|0\rangle$ is the higher state. Then, we introduce the interaction between the atom and the electromagnetic field in the standard approximations used in quantum optics. The first approximation is to take this interaction linear in the field operators, e.g. we take $\mathbf{p} \cdot \mathbf{A}$ or $\mathbf{d} \cdot \mathbf{E}$. The second step is to take the rotating wave–approximation. We assume the $|1\rangle \leftrightarrow |2\rangle$ transition to be prohibited. By expanding the field in plain waves and by using spherical coordinates for the wave–vector, in the interaction picture with respect to the free–field dynamics we get

$$H_{\mathrm{int}}(t) = \sum_{j=1}^{2} R_j^\dagger \sum_{\lambda=1}^{2} \frac{\hbar}{\sqrt{2\pi}} \int_0^{+\infty} \mathrm{d}\omega \int_\Sigma \mathrm{d}_2\sigma \,\overline{g_j(\omega, \sigma, \lambda)}\, \mathrm{e}^{-i\omega t} b(\omega, \sigma, \lambda) + \mathrm{h.c.}, \tag{2}$$

where $R_j = |j\rangle\langle 0|$, λ is the polarization index, σ is the direction of propagation, Σ is the full solid angle $\left(\int_\Sigma \mathrm{d}_2\sigma = 4\pi \right)$, $g_j(\omega, \sigma, \lambda)$ is the coupling intensity (it does not depend on σ and λ in the case of spherical symmetry of the atom), $b(\omega, \sigma, \lambda)$ is a Bose field in the Fock representation, an overbar means complex conjugation and h.c. means Hermitian conjugate.

A third approximation is to consider the coupling functions g_j flat around the transition frequencies ω_j and zero outside a neighborhood of ω_j:

$$H_{\text{int}}(t) = \hbar \sum_{j=1}^{2} R_j^\dagger \sum_{\lambda=1}^{2} \int_\Sigma \mathrm{d}_2\sigma \, \overline{g_j(\sigma, \lambda)} \, a_j(t, \sigma, \lambda) + \text{h.c.} \,, \tag{3}$$

$$a_j(t, \sigma, \lambda) = \frac{1}{\sqrt{2\pi}} \int_{\omega_j - \theta_j}^{\omega_j + \theta_j} \mathrm{d}\omega \, \mathrm{e}^{-\mathrm{i}\omega t} \, b(\omega, \sigma, \lambda) \,. \tag{4}$$

If the two frequencies ω_1 and ω_2 are well separated (the two frequency intervals do not overlap), we have

$$[a_i(t, \sigma, \lambda) \,, \, a_j^\dagger(t', \sigma', \lambda')] = 0 \,, \qquad \text{for } i \neq j \,. \tag{5}$$

The latest approximation is to consider θ_j very large ($\theta_j \to +\infty$: broadband approximation); in order to preserve eq. (5), this approximation has to be realized by adding independent fields for $j = 1, 2$. The final result is that the interaction Hamiltonian is given by eq. (3), where the $a_j(t, \sigma, \lambda)$ are Bose fields in the Fock representation and normalized in such a way that $[a_i(t, \sigma, \lambda) \,, \, a_j^\dagger(t', \sigma', \lambda')] = \delta_{ij} \delta_{\lambda\lambda'} \delta_2(\sigma, \sigma') \delta(t - t')$; $\delta_2(\sigma, \sigma')$ is a spherical Dirac delta with $\int_\Sigma \delta_2(\sigma, \sigma') \mathrm{d}_2\sigma = 1$, $\delta_2(\sigma, \sigma') = \delta_2(\sigma', \sigma)$.

The approximations we have made are a kind of singular coupling limit and it is known that, on the contrary of van Hove scaling (weak coupling limit), singular coupling limit does not give rise to energy shifts; therefore, H_A must contain the final physical frequencies.

Let us set now

$$A_j(t) = \frac{\mathrm{i}}{\sqrt{\gamma_j}} \sum_{\lambda=1}^{2} \int_0^t \mathrm{d}t' \int_\Sigma \mathrm{d}_2\sigma \, \overline{g_j(\sigma, \lambda)} \, a_j(t', \sigma, \lambda) \,; \tag{6}$$

the normalization constants $\sqrt{\gamma_j}$ are chosen in such a way that $[A_j(t) \,, \, A_i(t')] = 0$, $[A_j(t) \,, \, A_i^\dagger(t')] = \delta_{ij} \min(t, t')$. The list of all the derived constants used in the paper is given at the end in eq. (62). By using the fields A_j, we can write the evolution operator, in the interaction picture with respect to the free–field dynamics, as

$$U(t) = \overleftarrow{T} \exp\left\{ -\frac{\mathrm{i}}{\hbar} \int_0^t [H_A + H_{\text{int}}(t')] \mathrm{d}t' \right\} \tag{7}$$

$$= \overleftarrow{T} \exp\left\{ \int_0^t \left[-\frac{\mathrm{i}}{\hbar} H_A \, \mathrm{d}t' + \sum_{j=1}^{2} \sqrt{\gamma_j} \left(R_j \, \mathrm{d}A_j^\dagger(t') - R_j^\dagger \, \mathrm{d}A_j(t') \right) \right] \right\};$$

$\overleftarrow{T}$ is the usual time–ordering prescription. To handle such an evolution operator we need quantum stochastic calculus. The aim of such a calculus is just to define integrals with respect to $A_j(t)$, $A_j^\dagger(t)$ and other related operators and to give the rules to manipulate such integrals. An account of quantum stochastic calculus is given in Ref. [14]; I do not want to present this calculus here, but I shall follow Ref. [12], where the rules of quantum stochastic calculus are recalled and detection theory is developed. The relevance of the flat–spectrum and broadband approximations for the use of quantum stochastic calculus in quantum optics has been pointed out in Ref. [15].

The evolution operator U_t satisfies the quantum stochastic Schrödinger equation

$$\mathrm{d}U_t = \left\{ \left(-\frac{\mathrm{i}}{\hbar} H_A - \frac{1}{2} \sum_{j=1}^{2} \gamma_j R_j^\dagger R_j \right) \mathrm{d}t + \sum_{j=1}^{2} \sqrt{\gamma_j} \left(R_j \mathrm{d}A_j^\dagger(t) - R_j^\dagger \mathrm{d}A_j(t) \right) \right\} U_t \tag{8}$$

(cf Ref. [12], eqs. (3.1) and (3.2)).

Let us call $\mathcal{H}$ the Hilbert space where the emitting system lives; for us $\mathcal{H} = \mathbb{C}^3$. Let us take as initial state $\psi \otimes e(h)$, where $\psi \in \mathcal{H}$, $\|\psi\| = 1$ and $e(h)$ is a (normalized) coherent vector in Fock space: $a_j(t, \sigma, \lambda)e(h) = h_j(t, \sigma, \lambda)e(h)$; to describe nearly monochromatic lasers we take $h_j(t, \sigma, \lambda) \simeq e^{-i\alpha_j t} l_j(\sigma, \lambda)$, where α_j is near ω_j and $l_j(\sigma, \lambda)$ is different from zero only inside some solid angle S (the direction of the stimulating lasers).

The explicit time dependence due to the lasers can be removed by setting

$$U_\alpha(t) = \exp\left\{ -i \sum_{j=1}^{2} \alpha_j |j\rangle\langle j| t \right\} U_t ; \tag{9}$$

$U_\alpha(t)$ satisfies eq. (8) with the substitutions $-\omega_j \rightarrow \alpha_j - \omega_j \equiv \Delta_j$, $R_j \rightarrow \exp(-i\alpha_j t)R_j$. Then, the reduced density matrix of the atom, defined by

$$\varrho(t) = \text{Tr}_{\text{Fock}}\{ U_\alpha(t)|\psi \otimes e(h)\rangle\langle\psi \otimes e(h)|U_\alpha^\dagger(t) \}, \tag{10}$$

satisfies the master equation (cf Ref. [12], Sect. 3.2)

$$\frac{\mathrm{d}}{\mathrm{d}t} \varrho(t) = \mathcal{L}[\varrho(t)], \tag{11}$$

$$\mathcal{L}[\varrho] = -i\left[H_\Delta + \sum_{j=1}^{2} \sqrt{\gamma_j}\left(\overline{\lambda_j}\, R_j + \lambda_j R_j^\dagger \right), \varrho \right] + \frac{1}{2} \sum_{j=1}^{2} \gamma_j ([R_j, \varrho R_j^\dagger] + [R_j \varrho, R_j^\dagger])$$

$$= -iK\varrho + i\varrho K^\dagger + \sum_{j=1}^{2} \gamma_j |j\rangle\langle 0|\varrho|0\rangle\langle j|, \tag{12}$$

$$H_\Delta = \sum_{j=1}^{2} \Delta_j |j\rangle\langle j|, \qquad K = H_\Delta + \sum_{j=1}^{2}\left[\Omega_j \left(e^{i\beta_j}|0\rangle\langle j| + e^{-i\beta_j}|j\rangle\langle 0| \right) - \frac{i}{2}\gamma_j|0\rangle\langle 0| \right]. \tag{13}$$

Now we assume to have a detector able to count photons flying through a solid angle S_d; we take $S_\mathrm{d} \cap S = \emptyset$, so the lasers do not send light directly to the counter and only fluorescence light is detected. By neglecting the detector response function and the time of flight from the atom to the detector, we have that the detector performs a continual measurement of the observable

$$Z(t) = \sum_{j=1}^{2} \sum_{\lambda=1}^{2} \int_0^t \mathrm{d}s \int_{S_\mathrm{d}} \mathrm{d}_2\sigma \, a_j^\dagger(s, \sigma, \lambda)a_j(s, \sigma, \lambda); \tag{14}$$

the efficiency of the counter can be taken into account by choosing S_d smaller than the geometrical solid angle spanned by the detector. Note that $Z(t)$ is a number operator, with integer eigenvalues.

The first important point [3] is that

$$[Z(t), Z(s)] = 0, \qquad \forall t, s, \tag{15}$$

so that the family $\{Z(t), t \geq 0\}$ of selfadjoint commuting operators has a joint projection valued measure; the Fourier transform of such a measure (up to time t) is

$$F_t(k) = \exp\left\{ i \int_0^t k(s)\, \mathrm{d}Z(s) \right\}, \tag{16}$$

where k varies in a suitable space of real test functions. The second important point [4] is that

$$U_T^\dagger Z(t) U_T = U_t^\dagger Z(t) U_t, \qquad \forall T \geq t. \tag{17}$$

By introducing the Heisenberg picture $Z_H(t) = U_t^\dagger Z(t) U_t \equiv U_\alpha^\dagger(t) Z(t) U_\alpha(t)$, equation (17) implies

$$[Z_H(t), Z_H(s)] = 0, \qquad \forall t, s, \tag{18}$$

$$U_\alpha^\dagger(t) F_t(k) U_\alpha(t) = \exp\left\{ i \int_0^t k(s) \, \mathrm{d}Z_H(s) \right\}. \tag{19}$$

Equation (18) says that our observables are continually measurable even when the source is present; moreover, eq. (17) allows us to relate [4, 10] our Heisenberg–picture observables to the output fields of Ref. [15].

The whole information on the counting probabilities is contained in the characteristic functional

$$\Phi_t(k) = \langle u_t | F_t(k) | u_t \rangle, \qquad | u_t \rangle = U_\alpha(t) | \psi \otimes e(h) \rangle. \tag{20}$$

By construction $\Phi_t(k)$ is the Fourier transform of the probability measure; in the case of a (regular) counting process, such a characteristic functional has the structure (cf Ref. [10], Sect. 4)

$$\Phi_t(k) = P_t(0) + \sum_{m=1}^\infty \int_0^t \mathrm{d}t_m \int_0^{t_m} \mathrm{d}t_{m-1} \cdots \int_0^{t_2} \mathrm{d}t_1 \, \exp\left\{ i \sum_{n=1}^m k(t_n) \right\} p_t(t_m, \ldots, t_1), \tag{21}$$

where $P_t(m)$ is the probability of m counts up to time t and $p_t(t_m, \ldots, t_1)$ is the exclusive probability density of a count around t_1, a count around t_2, ... and no other count up to time t.

On the other side, as proved in Ref. [10], we have

$$F_t(k) = \, : \exp\left\{ \int_0^t \left(e^{ik(s)} - 1 \right) \mathrm{d}Z(s) \right\} : \tag{22}$$

$$= \, : e^{-Z(t)} \left\{ 1 + \sum_{m=1}^\infty \int_0^t \mathrm{d}Z(t_m) \int_0^{t_m} \mathrm{d}Z(t_{m-1}) \cdots \int_0^{t_2} \mathrm{d}Z(t_1) \, \exp\left[i \sum_{n=1}^m k(t_n) \right] \right\} : ,$$

where the symbol $:\ :$ denotes the normal ordering prescription. Therefore, by comparing eq. (21) with eqs. (20) and (22), we have

$$P_t(0) = \langle u_t | : e^{-Z(t)} : | u_t \rangle, \qquad p_t(t_m, \ldots, t_1) = \left\langle u_t \Big| : e^{-Z(t)} \frac{\mathrm{d}Z(t_1)}{\mathrm{d}t_1} \cdots \frac{\mathrm{d}Z(t_m)}{\mathrm{d}t_m} : \Big| u_t \right\rangle. \tag{23}$$

In particular we get

$$P_t(m) = \int_0^t \mathrm{d}t_m \int_0^{t_m} \mathrm{d}t_{m-1} \cdots \int_0^{t_2} \mathrm{d}t_1 \, p_t(t_m, \ldots, t_1)$$

$$= \left\langle u_t \Big| : e^{-Z(t)} \frac{1}{m!} \left(\int_0^t \mathrm{d}Z(s) \right)^m : \Big| u_t \right\rangle, \tag{24}$$

which is Kelley–Kleiner counting formula ([16] Sect. 5.5). Formulae (23) and (24) define consistent probabilities for a counting process, because they are derived from the Fourier transform of a projection valued measure. It is known that Kelley–Kleiner counting formula is not always consistent, e.g. if applied to a discrete–mode field. Our result shows that Kelley–Kleiner formula is consistent at least when applied to the fields involved in quantum stochastic calculus, which correspond ([10] Sect. 3.1) to the electromagnetic field in the quasimonochromatic paraxial approximation [17].

The formulae for the probabilities can be expressed also in terms of atomic quantities only, once the degrees of freedom of the fields have been traced out. Let us define an operator $G_t(k)$ acting on the trace–class operators on $\mathcal{H}$ by

$$G_t(k)[|\varphi_1\rangle\langle\varphi_2|] = \text{Tr}_{\text{Fock}}\left\{F_t(k)U_\alpha(t)|\varphi_1 \otimes e(h)\rangle\langle\varphi_2 \otimes e(h)|U_\alpha(t)\right\}, \qquad \forall \varphi_1, \varphi_2 \in \mathcal{H}; \tag{25}$$

note that we have $G_t(0) = \exp\{\mathcal{L}t\}$ and

$$\Phi_t(k) = \text{Tr}_{\mathcal{H}}\{G_t(k)[|\psi\rangle\langle\psi|]\}. \tag{26}$$

The adjoint of $G_t(k)$ acts on $\mathcal{B}(\mathcal{H})$ and is the Fourier transform of an instrument; the notion of instrument generalizes both the usual association of observables with selfadjoint operators and the reduction postulate [1]. Operators like $G_t(k)$ have been introduced in [2] and are at the basis of one of the formulations of continual measurement theory. By using quantum stochastic calculus, we can differentiate the r.h.s. of eq. (25) [3, 10] and we get

$$\frac{d}{dt} G_t(k) = \left[\widetilde{\mathcal{L}} + e^{ik(t)}J\right] G_t(k), \qquad G_0(t) = \mathbb{1}, \tag{27}$$

$$J[\varrho] = \sum_{j=1}^{2} \eta_j R_j \varrho R_j^\dagger = \sum_{j=1}^{2} \eta_j |j\rangle\langle 0|\varrho|0\rangle\langle j|, \tag{28}$$

$$\widetilde{\mathcal{L}}[\varrho] = \mathcal{L}[\varrho] - J[\varrho] = -iK\varrho + i\varrho K^\dagger + \sum_{j=1}^{2}(\gamma_j - \eta_j)|j\rangle\langle 0|\varrho|0\rangle\langle j|. \tag{29}$$

By expressing the solution of eq. (27) as a Dyson series we have

$$G_t(k) = e^{\widetilde{\mathcal{L}}t} + \sum_{m=1}^{\infty} \int_0^t dt_m \int_0^{t_m} dt_{m-1} \cdots \int_0^{t_2} dt_1 \exp\left\{i\sum_{n=1}^{m} k(t_n)\right\}$$
$$\times e^{\widetilde{\mathcal{L}}(t-t_m)} J e^{\widetilde{\mathcal{L}}(t_m - t_{m-1})} J \cdots e^{\widetilde{\mathcal{L}}(t_2 - t_1)} J e^{\widetilde{\mathcal{L}}t_1}. \tag{30}$$

By eqs. (22), (26) and (30) we obtain

$$P_t(0) = \text{Tr}_{\mathcal{H}}\left\{e^{\widetilde{\mathcal{L}}t}[|\psi\rangle\langle\psi|]\right\}, \tag{31}$$

$$\begin{aligned} p_t(t_m, \ldots, t_1) &= \text{Tr}_{\mathcal{H}}\left\{e^{\widetilde{\mathcal{L}}(t-t_m)} J \cdots e^{\widetilde{\mathcal{L}}(t_2-t_1)} J e^{\widetilde{\mathcal{L}}t_1}[|\psi\rangle\langle\psi|]\right\} \\ &= P_{t-t_m}(0|\varrho_0) \, w(t_m - t_{m-1}) \cdots w(t_2 - t_1) \, \eta\langle 0|e^{\widetilde{\mathcal{L}}t_1}[|\psi\rangle\langle\psi|]|0\rangle, \end{aligned} \tag{32}$$

$$P_\tau(0|\varrho_0) = \text{Tr}_{\mathcal{H}}\left\{e^{\widetilde{\mathcal{L}}\tau}[\varrho_0]\right\}, \qquad \varrho_0 = \sum_{j=1}^{2} \frac{\eta_j}{\eta}|j\rangle\langle j|, \qquad w(\tau) = \eta\langle 0|e^{\widetilde{\mathcal{L}}\tau}[\varrho_0]|0\rangle. \tag{33}$$

Moreover, we have $dP_t(0|\varrho_0)/dt = -w(t)$, which says that $w(t)$ is the interarrival waiting–time density. From the structure of the exclusive probability densities, we see that our detection process is a delayed renewal counting process; however, this property is specific of the present simple model.

The case $\Delta_1 = \Delta_2 \equiv \Delta$ is very peculiar, because $K|\varphi_0\rangle = \Delta|\varphi_0\rangle$, $\mathcal{L}[|\varphi_0\rangle\langle\varphi_0|] = 0$, $\widetilde{\mathcal{L}}[|\varphi_0\rangle\langle\varphi_0|] = 0$, where $|\varphi_0\rangle = \frac{1}{\sqrt{\Omega_1^2 + \Omega_2^2}}\left(\Omega_2 e^{-i\beta_1}|1\rangle - \Omega_1 e^{-i\beta_2}|2\rangle\right)$. Then, $\int_0^{+\infty} w(t)\, dt < 1$ and there is a non–zero probability that the fluorescence stop. When $\Delta_1 \neq \Delta_2$, $w(t)$ develops more decaying times and the discussion on bright and dark periods goes on in a similar way as in the V-system case [9, 13]. A more realistic model could be obtained by adding a weak $|1\rangle \leftrightarrow |2\rangle$ transition [18].

To introduce the stochastic representation of the measurement process [6, 7, 11], we need some new objects: the Weyl operators

$$W_1(t) = \exp\left\{ \sum_{j,\lambda=1}^{2} \int_0^t ds \int_\Sigma d_2\sigma\, e^{-i\alpha_j s}\, l_j(\sigma,\lambda) a_j^\dagger(s,\sigma,\lambda) - \text{h.c.} \right\}, \tag{34}$$

$$W_2(t) = \exp\left\{ \sum_{j,\lambda=1}^{2} \int_t^{+\infty} ds \int_\Sigma d_2\sigma\, h_j(s,\sigma,\lambda) a_j^\dagger(s,\sigma,\lambda) - \text{h.c.} \right\}, \tag{35}$$

$$W_3(t) = \exp\left\{ -i \sum_{j,\lambda=1}^{2} \int_0^t ds \int_\Sigma d_2\sigma \left[e^{-i\alpha_j s} g_j(\sigma,\lambda) a_j^\dagger(s,\sigma,\lambda) + \text{h.c.} \right] \right\}, \tag{36}$$

and the "quantum Poisson processes"

$$N_j^i(t) = \sum_{\lambda=1}^{2} \int_0^t ds \int_{C_i} d_2\sigma \left[a_j^\dagger(s,\lambda,\sigma) + i\, e^{i\alpha_j s}\, \overline{g_j(\sigma,\lambda)} \right] \left[a_j(s,\lambda,\sigma) - i\, e^{-i\alpha_j s}\, g_j(\sigma,\lambda) \right], \tag{37}$$

$$C_1 = S_d, \quad C_2 = \Sigma \backslash S_d, \quad N_d(t) = \sum_{j=1}^{2} N_j^1(t). \tag{38}$$

Let us stress again that the whole physical information is contained in $G_t(k)$ given in eq. (25). The strategy is to rewrite the r.h.s. of eq. (25) in such a way that the only Fock space operators involved are commuting selfadjoint operators, which can be simultaneously diagonalized and so can be interpreted as classical random variables [12]. First, by using the quantities (34)–(38), eq. (25) can be written as

$$G_t(k)[|\psi\rangle\langle\psi|] = \text{Tr}_{\text{Fock}}\left\{ \tilde{F}_t(k)|\psi_t\rangle\langle\psi_t| \right\}, \qquad |\psi_t\rangle = \tilde{U}_t|\psi \otimes e(0)\rangle, \tag{39}$$

$$\tilde{U}_t = W_3^\dagger(t) W_2^\dagger(t) W_1^\dagger(t) U_\alpha(t) W_1(t) W_2(t) = W_3^\dagger(t) W_1^\dagger(t) U_\alpha(t) W_1(t), \tag{40}$$

$$\tilde{F}_t(k) = W_3^\dagger(t) W_2^\dagger(t) W_1^\dagger(t) F_t(k) W_1(t) W_2(t) W_3(t) = W_3^\dagger(t) F_t(k) W_3(t)$$
$$= \exp\left\{ i \int_0^t k(s)\, dN_d(s) \right\}. \tag{41}$$

In getting eqs. (39)–(41) we have used the relation $W_1(t) W_2(t) e(0) = e(h)$ and the fact that $W_2(t)$ commutes with all the operators involved and $W_1(t)$ commutes with $F_t(k)$. Moreover, quantum stochastic calculus gives

$$d\tilde{U}_t = \left\{ \left[-iK + \sum_{j=1}^{2} \gamma_j \left(R_j - \tfrac{1}{2} \right) \right] dt + \sum_{j=1}^{2} \sqrt{\gamma_j} \left[e^{-i\alpha_j t} (R_j - 1)\, dA_j^\dagger(t) - \text{h.c.} \right] \right\} \tilde{U}_t. \tag{42}$$

The second step is to note that the increments of the various quantum processes commute with $\tilde{U}_t$ and that $a_j(s,\lambda,\sigma)$ annihilates the vacuum, so that we can write

$$\sum_{j=1}^{2} \sqrt{\gamma_j} \left[e^{-i\alpha_j t} (R_j - 1)\, dA_j^\dagger(t) - \text{h.c.} \right] \tilde{U}_t|\psi \otimes e(0)\rangle$$
$$= \sum_{j=1}^{2} \sqrt{\gamma_j}\, e^{-i\alpha_j t} (R_j - 1)\, \tilde{U}_t\, dA_j^\dagger(t)|\psi \otimes e(0)\rangle \tag{43}$$
$$= \sum_{j=1}^{2} (R_j - 1) \left(\sum_{i=1}^{2} dN_j^i(t) - \gamma_j\, dt \right) |\psi_t\rangle.$$

This allows us to write the evolution equation for ψ_t as

$$d\psi_t = \left\{ \sum_{i,j=1}^{2} (R_j - 1)\, dN_j^i(t) + \left[-iK + \tfrac{1}{2}(\gamma_1 + \gamma_2) \right] dt \right\} \psi_t. \tag{44}$$

To diagonalize the operators $N_j^i(t)$ appearing in $\widetilde{F}_t(k)$ and ψ_t, let us consider the trajectory space Ω of a Poisson point process of intensity $|g_j(\sigma, \lambda)|^2 \, \mathrm{d}_2 \sigma \mathrm{d}t$ with its Poisson probability measure P. Fock space is isomorphic to $L^2(\Omega, P)$ (where the inner product is the mathematical expectation of the product); under this isomorphism, the operators $N_j^i(t)$ become multiplication operators by independent Poisson processes: $N_j^1(t)$ has intensity $\eta_j \mathrm{d}t$ and $N_j^2(t)$ has intensity $(\gamma_j - \eta_j)\mathrm{d}t$. We take this isomorphic transformation and, without changing notation, we interpret eq. (44) as a classical stochastic differential equation for a process ψ_t with values in $\mathcal{H}$; such an equation enjoyes remarkable properties, which we shall discuss in the following. From now on, only classical stochastic calculus for counting processes is involved; the formal rules of this calculus are summarized by $(\mathrm{d}t)^2 = 0$, $\mathrm{d}t \mathrm{d}N_j^i(t) = 0$, $\mathrm{d}N_j^i(t)\mathrm{d}N_k^r(t) = \delta_{jk}\delta_{ir}\mathrm{d}N_j^i(t)$. Also the notion of conditional expectation will be essential. Norms and inner products will refer to $\mathcal{H}$.

Let $\mathcal{F}_t$ be the σ-algebra in Ω generated by the process $N_j^i(s)$, $0 \leq s \leq t$, $i, j = 1, 2$; $\mathcal{F}_t$, $t \geq 0$, is a filtration ($\mathcal{F}_s \subset \mathcal{F}_t$ for $s \leq t$) and, for a fixed t, $\mathcal{F}_t$ contains the events up to time t. The increments $\mathrm{d}N_j^i(t)$ "point into the future", they are independent of $\mathcal{F}_t$ and satisfy

$$\mathbb{E}_P\left[\mathrm{d}N_j^1 \middle| \mathcal{F}_t\right] = \eta_j \, \mathrm{d}t, \qquad \mathbb{E}_P\left[\mathrm{d}N_j^2 \middle| \mathcal{F}_t\right] = (\gamma_j - \eta_j) \, \mathrm{d}t. \tag{45}$$

The process ψ_t is $\mathcal{F}_t$–adapted (non–anticipating), i.e. $\mathbb{E}_P[\psi_t|\mathcal{F}_t] = \psi_t$. By the rules of stochastic calculus, we obtain easily from eq. (44)

$$\mathrm{d}|\psi_t\rangle\langle\psi_t| = \sum_{j=1}^{2}\left(R_j|\psi_t\rangle\langle\psi_t|R_j^\dagger - |\psi_t\rangle\langle\psi_t|\right)\left[\sum_{i=1}^{2}\mathrm{d}N_j^i(t) - \gamma_j\mathrm{d}t\right] + \mathcal{L}\left[|\psi_t\rangle\langle\psi_t|\right]\mathrm{d}t \tag{46}$$

and, by taking the trace,

$$\mathrm{d}\|\psi_t\|^2 = \|\psi_t\|^2 \sum_{j=1}^{2}\left(\left\|R_j\widehat{\psi}_t\right\|^2 - 1\right)\left[\sum_{i=1}^{2}\mathrm{d}N_j^i(t) - \gamma_j\mathrm{d}t\right], \qquad \widehat{\psi}_t = \psi_t/\|\psi_t\|. \tag{47}$$

By taking the expectation of eq. (46) and taking into account eq. (45), we obtain that $\mathbb{E}_P[|\psi_t\rangle\langle\psi_t|]$ satisfies the same master equation as $\varrho(t)$; because they coincide at time zero, we have the following stochastic representation of the reduced density matrix:

$$\varrho(t) = \mathbb{E}_P[|\psi_t\rangle\langle\psi_t|]. \tag{48}$$

By taking the trace of eq. (48) we have also $\mathbb{E}_P[\|\psi_t\|^2] = 1$. Moreover, from eq. (47), one has that $\|\psi_t\|^2$ is a martingale, i.e. $\mathbb{E}_P[\|\psi_t\|^2|\mathcal{F}_s] = \|\psi_s\|^2$, $s \leq t$. A mean–one and positive martingale can be used as a density with respect to P; we define a new probability measure $\widehat{P}$ by

$$\widehat{P}(F) = \mathbb{E}_P\left[1_F\|\psi_t\|^2\right], \qquad \forall F \in \mathcal{F}_t, \quad \forall t \geq 0. \tag{49}$$

Note that $\mathbb{E}_P\left[1_F\|\psi_T\|^2\right] = \mathbb{E}_P\left[1_F\|\psi_t\|^2\right]$, $\forall T \geq t$, $\forall F \in \mathcal{F}_t$, because $\|\psi_t\|^2$ is a martingale, and this implies that eq. (49) is a consistent definition of a unique probability measure $\widehat{P}$. Moreover, by eqs. (47)–(49), we have another stochastic representation of $\varrho(t)$:

$$\varrho(t) = \mathbb{E}_{\widehat{P}}\left[\left|\widehat{\psi}_t\right\rangle\left\langle\widehat{\psi}_t\right|\right]. \tag{50}$$

Under the new probability law $\widehat{P}$, the processes $N_j^i(t)$ are counting processes with stochastic intensities

$$\mathbb{E}_{\widehat{P}}\left[\mathrm{d}N_j^1(t) \middle| \mathcal{F}_t\right] = \eta_j\left\|R_j\widehat{\psi}_t\right\|^2 \mathrm{d}t, \qquad \mathbb{E}_{\widehat{P}}\left[\mathrm{d}N_j^2(t) \middle| \mathcal{F}_t\right] = (\gamma_j - \eta_j)\left\|R_j\widehat{\psi}_t\right\|^2 \mathrm{d}t. \tag{51}$$

249

Note that $\left\| R_j \widehat{\psi}_t \right\|^2 \equiv \left| \langle 0 | \widehat{\psi}_t \rangle \right|^2$ is a random quantity, so that the $N_j^i(t)$ are no more Poisson processes. The proof of eq. (51) needs some properties of conditional expectations under a change of measure; by such properties and eq. (47) one has

$$\mathbb{E}_{\widehat{P}} \left[dN_j^i(t) \middle| \mathcal{F}_t \right] = \frac{1}{\|\psi_t\|^2} \mathbb{E}_P \left[\|\psi_{t+dt}\|^2 dN_j^i(t) \middle| \mathcal{F}_t \right] = \left\| R_j \widehat{\psi}_t \right\|^2 \mathbb{E}_P \left[dN_j^i(t) \middle| \mathcal{F}_t \right],$$

from which eq. (51) follows.

From eqs. (44) and (47) one obtains, under the law $\widehat{P}$, a stochastic equation for the normalized vector $\widehat{\psi}_t$:

$$d\widehat{\psi}_t = \sum_{i,j=1}^{2} \left(\frac{R_j}{\left\| R_j \widehat{\psi}_t \right\|} - 1 \right) \widehat{\psi}_t \, dN_j^i(t) + \left[-iK + \frac{1}{2} \sum_{j=1}^{2} \gamma_j \left\| R_j \widehat{\psi}_t \right\|^2 \right] \widehat{\psi}_t \, dt . \quad (52)$$

The meaning of this equation is very simple. If at time t there is a jump of the process $N_j^i(t)$, then the wave–vector changes according to the rule

$$\widehat{\psi}_{t-} \rightarrow \widehat{\psi}_{t+} = \frac{R_j \widehat{\psi}_{t-}}{\left\| R_j \widehat{\psi}_{t-} \right\|} = |j\rangle \text{ (up to a phase).} \quad (53)$$

Between two jumps $\widehat{\psi}_t$ satisfies eq. (52) without the term containing $dN_j^i(t)$, which is equivalent to

$$\widehat{\psi}_t = \frac{\varphi_t}{\|\varphi_t\|}, \qquad \frac{d\varphi_t}{dt} = -iK\varphi_t . \quad (54)$$

The Monte–Carlo wavefunction method [19] is based on eqs. (50), (51), (53), (54).

Up to now, inside the stochastic formulation, we have not taken into account the fact that we observe only the process $N_d(t) = N_1^1(t) + N_2^1(t)$. Let $\mathcal{E}_t$ be the σ-algebra generated by $N_d(s)$, $0 \le s \le t$, and set $\mathcal{E}_\infty = \bigvee_{t \ge 0} \mathcal{E}_t$. By elementary properties of independent Poisson processes and conditional expectations, we have

$$\mathbb{E}_P \left[dN_j^1(t) \middle| \mathcal{E}_\infty \right] = \frac{\eta_j}{\eta} dN_d(t) , \qquad \mathbb{E}_P \left[dN_j^2(t) \middle| \mathcal{E}_\infty \right] = (\gamma_j - \eta_j) \, dt . \quad (55)$$

By taking the conditional expectation with respect to $\mathcal{E}_\infty$ in eq. (46), we obtain

$$d\kappa_t = \left(\sum_{j=1}^{2} \frac{\eta_j}{\eta} R_j \kappa_t R_j^\dagger - \kappa_t \right) (dN_d(t) - \eta dt) + \mathcal{L}[\kappa_t] dt , \quad (56)$$

$$\kappa_t = \mathbb{E}_P [|\psi_t\rangle\langle\psi_t| | \mathcal{E}_\infty] = \mathbb{E}_P [|\psi_t\rangle\langle\psi_t| | \mathcal{E}_t] \quad (57)$$

By normalizing the positive trace–class operator κ_t we get the random density matrix

$$\widehat{\kappa}_t = \kappa_t / \mathrm{Tr}_{\mathcal{H}} \{\kappa_t\} = \mathbb{E}_{\widehat{P}} \left[|\widehat{\psi}_t\rangle \langle\widehat{\psi}_t| \,\middle|\, \mathcal{E}_t \right] . \quad (58)$$

Note that $\mathrm{Tr}_{\mathcal{H}} \{\kappa_t\} = \mathbb{E}_P [\|\psi_t\|^2 | \mathcal{E}_t]$, so that eqs. (48), (50), (58) give

$$\varrho(t) = \mathbb{E}_P [\kappa_t] = \mathbb{E}_{\widehat{P}} [\widehat{\kappa}_t] . \quad (59)$$

Let us denote by $\widehat{P}_\mathcal{E}$ the probability measure $\widehat{P}$ restricted to $\mathcal{E}_\infty$. From eq. (56) one can derive an equation for $1/\mathrm{Tr}_{\mathcal{H}} \{\kappa_t\}$ and, then, for $\widehat{\kappa}_t$; the final result is that the random state $\widehat{\kappa}_t$, under the law $\widehat{P}_\mathcal{E}$, satisfies the non–linear stochastic equation

$$d\widehat{\kappa}_t = \left(\frac{\sum_j \eta_j R_j \widehat{\kappa}_t R_j^\dagger}{\sum_r \eta_r \mathrm{Tr}_{\mathcal{H}} \left\{ R_r \widehat{\kappa}_t R_r^\dagger \right\}} - \widehat{\kappa}_t \right) \left(dN_d(t) - \sum_l \eta_l \mathrm{Tr}_{\mathcal{H}} \left\{ R_l \widehat{\kappa}_t R_l^\dagger \right\} dt \right) + \mathcal{L}[\widehat{\kappa}_t]$$

$$= (\varrho_0 - \widehat{\kappa}_t) \, dN_d(t) + \widetilde{\mathcal{L}}[\widehat{\kappa}_t] \, dt + \eta \langle 0 | \widehat{\kappa}_t | 0 \rangle \, \widehat{\kappa}_t \, dt . \quad (60)$$

Moreover, we have

$$
\begin{aligned}
\mathbb{E}_{\widehat{P}}\left[\mathrm{d}N_{\mathrm{d}}(t)|\,\mathcal{E}_t\right] &= \mathbb{E}_{\widehat{P}}\left[\mathbb{E}_{\widehat{P}}\left[\mathrm{d}N_{\mathrm{d}}(t)|\,\mathcal{F}_t\right]\Big|\,\mathcal{E}_t\right] \\
&= \textstyle\sum_{j=1}^{2}\eta_j\,\mathbb{E}_{\widehat{P}}\left[\left\|R_j\widehat{\psi}_t\right\|^2\Big|\,\mathcal{E}_t\right]\mathrm{d}t = \sum_{j=1}^{2}\eta_j\,\mathrm{Tr}_{\mathcal{H}}\left\{R_j\widehat{\kappa}_t R_j^\dagger\right\}\mathrm{d}t = \eta\,\langle 0\,|\widehat{\kappa}_t|\,0\rangle\,\mathrm{d}t,
\end{aligned}
\tag{61}
$$

which says that $N_{\mathrm{d}}(t)$ is a counting process of stochastic intensity $\eta\,\langle 0\,|\widehat{\kappa}_t|\,0\rangle\,\mathrm{d}t$. Together with eq. (60), this implies that, under the law $\widehat{P}_{\mathcal{E}}$, $N_{\mathrm{d}}(t)$ is just the counting process described by the probabilities (31)–(33); moreover, $\widehat{\kappa}_t$ is a conditional state (a $posteriori$ state): the state of the source system at time t, having observed a certain trajectory for N_{d} (a sequence of counts) up to time t.

Let us end by the list of all the derived constants introduced in the paper:

$$
\gamma_j = \sum_{\lambda=1}^{2}\int_\Sigma |g_j(\sigma,\lambda)|^2 \mathrm{d}_2\sigma, \qquad \eta_j = \sum_{\lambda=1}^{2}\int_{S_{\mathrm{d}}} |g_j(\sigma,\lambda)|^2 \mathrm{d}_2\sigma,
$$

$$
\lambda_j = \frac{1}{\sqrt{\gamma_j}}\sum_{\lambda=1}^{2}\int_\Sigma \overline{g_j(\sigma,\lambda)}\,l_j(\sigma,\lambda)\,\mathrm{d}_2\sigma,
\tag{62}
$$

$$
\Delta_j = \alpha_j - \omega_j, \quad \Omega_j = \sqrt{\gamma_j}\,|\lambda_j|, \quad \beta_j = \arg\left(\lambda_j\sqrt{\gamma_j}\right), \quad \eta = \eta_1 + \eta_2.
$$

REFERENCES

[1] E. B. Davies, *Quantum Theory of Open Systems* (Academic, London, 1976).

[2] A. Barchielli, L. Lanz, G. M. Prosperi, Found. Phys. **13** (1983) 779–812.

[3] A. Barchielli, G. Lupieri, J. Math. Phys. **26** (1985) 2222–2230.

[4] A. Barchielli, Phys. Rev. A **34** (1986) 1642–1649.

[5] A. S. Holevo, in *Advances in Statistical Signal Processing*, vol. 1 (JAI Press, 1987) pp. 157–202.

[6] V. P. Belavkin, in *Modelling and Control of Systems*, edited by A. Blaquière, Lect. Notes Control Inform. Sciences **121** (Springer, Berlin, 1988) pp. 245–265.

[7] A. Barchielli, V. P. Belavkin, J. Phys. A: Math. Gen. **24** (1991) 1495–1514.

[8] P. Staszewski, *Quantum Mechanics of Continuously Observed Systems* (Nicholas Copernicus University Press, Toruń, 1993).

[9] A. Barchielli, J. Phys. A: Math. Gen. **20** (1987) 6341–6355.

[10] A. Barchielli, Quantum Opt. **2** (1990) 423–441.

[11] A. Barchielli, in *Stochastic Evolution of Quantum States in Open Systems and in Measurement Processes*, edited by L. Diósi et al. (World Scientific, Singapore, 1994) pp. 1–14.

[12] A. Barchielli, A. M. Paganoni, Quantum Semiclass. Opt. **8** (1996) 133–156.

[13] C. Cohen–Tannoudji, J. Dalibard, Europhys. Lett. **1** (1986) 441–448.

[14] K. R. Parthasarathy, *An Introduction to Quantum Stochastic Calculus* (Birkhäuser, Basel, 1992).

[15] C. W. Gardiner, M. J. Collet, Phys. Rev. A **31** (1985) 3761–3774.

[16] H. J. Carmichael, *An Open System Approach to Quantum Optics*, Lect. Notes Phys. **m18** (Springer, Berlin, 1993).

[17] H. P. Yuen, J. H. Shapiro, IEEE Trans. Inform. Theory **IT-24** (1978) 657–668.

[18] P. Zoller, M. Marte, D. F. Walls, Phys. Rev. A **35** (1987) 198–207.

[19] K. Mølmer, Y. Castin, J, Dalibard, J. Opt. Soc. Am. B **10** (1993) 524–538.

HOMODYNING AS UNIVERSAL DETECTION

Giacomo Mauro D'Ariano

Department of Electrical and Computer Engineering
Department of Physics and Astronomy
Northwestern University, Evanston, IL 60208
and
Istituto Nazionale di Fisica Nucleare, Sezione di Pavia
via A. Bassi 6, I-27100 Pavia, Italy

Homodyne tomography—i. e. homodyning while scanning the local oscillator phase—is now a well assessed method for "measuring" the quantum state. In this paper I will show how it can be used as a kind of universal detection, for measuring generic field operators, however at expense of some additional noise. The general class of field operators that can be measured in this way is presented, and includes also operators that are inaccessible to heterodyne detection. The noise from tomographical homodyning is compared to that from heterodyning, for those operators that can be measured in both ways. It turns out that for some operators homodyning is better than heterodyning when the mean photon number is sufficiently small. Finally, the robustness of the method to additive phase-insensitive noise is analyzed. It is shown that just half photon of thermal noise would spoil the measurement completely.

1. INTRODUCTION

Homodyne tomography is the only viable method currently known for determining the detailed state of a quantum harmonic oscillator—a mode of the electromagnetic field. The state measurement is achieved by repeating many homodyne measurements at different phases ϕ with respect to the local oscillator (LO). The experimental work of the group in Eugene-Oregon [1] undoubtedly established the feasibility of the method, even though the earlier data analysis were based on a filtered procedure that affected the results with systematic errors. Later, the theoretical group in Pavia-Italy presented an exact reconstruction algorithm [2], which is the method currently adopted in actual experiments (see, for example, Refs. [3] and [4]). The reconstruction algorithm of Ref. [2] was later greatly simplified [5], so that it was possible also to recognize the feasibility of the method even for nonideal quantum efficiency $\eta < 1$ at the homodyne detector, and, at the same time, establishing lower bounds for η for any given matrix representation. After these first results, further theoretical progress has been made, understanding the mechanisms that underly the generation of statistical errors [6], thus limiting the sensitivity of the method. More recently, for $\eta = 1$ non trivial factorization formulas have been recognized [7, 8] for the "pattern functions" [9] that are necessary to reconstruct the photon statistics.

In this paper I will show how homodyne tomography can also be used as a method for measuring generic field operators. In fact, due to statistical errors, the measured matrix elements cannot be used to obtain expectations of field operators, and a different algorithm for analyzing homodyne data is needed suited to the particular field operator whose expectation one wants to estimate. Here, I will present an algorithm valid for any operator that admits a normal ordered expansion, giving the general class of operators that can be measured in this way, also as a function of the quantum efficiency η. Hence, from the same bunch of homodyne experimental data, now one can obtain not only the density matrix of the state, but also the expectation value of various field operators, including some operators that are inaccessible to heterodyne detection. However, the price to pay for such detection flexibility is that all measured quantities will be affected by noise. But, if one compares this noise with that from heterodyning (for those operators that can be measured in both ways), it turns out that for some operators homodyning is less noisy than heterodyning, at least for small mean photon numbers.

Finally, I will show that the method of homodyne tomography is quite robust to sources of additive noise. Focusing attention on the most common situation in which the noise is Gaussian and independent on the LO phase, I will show that this kind of noise produces the same effect of nonunit quantum efficiency at detectors. Generalizing the result of Ref. [5], I will give bounds for the overall rms noise level below which the tomographical reconstruction is still possible. I will show that the smearing effect of half photon of thermal noise in average is sufficient to completely spoil the measurement, making the experimental errors growing up unbounded.

2. SHORT UP-TO-DATE REVIEW ON HOMODYNE TOMOGRAPHY

The homodyne tomography method is designed to obtain a general matrix element $\langle \psi | \hat{\varrho} | \varphi \rangle$ in form of expectation of a function of the homodyne outcomes at different phases with respect to the LO. In equations, one has

$$\langle \psi | \hat{\varrho} | \varphi \rangle = \int_0^\pi \frac{d\phi}{\pi} \int_{-\infty}^{+\infty} dx \, p(x; \phi) \, f_{\psi\varphi}(x; \phi) \,, \tag{1}$$

where $p(x; \phi)$ denotes the probability distribution of the outcome x of the quadrature $\hat{x}_\phi = \frac{1}{2} \left(a^\dagger e^{i\phi} + a e^{-i\phi} \right)$ of the field mode with particle operators a and $a^\dagger$ at phase ϕ with respect to the LO. Notice that it is sufficient to average only over $\phi \in [0, \pi]$, due to the symmetry $\hat{x}_{\phi+\pi} = -\hat{x}_\phi$. One wants the function $f_{\psi\varphi}(x; \phi)$ bounded for all x, whence every moment will be bounded for any possible (a priori unknown) probability distribution $p(x; \phi)$. Then, according to the central-limit theorem, one is guaranteed that the integral in Eq. (1) can be sampled statistically over a sufficiently large set of data, and the average values for different experiments will be Gaussian distributed, allowing estimation of confidence intervals. If, on the other hand, the kernel $f_{\psi\varphi}(x; \phi)$ turns out to be unbounded, then we will say that the matrix element cannot be measured by homodyne tomography.

The easiest way to obtain the integral kernel $f_{\psi\varphi}(x; \phi)$ is starting from the operator identity

$$\hat{\varrho} = \int \frac{d^2\alpha}{\pi} \, \mathrm{Tr}(\hat{\varrho} e^{-\bar{\alpha}a + \alpha a^\dagger}) \, e^{-\alpha a^\dagger + \bar{\alpha}a} \tag{2}$$

which, by changing to polar variables $\alpha = (i/2)ke^{i\phi}$, becomes

$$\hat{\varrho} = \int_0^\pi \frac{d\phi}{\pi} \int_{-\infty}^{+\infty} \frac{dk\,|k|}{4} \mathrm{Tr}(\hat{\varrho}e^{ik\hat{x}_\phi}) e^{-ik\hat{x}_\phi} . \tag{3}$$

Equation (2) is nothing but the operator form of the Fourier-transform relation between Wigner function and characteristic function: it can also be considered as an operator form of the Moyal identity

$$\int \frac{d^2z}{\pi} \langle k|\hat{D}^\dagger(z)|m\rangle\langle l|\hat{D}(z)|n\rangle = \langle k|n\rangle\langle l|m\rangle . \tag{4}$$

The trace-average in Eq. (3) can be evaluated in terms of $p(x,\phi)$, using the complete set $\{|x\rangle_\phi\}$ of eigenvectors of $\hat{x}_\phi$, and exchanging the integrals over x and k. One obtains

$$\hat{\varrho} = \int_0^\pi \frac{d\phi}{\pi} \int_{-\infty}^{+\infty} dx\, p(x;\phi)K(x - \hat{x}_\phi), \tag{5}$$

where the integral kernel $K(x)$ is given by

$$K(x) = -\frac{1}{2}\mathrm{P}\frac{1}{x^2} \equiv -\lim_{\varepsilon\to 0^+}\frac{1}{2}\mathrm{Re}\frac{1}{(x + i\varepsilon)^2}, \tag{6}$$

P denoting the Cauchy principal value. Taking matrix elements of both sides of Eq. (5) between vectors ψ and φ, we obtain the sampling formula we were looking for, namely

$$\langle\psi|\hat{\varrho}|\varphi\rangle = \int_0^\pi \frac{d\phi}{\pi} \int_{-\infty}^{+\infty} dx\, p(x;\phi)\langle\psi|K(x - \hat{x}_\phi)|\varphi\rangle . \tag{7}$$

Hence, the matrix element $\langle\psi|\hat{\varrho}|\varphi\rangle$ is obtained by averaging the function $f_{\psi\varphi}(x;\phi) \equiv \langle\psi|K(x - \hat{x}_\phi)|\varphi\rangle$ over homodyne data at different phases ϕ. As we will see soon, despite $K(x)$ is unbounded, for particular vectors ψ and φ in the Hilbert space the matrix element $\langle\psi|K(x - \hat{x}_\phi)|\varphi\rangle$ is bounded, and thus the integral (7) can be sampled experimentally.

Before analyzing specific matrix representations, I recall how the sampling formula (7) can be generalized to the case of nonunit quantum efficiency. Low efficiency homodyne detection simply produces a probability $p_\eta(x;\phi)$ that is a Gaussian convolution of the ideal probability $p(x;\phi)$ for $\eta = 1$ (see, for example, Ref. [10]). In terms of the generating functions of the $\hat{x}_\phi$-moments one has

$$\int_{-\infty}^{+\infty} dx\, p_\eta(x;\phi)e^{ikx} = \exp\left(-\frac{1 - \eta}{8\eta}k^2\right) \int_{-\infty}^{+\infty} dx\, p(x;\phi)e^{ikx} . \tag{8}$$

Upon substituting Eq. (8) into Eq. (3), and by following the same lines that lead us to Eq. (5), one obtains the operator identity

$$\hat{\varrho} = \int_0^\pi \frac{d\phi}{\pi} \int_{-\infty}^{+\infty} dx\, p_\eta(x;\phi)K_\eta(x - \hat{x}_\phi), \tag{9}$$

where now the kernel reads

$$K_\eta(x) = \frac{1}{2}\mathrm{Re} \int_0^{+\infty} dk\, k \exp\left(\frac{1 - \eta}{8\eta}k^2 + ikx\right) . \tag{10}$$

The desired sampling formula for $\langle\psi|\hat{\varrho}|\varphi\rangle$ is obtained again as in Eq. (7), by taking matrix elements of both sides of Eq. (10). Notice that now the kernel $K_\eta(x)$ is not even a tempered distribution: however, as we will see immediately, the matrix elements of $K_\eta(x - \hat{x}_\phi)$ are bounded for some representations, depending on the value of η. The matrix elements $\langle \psi | K_\eta(x - \hat{a}_\phi) | \varphi \rangle$ are bounded if the following inequality is satisfied for all phases $\phi \in [0, \pi]$

$$\eta > \frac{1}{1 + 4\varepsilon^2(\phi)} , \tag{11}$$

where $\varepsilon^2(\phi)$ is the harmonic mean

$$\frac{2}{\varepsilon^2(\phi)} = \frac{1}{\varepsilon_\psi^2(\phi)} + \frac{1}{\varepsilon_\varphi^2(\phi)} , \tag{12}$$

and $\varepsilon_v^2(\phi)$ is the "resolution" of the vector $|v\rangle$ in the $\hat{x}_\phi$-representation, namely:

$$|_\phi\langle x | v \rangle|^2 \simeq \exp\left[-\frac{x^2}{2\varepsilon_v^2(\phi)} \right] . \tag{13}$$

In Eq. (13) the symbol $\simeq$ stands for the leading term as a function of x, and $|x\rangle_\phi \equiv e^{ia^\dagger a\phi}|x\rangle$ denote eigen-ket of the quadrature $\hat{x}_\phi$ for eigenvalue x. Upon maximizing Eq. (11) with respect to ϕ one obtains the bound

$$\eta > \frac{1}{1 + 4\varepsilon^2} , \qquad \varepsilon^2 = \min_{\phi \in [0, \pi]} \{ \varepsilon^2(\phi) \} . \tag{14}$$

One can easily see that the bound is $\eta > 1/2$ for both number-state and coherent-state representations, whereas it is $\eta > (1 + s^2)^{-1} \geq 1/2$ for squeezed-state representations with minimum squeezing factor $s < 1$. On the other hand, for the quadrature representation one has $\eta > 1$, which means that this matrix representation cannot be measured. The value $\eta = 1/2$ is actually an absolute bound for all representations satisfying the "Heisenberg relation" $\epsilon(\phi)\epsilon(\phi + \frac{\pi}{2}) \geq \frac{1}{4}$ with the equal sign, which include all known representations (for a discussion on the existence of exotic representations see Ref. [11]). Here, I want to emphasize that the existence of such a lower bound for quantum efficiency is actually of fundamental relevance, as it prevents measuring the wave function of a single system using schemes of weak repeated indirect measurements on the same system [12].

At the end of this section, from Ref. [5] I report for completeness the kernel $\langle n | K(x - \hat{x}_\phi) | m \rangle$ for matrix elements between number eigenstates. One has

$$\langle n | K_\eta(x - \hat{x}_\phi) | n + d \rangle = e^{-id\phi} 2\kappa^{d+2} \sqrt{\frac{n!}{(n+d)!}} e^{-\kappa^2 x^2} \tag{15}$$

$$\times \sum_{\nu=0}^{n} \frac{(-)^\nu}{\nu!} \binom{n+d}{n-\nu} (2\nu + d + 1)! \kappa^{2\nu} \mathrm{Re}\left\{ (-i)^d D_{-(2\nu+d+2)}(-2i\kappa x) \right\} ,$$

where $\kappa = \sqrt{\eta/(2\eta - 1)}$, and $D_\sigma(z)$ denotes the parabolic cylinder function. For $\eta = 1$ the kernel factorizes as follows [7, 8]

$$\langle n | K(x - \hat{x}_\phi) | n + d \rangle =$$
$$e^{-id\phi}[2x u_n(x) v_{n+d}(x) - \sqrt{n+1} u_{n+1}(x) v_{n+d}(x) - \sqrt{m+1} u_n(x) v_{n+d+1}(x)] , \tag{16}$$

where $u_n(x)$ and $v_n(x)$ are the regular and irregular energy eigen-functions of the harmonic oscillator

$$u_j(x) = \frac{1}{\sqrt{j!}} \left(x - \frac{\partial_x}{2} \right)^j \left(\frac{2}{\pi} \right)^{1/4} e^{-x^2} ,$$
$$v_j(x) = \frac{1}{\sqrt{j!}} \left(x - \frac{\partial_x}{2} \right)^j (2\pi)^{1/4} e^{-x^2} \int_0^{\sqrt{2}x} dt \, e^{t^2} . \tag{17}$$

3. MEASURING GENERIC FIELD OPERATORS

Homodyne tomography provides the maximum achievable information on the quantum state, and, in principle, the knowledge of the density matrix should allow one to calculate the expectation value $\langle \hat{O} \rangle = \text{Tr}[\hat{O}\hat{\varrho}]$ of any observable $\hat{O}$. However, this is generally true only when one has an analytic knowledge of the density matrix, but it is not true when the matrix has been obtained experimentally. In fact, the Hilbert space is actually infinite dimensional, whereas experimentally one can achieve only a finite matrix, each element being affected by an experimental error. Notice that, even though the method allows one to extract *any* matrix element in the Hilbert space from the same bunch of experimental data, however, it is the way in which errors converge in the Hilbert space that determines the actual possibility of estimating the trace $\text{Tr}[\hat{O}\hat{\varrho}]$. To make things more concrete, let us fix the case of the number representation, and suppose we want to estimate the average photon number $\langle a^\dagger a \rangle$. In Ref. [13] it has been shown that for nonunit quantum efficiency the statistical error for the diagonal matrix element $\langle n|\hat{\varrho}|n \rangle$ diverges faster than exponentially versus n, whereas for $\eta = 1$ the error saturates for large n to the universal value $\varepsilon_n = \sqrt{2/N}$ that depends only on the number N of experimental data, but is independent on both n and on the quantum state. Even for the unrealistic case $\eta = 1$, one can see immediately that the estimated expectation value $\langle a^\dagger a \rangle = \sum_{n=0}^{H-1} n\varrho_{nn}$ based on the measured matrix elements ϱ_{nn}, is not guaranteed to converge versus the truncated-space dimension H, because the error on ϱ_{nn} is nonvanishing versus n. Clearly in this way I am not proving that the expectation $\langle a^\dagger a \rangle$ is unobtainable from homodyne data, because matrix errors convergence depends on the chosen representation basis, whence the ineffectiveness of the method may rely in the data processing, more than in the actual information contained in the bunch of experimental data. Therefore, the question is: is it possible to estimate a generic expectation value $\langle \hat{O} \rangle$ directly from homodyne data, without using the measured density matrix? As we will see soon, the answer is positive in most cases of interest, and the procedure for estimating the expectation $\langle \hat{O} \rangle$ will be referred to as *homodyning the observable* $\hat{O}$.

By *homodyning the observable* $\hat{O}$ I mean averaging an appropriate kernel function $\mathcal{R}[\hat{O}](x; \phi)$ (independent on the state $\hat{\varrho}$) over the experimental homodyne data, achieving in this way the expectation value of the observable $\langle \hat{O} \rangle$ for every state $\hat{\varrho}$. Hence, the kernel function $\mathcal{R}[\hat{O}](x; \phi)$ is defined through the identity

$$\langle \hat{O} \rangle = \int_0^\pi \frac{d\phi}{\pi} \int_{-\infty}^{+\infty} dx\, p(x; \phi)\mathcal{R}[\hat{O}](x; \phi) \,. \tag{18}$$

From the definition of $\mathcal{R}[\hat{O}](x; \phi)$ in Eq. (18), and from Eqs. (2) and (3)—which generally hold true for any Hilbert-Schmidt operator in place of $\hat{\varrho}$—one obtains

$$\hat{O} = \int_0^\pi \frac{d\phi}{\pi} \int_{-\infty}^{+\infty} dx\, \mathcal{R}[\hat{O}](x; \phi)|x\rangle_{\phi\phi}\langle x| \,, \tag{19}$$

with the kernel $\mathcal{R}[\hat{O}](x; \phi)$ given by

$$\mathcal{R}[\hat{O}](x; \phi) = \text{Tr}[\hat{O}K(x - \hat{x}_\phi)] \,, \tag{20}$$

and $K(x)$ given in Eq. (6). The validity of Eq. (20), however, is limited only to the case of a Hilbert-Schmidt operator $\hat{O}$, otherwise it is ill defined. Nevertheless, one can obtain the explicit form of the kernel $\mathcal{R}[\hat{O}](x; \phi)$ in a different way. Starting from the identity involving trilinear products of Hermite polynomials [14]

$$\int_{-\infty}^{+\infty} dx\, e^{-x^2}\, H_k(x)\, H_m(x)\, H_n(x) = \frac{2^{\frac{m+n+k}{2}}\,\pi^{\frac{1}{2}}\,k!m!n!}{(s-k)!(s-m)!(s-n)!}\,, \tag{21}$$
$$\text{for } k+m+n = 2s \text{ even},$$

Richter proved the following nontrivial formula for the expectation value of the normally ordered field operators [15]

$$\langle a^{\dagger n}a^m \rangle = \int_0^\pi \frac{d\phi}{\pi} \int_{-\infty}^{+\infty} dx\, p(x;\phi) e^{i(m-n)\phi} \frac{H_{n+m}(\sqrt{2}x)}{\sqrt{2^{n+m}\binom{n+m}{n}}}\,, \tag{22}$$

which corresponds to the kernel

$$\mathcal{R}[a^{\dagger n}a^m](x;\phi) = e^{i(m-n)\phi} \frac{H_{n+m}(\sqrt{2}x)}{\sqrt{2^{n+m}\binom{n+m}{n}}}\,. \tag{23}$$

This result can be easily extended to the case of nonunit quantum efficiency $\eta < 1$, as the normally ordered expectation $\langle a^{\dagger n}a^m \rangle$ just gets an extra factor $\eta^{\frac{1}{2}(n+m)}$. Therefore, one has

$$\mathcal{R}_\eta[a^{\dagger n}a^m](x;\phi) = e^{i(m-n)\phi} \frac{H_{n+m}(\sqrt{2}x)}{\sqrt{(2\eta)^{n+m}\binom{n+m}{n}}}\,, \tag{24}$$

where the kernel $\mathcal{R}_\eta[\hat{O}](x;\phi)$ is defined as in Eq. (18), but with the experimental probability distribution $p_\eta(x;\phi)$. From Eq. (24) by linearity on can obtain the kernel $\mathcal{R}_\eta[\hat{f}](x;\phi)$ for any operator function $\hat{f}$ that has normal ordered expansion

$$\hat{f} \equiv f(a, a^\dagger) = \sum_{nm=0}^\infty f_{nm}^{(n)} a^{\dagger n}a^m\,. \tag{25}$$

From Eq. (24) one obtains

$$\mathcal{R}_\eta[\hat{f}](x;\phi) = \sum_{s=0}^\infty \frac{H_s(\sqrt{2}x)}{s!(2\eta)^{s/2}} \sum_{nm=0}^\infty f_{nm}^{(n)} e^{i(m-n)\phi} n!m!\delta_{n+m,s} \tag{26}$$

$$= \sum_{s=0}^\infty \frac{H_s(\sqrt{2}x)i^s}{s!(2\eta)^{s/2}} \frac{d^s}{dv^s}\bigg|_{v=0} \mathcal{F}[\hat{f}](v;\phi)\,, \tag{27}$$

where

$$\mathcal{F}[\hat{f}](v;\phi) = \sum_{nm=0}^\infty f_{nm}^{(n)} \binom{n+m}{m}^{-1} (-iv)^{n+m} e^{i(m-n)\phi}\,. \tag{28}$$

Continuing from Eq. (27) one obtains

$$\mathcal{R}_\eta[\hat{f}](x;\phi) = \exp\left(\frac{1}{2\eta}\frac{d^2}{dv^2} + \frac{2ix}{\sqrt{\eta}}\frac{d}{dv}\right)\bigg|_{v=0} \mathcal{F}[\hat{f}](v;\phi)\,, \tag{29}$$

and finally

$$\mathcal{R}_\eta[\hat{f}](x;\phi) = \int_{-\infty}^{+\infty} \frac{dw}{\sqrt{2\pi\eta^{-1}}} e^{-\frac{\eta}{2}w^2} \mathcal{F}[\hat{f}](w + 2ix/\sqrt{\eta};\phi)\,. \tag{30}$$

Hence one concludes that the operator $\hat{f}$ can be measured by homodyne tomography if the function $\mathcal{F}[\hat{f}](v;\phi)$ in Eq. (28) grows slower than $\exp(-\eta v^2/2)$ for $v \to \infty$, and the integral in Eq. (30) grows at most exponentially for $x \to \infty$ (assuming $p(x;\phi)$ goes to zero faster than exponentially at $x \to \infty$).

In Table 1 I report the kernel $\mathcal{R}_\eta[\hat{O}](x;\phi)$ for some operators $\hat{O}$. One can see that for the raising operator $\hat{e}_+$ the kernel diverges at $\eta = 1/2^+$, namely it can be measured only for $\eta > 1/2$. The operator $\hat{W}_s$ in the same table gives the generalized Wigner function $W_s(\alpha, \bar{\alpha})$ for ordering parameter s through the identity $W_s(\alpha, \bar{\alpha}) = \text{Tr}[\hat{D}(\alpha)\hat{\varrho}\hat{D}^\dagger(\alpha)\hat{W}_s]$. From the expression of $\mathcal{R}_\eta[\hat{W}_s](x;\phi)$ it follows that by homodyning with quantum efficiency η one can measure the generalized Wigner function only for $s < 1 - \eta^{-1}$: in particular, as already noticed in Refs. [5], the usual Wigner function for $s = 0$ cannot be measured for any quantum efficiency [in fact one would have $\mathcal{R}_1[\hat{D}^\dagger(\alpha)\hat{W}_0\hat{D}(\alpha)](x;\phi) = K[x - \text{Re}(\alpha e^{-i\phi})]$, with $K(x)$ unbounded as given in Eq. (6)].

Table 1. Kernel $\mathcal{R}_\eta[\hat{O}](x;\phi)$, as defined in Eq. (18), for some operators $\hat{O}$. [The symbol $\Phi(a, b; x)$ denotes the customary confluent hypergeometric function.]

	$\hat{O}$	$\mathcal{R}_\eta[\hat{O}](x;\phi)$
(1)	$a^{\dagger n} a^m$	$e^{i(m-n)\phi} \dfrac{H_{n+m}(\sqrt{2}x)}{\sqrt{2^{n+m}} \binom{n+m}{n}}$
(2)	a	$2e^{i\phi}x$
(3)	a^2	$e^{2i\phi}(4x^2 - 1)$
(4)	$a^\dagger a$	$2x^2 - \frac{1}{2}$
(5)	$(a^\dagger a)^2$	$\frac{8}{3}x^4 - 2x^2$
(6)	$: \hat{D}^\dagger(\alpha) := e^{-\alpha a^\dagger} e^{\bar{\alpha} a}$	$\dfrac{\exp[-\frac{1}{2\eta}(\bar{\alpha}e^{i\phi})^2 + \frac{2x}{\sqrt{\eta}}\bar{\alpha}e^{i\phi}]}{1 + \frac{\alpha}{\bar{\alpha}}e^{-2i\phi}}$ $+\dfrac{\exp[-\frac{1}{2\eta}(\alpha e^{-i\phi})^2 - \frac{2x}{\sqrt{\eta}}\alpha e^{-i\phi}]}{1 + \frac{\bar{\alpha}}{\alpha}e^{2i\phi}}$
(7)	$\hat{e}_+ \doteq a^\dagger \dfrac{1}{\sqrt{1+a^\dagger a}}$	$2xe^{-i\phi}\dfrac{1}{\sqrt{2\pi\eta}}\displaystyle\int_{-\infty}^{+\infty} dv \dfrac{e^{-v^2}}{(1+z)^2}\Phi\left(2, \frac{3}{2}; \frac{x^2}{1+z^{-1}}\right),$ $z = \dfrac{e^{-v^2} - 1}{2\eta}$
(8)	$\hat{W}_s \doteq \dfrac{2}{\pi(1-s)}\left(\dfrac{s+1}{s-1}\right)^{a^\dagger a}$	$\displaystyle\int_0^\infty dt \dfrac{2e^{-t}}{\pi(1-s) - \frac{1}{\eta}}\cos\left(2\sqrt{\dfrac{2t}{(1-s) - \frac{1}{\eta}}}x\right)$
(9)	$|n + d\rangle\langle n|$	$\langle n|K(x - \hat{x}_\phi)|n + d\rangle$ in Eqs. (15) and (16)

3.1. COMPARISON BETWEEN HOMODYNE TOMOGRAPHY AND HETERO-DYNING

We have seen that from the same bunch of homodyne tomography data, not only one can recover the density matrix of the field, but also one can measure any field observable $\hat{f} \equiv f(a, a^\dagger)$ having *normal ordered* expansion $\hat{f} \equiv f^{(n)}(a, a^\dagger) = \sum_{nm=0}^\infty f^{(n)}_{nm}a^{\dagger n}a^m$ and bounded integral in Eq. (30)—this holds true in particular for any polynomial function of the annihilation and creation operators. This situation can be compared with the case of heterodyne detection, where again one measures general field observables, but admitting *anti-normal ordered* expansion $\hat{f} \equiv f^{(a)}(a, a^\dagger) = \sum_{nm=0}^\infty f^{(a)}_{nm}a^m a^{\dagger n}$, in which case the expectation value is obtained through the heterodyne average

$$\langle \hat{f} \rangle = \int \frac{d^2\alpha}{\pi} f^{(a)}(\alpha, \bar{\alpha}) \langle \alpha | \hat{\varrho} | \alpha \rangle . \tag{31}$$

For $\eta = 1$ the heterodyne probability is just the Q-function $Q(\alpha, \bar{\alpha}) = \frac{1}{\pi}\langle \alpha | \hat{\varrho} | \alpha \rangle$, whereas for $\eta = 1$ it will be Gaussian convoluted. As shown by Baltin [16], generally the anti-normal expansion either is not defined, or is *not consistent* on the Fock basis, namely $f^{(a)}(a, a^\dagger)|n\rangle$ has infinite norm or is different from $\hat{f}(a, a^\dagger)|n\rangle$ for some $n \geq 0$. In particular, let us focus attention on functions of the number operator $f(a^\dagger a) = \sum_{l=0}^\infty c_l (a^\dagger a)^l$, $f^{(n)}(a^\dagger a) = \sum_{l=0}^\infty c_l^{(n)} a^{\dagger l} a^l$, $f^{(a)}(a^\dagger a) = \sum_{l=0}^\infty c_l^{(a)} a^l a^{\dagger l}$. Baltin has shown that [16]

$$c_l^{(n)} = \frac{1}{l!} \int_{-\infty}^{+\infty} d\lambda\, g(\lambda)(e^{-i\lambda} - 1)^l = \sum_{k=0}^l \frac{(-)^{l-k} f(k)}{k!(l-k)!} ,$$

$$c_l^{(a)} = \frac{1}{l!} \int_{-\infty}^{+\infty} d\lambda\, e^{i\lambda} g(\lambda)(1 - e^{i\lambda})^l = \sum_{k=0}^l \frac{(-)^k f(-k-1)}{k!(l-k)!} , \tag{32}$$

$$g(\lambda) \doteq \int_{-\infty}^{+\infty} \frac{dx}{2\pi} f(x) e^{i\lambda x} .$$

From Eqs. (32) one can see that the normal ordered expansion is always well defined, whereas the anti-normal ordering needs extending the domain of f to negative integers. However, even though the anti-normal expansion is defined, this does not mean that the expectation of $f(a^\dagger a)$ can be obtained through heterodyning, because the integral in Eq. (31) may not exist. Actually, this is the case when the anti-normal expansion is not consistent on the Fock basis. In fact, for the exponential function $f(a^\dagger a) = \exp(-\mu a^\dagger a)$ one has $f^{(a)}(|\alpha|^2) = e^\mu \exp[(1 - e^\mu)|\alpha|^2]$; on the Fock basis $f^{(a)}(a^\dagger a)|n\rangle$ is a binomial expansion with finite convergence radius, and this gives the consistency condition $|1 - e^\mu| < 1$. However, one can take the analytic continuation corresponding for $1 - e^\mu < 1$, which coincides with the condition that the integral in Eq. (31) exists for any state $\hat{\varrho}$ (the Q-function vanishes as $\exp(-|\alpha|^2)$ for $\alpha \to \infty$, at least for states with limited photon number). This argument can be extended by Fourier transform to more general functions $f(a^\dagger a)$, leading to the conclusion that there are field operators that cannot be heterodyne-measured, even though they have well defined anti-normal expansion, but the expansion is not consistent on the Fock basis. As two examples, I consider the field operators $\hat{e}_+$ and $\hat{W}_s$ in Table 1. According to Eqs. (32) it follows that the operator $\hat{e}_+$ does not admit an anti-normal expansion, whence it cannot be heterodyne detected. This is in agreement with the fact that according to Table 1 we can homodyne $\hat{e}_+$ only for $\eta > 1/2$, and heterodyning is equivalent to homodyning with effective quantum efficiency $\eta = 1/2$ (which corresponds to the 3 dB noise due to the joint measurement [17]). The case of the operator $\hat{W}_s$ is different. It admits both normal-ordered and anti-normal-ordered forms: $\hat{W}_s = \frac{2}{\pi(1-s)} : \exp\left(-\frac{2}{1-s} a^\dagger a\right) :=$ $-\frac{2}{\pi(1+s)} : \exp\left(\frac{2}{1+s} a^\dagger a\right) :_A$, where $: \ldots :$ denotes normal ordering and $: \ldots :_A$ anti-normal. However, the consistency condition for anti-normal ordering is $2/(s+1) < 1$, with $s \leq 1$, which implies that one can heterodyne $\hat{W}_s$ for $s > -1$, again in agreement with the value of s achievable by homodyne tomography at $\eta = 1/2$.

Now I briefly analyze the additional noise from homodyning field operators, and compare them with the heterodyne noise. For a complex random variable $z = u + iv$ the noise is given by the eigenvalues $N^{(\pm)} = \overline{|z|^2} - |\bar{z}|^2 \pm |\overline{z^2} - \bar{z}^2|$ of the covariance matrix. When homodyning the field, the random variable is $z \equiv 2e^{i\phi}x$ [18] and the average over-line denotes the double integral over x and ϕ in Eq. (18). From Table (1) one has $\overline{z} = \langle a \rangle$, $\overline{z^2} = \langle a^2 \rangle$, $\overline{|z|^2} = 2\langle a^\dagger a \rangle + 1$, $\overline{e^{2i\phi}} = 0$ [19]. In this way one finds that the noise from homodyning the field is $N_{hom}^{(\pm)}[a] = 1 + 2\langle a^\dagger a \rangle - |\langle a \rangle|^2 \pm |\langle a^2 \rangle - \langle a \rangle^2|$. On the other hand, when heterodyning, z becomes the heterodyne output photocurrent, whence $\overline{z} = \langle a \rangle$, $\overline{z^2} = \langle a^2 \rangle$, $\overline{|z|^2} = \langle a^\dagger a \rangle + 1$, and one has $N_{het}^{(\pm)}[a] = 1 + \langle a^\dagger a \rangle - |\langle a \rangle|^2 \pm |\langle a^2 \rangle - \langle a \rangle^2|$, so that the tomographical noise is larger than the heterodyne noise by a term equal to the average photon number, i. e.

$$N_{hom}^{(\pm)}[a] = N_{het}^{(\pm)}[a] + \langle a^\dagger a \rangle . \tag{33}$$

Therefore, homodyning the field is always more noisy than heterodyning it. On the other hand, for other field observables it may happen that homodyne tomography is less noisy than heterodyne detection. For example, one can easily evaluate the noise $N_{hom}[\hat{n}]$ when homodyning the photon number $\hat{n} = a^\dagger a$. The random variable corresponding to the photon number is $\nu(z) = \frac{1}{2}(|z|^2 - 1) \equiv 2x^2 - \frac{1}{2}$, and from Table 1 we see that the noise $N_{hom}[\hat{n}] \doteq \overline{\Delta\nu^2(z)}$ can be written as $N_{hom}[\hat{n}] = \langle \Delta\hat{n}^2 \rangle + \frac{1}{2}\langle \hat{n}^2 + \hat{n} + 1 \rangle$ [13]. When heterodyning the field, the random variable corresponding to the photon number is $\nu(z) = |z|^2 - 1$, and from the relation $\overline{|z|^4} = \langle a^{\dagger 2}a^2 \rangle$ one obtains $N_{het}[\hat{n}] \doteq \overline{\Delta\nu^2(z)} = \langle \Delta\hat{n}^2 \rangle + \langle \hat{n} + 1 \rangle$, namely

$$N_{hom}[\hat{n}] = N_{het}[\hat{n}] + \frac{1}{2}\langle \hat{n}^2 - \hat{n} - 1 \rangle . \tag{34}$$

We thus conclude that homodyning the photon number is less noisy than heterodyning it for sufficiently low mean photon number $\langle \hat{n} \rangle < \frac{1}{2}(1 + \sqrt{5})$.

4. HOMODYNE TOMOGRAPHY IN PRESENCE OF ADDITIVE PHASE-INSENSITIVE NOISE

In this section I consider the case of additive Gaussian noise, in the typical situation in which the noise is phase-insensitive. This kind of noise is described by a density matrix evolved by the master equation

$$\partial_t \hat{\varrho}(t) = 2 \left[AL[a^\dagger] + BL[a] \right] \hat{\varrho}(t) , \tag{35}$$

where $L[\hat{c}]$ denotes the Lindblad super-operator $L[\hat{c}]\hat{\varrho} \doteq \hat{c}\hat{\varrho}\hat{c}^\dagger - \frac{1}{2}[\hat{c}^\dagger\hat{c}, \hat{\varrho}]_+$. Due to the phase invariance $L[ae^{-i\phi}] = L[a]$ the dynamical evolution does not depend on the phase, and the noise is phase insensitive. From the evolution of the averaged field $\langle a \rangle_{out} \equiv \text{Tr}[a\hat{\varrho}(t)] = g\langle a \rangle_{in} \equiv \text{Tr}[a\hat{\varrho}(0)]$ with $g = \exp[(A - B)t]$, we can see that for $A > B$ Eq. (35) describes phase-insensitive amplification with field-gain g, whereas for $B > A$ it describes phase-insensitive attenuation, with $g < 1$. Concretely, for $A > B$ Eq. (35) models unsaturated parametric amplification with thermal idler [average photon number $\bar{m} = B/(A - B)$], or unsaturated laser action [A and B proportional to atomic populations on the upper and lower lasing levels respectively]. For $B > A$, on the other hand, the same equation describes a field mode damped toward the thermal distribution [inverse photon lifetime $\Gamma = 2(B - A)$, equilibrium photon number $\bar{m} = A/(B - A)$], or a loss $g < 1$ along an optical fiber or at a beam-splitter, or even due to frequency conversion [20]. The borderline case $A = B$ leaves the average field invariant, but introduces noise that changes the average photon number as $\langle a^\dagger a \rangle_{out} = \langle a^\dagger a \rangle_{in} + \bar{n}$, where $\bar{n} = 2At$. In this case the solution of Eq. (35) can be cast into the simple form

$$\hat{\varrho}(t) = \int \frac{d^2\beta}{\pi\bar{n}} \exp\left(-|\beta|^2/\bar{n}\right) \hat{D}(\beta)\hat{\varrho}(0)\hat{D}^\dagger(\beta) . \tag{36}$$

This is the *Gaussian displacement noise* studied in Refs. [21,22] and commonly referred to as "thermal noise" [regarding the misuse of this terminology, see Ref. [22]], which can be used to model many kinds of undesired environmental effects, typically due to linear interactions with random classical fluctuating fields.

Eq. (35) has the following simple Fokker-Planck differential representation [23] in terms of the generalized Wigner function $W_s(\alpha, \bar{\alpha})$ for ordering parameter s

$$\partial_t W_s(\alpha, \bar{\alpha}; t) = \left[Q(\partial_\alpha \alpha + \partial_{\bar{\alpha}}\bar{\alpha}) + 2D_s\partial^2_{\alpha,\bar{\alpha}}\right] W_s(\alpha, \bar{\alpha}; t) , \tag{37}$$

where $Q = B - A$ and $2D_s = A + B + s(A - B)$. For nonunit quantum efficiency η and after a noise-diffusion time t the homodyne probability distribution $p_\eta(x; \phi; t)$ can be evaluated as the marginal distribution of the Wigner function for ordering parameter $s = 1 - \eta^{-1}$, namely

$$p_\eta(x; \phi; t) = \int_{-\infty}^{+\infty} dy W_{1-\eta^{-1}}\left((x + iy)e^{i\phi}, (x - iy)e^{-i\phi}; t\right) . \tag{38}$$

The solution of Eq. (37) is the Gaussian convolution [23]

$$W_s(\alpha, \bar{\alpha}; t) = \int \frac{d^2\beta}{\pi\delta_s^2} \exp\left[-\frac{|\alpha - g\beta|^2}{\delta_s^2}\right] W_s(\beta, \bar{\beta}; 0) , \qquad \delta_s^2 = \frac{D_s}{Q}(1 - e^{-2Qt}) , \tag{39}$$

and using Eq. (38) one obtains the homodyne probability distribution

$$p_\eta(x; \phi; t) = e^{Qt} \int_{-\infty}^{\infty} \frac{dx'}{\sqrt{2\pi\Delta_{1-\eta^{-1}}^2}} \exp\left[-\frac{(x' - g^{-1}x)^2}{2\Delta_{1-\eta^{-1}}^2}\right] p_\eta(x'; \phi) . \tag{40}$$

where $\Delta_\eta^2 = \frac{1}{2}g^{-2}\delta_{1-\eta^{-1}}^2$. It is easy to see that the generating function of the $\hat{x}_\phi$-moments with the experimental probability $p_\eta(x; \phi; t)$ can be written in term of the probability distribution $p(x; \phi)$ for perfect homodyning as follows

$$\int_{-\infty}^{+\infty} dx\, p_\eta(x; \phi; t)e^{ikx} = \exp\left(-\frac{1}{2}g^2\Delta_\eta^2 k^2 - \frac{1 - \eta}{8\eta}g^2 k^2\right) \int_{-\infty}^{+\infty} dx\, p(x; \phi)e^{igkx} , \tag{41}$$

Eq. (41) has the same form of Eq. (8), but with the Fourier variable k multiplied by g and with an overall *effective quantum efficiency* η_* given by

$$\eta_*^{-1} = \eta^{-1} + 4\Delta_\eta^2 = g^{-2}\eta^{-1} + \frac{2A}{B - A}(g^{-2} - 1) . \tag{42}$$

On the other hand, following the same lines that lead us to Eq. (9), we obtain the operator identity

$$\hat{\varrho} \equiv \hat{\varrho}(0) = \int_0^\pi \frac{d\phi}{\pi} \int_{-\infty}^{+\infty} dx\, p_{\eta_*}(x; \phi; t)K_{\eta_*}(g^{-1}x - \hat{x}_\phi) , \tag{43}$$

which also means that when homodyning the operator $\hat{O}$ one should use $\mathcal{R}_{\eta_*}(g^{-1}x; \phi)$ in place of $\mathcal{R}_\eta(x; \phi)$, namely, more generally, one needs to re-scale the homodyne outcomes by the gain and use the effective quantum efficiency η_* in Eq. (42). In terms of the gain g and of the input-output photon numbers, the effective quantum efficiency reads

$$\eta_*^{-1} = \eta^{-1} + g^{-2}(2\langle a^\dagger a \rangle_{out} + \eta^{-1}) - (2\langle a^\dagger a \rangle_{in} + \eta^{-1}) \,. \tag{44}$$

In the case of pure displacement Gaussian noise ($A = B$), Eq. (44) becomes

$$\eta_*^{-1} = \eta^{-1} + 2\bar{n} \,, \tag{45}$$

which means that the bound $\eta_* > 1/2$ is surpassed already for $\bar{n} \geq 1$: in other worlds, it is just sufficient to have half photon of thermal noise to completely spoil the tomographic reconstruction.

REFERENCES

[1] D. T. Smithey, M. Beck, M. G. Raymer, and A. Faridani, Phys. Rev. Lett. **70**, 1244 (1993).

[2] G. M. D'Ariano, C. Macchiavello and M. G. A. Paris, Phys. Rev. A**50**, 4298 (1994); Phys. Lett. A **195**, 31 (1994).

[3] M. Munroe, D. Boggavarapu, M. E. Anderson, and M. G. Raymer, Phys. Rev. A **52**, R924 (1995).

[4] S. Schiller, G. Breitenbach, S. F. Pereira, T. Müller, and J. Mlynek, Phys. Rev. Lett. **77** 2933 (1996); see also: G. Breitenbach, S. Schiller, and J. Mlynek, *Quantum state reconstruction of coherent light and squeezed light* on this volume.

[5] G. M. D'Ariano, U. Leonhardt and H. Paul, Phys. Rev. A **52** R1801 (1995).

[6] G. M. D'Ariano, Quantum Semiclass. Opt. **7**, 693 (1995).

[7] Th. Richter, Phys. Lett. A **221** 327 (1996).

[8] U. Leonhardt, M. Munroe, T. Kiss, Th. Richter, and M. G. Raymer, Opt. Comm. **127**, 144 (1996).

[9] U. Leonhardt, H. Paul and G. M. D'Ariano, Phys. Rev. A **52** 4899 (1995); H. Paul, U. Leonhardt, and G. M. D'Ariano, Acta Phys. Slov. **45**, 261 (1995).

[10] G. M. D'Ariano, *Quantum Estimation Theory and Optical Detection*, in *Concepts and Advances in Quantum Optics and Spectroscopy of Solids*, ed. by T. Hakioglu and A. S. Shumovsky. (Kluwer, Amsterdam 1996, in press).

[11] G. M. D'Ariano, *Measuring Quantum States*, in the same book of Ref. ([10]).

[12] G. M. D'Ariano and H. P. Yuen, Phys. Rev. Lett. **76** 2832 (1996).

[13] G. M. D'Ariano, C. Macchiavello, and N. Sterpi, *Systematic and statistical errors in homodyne measurements of the density matrix*, submitted to Phys. Rev. A.

[14] I. S. Gradshteyn and I. M. Ryzhik , *Table of integrals, series, and products* (Academic Press, 1980).

[15] Th. Richter, Phys. Rev. A **53** 1197 (1996).

[16] R. Baltin, J. Phys. A Math. Gen. **16** 2721 (1983); Phys. Lett. **102**A 332 (1984).

[17] H. P. Yuen, Phys. Lett. **91A**, 101 (1982).

[18] Notice that for the complex random variable $z = 2e^{i\phi}x$ the phase ϕ is a scanning parameter imposed by the detector. (Actually, the best way to experimentally scan the integral in Eq. (18) is just to pick up the phase ϕ at random.) Nevertheless, the argument of the complex number z is still a genuine random variable, because the sign of x is random, and depends on the value of ϕ. One has $\arg(z) = \phi + \pi(1 - \text{sgn}(x))$. For example, for any highly excited coherent state $|\alpha\rangle$ the probability distribution of $\arg(z)$ will approach a uniform distribution on $[\arg(\alpha) - \pi/2, \arg(\alpha) + \pi/2]$.

[19] One should remember that, the phase ϕ is imposed by the detector, and is uniformly scanned (randomly or not) in the interval $[0, \pi]$. This leads to $\overline{e^{2i\phi}} = 0$, independently on the state $\hat{\varrho}$.

[20] G. M. D'Ariano and C. Macchiavello, Phys. Rev. **A 48** 3947, (1993).

[21] M. J. W. Hall, *Phase and noise* in Quantum Communication and Measurement, ed. V. P. Belavkin, O. Hirota and R. L. Hudson, Plenum Press (New York and London 1995), p. 53-59.

[22] M. J. W. Hall, Phys. Rev. A **50** 3295 (1994).

[23] G. M. D'Ariano, C. Macchiavello, and M. G. A. Paris, *Information gain in quantum communication channels*, in *Quantum Communication and Measurement*, ed. V. P. Belavkin, O. Hirota and R. L. Hudson, Plenum Press (New York and London 1995), pag. 339.

RESOLUTIONS OF THE IDENTITY IN TERMS OF LINE INTEGRALS OF COHERENT STATES AND THEIR USE FOR QUANTUM STATE ENGINEERING

A. Vourdas

Dept. of Electrical Engineering and Electronics
University of Liverpool
Liverpool L69 3BX

Resolutions of the identity in terms of line integrals of coherent states and their complementary states are presented. The concept of complementary states is explained. The general technique is exemplified in the context of $SU(2)$ coherent states. It enables the construction of an arbitrary state within the Hilbert space H_{2j+1} in terms of $SU(2)$ coherent states. More general results for other types of coherent states are also presented.

1. INTRODUCTION

Coherent states form an overcomplete set of states. In fact it is known that if z_N is a convergent sequence to some point z_0 then the corresponding coherent states form an overcomplete set. This is a very powerful theorem. However, from a practical point of view in order to use the coherent states as a basis in the Hilbert space, we need to have a resolution of the identity which can be used for the expansion of an arbitrary state in terms of coherent states. And some times even a weaker concept than a resolution of the identity, like the concept of frames in the context of wavelets, might also be useful. The known resolutions of the identity are in terms of surface integrals. Here we study resolutions of the identity in terms of the line integrals of the type:

$$\int dl |s\rangle\langle s; \mathrm{com}| = 1, \tag{1}$$

where $|s\rangle$ are coherent states and $\langle s; \mathrm{com}|$ are "complementary" states which are not coherent states. The use of these states gives us great flexibility in constructing new resolutions of the identity; and at the same time there is no loss in the strength of the resulting resolution of the identity. Indeed (1) can be used to expand an arbitrary ket state $|f\rangle$ in terms of the coherent states $|s\rangle$ as:

$$|f\rangle = \int dl f(s) |s\rangle, \tag{2}$$

where

$$f(s) = \langle s; \mathrm{com}|f\rangle, \tag{3}$$

Quantum Communication, Computing, and Measurement
Edited by Hirota *et al.*, Plenum Press, New York, 1997

and the corresponding bra state $\langle f|$ in terms of the coherent states, $\langle s|$ as :

$$\langle f| = \int [dl f(s)]^* \langle s|. \tag{4}$$

The $\langle s; com|$ are auxiliary states which are used in the calculation of the coefficients $f(s)$. The above ideas have been inspired by recent work [1] where quantum states have been expressed as quantum superpositions of Glauber coherent states on a certain line in phase-space. The approximation of the exact expansion in terms of line integrals, by a discrete sum leads to the possibility of producing experimentally approximately any desired state as a superposition of Glauber coherent states. This is one approach within the more general frame work of quantum state engineering [2] and indicates one of the practical merits of expansions like (2),(4).

In this paper we construct a resolution of the identity using a line integral like Eq(1), which contains $SU(2)$ coherent states. We also study the properties of the complementary states $\langle s; com|$ that enter in this integral. Using this resolution of the identity we can expand an arbitrary state in the Hilbert space in terms of $SU(2)$ coherent states.

2. RESOLUTIONS OF THE IDENTITY IN TERMS OF $SU(2)$ COHERENT STATES AND THEIR COMPLEMENTARY STATES

We consider the angular momentum operators J_+, J_-, J_z, and the usual $|j, n >$ states $(j = 1, 2, 3, ... ; n = (-j), ..., j)$,

$$J^2|j, n >= j(j + 1)|j, n >, \tag{5}$$

$$J_z|j, n >= n|j, n > . \tag{6}$$

The states $|j, n >$ span a $(2j + 1)$-dimensional Hilbert space H. We also consider the $SU(2)$ operators:

$$T(\theta, \phi, \lambda) = \exp[-\frac{1}{2}\theta e^{-i\phi}J_+ + \frac{1}{2}\theta e^{i\phi}J_+] \exp[i\lambda J_z]. \tag{7}$$

$SU(2)$ coherent states are defined as

$$|z\rangle = (1 + |z|^2)^{-j} \sum_{n=-j}^{j} \delta(j, n)z^{j+n}|j, n\rangle, \tag{8}$$

$$\delta(j, n) = [\frac{(2j)!}{(j + n)!(j - n)!}]^{1/2}, \tag{9}$$

where z belongs to the extended complex plane which is stereographically related to a sphere. An alternative equivalent definition is

$$|\theta, \phi, \lambda\rangle = T(\theta, \phi, \lambda)|j, -j\rangle = \exp[-i\lambda j]|j, -j\rangle, \tag{10}$$

$$z = -\tan(\frac{1}{2}\theta)e^{-i\phi}. \tag{11}$$

The following resolution of the identity in terms of surface integrals of these states is well known:

$$\frac{2j + 1}{\pi} \int d\mu(z)|z\rangle\langle z| = 1, \tag{12}$$

$$d\mu(z) = (1 + |z|^2)^{-2}d^2z. \tag{13}$$

Here we are going to give an alternative resolution of the identity in terms of line integrals. We first define the "complementary" states to the $SU(2)$ coherent states as:

$$\langle z; \text{com}| = [\mathcal{N}(z)]^{-1} \sum_{n=-j}^{j} [\delta(j, n)z^{j+n+1}]^{-1} \langle j, n|, \tag{14}$$

$$\mathcal{N}(z) = [\sum_{n=-j}^{j} \frac{(j+n)!(j-n)!}{(2j)!} \frac{1}{|z|^{2(j+n+1)}}]^{1/2}, \tag{15}$$

where "com" in the notation indicates complementary states. They are auxiliary states that will be useful in the calculation of the coefficients, in the expansion of an arbitrary state in terms of $SU(2)$ coherent states. Some properties of the complementary states have been studied in [3]. Combining (8) and (14) we show the resolution of the identity

$$\oint_C \frac{dz}{2\pi i} (1 + |z|^2)^j \mathcal{N}(z)|z\rangle\langle z; \text{com}| = 1, \tag{16}$$

where C is a contour around the origin in the anticlockwise direction. Let $|f\rangle$ be an arbitrary (normalised) pure state

$$|f\rangle = \sum_{n=-j}^{j} f_n |j, n\rangle. \tag{17}$$

It can be expanded in terms of SU(2) coherent states on a contour C around the origin as:

$$|f\rangle = \oint_C \frac{dz}{2\pi i} f(z)|z\rangle, \tag{18}$$

where the coefficients $f(z)$ are given by

$$f(z) = (1 + |z|^2)^j \mathcal{N}(|z|)\langle z; \text{com}|f\rangle = (1 + |z|^2)^j \sum_{n=-j}^{j} \frac{f_n}{\delta(j, n)z^{j+n+1}}. \tag{19}$$

As an example of the above expansion we consider the states $|j, n\rangle$ for which we prove

$$f(z) = \frac{(1 + |z|^2)^j}{\delta(j, n)z^{j+n+1}}. \tag{20}$$

Another example are the $SU(2)$ coherent states $|w\rangle$ for which we prove

$$f(z) = \frac{1}{2} \frac{(1 + |z|^2)^j}{(1 + |w|^2)^j} S\left(\frac{w}{z}\right), \tag{21}$$

where

$$S(z) = \frac{z^{2j+1} - 1}{z - 1}, \tag{22}$$

if z is different than 1; and $S(z) = 2j + 1$ if $z = 1$.

3. RESOLUTIONS OF THE IDENTITY FOR OTHER TYPES OF CO-HERENT STATES: GENERAL METHOD

Above we have studied resolutions of the identity in terms of $SU(2)$ coherent states. Here we consider other types of coherent states (associated with a certain group) which we write in the general form:

$$|z\rangle = \sum_N a_N |N\rangle, \tag{23}$$

$$\sum_N |a_N|^2 = 1, \tag{24}$$

where $|N\rangle$ is an orthonormal basis. Their complementary states are defined as

$$\langle z; \mathrm{com}| = [\mathcal{N}(z)]^{-1} \sum_N [a_N z^{N+1}]^{-1} \langle N|, \tag{25}$$

where $\mathcal{N}(z)$ is a normalisation factor. We can now show the resolution of the identity

$$\oint_C dz \mathcal{N}(z)|z\rangle\langle z; \mathrm{com}| = \mathbf{1}, \tag{26}$$

where C is an anticlockwise contour around the origin. The difficulty with certain groups is that the normalisation factor diverges and this means that the complementary states do not belong in the usual Hilbert space but in some extension of it. In these cases extra work is required on how the complementary states are defined and in which space they belong. In the cases that the normalisation factor of the complementary states converges, the above formalism is complete and provides a resolution of the identity in terms of line integrals of coherent states.

4. DISCUSSION

Resolutions of the identity can be used for the expansion of an arbitrary state in terms of coherent states. The known resolutions of the identity are in terms of surface integrals. Here we have presented novel resolutions of the identity in terms of line integrals that involve both the coherent states and the so-called complementary states. The work has been presented primarily in the context of $SU(2)$ coherent states. But the formalism has also been generalised into other types of coherent states in section 3,where potential difficulties with the normalisation of the complementary states have been pointed out.

The formalism provides an expansion of an arbitrary state in terms of coherent states on a line. And if the line integral is approximated with a finite sum,then an arbitrary state can be represented approximately as a finite sum of coherent states(quantum state engineering).

REFERENCES

[1] J. Jansky, P. Adam, A.V. Vinogradov, Phys. Rev. Lett. 68, 3816 (1992),
 J. Jansky, P. Domokos, P. Adam, Phys. Rev. A48, 2213 (1993),
 J. Jansky, P. Domokos, S. Szabo, P. Adam Phys. Rev. A51, 4191 (1995),
 S. Szabo, P. Adam, J.Jansky, P. Domokos, Phys. Rev. A53, 2698 (1996),
 A. Wunsche (preprint).

[2] K. Vogel, V.M. Akulin, W.P. Schleich, Phys. Rev. Lett. 71, 1816 (1993).

[3] A. Vourdas, Phys.Rev.A(1996)to appear.

UNITARY CONTROL PROCESS
FOR QUANTUM OPTIMUM DETECTION

Masahide Sasaki[1] and Osamu Hirota[2]

[1] Communication Research Laboratory,
   Ministry of Posts & Telecommunications, Koganei, Tokyo 184, Japan
[2] Research Center for Quantum Communications, Tamagawa University
   Tamagawa-gakuen, Machida, Tokyo 194, Japan

It will be shown that the minimum error bound in binary decision of linearly-independent pure-state signals can be achieved for any given measurement process by installing an appropriate unitary transformation for the signal states in front of the measurement. The optimum decision problem can be viewed as how to find this transformation which modifies the received signals so as to cause the quantum interference optimally at the measurement. It will be discussed how the origin of the error reduction can be identified and how the required unitary control process can be constructed.

1. INTRODUCTION

In high-grade communication technology such as 1) high speed transmission over Tera bps, 2) high frequency modulation over THz, 3) high resolution for weak signals, ~ 10 photons/B, and so on, the quantum nature of light appears as a basic aspect. Namely, the uncertainty principle due to high frequency quanta directly limits the system performance. This limit had been known as the shot noise limit. But in 1967 Helstrom pioneered the new detection theory by taking quantum nature into account, and he showed that the fundamental limit is much superior to the shot noise limit [1].

Let us consider coherent light communication with binary-phase-shift-keyed (BPSK) signaling, $\{|\alpha\rangle, |-\alpha\rangle\}$. The conventional detection method is the homodyne detection which can almost reach the shot noise limit. The obtained error probability is represented by $P_e(\mathrm{SQL}) = \frac{1}{2}\mathrm{erfc}(\sqrt{2|\alpha|^2})$ with $\mathrm{erfc}(x) = \frac{2}{\sqrt{\pi}}\int_x^\infty dt\, e^{-t^2}$. But Helstrom predicted that we could reach a much lower bound given by the new formulas $\frac{1}{2}\left\{1 - \sqrt{1 - \exp(-4|\alpha|^2)}\right\}$.

Following Helstrom, Holevo [2], and Yuen, Kennedy, and Lax [3] developed the general framework to cope with M-ary signal detection. In particular, they formulated the problem by use of the probability operator measure (POM) and derived the necessary and sufficient conditions for optimum detection. Today this framework is called quantum detection theory.

Throughout this paper, the term *detection* means a process including quantum measurement and decision simultaneously. Such a process is described by the so-called detection operators on the Hilbert space which is in general the POM. This is non-negative

Hermite operators $\hat{\Pi}_i$ satisfying the resolution of the identity

$$\hat{\Pi}_i \geq 0, \quad \sum_i \hat{\Pi}_i = \hat{I}. \tag{1}$$

Demonstration is performed in the case of the binary pure-state signals $\{|\rho_1\rangle, |\rho_2\rangle\}$. We usually know prior probabilities $\{\xi_1, \xi_2\}$, respectively. Then $\{\hat{\Pi}_i\}$ can be derived by use of the Bayes procedure so as to minimize the error probability,

$$P_e = \xi_2 \text{Tr}\left(\hat{\Pi}_1 \hat{\rho}_2\right) + \xi_1 \text{Tr}\left(\hat{\Pi}_2 \hat{\rho}_1\right) = \xi_1 + \xi_2 \text{Tr}[(\hat{\rho}_2 - \lambda \hat{\rho}_1)\hat{\Pi}_1], \tag{2}$$

where $\hat{\rho}_j$ is the corresponding density operator $\hat{\rho}_j \equiv |\rho_j\rangle\langle\rho_j|$ and $\lambda \equiv \xi_1/\xi_2$. Minimization can be done by solving the eigenvalue problem for the Hermite matrix $\hat{\rho}_2 - \lambda \hat{\rho}_1$ which is of rank 2. We have two non-zero eigenvalues,

$$\omega_1 = \frac{1 - \lambda - \sqrt{(1+\lambda)^2 - 4\lambda|\kappa|^2}}{2} < 0, \quad \omega_2 = \frac{1 - \lambda + \sqrt{(1+\lambda)^2 - 4\lambda|\kappa|^2}}{2} > 0, \tag{3}$$

where κ is the overlap $\kappa \equiv \langle\psi_2|\psi_1\rangle$. Then $\{\hat{\Pi}_i\}$ can be constructed by the corresponding eigenvectors $|\omega_1\rangle$ and $|\omega_2\rangle$ as pure-state projectors:

$$\hat{\Pi}_1 = |\omega_1\rangle\langle\omega_1|, \quad \hat{\Pi}_2 = |\omega_2\rangle\langle\omega_2|, \tag{4}$$

where the $|\omega_i\rangle$'s are simply the linear superposition of $|\rho_1\rangle$ and $|\rho_2\rangle$. The minimum error probability is therefore,

$$P_e(\text{opt}) = \xi_1 + \xi_2\omega_1 = \frac{1}{2}(1 - \sqrt{1 - 4\xi_1\xi_2|\kappa|^2}), \tag{5}$$

which is now called the Helstrom bound.

Thus the quantum optimum detector is $\{\hat{\Pi}_i\}$ in Eq. (4). Although this result is beautiful, it dose not provide a recipe for achieving the optimum detector physically. A practical receiver structure achieving the Helstrom bound was first shown by Dolinar in the case of binary coherent-state signals [4]. It is based on a feedback arrangement. The signal states beat with local oscillator light via a beam splitter and are then detected by a photon counter where the signal states are discriminated by whether the total photon count is even or odd. In the feedback loop, every time a single photon is registered, the local oscillator light is readjusted depending on the accumulated outcomes. This was a big step to convince us that the corresponding physical process for the Helstrom bound surely existed, even though its implementation might still have difficulties. The corresponding detection operators, say $\{\hat{\Pi}_i^{\text{FB}}\}$, were derived by Holevo [5] and analyzed by the authors [6]. They can be represented by a normally ordered expression of creation and annihilation operators $\hat{a}^\dagger$ and $\hat{a}$ on the *whole Fock space*. These $\{\hat{\Pi}_i^{\text{FB}}\}$ are not pure-state projectors like the Helstrom solution $\{\hat{\Pi}_i\}$ which is uniquely determined in the plane spanned by the signal states. Only on the plane do $\{\hat{\Pi}_i^{\text{FB}}\}$ coincide with $\{\hat{\Pi}_i\}$ in matrix components. But they are physically different.

Actually, there are various kinds of physically different realizations for the optimum detection operators. Let $\{\hat{\Pi}_i^*\}$ be a physical solution for the signal states $\{|\rho_1\rangle, |\rho_2\rangle\}$. Then the condition for it can be given as,

$$\text{Tr}(\hat{R}\hat{\Pi}_i^*) = \omega_i, \quad (i = 1, 2), \quad \omega_1 < 0, \omega_2 > 0, \tag{6}$$

where $\hat{R} = \hat{\rho}_2 - \lambda\hat{\rho}_1$ and ω_i's are given in Eq. (3).

The problem addressed in this paper is *how to seek physically realizable* $\{\hat{\Pi}_i^*\}$? We shall answer that the above condition can be satisfied by the type of $\hat{\Pi}_i^* = \hat{U}^\dagger \hat{\Pi}_i^{SD} \hat{U}$ [9–11], where $\{\hat{\Pi}_i^{SD}\}$ can be an arbitrary projection valued measure(PVM), i.e., an orthogonal resolution of the identity, and $\hat{U}$ is a unitary operator which should satisfy a certain condition. Unlike Dolinar's scheme, this type of structure does not rely on a feedback process. As $\hat{\Pi}_i^*$, we may take the well-known detection processes like photon counting, homodyne detection, etc. The main concern is how to construct $\hat{U}$ on a physical basis. In the next section, we shall explain why the optimum detection operators may be pursued in such a structure of $\hat{U}^\dagger \hat{\Pi}_i^{SD} \hat{U}$.

2. THE SEMI-QUANTUM LIMIT

The structure of $\hat{U}^\dagger \hat{\Pi}_i^{SD} \hat{U}$ provides a natural extension from a classical detection scheme (the conventional receiver structure used at present) to a quantum detection scheme achieving the Helstrom bound. At first, we should explain the performance limit in classical detection theory.

In general, signal states $\{|\rho_1\rangle, |\rho_2\rangle\}$ are keyed with respect to a certain observable $\hat{X}$, called the signal observable . For phase modulation, $\hat{X}$ is the quadrature-phase amplitude, $\hat{X} = \frac{1}{2}(\hat{a} + \hat{a}^\dagger)$. For amplitude modulation, $\hat{X}$ is the photon number operator $\hat{X} = \hat{a}^\dagger \hat{a}$. The scheme used at present is based on direct measurement of the signal observable. In the ideal limit where noises due to imperfection of the system setup can be eliminated, the system performance is finally limited by the shot noise of the signal light itself, and the measurement process can be described by the projection $|x\rangle\langle x|$ with the eigenstate $|x\rangle$, i.e., $\hat{X}|x\rangle = x|x\rangle$. We then get the set of outcomes x, and its probability distributions $|\langle x|\rho_i\rangle|^2$ ($i = 1, 2$). Based on these distributions, binary decision is made by dividing the set $\{x\}$ into two subsets $\mathcal{A}$ and $\mathcal{B}$. If $x \in \mathcal{A}$, we decide the signal is $|\rho_1\rangle$, and if else, $|\rho_2\rangle$ is adopted.

The minimum error attained by adjusting this division is defined as the *semi-quantum limit* (Semi-QL). The corresponding detection operators can be defined as

$$\hat{\Pi}_A^{SD} \equiv \int_{\mathcal{A}} dx |x\rangle\langle x|, \quad \hat{\Pi}_B^{SD} \equiv \int_{\mathcal{B}} dx |x\rangle\langle x|, \quad \hat{\Pi}_A^{SD} + \hat{\Pi}_B^{SD} = \hat{I}. \tag{7}$$

They are especially called the *standard detection operators* and represent the ideal limit of the direct detection of the signal observable.

The Semi-QL is then given as

$$P_e(\text{SQL}) = \min_{\{\mathcal{A}, \mathcal{B}\}} \left[\xi_2 \text{Tr}(\hat{\Pi}_A^{SD} \hat{\rho}_2) + \xi_1 \text{Tr}(\hat{\Pi}_B^{SD} \hat{\rho}_1) \right], \tag{8}$$

The improvement from the Semi-QL is called *quantum gain*. As far as we rely on classical detection theory, no *quantum gain* is available.

In 1992, Usuda and Hirota found that the error probability in the homodyne scheme can be reduced simply by installing a Kerr medium in front of the detector, showing the Semi-QL can be broken simply [7]. They showed that error may be reduced only if the Kerr effect is considered quantum mechanically as caused by $\hat{U}_K = \exp(i\gamma \hat{a}^{\dagger 2} \hat{a}^2)$. If we use the squeezer $\hat{U}_S = \exp\gamma(\hat{a}^{\dagger 2} - \hat{a}^2)$ instead of the Kerr medium, error reduction will not occur.

Thus the control process should satisfy certain conditions for obtaining *quantum gain*. The detection operators $\hat{U}^\dagger \hat{\Pi}_i^{SD} \hat{U}$ provide a generalization of this scheme.

Fig. 1 shows the detection scheme. Into the standard detection for the signal observable $\hat{X}$, the unitary process $\hat{U}$ is installed in order to control the signal states adaptively. The next section is devoted to formulating a construction procedure for $\hat{U}$.

$$\{|\rho_1\rangle, |\rho_2\rangle\} \longrightarrow \boxed{\text{control process } \hat{U}} \longrightarrow \boxed{\hat{\Pi}_A^{\text{SD}}, \hat{\Pi}_B^{\text{SD}}}$$
$$\hat{X}\text{-keying} \qquad\qquad\qquad\qquad\qquad\qquad \hat{X}\text{-detection}$$

Figure 1. The detection scheme.

3. THE OPTIMUM RECEIVER STRUCTURE

Let $\mathcal{H}_A$ and $\mathcal{H}_B$ be the corresponding subspaces spanned by $\{|x\rangle\}$ with $\{x \in \mathcal{A}\}$ and $\{x \in \mathcal{B}\}$. Then the signal state $|\rho_1\rangle$ lies mainly in the subspace $\mathcal{H}_A$ but a part of it lies in the subspace $\mathcal{H}_B$ also. The state $|\rho_2\rangle$ does the same. So let us separate $|\rho_1\rangle$ into the main part $|A_1\rangle$ and small part $|B_1\rangle$ by projecting it by $\hat{\Pi}_A$ and $\hat{\Pi}_B$,

$$|\rho_1\rangle = (\hat{\Pi}_A^{\text{SD}} + \hat{\Pi}_B^{\text{SD}})|\rho_1\rangle = \sqrt{1 - \epsilon_1}|A_1\rangle + \sqrt{\epsilon_1}|B_1\rangle, \quad \epsilon_1 \equiv \text{Tr}\left(\hat{\Pi}_B^{\text{SD}} \hat{\rho}_1\right). \tag{9}$$

In the same way, the state $|\rho_2\rangle$ is decomposed into $|B_2\rangle$ and $|A_2\rangle$,

$$|\rho_2\rangle = (\hat{\Pi}_B^{\text{SD}} + \hat{\Pi}_A^{\text{SD}})|\rho_1\rangle = \sqrt{1 - \epsilon_2}|B_2\rangle + \sqrt{\epsilon_2}|A_2\rangle, \quad \epsilon_2 \equiv \text{Tr}\left(\hat{\Pi}_A^{\text{SD}} \hat{\rho}_2\right). \tag{10}$$

The states $|A_i\rangle$ and $|B_i\rangle$ are orthogonal to each other, while $|A_1\rangle$ and $|A_2\rangle$ are not and neither are $|B_1\rangle$ and $|B_2\rangle$. So we make the orthonormal sets $\{|e_1\rangle, |e_2\rangle\}$ on the subspace $\mathcal{H}_A$ and $\{|e_3\rangle, |e_4\rangle\}$ on the subspace $\mathcal{H}_B$ by the Schmidt orthogonalization;

$$|e_1\rangle \equiv \frac{|A_1\rangle - \kappa_A|A_2\rangle}{\sqrt{1 - |\kappa_A|^2}}, \quad |e_2\rangle \equiv |A_2\rangle, \quad \kappa_A \equiv \langle A_2|A_1\rangle, \tag{11}$$

$$|e_3\rangle \equiv |B_1\rangle, \quad |e_4\rangle \equiv \frac{|B_2\rangle - \kappa_B|B_1\rangle}{\sqrt{1 - |\kappa_B|^2}}, \quad \kappa_B \equiv \langle B_1|B_2\rangle. \tag{12}$$

Then the signal states can be expanded as,

$$|\rho_1\rangle = \sqrt{\epsilon_1}|e_3\rangle + \sqrt{1 - \epsilon_1}\kappa_A|e_2\rangle + \sqrt{1 - \epsilon_1}\sqrt{1 - |\kappa_A|^2}|e_1\rangle, \tag{13}$$

$$|\rho_2\rangle = \sqrt{1 - \epsilon_2}\sqrt{1 - |\kappa_B|^2}|e_4\rangle + \sqrt{1 - \epsilon_2}\kappa_B|e_3\rangle + \sqrt{\epsilon_2}|e_2\rangle. \tag{14}$$

The standard detection operators can be mapped into a PVM with simpler structure,

$$\hat{\Pi}_A^{\text{SD}} \equiv \int_{\mathcal{A}} dx|x\rangle\langle x| \quad \mapsto \quad |e_1\rangle\langle e_1| + |e_2\rangle\langle e_2|$$

$$\hat{\Pi}_B^{\text{SD}} \equiv \int_{\mathcal{B}} dx|x\rangle\langle x| \quad \mapsto \quad |e_3\rangle\langle e_3| + |e_4\rangle\langle e_4|$$

We are naturally led to the 4-dimensional matrix representation with this basis,

$$\hat{R} = \hat{\rho}_2 - \lambda\hat{\rho}_1 = \begin{bmatrix} R_{11} & R_{12} & R_{13} & R_{14} \\ R_{12}^* & R_{22} & R_{23} & R_{24} \\ R_{13}^* & R_{23}^* & R_{33} & R_{34} \\ R_{14}^* & R_{24}^* & R_{34}^* & R_{44} \end{bmatrix}, \tag{15}$$

where

$$\begin{aligned}
R_{11} &= -\lambda(1 - \epsilon_1)(1 - |\kappa_A|^2), & R_{23} &= \sqrt{\epsilon_2(1 - \epsilon_2)}\kappa_B^* - \lambda\sqrt{\epsilon_1(1 - \epsilon_1)}\kappa_A^*, \\
R_{12} &= -\lambda(1 - \epsilon_1)\kappa_A^*\sqrt{1 - |\kappa_A|^2}, & R_{24} &= \sqrt{\epsilon_2(1 - \epsilon_2)}\sqrt{1 - |\kappa_B|^2}, \\
R_{13} &= -\lambda\sqrt{\epsilon_1(1 - \epsilon_1)}\sqrt{1 - |\kappa_A|^2}, & R_{33} &= (1 - \epsilon_2)|\kappa_B|^2 - \lambda\epsilon_2, \\
R_{14} &= 0, & R_{34} &= (1 - \epsilon_2)\kappa_B^*\sqrt{1 - |\kappa_B|^2}, \\
R_{22} &= \epsilon_2 - \lambda(1 - \epsilon_1)|\kappa_A|^2, & R_{44} &= (1 - \epsilon_2)(1 - |\kappa_B|^2).
\end{aligned}$$

In this representation, the Semi-QL is given by the diagonal matrix elements as

$$P_e(\text{SQL}) = \xi_1 + \xi_2 \text{Tr}[(\hat{\rho}_2 - \lambda\hat{\rho}_1)\hat{\Pi}_A^{\text{SD}}] = \xi_1 + \xi_2(R_{11} + R_{22}) \tag{16}$$

Here it is worth mentioning the following property,

$$R_{11} + R_{22} \le 0 \le R_{33} + R_{44}, \tag{17}$$

which follows directly from the fact that the decision region $\{\mathcal{A}, \mathcal{B}\}$ is chosen so as to minimize Eq.(8).

On the other hand, the off-diagonal elements characterize the *quantum gain* which can not be achieved by the *standard detection operators*. In order to obtain the full quantum gain (to reach the Helstrom bound), one has to make the best use of these off-diagonal components. This is the key.

Let's move to the error improvement protocol. We consider the rotation $\hat{U}_{ij}$ in the plane spanned by $\{|e_i\rangle, |e_j\rangle\}$ where $(i = 1, 2; j = 3, 4)$, and transform the signal states. Let's denote the new matrix as $\hat{R}^{(1)} \equiv \hat{U}_{ij}\hat{R}\hat{U}_{ij}^{\dagger}$. $\hat{U}_{ij}$ is constructed as follows:

$$\hat{U}_{ij} \equiv \exp(-i\frac{\varphi}{2}\hat{Q}_{ij})\exp(\gamma\hat{P}_{ij})\exp(-i\frac{\varphi}{2}\hat{Q}_{ij}), \tag{18}$$

where $\hat{P}_{ij} \equiv |e_i\rangle\langle e_j| - |e_j\rangle\langle e_i|$, $\hat{Q}_{ij} \equiv |e_i\rangle\langle e_i| - |e_j\rangle\langle e_j|$, and $e^{i\varphi} \equiv R_{ij}/|R_{ij}|$, and the rotation angle γ is given by

$$\tan\gamma \equiv \sqrt{\frac{\sqrt{(R_{ii} - R_{jj})^2 + 4|R_{ij}|^2} + R_{ii} - R_{jj}}{\sqrt{(R_{ii} - R_{jj})^2 + 4|R_{ij}|^2} - R_{ii} + R_{jj}}}, \quad \frac{\pi}{2} < \gamma < \pi, \tag{19}$$

so that $R_{ij}^{(1)} = R_{ji}^{(1)} = 0$.

Diagonal components after the transformation are given as,

$$R_{ii}^{(1)} = \frac{1}{2}\left(R_{ii} + R_{jj} - \sqrt{(R_{ii} - R_{jj})^2 + 4|R_{ij}|^2}\right), \tag{20}$$

$$R_{jj}^{(1)} = \frac{1}{2}\left(R_{ii} + R_{jj} + \sqrt{(R_{ii} - R_{jj})^2 + 4|R_{ij}|^2}\right), \tag{21}$$

$$R_{kk}^{(1)} = R_{kk}, (k \ne i, j). \tag{22}$$

After the hybridization, the following inequality holds,

$$R_{11}^{(1)} + R_{22}^{(1)} < R_{11} + R_{22} < 0 < R_{33} + R_{44} < R_{33}^{(1)} + R_{44}^{(1)}. \tag{23}$$

which leads to,

$$P_e = \xi_1 + \xi_2 \text{Tr}[\hat{R}^{(1)}\hat{\Pi}_A^{\text{SD}}] = \xi_1 + \xi_2(R_{11}^{(1)} + R_{22}^{(1)}) \tag{24}$$

$$< \xi_1 + \xi_2(R_{11} + R_{22}) = \xi_1 + \xi_2 \text{Tr}[\hat{R}\hat{\Pi}_A^{\text{SD}}] = P_e(\text{SQL}). \tag{25}$$

The error probability can be lowered by replacing the matrix $\hat{R}$ with $\hat{R}^{(1)}$. This is the *quantum gain*. Its origin is the quantum interference R_{ij} between $|e_i\rangle$ and $|e_j\rangle$ components in $|\rho_1\rangle$ and $|\rho_2\rangle$. The transformed signal states are capable of causing quantum interference at the detection $\{\hat{\Pi}_A^{\text{SD}}, \hat{\Pi}_B^{\text{SD}}\}$.

The process could be repeated further. Successive applications of $\hat{U}_{ij}$ for possible pairs of (i, j) will finally lead to the following partially-diagonalized matrix form,

$$\hat{R}' \equiv \cdots \hat{U}_{i'j'}\hat{U}_{ij}\hat{R}\hat{U}_{ij}^{\dagger}\hat{U}_{i'j'}^{\dagger}\cdots = \begin{bmatrix} R'_{11} & R'_{12} & 0 & 0 \\ R'^{*}_{12} & R'_{22} & 0 & 0 \\ 0 & 0 & R'_{33} & R'_{34} \\ 0 & 0 & R'^{*}_{34} & R'_{44} \end{bmatrix}. \tag{26}$$

Our procedure automatically leads us to the situation where the trace of the upper-left block yields the negative eigenvalue ω_1 while the trace of the lower-right block yields the positive eigenvalue ω_2 because of the property Eq. (17). Thus we reach the Helstrom bound,

$$P_e(\text{opt}) = \xi_1 + \xi_2(R'_{11} + R'_{22}) = \xi_1 + \xi_2\omega_1. \tag{27}$$

The required unitary process is given as $\hat{U} = \cdots \hat{U}_{i'j'}\hat{U}_{ij}$. We shall call it *unitary control process*.

Thus we can reach the Helstrom bound by modifying the conventional detection scheme $\{\hat{\Pi}_A^{\text{SD}}, \hat{\Pi}_B^{\text{SD}}\}$ by installing the appropriate unitary control process $\hat{U}$ before the detection. In general, $\{\hat{\Pi}_A^{\text{SD}}, \hat{\Pi}_B^{\text{SD}}\}$ can be an arbitrary projection valued measure. The procedure is summarized in the following way:

Step 1: make an appropriate basis set $\{|e_i\rangle\}$ from $\{\hat{\Pi}_A^{\text{SD}}, \hat{\Pi}_B^{\text{SD}}\}$.

Step 2: derive the matrix representation of $\hat{R}$ based on $\{|e_i\rangle\}$.

Step 3: rotation $\hat{U}_{ij}$ in the plane $\{|e_i\rangle, |e_j\rangle\}$ is constructed.

Step 4: successive applications of $\hat{U}_{ij}$ for all possible pairs of (i,j), i=1,2;j=3,4.

We shall show what the states transformed by $\hat{U}$ are like in the case of equally probable BPSK signals. Let us start with the homodyne detection:

$$\hat{\Pi}_A^{\text{SD}} = \int_0^\infty dx|x\rangle\langle x|, \quad \hat{\Pi}_B^{\text{SD}} = \int_{-\infty}^0 dx|x\rangle\langle x|.$$

After applying the procedure, you can see the unitary control process can consist of two step rotations of $\hat{U}_{13} \equiv \exp(\gamma\hat{P}_{13})$ and $\hat{U}_{24} \equiv \exp[(\pi - \gamma)\hat{P}_{24}]$ as $\hat{U} = \hat{U}_{24}\hat{P}_{13}$.

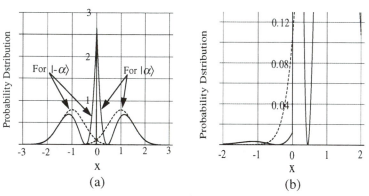

(a)   (b)

Figure 2. The probability distributions $|\langle x|\hat{U}|\pm\alpha\rangle|^2$ in the homodyne detection after transforming the signal states (solid lines). (a) In comparison, the ones in the direct homodyne detection $|\langle x|\pm\alpha\rangle|^2$ are shown by the dashed lines. (b) The distributions for $|\alpha\rangle$ are magnified in vertical scale.

The final probability distributions $|\langle x|\hat{U}|\pm\alpha\rangle|^2$ are shown in the Fig. 2 as the solid lines. Unlike the distributions in the direct homodyne detection (dashed lines), they have discontinuities at $x = 0$. To see this, the distribution for the signal state $|\alpha\rangle$ is magnified in vertical scale in Fig. 2 (b). The area of the skirt in $x < 0$ directly represents the error probabilities. The dashed line corresponds to the Semi-QL while the solid line gives the Helstrom bound. Drastic reduction of the error probability is apparent. This is direct result of the quantum interference induced by $\hat{U}$. Thus the role of the process $\hat{U}$ is to control probability distributions.

4. PHYSICAL CORRESPONDENCE TO $\hat{U}$

Our next concern is the physical correspondence to $\hat{U}$, particularly what the rotation $\hat{U}_{ij}$ means physically. It depends on what kind of signal states we consider. But by specifying the situation, we can make a more general statement. We assume that the signal states $\{|\rho_1\rangle, |\rho_2\rangle\}$ are generated from a non-degenerate vacuum state $|\Phi_0\rangle$ as $|\rho_k\rangle = e^{i\hat{G}_k}|\Phi_0\rangle$ $(k=1,2)$ where $\hat{G}_k$'s are Hermitian generators. Then the Fock space can be defined which is specified by the number states $\{|n\rangle\}$ of energy quanta created from the vacuum state $|\Phi_0\rangle$. The creation and annihilation operators $\hat{a}^\dagger$ and $\hat{a}$ describe dynamics of the system. In the Fock space representation, the projectors $\hat{P}_{ij}$ and $\hat{Q}_{ij}$ can be converted to a Hamiltonian $\hat{H} = \hbar f(\hat{a}^\dagger, \hat{a})$ of nonlinear processes of energy quanta.

To demonstrate all this, we consider BPSK signals again. In achieving the Helstrom bound for the signal states $\{|\alpha\rangle, |-\alpha\rangle\}$, the detection process could be any kind. If we take the homodyne detection, the unitary control process $\hat{U}$ can consist of the two step rotations $\hat{U}_{13}$ and $\hat{U}_{24}$. But instead we may take here the photon counting $\{\hat{\Pi}_A^{SD} = |0\rangle\langle 0|, \hat{\Pi}_B^{SD} = \sum_{n=1}^\infty |n\rangle\langle n|\}$. Then $\hat{U}$ becomes simpler and its physical meaning clearer. At first, let us transform the signal states into the on-off keyed (OOK) signal states $\{|0\rangle, |-2\alpha\rangle\}$ by combining a local oscillator light via a beam splitter which is represented by the operator $\hat{D}(-\alpha)$. The direct detection of these OOK signals with $\{|0\rangle\langle 0|, \sum_{n=1}^\infty |n\rangle\langle n|\}$ achieves an error probability very close to the Helstrom bound only leaving a small gap. This method has been known as Kennedy's method [8].

Now the gap can be further eliminated by inserting another unitary process $\hat{U}'$ like an *adaptor*:

$$
\begin{array}{ccccc}
|0\rangle & \rightarrow & \hat{U}'|0\rangle & \rightarrow & \hat{\Pi}_A = |0\rangle\langle 0|, \\
|-2\alpha\rangle & \rightarrow & \hat{U}'|-2\alpha\rangle & \rightarrow & \hat{\Pi}_B = \sum_{n=1}^\infty |n\rangle\langle n|.
\end{array} \tag{28}
$$

Let us focus on the physical meaning of $\hat{U}'$.

Our procedure being applied, the 4 bases reduce to the 2 components $|e_2\rangle = |0\rangle$ and $|e_4\rangle = (|-2\alpha\rangle - \sqrt{\epsilon}|0\rangle)/\sqrt{1-\epsilon}$ with $\epsilon = |\langle 0|-2\alpha\rangle|^2$ and the required unitary control process $\hat{U}'$ is simply,

$$
\hat{U}' \equiv \exp(\gamma \hat{P}_{24}), \quad \hat{P}_{24} \equiv |e_2\rangle\langle e_4| - |e_4\rangle\langle e_2|.
$$

The projector $\hat{P}_{24}$ can be converted to the series of $\hat{a}$ and $\hat{a}^\dagger$,

$$
\hat{P}_{24} = |e_2\rangle\langle e_4| - |e_4\rangle\langle e_2| = \sum_{n=1}^\infty d_n(|0\rangle\langle n| - |n\rangle\langle 0|) = \sum_{l=0}^\infty \frac{(-\hat{a}^\dagger)^l \hat{a}^l}{l!} \sum_{n=1}^\infty d_n \frac{\hat{a}^n}{\sqrt{n!}} - \text{h.c.},
$$

where $d_n = c_n/\sqrt{1-\epsilon}$ and $c_n = e^{-2\alpha^2}(2\alpha)^n/\sqrt{n!}$.

Though $\hat{P}_{24}$ includes infinite series of $\hat{a}$ and $\hat{a}^\dagger$, we can reduce this higher nonlinearity. The on-state signal can be decomposed into two parts,

$$
|-2\alpha\rangle = \sum_{n=0}^\infty c_n|n\rangle = \sqrt{1-\delta_M}|\psi_M\rangle + \sqrt{\delta_M}|\phi_M\rangle
$$

where

$$
|\psi_M\rangle = \frac{1}{\sqrt{1-\delta_M}} \sum_{n=0}^M c_n|n\rangle, \quad |\phi_M\rangle = \frac{1}{\sqrt{\delta_M}} \sum_{n=M+1}^\infty c_n|n\rangle, \quad \delta_M = 1 - \sum_{n=0}^M c_n^2,
$$

and for given signal power $|\alpha|^2$, M can be taken such that $\delta_M \ll 1$. Then the signal states can be approximated by $\{|0\rangle, |\psi_M\rangle\}$. In other words, $\{|M\rangle, |M+1\rangle, \cdots\}$ do not enter the receiver. In such a situation the higher-order terms in $\hat{P}_{24}$ can be neglected. Consequently, $\hat{U}'$ can be given as $\sim e^{\gamma \hat{P}_M}$ with

$$\hat{P}_M = \sum_{l=0}^{M} \frac{(-\hat{a}^\dagger)^l \hat{a}^l}{l!} \sum_{n=1}^{M} d'_n \frac{\hat{a}^n}{\sqrt{n!}} - \text{h.c.},$$

which represents multiphoton processes up to $3M$-th order. The attained error probability can be written as

$$P'_e = \frac{1}{2} \left\{ \xi_1 + \xi'_2 - \sqrt{(\xi_1 + \xi'_2)^2 - 4\xi_1 \xi'_2 c'^2_0} \right\}, \tag{29}$$

where ξ'_2 is defined by $\xi_2 = (1 - \delta_M)\xi_2$. So $\xi_1 + \xi'_2 < 1$, which represents the degradation by neglecting the higher order terms. Numerical results for several truncations of M are shown in Fig. 3.

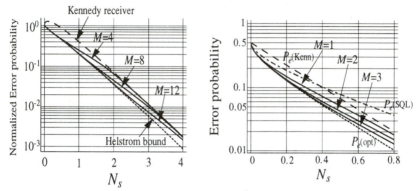

Figure 3. The error probabilities versus the signal power, obtained by using $\hat{U}' \sim e^{\gamma \hat{P}_M}$ in the diagram (28).

Fig. 3(a) shows the normalized error probabilities by the Semi-QL $P_e(\text{SQL}) = \frac{1}{2}\text{erfc}(\sqrt{2|\alpha|^2})$. The effect of neglecting the higher order terms appears as deviations of the solid lines from the Helstrom bound (dotted line, $P_e(\text{opt})$) at the larger side of the signal power. Fig. 3(b) is the error performance in the weak signal region. The lowest nonlinearity in $\hat{P}_M$ is capable of overcoming Kennedy's method($P_e(\text{Kenn})$) and direct homodyne detection($P_e(\text{SQL})$).

For implementations of $\hat{P}_M$, we could find two possible candidates which were proposed by Kilin and Horoshko [12], and Law and Eberly [13]. The former is the combination of Pockel, Kerr, and Faraday effects. The Hamiltonian given there is actually the same as P_M with $M = 1$ although the purpose is different. The latter is the cavity QED scheme using the two channel Raman transition, where higher nonlinearity is available keeping pure-state evolution of the signal field and the atom. These two are theoretical proposal and further practical studies are strongly desired.

5. SUMMARY

In this paper, it is shown that the optimum detection operators achieving the minimum error bound in binary pure-state signals can be constructed as $\hat{U}^\dagger \hat{\Pi}_i^{\text{SD}} \hat{U}$, where $\hat{\Pi}_i^{\text{SD}}$ can be an arbitrary PVM while the unitary operator $\hat{U}$ should satisfy a certain condition. A systematic construction procedure for such $\hat{U}$ has been given. Physically, the unitary process $\hat{U}$ can be generated by nonlinear processes of energy quanta related with the physical source of the signal states.

The above results leads us to a design theory of the quantum receiver based on how to modify the conventional detection methods used at present. The required modification is just installing the unitary process $\hat{U}$ in front of the detection $\hat{\Pi}_i^{\text{SD}}$. In future, generalization to M-ary signals even including mixed states is needed. We hope this study gives a step toward a design theory of the quantum receiver, of the engineer, by the engineer, for the engineer.

ACKNOWLEDGMENTS

The authors would like to thank Dr. M. Ban of Hitachi Advanced Research Laboratory, Dr. K. Yamazaki and Dr. M. Osaki of Tamagawa University, Tokyo, for their helpful discussions

REFERENCES

[1] C. W. Helstrom : *Quantum Detection and Estimation Theory* (Academic Press, New York, 1976).

[2] A. S. Holevo: J. Multivar. Anal. **3**, pp337-394, (1973).

[3] H. P. Yuen, R. S. Kennedy, and M. Lax, IEEE Trans., **IT-21**, 125, (1975).

[4] S. J. Dolinar: Quarterly Progress Report No. 111, Research Laboratory of Electronics, MIT, pp115-120, (1973).

[5] A. S. Holevo, Soviet Mathematics(IZV. VUZ.), Vol. **26**, pp3-9, (1982).

[6] M. Sasaki and O. Hirota: to appear in Phys. Rev. A**54** (1996).

[7] T. S. Usuda and O. Hirota, *Quantum Communication and Measurement*, pp419-427, (ed. by Belavkin, Hirota, and Hudson, Plenum Publishing, New York, 1995).

[8] R. S. Kennedy: Quarterly Progress Report No. 108, Research Laboratory of Electronics, MIT, pp219-225, (1973).

[9] M. Sasaki, T. S. Usuda, and O. Hirota, Phys. Rev. A**51**, 1702 (1995).

[10] M. Sasaki and O. Hirota: Phys. Lett. **A210**, pp21-25 (1996).

[11] M. Sasaki, T. S. Usuda, and O. Hirota, A. S. Holevo : Phys. Rev. A**53**, 1273 (1996).

[12] S. Y. Kilin and D. B. Horoshko, Phys. Rev. Lett **74**, 5206(1995).

[13] C. K. Law and J. H. Eberly, Phys. Rev. Lett **76**, 1055(1996).

QUANTUM ZENO EFFECT AND "DOMINATION" OF THE TEMPORAL EVOLUTION OF QUANTUM SYSTEMS

S. Pascazio

Dipartimento di Fisica, Università di Bari
Istituto Nazionale di Fisica Nucleare, Sezione di Bari
I-70126 Bari, Italy

The temporal behavior of quantum mechanical systems is analyzed and compared to the exponential decay law. The notion of quantum Zeno effect is discussed and a recent experimental test is critically reviewed: The presence of a subtle repopulation effect requires a reinterpretation of the experimental results. A new experiment is proposed, in which the lifetime of an unstable atom is extended by illuminating it with an intense and suitable EM field. This is a purely dynamical effect and is related to the notion of "dominated" evolution.

1. HISTORICAL INTRODUCTION

The temporal behaviour of quantum mechanical systems was widely investigated in the past and is recently attracting increasing attention due to, in particular, to the curious features of the short-time region. The seminal work by Gamow [1] on the exponential decay law, as well as its derivation by Weisskopf and Wigner [2] are based on the assumption that a pole near the real axis of the complex energy plane essentially determines the temporal evolution of the quantum system. It is well known that this assumption leads to a spectrum of the Breit-Wigner type [3].

However, it was soon understood that a purely exponential decay law can neither be expected for very short [4,5] nor for very long [6,7] times. The first estimates for the domain of validity of the exponential law came only later, when it became clear [8] that the long-time power tails are a consequence of the Paley-Wiener theorem [9] on Fourier transforms and that the short-time quadratic behavior can be exploited in order to increase the "survival probability" of an unstable quantum system [10–12]. The latter idea hinged upon the notion of quantum measurement—a projection à la von Neumann, in the orthodox Copenhagen interpretation.

A few years later Misra and Sudarshan proved, by a well known theorem [13], that the temporal evolution of a quantum system can be halted in the so-called limit of continuous observation and introduced the notion of "quantum Zeno paradox"— Zeno was the Eleatic philosopher famous for his paradoxical arguments against the philosophical notion of becoming: His sped arrows would never reach their target, if closely looked at. It is remarkable that von Neumann had realized (already in 1932!) that a quantum mechanical state can be "steered" into other states by a series of measurements in rapid succession [14], so that, if the final state coincides with the initial one, the evolution of a quantum system is halted (or at least slowed down).

However, it is *not* necessary to make use of the controversial notion of quantum measurement, in order to obtain a Zeno-type dynamics. The first (to our knowledge) who shed light on this important point was Peres [15] who realized that the quantum Zeno effect (QZE) can be given a dynamical explanation, without making use of projection operators.

Review articles on the QZE and the interesting features of the temporal evolution of quantum mechanical systems are given in Refs. [16,17]. In this paper we shall review the main features of the quantum mechanical evolution law and shall critically analyze a recent experimental test of the QZE. Finally, we shall put forward a new proposal for an experimental test of the QZE on a truly unstable system.

2. PRELIMINARIES

Let us outline the differences between the classical and the quantum evolution laws. In classical physics one follows a heuristic approach, by assuming that the "decay probability per unit time" is a constant Γ (the inverse lifetime) that does not depend on the total number N of unstable systems, on their past history and on the environment surrounding them. Let the (very large) number of systems at time t be $N(t)$; the number of systems that will decay in the time interval dt is

$$- dN = N\Gamma dt, \tag{2.1}$$

which yields

$$N(t) = N_0 e^{-\Gamma t}, \tag{2.2}$$

where $N_0 = N(0)$. The "survival" or "nondecay probability" reads

$$P(t) = \frac{N(t)}{N_0} = e^{-\Gamma t} \simeq 1 - \Gamma t + \cdots, \tag{2.3}$$

where the expansion holds at short times. The above derivation is usually found in elementary textbooks. However, the assumptions underpinning it are delicate, for they reflect the basic features of a Markoffian process, in which memory and/or collective effects are absent.

What about quantum mechanics? Let $|a\rangle$ be the wave function of a given quantum system at time $t = 0$. The evolution is governed by the unitary operator $U(t) = \exp(-iHt)$, where H is the Hamiltonian. The survival or nondecay probability at time t is defined as the square modulus of the survival amplitude

$$P(t) = |\langle a|e^{-iHt}|a\rangle|^2. \tag{2.4}$$

By assuming that $|a\rangle$ is normalizable and belongs to the domain of definition of H (so that all moments of H in the state $|a\rangle$ are finite) one gets the short-time expansion

$$P(t) = 1 - t^2/\tau_Z^2 + \cdots, \tag{2.5}$$

$$\tau_Z^{-1} \equiv \triangle H = \left(\langle a|H^2|a\rangle - \langle a|H|a\rangle^2\right)^{1/2}, \tag{2.6}$$

which is quadratic in t and therefore yields a vanishing decay rate for $t \to 0$. (It is assumed that $\triangle H$ is nonvanishing, or, in other words, that $|a\rangle$ is not an eigenstate of H. Otherwise one simply gets $P(t) = 1$.) The short-time quadratic behavior is in manifest contradiction with the exponential law (2.3), that predicts a nonvanishing decay rate Γ.

The quantum mechanical vanishing decay rate at short times can be exploited in order to slow down the decay process. Suppose we perform N measurements at equal time intervals $t = T/N$, in order to ascertain whether the system is still in its initial state. After each measurement, the system is "projected" onto the quantum mechanical state representing the result of the measurement and the evolution starts anew according to (2.5). The probability of observing the initial state at the final time $T = Nt$, after having performed the above-mentioned N measurements, reads

$$P^{(N)}(T) = [P(t)]^N = [P(T/N)]^N \simeq \left(1 - \frac{1}{\tau_Z^2}\left(\frac{T}{N}\right)^2\right)^N \underset{\sim}{\overset{N \text{ large}}{\sim}} e^{-T^2/\tau_Z^2 N}. \qquad (2.7)$$

Notice that both T and N are finite, in the above. We shall refer to (2.7) as quantum Zeno effect: Repeated observations "slow down" the evolution and increase the probability that the system is still in the initial state at time T. In the limit of continuous observation ($N \to \infty$) one obtains

$$P^{(N)}(T) \simeq \left(1 - \frac{1}{\tau_Z^2}\left(\frac{T}{N}\right)^2\right)^N \xrightarrow{N \to \infty} 1. \qquad (2.8)$$

Infinitely frequent observations halt the evolution and completely "freeze" the initial state of the quantum system. This is the quantum mechanical version of the Zeno paradox: The quantum "arrow," although sped under the action of its Hamiltonian, does not move, if it is continuously observed.

We showed in Ref. [18] that the $N \to \infty$ limit is unphysical, for it is in contradiction with Heisenberg's uncertainty principle. In this sense, we shall say that the quantum Zeno *effect*, with N finite, becomes a quantum Zeno *paradox* when $N \to \infty$.

3. AN EXPERIMENTAL TEST

The QZE was not thought to be subject to experimental investigation due to the lack of precise estimates for the temporal scales involved. Observe that while the lifetime Γ^{-1} is defined, via Fermi's Golden rule [19], in terms of the "on-shell matrix elements—those at the same energy as the initial state," the definition of the Zeno time τ_Z involves all "accessible energies, so it is substantially off-shell." This remark was made by Schulman [20] (see also Refs. [21,22]). A comparison between the relative time scales depends therefore on the interaction Hamiltonian, and is in general a difficult task.

Renewed interest in the QZE was motivated by an idea proposed by Cook [23] and the subsequent experiment performed by Itano et al. [24]. The meaning of this experiment has been hotly debated [25–27]: It is now widely believed that the experimental results can be explained by making use of a unitary dynamics [25,27].

However, curiously enough, few people have realized that the experiment is at variance with the original definition of QZE as given by Misra and Sudarshan. Indeed, the interesting proposal by Cook, that makes use of a two-level system undergoing Rabi oscillations, as well as the beautiful experiment performed by Itano et al., investigate the probability of finding the initial state *at time* t, *regardless* of the state of the system in the time interval $\triangle$. Let us briefly discuss this point (a more exhaustive analysis is given in [28]).

In their seminal paper [13], Misra and Sudarshan endeavoured to define "the probability $\mathcal{P}(0, T)$ that no decay is found *throughout the interval* $\triangle = [0, T]$ when the initial state of the system was known to be ρ_0." (Italics in the original. Some symbols have been changed. If the initial state is pure [as in (2.4)-(2.6)], then $\rho_0 = |a\rangle\langle a|$.) Their definition is

$$\mathcal{P}(0,T) \equiv \lim_{N\to\infty} P^{(N)}(T), \tag{3.1}$$

where $P^{(N)}(T)$ is essentially the quantity defined in Eq. (2.7).

Cook's proposal and Itano et al.'s experiment involve a three-level atomic system, on which an rf field of frequency ω provokes Rabi oscillations between levels 1 and 2. In the rotating wave approximation and in absence of detuning, the Block vector $\boldsymbol{R} \equiv (R_1, R_2, R_3)$ undergoes a precession around $\boldsymbol{\omega} \equiv (\omega, 0, 0)$ according to the equation

$$\dot{\boldsymbol{R}} = \boldsymbol{\omega} \times \boldsymbol{R}. \tag{3.2}$$

As is well known, the third component of the Bloch vector simply expresses the difference between the populations of levels 1 and 2: $R_3 = P_2 - P_1$, while its first two components $R_{1,2}$ are expressed in terms of the off-diagonal elements of the density matrix.

The solution of the above equation, with initial condition $\boldsymbol{R}(0) \equiv (0,0,-1)$ (only level 1 is initially populated) reads

$$\boldsymbol{R}(t) = (0, \sin\omega t, -\cos\omega t) \tag{3.3}$$

and if the transition beween the two levels is driven by an on-resonant π pulse, of duration $T = \pi/\omega$, only level 2 is populated at time T:

$$P_2(T) = 1. \tag{3.4}$$

On the other hand, assume you perform N measurements at equal time intervals $\tau = \pi/N\omega$ by shining on the system very short "measurement" pulses, that provoke transitions from level 1 to level 3, followed by rapid spontaneous emissions of photons. Every measurement pulse "projects" the atom into level 1 or 2 and rapidly makes $R_{1,2}$ vanish (remember that $R_{1,2}$ depend on the the off-diagonal elements of the density matrix), while it leaves R_3 (that depends on the populations) unaltered. It is not difficult to see that after N measurements, at time $T = N\tau = \pi/\omega$,

$$\boldsymbol{R}(T) = [0,0,-\cos^N(\pi/N)] \equiv \boldsymbol{R}^{(N)}, \tag{3.5}$$

so that the probability that the atom is in level 2 at time T, after the N measurements, reads

$$P_2^{(N)}(T) = \frac{1}{2}\left[1 + R_3^{(N)}\right] = \frac{1}{2}\left[1 - \cos^N(\pi/N)\right]. \tag{3.6}$$

Since $P_2^{(N)}(T) \to 0$ as $N \to \infty$, this is interpreted as quantum Zeno effect. The experimental result [24] are in very good agreement with the above formula. However, this is *not* the quantum Zeno effect, according to the definition (3.1): Equation (3.6) expresses only the probability that the atom is in level 2 at time T, after N measurements, *independently* of its past history. As a matter of fact, repopulation effects of level #2 from level #1 and *vice versa* are not prevented: In order to understand this (rather subtle) point, let us look explicitly at the first two measurements.

After the first measurement, Eq. (3.5) yields

$$R_3^{(1)} = -\cos\frac{\pi}{N} = P_2^{(1)} - P_1^{(1)}, \tag{3.7}$$

$$P_1^{(1)} \equiv \cos^2\frac{\pi}{2N}, \qquad P_2^{(1)} \equiv \sin^2\frac{\pi}{2N}, \tag{3.8}$$

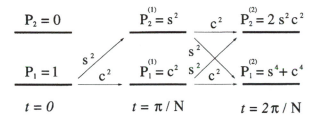

Figure 1: Transition probabilities after the first two measurements ($s \equiv \sin \frac{\pi}{2N}$ and $c \equiv \cos \frac{\pi}{2N}$).

where $P_j^{(1)}$ is the occupation probability of level j ($j = 1, 2$) at time $\tau = \pi/N\omega$, after the first measurement pulse. After the second measurement, one obtains

$$R_3^{(2)} = -\cos^2 \frac{\pi}{N} = P_2^{(2)} - P_1^{(2)}, \tag{3.9}$$

$$P_1^{(2)} \equiv \cos^4 \frac{\pi}{2N} + \sin^4 \frac{\pi}{2N}, \qquad P_2^{(2)} \equiv 2\sin^2 \frac{\pi}{2N} \cos^2 \frac{\pi}{2N}, \tag{3.10}$$

where $P_j^{(2)}$ ($j = 1, 2$) are the occupation probabilities at time $2\tau = 2\pi/N\omega$. Look at Figure 1: $P_1^{(2)}$, in Eq. (3.10) is *not the survival probability* of level 1: It is the probability that level 1 is populated at time $t = 2\pi/N$, including the possibility that the transition $1 \rightarrow 2 \rightarrow 1$ took place, with probability $\sin^2 \frac{\pi}{2N} \cdot \sin^2 \frac{\pi}{2N} = \sin^4 \frac{\pi}{2N}$. The survival probability, according to (3.1), is the probability that the atom is found in level 1 *both* in the first and second measurements, and is given by $\cos^4 \frac{\pi}{2N}$.

The repopulation effect that takes place after N measurements is described in [28] and brings to light a binomial distribution for the probability (3.6).

4. PROPOSAL FOR A NEW EXPERIMENT: HINDERED DECAY

The original ideas on the QZE involved truly *unstable* systems [10–12] rather than systems undergoing oscillations of some sort. More to this, as we have just seen, one should prevent repopulation effects on oscillating systems. It is therefore interesting to study the properties of an atomic system that (unlike in the case described in the previous section) is initially prepared in an excited state and undergoes a "measurement" of some sort. The question is: Would the "measurement" hinder decay?

Let us be more specific, and consider the following situation: Prepare a 3-level atom in the excited level #2. The atom, if left undisturbed, would naturally decay to its ground state (assumed to be level #1) according to an (approximately) exponential law. Suppose now that you shine on the atom a very intense laser beam whose frequency is approximately equal to $E_3 - E_1$ [where E_j is the energy of level #j(= 1, 2, 3)]. The atom, being continuously "monitored" by the laser beam, undergoes a sort of "continuous observation," in the following sense: If the electron makes a transition from level #2 to level #1, it is rapidly "snatched" away to level #3, so that any evidence that level #3 is populated would mean that level #2 has decayed. Level #2 is therefore continuosly "observed" and we intuitively expect its decay to be hindered. [Notice that, in principle, it is *not* necessary that an experimenter *observes* the atom in level #3 (e.g. by detecting a photon spontaneously emitted by level #3): For all practical and computational purposes, it is enough to apply von Neumann's projection rules.] It is interesting to notice that Peres arrived at a similar conclusion, although in

283

a different context. In Ref. [15] he wrote: "If the decay products are quickly removed by some external mechanism, [the survival amplitude] will remain constant."

A detailed calculation, following the above idea, has been presented in [29]: Consider the Hamiltonian ($\hbar = 1$)

$$
\begin{aligned}
H = \sum_{j=1}^{3} E_j |j\rangle\langle j| + \sum_k \omega_k a_k^\dagger a_k + \sum_k \Omega_k A_k^\dagger A_k \\
+ \sum_k (\phi_k a_k^\dagger |1\rangle\langle 2| + \text{H.c.}) + \sum_k (\Phi_k A_k^\dagger |1\rangle\langle 3| + \text{H.c.}),
\end{aligned}
\tag{4.1}
$$

where $|j\rangle$ ($j = 1, 2, 3$) is the atomic state, the first term is the free Hamiltonian of the 3-level atom, the second and third terms are the free Hamiltonians of the photons associated with the $1 \leftrightarrow 2$ and $1 \leftrightarrow 3$ transitions, respectively ($\omega_k \approx E_2 - E_1$ and $\Omega_k \approx E_3 - E_1$), and the fourth and fifth terms are the interaction Hamiltonians describing, in the rotating wave approximation, the $1 \leftrightarrow 2$ and $1 \leftrightarrow 3$ transitions, respectively. The operators a_k and A_k obey boson commutation relations and the c-numbers ϕ_k, Φ_k are the matrix elements for the atomic transitions.

We prepare our system in the initial state $|\Psi_0\rangle = |2\rangle \otimes |0_k\rangle \otimes |N_0\rangle$ (atom in level #2, no photons of energy $\omega_k \approx E_2 - E_1$ and $N_0(\gg 1)$ photons of energy $\Omega_0 = E_3 - E_1$) and solve the time-dependent Schrödinger equation $i\partial\Psi_t/\partial t = H\Psi_t$. In the continuum limit, the survival amplitude can be expressed as an inverse Laplace transform

$$
\langle\Psi_0|\Psi_t\rangle = \frac{1}{2\pi i} \int_{\epsilon-i\infty}^{\epsilon+i\infty} \frac{e^{st}}{s + Q(s)} ds,
\tag{4.2}
$$

$$
Q(s) = \int dE \rho(E) |\varphi(E)|^2 \frac{s + iE}{(s+iE)^2 + B^2}.
\tag{4.3}
$$

where $B^2 = N_0 |\Phi_0|^2$, $\rho(E)$ is the density of states at energy E and $\varphi(E)$ are the scaled matrix elements of the $1 \leftrightarrow 2$ transition. The evolution is dominated by the poles of the integrand, namely the zeros of the equation $s + Q(s) = 0$.

Let us first consider the case $B = 0$. It is easily inferred that there is one pole of coordinates

$$
s = -\gamma/2 + i\triangle E,
\tag{4.4}
$$

$$
\triangle E = P \int dE \frac{g(E)}{E},
$$

$$
\gamma = 2\pi\rho(E_0)|\varphi(E_0)|^2,
\tag{4.5}
$$

where E_0 is the energy of the initial state Ψ_0. This is nothing but the Fermi Golden Rule [19]. Substitution in (4.2) yields the exponential decay law:

$$
\langle\Psi_0|\Psi_t\rangle \simeq e^{(-\gamma/2 + i\triangle E)t}.
\tag{4.6}
$$

Consider now the case $B \neq 0$. One obtains

$$
s = -\gamma'/2 + i\triangle E',
\tag{4.7}
$$

$$
\triangle E' = P \int dE g(E) \frac{E}{E^2 - B^2},
$$

$$
\gamma' = \pi \left[\rho(E_0 + B)|\varphi(E_0 + B)|^2 + \rho(E_0 - B)|\varphi(E_0 - B)|^2 \right].
\tag{4.8}
$$

The presence of the B-field (which is associated with the $1 \leftrightarrow 3$ transition) modifies the lifetime of level #2 ! In particular,

$$
\frac{\gamma}{\gamma'} = \frac{2\rho(E_0)|\varphi(E_0)|^2}{\rho(E_0 + B)|\varphi(E_0 + B)|^2 + \rho(E_0 - B)|\varphi(E_0 - B)|^2}.
\tag{4.9}
$$

A quantitative estimate of the above ratio requires evaluation of the matrix elements φ and the phase space factor ρ and is given in [29]. However, it is natural to expect that $\gamma' \ll \gamma$, as B becomes large: The decay is "hindered" by the presence of the B-field.

This proposal is a direct test of QZE on a truly decaying system and prevents repopulation effects of the type described in Sec. 3.

5. COMMENTS AND MORAL

Most of the previous analysis on the QZE focussed on the quadratic early-time behavior (2.5) and on the delicate notion of quantum measurement [30]. On the other hand, in the last section, we saw that it is possible, at least in principle, to increase the lifetime of an excited atom *without* exploiting the short-time nonexponential behavior. By contrast, our atom simply settles into a slower exponential: It is just the change in the lifetime that displays the new features of the evolution. This temporal evolution is "dominated" by the presence of the EM ("B") field [29,31]. This effect is a purely dynamical one [27] and is explainable in terms of Schrödinger's equation.

One might wonder whether the B field in (4.2)-(4.3) is actually performing a *bona fide* quantum "measurement." This is because physicists are used in thinking of a measurement process as a quick interaction, that strongly and rapidly affects the system and provokes a spectral decomposition (in Wigner's sense [32]). This view, although widespread, is somewhat misleading. For example, the situation outlined in Sec. 4 is to be contrasted to the above-mentioned viewpoint: The interaction takes some time and looks more and more like a "measurement" as B increases. Loosely speaking, the measurement is "slowly" performed during a certain elapse of time and B yields, in some sense, a measure of the effectiveness of such a measurement.

It is difficult, in our opinion, to maintain the philosophical position that a quantum measurement is a very peculiar physical process, that involves "classical" apparata (whatever that means), many universes or sentient beings. The above analysis forces us to view the measurement process as a dynamical process of some sort. It is nothing but a physical interaction, that takes place during a certain elapse of time and follows (as far as we know) the laws of quantum mechanics. By stating this, we are by no means implying that all problems are solved: On the contrary, the quantum theory of measurement is still full of pitfalls and conceptual difficulties: von Neumann's projection rules should never be applied lightheartedly, because by virtue (and in spite) of their effectiveness, they may lead physicists astray.

Acknowledgements: I wish to thank H. Nakazato, M. Namiki, H. Rauch, L.S. Schulman and L. Vaidman for their comments and the High Energy Physics Group of Waseda University for their warm hospitality. This work was partially supported by the Japanese Society for the Promotion of Science, under a bilateral exchange program with Italian Consiglio Nazionale delle Ricerche, and by the Administration Council of the University of Bari.

REFERENCES

[1] G. Gamow, Z. Phys. **51** (1928) 204.

[2] V. Weisskopf and E.P. Wigner, Z. Phys. **63** (1930) 54; **65** (1930) 18.

[3] G. Breit and E.P. Wigner, Phys. Rev. **49** (1936) 519.

[4] L. Mandelstam and I. Tamm, J. Phys. **9** (1945) 249.

[5] V. Fock and N. Krylov, J. Phys. **11** (1947) 112.

[6] E.J. Hellund, Phys. Rev. **89** (1953) 919.

[7] M. Namiki and N. Mugibayashi, Prog. Theor. Phys. **10** (1953) 474.

[8] L.A. Khalfin, Dokl. Acad. Nauk USSR **115** (1957) 277 [Sov. Phys. Dokl. **2** (1957) 340]; Zh. Eksp. Teor. Fiz. **33** (1958) 1371 [Sov. Phys. JETP **6** (1958) 1053].

[9] R.E.A.C. Paley and N. Wiener, *Fourier Transforms in the Complex Domain* (American Mathematical Society Colloquium Publications Vol. XIX, New York, 1934).

[10] A. Beskow and J. Nilsson, Arkiv für Fysik **34** (1967) 561.

[11] L.A. Khalfin, Zh. Eksp. Teor. Fiz. Pis. Red. **8** (1968) 106 [JETP Letters **8** (1968) 65]; Phys. Lett. **112B** (1982) 223; Usp. Fiz. Nauk. **160** (1990) 185 [Sov. Phys. Usp. **33** (1990) 10].

[12] L. Fonda, G. C. Ghirardi, A. Rimini and T. Weber, Nuovo Cim. **A15** (1973) 689; **A18** (1973) 805; A. DeGasperis, L. Fonda and G. C. Ghirardi, Nuovo Cim. **A21** (1974) 471.

[13] B. Misra and E.C.G. Sudarshan, J. Math. Phys. **18** (1977) 756.

[14] J. von Neumann, *Die Mathematische Grundlagen der Quantenmechanik* (Springer, Berlin, 1932), p. 195 [English translation: *Mathematical Foundations of Quantum Mechanics*, translated by E.T. Beyer (Princeton University Press, Princeton, 1955) p. 366].

[15] A. Peres, Am. J. Phys. **48** (1980) 931.

[16] L. Fonda, G. C. Ghirardi and A. Rimini, Rep. Prog. Phys. **41** (1978) 587; G-C. Cho, H. Kasari and Y. Yamaguchi, Prog. Theor. Phys. **90** (1993) 803.

[17] H. Nakazato, M. Namiki and S. Pascazio, Int. J. Mod. Phys. **B10** (1996) 247.

[18] H. Nakazato, M. Namiki, S. Pascazio and H. Rauch, Phys. Lett. **A199** (1995) 27.

[19] E. Fermi, *Nuclear Physics* (Univ. Chicago, Chicago, 1950) pp. 136, 148; See also *Notes on Quantum Mechanics. A Course Given at the University of Chicago in 1954*, ed. E. Segré (Univ. Chicago, Chicago, 1960) Lec. 23; also Rev. Mod. Phys. **4** (1932) 87.

[20] L.S. Schulman, Proc. of the Adriatico Research Conf. on "Tunnelling and its Implications," ed. D. Mugnai et al. (World Sci., Singapore, 1996).

[21] A. Peres, Ann. Phys. **129** (1980) 33.

[22] L.S. Schulmann, A. Ranfagni and D. Mugnai, Phys. Scr. **49** (1994) 536.

[23] R.J. Cook, Phys. Scr. **T21** (1988) 49.

[24] W.H. Itano, D.J. Heinzen, J.J. Bollinger and D.J. Wineland, Phys. Rev. **A41** (1990) 2295.

[25] T. Petrosky, S. Tasaki and I. Prigogine, Phys. Lett. **A151** (1990) 109; Physica **A170** (1991) 306.

[26] A. Peres and A. Ron, Phys. Rev. **A42** (1990) 5720; L. E. Ballentine, Phys. Rev. **A43** (1991) 5165; W. H. Itano, D. J. Heinzen, J. J. Bollinger, and D. J. Wineland, Phys. Rev. **A43** (1991) 5168; V. Frerichs and A. Schenzle, in *Foundations of Quantum Mechanics*, T. D. Black, M. M. Nieto, H. S. Pilloff, M. O. Scully and R. M. Sinclair, eds., World Scientific, Singapore (1992); S. Inagaki, M. Namiki and T. Tajiri, Phys. Lett. **A166** (1992) 5; D. Home and M. A. B. Whitaker, J. Phys. **A25** (1992) 657; Phys. Lett. **A173** (1993) 327; R. Onofrio, C. Presilla and U. Tambini, Phys. Lett. **A183** (1993) 135; Ph. Blanchard and A. Jadczyk, Phys. Lett. **A183** (1993) 272; T. P. Altenmuller and A. Schenzle, Phys. Rev. A **49** (1994) 2016; M. Berry, in *Fundamental Problems in Quantum Theory*, eds., D. M. Greenberger and A. Zeilinger (*Ann. N.Y. Acad. Sci.* **Vol. 755**, New York, 1995), p. 303; A. Beige and G. Hegerfeldt, Phys. Rev. **A53** (1996) 53.

[27] S. Pascazio, M. Namiki, G. Badurek and H. Rauch, Phys. Lett. **A179** (1993) 155; S. Pascazio and M. Namiki, Phys. Rev. **A50** (1994) 4582.

[28] H. Nakazato, M. Namiki, S. Pascazio, and H. Rauch, Phys. Lett. **A217** (1996) 203.

[29] E. Mihokova, S. Pascazio, and L.S. Schulman, "Hindered decay: Quantum Zeno effect through electromagnetic field domination," preprint BA-TH/96-242.

[30] For a review, see *Quantum Theory and Measurement*, eds. J.A. Wheeler and W.H. Zurek (Princeton University Press, 1983); P. Busch, P.J. Lahti and P. Mittelstaedt, *The quantum theory of measurement* (Springer Verlag, Berlin, 1991); M. Namiki and S. Pascazio, Phys. Rep. **232** (1993) 301.

[31] B. Gaveau and L. S. Schulman, J. Stat. Phys. **58** (1990) 1209; J. Phys. A **28** (1995) 7359.

[32] E.P. Wigner, Am. J. Phys. **31**, 6 (1963).

PHYSICAL INTERPRETATION OF OPTIMUM QUANTUM DETECTION OPERATORS

R. Momose[1], M. Sasaki[2], and O. Hirota[1]

[1] Research Center for Quantum Communications,
Tamagawa University, Machida, Tokyo, Japan
[2] Communication Research Laboratory,
Ministry of Posts and Telecommunications, Koganei, Tokyo, Japan

In this paper, it will be clarified why quantum detection theory may predict superior performance in comparison with semi-classical detection theory. The reason is based on the fact that in the quantum formulation the reduction of probabilities of the cross over regions among decision symbols is allowed by the quantum interference induced by quantum measurement processes. The superior performance for optimum and Kennedy's receivers is explained by the compression of probability amplitude of signal state by the projectors. Furthermore we show the general realization theorem of the optimum projectors.

1. INTRODUCTION

Quantum communication theory predicts the existence of systems the so called quantum receiver, which can overcome the performance of the conventional receiver systems [1–3]. The physical interpretation of the quantum receivers in the general case is not yet clarified. We are concerned with the physical meaning of such an effect in quantum measurement processes as a model of the optical receivers. The general approach is, however, still difficult. Our discussion will be devoted to only systems with signals of pure states.

It is well-known that the general quantum measurement processes can be described by the positive operator valued measure (POM) or semi-observable [2]. In addition, the general detection operators are also described by the POM. However, in the case of linear independent states, quantum detection theory show that the optimum quantum detection processes can be given by orthogonal projectors with a finite dimension which is equal to the number of the signal states [4], and non-orthogonal projectors (POM) increases error probability. On the other hand, in the case of linear dependent states, POM gives an improvement [2]. For the design of such quantum measurement devices, we should clarify the physical phenomena corresponding to the optimum quantum detection processes. In order to discuss such a problem, we have shown in Ref. [5,6] an idea of classification of the quantum detection operators which involve a definition of the semi-quantum limit: SemiQL corresponding to the bound for the classical detection theory. If we wish to overcome the bound, then the conventional probability formula for the signal detection becomes inapplicable.

Quantum Communication, Computing, and Measurement
Edited by Hirota *et al.*, Plenum Press, New York, 1997

In this paper, we first survey the Helstrom-Holevo-Yuen formalism in quantum detection theory, then we introduce the content of the former paper: [6] on the semi-classical formalism. Finally we will show that the optimum detection process derived from the Helstrom-Holevo-Yuen formalism automatically induces a quantum interference. That is, the reason of why it is so difficult to find the physical correspondence of the optimum projectors arises from the fact that they are representing the quantum interference. This result cannot be deduced from Naimark's theorem which is known as a kind of realization of the POM or the semi-observable. Our result provides a powerful guide to the realization of abstract description of quantum detection processes for the technological advance.

2. QUANTUM DETECTION THEORY

2.1. DEFINITION OF THE DETECTION OPERATOR

In quantum detection theory, the detection processes are represented as follows:

$$\hat{I} = \sum_{j \in J} \hat{\Pi}_j$$

$$\hat{\Pi}_j = \int_{R_j} d\hat{X}(x) \geq 0 \tag{1}$$

where $d\hat{X}(x)$ is positive operator valued measure (POM) defined as $\left\{ x \in \Omega \rightarrow d\hat{X}(x) \right\}$ such that $d\hat{X}(\Omega) = \hat{I}$. These operators describe simultaneously the quantum measurement process and decision process. It means that the detection operator outputs directly the decision symbols corresponding to the hypothesis. That is, $\hat{\Pi} : \left\{ j \in J \rightarrow \hat{\Pi}(j) \right\}$ such that $\hat{\Pi}(J) = \hat{I}$. These are regarded as semi-observable with value space (J, j). As a result, we cannot recognize what kind of physical quantum measurement processes do these detection operators involve in such an abstract description. Such an abstract theory is called Helstrom-Holevo-Yuen formalism. Thus we should investigate the physical correspondence of the formalism. The importance of this problem was pointed out by Holevo.

2.2. FORMULATION OF THE OPTIMIZATION PROBLEM

In order to find the best quantum measurement and decision making, Helstrom formulated the optimization problem with respect to the detection operator as the detection theory with analogy for the classical communication theory. By the pioneering works of Holevo, Yuen, and others, we have the following well-known results:

Theorem 1:

Quantum Bayes [2,3], Necessary and sufficient conditions

$$\hat{\Pi}_j \left[\xi_j \hat{\rho}_j - \xi_i \hat{\rho}_i \right] \hat{\Pi}_i = 0, \ \forall i, j$$

$$\hat{\Gamma} - \xi_i \hat{\rho}_i \geq 0, \ \forall i \tag{2}$$

Theorem 2:
Quantum minimax [7,8], Necessary and sufficient conditions

$$\hat{\Pi}_j \left[\xi_j \hat{\rho}_j - \xi_i \hat{\rho}_i \right] \hat{\Pi}_i = 0, \ \forall i, j$$

$$\hat{\Gamma} - \xi_i \hat{\rho}_i \geq 0, \ \forall i \tag{3}$$

$$\mathrm{Tr} \hat{\rho}_i \hat{\Pi}_i = \mathrm{Tr} \hat{\rho}_j \hat{\Pi}_j, \ \forall i, j$$

2.3. SOLUTION OF THE OPTIMIZATION PROBLEM

In general, it is very difficult to solve the above optimization problems. Kennedy gave the most important lemma for solving the optimization problems as follows:

Lemma 1 (R. S. Kennedy) [4]:
The optimum detection operators for the linear independent pure state (LIPS) are orthogonal projectors in the finite dimensional space.

However, still we have difficulties to solve them. Recently, Osaki, Ban, and Hirota [8] showed the analytical solutions for these problems by applying the quantum minimax formula and Kennedy's lemma. Here we give the minimum error probability and the corresponding detection operator in the case of binary pure states: $\{ |\alpha\rangle, |-\alpha\rangle \}$.

$$\begin{aligned}
\hat{\Pi}_1 &= |\omega_1\rangle\langle\omega_1| \\[2mm]
&= \frac{1}{2(1-\kappa^2)} \left\{ \left(1 + \sqrt{1-\kappa^2}\right) |\alpha\rangle\langle\alpha| + \left(1 - \sqrt{1-\kappa^2}\right) |-\alpha\rangle\langle-\alpha| \right. \\[2mm]
&\quad \left. -\kappa \left(|\alpha\rangle\langle-\alpha| + |-\alpha\rangle\langle\alpha| \right) \right\}
\end{aligned}$$

$$\begin{aligned}
\hat{\Pi}_2 &= |\omega_2\rangle\langle\omega_2| \\[2mm]
&= \frac{1}{2(1-\kappa^2)} \left\{ \left(1 - \sqrt{1-\kappa^2}\right) |\alpha\rangle\langle\alpha| + \left(1 + \sqrt{1-\kappa^2}\right) |-\alpha\rangle\langle-\alpha| \right. \\[2mm]
&\quad \left. -\kappa \left(|\alpha\rangle\langle-\alpha| + |-\alpha\rangle\langle\alpha| \right) \right\}
\end{aligned} \tag{4}$$

So far, several realizations of the Helstrom bound by means of heuristic manner have been proposed by Dolinar [9] and others, but still there is no general interpretation of the optimum detection operator. Because there is no simple relation between the detection operator and them.

3. SEMI-CLASSICAL FORMALISM FOR QUANTUM DETECTION

3.1. ROLE OF THE SEMI-CLASSICAL FORMALISM

It is well-known that the mathematical formulation of quantum detection theory has been given by Helstrom, Holevo, and Yuen. They employed the positive operator valued measure (POM) to describe the signal detection processes which involve both quantum measurement and decision making. As a result, the optimizations on error performance under the most general mathematical basis in quantum mechanics could be discussed.

However, it brought us a new problem the so called realization problem of the optimum detection operators. In order to cope with this problem, we have proposed a discrimination of the class of detection operators [6]. This corresponds to going back to the age before Helstrom's work. The first attempt is to limit the mathematical back ground (measurement process and detection theory) to the von Neumann measurement and classical detection theory. In engineering science, it is called semi-classical formalism or standard formalism [6,8]. In order to use classical detection theory, we need probability densities describing the results of measurements. The probability densities can be given based on the von Neumann formula for measuring the signal observables. The decision making will be done based on the likelihood ratio of the densities when we measure a certain eigenvalue of the observable. Thus the semi-classical formalism corresponds to a simple application of classical detection theory to the quantum systems. Helstrom skipped this stage when he formulated the quantum detection theory. As a result, we were able to predict a new quantum bound at the sacrifice of the difficulty of the interpretation and the realization of such an abstract description as mentioned above. Our purpose is to pursue a realization method by revealing the explicit difference between the classical and the quantum detection theories. So we expect to encounter different physical phenomena when we leave the classical domain. The semi-classical formalism offers the border between the classical and quantum detection theories, though the later one involves the former one.

3.2. DEFINITION OF STANDARD DETECTION OPERATOR

In practical communication systems, the physical quantity conveying signals with the quantum states are prepared. Here we limit the mathematical back ground (measurement process and detection theory) to the standard measurements like photon counting, homodyne, and heterodyne for the admitted observable and classical detection theory. The probability densities we need in the classical detection theory are defined by the von Neumann formula by using the physical quantity of signal (observable) and the quantum states. By combining classical detection theory and quantum measurement of the signal observable, we can define the detection operators as follows:

$$\hat{\Pi}_{j(\text{SD})} = \int_{\text{R}_j} |x\rangle\langle x| \mathrm{d}x$$

$$\sum_j \hat{\Pi}_{j(\text{SD})} = \hat{\text{I}}, \ \hat{\Pi}_{j(\text{SD})} \geq 0$$

(5)

They are called the standard detection operators [6]. Since these are the detection operators, they satisfy $\hat{\Pi} : \{ j \in J \rightarrow \hat{\Pi}(j) \}$ such that $\hat{\Pi}(J) = \hat{\text{I}}$. But they are constructed by a projection valued measure (PVM) with the value space (Ω, x) of the signal observable. Of course, these are subset of $\mathcal{L}$: the class of the detection operators based on the POM theory. In this point of view, we can classify the detection operator into the standard detection operator and others. The set subtracted the class of the standard detection operators from whole detection operators: $\mathcal{L}$ which can be defined by the POM theory is called the generalized detection operator. Now we can define the semi-quantum limit (SemiQL) in the detection theory based on the above formalism. The following is the definition of the SemiQL in the detection theory. The best performance based on only the class of the standard quantum detection operators is called the semi-quantum limit (SemiQL) in the detection theory. If the signal observable is a set of non-commuting observables, then the minimum error probability based on the simultaneous measurement for such non-commuting observables is called the SemiQL.

This corresponds to heterodyne process. Or it is equivalent to that based on standard detection operator on the Naimark extension space. In this case, the standard detection operator is constructed by PVM of corresponding signal observables on the extended space. By this simple definition of the semi-quantum limit (SemiQL) in the detection theory, we can consider the difference of physical phenomena which are incorporated by the standard detection and generalized detection processes. Recently we showed the following.

Remark 1 [6]:
A physical condition for overcoming the SemiQL in the case of binary pure states is an effect of quantum interference between signal state and measurement state.

4. STRUCTURE OF OPTIMUM DETECTION OPERATORS

4.1. RELATION BETWEEN OPTIMUM DETECTION AND KENNEDY'S IDEA

It is well-known that Kennedy [10] proposed a near optimum scheme as an example for the realization of the optimum quantum detection process. The detection operators were derived by Shapiro as follows [11]:

$$\hat{\Pi}_1 = \hat{I} - |-\alpha\rangle\langle-\alpha|$$

$$\hat{\Pi}_2 = |-\alpha\rangle\langle-\alpha| \tag{6}$$

Recently, Osaki, Ban, and Hirota [8] also showed that the difference between detection operators of optimum and Kennedy's system is the conventional quantum interference based on Sasaki's work [12] who first clarified the role of the quantum interference for overcoming the SemiQL. However, we have not yet general interpretation of the two-dimensional projector like Kennedy's detection operator: Eq.(6). By the optimization with respect to detection operators, we have had a new quantum bound so called Helstrom's bound. This overcome the SemiQL. Thus we can understand that projectors on the finite dimensional space are the generalized detection operators. So they have no simple correspondence to the signal observable, even it belongs to the class of orthogonal projections. Now our main problem for the physical meaning of the projectors is addressed.

Remark 2:
The optimum quantum detection operators (orthogonal projectors) for the binary pure states induce two kinds of quantum interference.

We shall explain the above statement. The optimum projectors are constructed by the signal states. They belong to the generalized detection operators which have, in general, no simple correspondence to the conventional optical receiver, and they are sometimes called semi-observable with value space (J, j) in the mathematics. We want to know the physical meaning of "quantum gain by the optimum quantum detection process" which means the reduction of the error probability by the quantum detection theory in comparison with the classical detection theory.

Let us go back to the definition of the standard detection operator constructed by PVM with value space (Ω, β). By the spectral theory, it is corresponding to a self adjoint operator as an observable. The value space is essential in this case, because they are eigenvalues or measurement results of the observable and also it implies variables for the decision making. It is called the decision space. Here if the optimum projectors belong to the standard detection operator, then the decision error performance must become the SemiQL from the definition of the SemiQL. Here $P_e < P_{e(SemiQL)}$ is allowed if and only if the reduction of the probabilities for overlapped set of the measurement values under two hypothesis is actually possible in the sense of the classical detection theory. However, this is not allowed in classical detection theory, because it is not able to describe by the formalism of the conventional probability theory. Here the meanings of the difference from the classical formulation of probability in the quantum formalism will play an essential role.

In the reference [8], we showed that the difference between the optimum and Kennedy's processes is based on the conventional quantum interference caused by the superposition of the states in the optimum projectors consisting of signal states. And if the power of signals increases, then the optimum projectors go toward the Kennedy's projectors. So if we can clarify the physical meaning of the Kennedy's projectors, finally we can clarify the physical meaning of the optimum projectors on two dimensional space. The probability of the decision error based on the Kennedy's projector is

$$P_{e(Kennedy)} = \frac{1}{2}\text{Tr}|\alpha\rangle\langle\alpha|\Pi_2 = \frac{1}{2}|\langle\alpha| - \alpha\rangle|^2 \tag{7}$$

This seems an inner product between the signal state and the projector. If it is only an inner product, $P_{e(Kennedy)}$ can take arbitrary value: $0 \leq P_{e(Kennedy)} = \frac{1}{2}|\langle\alpha| - \alpha\rangle|^2 \leq 1$.

If it is so, it is not important to give it any physical interpretation. However, even if it has the form of inner product, it has different meaning when these have the next constraint:

$$\hat{\Pi}_1 + \hat{\Pi}_2 = \hat{I} \tag{8}$$

This means that the inner product gives the probabilities for the decisions of error or correct. In this case, the total probability should be unity and the range of $P_{e(Kennedy)} = \frac{1}{2}|\langle\alpha| - \alpha\rangle|^2$ is bounded. Kennedy's projector is truly this case. If it gives below the SemiQL, it is clear that it means the rate of compression of the probabilities for the error decisions. Let us describe the role of Eq.(6) as follows:

$$\langle\alpha|\Pi_2|\alpha\rangle = |\langle\alpha| - \alpha\rangle|^2 = \left|\int f(x) \cdot g(x)\mathrm{d}x\right|^2 < \text{SemiQL} \tag{9}$$

$$\langle-\alpha|\Pi_1| - \alpha\rangle = 0 \tag{10}$$

where $\{x\}$ is the eigenvalue of the signal observable. The function $\langle x| - \alpha\rangle = g(x)$ is interpreted as the weight function to compress the probability on the classical decision space. The case of Eq.(10) corresponds to a perfect elimination of quantum fluctuation by the projector. There is no such a rule in the classical probability theory. So it may be also regarded as the degree of the interference, because it directly controls the probability amplitude of the wave function. Although this type of the interference is different from the form of the conventional definition of the quantum interference, the origin is the same one. In this case, the quantum interference must appear as the effect of the quantum measurement. Thus we can understand that the optimum projectors induce the quantum interference between signal state and measurement state. □

Remark 3:

Can we realize the projectors on finite dimensional space by real physical devices? Detection operators corresponding to real physical devices are in infinite dimensional space in general.

4.2. REALIZATION THEOREM AND RELATION WITH NAIMARK'S THEOREM

In the above section, we showed the physical interpretation of the optimum projector. The problem is how to realize the quantum interference based on optimum projectors. Recently we gave a method for physical realization for the specific optimum projectors.

Theorem 3 [13, 14]:

The optimum projectors for any binary pure states can be realized by a unitary operator and a standard detection operator which is called the received quantum state control.

Here we can generalize the above theorem.

Theorem 4:

Optimum projectors for arbitrary M-ary linear independent states can be realized by quantum state control using a unitary operator representing quantum interference and a standard quantum measurement.

Proof:

Let the optimum detector basis $\{|\omega_i\rangle\}$ span H_M. Let the standard discrete measurement be $\{|n\rangle\}$ which is complete orthonormal in H, $H_M \subseteq H$. Let $H = H_M \oplus H'$ define H'. $\{|\omega_i\rangle\}$ is complete orthonormal in H_M. Pick any orthonormal basis $\{|v_j\rangle\}$ in H'. $\{|\omega_i\rangle\} \cup \{|v_j\rangle\}$ are complete orthonormal in H. There are many $\hat{U}$ mapping from $\{|n\rangle\}$ to $\{|\omega_i\rangle\} \cup \{|v_j\rangle\}$. Let $\hat{U}|\omega_i\rangle = |n_i\rangle$, $n_i \in N$. Then an optimum detection operator can be realized by $\{|n_i\rangle\}$, because $\langle \omega_i|\rho|\omega_i\rangle = \langle n_i|\hat{U}\rho\hat{U}^\dagger|n_i\rangle$.

This result is not equivalent with Naimark theorem, because unitary operator of our type has no meanings in such a theorem [15]. So this provides a new concept for realization of optimum projectors in quantum detection theory.

That is, the sense of our realization of the optimum projector is completely different from that of Naimark theorem which provides the mathematical equivalence in the extension space. However, theorems 3 and 4 mean the physical realization in the sense that the optimum projector in the finite dimensional space and the corresponding combined system of unitary operator and standard detection operator provides the same performance for the error probability as the criterion. Furthermore, from the theorem 3 and 4, we can say that the quantum gain in the detection theory can be realized by using quantum state control even if we employ the classical detection theory. However, quantum state control must generate a superposition of quantum states in order to induce the proper quantum interference.

5. CONCLUSIONS

We have discussed the physical interpretation of the optimum detection operators for the binary pure states signals. In spite that they are orthogonal projector, they are required to induce a quantum interference. Thus it has been clarified that the optimum projectors involve the quantum interference as an operation effect. This result provides powerful guide to the realization problem. In fact, several realization methods have been proposed under this concept by us [13, 14]. Also we gave a general realization theorem for M-ary LIPS. Finally, we summarize our works in the figure 1.

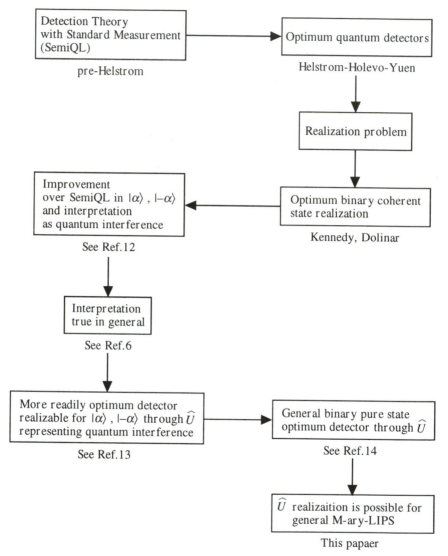

Figure 1. History of Quantum Detection Theory

ACKNOWLEDGMENT

We are grateful to Professor Yuen and Professor Ozawa for their kind suggestions.

REFERENCES

[1] C. W. Helstrom, *Quantum detection and estimation theory*, Academic Press, New York, (1976).

[2] A. S. Holevo, *Probabilistic and statistical aspect of quantum theory*, North Holland, Amsterdam, (1976).

[3] H. P. Yuen, R. S. Kennedy, and M. Lax, Trans. IEEE IT-21, 125, (1975).

[4] R. S. Kennedy, Quart. Progr. Rep. **110**, Res.Lab.Electron, M.I.T., (1973).

[5] O. Hirota, Research Review of Tamagawa University Research Institute, **1**, 1, (1995).

[6] R. Momose, M. Osaki, M. Ban, M. Sasaki, and O. Hirota, Proc. 4th International Conf. on Squeezed State and Uncertainty Relation, NASA Proc. Seri. (1995).

[7] O. Hirota and S. Ikehara, The Trans. IEICE of Japan, E-65, 627, (1982).

[8] M. Osaki, M. Ban, and O. Hirota, Phys. Rev. A-54, Aug. (1996).

[9] S. J. Dolinar, Quart. Progr. Rep. **111**, Res.Lab.Electron, M.I.T., (1973).

[10] R. S. Kennedy, Quart. Progr. Rep. **108**, Res.Lab.Electron, M.I.T., (1973).

[11] J. H. Shapiro, IEEE Trans. Inform. Theory, IT-26, 490, (1980).

[12] M. Sasaki, T. Usuda and O. Hirota, Phys. Rev. A-51, Feb., (1995).

[13] M. Sasaki, T. Usuda, and O. Hirota and A. S. Holevo, Phys. Rev. A-53, Mar., (1996).

[14] M. Sasaki, and O. Hirota, To be Published in Phys. Lett. A.

[15] M. Ozawa, Private communication.

GENERALISED UNCERTAINTIES FOR QUANTUM SIGNAL PROCESSING

Dorje C. Brody[1] and Bernhard K. Meister[2]

[1] Blackett Laboratory, Imperial College
South Kensington, London SW7 2BZ, U.K.
[2] Physics Department, Tokyo Institute of Technology
Meguro, Tokyo 152, Japan

Generalised uncertainty relations based upon Fourier transforms of discrete functions are reviewed. A new discrete version of the angular momentum uncertainty relations, based upon SU(2) transformations, is proved. Possible applications in quantum signal processing are also discussed.

1. INTRODUCTION

It is well known that the Heisenberg uncertainty relation for momentum p and position q, given by

$$\Delta q \Delta p \geq 1 , \tag{1}$$

can be viewed as a direct consequence of Fourier analysis. That is, a function and its Fourier transform cannot both be highly concentrated. Physically, this implies that the less the uncertainty in q, the greater the uncertainty in p, and conversely. In his original introduction to the quantum mechanical uncertainties, Heisenberg [1] implicitly introduced two distinct interpretations to the relation (1): the first one is that discussed in conventional quantum mechanics textbooks, namely, the variance-based uncertainty approach, whereby for example Δq in (1) above is understood as the standard deviation

$$\Delta q^2 \equiv \Delta_\psi q^2 \equiv \langle \psi | (q - \bar{q}_\psi)^2 | \psi \rangle , \tag{2}$$

with $\bar{q}_\psi \equiv \langle \psi | q | \psi \rangle$ for some state vector $|\psi\rangle$. A similar interpretation applies to Δp. The second view, which in some sense has been overlooked until recently [2], arises out of what we now understand as the effect of filtering. In other words, uncertainties arise from the limitation of the measurements. For example, that a Gaussian state saturates the uncertainty lower bound is a well known fact; however, for practical purposes it is not possible to actually 'measure' the entire Gaussian distribution from minus to plus infinity, but instead one is confined to a finite set of intervals.

Since Heisenberg's intuitive, physically motivated derivation of the uncertainty relations, a number of other approaches to such relations have been pursued. For example, in the information theoretic (or entropic) uncertainty relations, as discussed briefly below, one associates the Shannon information entropy with the measure of uncertainties.

Another attractive approach is a quantum extension of the classical Cramer-Rao inequality for parameter estimation [3]. These approaches do not require the association of self-adjoint operators to the parameters, and therefore yields more general results than the standard uncertainty relations in the sense that a large variety of physically important measurements can be treated systematically.

Although such approaches resolve some of the difficulties in obtaining various types of uncertainty relations within the conventional description of quantum mechanics, it is not obvious whether one can thereby recover operator uncertainty relations such as those concerning angular momentum. Also, the assignment of uncertainty to discrete outcomes of the measurements of observables such as spin or angular momentum has remained an open problem up to now. Recently, however, Donoho and Stark [4] provided, in the setting of signal processing analysis, uncertainty relations involving filtering processes. Their analysis also extends to the case of discrete Fourier transforms. It was noticed that, in a mathematical sense, the results of Donoho and Stark constituted the first demonstration of the proof for Heisenberg's second interpretation to the uncertainty relations [2,5].

In the present article, we first briefly outline, for a comparison, the results from entropic uncertainty relations. These results are of considerable interest in their own right since in some circumstances they are 'stronger' than the conventional Heisenberg relations. We then present the results that have been obtained in the area of signal processing on generalised uncertainty relations. These notions are then extended in order to obtain a new discrete versions of angular-momentum uncertainty relation, which takes the form $N_1 N_2 \geq 2j + 1$, where N_i is the nonzero component of the angular momentum for a spin-j particle in the i-th direction.

2. ENTROPIC UNCERTAINTY RELATIONS

In quantum theory, any single observable or a commuting set of observables can in principle be measured with arbitrary accuracy. However, there is in general an irreducible lower bound on the uncertainty in the result of a simultaneous measurement of noncommuting observables. Heisenberg's relation is one such example, however, Bialynicki-Birula [6] and Deutsch [7] argued that, in a sense, the inequality is 'too weak' for practical purposes, which led them to the establishment of an information theoretic uncertainty relation.

In the entropic uncertainty relations the information entropy $H(p) = -\int p(x) \ln p(x)\, dx$ for a given probability distribution $p(x)$, serves as an accurate measure of uncertainties. Within the context of Fourier theory, Hirschman [8] has shown that if $\psi(x)$ and $\tilde{\psi}(k)$ are related through a Fourier transform

$$\tilde{\psi}(k) = \frac{1}{\sqrt{2\pi\hbar}} \int dx\, e^{-ikx/\hbar} \psi(x) , \qquad (3)$$

then the following inequality holds: $H(|\tilde{\psi}|^2) + H(|\psi|^2) \geq 1 + \ln \pi$. Since then, a number of improvements upon the lower bound has been made and the results have also applied in quantum mechanics.

For example, one of Bialynicki-Birula extended the argument to cover an entropic uncertainty relation for angle and angular momentum given by

$$H(p_\phi^m) + H(p_{J_z}^m) \geq -\ln \frac{\Delta\phi}{2\pi} , \qquad (4)$$

where the probabilities p_ϕ^m and $p_{J_z}^m$ are given respectively by

$$p_\phi^m = \int_{\Delta\phi_m} d\phi |\psi(\phi)|^2 , \quad \text{and} \quad p_{J_z}^m = |c_m|^2 , \tag{5}$$

where the wave function

$$\psi(\phi) = \frac{1}{\sqrt{2\pi}} \sum_{m=-\infty}^{\infty} e^{im\phi} c_m \tag{6}$$

depends upon the angular variable ϕ and its expansion coefficients c_m when expanded into the set of eigenfunctions of J_z.

It is interesting to note that recently, Steane [9] (see, also Ekert and Macchiavello [10]) has extended the entropic uncertainty relation in order to obtain a discrete form of uncertainty relation, from which he made a link between basic quantum theory and the linear error correcting codes of classical information theory. He considered a 'binary' basis called "basis 1" and another basis "basis 2" which is obtained by rotating the original basis 1. Now, suppose a state can be written as a superposition of M_1 of the product states of basis 1 and a superposition of M_2 of the product states of basis 2. Then, Steane's inequality gives a lower bound on the product of these two numbers:

$$M_1 M_2 \geq 2^n , \tag{7}$$

where n is the total number of 'binary states'. For further details on entropic inequalities, we refer to the above mentioned references. Here, instead, we shall first review some recent developments in signal processing, then extend these notions in order to obtain new discrete versions of the angular momentum uncertainty relations.

3. FOURIER-BASED INEQUALITIES

Let us start by providing a number of standard definitions and theorems. The functions and sequences used are all elements of L_2 or l_2, with unit norm, unless otherwise specified. The discrete Fourier transform of a sequence $\{x_t\}$ of length N is defined as

$$\tilde{x}_\omega \equiv \frac{1}{\sqrt{N}} \sum_{t=0}^{N-1} x_t e^{-2\pi i\omega t/N} , \tag{8}$$

and for the continuous Fourier transform, we have

$$\tilde{f}(\omega) \equiv \int_{-\infty}^{\infty} dt f(t) e^{-2\pi i\omega t} . \tag{9}$$

Now, we introduce two operators $\hat{P}_T$ and $\hat{P}_\Omega$. The time limiting operator $\hat{P}_T$ is defined by

$$(\hat{P}_T f)(t) = \begin{cases} f(t) & t \in T, \\ 0 & \text{otherwise.} \end{cases} \tag{10}$$

and the frequency limiting operator $\hat{P}_\Omega$ is

$$(\hat{P}_\Omega f)(t) = \int_\Omega d\omega e^{2\pi i\omega t} \tilde{f}(\omega) , \tag{11}$$

where T and Ω are measurable subsets on the real line.

We say that a function f is ϵ_T-concentrated if $\|f - \hat{P}_T f\| \leq \epsilon_T$ for a real number ϵ_T and similarly $\tilde{f}$ is said to be ϵ_Ω-concentrated if $\|f - \hat{P}_\Omega f\| \leq \epsilon_\Omega$. Hence if f is

ϵ_T-concentrated on a measurable set T and $\tilde{f}$ is ϵ_Ω-concentrated on a measurable set Ω, we have

$$\|f - \hat{P}_\Omega \hat{P}_T f\| \leq \epsilon_T + \epsilon_\Omega \ . \tag{12}$$

Next, defining the operator Q by

$$(Qf)(t) \equiv \int_{-\infty}^{\infty} q(s,t)f(s)ds \ , \tag{13}$$

the Hilbert-Schmidt norm of Q is then given by

$$\|Q\|_{HS} \equiv \left(\int_{-\infty}^{\infty} \int_{-\infty}^{\infty} dt ds |q(s,t)|^2 \right)^{1/2} \ . \tag{14}$$

Note that the two norms are related by $\|Q\| \leq \|Q\|_{HS}$. The following result can then be easily verified:

Lemma 3.1 *(Donoho and Stark, 1989) The Hilbert-Schmidt norm of $\hat{P}_\Omega \hat{P}_T$ is given by*

$$\|\hat{P}_\Omega \hat{P}_T\|_{HS}^2 = |T||\Omega| \ . \tag{15}$$

Using the relations introduced above, we are now in a position to note a number of generalised uncertainty relations. First, we note the following lemma for discrete functions.

Lemma 3.2 *(Donoho and Stark, 1989) If the sequence $\{x_t\}$ of length N has N_t nonzero elements, then $\{\tilde{x}_\omega\}$ cannot have N_t consecutive zeros.*

Theorem 3.1 (Donoho and Stark, 1989) *Suppose that $\{x_t\}$ is nonzero at N_t points and that $\{\tilde{x}_\omega\}$ is nonzero at N_ω points. Then, the following inequalities hold:*

$$N_t \cdot N_\omega \geq N \ , \tag{16}$$

$$N_t + N_\omega \geq 2\sqrt{N} \ . \tag{17}$$

A useful theorem for the continuous functions can be obtained as follows:

Theorem 3.2 (Donoho and Stark, 1989) *Let T and Ω be measurable sets on the real line, and suppose there is a Fourier transform pair $(f, \tilde{f})$ such that f is ϵ_T-concentrated on T and $\tilde{f}$ is ϵ_Ω-concentrated on Ω. Then,*

$$|\Omega||T| \geq (1 - (\epsilon_T + \epsilon_\Omega))^2 \ . \tag{18}$$

An analogous result can be obtained for the discrete cases, which will be discussed in the following section together with the results for angular-momentum transformations.

4. ANGULAR-MOMENTUM UNCERTAINTY RELATIONS

In this section we shall now demonstrate that the uncertainty relations discussed above can be generalised to provide discrete analogues of the standard angular momentum uncertainty relations, for example,

$$\langle \Delta \hat{J}_x^2 \rangle \langle \Delta \hat{J}_y^2 \rangle \geq \frac{\hbar^2}{4} \langle \hat{J}_z^2 \rangle \ . \tag{19}$$

Note that the average $\langle \ \rangle$ depends upon the state of the system. Hence, if one chooses an eigenstate of $\hat{J}_z$, for example, then the right-hand side is just $m^2 \hbar^4 / 4$.

As an illustration, consider now the situation where one observes an ensemble of polarised spin particles with unknown polarisation direction, but knows that all the particles are identically prepared. These particles may be regarded, for example, as hydrogen atoms or alkaline-earth metal atoms which do not exhibit the anomalous Zeeman effect. For simplicity, we assume that the observer uses Stern-Gerlach devices with magnetic fields directed at angles θ_1 or θ_2 relative to the x-axis. The detectors are then just screens along the θ_1- and θ_2-axes. Each screen is divided into $2j + 1$ intervals (i.e., one dimensional boxes) where j is the highest spin of the atom, which is assumed known. After observations of the ensemble (where the number of particles is assumed to be $>> 2j + 1$) along, say, the direction of the θ_2-axis, one obtains an assignment of numbers to the respective boxes.

Suppose that, as a result of the observations, one obtains a distribution sharply peaked somewhere along the θ_2-axis. The commutation relations between angular momentum operators imply the impossibility of simultaneously determining more than one component of the angular momentum. Hence, if we measure the θ_1-component of the same atoms, we intuitively expect to obtain a widely spread distribution. If these (θ_1 and θ_2) distributions were related by a Fourier transform, then from the above arguments we would obtain

$$N_1 \cdot N_2 \geq 2j + 1 , \qquad (20)$$

where N_i ($i = 1, 2$) denotes the number of nonzero elements (nonempty boxes) along the θ_i-axis. However, the spinor components with squared amplitudes defining these two distributions are related by the following rotation matrix [11]

$$d_{m'm}^{(j)}(\beta) = \left[\frac{(j + m')!(j - m')!}{(j + m)!(j - m)!} \right]^{\frac{1}{2}} \left(\cos \frac{\beta}{2} \right)^{m'+m}$$
$$\times \left(\sin \frac{\beta}{2} \right)^{m'-m} P_{j-m'}^{m'-m,m'+m}(\cos \beta) , \qquad (21)$$

rather than by a Fourier transform. Here, P is the Jacobi polynomial

$$P_n^{a,b}(x) = \frac{(-1)^n}{2^n n!}(1 - x)^{-a}(1 + x)^{-b} \times \frac{d^n}{dx^n}\left[(1 - x)^{a+n}(1 + x)^{b+n} \right] , \qquad (22)$$

and the angle β in our case is just $\theta_2 - \theta_1$. Hence, it is not clear that an inequality such as (20) should hold. However, one can prove that all the relevant submatrices of $d_{m'm}^{(j)}$ have nonvanishing determinants except for a few values of β belonging to a set of measure zero, and hence, following the same argument as in the Fourier transform case, we obtain the following result:

Theorem 4.1 Let N_1 be the number of nonzero spin-components of a spin-j particle in any given one direction, and let N_2 be the number of nonzero spin-components in a different direction. Then, the following inequality holds:

$$N_1 \cdot N_2 \geq 2j + 1 . \qquad (23)$$

As a trivial extension, we can obtain the following bound for simultaneous measurements of k different components of the angular momentum of the atoms:

Corollary 4.1 Let $\{N_k\}$ be the set of numbers of nonzero spin-components in k distinct directions. Then,

$$N_1 \cdot N_2 \cdots N_k \geq (2j + 1)^{k/2} . \qquad (24)$$

Note that, although the above proof follows for almost any angle β, in order that the inequality be valid for the case $\beta << 1$, the required sample size must approach infinity. Also, as mentioned above, the set of angles where the determinants of some submatrices vanish is of measure zero. For example, the inequality (20) does not hold for any nonzero spin j if the angle $\beta = n\pi$.

5. BANDLIMITED UNCERTAINTY RELATIONS

In the foregoing discussion, we have assumed an ideal situation where the number of the particles is large, and the observer can ascertain with sufficient certainty whether or not any particles have arrived at any given box. Otherwise, we can block some of the detector boxes and confine our attention to the particles passing through the remaining boxes. After these particles have passed through the field of the Stern-Gerlach magnet in the first direction, we recombine the beams and then measure the components in another direction. For such cases, as well as in general, an approximate version of the above inequality is useful. We shall consider this for both Fourier transforms and spinor rotations in the following.

Again, we consider two distributions f_m and $\tilde{f}_{m'} = \sum_m d_{m'm} f_m$. If $d_{m'm}$ is an element of U(1), then this is just a discrete Fourier transform, and if $d_{mm'} \in$ SU(2), then f_m denotes the normalised spinor components corresponding to one axis and $\tilde{f}_{m'}$ those corresponding to another axis, rotated by the angle β relative to the first. We now define two projection operators,

$$\hat{P}_T f_n = \begin{cases} f_n & n \in T, \\ 0 & \text{otherwise.} \end{cases} \tag{25}$$

and

$$\hat{P}_\Omega f_n = \sum_{m \in \Omega} d^\dagger_{nm} \tilde{f}_m , \tag{26}$$

for some index sets T and Ω. The sequence f_n is said to be ϵ_T-concentrated on an index set T, if

$$\|f - \hat{P}_T f\| = \sum_n |f_n - \hat{P}_T f_n| \leq \epsilon_T ,$$

and similarly, $\tilde{f}$ is ϵ_Ω-concentrated on Ω, if $\|f - \hat{P}_\Omega f\| \leq \epsilon_\Omega$. Therefore, if f is ϵ_T-concentrated on T and $\tilde{f}$ is ϵ_Ω-concentrated on Ω, we have

$$\|\hat{P}_\Omega \hat{P}_T\| \geq 1 - \epsilon_T - \epsilon_\Omega . \tag{27}$$

We shall now find an upper bound for the norm of $\hat{P}_\Omega \hat{P}_T$. First consider Fourier transforms. In this case, the bound can simply be obtained by introducing the Frobenius matrix norm

$$\|\hat{Q}\|^2_F \equiv \sum_{m,k} q^*_{mk} q_{mk},$$

of an operator $\hat{Q}$, which is defined by $\hat{Q} f_m \equiv \sum_n q_{mn} f_n$. Since the conventional norm of an operator satisfies the inequality $\|\hat{Q}\| \leq \|\hat{Q}\|_F$ [4], we now calculate the norm $\|\hat{P}_T \hat{P}_\Omega\|_F$. In terms of the matrix elements, one obtains

$$\hat{P}_\Omega \hat{P}_T f_k = \sum_m q_{km} f_m ,$$

with

$$q_{km} = \begin{cases} \frac{1}{N} \sum_{m' \in \Omega} e^{2\pi i m'(k-m)/N} & m \in T, \\ 0 & \text{otherwise.} \end{cases}$$

Using Parseval's equality (i.e., the norm of an operator is the same as that of its Fourier transform), the Frobenius matrix norm can easily be calculated as

$$\|\hat{P}_\Omega \hat{P}_T\|_F^2 = \frac{N_T \cdot N_\Omega}{N} .$$

Hence, we are led to the following result:

Theorem 5.1 (Donoho and Stark, 1989) *Let* $\{(f_t), (\tilde{f}_\omega)\}$ *be a Fourier transform pair with* (f_t) ϵ_T-*concentrated on the index set* T *and* $(\tilde{f}_\omega)$ ϵ_Ω-*concentrated on the index set* Ω. *Let* N_T *and* N_Ω *denote the number of elements of* T *and* Ω, *respectively. Then,*

$$N_T \cdot N_\Omega \geq N(1 - (\epsilon_T + \epsilon_\Omega))^2 . \tag{28}$$

Now, suppose we have a measurement that is restricted to the set T containing N_T elements (boxes), from which ϵ_T can be evaluated. After choosing N_Ω boxes for the second measurement, we find the following upper bound for the observed intensity $1 - \epsilon_\Omega$ as

$$1 - \epsilon_\Omega \leq \sqrt{\frac{N_T N_\Omega}{N}} + \epsilon_T , \tag{29}$$

assuming $1 - (\epsilon_T + \epsilon_\Omega) \geq 0$.

Returning to the case of angular momentum, in terms of the matrix elements $d_{m'm}$ given in (21), one obtains

$$\hat{P}_\Omega \hat{P}_T f_k = \sum_{m' \in \Omega} d_{km'}^\dagger \sum_{m \in T} d_{m'm} f_m$$

$$= \sum_{m \in T} \left(\sum_{m' \in \Omega} d_{km'}^\dagger d_{m'm} \right) f_m$$

$$= \sum_m q_{km} f_m ,$$

with

$$q_{km} = \begin{cases} \sum_{m' \in \Omega} d_{km'}^\dagger d_{m'm} & m \in T, \\ 0 & \text{otherwise.} \end{cases}$$

The resulting bound obtained by the Frobenius matrix norm in this case is not sharp and thus one must consider different methods. In particular, it is clear that the norm depends not only upon N_T and N_Ω but also upon the turning angle β. Moreover, if $\beta \ll 1$, then it is always possible to find an example where (28) does not hold. Therefore, we restrict our attention to the case $\beta \sim \pi/2$. In this case, the bound can easily be obtained by finding the largest element of the matrix, with the result

$$\binom{N}{N/2} N_T N_\Omega \left(\sin\frac{\beta}{2} \cos\frac{\beta}{2} \right)^N \geq (1 - (\epsilon_T + \epsilon_\Omega))^2 . \tag{30}$$

6. APPLICATIONS IN SIGNAL PROCESSING

Now, let us consider the received signal r taking the form

$$r = s + P_T \eta , \tag{31}$$

which is produced by adding to the original signal s the modified noise given by $P_T \eta$, where η is the noise and P_T denotes the operator limiting of the noise to a fixed time interval or a wave band T. Assuming such a form of the signal is not always unrealistic, since, for example, in astronomy, signals are only distorted significantly if clouds cover the particular region of the sky studied by the telescope. The same could be said for spectroscopy, where noise can be on different scales, for example, small noise for most of the waveband and significant noise confined to a few special wavelengths. In these situations we can apply the following theorem:

Theorem 6.1 (Donoho and Stark, 1989) *If $|\Omega|\,|T| < \frac{1}{2}$, then the signal can be recovered perfectly, independent of the noise function η.*

This idealised case, however, is of course not often encountered in more realistic situations. Nonetheless, the following theorem would be more useful:

Theorem 6.2 (Donoho and Stark, 1989) *Let $|\Omega|\,|T| < \frac{1}{2}$. If η vanishes outside the set T, then its best approximation from $B_1(\Omega)$ is zero, where $B_1(\Omega)$ denotes the set of functions $f \in L_1$ that are bandlimited in Ω.*

This leads naturally to the following conjecture, namely, the norm of the product of operators $\|P_\Omega P_T\|$, where Ω is an interval and T ranges over measurable sets, is maximised when both $|T|$ and $|\Omega|$ are continuous intervals. Daubechies [12] has shown, using perturbative arguments, that this statement holds 'infinitesimally'. In other words, $\|P_\Omega P_T\|$ decreases as T is perturbed away from an interval to a union of intervals. The conjecture has also been proven, if $|T|\,|\Omega| < 0.8$.

A standard question in spectroscopy is to ask what are the effects of filters. For example, standard procedures in various experiments involve the use of the whole range of different filters in order to obtain data for analysis. This creates a host of problems which are not adequately dealt with in terms of conventional 'error bars'. The theorems stated above, however, already provide a hint of how to tackle this problem, since they demonstrate how the uncertainty principle is weakened by introducing 'cut-offs'. These results thus indirectly tell us how the data itself is affected.

We can, for example, deduce how much of the signal has been lost through the introduction of filters by giving bounds for ϵ_T or ϵ_Ω. Perhaps an example will demonstrate more clearly the role of the approximate uncertainty relations. If we choose the product $c = |T|\,|\Omega|$ of $|T|$ and $|\Omega|$ to be small, i.e., $c < 1$, then we know that $c \geq (1-(\epsilon_T+\epsilon_\Omega))^2$. If we further assume that in a particular given experiment one of the ϵ's, say ϵ_T, is small, then it follows that

$$\epsilon_\Omega \geq 1 - \sqrt{c}\,. \tag{32}$$

This simple inequality already provides an upper bound for the losses caused by a frequency filter. This result, despite its simplicity, would have immediate consequences in spectroscopy. We assume, without being aware of particular publications, that results like these in one form or another are already known to the researchers in the field of spectroscopy. Note that a more general bound for the losses caused by filters is given by

$$\epsilon_T + \epsilon_\Omega \geq 1 - \sqrt{c}\,, \tag{33}$$

if $\epsilon_T + \epsilon_\Omega < 1$.

7.   DISCUSSION

We have generalised the uncertainty relations that have previously been developed for Fourier transforms to $SU(2)$ transformations in order to derive discrete angular momentum uncertainty relations. However, there are many possible applications within the framework of Fourier transform theory, including position-momentum or time-energy uncertainty relations. While conventional uncertainty relations assume the concentration of the function (distribution) and its Fourier transform on continuous intervals, the above results (16) and (17) are valid for concentrations on arbitrary measurable sets. Moreover, as shown in [4] for the case of Fourier transforms, the inequality (28) also holds for continuous functions. These inequalities also have important applications to signal recovery in quantum communication theory and quantum spectroscopy.

Another obvious application would be to discrete quantum mechanics, where generalised uncertainty relations for Fourier theory discussed above can be applied without any modification of the proofs. Also, these generalisations can be further extended to obtain uncertainty relations on Lie groups, with obvious applications in the field of particle physics, including measurements of discrete quantities such as isospin or hypercharge, etc. Such extensions can be studied using the Peter-Weyl theorem [13], however, this topic is beyond the scope of the present discussion, and will be studied elsewhere.

REFERENCES

[1] Heisenberg, W., Zeits. f. Phys. **43**, 172 (1927).

[2] Meister, B.K., PhD Thesis, Imperial College, London (1996).

[3] Brody, D.C. and Hughston, L.P., Phys. Rev. Lett. **77**, 2851 (1996).

[4] Donoho, D.L. and Stark, P.B., SIAM J. App. Math. **49**, 906 (1989).

[5] Brody, D.C. and Meister, B.K., "Discrete Uncertainty Principle" Imperial College Preprint IC/TP/94-95/60.

[6] Bialynicki-Birula, I., Lecture Notes in Mathematics **1136**, 90 (1984).

[7] Deutsch, D., Phys. Rev. Lett., **50**, 631 (1983).

[8] Hirshman, I.I., Amer. J. Math., **79**, 152 (1957).

[9] Steane, A.M., Phys. Rev. Lett., **77**, 793 (1996).

[10] Ekert, A. and Macchiavello, C., Phys. Rev. Lett. **77**, 2585 (1996).

[11] Edmonds, A. R., *Angular Momentum in Quantum Mechanics* (Princeton Univ. Press, NJ, 1968), Landau, L. D. and Lifshitz, E. M., *Quantum Mechanics* (Pergamon Press, Oxford, 1977).

[12] Daubechies, I., *Ten Lectures on Wavelets*, (SIAM, Philadelphia PA, 1992).

[13] Varadarajan, V. S., *An Introduction to Harmonic Analysis on Semisimple Lie Groups* (Cambridge University Press, Cambridge, 1989); Brody, D.C., Physica A, **213**, 315 (1995).

OPTIMAL QUANTUM MEASUREMENTS FOR PHASE ESTIMATION IN INTERFEROMETRY

B. C. Sanders[1], G. J. Milburn[2], and Zhongxi Zhang[2]

[1] School of Mathematics, Physics, Computing and Electronics
Macquarie University, New South Wales 2109, Australia
[2] Department of Physics, The University of Queensland
Queensland 4072, Australia

Optimal quantum measurements in optical interferometry yield a $1/n$ scaling of phase uncertainty $\Delta\phi$, where n is the number of photons in the interferometer, for both passive (linear) and active (nonlinear) interferometers. The phase uncertainty is *independent* of applied phase shift for the optimal measurement scheme, and we identify the coefficient of proportionality in each case.

1. INTRODUCTION

Interferometers are highly successful as precise measuring tools, so much so that the principle of complementarity imposes genuine performance limits [1]. With classical light there is no intrinsic obstacle to measuring the interferometric phase shift, but quantum limits to precision exist due to constraints on the energy of the field in the interferometer. We employ quantum measurement theory to extract a precise estimate of the interferometric phase shift subject to a constraint on photon number within the interferometer.

The interferometer input state is assumed to be known. Much work, both experimental and theoretical, has been directed towards determining the quantum state of light [2], and we assume that the state of light entering the interferometer has been fully characterised; *i.e.*, its density matrix $\hat{\rho}$ is fully known. Furthermore, the interferometer is assumed to be lossless and transforms a two–mode input field into a two–mode output field by a unitary transformation $\hat{\mathcal{I}}(\phi)$. The c-number phase shift ϕ is not known and must be estimated by performing appropriate measurements on the output field.

Quantum measurement theory [3,4], which provides the techniques for determining the optimal measurement scheme, has been applied to the problem of measuring the phase shift of a harmonic oscillator [5,6], and these methods generalise to the case of interferometric phase shifts. In fact the harmonic oscillator phase shift is an interferometric phase shift, but the phase shift is measured against a classical reference oscillator. In practice this measurement is achieved using an interferometer with a strong local oscillator, generally achieved by directing a very strong coherent field into the interferometer and partitioning the field unequally between a weak signal field and a very strong local oscillator field which can be treated classically. However, energy constraints on the field within the interferometer apply equally to both signal and local oscillator modes. A self–consistent treatment of estimating interferometric phase shifts is necessarily a two–mode analysis with both signal and local oscillator fields quantised.

Yurke *et al* [7] introduced two classes of interferometers: passive interferometers which can be characterised by an SU(2) symmetry and active interferometers which are characterised by an SU(1,1) symmetry. Passive interferometers include a broad class of interferometers which use mirrors, beam splitters and phase shifters, but the most convenient configuration for interpreting the mathematics is the Mach–Zehnder interferometer: the two–mode input field is first mixed at a beam splitter, then subjected to a mutual phase shift between the two internal fields of the interferometer, and mixed at a second beam splitter before exiting the interferometer. The active interferometer replaces each of the two beam splitters, at the input and output ports of the interferometer, by a nonlinear optical element. The nonlinear optical element converts the classical input field into photon pairs, such as that produced by parametric fluorescence [8], and the two photons, which travel down the two distinct paths in the interferometer and subjected to a mutual phase shift, are recombined at a second nonlinear element where a photon pair upconversion takes place.

These two classes of interferometers are analysed here to determine the scaling of phase uncertainty $\Delta\phi$ with total photon number n within the interferometer. Yurke *et al* [7] demonstrated the scaling

$$\Delta\phi \propto 1/n \tag{1}$$

for both passive and active interferometers based on photon counting techniques at the two output ports. However, the measurement scheme, based on photon counting methods, is not optimal as the phase sensitivity $\Delta\phi$ varies with the applied interferometric phase shift ϕ[9].

The optimal measurement scheme for SU(2) interferometry, identified by Sanders and Milburn [10], demonstrates a $1/n$ scaling independent of the applied phase shift. Here we establish the coefficient of proportionality for that scaling formula. The coefficient is established by analysing the distribution of phase data in the context of the fiducial distribution as well as by employing the Cramèr-Rao lower bound (CRLB)[5]. We also show that $1/n$ scaling applies to the SU(1,1) interferometer and determine the scaling coefficient as well.

2. UNITARY INTERFEROMETER TRANSFORMATIONS

The interferometer transforms two input fields a and b, with annihilation operators $\hat{a}$ and $\hat{b}$, respectively, into two output fields. Losses are assumed to be negligible. The interferometer transformation is represented by the unitary operator

$$\hat{\mathcal{I}}(\phi) = \exp\left(-i\phi\hat{G}\right), \tag{2}$$

for $\hat{G}$ the generator of the phase shift. The Schwinger representation [7,11] is used for the passive interferometer which exhibits an SU(2) symmetry, and $\hat{G} = \hat{J}_y$ in this case [10], for $\hat{J}^2$ the Casimir invariant. The transformation (2) is equivalent to a beam splitter transformation with variable reflectivity [7,12]. The number difference operator is given by

$$\hat{J}_z = \left(\hat{a}^\dagger\hat{a} - \hat{b}^\dagger\hat{b}\right)/2, \tag{3}$$

and the Fock state $|m\rangle_a \otimes |n\rangle_b$ can be written as the $\hat{J}_z$ eigenstate $|j\,\mu\rangle_z$ with eigenvalue μ where $2j = m + n$ and $2\mu = m - n$.

The transformation for the active interferometer is generated by elements of the su(1,1) algebra [7]. Again for $\hat{a}$ and $\hat{b}$ the annihilation operators for the input modes, the three independent generators for the ideal active interferometer are

$$\hat{K}_x = \frac{1}{2}\left(\hat{a}\hat{b} + \hat{a}^\dagger\hat{b}^\dagger\right),\tag{4}$$

$$\hat{K}_y = \frac{i}{2}\left(\hat{a}\hat{b} - \hat{a}^\dagger\hat{b}^\dagger\right),\tag{5}$$

$$\hat{K}_z = \frac{1}{2}\left(\hat{a}^\dagger\hat{a} + \hat{b}\hat{b}^\dagger\right),\tag{6}$$

which obey the su(1,1) algebra:

$$[\hat{K}_x, \hat{K}_y] = -i\hat{K}_z, \ [\hat{K}_y, \hat{K}_z] = i\hat{K}_x, \ [\hat{K}_z, \hat{K}_x] = i\hat{K}_y.\tag{7}$$

The eigenstate of $\hat{K}^2$, with eigenvalue $k(k-1)$, and of $\hat{K}_z$, with eigenvalue μ, is

$$|k = 1/2 \ \mu\rangle_z = |n\rangle_a \otimes |n\rangle_b\tag{8}$$

where $\mu = 1/2 + n$.

The overall transformation for the interferometer corresponds to two–photon generation by a classical pump field, and the internal fields are subject to a relative phase shift ϕ between the two internal modes, followed by two–photon recombination at the second parametric amplifier [7]. The total photon number in both arms of the interferometer is, for a vacuum state input $|0\rangle_a \otimes |0\rangle_b$,

$$n = 2\sinh^2(\beta/2),\tag{9}$$

or, equivalently, $\beta = \cosh^{-1}(2n+1)$. The unitary transformation for the active interferometer,

$$\hat{\mathcal{I}}_\beta(\phi) = e^{-i\beta\hat{K}_y}e^{i\phi\hat{K}_z}e^{i\beta\hat{K}_y},\tag{10}$$

commutes with the Casimir invariant

$$\hat{K}^2 \equiv \hat{K}_z^2 - \hat{K}_x^2 - \hat{K}_y^2 = \frac{1}{4}\left[\left(\hat{a}^\dagger\hat{a} - \hat{b}^\dagger\hat{b}\right)^2 - 1\right] = k(k-1).\tag{11}$$

where k corresponds to the photon number difference for the two output modes. For the case of interest here, where the two input modes are in the vacuum state, we treat the principle discrete series representation of SU(1,1) with $k = 1/2$.

3. OPTIMAL MEASUREMENTS

The optimal measurement strategy corresponds to projections onto the phase states $\{|\theta\rangle\}$ for which $\hat{G}$ of eq (2) acts as a pure differential operator [13]:

$$\hat{G}|\theta\rangle = \frac{1}{i}\frac{d}{d\theta}|\theta\rangle.\tag{12}$$

Equivalently the interferometer operator (2) is an exponentiated differential operator in the phase representation:

$$\hat{\mathcal{I}}(\phi)|\theta\rangle = \exp\left(-i\phi\frac{d}{d\theta}\right)|\theta\rangle.\tag{13}$$

In the eigenbasis of $\hat{G}$, where $\hat{G}|g\rangle = g|g\rangle$, the phase state can be written as the superposition

$$|\theta\rangle = \sum_{g} e^{ig\theta}|g\rangle. \tag{14}$$

The optimal positive operator–valued measure is thus the projection operator,

$$\hat{E}(\theta)d\theta = \mathcal{N}|\theta\rangle\langle\theta|d\theta \tag{15}$$

for $\mathcal{N}$ a normalisation factor such that

$$\int_{-\pi}^{\pi} \hat{E}(\theta)d\theta = \hat{1}. \tag{16}$$

For an input state with density matrix $\hat{\rho}$, the measured distribution is given by

$$P(\theta|\phi) = P(\theta - \phi) = \text{Tr}\left(\hat{\rho}\hat{E}(\theta - \phi)\right) = \mathcal{N}\langle\theta - \phi|\hat{\rho}|\theta - \phi\rangle. \tag{17}$$

Without loss of generality, $\phi = 0$ can be assumed as the distribution is shift–invariant; hence the precision of the estimate for $\phi = 0$ is equal to the precision for any value of ϕ.

For the passive interferometer, $\hat{J}_y$ acts on the SU(2) phase states [14]

$$|j\,\theta\rangle = (2j + 1)^{-1/2} \sum_{\mu=-j}^{j} e^{i\mu\theta}|j\,\mu\rangle_y \tag{18}$$

as a pure differential operator,

$$\hat{J}_y|j\,\theta\rangle = \frac{1}{i}\frac{d}{d\theta}|j\,\theta\rangle, \tag{19}$$

where $\hat{J}_y|j\,\mu\rangle_y = \mu|j\,\mu\rangle_y$. For the active interferometer, on the other hand, the eigenstates of the unitary operator (10) are

$$|k\mu\rangle_\beta \equiv e^{-i\beta\hat{K}_y}|k\mu\rangle_z. \tag{20}$$

Equation (20) indicates that the eigenstates of the generator of the unitary transformation are simply squeezed two-mode number states. The conjugate representation is defined by the phase states

$$|k\,\theta\rangle_\beta = \sum_{\mu} e^{i\mu\theta}|k\mu\rangle_\beta \tag{21}$$

which, for $k = 1/2$, is given by

$$|k = 1/2\,\mu\rangle_\beta = e^{i\theta/2} \sum_{n=0}^{\infty} e^{in\theta} e^{-\frac{\beta}{2}(\hat{a}^\dagger\hat{b}^\dagger - \hat{a}\hat{b})} \left(|n\rangle_a \otimes |n\rangle_b\right). \tag{22}$$

The optimum POVM is the projection

$$\hat{E}_\beta(\theta)d\theta = |k\theta\rangle_\beta\langle k\theta| \, d\theta/2\pi \tag{23}$$

which is normalised to unity on the interval $[-\pi, \pi)$.

4.   PHASE UNCERTAINTY

For passive and active interferometers, expressions for the phase distributions (17) can be calculated. The distribution can then be analysed by the standard techniques of probability theory. Such techniques include the fiducial distribution and the Cramèr-Rao lower bound (CRLB) [5].

312

4.1. THE FIDUCIAL DISTRIBUTION

The fiducial distribution, for a symmetric distribution $P(\theta)$, is

$$\Phi(\sigma) = 2 \int_0^\sigma P(\theta) \frac{d\theta}{2\pi}, \tag{24}$$

and $\Phi(\pi) = 1$. For $\kappa = \Phi(\sigma)$ for some κ, a randomly measured point θ has a probability of κ to be in the interval $(\phi - \sigma, \phi + \sigma)$. Thus, the value of σ for $\kappa = 2/3$ is the half–width of the distribution which contains $2/3$ of the area. The choice $\kappa = 2/3$ agrees closely with the 68% confidence level used for studies of harmonic oscillator phase [5].

For each interferometer case, passive and active, an optimal input state is necessary to achieve maximum phase sensitivity. The dual Fock state input is assumed for the passive interferometer [9,10] and a classical coherent state input is assumed for the active interferometer [7].

For the passive interferometer the asymptotic probability distribution

$$P_j(\theta) = |\langle j\, \theta | j\, 0 \rangle_y|^2 = \frac{2j+1}{2\pi} \frac{[\Gamma(3/4)]^2}{2^{3/2}} \frac{\left[J_{1/4}(j\theta)\right]^2}{\sqrt{j\theta}} \tag{25}$$

has been calculated for large j [10]. The distribution $P_j(\theta)$ depends, not on j and θ independently, but rather on the product. Thus, any estimate of where the centre of the distribution is must improve proportionally with $1/j$ and hence with $1/n$ where $n = 2j$.

The fiducial distribution can be calculated using the asymptotic (large σ) Bessel function expansion to the integral

$$\int_0^\sigma \frac{J_{1/4}^2(x)}{\sqrt{x}} dx \approx \frac{\pi}{\sqrt{2}\Gamma^2(3/4)} - \frac{2}{\pi\sqrt{\sigma}}. \tag{26}$$

Replacing $n = 2j$ gives the result

$$\Phi_n(\sigma) \approx 1 - \left(\frac{2\Gamma(3/4)}{\pi}\right)^2 (n\sigma)^{-1/2}. \tag{27}$$

The probability that a datum $\theta_i \in (-\sigma, \sigma)$ is κ is given by $\kappa = 2\Phi_n(\sigma)$ which can be solved:

$$j\sigma = \frac{16\Gamma^4(3/4)}{\pi^4(1-\kappa)^2} \tag{28}$$

which leads to

$$\Delta\phi \approx 3.36/n \tag{29}$$

for $\kappa = 2/3$ and is smaller than the estimate involving the separations of the first zeroes for the multipeaked phase distribution (25) [10].

For the active interferometer, we can get an explicit expression for $P_\beta(\theta|\phi)$ when the input state is the two-mode vacuum state $|0\rangle \equiv |k = 1/2\ \mu = 0\rangle = |0\rangle_a \otimes |0\rangle_b$. The su(1,1) disentangling theorem [7]

$$e^{-i(\beta/2)\hat{K}_y} = e^{-\tanh(\beta/2)a^\dagger b^\dagger} \exp\left(-\hat{K}_z \ln\left[\cosh^2(\beta/2)\right]\right) e^{\tanh(\beta/2)ab} \tag{30}$$

gives

$$\begin{aligned} P_\beta(\theta|\phi) = P_\beta(\theta - \phi) &= \left|\cosh(\beta/2) - e^{-i(\theta-\phi)}\sinh(\beta/2)\right|^{-2} \\ &= \left[\cosh\beta - \cos(\theta-\phi)\sinh\beta\right]^{-1}. \end{aligned} \tag{31}$$

313

For $\kappa = 2/3$, the fiducial distribution

$$\Phi_\beta(\sigma) = \frac{2}{\pi} \tan^{-1}\left(e^\beta \tan \frac{\sigma}{2}\right) \tag{32}$$

gives the result

$$\sigma = 2 \tan^{-1}\left(\sqrt{3}e^{-\beta}\right). \tag{33}$$

For $\beta \gg 1$ we have $\sigma \approx 2\sqrt{3}e^{-\beta}$ or $\sigma \approx \sqrt{3}/n$, i.e., a $1/n$ scaling and superior to the scaling (29) for the passive interferometer with respect to the number of photons *within* the interferometer.

4.2. CRAMÈR-RAO LOWER BOUND

The fiducial distribution gives a measure for the scatter of points. Also of importance is the question of how the phase shift estimate scales with photon number. The CRLB establishes the lowest uncertainty which could be achieved for a given phase distribution. Specifically the phase uncertainty scales as

$$\Delta\phi = 1/\sqrt{F} \tag{34}$$

for

$$F = 2 \int_0^\pi \left[\frac{d}{d\theta}\ln P_n(\theta)\right]^2 P(\theta)\frac{d\theta}{2\pi} \tag{35}$$

the Fisher information.

For the passive interferometer,

$$F_j = 2^{3/2}\pi^{-1}\Gamma^2(3/4)j^2 \int_0^\infty x^{-1/2}J_{5/4}^2 dx. \tag{36}$$

Using the integral [15]

$$\int_0^\infty \frac{J_{5/4}^2}{\sqrt{x}}dx = 2^{-3/2}\pi/\Gamma^2(3/4) \tag{37}$$

the Fisher information simplifies to

$$F_j = j^2. \tag{38}$$

The CRLB for the phase uncertainty is, therefore,

$$(\Delta\phi)_n = F^{-1} = j^{-1} = 2/n. \tag{39}$$

which sets an absolute lower bound to the uncertainty achievable using this non–Gaussian distribution.

For the active interferometer

$$F_\beta = \pi^{-1}\sinh^2\beta \int_0^\pi \frac{\sinh^2\beta\sin^2\theta}{(\cosh\beta - \sinh\beta\cos\theta)^3}d\theta. \tag{40}$$

The integral may be performed to give the Fisher information exactly by

$$F_\beta = \frac{1}{2}\sinh^2\beta = 2n(n+1); \tag{41}$$

thus, for large n, the phase uncertainty scales according to

$$\Delta\phi \approx \frac{1}{\sqrt{2n}}. \tag{42}$$

5. CONCLUSIONS

Choosing the optimal POVM guarantees that the precision of the phase shift measurement does not depend on the applied phase shift for both passive and active interferometers. The phase uncertainty is smaller for the active interferometer than for the passive interferometer for a fixed number of photons n within the interferometer, but this advantage is mitigated by the low photon pair production efficiency which requires a higher power input in the case of the active interferometer. The passive interferometer, which requires n photons in the input field to obtain n photons within the interferometer, is ideally 100% efficient at converting input photons into photons within the interferometer, but requires a nonclassical input state. Optimal phase measurements can be used to determine interferometric phase shifts with uncertainties that scale as $1/n$ for n the number of photons within the (passive or active) interferometer. This precision is independent of the applied phase shift.

This research has been supported by a Macquarie University Research Grant.

REFERENCES

[1] C. M. Caves, Phys. Rev. D **23**, 1693 (1981).

[2] *See* U. Leonhardt and H. Paul, *Prog. Quant. Electr.* **19**, 89-130 (1995) and refs. therein.

[3] C. W. Helstrom, *Quantum Detection and Estimation Theory* (Academic, New York, 1976).

[4] S. L. Braunstein, C. M. Caves and G. J. Milburn, Ann. Phys. (N.Y.) **247**, 135 (1996).

[5] S. L. Braunstein, A. S. Lane and C. M. Caves, Phys. Rev. Lett. **69**, 2153 (1992); S. L. Braunstein, Phys. Rev. Lett. **69**, 3598 (1992).

[6] M. J. W. Hall, J. Mod. Opt. **40**, 809 (1993).

[7] B. Yurke, S. L. McCall, and J. R. Klauder, Phys. Rev. A **33**, 4033 (1986).

[8] D. C. Burnham and D. L. Weinberg, Phys. Rev. Lett. **25**, 84 (1970).

[9] The scaling law (1) for passive interferometers has also been shown by M. J. Holland and K. Burnett, Phys. Rev. Lett. **71**, 1355 (1993).

[10] B. C. Sanders and G. J. Milburn, Phys. Rev. Lett. **75**, 2944 (1995).

[11] J. Schwinger, US Atomic Energy Commission Report No. NYO-3071 (U. S. GPO, Washington, D. C., 1952); reprinted in *Quantum Theory of Angular Momentum*, L. C. Biedenharn and H. van Dam, eds. (Academic, New York, 1965).

[12] R. A. Campos, B. E. A. Saleh, and M. C. Teich, Phys. Rev. A **40**, 1371 (1989).

[13] G. J. Milburn, W.-Y. Chen, and K. R. Jones, Phys. Rev. A **50**, 801 (1994).

[14] A. Vourdas, Phys. Rev. A **41**, 1653 (1990).

[15] G. N. Watson *A Treatise on the Theory of Bessel Functions* (Cambridge Univ. Press, London, 1922).

HYPERSENSITIVITY TO PERTURBATION:
AN INFORMATION-THEORETICAL CHARACTERIZATION OF
CLASSICAL AND QUANTUM CHAOS

Rüdiger Schack[1], and Carlton M. Caves[2]

[1] Department of Mathematics
Royal Holloway, University of London
Egham, Surrey TW20 0EX, United Kingdom
E-mail: r.schack@rhbnc.ac.uk
[2] Center for Advanced Studies
Department of Physics and Astronomy, University of New Mexico
Albuquerque, New Mexico 87131–1156, USA
E-mail: caves@tangelo.phys.unm.edu

Hypersensitivity to perturbation is a criterion for chaos based on the question of how much information about a perturbing environment is needed to keep the entropy of a Hamiltonian system from increasing. In this paper we give a brief overview of our work on hypersensitivity to perturbation in classical and quantum systems.

1. INTRODUCTION

In both classical and quantum physics isolated systems can display unpredictable behavior, but the reasons for the unpredictability are quite different. In classical (Hamiltonian) mechanics unpredictability is a consequence of chaotic dynamics, or exponential sensitivity to initial conditions, which makes it impossible to predict the phase-space trajectory of a system to a certain accuracy from initial data given to the same accuracy. This unpredictability, which comes from not knowing the system's initial conditions precisely, is measured by the Kolmogorov-Sinai (KS) entropy, which is the rate at which initial data must be supplied in order to continue predicting the coarse-grained phase-space trajectory [1]. In quantum mechanics there is no sensitivity to initial conditions in predicting the evolution of a state vector, because the unitary evolution of quantum mechanics preserves the inner product between state vectors. The absence of sensitivity to initial conditions seems to suggest that there is no quantum chaos. Yet quantum mechanics has an even more fundamental kind of unpredictability, which has nothing to do with dynamics: even if a system's state vector is known precisely, the results of measurements are generally unpredictable.

To compare the unpredictability of classical and quantum dynamics, we first remove the usual sources of unpredictability from consideration and then introduce a new source of unpredictability that is the same in both classical and quantum dynamics. The first step is to focus in classical physics on the evolution of phase-space distributions, governed by the Liouville equation, instead of on phase-space trajectories, and to focus in quantum physics on the evolution of state vectors, governed by the Schrödinger equation. The Liouville equation preserves the overlap between distributions, so there is no sensitivity to initial conditions in predicting the evolution of a phase-space distribution. By shifting attention from phase-space trajectories to distributions, we remove lack of knowledge of initial conditions as a source of unpredictability. Moreover, by considering only Schrödinger evolution of state vectors, i.e., evolution uninterrupted by measurements, we eliminate the intrinsic randomness of quantum measurements as a source of unpredictability.

The conclusion that there is no chaos in quantum evolution is now seen to be too facile. Were things so simple, one would have to conclude that there is no chaos in classical Liouville evolution either [2]. Having taken both classical and quantum unpredictability out of the picture, we introduce a new source of unpredictability to investigate chaos in the dynamics. We do this by adding to the system Hamiltonian, either classical or quantum mechanical, a stochastic perturbation. We measure the unpredictability introduced by the perturbation in terms of the increase of system entropy. By gathering information about the history of the perturbation, one can make the increase of system entropy smaller. To characterize the resistance of the system to predictability, we compare the information gathered about the perturbation with the entropy reduction that this information purchases. We say that a system is *hypersensitive to perturbation* [3] if the perturbation information is much larger than the associated system-entropy reduction, and we regard hypersensitivity to perturbation as the signature of chaos in Liouville or Schrödinger evolution (see Sec. 2).

For classical systems we have shown that systems with chaotic dynamics display an *exponential* hypersensitivity to perturbation [4,5], in which the ratio of perturbation information to entropy reduction grows exponentially in time, with the exponential rate of growth given by the KS entropy. Thus, for classical systems, we have established that exponential hypersensitivity to perturbation characterizes chaos in Liouville evolution in a way that is exactly equivalent to the standard characterization of chaos in terms of the unpredictability of phase-space trajectories (see Sec. 3).

For a variety of quantum systems we have used numerical simulations to investigate hypersensitivity to perturbation [6–8]. The simulations suggest that hypersensitivity to perturbation provides a characterization of chaos in quantum dynamics: quantum systems whose classical dynamics is chaotic display a quantum hypersensitivity to perturbation, which comes about because the perturbation generates state vectors that are nearly randomly distributed in the system Hilbert space, whereas quantum systems whose classical dynamics is not chaotic do not display hypersensitivity to perturbation (see Sec. 4).

2. HYPERSENSITIVITY TO PERTURBATION

Hypersensitivity to perturbation, in either classical or quantum mechanics, is defined in terms of information and entropy. The entropy H of an isolated physical system (Gibbs entropy for a classical system, von Neumann entropy for a quantum system) does not change under Hamiltonian time evolution. If the time evolution of the system is perturbed through interaction with an incompletely known environment, however, averaging over the perturbation typically leads to an entropy increase ΔH_S. Throughout this paper, we make the simplifying assumption that the interaction with the environment is equivalent to a stochastic perturbation of the Hamiltonian, a restriction we hope to be able to remove in the future. Conditions under which this assumption is valid are discussed in [8]. The increase of the system entropy can be limited to an amount ΔH_{tol}, the *tolerable entropy increase*, by obtaining, from the environment, information about the perturbation. We denote by $\Delta I_{\min}$ the minimum information about the perturbation needed, on the average, to keep the system entropy below the tolerable level ΔH_{tol}. A formal definition of the quantities ΔH_S, ΔH_{tol}, and $\Delta I_{\min}$ can be found in [5] for the classical case and in [8] for the quantum case.

Entropy and information acquire physical content in the presence of a heat reservoir at temperature T. If all energy in the form of heat is ultimately exchanged with the heat reservoir, then each bit of entropy, i.e., each bit of *missing information* about the system state, reduces by the amount $k_B T \ln 2$ the energy that can be extracted from the system in the form of useful work. The connection between *acquired* information and work is provided by Landauer's principle [9,10], according to which not only each bit of missing information, but also each bit of acquired information, has a free-energy cost of $k_B T \ln 2$. This cost, the *Landauer erasure cost*, is paid when the acquired information is erased. Acquired information can be quantified by algorithmic information [11–15].

We now define that a system is hypersensitive to perturbation if the information $\Delta I_{\min}$ required to reduce the system entropy from ΔH_S to ΔH_{tol} is large compared to the entropy reduction $\Delta H_S - \Delta H_{\text{tol}}$, i.e.,

$$\frac{\Delta I_{\min}}{\Delta H_S - \Delta H_{\text{tol}}} \gg 1 \,. \tag{1}$$

The information $\Delta I_{\min}$ purchases a reduction $\Delta H_S - \Delta H_{\text{tol}}$ in system entropy, which is equivalent to an increase in the useful work that can be extracted from the system; hypersensitivity to perturbation means that the Landauer erasure cost of the information is much larger than the increase in available work.

Hypersensitivity to perturbation means that the inequality (1) holds for almost all values of ΔH_{tol}. The inequality (1) tends always to hold, however, for sufficiently small values of ΔH_{tol}. The reason is that for these small values of ΔH_{tol}, one is gathering enough information from the perturbing environment to track a particular system state whose entropy is nearly equal to the initial system entropy. In other words, one is essentially tracking a particular realization of the perturbation among all possible realizations. Thus, for small values of ΔH_{tol}, the information $\Delta I_{\min}$ becomes a property of the perturbation; it is the information needed to specify a particular realization of the perturbation. The important regime for assessing hypersensitivity to perturbation is where ΔH_{tol} is fairly close to ΔH_S, and it is in this regime that one can hope that $\Delta I_{\min}$ reveals something about the system dynamics, rather than properties of the perturbation.

3. CLASSICAL CHAOS

In this section we do not aim for rigor; many statements in this section are without formal proof. Instead, our objective here is to extract the important ideas from the rigorous analysis given in [5] and to use them to develop a heuristic physical picture of why chaotic systems display exponential hypersensitivity to perturbation. For a simple illustration and a system where exact solutions exist, see [4]. This section is an abbreviated version of the discussion section of [5].

Consider a classical Hamiltonian system whose dynamics unfolds on a $2F$-dimensional phase space, and suppose that the system is perturbed by a stochastic Hamiltonian whose effect can be described as diffusion on phase space. Suppose that the system is globally chaotic with KS entropy K. For such a system a phase-space density is stretched and folded by the chaotic dynamics, developing exponentially fine structure as the dynamics proceeds. A simple picture is that the phase-space density stretches exponentially in half the phase-space dimensions and contracts exponentially in the other half of the dimensions.

The perturbation is characterized by a perturbation strength and by correlation cells. We can take the perturbation strength to be the typical distance (e.g., Euclidean distance with respect to some fixed set of canonical coördinates) that a phase-space point diffuses under the perturbation during an e-folding time, $F/K \ln 2$, in a typical contracting dimension. The perturbation becomes effective (in a sense defined precisely in Ref. [5]) when the phase-space density has roughly the same size in the contracting dimensions as the perturbation strength. Once the perturbation becomes effective, the effects of the diffusive perturbation and of the further exponential contraction roughly balance one another, leaving the *average* phase-space density with a constant size in the contracting dimensions.

The correlation cells are phase-space cells over which the effects of the perturbation are well correlated and between which the effects of the perturbation are essentially uncorrelated. We assume that all the correlation cells have approximately the same phase-space volume. We can get a rough idea of the effect of the perturbation by regarding the correlation cells as receiving independent perturbations. Moreover, the diffusive effects of the perturbation during an e-folding time $F/K \ln 2$ are compressed exponentially during the next such e-folding time; this means that once the perturbation becomes effective, the main effects of the perturbation at a particular time are due to the diffusion during the immediately preceding e-folding time.

Since a chaotic system cannot be shielded forever from the effects of the perturbation, we can choose the initial time $t = 0$ to be the time at which the perturbation is just becoming effective. We suppose that at $t = 0$ the unperturbed density is spread over 2^{-Kt_0} correlation cells, t_0 being the time when the unperturbed density occupies a single correlation cell. The essence of the KS entropy is that for large times t the unperturbed density spreads over

$$\mathcal{R}(t) \sim 2^{K(t-t_0)} \tag{2}$$

correlation cells, in each of which it occupies roughly the same phase-space volume. The exponential increase of $\mathcal{R}(t)$ continues until the unperturbed density is spread over essentially all the correlation cells. We can regard the unperturbed density as being made up of *subdensities*, one in each occupied correlation cell and all having roughly the same phase-space volume.

After $t = 0$, when the perturbation becomes effective, the *average* density continues to spread exponentially in the expanding dimensions. As noted above, this spreading is not balanced by contraction in the other dimensions, so the phase-space volume occupied by the average density grows as 2^{Kt}, leading to an entropy increase

$$\Delta H_{\mathcal{S}} \sim \log_2(2^{Kt}) = Kt . \tag{3}$$

Just as the unperturbed density can be broken up into subdensities, so the average density can be broken up into *average subdensities*, one in each occupied correlation cell. Each average subdensity occupies a phase-space volume that is 2^{Kt} times as big as the volume occupied by an unperturbed subdensity.

The unperturbed density is embedded within the phase-space volume occupied by the average density and itself occupies a volume that is smaller by a factor of 2^{-Kt}. We can picture a *perturbed* density crudely by imagining that in each occupied correlation cell the unperturbed subdensity is moved rigidly to some new position within the volume occupied by the *average* subdensity; the result is a *perturbed subdensity*. A *perturbed density* is made up of perturbed subdensities, one in each occupied correlation cell. All of the possible perturbed densities are produced by the perturbation with roughly the same probability.

Suppose now that we wish to hold the entropy increase to a tolerable amount ΔH_{tol}. We must first describe what it means to specify the phase-space density at a level of resolution set by a tolerable entropy increase ΔH_{tol}. An approximate description can be obtained in the following way. Take an occupied correlation cell, and divide the volume occupied by the average subdensity in that cell into $2^{\Delta H_S - \Delta H_{\text{tol}}}$ nonoverlapping volumes, all of the same size. Aggregate all the perturbed subdensities that lie predominantly within a particular one of these nonoverlapping volumes to produce a *coarse-grained subdensity*. There are $2^{\Delta H_S - \Delta H_{\text{tol}}}$ coarse-grained subdensities within each occupied correlation cell, each having a phase-space volume that is bigger than the volume occupied by a perturbed subdensity by a factor of

$$\frac{2^{Kt}}{2^{\Delta H_S - \Delta H_{\text{tol}}}} = 2^{\Delta H_{\text{tol}}} \, . \tag{4}$$

A *coarse-grained density* is made up by choosing a coarse-grained subdensity in each occupied correlation cell. A coarse-grained density occupies a phase-space volume that is bigger than the volume occupied by the unperturbed density by the factor $2^{\Delta H_{\text{tol}}}$ of Eq. (4) and hence represents an entropy increase

$$\log_2 \left(2^{\Delta H_{\text{tol}}} \right) = \Delta H_{\text{tol}} \, . \tag{5}$$

Thus to specify the phase-space density at a level of resolution set by ΔH_{tol} means roughly to specify a coarse-grained density. The further entropy increase on averaging over the perturbation is given by

$$\log_2 \left(2^{\Delta H_S - \Delta H_{\text{tol}}} \right) = \Delta H_S - \Delta H_{\text{tol}} \, . \tag{6}$$

What about the information $\Delta I_{\min}$ required to hold the entropy increase to ΔH_{tol}? Since there are $2^{\Delta H_S - \Delta H_{\text{tol}}}$ coarse-grained subdensities in an occupied correlation cell, each produced with roughly the same probability by the perturbation, it takes approximately $\Delta H_S - \Delta H_{\text{tol}}$ bits to specify a particular coarse-grained subdensity. To describe a coarse-grained density, one must specify a coarse-grained subdensity in each of the $\mathcal{R}(t)$ occupied correlation cells. Thus the information required to specify a coarse-grained density—and, hence, the information required to hold the entropy increase to ΔH_{tol}—is given by

$$\Delta I_{\min} \sim \mathcal{R}(t)(\Delta H_S - \Delta H_{\text{tol}}) \, , \tag{7}$$

corresponding to there being a total of $(2^{\Delta H_S - \Delta H_{\text{tol}}})^{\mathcal{R}(t)}$ coarse-grained densities. The entropy increase (6) comes from counting the number of *nonoverlapping* coarse-grained densities that are required to fill the volume occupied by the average density, that number being $2^{\Delta H_S - \Delta H_{\text{tol}}}$. In contrast, the information $\Delta I_{\min}$ comes from counting the exponentially greater number of ways of forming *overlapping* coarse-grained densities by choosing one of the $2^{\Delta H_S - \Delta H_{\text{tol}}}$ nonoverlapping coarse-grained subdensities in each of the $\mathcal{R}(t)$ correlation cells.

The picture developed in this section, summarized neatly in Eq. (7), requires that ΔH_{tol} be big enough that a coarse-grained subdensity is much larger than a perturbed subdensity, so that we can talk meaningfully about the perturbed subdensities that lie predominantly *within* a coarse-grained subdensity. If ΔH_{tol} becomes too small, Eq. (7)

breaks down, and the information $\Delta I_{\min}$, rather than reflecting a property of the chaotic dynamics as in Eq. (7), becomes essentially a property of the perturbation, reflecting a counting of the number of possible realizations of the perturbation.

The boundary between the two kinds of behavior of $\Delta I_{\min}$ is set roughly by the number F of contracting phase-space dimensions. When $\Delta H_{\mathrm{tol}}/F \gtrsim 1$, the characteristic scale of a coarse-grained subdensity in the contracting dimensions is a factor of

$$\left(2^{\Delta H_{\mathrm{tol}}}\right)^{1/F} = 2^{\Delta H_{\mathrm{tol}}/F} \gtrsim 2 \tag{8}$$

larger than the characteristic size of a perturbed subdensity in the contracting dimensions. In this regime the picture developed in this section is at least approximately valid, because a coarse-grained subdensity can accommodate several perturbed subdensities in each contracting dimension. The information $\Delta I_{\min}$ quantifies the effects of the perturbation on scales as big as or bigger than the finest scale set by the system dynamics. These effects, as quantified in $\Delta I_{\min}$, tell us directly about the size of the exponentially fine structure created by the system dynamics. Thus $\Delta I_{\min}$ becomes a property of the system dynamics, rather than a property of the perturbation.

In contrast, when $\Delta H_{\mathrm{tol}}/F \lesssim 1$, we are required to keep track of the phase-space density on a very fine scale in the contracting dimensions, a scale smaller than the characteristic size of a perturbed subdensity in the contracting dimensions. Subdensities are considered to be distinct, even though they overlap substantially, provided that they differ by more than this very fine scale in the contracting dimensions. The information $\Delta I_{\min}$ is the logarithm of the number of realizations of the perturbation which differ by more than this very fine scale in at least one correlation cell. The information becomes a property of the perturbation because it reports on the effects of the perturbation on scales finer than the finest scale set by the system dynamics—i.e., scales that are, at the time of interest, irrelevant to the system dynamics.

We are now prepared to put in final form the exponential hypersensitivity to perturbation of systems with a positive KS entropy:

$$\frac{\Delta I_{\min}}{\Delta H_{\mathcal{S}} - \Delta H_{\mathrm{tol}}} \sim \mathcal{R}(t) \sim 2^{K(t-t_0)} \quad \text{for } \Delta H_{\mathrm{tol}} \gtrsim F. \tag{9}$$

Once the chaotic dynamics renders the perturbation effective, this exponential hypersensitivity to perturbation is essentially independent of the form and strength of the perturbation. Its essence is that within each correlation cell there is a roughly even trade-off between entropy reduction and information, but for the entire phase-space density the trade-off is exponentially unfavorable because the density occupies an exponentially increasing number of correlation cells, in each of which it is perturbed independently.

What about systems with regular, or integrable dynamics? Though we expect no universal behavior for regular systems, we can get an idea of the possibilities from the heuristic description developed in this section. Hypersensitivity to perturbation requires, first, that the phase-space density develop structure on the scale of the strength of the perturbation, so that the perturbation becomes effective, and, second, that after the perturbation becomes effective, the phase-space density spread over many correlation cells.

For many regular systems there will be no hypersensitivity simply because the phase-space density does not develop fine enough structure. Regular dynamics can give rise to nonlinear shearing, however, in which case the density can develop structure on the scale of the strength of the perturbation and can spread over many correlation cells. In this situation, one expects the picture developed in this section to apply at least approximately: to hold the entropy increase to ΔH_{tol} requires giving $\Delta H_S - \Delta H_{\text{tol}}$ bits per occupied correlation cell; $\Delta I_{\min}$ is related to ΔH_{tol} by Eq. (7), with $\mathcal{R}(t)$ being the number of correlation cells occupied at time t. Thus regular systems can display hypersensitivity to perturbation if $\mathcal{R}(t)$ becomes large (although this behavior could be eliminated by choosing correlation cells that are aligned with the nonlinear shearing produced by the system dynamics), but they cannot display *exponential* hypersensitivity to perturbation because the growth of $\mathcal{R}(t)$ is slower than exponential.

A more direct way of stating this conclusion is to reiterate what we have explained in this section and shown in Ref. [5]: Exponential hypersensitivity to perturbation is equivalent to the spreading of phase-space densities over an exponentially increasing number of phase-space cells; such exponential spreading holds for chaotic, but not for regular systems and is quantified by a positive value of the Kolmogorov-Sinai entropy.

4. QUANTUM CHAOS

4.1. DISTRIBUTION OF VECTORS IN HILBERT SPACE

The simplifying restriction on the interaction with the environment made in Sec. 2 means, for the quantum case, that the interaction with the environment is equivalent to a stochastic unitary time evolution. Given this assumption, we can proceed as follows. At a given time, we describe the result of the perturbed time evolution by a list $\mathcal{L} = (|\psi_1\rangle, \ldots, |\psi_N\rangle)$ of N vectors in D-dimensional Hilbert space, with probabilities $q_1, \ldots, q_N$, each vector in the list corresponding to a particular realization of the perturbation, which we call a *perturbation history*. Averaging over the perturbation leads to a system density operator

$$\hat{\rho}_S = \sum_{j=1}^{N} q_j |\psi_j\rangle\langle\psi_j| \,, \tag{10}$$

with entropy

$$\Delta H_S = -\text{tr}\!\left(\hat{\rho}_S \log_2 \hat{\rho}_S\right). \tag{11}$$

Consider the class of measurements on the environment whose outcomes partition the list $\mathcal{L}$ into R groups labeled by $r = 1, \ldots, R$. We denote by N_r the number of vectors in the rth group ($\sum_{r=1}^{R} N_r = N$). The N_r vectors in the rth group and their probabilities are denoted by $|\psi_1^r\rangle, \ldots, |\psi_{N_r}^r\rangle$ and $q_1^r, \ldots, q_{N_r}^r$, respectively. The measurement outcome r, occurring with probability

$$p_r = \sum_{i=1}^{N_r} q_i^r \,, \tag{12}$$

indicates that the system state is in the rth group. The system state conditional on the measurement outcome r is described by the density operator

$$\hat{\rho}_r = p_r^{-1} \sum_{i=1}^{N_r} q_i^r |\psi_i^r\rangle\langle\psi_i^r| \,. \tag{13}$$

We define the conditional system entropy

$$\Delta H_r = -\text{tr}\!\left(\hat{\rho}_r \log_2 \hat{\rho}_r\right), \tag{14}$$

the average conditional entropy

$$\Delta H = \sum_r p_r \Delta H_r \,, \tag{15}$$

and the average information

$$\Delta I = -\sum_r p_r \log_2 p_r \; . \tag{16}$$

We now describe nearly optimal measurements, i.e., nearly optimal groupings, for which ΔI is a close approximation to $\Delta I_{\min}$, the minimum information about the environment needed, on the average, to keep the system entropy below a given tolerable entropy ΔH_{tol}, as described in Sec. 2. Given ΔH_{tol}, we want to partition the list of vectors $\mathcal{L}$ into groups so as to minimize the information ΔI without violating the condition $\Delta H \le \Delta H_{\text{tol}}$. To minimize ΔI, it is clearly favorable to make the groups as large as possible. Furthermore, to reduce the contribution to ΔH of a group containing a given number of vectors, it is favorable to choose vectors that are as close together as possible in Hilbert space. Here the distance between two vectors $|\psi_1\rangle$ and $|\psi_2\rangle$ can be quantified in terms of the Hilbert-space angle [16]

$$\phi = \cos^{-1}\big(|\langle\psi_1|\psi_2\rangle|\big) \; . \tag{17}$$

Consequently, to find a nearly optimal grouping, we choose an arbitrary *resolution angle* ϕ ($0 \le \phi \le \pi/2$) and group together vectors that are less than an angle ϕ apart. More precisely, groups are formed in the following way. Starting with the first vector, $|\psi_1\rangle$, in the list $\mathcal{L}$, the first group is formed of $|\psi_1\rangle$ and all vectors in $\mathcal{L}$ that are within an angle ϕ of $|\psi_1\rangle$. The same procedure is repeated with the remaining vectors to form the second group, then the third group, continuing until no ungrouped vectors are left. This grouping of vectors corresponds to a partial averaging over the perturbations. To describe a vector at resolution level ϕ amounts to averaging over those details of the perturbation that do not change the final vector by more than an angle ϕ.

For each resolution angle ϕ, the grouping procedure described above defines an average conditional entropy $\Delta H \equiv \Delta H(\phi)$ and an average information $\Delta I \equiv \Delta I(\phi)$. If we choose, for a given ϕ, the tolerable entropy $\Delta H_{\text{tol}} = \Delta H(\phi)$, then to a good approximation, the information $\Delta I_{\min}$ is given by $\Delta I_{\min} \simeq \Delta I(\phi)$. By determining the entropy $\Delta H(\phi)$ and the information $\Delta I(\phi)$ as functions of the resolution angle ϕ, there emerges a rather detailed picture of how the vectors are distributed in Hilbert space. If $\Delta I(\phi)$ is plotted as a function of $\Delta H(\phi)$ by eliminating the angle ϕ, one obtains a good approximation to the functional relationship between $\Delta I_{\min}$ and ΔH_{tol}.

As a further characterization of our list of vectors, we calculate the distribution $g(\phi)$ of Hilbert-space angles $\phi = \cos^{-1}(|\langle\psi|\psi'\rangle|)$ between all pairs of vectors $|\psi\rangle$ and $|\psi'\rangle$. For vectors distributed randomly in D-dimensional Hilbert space, the distribution function $g(\phi)$ is given by [7]

$$g(\phi) = 2(D-1)(\sin\phi)^{2D-3}\cos\phi \; . \tag{18}$$

The maximum of this $g(\phi)$ is located at $\phi = \arccos\big(\sqrt{2(D-1)}\big)$; for large-dimensional Hilbert spaces, $g(\phi)$ is very strongly peaked near the maximum, which is located at $\phi \simeq \pi/2 - 1/\sqrt{2D}$, very near $\pi/2$.

To investigate if a quantum map shows hypersensitivity to perturbation, we use the following numerical method. We first compute a list of vectors corresponding to different perturbation histories. Then, for about 50 values of the angle ϕ ranging from 0 to $\pi/2$, we group the vectors in the nearly optimal way described above. Finally, for each grouping and thus for each chosen angle ϕ, we compute the information $\Delta I(\phi)$ and the entropy $\Delta H(\phi)$. In addition, we compute the angles between all pairs of vectors in the list and plot them as a histogram approximating the distribution function $g(\phi)$.

4.2. A TYPICAL NUMERICAL RESULT

In this section, we present a typical numerical result for the quantum kicked top taken from [8], where more details can be found. We look at the time evolution of an initial Hilbert-space vector $|\psi_0\rangle$ at discrete times nT. After n time steps, the unperturbed vector is given by

$$|\psi_n\rangle = \hat{T}^n |\psi_0\rangle \,, \tag{19}$$

where $\hat{T}$ is the unitary Floquet operator [17,18]

$$\hat{T} = e^{-i(k/2J)\hat{J}_x^2} e^{-i\pi\hat{J}_z/2} \,, \tag{20}$$

and where $\hbar\hat{\mathbf{J}} = \hbar(\hat{J}_x, \hat{J}_y, \hat{J}_z)$ is the angular momentum vector for a spin-J particle evolving in $(2J + 1)$-dimensional Hilbert space.

Depending on the initial condition, the classical map corresponding to the Floquet operator (20) displays regular as well as chaotic behavior [18]. Following [19], we choose initial Hilbert-space vectors for the quantum evolution that correspond to classical initial conditions located in regular and chaotic regions of the classical dynamics, respectively. For this purpose, we use *coherent states* [20–22]. In this section, we consider two initial states. The first one is a coherent state centered in a regular region of the classical dynamics; we refer to it as the *regular initial state*. The second one, referred to as the *chaotic initial state*, is a coherent state centered in a chaotic region of the classical dynamics.

The perturbation is modeled as an additional rotation by a small random angle about the z axis. The system state after n perturbed steps is thus given by

$$|\psi_n\rangle = \hat{T}(l_n) \cdots \hat{T}(l_1) |\psi_0\rangle \,, \tag{21}$$

where $\hat{T}(l_m) = e^{-igl_m\hat{J}_z}\hat{T}$, with $l_m = \pm 1$, is the unperturbed Floquet operator (20) followed by an additional rotation about the z axis by an angle $l_m g = \pm g$, the parameter g being the *perturbation strength*. There are 2^n different perturbation histories obtained by applying every possible sequence of perturbed unitary evolution operators $\hat{T}(-1)$ and $\hat{T}(+1)$ for n steps. We have applied the method described in Sec. 4.1 to find numerically a nearly optimal grouping of the list $\mathcal{L}$ of 2^n vectors generated by all perturbation histories.

Figure 1 shows results for spin $J = 511.5$ and a total number of $2^{12} = 4\,096$ vectors after $n = 12$ perturbed steps [8]. We used a *twist parameter* $k = 3$ and perturbation strength $g = 0.003$. For Fig. 1(a), the chaotic initial state was used. The distribution of Hilbert-space angles, $g(\phi)$, is concentrated at large angles; i.e., most pairs of vectors are far apart from each other. The information ΔI needed to track a perturbed vector at resolution level ϕ is 12 bits at small angles, where each group contains only one vector. At $\phi \simeq \pi/16$ the information suddenly drops to 11 bits, which is the information needed to specify one pair of vectors out of 2^{11} pairs, the two vectors in each pair being generated by perturbation sequences that differ only at the first step. The sudden drop of the information to 10 bits at $\phi \simeq \pi/8$ similarly indicates the existence of 2^{10} quartets of vectors, generated by perturbation sequences differing only in the first two steps. Figure 1(a) suggests that, apart from the organization into pairs and quartets, there is not much structure in the distribution of vectors for a chaotic initial state. The 2^{10} quartets seem to be rather uniformly distributed in a $n_d = 46$-dimensional Hilbert space (see [8] for a definition of the number of explored Hilbert-space dimensions, n_d).

The inset in Fig. 1(a) shows the approximate functional dependence of the information needed about the perturbation, $\Delta I_{\min}$, on the tolerable entropy ΔH_{tol}, based on

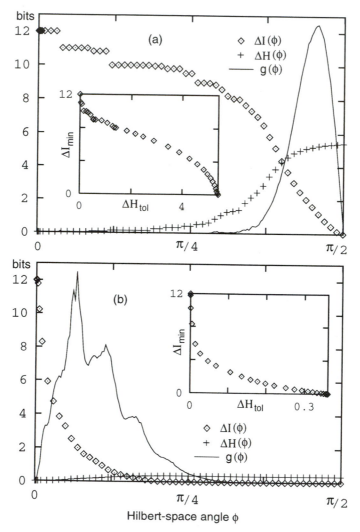

Figure 1. Results characterizing the distribution of Hilbert-space vectors for the perturbed kicked top. (a) Chaotic case, (b) regular case. For details see the text.

the data points $\Delta I(\phi)$ and $\Delta H(\phi)$. There is an initial sharp drop of the information, reflecting the grouping of the vectors into pairs and quartets. Then there is a roughly linear decrease of the information over a wide range of ΔH_{tol} values, followed by a final drop with increasing slope down to zero at the maximum value of the tolerable entropy, $\Delta H_{tol} = \Delta H_S$. The large slope of the curve near $\Delta H_{tol} = \Delta H_S$ can be regarded as a signature of hypersensitivity to perturbation. The linear regime at intermediate values of ΔH_{tol} is due to the finite size of the sample of vectors: in this regime the entropy ΔH_r of the rth group is limited by $\log_2 N_r$, the logarithm of the number of vectors in the group.

Figure 1(b) shows data for 2^{12} vectors after 12 perturbed steps in the regular case. The distribution of perturbed vectors starting from the regular initial state is completely different from the chaotic initial condition of Fig. 1(a). The angle distribution $g(\phi)$ is conspicuously nonrandom: it is concentrated at angles smaller than roughly $\pi/4$, and there is a regular structure of peaks and valleys. Accordingly, the information drops rapidly with the angle ϕ. The number of explored dimensions is $n_d = 2$, which agrees with results of Peres [19] that show that the quantum evolution in a regular region of the kicked top is essentially confined to a 2-dimensional subspace. The ΔI_{min} vs. ΔH_{tol} curve in the inset bears little resemblance to the chaotic case. Summarizing, one can say that, in the regular case, the vectors do not get far apart in Hilbert space, explore only few dimensions, and do not explore them randomly.

To obtain better numerical evidence for hypersensitivity in the chaotic case and for the absence of it in the regular case would require much larger samples of vectors, a possibility that is ruled out by restrictions on computer memory and time. The hypothesis most strongly supported by our data is the random character of the distribution of vectors in the chaotic case. In the following section we show that randomness in the distribution of perturbed vectors implies hypersensitivity to perturbation.

4.3. DISCUSSION

Guided by our numerical results we now present an analysis of hypersensitivity to perturbation for quantum systems based on the conjecture that, for chaotic systems, Hilbert space is explored randomly by the perturbed vectors. We consider a Hamiltonian quantum system whose classical phase-space dynamics is chaotic and assume the system is perturbed by a stochastic Hamiltonian that classically gives rise to diffusion on phase space. We suppose that at time $t = 0$ the system's state vector has a Wigner distribution that is localized on phase space. We further assume that at $t = 0$ the perturbation is just becoming effective in the classical sense described in Sec. 3.

Our numerical analyses [6–8] suggest the following picture. For times $t > 0$, the entropy ΔH_S of the average density operator $\hat{\rho}_S$ (10) increases linearly with time. This is in accordance with an essentially classical argument given by Zurek and Paz [23]. Denoting the proportionality constant by κ, we have

$$\Delta H_S \simeq \kappa t . \qquad (22)$$

Since the von Neumann entropy of a density operator is bounded by the logarithm of the dimension of Hilbert space, it follows that the realizations of the perturbation—i.e., the state vectors that result from the different perturbation histories—explore at least a number

$$\mathcal{D}(t) \equiv 2^{\Delta H_S} \simeq 2^{\kappa t} \qquad (23)$$

of Hilbert-space dimensions, which increases exponentially. Our main conjecture now is that these dimensions are explored quasi-randomly, i.e., that the realizations of the perturbation at time t are distributed essentially like random vectors in a $\mathcal{D}(t)$-dimensional Hilbert space.

Starting from this main conjecture, we will now derive an estimate of the information $\Delta I_{\min}$ needed to keep the system-entropy increase below the tolerable amount ΔH_{tol}. Following the discussion on grouping vectors in Sec. 4.1, a tolerable entropy increase ΔH_{tol} corresponds to gathering the realizations of the perturbation into Hilbert-space spheres of radius ϕ. The state vectors in each such sphere fill it randomly (since the perturbation is diffusive, there are plenty of vectors), so the entropy of their density operator—which is the tolerable entropy—is

$$\Delta H_{\text{tol}} = -\left(1 - \frac{\mathcal{D} - 1}{\mathcal{D}} \sin^2 \phi\right) \log_2\left(1 - \frac{\mathcal{D} - 1}{\mathcal{D}} \sin^2 \phi\right) - \frac{\mathcal{D} - 1}{\mathcal{D}} \sin^2 \phi \, \log_2\left(\frac{\sin^2 \phi}{\mathcal{D}}\right) \tag{24}$$

(Eq. (B6) of [7]). The number of spheres of radius ϕ in $\mathcal{D}$-dimensional Hilbert space is $(\sin \phi)^{-2(\mathcal{D}-1)}$ (Eq. (5.1) of [7]), so the information needed to specify a particular sphere is

$$\Delta I_{\min} \simeq \Delta \tilde{I}_{\min} \equiv \log_2\left((\sin \phi)^{-2(\mathcal{D}-1)}\right) = -(\mathcal{D} - 1) \log_2(\sin^2 \phi) . \tag{25}$$

The information $\Delta \tilde{I}_{\min}$ consistently underestimates the actual value of $\Delta I_{\min}$, which comes from an optimal grouping of the random vectors; the reason is that the perfect grouping into nonoverlapping spheres of uniform size assumed by Eq. (25) does not exist.

Using Eq. (25) to eliminate ϕ from Eq. (24) gives an expression for ΔH_{tol} as a function of $\Delta \tilde{I}_{\min}$,

$$\Delta H_{\text{tol}} = -\left(1 - \frac{\mathcal{D} - 1}{\mathcal{D}} 2^{-\Delta \tilde{I}_{\min}/(\mathcal{D}-1)}\right) \log_2\left(1 - \frac{\mathcal{D} - 1}{\mathcal{D}} 2^{-\Delta \tilde{I}_{\min}/(\mathcal{D}-1)}\right)$$
$$- \frac{\mathcal{D} - 1}{\mathcal{D}} 2^{-\Delta \tilde{I}_{\min}/(\mathcal{D}-1)} \log_2\left(\frac{2^{-\Delta \tilde{I}_{\min}/(\mathcal{D}-1)}}{\mathcal{D}}\right) , \tag{26}$$

from which $\mathcal{D}$ could be eliminated in favor of ΔH_S by invoking Eq. (23). The behavior of $\Delta \tilde{I}_{\min}$ as a function of ΔH_{tol} expressed in Eq. (26) is the universal behavior that we conjecture for chaotic systems, except for when ΔH_{tol} is so close to ΔH_S that $\Delta \tilde{I}_{\min} \lesssim 1$, as the spheres approximation used above breaks down for angles ϕ for which Hilbert space can accommodate only one sphere. Since ΔH_{tol} increases and $\Delta \tilde{I}_{\min}$ decreases with ϕ, $\Delta \tilde{I}_{\min}$ increases as ΔH_{tol} decreases from its maximum value of ΔH_S.

To gain more insight into Eq. (26), we calculate the derivative

$$\frac{d\Delta \tilde{I}_{\min}}{d\Delta H_{\text{tol}}} = -\frac{\mathcal{D}}{\sin^2 \phi \ln(1 + \mathcal{D} \cot^2 \phi)} , \tag{27}$$

which is the marginal tradeoff between between information and entropy. For ϕ near $\pi/2$, so that $\epsilon = \pi/2 - \phi \ll 1$, the information becomes $\Delta \tilde{I}_{\min} = (\mathcal{D} - 1)\epsilon^2 / \ln 2$, and the derivative (27) can be written as

$$\frac{d\Delta \tilde{I}_{\min}}{d\Delta H_{\text{tol}}} \simeq -\frac{\mathcal{D}}{\ln(1 + \mathcal{D}\epsilon^2)} = -\frac{\mathcal{D}}{\ln\left(1 + \frac{\mathcal{D}}{\mathcal{D} - 1} \Delta \tilde{I}_{\min} \ln 2\right)} . \tag{28}$$

For $\Delta I_{\min} \gtrsim 1$, i.e., when Eq. (26) is valid, the size of the derivative (28) is determined by $\mathcal{D}(t) = 2^{\Delta H_S} \simeq 2^{\kappa t}$, with a slowly varying logarithmic correction. This behavior, characterized by the typical slope $\mathcal{D}(t)$, gives an exponential hypersensitivity to perturbation, with the classical number of correlation cells, $\mathcal{R}(t)$, roughly replaced by the number of explored Hilbert-space dimensions, $\mathcal{D}(t)$.

It is a remarkable fact that the concept of perturbation cell or perturbation correlation length (see Sec. 3) did not enter this quantum-mechanical discussion. Indeed, our numerical results suggest that our main conjecture holds for a single correlation cell, i.e., for a perturbation that is correlated over all of the relevant portion of phase space. That we find this behavior indicates that we are dealing with an intrinsically quantum-mechanical phenomenon. What seems to be happening is the following. For tolerable entropies $\Delta H_{\text{tol}} \gtrsim F$, where $2F$ is the dimension of classical phase space as in Sec. 3, we can regard a single-cell perturbation as perturbing a classical system into a set of nonoverlapping densities. In a quantum analysis these nonoverlapping densities can be crudely identified with orthogonal state vectors. The single-cell quantum perturbation, in conjunction with the chaotic quantum dynamics, seems to be able to produce arbitrary linear superpositions of these orthogonal vectors, a freedom not available to the classical system. The result is a much bigger set of possible realizations of the perturbation.

5. CONCLUSION

This paper compares and contrasts hypersensitivity to perturbation in classical and quantum dynamics. Although hypersensitivity provides a characterization of chaos that is common to both classical and quantum dynamics, the mechanisms for hypersensitivity are different classically and quantum mechanically. The classical mechanism has to do with the information needed to specify the phase-space distributions produced by the perturbation—this is classical information—whereas the quantum mechanism has to do with the information needed to specify the random state vectors produced by the perturbation—this is quantum information because it relies on the superposition principle of quantum mechanics. Captured in a slogan, the difference is this: *a stochastic perturbation applied to a classical chaotic system generates classical information, whereas a stochastic perturbation applied to a quantum system generates quantum information.*

REFERENCES

[1] V. M. Alekseev and M. V. Yakobson, Phys. Reports **75**, 287 (1981).

[2] M. V. Berry, in *New Trends in Nuclear Collective Dynamics*, edited by Y. Abe, H. Horiuchi, and K. Matsuyanagi (Springer, Berlin, 1992), p. 183.

[3] C. M. Caves, in *Physical Origins of Time Asymmetry*, edited by J. J. Halliwell, J. Pérez-Mercader, and W. H. Zurek (Cambridge University Press, Cambridge, UK, 1993), p. 47.

[4] R. Schack and C. M. Caves, Phys. Rev. Lett. **69**, 3413 (1992).

[5] R. Schack and C. M. Caves, Phys. Rev. E **53**, 3387 (1996).

[6] R. Schack and C. M. Caves, Phys. Rev. Lett. **71**, 525 (1993).

[7] R. Schack, G. M. D'Ariano, and C. M. Caves, Phys. Rev. E **50**, 972 (1994).

[8] R. Schack and C. M. Caves, Phys. Rev. E **53**, 3257 (1996).

[9] R. Landauer, IBM J. Res. Develop. **5**, 183 (1961).

[10] R. Landauer, Nature **355**, 779 (1988).

[11] G. J. Chaitin, *Algorithmic Information Theory* (Cambridge University Press, Cambridge, UK, 1987).

[12] W. H. Zurek, Nature **341**, 119 (1989).

[13] W. H. Zurek, Phys. Rev. A **40**, 4731 (1989).

[14] C. M. Caves, in *Complexity, Entropy, and the Physics of Information*, edited by W. H. Zurek (Addison Wesley, Redwood City, California, 1990), p. 91.

[15] R. Schack, to appear in Int. J. Theor. Phys. [e-print hep-th/9409022].

[16] W. K. Wootters, Phys. Rev. D **23**, 357 (1981).

[17] H. Frahm and H. J. Mikeska, Z. Phys. B **60**, 117 (1985).

[18] F. Haake, M. Kuś, and R. Scharf, Z. Phys. B **65**, 381 (1987).

[19] A. Peres, in *Quantum Chaos*, edited by H. A. Cerdeira, R. Ramaswamy, M. C. Gutzwiller, and G. Casati (World Scientific, Singapore, 1991), p. 73.

[20] J. M. Radcliffe, J. Phys. A **4**, 313 (1971).

[21] P. W. Atkins and J. C. Dobson, Proc. R. Soc. Lond. A **321**, 321 (1971).

[22] A. M. Perelomov, *Generalized Coherent States* (Springer, Berlin, 1986).

[23] W. H. Zurek and J. P. Paz, Phys. Rev. Lett. **72**, 2508 (1994).

A TOPOLOGICAL APPROACH TO PHASE OF QUANTUM CHAOS

Mikito Toda

Physics Department, Kyoto University
toda@ton.scphys.kyoto-u.ac.jp

We explain the underlying ideas in our study of the relationship between quantum chaos and statistical mechanics.

This study consists of the following two steps. The first is to focus attention to topological defects of phase in the Husimi representation for quantum dynamics corresponding to chaos. This reveals characteristic features of quantum chaos corresponding to the folding of horseshoe dynamics in classical chaos. The second is to investigate the phase retrieval problem of quantum chaos. This shows a close connection between the difficulty of phase retrieval and the characteristics of topological defects of quantum chaos.

Based on these results, we suggest that the difficulty of phase retrieval is crucial for the loss of phase information in quantum statistical mechanics, when we take into account not only measurement but also information processes on statistical ensembles.

1. INTRODUCTION

The motivation of this study comes from the following ideas. In classical mechanics, the origin of irreversibility is understood to result from intrinsic properties of dynamics, i.e., irregular behavior of chaos. On the other hand, in quantum mechanics, the origin has been attributed to extrinsic aspects such as interaction with environment and insufficient knowledge. The most serious drawback of these ideas is that they fail to give objective meaning to irreversibility.

To the contrary, we will suggest that close connection exists between loss of phase information and intrinsic features of quantum states. Showing this connection involves the following two steps.

The first is to study the dynamical properties of quantum systems corresponding to chaos. In particular, we focus our attention on topological defects of phase in the Husimi representation. Then, we can see a clear correspondence of classical chaos in the dynamical features leading to random distribution of topological defects. These features constitute the basis of our study when we discuss the foundation of statistical mechanics.

The second is the phase retrieval problem. Measurement processes leave us with the absolute values $|\Psi|^2$ of a wavefunction Ψ. Conventional ideas on statistical mechanics attribute the loss of phase information to this. However, we can somehow recover a part of phase information *after a measurement is done*. Phase retrieval is *information processing* to achieve this purpose. Then, our question is whether quantum chaos resists phase retrieval, and if so, how and to what extent. Concerning this question, we show that the random distribution of topological defects causes difficulty in phase retrieval.

With these results, we will discuss the implications of the difficulty of phase retrieval for the foundation of statistical mechanics. Our standpoint is the following: Information processes for phase retrieval reveal that the loss of phase information is closely related to the intrinsic features of quantum chaos.

Here, we will concentrate on explaining the basic ideas and conjectures for future study, since some of the material is already published elsewhere [1] [2] [3].

2. DYNAMICAL FEATURES OF CHAOS

The basic mechanism of classical chaos is Smale's horseshoe, i.e., repetition of stretching and folding. Through this mechanism, phase space distributions of a classical system exhibit complicated structure.

In order to see the corresponding behavior in quantum mechanics, we use a phase space distribution of wavefunctions. As will be shown later, the Husimi representation is appropriate to study the relation between characteristics of quantum chaos and the phase retrieval problem.

The Husimi representation is defined as an inner product $\langle X, P | \Psi \rangle$ between a wave function $|\Psi\rangle$ and the minimum uncertainty wave packets $|X, P\rangle$,

$$\langle X, P | \Psi \rangle = (\pi \hbar \sigma^2)^{-1/4} \int \exp \left\{ -\frac{(x - X)^2}{2\hbar \sigma^2} - \frac{iPx}{\hbar} \right\} \Psi(x) \, dx, \qquad (1)$$

where σ is an arbitrary constant called the squeezing parameter [4] [5]. Its absolute square is a probability distribution concerning approximate and simultaneous measurement of both position and momentum using minimum uncertainty wavepackets. In other words, it describes a measurement which corresponds to coarse graining in classical statistical mechanics.

Moreover, the Husimi representation makes possible a new approach to characterize phase of wave functions, that is, to study topological defects of phase [6] [7]. This comes from the following property of the Husimi representation. It is an entire function of the variable $z = x + ip$, where x is position and p is momentum. Therefore, its zeros are topological defects of phase, i.e., traversing around a zero gives a phase change of 2π. This property offers an efficient method to study topological characteristics of phase [10].

The first step in our work is to investigate the dynamical behavior of topological defects [2]. In the process corresponding to folding, a wavefunction in the Husimi representation is also folded. Phase difference between these folded parts brings about topological defects of phase. In the initial stage of time evolution where the wavefunction corresponds to the Lagrangian manifold, its defects distribute smoothly on curves. However, in the later stage, the distribution of defects changes from the smoothly lined one to more randomly scattered one. This change is caused by multiple interference of the folded parts. Thus, the process of generating topological defects of phase corresponds to the folding of Smale horseshoe dynamics. In particular, the change of the distribution to random one plays a crucial role in the following.

3. PHASE RETRIEVAL PROBLEM

Let us briefly explain the phase retrieval problem [11]. Suppose we are measuring a certain observable of a wave function Ψ. After repeating this measurement for an ensemble of the same wavefunction, we obtain the probability distribution $|\Psi|^2$. The problem is how to guess the observed wave function Ψ based on the probability distribution $|\Psi|^2$, that is, how to retrieve phase information. In order to do this, we need some additional assumptions concerning the wave functions we observe; otherwise any phase variation can give the same probability distribution. These assumptions should be sufficiently general such that we do not need detailed information about the observed wave function. Whether we can find such a general assumption is one of the factors which determine the degree of difficulty in retrieving phase.

To be definite, we consider the following case. Suppose, after measurement of position x, we have $|\Psi(x_j)|$, where x_j are equi-distanced from $j = 0$ to $j = n$. The additional assumption in this case is the following. *The support of wave functions $\tilde{\Psi}(p)$ is finite*, i.e.,

$$\tilde{\Psi}(p) = 0 \qquad \text{for} \quad p \notin [a, b], \tag{2}$$

where $\tilde{\Psi}(p)$ is the Fourier transformation of $\Psi(x)$. Functions of this property are called band-limited. In actual experimental situations, this property would be fulfilled because the measurement range of apparatus is finite.

We call the following two types of loss of phase information "trivial" loss: (i) $\Psi(x)$ or $\Psi(x)e^{i(p_0 x + \theta_0)}$ where p_0 and θ_0 are constants, (ii) $\Psi(x)$ or its complex conjugate $\Psi(x)^*$. Our question is whether we can recover phase information other than the trivial ones.

In order to investigate the above question, the following two theorems play a crucial role [8] [9]. The Paley-Wiener theorem says that band-limited functions $\Psi(x)$ can be analytically continued to the complex x plane, and is an entire function of order not exceeding 1. Then the Hadamard factorization theorem says that an entire function of order 1 is represented by an infinite product as

$$\Psi(x) = x^m e^{C_0 + C_1 x} \prod_{n=1}^{\infty} \left(1 - \frac{x}{x_n}\right) e^{x/x_n}, \tag{3}$$

where $\{x_n\}_{n=1}^{\infty}$ are its zeros other than the origin, m is the number of degenerate zeros at the origin, and C_0 and C_1 are complex coefficients. In phase retrieval problem, what we concern is the part of this expansion which involves zeros.

In the phase retrieval problem, what we have at hand is

$$|\Psi(x)|^2 \propto \prod_{n=1}^{\infty} \left(1 - \frac{x}{x_n}\right) \left(1 - \frac{x}{x_n^*}\right). \tag{4}$$

Thus we have to determine, for each n, whether x_n or x_n^* belongs to the zeros of the original wave function. However we do not have, in general, such information which enables us to make this decision.

Our next question in phase retrieval is whether we can reduce the number of these possibilities. In this reduction, we make use of the results in the previous section, i.e., characteristic features of topological defects.

First of all, note the relation between complex zeros in phase retrieval and zeros of the Husimi representation. Complex zeros of $\Psi(x)$ can be obtained from zeros of the Husimi representation as we take the limiting process where the minimum uncertainty wavepackets are squeezed into the eigenstates of position. This limiting process would not change seriously the qualitative features of the distribution of zeros since it is a linear transformation involving the squeezing parameter.

The second point to notice is that zeros of the Husimi representation distribute smoothly on curves when the original wavefunction corresponds to a Lagrangian manifold. Then, for such wavefunctions, we expect that this property also holds for complex zeros of Ψ. This limits the range of possible wavefunctions in phase retrieval for these wavefunctions, and thus can be utilized for reducing the possibilities.

For wavefunctions of integrable systems, it can be shown that the reduction process actually works. To the contrary, for wavefunctions with random distribution of defects, we do not have additional information for the reduction. This difference in difficulty of phase retrieval implies that quantum chaos would be the cause of the loss of phase information.

4. ZERO TRACKING

We will investigate further the loss of phase information and its relation to quantum chaos. The next case for phase retrieval is the following. Suppose we know the initial wavefunction $\Psi(t = 0, x_j)$. As the system evolves, we will do the measurement and obtain the results $|\Psi(t_i, x_j)|$ for each time step $t = t_i$. We assume that $\Psi(t_i, x)$ is also band-limited. Then, the question is whether and how phase retrieval is achieved for the wavefunction, which evolves under certain time development.

Experimental situations corresponding to this case would be, for example, the following. Suppose a molecule is electronically excited. Then, the nuclear wavefunction of the molecule starts evolving on the electronically excited potential surface, and we observe this wavefunction afterward. We know the initial wavefunction of this time evolution, since the ground state of the molecule is a Gaussian wavepacket. Therefore, phase retrieval problem in this experiment would correspond to the above case.

The idea for phase retrieval is zero tracking, that is, keeping track of the orbits of zeros from their initial positions. Given the initial state, the initial position of the complex zeros are known. At the following times, pairs of zeros and their complex conjugates are known from the data $|\Psi|^2$. From each pair of a zero and its conjugate, we choose the nearest to the zeros of the wavefunction at the previous time. Thus, the wavefunction at the next time step is recovered from the one at the previous time. This process is repeated until the final time is reached.

Note that zeros neither appear nor disappear locally since they are topological defects of phase with phase difference 2π. Therefore, orbits of zeros are continuous, and we can keep track of them as far as time step is short enough.

The question in this case is the following, *What causes difficulty of zero tracking ?*

The first difficulty arises when a zero crosses the real axis. Then we cannot, in general, decide on whether the orbit is tracked to the upper half plane or the lower one. A probable guess, if not justified, would be to extrapolate the orbit of the zero. As will be discussed later, the orbit of a zero is expected to exhibit smooth behavior as far as another zero does not come near to the one. Thus, the extrapolation would be a reasonable choice.

The second difficulty arises when the orbit of zeros are not smooth. This happens when zeros come near to each other and exhibit avoided crossing. The fact that zeros exhibit avoided crossing can be understood similarly to the avoided crossing of energy levels. The discussion is based on the number of parameters for two zeros to coincide. In order to have two zeros coincide, we need two parameters, one for the real part and the other for the imaginary. Since time is one parameter, zeros do not coincide under time evolution unless certain symmetry exists.

When avoided crossing occurs near the real axis, extrapolation of the orbit would be erroneous. Thus, we can suggest that avoid crossing of zeros near the real axis would be the difficulty of zero tracking.

Our next question concerns with the relation between quantum chaos and the difficulty of zeros tracking. *Does quantum chaos resist the processes of zero tracking ?* At present, we do not have definite answer to this question.

Preliminary results for time development of zeros of the Husimi representation would be suggestive concerning this question [3]. Time evolution of integrable systems exhibit collective and coherent movement of zeros. Although avoided crossing of zeros takes place, we can extrapolate the movement of zeros beyond the avoided crossing. This is similar to the avoided crossing of energy levels for nearly integrable systems. For quantum chaos, zeros exhibit collective but less coherent movement. We can also see entanglement of orbits of zeros which come closer to each other. This would be a precursor of avoided crossing characteristic to quantum chaos.

Based on the above results, we expect that zero tracking works for integrable systems. Coherent movement of zeros enables us to extrapolate orbits of zeros. Moreover, it would give the method tolerance toward external noise and numerical errors. For quantum chaos, this method would also work for a part of the wavefunction since some zeros exhibit smooth behavior. It would be interesting to study to what extent zeros tracking works for quantum chaos. Such study would give some insight as to the dynamical mechanism of the loss of phase information.

5. PHASE RETRIEVAL FOR MULTIPLE VARIABLES

For entire functions of more than one variable, the Hadamard factorization theorem does not hold. This provides a completely new situation for phase retrieval problem [12].

Suppose we have the data $|\Psi(x_1, x_2)|^2$. Then, this can be factorized into two irreducible functions $\Psi(x_1, x_2)$ and $\Psi^*(x_1, x_2)$ where Ψ^* indicates the complex conjugate of Ψ. Thus, there is no loss of phase information other than the trivial one. However, practice of phase retrieval would be difficult because factorization is sensitive to noise and error. For example, adding a extra noise to get $|\Psi(x_1, x_2)|^2 + \epsilon$ makes the data irreducible, i.e., even the factorization into Ψ and Ψ^* becomes impossible. Therefore, our question in this case concerns difficulty of the practice of phase retrieval.

The basic idea of the methods for phase retrieval is zero tracking [13]. At a fixed value of x_1, $|\Psi|^2$ is considered as an entire function of one variable x_2. Therefore, it is factorized into linear factors. These linear factors are somehow connected in the complex plane of x_1 to form Ψ and Ψ^*. Connecting these factors needs zero tracking; starting from an arbitrary value of x_1, find orbits of the zeros of $|\Psi(x_1, x_2)|^2$ as the function of x_1 along an appropriate path on the x_1 plane. Then the question arises as follows. *Where does zero tracking become difficult?*

It is known that zero tracking is sensitive to errors when zeros become degenerate. These degenerate zeros constitute a singularity of the zero surface $|\Psi(x_1, x_2)|^2 = 0$, i.e., the intersection points of this surface with itself. In particular, the intersection of the surface $\Psi = 0$ with the one $\Psi^* = 0$ is dangerous, because zero tracking would erroneously go on from Ψ to Ψ^* leading to a wrong solution. Note that this difficulty corresponds to that of the zero tracking for time evolution of one variable case.

Our next question is *whether quantum chaos in more than one variable exhibits singularity of the zero surface*. Work on this direction is in progress and will be published elsewhere. It would be interesting to study the relation between the singularity and folding mechanism in more than one degree of freedom. This study would shed light on the problem of how a system coupled with additional degrees of freedom loses phase information.

Recently, Shub and Smale are studying computational complexity of zero tracking [14]. Their idea is to estimate the probability that tracking paths of zeros encounter singularities of the zero surface for general random polynomials. They also calculate the conditional number, i.e., the distance from singularities, where zero tracking becomes ill-conditioned. These ideas can be also applied to phase retrieval problem. A slight difference in approach would be that we are interested in an individual wavefunction rather than the average case. Then it would be interesting to compare wavefunctions of quantum chaos to the average case, where general polynomials are concerned. The crucial point of their method is to formulate the problem so that it is unitarily invariant. This invariance makes their method even more suitable for application to quantum mechanics.

6. DISCUSSION

Here we will discuss the loss of phase information in the light of phase retrieval problem. Our results strongly suggest the following: Intrinsic properties of the dynamics is crucial for the loss of phase information, when we take into account information processes of phase retrieval.

Considering the information processes might appear unfamiliar to some readers. However, the relations between statistical mechanics and information processes have been an active research area since Maxwell discussed his famous demon. His argument was further developed by Szilard leading to the relation between information and entropy. Our study can be considered as a further development of these studies into quantum mechanics.

In quantum mechanics, measurement processes have been thought of as the major source of irreversibility. However, from the standpoint of statistical ensemble, information processes can be applied to reduce entropy of the system. In other words, we can reduce ambiguity of the knowledge about the system through phase retrieval. How much this reduction is feasible is not arbitrary; It is limited by the intrinsic properties of the system. This would be expressed as the following relation.

$$S_I = S_M - S_P, \tag{5}$$

where S_M is the entropy increase caused by measurement, S_P is the entropy which cannot be reduced by phase retrieval and S_I is the amount of information we can obtain by phase retrieval. Then, S_P would be expressed as $S_P = \log \Omega_P$ by the phase space volume Ω_P where zero tracking becomes ill-conditioned.

Another way to connect phase retrieval problem with the foundations of statistical mechanics would be the following thought experiment. Suppose we are trying to reverse the dynamics of a system. Available information for the dynamics is data $|\Psi(t_i)|^2$ for consecutive times t_i. The initial state for the reversal is the complex conjugate of the wavefunction at the final time. Then, difficulty of phase retrieval is an obstruction to prepare the initial state for the reversal. Thus, irreversibility of the dynamics is closely connected with difficulty of phase retrieval.

The above discussions implies the relationship between phase retrieval problem and the foundation of statistical mechanics. To make them more convincing will be done in future publications.

REFERENCES

[1] A part of the material was also presented in Conference on Quantum Chaos and Dissipation held at Guntzburg Germany on 9-12 September 1996.

[2] M.Toda, Physica D59(1992) 121.

[3] M.Toda, in Proceeding of the International Conference on Dynamical Systems and Chaos, Vol.2, p532, ed.,Y.Aizawa et al.,(World Scientific,1995).

[4] K.Husimi,
Proc.Phys.Math.Soc.22(1940) 264.

[5] K.Takahashi,
J.Phys.Soc.Jpn.55(1986) 762.

[6] A.M.Perelomov,
Theor.Math.Phys. 6(1971) 156.

[7] V.Bergmann,P.Butera,L.Girardello, and J.R.Klauder,
Rep.Math.Phys. 2(1971) 221.

[8] L.V.Ahlfors, Complex Analysis, 3rd ed. (McGraw-Hill, Singapore, 1979).

[9] E.C.Titchmarsh, The Theory of Functions, 2nd ed. (Oxford Univ. Press, Oxford, 1986).

[10] P.Leboeuf and A.Voros,
J.Phys.A23(1990) 1765.

[11] For review on phase retrieval problem in general, see, e.g.,
(a)R.H.T.Bates and D.Mnyama, in: Advances in Electronics and Electron Physics, Vol.67,
ed. P,W.Hawkes, (Academic Press, New York, 1986) p.1;
(b)Image Recovery:Theory and Application, ed. H.Stark, (Academic Press, New York, 1987);
(c) N.H.Hurt, Phase Retrieval and Zero Crossings, (Kluwer Academic, Dordrecht, 1989).

[12] (a)Yu.M.Bruck and L.G.Dodin, Opt.Comm.30(1979) 304.
(b)I.Manolitsakis, J.Math.Phys.23(1982) 2291.

[13] (a)D.Izraelevitz and J.S.Lim, IEEE trans. ASSP35(1987) 511.
(b)R.G.Lane, W.R.Fright and R.H.T.Bates, IEEE trans. ASSP35(1987) 515.
(c)P.J.Bones et al. J.Opt.Soc.Am.12A(1995)1842.

[14] (a)M.Shub and S.Smale, J.Am.Math.Soc.6(1993) 459.
(b)M.Shub and S.Smale, in Computational Algebraic Geometry, F.Eysette and A.Galliger,eds.,Progress in Mathematics,Vol.109,(Birkhauser,1993),p267.
(c) M.Shub and S.Smale, J.Complexity 9(1993) 4.

SUBDYNAMICS THROUGH TIME SCALES AND SCATTERING MAPS IN QUANTUM FIELD THEORY*

Ludovico Lanz[1], Olaf Melsheimer[2], and Bassano Vacchini[1]

[1] Dipartimento di Fisica dell'Università di Milano
INFN, Sezione di Milano,
Via Celoria 16, I-20133, Milano, Italy
[2] Fachbereich Physik, Philipps-Universität
Renthof 7, D-3550 Marburg, Germany

It is argued that the dynamics of an isolated system, due to the concrete procedure by which it is separated from the environment, has a non-Hamiltonian contribution. By a unified quantum field theoretical treatment of typical subdynamics, e.g., hydrodynamics, kinetic theory, master equation for a particle interacting with matter, we look for the structure of this more general dynamics.

1. THE CONCEPT OF PHYSICAL SYSTEM

Quantum mechanics (QM) has non-separability as its most striking feature, i.e., one cannot attribute "properties" to parts of a system and therefore typical problems like the measurement process and EPR situations arise. This feature is so deeply rooted in the mathematical structure of QM that we believe one should not try to make it less stringent, e.g., by attempts like "spontaneous reduction" [1]. We prefer instead to weaken the very concept of physical system: usually the "isolation" of a physical system is taken for granted, while in our opinion the way in which isolation is achieved belongs to the very definition of the system. Any attempt inside QM to obtain the subdynamics for a subsystem enforces the introduction of a suitable time scale in order to break the correlations with the environment; in a completely sharp description of the dynamics of a subsystem the physics of the whole universe would enter. The preparation procedure leading to a system, isolated during a time interval $[t_0, t_1]$ and confined in a spatial region ω, covers a time interval $[T, t_0]$, that will be called "preparation time". Due to the confinement the basic space-time symmetries are broken and by suitable boundary conditions "peculiar" properties of the system are introduced. This obviously reduces the universal character of the dynamical description, however an important universal behaviour still remains due to symmetry and locality (or short range character) of effective interactions, whose relevance becomes particularly evident in the quantum field theoretical approach. We thus regard a physical system as a part of the world under control by a suitable preparation, whose local behaviour is explained in terms of

---

*THIS CONTRIBUTION TO THE PROCEEDINGS REFERS TO TWO DISTINCT LECTURES PRESENTED BY PROF. L. LANZ AND PROF. O. MELSHEIMER.

locally interacting quantum fields. The choice of these fields depends on the level of description of the system. A large part of physics can be explained in terms of quantum fields related to molecules with a typical time scale of the order $\approx 10^{-13}$ s; a much more refined description arises if the basic fields are related to nuclei and electrons, then the basic theory would be QED and a much smaller time scale $\approx 10^{-23}$ s could be considered: however such role of QED as basic theory of macrosystems is far from being exploited.

In a sense our viewpoint can appear as opposite to the most widely spread one, which we synthetise as follows: particles are the primary systems, related to non-confined quantum fields and to basic symmetries, all other systems are structure of particles; one then tries to obtain a typical macroscopic behaviour in some suitable thermodynamic limit. According to us, on the contrary, macroscopic systems are to be taken as the primary systems, even if in their definition time scales and spatial confinement must be carefully taken into account; the theoretical framework for their description is quantum field theory, locality and quantisation taking the place of the atomistic model. In this context particles are a derived concept. The description of non-equilibrium systems is put in the foreground and at least in principle should be performed taking boundary effects into account; procedures like "continuous" limit should be applied only at the end, if one wants to get rid of boundary effects. This standpoint is closer to thermodynamics and electromagnetism, while the former one originates from classical mechanics. The relevance of macroscopic systems for the foundations of QM is the starting point of Ludwig's axiomatic approach to QM [2]. The insistence on the distinction between these two attitudes is due to the fact that they lead in a natural way to two different formulations of the dynamics. In the first approach one associates a wave function ψ to each system ($\psi(\mathbf{x}, t)$ for one particle, ..., $\psi(\mathbf{x}_1, \mathbf{x}_2, \ldots, \mathbf{x}_N, t)$ for N particles); obviously if one describes situations like "unpolarised" particles it is appropriate to use a statistical operator, in order to take a lack of control of the experimental specification into account. This aspect becomes increasingly important for large N, so that statistical operators are very useful for macroscopic systems, nevertheless the basic dynamics is given by an evolution operator for the wavefunction ψ. On the other hand, starting with a macroscopic system, one is led to assume a statistical operator $\hat{\varrho}_t$ as the most appropriate mathematical representation of the preparation procedure until time t. The set $\mathcal{K}(\mathcal{H})$ of statistical operators on the Hilbert space $\mathcal{H}$ becomes most important and the space $\mathcal{T}(\mathcal{H})$ of trace-class operators, which is generated in a natural way by $\mathcal{K}(\mathcal{H})$ [$\mathcal{K}(\mathcal{H})$ is the base of the base-norm space $\mathcal{T}(\mathcal{H})$], plays a role similar to that of $\mathcal{H}$ in the previous formalism. Correspondingly unitary operators on $\mathcal{H}$ in the first approach are replaced by affine maps of $\mathcal{K}(\mathcal{H})$ in $\mathcal{K}(\mathcal{H})$, i.e. by positive, trace-preserving maps on $\mathcal{T}(\mathcal{H})$. If the system is isolated in the time interval $[t_0, t_1]$ the spontaneous repreparations $\hat{\varrho}_t$, $t \in [t_0, t_1]$, are related together by $\hat{\varrho}_t = \mathcal{M}_{tt'}\hat{\varrho}_{t'}$ ($t \geq t'$), where the evolution system $\{\mathcal{M}_{t''t'} \ t'' \geq t'\}$ satisfies the composition rule $\mathcal{M}_{t'''t'} = \mathcal{M}_{t'''t''}\mathcal{M}_{t''t'}$ ($t' \leq t'' \leq t'''$). We stress the fact that there is no reason to assume that $\mathcal{M}_{t''t'}$ has an inverse. If $\mathcal{M}_{t''t'}^{-1}$ exists then $\mathcal{M}_{t''t'} = \hat{U}_{t''t'} \cdot \hat{U}_{t''t'}^{\dagger}$ (see for example [3]), with $\hat{U}_{t''t'}$ unitary or antiunitary operator and one is brought back to the Hilbert space formalism: $\psi_{t''} = \hat{U}_{t''t'}\psi_{t'}$. The dynamics in the present framework is indeed more general and has irreversibility as typical phenomenon.

To determine the maps $\mathcal{M}_{t''t'}$ a choice of relevant observables is necessary: when a time scale is introduced, only those observables should be considered, whose expectation values do not appreciably vary in a time interval of the order of the time scale. It is thus necessary to work in the Heisenberg picture, i.e. with the adjoint map $\mathcal{M}'_{tt_0}$, and consider expressions of the form $\mathcal{M}'_{tt_0}\hat{A}$, $\hat{A}$ being a relevant observable. For the same system different descriptions can be given by different choices of relevant observables and corresponding time scales: e.g., hydrodynamic or kinetic description of a continuum. Skipping questions of mathematical rigour we can assume the differential equation

$$\frac{d}{dt}\mathcal{M}'_{tt_0} = \mathcal{L}'_t \mathcal{M}'_{tt_0},\tag{1.1}$$

and represent $\mathcal{M}'_{tt_0}$ in the form $\mathcal{M}'_{tt_0} = T\left(e^{\int_{t_0}^t dt' \, \mathcal{L}'_{t'}}\right)$ in terms of the generator $\mathcal{L}'_t$. It is well known (rigorously for bounded $\mathcal{L}'_t$) that if $\mathcal{M}'_{t''t'}$ has the additional property of complete positivity (CP), $\mathcal{L}'_t$ has the Lindblad structure [4]:

$$\mathcal{L}'_t \hat{B} = +\frac{i}{\hbar}\left(\hat{H}_t \hat{B} - \hat{B}\hat{H}_t\right) - \frac{1}{\hbar}\left(\hat{A}_t \hat{B} + \hat{B}\hat{A}_t\right) + \frac{1}{\hbar}\sum_j \hat{L}^\dagger_{tj}\hat{B}\hat{L}_{tj},\tag{1.2}$$

$$\hat{H}_t = \hat{H}^\dagger_t, \qquad \hat{A}_t = \frac{1}{2}\sum_j \hat{L}_{tj}\hat{L}^\dagger_{tj}.$$

In our framework the assumption of CP can appear too restrictive since only a suitable subset of observables is relevant and one expects that a modified concept of CP of $\mathcal{M}'_{t''t'}$ relatively to these observables should be given, leading to a more general structure of $\mathcal{L}'_t$; we shall return to this point in the sequel.

The more general description of the dynamics that we are considering allows the introduction of the concept of trajectory in quantum theory. In fact in the general formalism of continuous measurement approach [5] one has that an evolution system $\{\mathcal{M}_{t''t'} \quad t'' \geq t'\}$ with $\mathcal{L}_t$ having the Lindblad structure can be decomposed on a space $Y_{t_0}^{t_1}$ of trajectories for stochastic variables $\xi(t)$. The concept of trajectory is particularly useful in the field of quantum optics, as is shown by the many interesting applications to be found in the literature. More precisely one can consider Wiener and jump processes related to the operators $\hat{L}_{tj}$ in the sense that the expectations of the increments for example in the case of jump processes are given by [6]:

$$\langle d\xi_j(t)\rangle = dt\,\mathrm{Tr}\left((\hat{L}^\dagger_{tj}\hat{L}_{tj})\hat{\varrho}(t)\right).$$

One can define σ-algebras $\mathcal{B}(Y_{t'}^{t''})$ of subsets $\Omega_{t'}^{t''}$ of $Y_{t'}^{t''}$ and construct operation valued measures $\mathcal{F}_{t'}^{t''}(\Omega_{t'}^{t''})$ on $\mathcal{B}(Y_{t'}^{t''})$ in such a way that $\mathcal{M}_{t''t'} = \mathcal{F}(Y_{t'}^{t''})$. Then for any decomposition $Y_{t'}^{t''} = \cup_\alpha(\Omega_{t'}^{t''}{}_\alpha)$ with disjoint subsets $\Omega_{t'}^{t''}{}_\alpha$ one has

$$\mathcal{M}_{t''t'} = \sum_\alpha \mathcal{F}(\Omega_{t'}^{t''}{}_\alpha).\tag{1.3}$$

One can therefore claim that the quantum dynamics of the system is compatible with the evolution of classical stochastic variables; typically the probability that the trajectory of these variables for $t' \leq t \leq t''$ belongs to a subset $\Omega_{t'}^{t''}{}_\alpha$ is given by $p(\Omega_{t'}^{t''}{}_\alpha) = \mathrm{Tr}\left(\mathcal{F}_{t'}^{t''}(\Omega_{t'}^{t''}{}_\alpha)\hat{\varrho}(t')\right)$. The decomposition of $\mathcal{M}_{t''t'}$ by operation valued stochastic processes $\mathcal{F}_{t'}^{t''}$ on a suitable trajectory space $Y_{t'}^{t''}$ is not unique, i.e. there are many compatible objective "classical" pictures which are consistent with the quantum evolution, a feature that can be linked with a generalised "concept of complementarity". The very possibility of recovering some kind of classical insight into QM is due to the non-Hamiltonian evolution; obviously (1.3) would be inconsistent with $\mathcal{M}_{t''t'} = \hat{U}_{t''t'} \cdot \hat{U}^\dagger_{t''t'}$, since for $\hat{\varrho}_{t'} = |\psi_{t'}\rangle\langle\psi_{t'}|$ the l.h.s. of (1.3) is a pure state and the r.h.s. is a mixture.

In the framework we have now presented dynamics is given by $\mathcal{L}'_t$ [7]; while one expects that the Hamiltonian part is fixed by the local interactions, the remaining part is connected to the preparation procedure of the isolated system: it cannot be strictly derived from a Hamiltonian theory of a larger system surrounding it (in fact also for this larger system an $\mathcal{L}'_t$ should be determined). The problem arises to give reasonable criteria for the construction of $\mathcal{L}'_t$. One can expect that near to equilibrium only the Hamiltonian part $\frac{i}{\hbar}[\hat{H}, \cdot]$ is important, as it is clearly indicated by the great success of equilibrium statistical mechanics; however the non-Hamiltonian part of $\mathcal{L}'_t$ is relevant for irreversible behaviour and for a full explanation of approach to equilibrium: in fact energy conservation $\mathcal{L}'_t \hat{H} = 0$ (at least on the relevant time scale) grants for the existence of an "eigenstate" of $\mathcal{L}'_t$ with practically zero eigenvalue, while one expects that the other eigenvalues of $\mathcal{L}'_t$ have a negative real part.

2. A MICROSYSTEM INTERACTING WITH MATTER

We shall take on later the problem of an explicit construction of $\hat{\varrho}(t)$ for a macrosystem $\mathcal{S}_{\mathrm{M}}$. We assume now that $\hat{\varrho}(t)$ is given (e.g., the system is at equilibrium) and consider the problem of describing the new system $\mathcal{S} = \mathcal{S}_{\mathrm{M}} +$ a microsystem, $\mathcal{S}$ still being confined inside a region ω. The Hamiltonian of $\mathcal{S}$ is:

$$\hat{H} = \hat{H}_0 + \hat{H}_{\mathrm{M}} + \hat{V}, \qquad \hat{H}_0 = \sum_f E_f \hat{a}_f^\dagger \hat{a}_f, \qquad \left[\hat{a}_f, \hat{a}_g^\dagger\right]_{\mp} = \delta_{fg},$$

where E_f are the eigenvalues of the operator $-\frac{\hbar^2}{2m}\Delta_2$:

$$-\frac{\hbar^2}{2m}\Delta_2 u_f(\mathbf{x}) = E_f u_f(\mathbf{x}), \qquad u_f(\mathbf{x}) = 0, \qquad \mathbf{x} \in \partial\omega.$$

Let us assume for the statistical operator of $\mathcal{S}$ the following structure:

$$\hat{\varrho}(t) = \sum_{gf} \hat{a}_g^\dagger \hat{\varrho}_{\mathrm{M}}(t) \hat{a}_f \varrho_{gf}(t), \tag{2.1}$$

$$\hat{a}_f \hat{\varrho}_{\mathrm{M}} = 0. \tag{2.2}$$

The coefficients ϱ_{gf} build a positive, trace one matrix, which can be considered as the representative of a statistical operator $\hat{\varrho}^{(1)}(t)$ in the Hilbert space $\mathcal{H}^{(1)}$ spanned by the states u_f ($\varrho_{gf} = \langle u_g | \hat{\varrho}^{(1)} | u_f \rangle$). Equation (2.2) indicates that the system $\mathcal{S}_{\mathrm{M}}$ has charge $\hat{Q} = \sum_f \hat{a}_f^\dagger \hat{a}_f$ with value zero, i.e. it does not contain the microsystem. Equation (2.1) represents the fact that $\mathcal{S}_{\mathrm{M}}$ has been perturbed by the additional particle and therefore presents a new dynamical behaviour contained in the coefficients $\varrho_{gf}(t)$ that can be picked out studying the time evolution of the observables $\hat{A} = \sum_{h,k} \hat{a}_h^\dagger A_{hk} \hat{a}_k$; in fact the subdynamics of these observables provides the QM of a one-particle system with Hilbert space $\mathcal{H}^{(1)}$, statistical operator $\hat{\varrho}^{(1)}$ and observables $\hat{\mathsf{A}}^{(1)}$, with matrix elements $A_{hk} = \langle u_h | \hat{\mathsf{A}}^{(1)} u_k \rangle_{\mathcal{H}^{(1)}}$, through the formula

$$\mathrm{Tr}_{\mathcal{H}}\left(\hat{A}\hat{\varrho}(t)\right) = \sum_{hk} \mathrm{Tr}_{\mathcal{H}}\left(e^{\frac{i}{\hbar}\hat{H}t}\hat{a}_h^\dagger \hat{a}_k e^{-\frac{i}{\hbar}\hat{H}t}\hat{\varrho}\right) A_{hk} = \mathrm{Tr}_{\mathcal{H}^{(1)}}\left(\hat{\mathsf{A}}^{(1)}\hat{\varrho}^{(1)}(t)\right). \tag{2.3}$$

One has to study the expression $e^{\frac{i}{\hbar}\hat{H}t}\hat{a}_h^\dagger \hat{a}_k e^{-\frac{i}{\hbar}\hat{H}t}$, exploiting the fact that the expectation values $\langle \hat{A} \rangle_t$ are "slowly varying" if the matrix A_{hk} is "quasi-diagonal" (if $A_{hk} = \delta_{hk}$, $\hat{A}$ is a conserved charge). We give here only a sketchy account of the main points (for details see [8]). It proves useful to use in the Heisenberg picture a formalism in $\mathcal{B}(\mathcal{H})$ reminiscent of usual scattering theory in $\mathcal{H}$, by means of superoperators, typically:

$$\mathcal{H}' = \frac{i}{\hbar}[\hat{H}, \cdot], \qquad \mathcal{H}'_0 = \frac{i}{\hbar}[\hat{H}_0 + \hat{H}_{\mathrm{M}}, \cdot], \qquad \mathcal{V}' = \frac{i}{\hbar}[\hat{V}, \cdot].$$

In such a context operators of the form $\hat{a}_h^\dagger \hat{a}_k$ are "eigenstates" of $\mathcal{H}_0'$ with eigenvalues $\frac{i}{\hbar}(E_h - E_k)$. Setting $\mathcal{U}'(t) = e^{\mathcal{H}'t}$ one has:

$$\mathcal{U}'(t)\left(\hat{a}_h^\dagger \hat{a}_k\right) = \left(\mathcal{U}'(t)\hat{a}_h^\dagger\right)\left(\mathcal{U}'(t)\hat{a}_k\right) \tag{2.4}$$

$$= \int_{-i\infty+\eta}^{+i\infty+\eta} \frac{dz_1}{2\pi i} e^{z_1 t}\left(\frac{1}{z_1 - \mathcal{H}'}\hat{a}_h^\dagger\right) \int_{-i\infty+\eta}^{+i\infty+\eta} \frac{dz_2}{2\pi i} e^{z_2 t}\left(\frac{1}{z_2 - \mathcal{H}'}\hat{a}_k\right),$$

$$\frac{1}{z - \mathcal{H}'} = \frac{1}{z - \mathcal{H}_0'} + \frac{1}{z - \mathcal{H}_0'}\mathcal{T}(z)\frac{1}{z - \mathcal{H}_0'}, \quad \text{where} \quad \mathcal{T}(z) \equiv \mathcal{V}' + \mathcal{V}'\frac{1}{z - \mathcal{H}'}\mathcal{V}'. \tag{2.5}$$

$\mathcal{T}(z)$ is reminiscent of the usual T-matrix of scattering theory and plays a central role in this treatment: it will be called "scattering map". The operator $\mathcal{T}(z)$ has poles on the imaginary axis for $z = \frac{i}{\hbar}(e_\alpha - e_\beta)$, e_α being the eigenvalues of $\hat{H}$. In the calculation of expression (2.4) we shall assume that the function $\mathcal{T}(z)$ for $Re z \approx \varepsilon$ with $\varepsilon \gg \delta$ (δ typical spacing between the poles) is smooth enough, so that the only relevant contribution from the singularities of $(z - \mathcal{H}')^{-1}$ stems from the singularities of $(z - \mathcal{H}_0')^{-1}$; this smoothness property is linked to the fact that the set of poles of $(z - \mathcal{H}')^{-1}$ goes over to a continuum if the confinement is removed yielding an analytic function with a cut along the imaginary axis, that can be continued across the cut without singularities if no absorption of the microsystem occurs. More precisely $\mathcal{T}(iy + \varepsilon)$ is considered as practically constant for variations $\Delta y \approx \frac{\hbar}{\tau_0}$, where τ_0 has to be interpreted as a collision time. Treating expression (2.4) we make use of the inequality

$$|E_h - E_k| \ll \frac{\hbar}{\tau_0}, \tag{2.6}$$

whose physical meaning is that the typical variation time τ_1 of the quantities $\langle \hat{A} \rangle_t$ is much larger than τ_0. One then arrives at the following very perspicuous structure for $\mathcal{U}'(t)\left(\hat{a}_h^\dagger \hat{a}_k\right)$:

$$\mathcal{U}'(t)\left(\hat{a}_h^\dagger \hat{a}_k\right) = \hat{a}_h^\dagger \hat{a}_k + t\mathcal{L}'\left(\hat{a}_h^\dagger \hat{a}_k\right),$$

$$\mathcal{L}'\left(\hat{a}_h^\dagger \hat{a}_k\right) = \frac{i}{\hbar}\left[\hat{H}_{\text{eff}}, \hat{a}_h^\dagger \hat{a}_k\right] - \frac{1}{\hbar}\left(\left[\hat{\Gamma}^{(1)}, \hat{a}_h^\dagger\right]\hat{a}_k - \hat{a}_h^\dagger\left[\hat{\Gamma}^{(1)}, \hat{a}_k\right]\right) + \frac{1}{\hbar}\sum_\lambda \hat{R}_{h\lambda}^{(1)\dagger}\hat{R}_{k\lambda}^{(1)}, \tag{2.7}$$

where $\hat{H}_{\text{eff}} = \hat{H}_0 + \hat{V}^{\text{eff}}$ and

$$\hat{V}^{\text{eff}} = \sum_{gr} \hat{a}_r^\dagger \hat{V}_{rg}^{\text{eff}}\hat{a}_g$$

$$= i\hbar \sum_{\substack{\lambda\lambda'\\gr}} \hat{a}_r^\dagger |\lambda\rangle\langle\lambda|\frac{1}{2}\left[\left(\mathcal{T}\left(-\frac{i}{\hbar}E_r + \varepsilon\right)\hat{a}_r\right)\hat{a}_g^\dagger + \hat{a}_r\left(\mathcal{T}\left(\frac{i}{\hbar}E_g + \varepsilon\right)\hat{a}_g^\dagger\right)\right]|\lambda'\rangle\langle\lambda'|\hat{a}_g,$$

$$\hat{\Gamma}^{(1)} = \sum_{gr} \hat{a}_r^\dagger \hat{\Gamma}_{rg}\hat{a}_g$$

$$= i\hbar \sum_{\substack{\lambda\lambda'\\gr}} \hat{a}_r^\dagger |\lambda\rangle\langle\lambda|\frac{i}{2}\left[\left(\mathcal{T}\left(-\frac{i}{\hbar}E_r + \varepsilon\right)\hat{a}_r\right)\hat{a}_g^\dagger - \hat{a}_r\left(\mathcal{T}\left(\frac{i}{\hbar}E_g + \varepsilon\right)\hat{a}_g^\dagger\right)\right]|\lambda'\rangle\langle\lambda'|\hat{a}_g,$$

$$\hat{R}_{k\lambda}^{(1)} = \sqrt{2\varepsilon\hbar^3} \sum_{g\lambda'} \frac{\langle\lambda|\left(\mathcal{T}\left(-\frac{i}{\hbar}E_g + \varepsilon\right)\hat{a}_g\right)\hat{a}_k^\dagger|\lambda'\rangle}{E_g + E_\lambda - E_k - E_{\lambda'} - i\hbar\varepsilon}\langle\lambda'|\hat{a}_g,$$

and $|\lambda\rangle$ denotes an eigenvector of $\hat{H}_M$ with eigenvalue E_λ and of $\hat{H}_0$ with eigenvalue zero. Eq.(2.7) shows a typical structure arising in the calculation, which we will also find in the more complex situation examined in §3, where the form of the different operators is

343

further commented on. Let us observe that $\hat{V}^{\text{eff}}_{rg}$ and $\hat{\Gamma}_{rg}$ are not c-number coefficients, but operators acting in the Fock space for the macrosystem, as stressed by the hats; they are connected respectively to the self-adjoint and anti-self-adjoint part of what can be considered as an operator valued T-matrix. The last contribution displays the "bilinear structure" of the third term in the r.h.s. of (1.2), connected to irreversibility and CP and not reproducible in the Hilbert space formalism, even resorting to an interaction potential which is not self-adjoint. Within the approximation leading to (2.7) one has $\hat{\Gamma}^{(1)} \approx \frac{1}{2}\sum_{h\lambda} \hat{R}^{(1)\dagger}_{h\lambda} \hat{R}^{(1)}_{h\lambda}$ and therefore $\mathcal{L}'\hat{N} = 0$. Appealing to (2.3) we may obtain an evolution equation for the matrix elements ϱ_{fg} which is meaningful on a time scale much longer than the correlation time for $\mathcal{S}_{\text{M}}$:

$$\frac{d\varrho_{gf}}{dt} = -\frac{i}{\hbar}\left(E_g - E_f\right)\varrho_{gf} + \frac{1}{\hbar}\sum_h \varrho_{gh}Q^{\dagger}_{hf} + \frac{1}{\hbar}\sum_k Q_{gk}\varrho_{kf} + \frac{1}{\hbar}\sum_{\substack{hk \\ \lambda\xi}} (\mathsf{L}_{\lambda\xi})_{gk}\, \varrho_{kh}\, (\mathsf{L}_{\lambda\xi})^*_{fh}$$

with

$$Q_{kf} = \hbar\text{Tr}_{\mathcal{H}}\left[\left(\mathcal{T}\left(-\frac{i}{\hbar}E_k + \varepsilon\right)\hat{a}_k\right)\hat{a}^{\dagger}_f\hat{\varrho}_{\text{M}}(t)\right],$$

$$(\mathsf{L}_{\lambda\xi})_{kf} = \sqrt{2\varepsilon\hbar^3\pi_{\xi}}\langle\lambda|\left[\left(\mathcal{T}\left(-\frac{i}{\hbar}E_k + \varepsilon\right)\hat{a}_k\right)\hat{a}^{\dagger}_f\right]\frac{1}{E_k + E_{\lambda} - E_f - H_{\text{M}} - i\hbar\varepsilon}|\xi(t)\rangle;$$

$\xi(t)$ is a complete system of eigenvectors of $\hat{\varrho}_{\text{M}}(t)$, $(\hat{\varrho}_{\text{M}}(t) = \sum_{\xi(t)}\pi_{\xi(t)}|\xi(t)\rangle\langle\xi(t)|)$. To show the connection with (1.2) we introduce in $\mathcal{H}^{(1)}$ the operators $\hat{Q}^{(1)}, \hat{L}^{(1)}_{\lambda\xi}$:

$$\langle k|\hat{Q}^{(1)}|f\rangle = Q_{kf} \quad , \quad \langle k|\hat{L}^{(1)}_{\lambda\xi}|f\rangle = (\mathsf{L}_{\lambda\xi})_{kf},$$

thus attaining in the Schrödinger picture the full evolution of $\varrho^{(1)}$, given by the typical Lindblad generator:

$$\frac{d\hat{\varrho}^{(1)}}{dt} = -\frac{i}{\hbar}\left[\hat{\mathsf{H}}_{\text{eff}}, \hat{\varrho}^{(1)}\right] + \frac{1}{2\hbar}\left\{\left(\hat{Q}^{(1)} + \hat{Q}^{(1)\dagger}\right), \hat{\varrho}^{(1)}\right\} + \frac{1}{\hbar}\sum_{\xi,\lambda}\hat{L}^{(1)}_{\lambda\xi}\hat{\varrho}^{(1)}\hat{L}^{(1)\dagger}_{\lambda\xi}, \tag{2.8}$$

where $\hat{\mathsf{H}}^{(1)}_{\text{eff}} = \hat{\mathsf{H}}^{(1)}_0 + \frac{i}{2}\left(\hat{Q}^{(1)} - \hat{Q}^{(1)\dagger}\right)$. Furthermore according to preservation of trace we have $\hat{Q}^{(1)} + \hat{Q}^{(1)\dagger} = -\sum_{\lambda\xi}\hat{L}^{(1)\dagger}_{\lambda\xi}\hat{L}^{(1)}_{\lambda\xi}$.

As it is well-known (2.8) is apt to describe very different physical situations. If the last contribution, which we will call "incoherent", may be neglected, at least as a first approximation, eq.(2.8) is equivalent to a Schrödinger equation with a possibly complex potential. In the case of a particle interacting with matter this equation is well-suited to describe a coherent optical behaviour, for example in terms of a refractive index, as it is usually done in neutron optics [9, 10] and recently also in atom optics [11, 12]. In this framework the operator $\hat{Q}^{(1)}$ is to be interpreted as an optical potential, which in our formalism is naturally linked to matrix elements of the T-operator, thus showing the connection between the effective, macroscopic description through an index of refraction and quantities characterising the local interactions. The T-operator may be replaced by phenomenological expressions (for example the Fermi pseudo-potential in the case of neutron optics). This picture is particularly useful to deal with particle interferometry. To see how the last contribution may be linked to an interaction having a measuring character let us introduce the reversible mappings $\mathcal{A}_{t''t'} = \hat{U}^{(1)}_{t''t'} \cdot \hat{U}^{(1)\dagger}_{t''t'}$, where $\hat{U}^{(1)}_{t''t'} = T\exp(-\frac{i}{\hbar}\int_{t'}^{t''} dt\,(\hat{\mathsf{H}}^{(1)}_0(t) + i\hat{Q}^{(1)}(t)))$, corresponding to a coherent contractive

344

evolution of the microsystem during the time interval $[t', t'']$, and the CP mappings $\mathcal{L}_{\lambda\xi} = \hat{L}^{(1)}_{\lambda\xi}(t) \cdot \hat{L}^{(1)}_{\lambda\xi}{}^{\dagger}(t)$, having a measuring character, as it is clear from their very structure, reminiscent of the reduction postulate. The expression of the operators $\hat{L}^{(1)}_{\lambda\xi}$ shows how these mappings may be linked with a transition inside the macrosystem specified by the pair of indexes ξ, λ, as a result of scattering with the microsystem. These transitions are in general not detectable, but under suitable conditions they could prime real events. The solution of (2.8) may be written in the form:

$$\varrho_t = \mathcal{A}_{tt_0}\varrho_{t_0} + \sum_{\lambda_1\xi_1} \int_{t_0}^{t} dt_1\, \mathcal{A}_{tt_1}\mathcal{L}_{\lambda_1\xi_1}(t_1)\mathcal{A}_{t_1 t_0}\varrho_{t_0} + \dots, \tag{2.9}$$

that is a sum over subcollections corresponding to the realization of no event, one event and so on. The set of variables $N_{\lambda\xi}(\tau)$, $\tau \geq t_0$, (number of transitions up to time τ), define a multicomponent classical stochastic process, and (2.9) corresponds to the decomposition of the evolution map on the space of trajectories for $N_{\lambda\xi}(\tau)$. This is a straightforward generalization of the typical "counting process" considered by Srinivas and Davies [13]. Of course other decompositions in terms of operation valued maps are possible on trajectory spaces related to different observables, as indicated in § 1. When the first term in (2.9) is largely predominant a wavelike description as given by the Schrödinger equation is sufficiently accurate and small disturbances, conveyed by the other terms, play no significant role. In a different physical context however, as would be the case for the Brownian motion of a particle interacting with an ideal gas, the interplay between the contractive and the incoherent part has a major role. Being interested in the dynamics far away from the walls the quantum number h corresponds to the momentum variable $\mathbf{p}_h$, and supposing that momentum transfers are small (Fokker-Planck approximation) one arrives at an equation describing diffusion in phase-space which has the following form (see [14]):

$$\frac{d\hat{\varrho}}{dt} = -\frac{i}{\hbar}\left[\hat{H}_{\text{eff}}, \hat{\varrho}\right] - D_{pp}\left[\hat{x}, [\hat{x}, \hat{\varrho}]\right] - D_{qq}\left[\hat{p}, [\hat{p}, \hat{\varrho}]\right] - \frac{i\eta}{2M}\left[\hat{x}, \{\hat{p}, \hat{\varrho}\}\right],$$

D_{qq}, D_{qq} and η being diffusion coefficients linked in different ways to the operators $\hat{L}^{(1)}_{\lambda\xi}$ and M the mass of the particle.

3. THEORY OF A MACROSYSTEM: THERMODYNAMIC EVOLUTION BY A SCATTERING MAP

We consider a very schematic model of macrosystem in the non-relativistic case built by one type of molecules with mass m confined inside a region ω, interacting by a two body potential $V(|\mathbf{x} - \mathbf{y}|)$; for the sake of simplicity no internal structure of the molecules is taken into account. In the field theoretical language the system is described by a quantum Schrödinger field (QSF):

$$\hat{\psi}(\mathbf{x}) = \sum_{f} u_f(\mathbf{x})\hat{a}_f, \qquad \left[\hat{a}_f, \hat{a}_g^{\dagger}\right]_{\pm} = \delta_{fg}, \tag{3.1}$$

$$-\frac{\hbar^2}{2m}\Delta_2 u_f(\mathbf{x}) = E_f u_f(\mathbf{x}), \qquad u_f(\mathbf{x}) = 0 \quad \mathbf{x} \in \partial\omega.$$

We shall assume the following Hamiltonian to take local interactions and confinement into account:

$$\hat{H} = \sum_{f} E_f \hat{a}_f^{\dagger}\hat{a}_f + \frac{1}{2}\sum_{\substack{l_1 l_2 \\ f_1 f_2}} \hat{a}_{l_1}^{\dagger}\hat{a}_{l_2}^{\dagger} V_{l_1 l_2 f_2 f_1}\hat{a}_{f_2}\hat{a}_{f_1}, \tag{3.2}$$

$$V_{l_1 l_2 f_2 f_1} = \int_\omega d^3\mathbf{x} \int_\omega d^3\mathbf{y}\, u_{l_1}^*(\mathbf{x}) u_{l_2}^*(\mathbf{y}) V(|\mathbf{x} - \mathbf{y}|) u_{f_2}(\mathbf{y}) u_{f_1}(\mathbf{x}). \qquad (3.3)$$

Eq.(3.1) is linked to the basic "local" Hamiltonian for the non-confined field (NC)

$$\hat{H}_{\mathrm{NC}} = \int d^3\mathbf{x}\, \frac{\hbar^2}{2m} \mathrm{grad}\hat{\psi}_{\mathrm{NC}}^\dagger(\mathbf{x}) \cdot \mathrm{grad}\hat{\psi}_{\mathrm{NC}}(\mathbf{x})$$
$$+ \frac{1}{2} \int d^3\mathbf{x} d^3\mathbf{r}\, \hat{\psi}_{\mathrm{NC}}^\dagger \left(\mathbf{x} - \frac{\mathbf{r}}{2}\right) \hat{\psi}_{\mathrm{NC}}^\dagger \left(\mathbf{x} + \frac{\mathbf{r}}{2}\right) V(r) \hat{\psi}_{\mathrm{NC}} \left(\mathbf{x} + \frac{\mathbf{r}}{2}\right) \hat{\psi}_{\mathrm{NC}} \left(\mathbf{x} - \frac{\mathbf{r}}{2}\right),$$

$$\left[\hat{\psi}_{\mathrm{NC}}(\mathbf{x}), \hat{\psi}_{\mathrm{NC}}^\dagger(\mathbf{x}')\right]_\pm = \delta(\mathbf{x} - \mathbf{x}'),$$

simply selecting the part of $\hat{H}_{\mathrm{NC}}$ related to the "normal modes" u_f typical of the confinement: in fact the preparation procedure should imply a kind of relaxation of $\hat{\psi}_{\mathrm{NC}}(\mathbf{x})$ to $\hat{\psi}(\mathbf{x})$. Skipping this problem and also the related question of the full explicit structure of $\mathcal{L}'$ for a realistic system, we shall simply take the Hamiltonian (3.2) containing only the normal modes of the field inside ω. If we are interested in a hydrodynamic description, relevant observables are constructed starting with the densities of the typical constants of motion, mass and energy:

$$\hat{\rho}_m(\mathbf{x}) = m\hat{\psi}^\dagger(\mathbf{x})\hat{\psi}(\mathbf{x}), \qquad (3.4)$$
$$\hat{e}(\mathbf{x}) = \frac{\hbar^2}{2m} \mathrm{grad}\hat{\psi}^\dagger(\mathbf{x}) \cdot \mathrm{grad}\hat{\psi}(\mathbf{x})$$
$$+ \frac{1}{2} \int_{\omega_x} d^3\mathbf{r}\, \hat{\psi}^\dagger \left(\mathbf{x} - \frac{\mathbf{r}}{2}\right) \hat{\psi}^\dagger \left(\mathbf{x} + \frac{\mathbf{r}}{2}\right) V(r) \hat{\psi} \left(\mathbf{x} + \frac{\mathbf{r}}{2}\right) \hat{\psi} \left(\mathbf{x} - \frac{\mathbf{r}}{2}\right),$$

where the dependence of ω_x on $\mathbf{x}$ is generally negligible if $V(r)$ is a short range potential. In the case of a kinetic description we replace (3.4) by the "Boltzmann" operator density $\hat{f}(\mathbf{x}, \mathbf{p}) = m \sum_{hk} \hat{a}_h^\dagger \langle u_h | \hat{\mathsf{F}}^{(1)}(\mathbf{x}, \mathbf{p}) | u_k \rangle \hat{a}_k$, where $\hat{\mathsf{F}}^{(1)}$ is the density of joint one particle position-momentum observables [15,16]. These densities lead to slowly varying quantities if they are integrated over regions large enough in space or phase-space, since one has constants if the integration is extended over the whole space. The constants of motion leading to this subdynamics are linked to very fundamental symmetries: time translation invariance and gauge symmetry. Our relevant observables have the general structure:

$$\sum_{hk} \hat{a}_h^\dagger A_{hk}(\xi)\hat{a}_k \quad , \quad \sum_{\substack{k_1 k_2 \\ h_1 h_2}} \hat{a}_{h_1}^\dagger \hat{a}_{h_2}^\dagger A_{h_1 h_2 k_2 k_1}(\mathbf{x})\hat{a}_{k_2}\hat{a}_{k_1}, \qquad (3.5)$$

$$A_{h_1 h_2 k_2 k_1}(\mathbf{x}) = \frac{1}{2} \int_{\omega_x} d^3\mathbf{r}\, u_{h_1}^* \left(\mathbf{x} - \frac{\mathbf{r}}{2}\right) u_{h_2}^* \left(\mathbf{x} + \frac{\mathbf{r}}{2}\right) V(r) u_{k_2} \left(\mathbf{x} + \frac{\mathbf{r}}{2}\right) u_{k_1} \left(\mathbf{x} - \frac{\mathbf{r}}{2}\right).$$

We thus have to study in Heisenberg picture the expressions:

$$\sum_{hk} e^{\frac{i}{\hbar}\hat{H}t} \hat{a}_h^\dagger \hat{a}_k e^{-\frac{i}{\hbar}\hat{H}t} A_{hk}(\xi), \qquad \sum_{\substack{h_1 h_2 \\ k_1 k_2}} e^{\frac{i}{\hbar}\hat{H}t} \hat{a}_{h_1}^\dagger \hat{a}_{h_2}^\dagger \hat{a}_{k_2} \hat{a}_{k_1} e^{-\frac{i}{\hbar}\hat{H}t} A_{h_1 h_2 k_2 k_1}(\mathbf{x}), \qquad (3.6)$$

and shall take into account that by the slow variability only terms that are "diagonal enough" are really relevant; the sums should be restricted to indexes such that:

$$\frac{1}{\hbar}|E_h - E_k| < \frac{1}{\tau_1}, \qquad \frac{1}{\hbar}|E_{h_1} + E_{h_2} - E_{k_1} - E_{k_2}| < \frac{1}{\tau_1},$$

where τ_1 is the characteristic variation time of the relevant quantities. We would like to stress the fact that the QSF is the basic tool to describe a massive continuum, just like the quantum electromagnetic field describes a massless continuum. The dynamics of the QSF, $\hat{\psi}(\mathbf{x}, t) = e^{\frac{i}{\hbar}\hat{H}t}\hat{\psi}(\mathbf{x})e^{-\frac{i}{\hbar}\hat{H}t}$, in terms of which one can rewrite (3.6), is given by the simple field equation

$$i\hbar\frac{\partial}{\partial t}\hat{\psi}(\mathbf{x}, t) = -\frac{\hbar^2}{2m}\Delta_2\hat{\psi}(\mathbf{x}, t) + \int d^3\mathbf{y}\,\hat{\psi}^\dagger(\mathbf{y}, t)V(|\mathbf{x}-\mathbf{y}|)\hat{\psi}(\mathbf{y}, t)\hat{\psi}(\mathbf{x}, t), \qquad (3.7)$$

however no such equation holds for the expectation value of the field $\psi(\mathbf{x}, t) = \langle\hat{\psi}(\mathbf{x}, t)\rangle$ due to correlations in the non-linear term; $\psi(\mathbf{x}, t)$ is not useful to calculate the expectations of operators (3.6) and therefore a classical Schrödinger field equation for $\psi(\mathbf{x}, t)$ has no physical meaning in general. In this respect the case of electromagnetism, where no self-interaction of the field occurs, is deeply different and allows classical electrodynamics to play an important role. To the macrosystem one associates typical "thermodynamic state" parameters: the velocity field $\mathbf{v}(\mathbf{x}, t)$, the temperature field $\beta(\mathbf{x}, t)$, the chemical potential field $\mu(\mathbf{x}, t)$ in the case of the hydrodynamic description or more generally a field $\mu(\mathbf{x}, \mathbf{p}, t)$ on the one-particle phase-space in the kinetic case [17]. The parameters $\beta(\mathbf{x}, t)$ and $\mu(\mathbf{x}, t)$ ($\mu(\mathbf{x}, \mathbf{p}, t)$) determine the expectation values of energy density and mass density (the Boltzmann operator); let us briefly recall how the relation between state variables and expectation values is established [18]. At any time t one considers the whole set of statistical operators $\{\hat{w}\}$ which yield the expectation values assigned at that time:

$$\langle\hat{e}^{(0)}(\mathbf{x})\rangle_t = \mathrm{Tr}\left(\hat{e}^{(0)}(\mathbf{x})\hat{w}\right), \quad \langle\hat{\rho}_m(\mathbf{x})\rangle_t = \mathrm{Tr}(\hat{\rho}_m(\mathbf{x})\hat{w}), \quad \langle\hat{f}^{(0)}(\mathbf{x}, \mathbf{p})\rangle_t = \mathrm{Tr}\left(\hat{f}^{(0)}(\mathbf{x}, \mathbf{p})\hat{w}\right),$$

$$\hat{e}^{(0)}(\mathbf{x}) = \frac{1}{2m}\left(i\hbar\frac{\partial}{\partial\mathbf{x}} - m\mathbf{v}(\mathbf{x}, t)\right)\hat{\psi}^\dagger(\mathbf{x})\cdot\left(-i\hbar\frac{\partial}{\partial\mathbf{x}} - m\mathbf{v}(\mathbf{x}, t)\right)\hat{\psi}(\mathbf{x}) \qquad (3.8)$$

$$+ \frac{1}{2}\int_{\omega_x} d^3\mathbf{r}\,\hat{\psi}^\dagger\left(\mathbf{x} - \frac{\mathbf{r}}{2}\right)\hat{\psi}^\dagger\left(\mathbf{x} + \frac{\mathbf{r}}{2}\right)V(r)\hat{\psi}\left(\mathbf{x} + \frac{\mathbf{r}}{2}\right)\hat{\psi}\left(\mathbf{x} - \frac{\mathbf{r}}{2}\right),$$

$$\hat{\rho}_m(\mathbf{x}) = \hat{\rho}_m^{(0)}(\mathbf{x}) = m\hat{\psi}^\dagger(\mathbf{x})\hat{\psi}(\mathbf{x}), \qquad \hat{f}^{(0)}(\mathbf{x}, \mathbf{p}) = \hat{f}(\mathbf{x}, \mathbf{p} - m\mathbf{v}(\mathbf{x}, t)),$$

where the quantities indexed by (0) (depending explicitly on the velocity field $\mathbf{v}(\mathbf{x}, t)$) represent densities in the reference frame in which the continuum is locally at rest. The velocity field is related to the expectation value of the momentum density $\hat{\mathbf{p}}(\mathbf{x})$ through the relation $\langle\hat{\mathbf{p}}^{(0)}(\mathbf{x})\rangle = 0$, where

$$\hat{\mathbf{p}}^{(0)}(\mathbf{x}) = \frac{1}{2}\left\{\hat{\psi}^\dagger(\mathbf{x})\left(-i\hbar\frac{\partial}{\partial\mathbf{x}} - m\mathbf{v}(\mathbf{x}, t)\right)\hat{\psi}(\mathbf{x}) + \left[\left(i\hbar\frac{\partial}{\partial\mathbf{x}} - m\mathbf{v}(\mathbf{x}, t)\right)\hat{\psi}^\dagger(\mathbf{x})\right]\hat{\psi}(\mathbf{x})\right\}$$

or equivalently $\langle\hat{\mathbf{p}}(\mathbf{x})\rangle_t = \mathbf{v}(\mathbf{x}, t)\langle\hat{\rho}_m(\mathbf{x})\rangle_t$. Then one looks for a statistical operator in the set $\{\hat{w}\}$ such that the von Neumann entropy $S = -k\mathrm{Tr}(\hat{w}\log\hat{w})$ is maximal, i.e. the most unbiased choice of a statistical operator leading to the given expectation values. The unique solution of this problem is

$$\hat{w}[\beta(t), \mu(t), \mathbf{v}(t)] = \frac{e^{-\int_\omega d^3\mathbf{x}\,\beta(\mathbf{x}, t)\left[\hat{e}^{(0)}(\mathbf{x}) - \mu(\mathbf{x}, t)\hat{\rho}_m(\mathbf{x})\right]}}{\mathrm{Tr}\,e^{-\int_\omega d^3\mathbf{x}\,\beta(\mathbf{x}, t)\left[\hat{e}^{(0)}(\mathbf{x}) - \mu(\mathbf{x}, t)\hat{\rho}_m(\mathbf{x})\right]}} \qquad (3.9)$$

and analogously in the kinetic case.

The corresponding $S = -k\mathrm{Tr}(\hat{w}[\beta(t), \mu(t), \mathbf{v}(t)]\log\hat{w}[\beta(t), \mu(t), \mathbf{v}(t)])$ is the thermodynamic entropy of the macrosystem. If the time evolution of the expectation values $\langle\hat{e}^{(0)}(\mathbf{x})\rangle_t, \langle\hat{\rho}_m(\mathbf{x})\rangle_t, (\langle\hat{f}(\mathbf{x}, \mathbf{p})\rangle_t)$ is given by the Hamiltonian evolution (3.6) or more generally by a map $\mathcal{M}'_{tt_0}$, having a preadjoint $\mathcal{M}_{tt_0}$ which does not decrease the

347

von Neumann entropy, one immediately has that the thermodynamic entropy is non-decreasing. In this way one establishes the second principle of thermodynamics on a very clear dynamical basis.

In the simplest scheme of macroscopic dynamics the thermodynamic state parameters $\mathbf{v}(\mathbf{x}, t)$, $\beta(\mathbf{x}, t)$, $\mu(\mathbf{x}, t)$ $(\mu(\mathbf{x}, \mathbf{p}, t))$ at time t_0 determine its evolution for $t > t_0$, e.g., by differential equations. Phenomenology shows that this is very often the case. Tackling the problem from the theoretical viewpoint one is induced, considering the operators

$$
\begin{aligned}
\dot{\hat{\rho}}_m(\mathbf{x}) &= \tfrac{i}{\hbar}[\hat{H}, \hat{\rho}_m(\mathbf{x})], & \dot{\hat{p}}(\mathbf{x}) &= \tfrac{i}{\hbar}[\hat{H}, \hat{p}(\mathbf{x})], \\
\dot{\hat{e}}(\mathbf{x}) &= \tfrac{i}{\hbar}[\hat{H}, \hat{e}(\mathbf{x})], & (\dot{\hat{f}}(\mathbf{x}, \mathbf{p}) &= \tfrac{i}{\hbar}[\hat{H}, \hat{f}(\mathbf{x}, \mathbf{p})]),
\end{aligned}
$$

to calculate their expectations with the statistical operator given by (3.9). This leads to wrong results as can be seen from the fact that the expectation values of the currents which can be associated, through a conservation equation, to these operators would vanish [19], due to time reversal invariance of microphysics, thus failing to describe any dissipative flow (e.g., heat conduction, viscosity, etc.). The idea of a time scale for the thermodynamic evolution and of a related subdynamics for the basic densities leads to a refinement of the aforementioned procedure: assume that $\tfrac{i}{\hbar}[\hat{H}, \cdot]$ can be replaced by a mapping $\mathcal{L}'$, initially defined on the linearly independent elements $\hat{a}_h^\dagger \hat{a}_k$, $\hat{a}_{h_1}^\dagger \hat{a}_{h_2}^\dagger \hat{a}_{k_2} \hat{a}_{k_1}$, giving the slow time evolution of the relevant variables. In this way not only the statistical operator $\hat{w}[\beta(t), \mu(t), \mathbf{v}(t)]$, but also the evolution operator is tuned to the relevant observables. Then one has the following set of closed evolution equations for the thermodynamic fields $\mathbf{v}(\mathbf{x}, t)$, $\beta(\mathbf{x}, t)$, $\mu(\mathbf{x}, t)$, $(\mu(\mathbf{x}, \mathbf{p}, t))$ related to the basic observables $\hat{A} = \hat{\rho}_m(\mathbf{x})$, $\hat{p}(\mathbf{x})$, $\hat{e}(\mathbf{x})$, $(\hat{f}(\mathbf{x}, \mathbf{p}))$:

$$
\frac{d}{dt} \operatorname{Tr}\left(\hat{A} \hat{w}[\beta(t), \mu(t), \mathbf{v}(t)] \right) = \operatorname{Tr}\left((\mathcal{L}' \hat{A}) \hat{w}[\beta(t), \mu(t), \mathbf{v}(t)] \right). \tag{3.10}
$$

The non-Hamiltonian form of the map $\mathcal{L}'$ eliminates the aforementioned difficulties with vanishing dissipative flows; preliminary investigations of the consequences of (3.10) in the case of a dilute gas indicate that it could be the right solution. The map $\mathcal{L}'$ that adequately replaces $\tfrac{i}{\hbar}[\hat{H}, \cdot]$ for the slow variables must generate an evolution of the relevant observables that preserves their positivity properties (e.g., $\hat{\rho}_m(\mathbf{x})$, $\hat{f}(\mathbf{x}, \mathbf{p})$) and also conservation of mass ($\hat{M} = \int d^3\mathbf{x}\, \hat{\rho}_m(\mathbf{x}) = \int d^3\mathbf{x} d^3\mathbf{p}\, \hat{f}(\mathbf{x}, \mathbf{p})$) and of energy ($\hat{E} = \int d^3\mathbf{x}\, \hat{e}(\mathbf{x})$). Then $\mathcal{L}' \hat{M} = 0$ and $\mathcal{L}' \hat{E} = 0$, while positivity with respect to observables constructed in terms of creation and annihilation operators could arise by a stronger property, reminding CP:

$$
\sum_{hk} \langle \psi_h | \mathcal{U}' \left(\hat{a}_h^\dagger \hat{a}_k \right) \psi_k \rangle > 0, \qquad \sum_{\substack{h_1 h_2 \\ k_1 k_2}} \langle \psi_{h_1 h_2} | \mathcal{U}' \left(\hat{a}_{h_1}^\dagger \hat{a}_{h_2}^\dagger \hat{a}_{k_2} \hat{a}_{k_1} \right) \psi_{k_1 k_2} \rangle > 0, \tag{3.11}
$$

for any choice of $\{\psi_h\}$ and $\{\psi_{h_1 h_2}\}$.

The time evolution of the typical expressions (3.6) can be studied by a procedure quite similar to that already shown in § 2, based on the representation (2.4) in terms of the "superoperator" $\mathcal{H}_0$, having $\hat{a}_h^\dagger \hat{a}_k$, $\hat{a}_{h_1}^\dagger \hat{a}_{h_2}^\dagger \hat{a}_{k_2} \hat{a}_{k_1}$ as eigenstates and of the superoperator $\mathcal{T}(z)$, which was called scattering map. If suitable smoothness properties of $\mathcal{T}(z)$ occur, essentially only the poles of $(z - \mathcal{H}_0')^{-1}$ contribute to the calculation of (2.4), so that the following asymptotic representation holds:

$$
\mathcal{U}'(t) \left(\hat{a}_h^\dagger \hat{a}_k \right) = \hat{a}_h^\dagger \hat{a}_k + t \mathcal{L}' \left(\hat{a}_h^\dagger \hat{a}_k \right), \qquad \tau_0 \ll t \ll \frac{\hbar}{|E_h - E_k|}; \tag{3.12}
$$

τ_0 is linked to smoothness properties of $\mathcal{T}(z)$ and can be interpreted as the typical duration of a collision between two particles interacting through the potential $V(|\mathbf{x} - \mathbf{y}|)$; τ_0 fixes a time scale that is assumed to be much smaller than the typical variation time τ_1 of our relevant observables. $\mathcal{L}'$ is a linear mapping defined initially on the linearly independent elements $\hat{a}_h^\dagger \hat{a}_k$, $\hat{a}_{h_1}^\dagger \hat{a}_{h_2}^\dagger \hat{a}_{k_2} \hat{a}_{k_1}$. For brevity we simply describe the structure of $\mathcal{L}'$, skipping the derivation. The formalism produces the typical structure of two-particle QM, with an N-body correction due to the Pauli principle. A two-particle scattering operator is defined by

$$\hat{\mathsf{T}}^{(2)}(z) = \hat{V}^{(2)} + \hat{V}^{(2)} \frac{1}{z - \hat{H}_L^{(2)}} \hat{V}_L^{(2)}, \qquad \hat{H}_L^{(2)} = \hat{H}_0^{(2)} + \hat{V}_L^{(2)}, \tag{3.13}$$

where these operators, labelled by the index (2), are defined in the Hilbert space $\mathcal{H}^{(2)}$ of two identical particles by matrix elements in the two-particle (symmetric or antisymmetric) basis $|l_2 l_1\rangle$; the matrix elements are:

$$\langle l_2 l_1 | \hat{H}_0^{(2)} | f_2 f_1 \rangle = (E_{f_1} + E_{f_2}) \frac{1}{2!} \left(\delta_{l_2 f_2} \delta_{l_1 f_1} \pm \delta_{l_2 f_1} \delta_{l_1 f_2} \right),$$

$$\langle l_2 l_1 | \hat{V}^{(2)} | f_2 f_1 \rangle = V_{l_1 l_2 f_2 f_1}, \tag{3.14}$$

$$\langle l_2 l_1 | \hat{V}_L^{(2)} | f_2 f_1 \rangle = (1 \pm \hat{n}_{l_1} \pm \hat{n}_{l_2}) V_{l_1 l_2 f_2 f_1}, \tag{3.15}$$

the coefficients $E_f, V_{l_1 l_2 f_2 f_1}$ are given in (3.2) and (3.3), the factor $(1 \pm \hat{n}_{l_1} \pm \hat{n}_{l_2})$ is given in a more indirect way: the "two-particle" QM expressed by the aforementioned operators provides c-number coefficients in Fock space operator expressions initially defined on the Fock space basis $| \ldots n_f \ldots \rangle$, n_f being the occupation numbers of the different field modes f: $n_f \in \mathbb{N}$ in the Bose case, $n_f = 0, 1$ in the Fermi case; therefore the factor $(1 \pm \hat{n}_{l_1} \pm \hat{n}_{l_2})$ depends on the Fock space basis elements on which the final Fock space operator is acting. Also the adjoint operator in the two-particle Hilbert space will be useful:

$$\hat{V}_R^{(2)} = \hat{V}_L^{(2)\dagger}, \quad \hat{H}_R^{(2)} = \hat{H}_L^{(2)\dagger}, \quad \left[\hat{\mathsf{T}}^{(2)}(z) \right]^\dagger = \hat{V}^{(2)} + \hat{V}_R^{(2)} \frac{1}{z^* - \hat{H}_R^{(2)}} \hat{V}^{(2)}. \tag{3.16}$$

The superoperator $\mathcal{L}'$ consists of an Hamiltonian part $\frac{i}{\hbar}[\hat{H}_{\text{eff}}, \cdot]$ and of a part, analogous to the one in (2.7), reminding the Lindblad structure (1.2). The formally self-adjoint Hamilton operator $\hat{H}_{\text{eff}}$ is initially defined on the Fock space basis $| \ldots n_f \ldots \rangle$ by the following expression:

$$\hat{H}_{\text{eff}} = \sum_f E_f \hat{a}_f^\dagger \hat{a}_f + \frac{1}{2} \sum_{\substack{l_1 l_2 \\ f_1 f_2}} \hat{a}_{l_1}^\dagger \hat{a}_{l_2}^\dagger V_{l_1 l_2 f_2 f_1}^{eff} \hat{a}_{f_2} \hat{a}_{f_1}, \tag{3.17}$$

$$V_{l_1 l_2 f_2 f_1}^{eff} = \langle l_2 l_1 | \frac{1}{2} \left(\hat{\mathsf{T}}^{(2)}(E_{f_1} + E_{f_2} + i\hbar\varepsilon) + \left[\hat{\mathsf{T}}^{(2)}(E_{l_1} + E_{l_2} + i\hbar\varepsilon) \right]^\dagger \right) | f_2 f_1 \rangle.$$

By comparison with (3.1) one can notice that introducing the time scale $\tau \gg \tau_0$ the coefficients $V_{l_1 l_2 f_2 f_1}$ related to the basic interaction between the field modes is replaced by $V_{l_1 l_2 f_2 f_1}^{eff}$, linked with a full, Pauli principle corrected description of the two body collisions in the medium, expressed in terms of the self-adjoint part of the operator $\hat{\mathsf{T}}^{(2)}(z)$. The anti-self-adjoint part $\frac{i}{2}(\hat{\mathsf{T}}^{(2)}(z) - \hat{\mathsf{T}}^{(2)}(z)^\dagger)$ is not zero if one goes beyond Born approximation and provides a contribution to $\mathcal{L}'$ analogous to the second term in the l.h.s. of (1.2), of the form $-\frac{1}{\hbar} \left(\left[\hat{\Gamma}^{(2)}, \hat{a}_h^\dagger \right] \hat{a}_k - \hat{a}_h^\dagger \left[\hat{\Gamma}^{(2)}, \hat{a}_k \right] \right)$, that due to sign "-"

cannot be rewritten as $\left[\hat{\Gamma}^{(2)}, \cdot \right]$; the operator $\hat{\Gamma}^{(2)}$ is defined on the Fock space basis by

$$\frac{1}{2} \sum_{\substack{f_1 f_2 \\ l_1 l_2}} \hat{a}_{l_1}^\dagger \hat{a}_{l_2}^\dagger \langle l_2 l_1 | \frac{i}{2} \left(\hat{\mathsf{T}}^{(2)}(E_{f_1} + E_{f_2} + i\hbar\varepsilon) - \left[\hat{\mathsf{T}}^{(2)}(E_{l_1} + E_{l_2} + i\hbar\varepsilon) \right]^\dagger \right) | f_2 f_1 \rangle \hat{a}_{f_2} \hat{a}_{f_1}.$$

At this point one immediately expects a third contribution to $\mathcal{L}'$ related to the product structure $\hat{a}_h^\dagger \hat{a}_k$ and involving both $\hat{\mathsf{T}}^{(2)}$ and $\hat{\mathsf{T}}^{(2)\dagger}$; this contribution is given by $\frac{1}{\hbar} \sum_\lambda \hat{R}_{h\lambda}^{(2)\dagger} \hat{R}_{k\lambda}^{(2)}$ and reminds the structure of the third term at the l.h.s. of the Lindblad expression (1.2), where it accounted for decoherence (or state reduction, or event production). The operators $\hat{R}_{k\lambda}^{(2)}$ are defined on the Fock space basis by:

$$\hat{R}_{k\lambda}^{(2)} = -i\sqrt{2\varepsilon(1 \pm \hat{n}_\lambda \pm \hat{n}_k)} \sum_{f_1 f_2} \frac{\langle k\lambda | \hat{\mathsf{T}}^{(2)}(E_{f_1} + E_{f_2} + i\hbar\varepsilon) | f_2 f_1 \rangle}{E_k + E_\lambda - E_{f_1} - E_{f_2} - i\hbar\varepsilon} \hat{a}_{f_2} \hat{a}_{f_1}.$$

The factor $\sqrt{2\varepsilon(1 \pm \hat{n}_\lambda \pm \hat{n}_k)}$ arises in the approximate factorisation of a Pauli correction term depending both on $\hat{n}_k$ and $\hat{n}_h$:

$$2\varepsilon \left(1 \pm \hat{n}_\lambda \pm \frac{1}{2}(\hat{n}_h + \hat{n}_k) \right) \approx \sqrt{2\varepsilon(1 \pm \hat{n}_\lambda \pm \hat{n}_h)} \sqrt{2\varepsilon(1 \pm \hat{n}_\lambda \pm \hat{n}_k)}, \tag{3.18}$$

this factorisation, which is a good approximation if the Pauli corrections are not very large, is a typical quantum condition, which together with $\tau_0 \ll \tau_1$ must be satisfied for the validity of the simple thermodynamic behaviour that we are considering in this section. The final structure of $\mathcal{L}'$ is formally the same as in (2.7)

$$\mathcal{L}' \hat{a}_h^\dagger \hat{a}_k = \frac{i}{\hbar} \left[\hat{H}_{\text{eff}}, \hat{a}_h^\dagger \hat{a}_k \right] - \frac{1}{\hbar} \left(\left[\hat{\Gamma}^{(2)}, \hat{a}_h^\dagger \right] \hat{a}_k - \hat{a}_h^\dagger \left[\hat{\Gamma}^{(2)}, \hat{a}_k \right] \right) + \frac{1}{\hbar} \sum_\lambda \hat{R}_{h\lambda}^{(2)\dagger} \hat{R}_{k\lambda}^{(2)}, \tag{3.19}$$

the main difference lying in the space in which these operators act, according to the two different physical situations. As a consequence of unitarity of $\mathcal{U}'$ one can prove that within the approximation leading to expression (3.19) one has:

$$\hat{\Gamma}^{(2)} \approx \frac{1}{4} \sum_{h\lambda} \hat{R}_{h\lambda}^{(2)\dagger} \hat{R}_{h\lambda}^{(2)}, \tag{3.20}$$

therefore one can replace the expression $\hat{\Gamma}^{(2)} \approx \frac{1}{4} \sum_{h\lambda} \hat{R}_{h\lambda}^{(2)\dagger} \hat{R}_{h\lambda}^{(2)}$ in (3.19): in this way the conservation relation $\mathcal{L}' \hat{M} = 0$ is exactly satisfied. It can be easily shown that $\sum_{hk} \langle \psi_h | ([1 + \tau \mathcal{L}'] \hat{a}_h^\dagger \hat{a}_k) \psi_k \rangle \geq 0$ to first order in τ, so that the positivity property (3.11) is satisfied.

As a preliminary check of the formalism let us report that the calculation of $\mathcal{L}'(\hat{a}_h^\dagger \hat{a}_k)$ yields the typical structure of the collision term of the Boltzmann equation with the Pauli principle corrections: $\frac{1}{\hbar} \hat{R}_{h\lambda}^{(2)\dagger} \hat{R}_{h\lambda}^{(2)}$ and $-\frac{1}{\hbar} \left[\hat{\Gamma}^{(2)}, \hat{a}_h^\dagger \right] \hat{a}_h + \text{c.c.}$ are respectively the "gain" and the "loss" part of the collision term; $\mathcal{L}'(\hat{a}_h^\dagger \hat{a}_k)$ yields also the streaming term of the Boltzmann equation. The study of $\mathcal{L}'(\hat{a}_{h_1}^\dagger \hat{a}_{h_2}^\dagger \hat{a}_{k_2} \hat{a}_{k_1})$ is not yet finished, it should end up with a full hydrodynamic and kinetic description of a one component continuum. The approximations leading to $\mathcal{L}'$ are based on the smoothness assumption related to the condition $\tau_0 \ll \tau_1$ and to a "one mode" approximation for the description of the dynamics in the time interval τ_0. A finite parameter $\varepsilon \simeq \hbar\tau_0$ appears in the formal expression of $\mathcal{L}'$; the final results do not appreciably depend on this by-product of the approximations if $\tau_0 \ll \tau_1$. In a sense the simple thermodynamic behaviour expressed by (3.10) arises by an approximation and this is indicated by the presence of

ε: an appreciable dependence of the results on ε indicates a failure of the smoothness assumption and of the related approximations. Let us stress finally that in this approach existence of closed evolution equations for the thermodynamic state variables avoids any factorisation assumption for the distribution functions and therefore goes far beyond the approach based on the truncation of a hierarchy.

4. DYNAMICS WITH MEMORY EFFECTS

According to § 3, when $\frac{i}{\hbar}[\hat{H}, \cdot]$ can be replaced by the map $\mathcal{L}'$ given by (3.19) the family of generalised Gibbs states $\hat{w}(t)$ replaces the family of statistical operators $\hat{\varrho}_t = \mathcal{U}(t - t_0)\hat{\varrho}_{t_0}$ (for simplicity we assume now time-translation invariance). This means that to determine the evolution of the thermodynamic state from a given time $\bar{t}$ onwards nothing else than β, μ, $\mathbf{v}$ at that time has to be taken into account: i.e. no bias comes by the previous history $\beta(\mathbf{x}, t')$, $\mu(\mathbf{x}, t')$, $\mathbf{v}(\mathbf{x}, t')$, $t' < \bar{t}$. This is no longer true if the condition $\tau_1 \gg \tau_0$ [see eq. (3.12)] is not satisfied. Let us assume that at an initial time T the statistical operator $\hat{\varrho}_T$ can be identified with the Gibbs state $\hat{w}(T)$ related to it:

$$\hat{\varrho}_T = \hat{w}(T). \tag{4.1}$$

By a straightforward calculation [18] one has:

$$\hat{\varrho}_t = e^{-\frac{i}{\hbar}\hat{H}(t-T)}\hat{\varrho}_T e^{\frac{i}{\hbar}\hat{H}(t-T)} = \frac{e^{-\langle\beta(T)\cdot\hat{e}^{(0)}[-(t-T)]\rangle + \langle[\mu(T)\beta(T)]\cdot\hat{\rho}_m[-(t-T)]\rangle}}{\operatorname{Tr} e^{-\langle\beta(T)\cdot\hat{e}^{(0)}[-(t-T)]\rangle + \langle[\mu(T)\beta(T)]\cdot\hat{\rho}_m[-(t-T)]\rangle}} \tag{4.2}$$

$$= \frac{e^{-\langle\beta(t)\cdot\hat{e}^{(0)}\rangle + \langle[\mu(t)\beta(t)]\cdot\hat{\rho}_m\rangle - \int_0^{t-T} d\tau \frac{d}{d\tau}\left(\langle\beta(t-\tau)\cdot\hat{e}^{(0)}(-\tau)\rangle - \langle[\mu(t-\tau)\beta(t-\tau)]\cdot\hat{\rho}_m(-\tau)\rangle\right)}}{\operatorname{Tr} e^{-\langle\beta(t)\cdot\hat{e}^{(0)}\rangle + \langle[\mu(t)\beta(t)]\cdot\hat{\rho}_m\rangle - \int_0^{t-T} d\tau \frac{d}{d\tau}\left(\langle\beta(t-\tau)\cdot\hat{e}^{(0)}(-\tau)\rangle - \langle[\mu(t-\tau)\beta(t-\tau)]\cdot\hat{\rho}_m(-\tau)\rangle\right)}},$$

where $\hat{A}(\tau) = e^{\frac{i}{\hbar}\hat{H}\tau}\hat{A}e^{-\frac{i}{\hbar}\hat{H}\tau}$ and $\langle\beta(t)\cdot\hat{A}\rangle = \int_\omega d^3\mathbf{x}\,\beta(t, \mathbf{x})\hat{A}(\mathbf{x})$. In the last term of the exponent the history of the thermodynamic state during the time interval $[T, t]$ appears; by $\dot{\hat{\rho}}_m = -\operatorname{div}\hat{\mathbf{J}}_m^{(0)}$, $\dot{\hat{e}} = -\operatorname{div}\hat{\mathbf{J}}_l^{(0)}$ it can be rewritten in the more perspicuous form:

$$-\int_0^{t-T} d\tau \frac{d}{d\tau}\left(\langle\beta(t-\tau)\cdot\hat{e}^{(0)}(-\tau)\rangle - \langle[\mu(t-\tau)\beta(t-\tau)]\cdot\hat{\rho}_m(-\tau)\rangle\right) \tag{4.3}$$

$$= \int_T^t d\tau'\left[\langle\frac{d}{d\tau'}\beta(\tau')\cdot\hat{e}^{(0)}(\tau'-t)\rangle - \langle\frac{d}{d\tau'}[\beta(\tau')\mu(\tau')]\cdot\hat{\rho}_m^{(0)}(\tau'-t)\rangle\right.$$

$$\left. - \langle\operatorname{grad}\beta(\tau')\cdot\hat{\mathbf{J}}_l^{(0)}(\tau'-t)\rangle + \langle\operatorname{grad}(\beta(\tau')\mu(\tau'))\cdot\hat{\mathbf{J}}_m^{(0)}(\tau'-t)\rangle\right]$$

$$+ \int_T^{t_0} d\tau' \int_{\partial\omega} d\sigma\,\mathbf{n}\cdot\left(\langle\beta(\tau', \mathbf{x})\hat{\mathbf{J}}_l^{(0)}(\mathbf{x}, \tau'-t)\rangle - \langle\beta(\tau', \mathbf{x})\mu(\tau', \mathbf{x})\hat{\mathbf{J}}_m^{(0)}(\mathbf{x}, \tau'-t)\rangle\right),$$

where time and space derivatives of the thermodynamic fields appear on the same footing; by the last term also matter and energy exchanges with the environment during the preparation time $[T, t_o]$ can be described. Taking expression (4.2) for $\hat{\varrho}_t$ to calculate the basic expectation values and thus determining the thermodynamic state variables for $t > t_0$ as in (3.10), one has for them closed evolution equations having as input $\beta(\mathbf{x}, \tau')$, $\mu(\mathbf{x}, \tau')$, $\mathbf{v}(\mathbf{x}, \tau')$, $\tau' \in [T, t_0]$. Such equations are generally used and work under the hypothesis that memory decays within a typical correlation time. This also helps to attenuate the problem of the initial choice (4.1). We mention in passing that no problem about condition (4.1) exists if one assumes the point of view of "informational thermodynamics": then $\hat{\varrho}_T = \hat{w}(T)$ is just dictated by the measured values of the relevant variables at time T; however this approach does not explain why the previous history of a concrete collection of macrosystems is irrelevant just before T. Let us also mention the solution given by Zubarev: T is shifted to $-\infty$, thus taking off any previous history; however this limit is highly critical and since also a thermodynamic limit is involved, it shifts the problem of thermodynamic evolution to a cosmological one. In our framework a time scale is associated to the system and the generator $\mathcal{L}'$ should have a non-Hamiltonian part. This provides a mechanism by which memory can decay. Let us assume that the preparation time $t_o - T$ is larger than the decay time of the memory: at this point the history that comes before T is irrelevant for the dynamics that $\mathcal{L}'$ is able to describe. Then the choice (4.1), that is not biased by this history, is adequate. When $\mathcal{L}' = \frac{i}{\hbar}[\hat{H},\cdot] + \tilde{\mathcal{L}}'$, calling $\hat{\varrho}([\beta,\mu,\mathbf{v}],t,T)$ the operator on the l.h.s. of (4.2) one has:

$$\mathrm{Tr}\left(\hat{A}\mathcal{U}(t,T)\hat{\varrho}_T\right) = \mathrm{Tr}\left[\left(Te^{\int_T^t d\tau\,\tilde{\mathcal{L}}'(\tau)}\hat{A}\right)\hat{\varrho}([\beta,\mu,\mathbf{v}],t,T)\right],$$

$$\tilde{\mathcal{L}}'(\tau) = e^{\mathcal{L}_0'(T-\tau)}\tilde{\mathcal{L}}'e^{-\mathcal{L}_0'(T-\tau)}, \qquad \mathcal{L}_0' = \frac{i}{\hbar}[\hat{H},\cdot].$$

REFERENCES

[1] G. C. Ghirardi, P. Pearle and A. Rimini, *Phys. Rev. A* **42**, 78 (1990).

[2] G. Ludwig, *Foundations of Quantum Mechanics* (1983, Springer, Berlin).

[3] E. B. Davies, *Quantum Theory of Open Systems* (1976, Academic Press, London).

[4] G. Lindblad, *Commun. Math. Phys.* **48**, 119 (1976).

[5] E. B. Davies, *Commun. Math. Phys.* **15** (1969) 277; **19** (1970) 83; **22** (1971) 51. A. Barchielli, L. Lanz, G. M. Prosperi, *Nuovo Cimento* **72B** (1982) 79; *Found. Phys.* **13** (1983) 779; *Proceedings of the International Symposium: Foundations of Quantum Mechanics in the Light of New Technology* (Tokyo, 1983), p.165; A. Barchielli, G. Lupieri, *J. Math. Phys.* **26** (1985) 2222; A. S. Holevo, in *Lect. Notes in Mathematics* (1988, Springer, Berlin), vol. 1303, p.128; *Lect. Notes in Mathematics* (1989, Springer, Berlin), vol. 1396, p.229; L. Lanz and O. Melsheimer, in *Quantum Mechanics and Trajectories – Symposium On the Foundations of Modern Physics*, edited by P. Busch, P.J. Lahti and P. Mittelstaedt (World Scientific, 1993) p.233-241; V. P. Belavkin, in A. Blaquière (ed.), *Modelling and Control of Systems*, Lect. Notes in Control and Information Sciences, (1988, Springer, Berlin), vol. 121, p.245; V. P. Belavkin, *Phys. Lett.* **140A** (1989) 355; V. P. Belavkin and P. Staszewski, *Phys. Lett.* **140A** (1989) 359.

[6] L. Lanz, *Int. J. Theor. Phys.* **33**, 19 (1994).

[7] L. Lanz and O. Melsheimer, *Nuovo Cimento* **108B**, 511 (1993).

[8] L. Lanz and B. Vacchini, *Int. J. Theor. Phys.* **36**, 67 (1997).

[9] H. Rauch, in *Advances in Quantum Phenomena*, edited by E. G. Beltrametti and J.-M. Lévy-Leblond, NATO ASI series, Vol. B347, (Plenum Press, New York, 1995) p.113.

[10] V. F. Sears, *Neutron Optics* (Oxford University Press, Oxford, 1989).

[11] C. S. Adams, M. Siegel, J. Mlynek, *Phys. Rep.* **240**, 143 (1994).

[12] J. Vigué, *Phys. Rev. A* **52**, 3973 (1995).

[13] M. D. Srinivas and E. B. Davies, *Optica Acta* **28**, 981 (1981).

[14] L. Diósi, *Europhys. Lett.* **30**, 63 (1995).

[15] L. Lanz, O. Melsheimer and E. Wacker, *Physica* **131A**, 520 (1985).

[16] A. S. Holevo, *Probabilistic and Statistical Aspects of Quantum Theory* (1982, North Holland, Amsterdam).

[17] V. G. Morozov and G. Roepke, *Physica* **221A**, 511 (1995).

[18] W. A. Robin, *J. Phys. A* **23**, 2065 (1990).

[19] D. N. Zubarev, *Non-equilibrium Statistical Thermodynamics,* (Consultant Bureau, New York, 1974).

TIME-ORDERED WICK EXPONENTIAL AND QUANTUM STOCHASTIC DIFFERENTIAL EQUATIONS

Nobuaki Obata

Graduate School of Polymathematics
Nagoya University
Nagoya 464-01, Japan

1. INTRODUCTION

Let $H = L^2(\mathbb{R}, dt)$ be the real Hilbert space of L^2-functions on $\mathbb{R}$ and let $\Gamma(H_{\mathbb{C}})$ be the Boson Fock space over $H_{\mathbb{C}}$, the complexification of H. Let $\mathcal{H}$ be another complex Hilbert space. Given a one-parameter family of operators $\{L_t\}$ acting in $\Gamma(H_{\mathbb{C}}) \otimes \mathcal{H}$, we consider the initial value problem of the form:

$$\frac{d\Xi_t}{dt} = L_t \diamond \Xi_t, \qquad \Xi|_{t=0} = \Xi_0, \tag{1}$$

where $\diamond$ is the Wick product. The main purpose of this paper is to prove the unique existence of a solution to equation (1) in the sense of distributions. The main statement will be found in §5.

In some applications $\Gamma(H_{\mathbb{C}})$ and $\mathcal{H}$ are considered as a noise space and a system space, respectively. The annihilation operator a_t and the creation operator a_t^*, t running over $\mathbb{R}$, are fundamental in the Fock space $\Gamma(H_{\mathbb{C}})$ and, in particular, are considered as "primary" noise in quantum statistics (sometimes referred to as quantum white noise). However, they are not proper operators whenever only the Hilbert space $\Gamma(H_{\mathbb{C}})$ is taken into account. To overcome this difficulty we adopt in this paper the white noise distribution theory (WNDT for short; see e.g., [9] for recent development) and the general theory of operators on white noise functions established in [11, 12]. Our approach includes quantum stochastic differential equations discussed by Hudson and Parthasarathy [6] and their generalizations.

This paper is intended for a continuation of [16, 17]. There are another topics concerning "white noise approach" to quantum stochastic analysis: see [5] for quantum Itô formula; [13,15] for quantum stochastic processes and integrals; and [14] for quantum martingales.

General Notation: For a real vector space $\mathfrak{X}$ the complexification is denoted by $\mathfrak{X}_{\mathbb{C}}$. For two locally convex spaces $\mathfrak{X}$, $\mathfrak{Y}$ let $\mathcal{L}(\mathfrak{X}, \mathfrak{Y})$ denote the space of continuous linear operators from $\mathfrak{X}$ into $\mathfrak{Y}$. Unless otherwise stated, $\mathcal{L}(\mathfrak{X}, \mathfrak{Y})$ is endowed with the topology of bounded convergence. For simplicity we also write $\mathcal{L}(\mathfrak{X}) = \mathcal{L}(\mathfrak{X}, \mathfrak{X})$.

Quantum Communication, Computing, and Measurement
Edited by Hirota *et al.*, Plenum Press, New York, 1997

2. WNDT AND QUANTUM WHITE NOISE

Let $\mathcal{S}(\mathbb{R})$ be the space of $\mathbb{R}$-valued rapidly decreasing functions on the real line $\mathbb{R}$ and $\mathcal{S}'(\mathbb{R})$ its dual space, i.e., the space of tempered distributions. Then we come to a real Gelfand triple:

$$E = \mathcal{S}(\mathbb{R}) \subset H = L^2(\mathbb{R}, dt) \subset E^* = \mathcal{S}'(\mathbb{R}).$$

The real inner product of H and the canonical bilinear form on $E^* \times E$ are compatible and denoted by the same symbol $\langle \cdot, \cdot \rangle$. Let μ be the standard Gaussian measure on E^* and $L^2(E^*, \mu)$ the Hilbert space of $\mathbb{C}$-valued L^2-functions on E^*. There is a unitary isomorphism between $L^2(E^*, \mu)$ and the Boson Fock space $\Gamma(H_{\mathbb{C}})$ determined uniquely by the correspondence

$$\phi_\xi(x) = e^{\langle x, \xi \rangle - \langle \xi, \xi \rangle / 2} \quad \longleftrightarrow \quad \left(1, \xi, \frac{\xi^{\otimes 2}}{2!}, \cdots, \frac{\xi^{\otimes n}}{n!}, \cdots \right), \qquad \xi \in E_{\mathbb{C}}.$$

This is the celebrated *Wiener–Itô–Segal isomorphism*. If $\phi \in L^2(E^*, \mu)$ and $(f_n)_{n=0}^{\infty} \in \Gamma(H_{\mathbb{C}})$ are related in this manner, we write $\phi \sim (f_n)$ for simplicity. It is then noted that

$$\| \phi \|_0^2 = \sum_{n=0}^{\infty} n! \, | f_n |_0^2, \qquad \phi \sim (f_n), \tag{2}$$

where $\| \phi \|_0$ is the L^2-norm of $\phi \in L^2(E^*, \mu)$.

Extending identity (2), we introduce a family of norms with indices $-1 < \beta < 1$ and $p \in \mathbb{R}$ by setting

$$\| \phi \|_{p,\beta}^2 = \sum_{n=0}^{\infty} (n!)^{1+\beta} \, | f_n |_p^2, \qquad \phi \sim (f_n),$$

where $| f_n |_p = | (A^{\otimes n})^p f_n |_0$, $A = 1 + t^2 - d^2/dt^2$. Suppose $p \geq 0$ and $0 \leq \beta < 1$. Then $(E_p)_\beta = \{ \phi ; \| \phi \|_{p,\beta} < \infty \}$ becomes a Hilbert space and

$$(E)_\beta = \operatorname*{proj\,lim}_{p \to \infty} (E_p)_\beta \left(= \bigcap_{p \geq 0} (E_p)_\beta \text{ as vector spaces} \right)$$

becomes a countable Hilbert nuclear space. On the other hand, $\| \cdot \|_{-p,-\beta}$ is a Hilbertian norm on $L^2(E^*, \mu)$ and we denote by $(E_{-p})_{-\beta}$ the completion. It then holds that

$$(E)_\beta^* \cong \operatorname*{ind\,lim}_{p \to \infty} (E_{-p})_{-\beta} \left(= \bigcup_{p \geq 0} (E_{-p})_{-\beta} \text{ as vector spaces} \right).$$

For each $0 \leq \beta < 1$ we thus obtain a Gelfand triple:

$$(E)_\beta \subset L^2(E^*, \mu) \cong \Gamma(L^2(\mathbb{R})) \subset (E)_\beta^*, \qquad 0 \leq \beta < 1, \tag{3}$$

which is called the *Kondratiev–Streit space*, see [9]. The canonical bilinear form on $(E)_\beta^* \times (E)_\beta$ will be denoted by $\langle\!\langle \cdot, \cdot \rangle\!\rangle$. Then we have

$$\langle\!\langle \Phi, \phi \rangle\!\rangle = \sum_{n=0}^{\infty} n! \, \langle F_n, f_n \rangle, \qquad \Phi \sim (F_n) \in (E)_\beta^*, \quad \phi \sim (f_n) \in (E)_\beta,$$

where $\langle \cdot, \cdot \rangle$ is the canonical $\mathbb{C}$-bilinear form on $(E_{\mathbb{C}}^{\otimes n})^* \times E_{\mathbb{C}}^{\otimes n}$. The case of $\beta = 0$ in (3) is called the *Hida–Kubo–Takenaka space* [8] and denoted by $(E) \subset L^2(E^*, \mu) \subset (E)^*$.

With each t we associate an operator $a_t \in \mathcal{L}((E)_\beta, (E)_\beta)$ uniquely determined by $a_t \phi_\xi = \xi(t)\phi_\xi$, $\xi \in E_\mathbb{C}$. This is called the *annihilation operator at a point $t \in \mathbb{R}$*. Its adjoint $a_t^* \in \mathcal{L}((E)_\beta^*, (E)_\beta^*)$ is called the *creation operator at a point t*. These are *not* operator-valued distributions but continuous operators for themselves. Moreover, the map $t \mapsto a_t \in \mathcal{L}((E)_\beta, (E)_\beta)$ is infinitely differentiable; hence so is $t \mapsto a_t^* \in \mathcal{L}((E)_\beta^*, (E)_\beta^*)$. Since the natural inclusions

$$\mathcal{L}((E)_\beta, (E)_\beta) \subset \mathcal{L}((E)_\beta, (E)_\beta^*), \qquad \mathcal{L}((E)_\beta^*, (E)_\beta^*) \subset \mathcal{L}((E)_\beta, (E)_\beta^*)$$

are continuous, $t \mapsto W_t = a_t + a_t^* \in \mathcal{L}((E)_\beta, (E)_\beta^*)$ is also infinitely differentiable. It is known that $\{W_t\}$ is nothing but the one-parameter family of multiplication operators by the classical white noise process which lives in $(E)_\beta^*$, see e.g., [11, §4.1]. The pair $\{(a_t, a_t^*)\}$ or $\{W_t\}$ is called the *quantum white noise*.

3. QUANTUM STOCHASTIC PROCESSES

Let $\mathcal{H}$ be another Hilbert space which is sometimes referred to as a *system Hilbert space* and we need $\mathcal{H}$-valued white noise functions. Namely, we consider

$$(E)_\beta \otimes \mathcal{H} \subset L^2(E^*, \mu) \otimes \mathcal{H} \subset ((E)_\beta \otimes \mathcal{H})^* \cong (E)_\beta^* \otimes \mathcal{H},$$

where $\mathcal{H}$ and $\mathcal{H}^*$ are identified. Note that

$$\mathcal{L}((E)_\beta \otimes \mathcal{H}, (E)_\beta^* \otimes \mathcal{H}) \cong \mathcal{L}((E)_\beta \otimes (E)_\beta, \mathcal{L}(\mathcal{H})) \qquad \text{as vector spaces.}$$

Moreover, for a sequence the convergences in $\mathcal{L}((E)_\beta \otimes \mathcal{H}, (E)_\beta^* \otimes \mathcal{H})$ and in $\mathcal{L}((E)_\beta \otimes (E)_\beta, \mathcal{L}(\mathcal{H}))$ are equivalent. On the other hand, we have the topological isomorphisms:

$$\mathcal{L}((E)_\beta \otimes (E)_\beta, \mathcal{L}(\mathcal{H})) \cong ((E)_\beta \otimes (E)_\beta)^* \otimes \mathcal{L}(\mathcal{H})$$
$$\cong (((E)_\beta \otimes (E)_\beta) \otimes_\pi (\mathcal{H} \otimes_\pi \mathcal{H}))^*,$$

which follow from well-known properties of the π-tensor product and the kernel theorem.

A one-parameter family of operators $\{\Xi_t\}_{t \in T} \subset \mathcal{L}((E)_\beta \otimes \mathcal{H}, (E)_\beta^* \otimes \mathcal{H})$ is called a *quantum stochastic process* if $t \mapsto \Xi_t$ is continuous, where t runs over an interval $T \subset \mathbb{R}$. By definition $\{a_t\}$, $\{a_t^*\}$ and $\{W_t\}$ are quantum stochastic processes. If $\{\Xi_t\} \subset \mathcal{L}((E)_\beta, (E)_\beta^*)$ is a quantum stochastic process, so is the amplification $\{\Xi_t \otimes I\}$. We often write Ξ_t for $\Xi_t \otimes I$ for brevity.

If $\{L_t\} \subset \mathcal{L}((E)_\beta \otimes \mathcal{H}, (E)_\beta^* \otimes \mathcal{H})$ is a quantum stochastic process, so is the integral

$$\Xi_t = \int_0^t L_s \, ds,$$

where the integral is defined through the canonical bilinear form. In that case it holds that

$$\frac{d}{dt}\Xi_t = L_t \qquad \text{in} \quad \mathcal{L}((E)_\beta \otimes \mathcal{H}, (E)_\beta^* \otimes \mathcal{H}).$$

Moreover, it is known [16] that $\{L_t a_t\}$ and $\{a_t^* L_t\}$ are again quantum stochastic processes, hence so are

$$\int_0^t a_s^* L_s \, ds, \qquad \int_0^t L_s^* a_s \, ds.$$

These are called quantum stochastic integrals against the creation and the annihilation processes, respectively. In particular,

$$A_t = \int_0^t a_s \, ds, \qquad A_t^* = \int_0^t a_s^* \, ds, \qquad \Lambda_t = \int_0^t a_s^* a_s \, ds, \tag{4}$$

are respectively the *annihilation process*, the *creation process* and the *number process* of Hudson–Parthasarathy [6]. Contrary to their theory we consider the number process as being not independent of $\{A_t\}$ and $\{A_t^*\}$. In fact, we proved in [13] that any quantum stochastic process in $\mathcal{L}((E), (E)^*)$ can be decomposed into a sum of "generalized" quantum stochastic integrals against the annihilation process, against the creation process and against the time. We are thus convinced that $\{a_t\}$ and $\{a_t^*\}$ are the "primary" quantum noises. The situation for a quantum stochastic process in $\mathcal{L}((E)_\beta \otimes \mathcal{H}, (E)_\beta^* \otimes \mathcal{H})$ is expected to be similar.

4. OPERATOR SYMBOL AND WICK PRODUCT

For $\Xi \in \mathcal{L}((E)_\beta \otimes \mathcal{H}, (E)_\beta^* \otimes \mathcal{H})$ an $\mathcal{L}(\mathcal{H})$-valued function $\widehat{\Xi}$ on $E_{\mathbb{C}} \times E_{\mathbb{C}}$ defined by

$$\langle \widehat{\Xi}(\xi, \eta) u, v \rangle = \langle\!\langle \Xi(\phi_\xi \otimes u), \phi_\eta \otimes v \rangle\!\rangle, \qquad \xi, \eta \in E_{\mathbb{C}}, \quad u, v \in \mathcal{H},$$

is called the *symbol* of Ξ. The symbol determines an operator $\Xi \in \mathcal{L}((E)_\beta \otimes \mathcal{H}, (E)_\beta^* \otimes \mathcal{H})$ uniquely. The above definition is due to [3,7], see also [11,12] for a detailed study in terms of WNDT.

The following two theorems are fundamental and are proved by modifying similar results for $\beta = 0$ obtained in [11,12,16].

Theorem 4.1: *An $\mathcal{L}(\mathcal{H})$-valued function Θ defined on $E_{\mathbb{C}} \times E_{\mathbb{C}}$ is the symbol of an operator $\mathcal{L}((E)_\beta \otimes \mathcal{H}, (E)_\beta^* \otimes \mathcal{H})$ if and only if*

(i) for any $\xi, \xi_1, \eta, \eta_1 \in E_{\mathbb{C}}$ and $u, v \in \mathcal{H}$ the function

$$(z, w) \mapsto \langle \Theta(z\xi + \xi_1, w\eta + \eta_1) u, v \rangle$$

is entire holomorphic on $\mathbb{C} \times \mathbb{C}$;

(ii) there exist constant numbers $C \geq 0$, $K \geq 0$ and $p \geq 0$ such that

$$\| \Theta(\xi, \eta) \|_{OP} \leq C \exp K \left(|\xi|_p^{\frac{2}{1-\beta}} + |\eta|_p^{\frac{2}{1-\beta}} \right), \qquad \xi, \eta \in E_{\mathbb{C}}.$$

Theorem 4.2: *Let $\{\Xi_n\}$ be a sequence of operators in $\mathcal{L}((E)_\beta \otimes \mathcal{H}, (E)_\beta^* \otimes \mathcal{H})$. Then $\{\Xi_n\}$ converges to 0 in $\mathcal{L}((E)_\beta \otimes \mathcal{H}, (E)_\beta^* \otimes \mathcal{H})$ or equivalently in $\mathcal{L}((E)_\beta \otimes (E)_\beta, \mathcal{L}(\mathcal{H}))$ if and only if there exist a sequence $\{\epsilon_n\}$ of positive numbers converging to 0, constant numbers $K \geq 0$ and $p \geq 0$ such that*

$$\| \widehat{\Xi}_n(\xi, \eta) \|_{OP} \leq \epsilon_n \exp K \left(|\xi|_p^{\frac{2}{1-\beta}} + |\eta|_p^{\frac{2}{1-\beta}} \right), \qquad \xi, \eta \in E_{\mathbb{C}}, \quad n = 1, 2, \cdots.$$

We now introduce the Wick product in $\mathcal{L}((E)_\beta, (E)_\beta^*)$. It follows from Theorem 4.1 that for two operators $\Xi_1, \Xi_2 \in \mathcal{L}((E)_\beta, (E)_\beta^*)$ there exists a unique operator in $\mathcal{L}((E)_\beta, (E)_\beta^*)$, denoted by $\Xi_1 \diamond \Xi_2$ and called the *Wick product*, such that

$$(\Xi_1 \diamond \Xi_2)\widehat{}(\xi, \eta) = e^{-\langle \xi, \eta \rangle} \widehat{\Xi}_1(\xi, \eta) \widehat{\Xi}_2(\xi, \eta), \qquad \xi, \eta \in E_{\mathbb{C}}. \tag{5}$$

Here are some algebraic properties:

$$I \diamond \Xi = \Xi \diamond I = \Xi, \quad (\Xi_1 \diamond \Xi_2) \diamond \Xi_3 = \Xi_1 \diamond (\Xi_2 \diamond \Xi_3), \quad (\Xi_1 \diamond \Xi_2)^* = \Xi_2^* \diamond \Xi_1^*. \tag{6}$$

Moreover, we note that

$$\Xi_1 \diamond \Xi_2 = \Xi_2 \diamond \Xi_1.$$

Namely, equipped with the Wick product, $\mathcal{L}((E)_\beta, (E)_\beta^*)$ becomes a commutative algebra. As for the annihilation and creation operators we have

$$a_s \diamond a_t = a_s a_t, \qquad a_s^* \diamond a_t = a_s^* a_t, \qquad a_s \diamond a_t^* = a_t^* a_s, \qquad a_s^* \diamond a_t^* = a_s^* a_t^*. \qquad (7)$$

More generally, it holds that

$$a_{s_1}^* \cdots a_{s_l}^* \Xi a_{t_1} \cdots a_{t_m} = \Xi \diamond (a_{s_1}^* \cdots a_{s_l}^* a_{t_1} \cdots a_{t_m}), \qquad \Xi \in \mathcal{L}((E)_\beta, (E)_\beta^*).$$

It is known [17] that the Wick product is a unique bilinear map from $\mathcal{L}((E)_\beta, (E)_\beta^*) \times \mathcal{L}((E)_\beta, (E)_\beta^*)$ into $\mathcal{L}((E)_\beta, (E)_\beta^*)$ which is (i) separately continuous; (ii) associative; and (iii) satisfies (7).

For $\Xi_1, \Xi_2 \in \mathcal{L}((E)_\beta \otimes \mathcal{H}, (E)_\beta^* \otimes \mathcal{H})$, again the Wick product $\Xi_1 \diamond \Xi_2$ is defined by (5) though $\hat{\Xi}_1(\xi, \eta) \hat{\Xi}_2(\xi, \eta)$ in the right hand side is the usual product (composition) of two operators in $\mathcal{L}(\mathcal{H})$. The algebraic properties in (6) are again valid; however, contrary to the case of $\mathcal{H} = \mathbb{C}$ the Wick product in the vector-valued case is not commutative. In fact, by definition we have

$$(\Xi_1 \otimes L_1) \diamond (\Xi_2 \otimes L_2) = (\Xi_1 \diamond \Xi_2) \otimes (L_1 L_2), \qquad \Xi_i \in \mathcal{L}((E)_\beta, (E)_\beta^*), \; L_i \in \mathcal{L}(\mathcal{H}).$$

5. MAIN THEOREM

We need a notation. Any operator $\Xi \in \mathcal{L}((E)_\beta \otimes \mathcal{H}, (E)_\beta^* \otimes \mathcal{H})$ admits an infinite series expansion in terms of integral kernel operators:

$$\Xi = \sum_{l,m=0}^{\infty} \Xi_{l,m}(\kappa_{l,m}), \qquad \kappa \in (E_{\mathbb{C}}^{\otimes(l+m)})^* \otimes \mathcal{L}(\mathcal{H}), \qquad (8)$$

where the series converges in $\mathcal{L}((E)_\beta \otimes \mathcal{H}, (E)_\beta^* \otimes \mathcal{H})$. Recall that an integral kernel operator has a formal integral expression:

$$\Xi_{l,m}(\kappa_{l,m}) = \int_{\mathbb{R}^{l+m}} \kappa_{l,m}(s_1, \cdots, s_l, t_1, \cdots, t_m) a_{s_1}^* \cdots a_{s_l}^* a_{t_1} \cdots a_{t_m} \, ds_1 \cdots ds_l dt_1 \cdots dt_m.$$

If an operator $\Xi \in \mathcal{L}((E)_\beta \otimes \mathcal{H}, (E)_\beta^* \otimes \mathcal{H})$ is expressed as in (8), we put

$$\deg \Xi = \sup \{l + m \,;\, \kappa_{l,m} \neq 0\} \leq \infty.$$

If $\Xi \in \mathcal{L}((E)_\beta \otimes \mathcal{H}, (E)_\beta^* \otimes \mathcal{H})$ has a finite degree $\deg \Xi < \infty$, i.e., if Ξ is a finite sum of integral kernel operators, then $\Xi \in \mathcal{L}((E) \otimes \mathcal{H}, (E)^* \otimes \mathcal{H})$. Namely, for an operator of finite degree β is superfluous.

Theorem 5.1: *Let $\{L_t\}$ be a quantum stochastic process, where t runs over an interval $T \subset \mathbb{R}$. Assume (i) there exists $0 \leq \beta < 1$ such that $\deg L_t \leq 2/(1 - \beta)$; (ii) there exist $K_1 \geq 0$ and $p \geq 0$ such that*

$$|\kappa_{l,m}(t)|_{-p} \leq K_1, \qquad t \in T, \quad l, m = 0, 1, 2, \cdots. \qquad (9)$$

Then the initial value problem

$$\frac{d\Xi_t}{dt} = L_t \diamond \Xi_t, \qquad \Xi|_{t=0} = \Xi_0 \in \mathcal{L}((E) \otimes \mathcal{H}, (E)^* \otimes \mathcal{H}), \qquad (10)$$

has a unique solution in $\mathcal{L}((E)_\beta \otimes \mathcal{H}, (E)_\beta^* \otimes \mathcal{H})$.

Proof. If Ω_t is a solution of (10) with $\Omega_0 = I$, then $\Xi_t = \Omega_t \diamond \Xi_0$ is a solution to the original equation. Thus it is sufficient to prove the assertion with the initial condition $\Xi_0 = I$. We put

$$Y_n = Y_n(t) = \int_0^t dt_1 \int_0^{t_1} dt_2 \cdots \int_0^{t_{n-1}} dt_n \, L_{t_1} \diamond L_{t_2} \diamond \cdots \diamond L_{t_n}.$$

Then by the definition of Wick product we obtain

$$\widehat{Y}_n(\xi, \eta) = e^{\langle \xi, \eta \rangle} \int_0^t dt_1 \int_0^{t_1} dt_2 \cdots$$
$$\cdots \int_0^{t_{n-1}} dt_n \, e^{-\langle \xi, \eta \rangle} \widehat{L}_{t_1}(\xi, \eta) e^{-\langle \xi, \eta \rangle} \widehat{L}_{t_2}(\xi, \eta) \cdots e^{-\langle \xi, \eta \rangle} \widehat{L}_{t_n}(\xi, \eta).$$

On the other hand, in view of

$$L_t = \sum_{l+m \leq d} \Xi_{l,m}(\kappa_{l,m}(t)), \qquad \deg L_t \leq d < \infty,$$

we have

$$\widehat{L}_t(\xi, \eta) = e^{\langle \xi, \eta \rangle} \sum_{l+m \leq d} \left\langle \kappa_{l,m}(t), \eta^{\otimes l} \otimes \xi^{\otimes m} \right\rangle.$$

Hence by assumption

$$\left\| e^{-\langle \xi, \eta \rangle} \widehat{L}_t(\xi, \eta) \right\|_{OP} \leq \sum_{l+m \leq d} \left\| \left\langle \kappa_{l,m}(t), \eta^{\otimes l} \otimes \xi^{\otimes m} \right\rangle \right\|_{OP}$$
$$\leq C_1 + K_2 \left(|\xi|_p^{\frac{2}{1-\beta}} + |\eta|_p^{\frac{2}{1-\beta}} \right), \qquad t \in T, \quad \xi, \eta \in E_{\mathbb{C}},$$

for some $C_1 \geq 0$ and $K_2 \geq 0$. Thus

$$\left\| \widehat{Y}_n(\xi, \eta) \right\|_{OP} \leq \left| e^{\langle \xi, \eta \rangle} \right| \frac{t^n}{n!} \left\{ C_1 + K_2 \left(|\xi|_p^{\frac{2}{1-\beta}} + |\eta|_p^{\frac{2}{1-\beta}} \right) \right\}^n,$$

and

$$\sum_{n=0}^{\infty} \left\| \widehat{Y}_n(\xi, \eta) \right\|_{OP} \leq \left| e^{\langle \xi, \eta \rangle} \right| \exp t \left\{ C_1 + K_2 \left(|\xi|_p^{\frac{2}{1-\beta}} + |\eta|_p^{\frac{2}{1-\beta}} \right) \right\}$$
$$\leq C \exp K \left(|\xi|_p^{\frac{2}{1-\beta}} + |\eta|_p^{\frac{2}{1-\beta}} \right)$$

for some $C \geq 0$ and $K \geq 0$. Then, applying Theorem 4.2, we see that $\Xi_t \equiv \sum_{n=0}^{\infty} Y_n$ converges in $\mathcal{L}((E)_\beta \otimes \mathcal{H}, (E)_\beta^* \otimes \mathcal{H})$. It is easily shown that Ξ_t is a solution of (10). The uniqueness is almost clear. QED

Remark: It follows from [13] that condition (9) follows from the continuity of $t \mapsto L_t$ if $\dim \mathcal{H} < \infty$ and if T is a compact interval. (For the existence of a solution we may assume without loss of generality T to be compact.) However, it is not known whether or not condition (9) is superfluous for a general $\mathcal{H}$.

The infinite series

$$\Xi_t = I + \sum_{n=1}^{\infty} \int_0^t dt_1 \int_0^{t_1} dt_2 \cdots \int_0^{t_{n-1}} dt_n \, L_{t_1} \diamond L_{t_2} \diamond \cdots \diamond L_{t_n}, \tag{11}$$

which gives the solution to (10), is called the *time-ordered Wick exponential.* A particular case where

$$\Omega_t \diamond L_t = L_t \diamond \Omega_t, \qquad \Omega_t = \int_0^t L_s ds, \tag{12}$$

is discussed in [16]. In that case, since

$$\int_0^t dt_1 \int_0^{t_1} dt_2 \cdots \int_0^{t_{n-1}} dt_n \, L_{t_1} \diamond L_{t_2} \diamond \cdots \diamond L_{t_n} = \frac{1}{n!} \underbrace{\Omega_t \diamond \cdots \diamond \Omega_t}_{n \text{ times}} = \frac{1}{n!} \Omega_t^{\diamond n},$$

the time-ordered Wick exponential (11) becomes the Wick exponential:

$$\Xi_t = \text{wexp} \, \Omega_t = \sum_{n=0}^{\infty} \frac{1}{n!} \Omega_t^{\diamond n}. \tag{13}$$

Under the commutativity condition (12) we can discuss a non-homogeneous case

$$\frac{d\Xi}{dt} = L_t \diamond \Xi + M_t, \qquad \Xi\big|_{t=0} = \Xi_0 \in \mathcal{L}((E) \otimes \mathcal{H}, (E)^* \otimes \mathcal{H}), \tag{14}$$

see [16] for more details. Note that the commutativity condition is automatically satisfied when $\mathcal{H} = \mathbb{C}$.

6. EXAMPLES

Before illustrating some examples, we note relation between the Wick product and the usual product (composition) of operators. Let $\mathfrak{A}$ be the space of all $\Xi \in \mathcal{L}((E)_\beta \otimes \mathcal{H}, (E)_\beta^* \otimes \mathcal{H})$ which admit expansions of the form: $\Xi = \sum_{m=0}^{\infty} \Xi_{0,m}(\kappa_{0,m})$, i.e., contain no creation operators. It is then known [16] that

$$\Xi \diamond \Omega = \Xi \Omega, \qquad \Omega \in \mathfrak{A} \cap \mathcal{L}((E)_\beta \otimes \mathcal{H}), \ \Xi \in \mathcal{L}((E)_\beta \otimes \mathcal{H}, (E)_\beta^* \otimes \mathcal{H}). \tag{15}$$

Note also that

$$(H \otimes I) \diamond \Xi = \Xi \diamond (H \otimes I),$$
$$H \in \mathcal{L}((E)_\beta, (E)_\beta^*), \qquad \Xi \in \mathcal{L}((E)_\beta \otimes \mathcal{H}, (E)_\beta^* \otimes \mathcal{H}). \tag{16}$$

By virtue of (15) and (16) a wide class of quantum stochastic differential equations comes into our discussion.

Example 1: Let $L_i \in \mathcal{L}(\mathcal{H})$, $i = 1, 2, 3, 4$, and consider the initial value problem:

$$\frac{d\Xi}{dt} = L_1 a_t^* \Xi a_t + L_2 \Xi a_t + L_3 a_t^* \Xi + L_4 \Xi, \qquad \Xi\big|_{t=0} = \Xi_0 \in \mathcal{L}((E) \otimes \mathcal{H}, (E)^* \otimes \mathcal{H}), \tag{17}$$

where L_i stands for $I \otimes L_i$, a_t for $a_t \otimes I$, and so forth. It follows from (15) and (16) that

$$L_1 a_t^* \Xi a_t + L_2 \Xi a_t + L_3 a_t^* \Xi + L_4 \Xi = (L_1 a_t^* a_t + L_2 a_t + L_3 a_t^* + L_4) \diamond \Xi,$$

for any $\Xi \in \mathcal{L}((E)_\beta \otimes \mathcal{H}, (E)_\beta^* \otimes \mathcal{H})$. Then equation (17) is brought into a particular case of (14) where

$$L_t = L_1 a_t^* a_t + L_2 a_t + L_3 a_t^* + L_4, \qquad M_t = 0.$$

Moreover, the commutativity condition (12) is obviously satisfied, and $\deg L_t = 2$ implies $\beta = 0$. Consequently, (17) has a unique solution in $\mathcal{L}((E) \otimes \mathcal{H}, (E)^* \otimes \mathcal{H})$.

Example 2: A similar argument as in Example 1 can be applied to an equation involving higher powers of quantum white noises such as

$$\frac{d\Xi}{dt} = \sum_{m,n} L_{m,n} a_t^{*m} \Xi a_t^n, \qquad L_{m,n} \in \mathcal{L}(\mathcal{H}). \tag{18}$$

The unique solution lies in $\mathcal{L}((E)_\beta \otimes \mathcal{H}, (E)^*_\beta \otimes \mathcal{H})$, where $0 \le \beta < 1$ should be chosen as $\sup\{m+n \,;\, L_{m,n} \ne 0\} \le 2/(1-\beta)$. Quantum stochastic differential equations involving higher powers of quantum white noises have been recently discussed by Accardi [1]. Note that such equations are fairly singular from the usual aspect and are considered as Schrödinger equations with singular Hamiltonians in interaction representation.

We finally recall quantum stochastic differential equations of Hudson–Parthasarathy type [6]. For $i = 1, 2, 3, 4$ let $\{L_t^{(i)}\} \subset \mathcal{L}((E) \otimes \mathcal{H}, (E)^* \otimes \mathcal{H})$ be an adapted quantum stochastic process and consider

$$d\Xi = (L_t^{(1)} d\Lambda_t + L_t^{(2)} dA_t + L_t^{(3)} dA_t^* + L_t^{(4)} dt)\Xi, \qquad \Xi\big|_{t=0} = \Xi_0, \qquad (19)$$

where $\{\Lambda_t\}$, $\{A_t\}$, $\{A_t^*\}$ are defined in (4). In fact, equation (19) is understood as a formal representation of the integral equation

$$\Xi_t = \Xi_0 + \int_0^t (L_1 \Xi_s d\Lambda_s + L_2 \Xi_s dA_s + L_3 \Xi_s dA_s^* + L_4 \Xi_s ds), \qquad (20)$$

where the integrals are Itô type quantum stochastic integrals of adapted processes. As a result, the solution should be an adapted process. (In short, the role of an infinitesimal increment of the Brownian motion dB_t in the classical Itô theory is played by dA_t, dA_t^* and $d\Lambda_t$. For comprehensive account see [10,18].) Equation (19) is brought into a usual differential equation by means of symbols:

$$\frac{d}{dt}\,\widehat{\Xi}_t(\xi, \eta) = \xi(t)\eta(t)(L_t^{(1)}\Xi_t)\widehat{}(\xi, \eta) + $$

$$+ \xi(t)(L_t^{(2)}\Xi_t)\widehat{}(\xi, \eta) + \eta(t)(L_t^{(3)}\Xi_t)\widehat{}(\xi, \eta) + (L_t^{(4)}\Xi_t)\widehat{}(\xi, \eta). \qquad (21)$$

On the other hand, we can consider the initial value problem:

$$\frac{d\Xi}{dt} = (a_t^* L_t^{(1)} a_t + L_t^{(2)} a_t + a_t^* L_t^{(3)} + L_t^{(4)}) \diamond \Xi, \qquad \Xi\big|_{t=0} = \Xi_0. \qquad (22)$$

Contrary to (19), equation (22) is a readily well-posed differential equation for operators. Obviously, in terms of operator symbols (22) becomes

$$\frac{d}{dt}\,\widehat{\Xi}_t(\xi, \eta) = e^{-\langle \xi, \eta \rangle} \Big\{ \xi(t)\eta(t)\widehat{L_t^{(1)}}(\xi, \eta) + $$

$$+ \xi(t)\widehat{L_t^{(2)}}(\xi, \eta) + \eta(t)\widehat{L_t^{(3)}}(\xi, \eta) + \widehat{L_t^{(4)}}(\xi, \eta) \Big\} \widehat{\Xi}_t(\xi, \eta). \qquad (23)$$

Then equations (21) and (23) coincide if

$$(L_t^{(i)}\Xi_t)\widehat{}(\xi, \eta) = e^{-\langle \xi, \eta \rangle}\widehat{L_t^{(i)}}(\xi, \eta)\widehat{\Xi}_t(\xi, \eta), \qquad i = 1, 2, 3, 4,$$

or equivalently if

$$L_t^{(i)}\Xi_t = L_t^{(i)} \diamond \Xi_t, \qquad i = 1, 2, 3, 4. \qquad (24)$$

A sufficient condition for (24) is that $(L_t^{(i)})^* \in \mathfrak{A} \cap \mathcal{L}((E)_\beta \otimes \mathcal{H})$, see (15).

Consider a particular case where $L_t^{(i)} = I \otimes L_i$, $L_i \in \mathcal{L}(\mathcal{H})$. Then $\{L_t^{(i)}\}$ is an adapted (constant) process and $L_t^{(i)}\Xi = L_t^{(i)} \diamond \Xi$ for any $\Xi \in \mathcal{L}((E)_\beta \otimes \mathcal{H}, (E)^*_\beta \otimes \mathcal{H})$. In that case equations (19) and (22) become equivalent; and the latter has been discussed in Example 1. In other words, a typical quantum stochastic differential equation of Hudson–Parthasarathy is included in our framework.

REFERENCES

[1] L. Accardi: "Applications of Quantum Probability to Quantum Theory," Lectures delivered at Nagoya University, 1996.

[2] V. P. Belavkin: *A quantum nonadapted Ito formula and stochastic analysis in Fock scale*, J. Funct. Anal. **102**, 414–447 (1991).

[3] F. A. Berezin: *Wick and anti-Wick operator symbols*, Math. USSR Sbornik **15** (1971), 577–606.

[4] T. Hida: "Analysis of Brownian Functionals," Carleton Math. Lect. Notes No. 13, Carleton Univ. Ottawa, 1975.

[5] Z.-Y. Huang: *Quantum white noises – White noise approach to quantum stochastic calculus*, Nagoya Math. J. **129** (1993), 23–42.

[6] R. L. Hudson and K. R. Parthasarathy: *Quantum Ito's formula and stochastic evolutions*, Commun. Math. Phys. **93** (1984), 301–323.

[7] P. Krée and R. Rączka: *Kernels and symbols of operators in quantum field theory*, Ann. Inst. Henri Poincaré **28** (1978), 41–73.

[8] I. Kubo and S. Takenaka: *Calculus on Gaussian white noise*, Proc. Japan Acad. **56A** (1980), 376–380.

[9] H.-H. Kuo: "White Noise Distribution Theory," CRC Press, 1996.

[10] P. A. Meyer: "Quantum Probability for Probabilists," Lect. Notes in Math. Vol. 1538, Springer–Verlag, 1993.

[11] N. Obata: "White Noise Calculus and Fock Space," Lect. Notes in Math. Vol. 1577, Springer–Verlag, 1994.

[12] N. Obata: *Operator calculus on vector-valued white noise functionals*, J. Funct. Anal. **121** (1994), 185–232.

[13] N. Obata: *Generalized quantum stochastic processes on Fock space*, Publ. RIMS **31** (1995), 667–702.

[14] N. Obata: *White noise approach to quantum martingales*, in "Probability Theory and Mathematical Statistics (S. Watanabe et al. Eds.)," pp. 379–386, World Scientific, 1996.

[15] N. Obata: *Integral kernel operators on Fock space – Generalizations and applications to quantum dynamics*, Acta Appl. Math. in press.

[16] N. Obata: *Quantum stochastic differential equations in terms of quantum white noise*, to appear in "Proc. Second World Congress of Nonlinear Analysts."

[17] N. Obata: *Wick product of white noise operators and its application to quantum stochastic differential equations*, RIMS Kokyuroku **957** (1996), 167–185.

[18] K. R. Parthasarathy: "An Introduction to Quantum Stochastic Calculus," Birkhäuser, 1992.

"NONLOCAL" INTERFERENCE EFFECTS IN FREQUENCY DOMAIN

Miloslav Dušek

Department of Optics, Palacký University, 17. listopadu 50
772 07 Olomouc, Czech Republic
e-mail: dusek@optnw.upol.cz

It is a well known fact that interference is observable as a variation of intensity only when the path difference between two arms of an interferometer is shorter than the coherence length of the light. Nevertheless, interference effects do not vanish in such case, but they manifest themselves as a modulation of the spectrum. It is also known that the photon pairs produced by spontaneous parametric down-conversion show energy correlation (entanglement). A quantum measurement on one photon of the entangled pair affects considerably the whole system due to the "collapse" of the wave function. The correlation in entangled states is purely a quantum effect. It will be shown that the interference in the frequency domain and the "nonlocality" of quantum mechanics may appear simultaneously. An experiment is proposed which should demonstrate that if a filter providing spectral selection is placed in the route of one photon of the entangled pair and the photon is detected behind it, then interference appears in the (distant) Mach-Zehnder interferometer placed in the route of the other photon of the pair even if the optical path difference through the interferometer exceeds the coherence length of the light and if the spectra of these two photons do not overlap. The effect described represents a very graphical illustration of strong frequency correlation of the considered two-photon entangled state.

1. INTRODUCTION

In the recent past there was a good deal of research concerning experimental tests of quantum nonlocality on the basis of quantum optics. Various experiments were performed demonstrating violation of Bell's inequalities (and other classical inequalities) and showing evidence of quantum entanglement [1]. In these experiments, both the states exhibiting nonlocal spin or polarization correlations [2] and entangled states with frequency and momentum correlations [3] were used, the latter usually in the form of two entangled photons produced by spontaneous parametric down-conversion. These experiments play an important role in physics. They deepen understanding of the fundamental features of quantum mechanics and they indicate the impossibility to replace quantum mechanics by a classical theory with local hidden variables [4]. Besides, nonlocal phenomena and related experimental techniques find an interesting practical application in quantum cryptography [5].

Many experiments are based on various artfully chosen interference effects of different orders. However, if the path difference between two arms of an interferometer

Quantum Communication, Computing, and Measurement
Edited by Hirota *et al.*, Plenum Press, New York, 1997

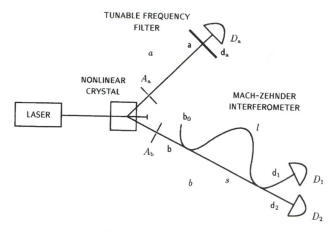

Figure 1. Proposed experimental setup. A_a and A_b are apertures selecting photon-pair beams; D_a, D_1, and D_2 are photodetectors; a denotes the route of the signal photon, b the route of the idler photon; l and s denote long and short arms of the interferometer.

is greater than the longitudinal coherence length of the light, the interference (of the 2nd order) cannot be observed as a variation of intensity. Nevertheless, interference effects do not vanish when the path difference is greater than the coherence length, but they manifest themselves as a modulation of the spectrum. Classical optics has long been familiar with this effect [6] and recently increased attention has been paid to it [7]. However, only a few authors have dealt with this phenomenon in a quantum context (e.g. [8–10]).

In this contribution we will show that both these phenomena (nonlocality or "contextuality" [11] of quantum mechanics and interference effects in spectral domain) may appear together.

2. PRINCIPLE OF THE EXPERIMENT

An outline of the proposed experimental scheme is shown in Fig. 1. Correlated photon pairs are produced by a parametric down-conversion process in a suitably cut nonlinear crystal pumped by a short-wavelength laser at frequency ω_0. Two apertures select a pair of energy correlated photons from the broadband cone behind the crystal. The signal photon beam propagates in the direction denoted by a and falls on a narrowband tunable frequency filter (e.g. Fabry-Perot) with amplitude frequency transmissivity $T_f(\omega)$. The filter can be regarded as a beam-splitter with frequency dependent transmissivity $T_f(\omega)$ and reflectivity $R_f(\omega)$. Than the annihilation operator of the output field may be written as

$$d_a(\omega) = T_f(\omega)a(\omega) + R_f(\omega)a_0(\omega), \tag{1}$$

where $a_0(\omega)$ is the operator of the mode at the unused port. The detector D_a is assumed to be placed just behind the filter.

In the route of the idler photon, referred to as b, a Mach-Zehnder interferometer is mounted, at a distance that is arbitrary. The annihilation operators of the input and output modes of the interferometer are related by the the following unitary transformation ($b_0(\omega)$ represents the field at the unused input port)

$$\begin{bmatrix} d_1(\omega) \\ d_2(\omega) \end{bmatrix} = \begin{bmatrix} \mathcal{R} & \mathcal{T} \\ \mathcal{T} & \mathcal{R} \end{bmatrix} \begin{bmatrix} \exp(-i\omega t_l) & 0 \\ 0 & \exp(-i\omega t_s) \end{bmatrix} \begin{bmatrix} \mathcal{R} & \mathcal{T} \\ \mathcal{T} & \mathcal{R} \end{bmatrix} \begin{bmatrix} b(\omega) \\ b_0(\omega) \end{bmatrix}, \tag{2}$$

where $\mathcal{R}$ and $\mathcal{T}$ are the amplitude reflection and transmission coefficients, respectively, which are considered the same for both beam-splitters and which are assumed to be frequency independent and to satisfy the usual unitarity relations

$$|\mathcal{R}|^2 + |\mathcal{T}|^2 = 1, \tag{3}$$

$$\mathcal{R}^*\mathcal{T} + \mathcal{R}\mathcal{T}^* = 0.$$

The quantities t_l and t_s are the transit times through the longer and shorter arms. Assuming symmetrical beam-splitters with $\mathcal{R} = i/\sqrt{2}$ and $\mathcal{T} = 1/\sqrt{2}$, one obtains the following expression for the operators $d_j(\omega)$ [$j = 1, 2$] in terms of the input fields

$$d_j(\omega) = B_j b(\omega) + B_{0j} b_0(\omega), \tag{4}$$

where

$$B_1(\omega) = -B_{02}(\omega) = \tfrac{1}{2} \exp(-i\omega t_l)[\exp(i\omega\Delta t) - 1], \tag{5}$$

$$B_{01}(\omega) = B_2(\omega) = i\tfrac{1}{2} \exp(-i\omega t_l)[\exp(i\omega\Delta t) + 1],$$

and $\Delta t = t_l - t_s$.

Let us suppose that the level of excitation of the field is low enough so that there is a very low probability for more than one photon pair to appear (at one time). We will assume for our calculations that just one pair of photons is present. The state of the field generated in the nonlinear crystal may then be written as

$$|\psi\rangle = (\delta\omega)^2 \sum_\omega \sum_{\omega'} \xi(\omega, \omega')\, a^\dagger(\omega) b^\dagger(\omega')\, |\text{vac}\rangle, \tag{6}$$

where $\delta\omega$ is the mode spacing [12]; $a^\dagger(\omega)$ and $b^\dagger(\omega)$ are the appropriate creation operators. The function $\xi(\omega, \omega')$ characterizes the correlation between the modes a and b. This function also includes the influence of the finite width of the laser spectral line and of the finite interaction volume.

From the requirement of normalization it follows that [13]

$$(\delta\omega)^2 \sum_\omega \sum_{\omega'} |\xi(\omega, \omega')|^2 = 1. \tag{7}$$

Further let us consider perfect energy correlation between the signal and idler photons.

$$\xi(\omega, \omega') = \begin{cases} \eta(\omega)(\delta\omega)^{-1/2} & \text{if } \omega' = \omega_0 - \omega, \\ 0 & \text{otherwise.} \end{cases} \tag{8}$$

From Eq.(7) one finds that

$$\delta\omega \sum_\omega |\eta(\omega)|^2 = 1. \tag{9}$$

3. CALCULATION OF DETECTION RATES

First we find the expressions for the electric fields operators $E_a(t)$ and $E_j(t)$ at the detectors D_a and D_j $[j = 1, 2]$. Designating t_a the propagation time from the crystal to the frequency filter and t_b the propagation time from the crystal to the interferometer, one may write the positive frequency parts of the mentioned operators as follows

$$E_a^{(+)}(t) = \frac{\delta\omega}{(2\pi)^{1/2}} \sum_\omega d_a(\omega) \exp[-i\omega(t - t_a)]$$

$$= \frac{\delta\omega}{(2\pi)^{1/2}} \sum_\omega [T_f(\omega)a(\omega) + R_f(\omega)a_0(\omega)] \exp[-i\omega(t - t_a)], \qquad (10)$$

$$E_j^{(+)}(t) = \frac{\delta\omega}{(2\pi)^{1/2}} \sum_\omega d_j(\omega) \exp[-i\omega(t - t_b)]$$

$$= \frac{\delta\omega}{(2\pi)^{1/2}} \sum_\omega [B_j(\omega)b(\omega) + B_{0j}(\omega)b_0(\omega)] \exp[-i\omega(t - t_b)]. \qquad (11)$$

The fields are normalized so that $E^{(-)}E^{(+)}$ is in units of photons per second.

Let us suppose that the detectors D_a and D_j have quantum efficiencies α_a and α_j, respectively. Then, given the state of the field described above, the average rates of photon counting at detectors D_1 and D_2, irrespective of whether the detector D_a registers a photon or not, are given by [14]

$$R_j(t) = \alpha_j \langle\psi| E_j^{(-)}(t)E_j^{(+)}(t) |\psi\rangle$$

$$= \alpha_j \frac{(\delta\omega)^2}{2\pi} \sum_\omega |\eta(\omega)B_j(\omega_0 - \omega)|^2. \qquad (12)$$

For our purposes it is interesting to suppose that the transit time difference Δt arising in the interferometer is much longer than the coherence time t_{coh} of the field. In such a case no interference is expected. Using Eqs. (5) and (9), and changing the sum to an integral, one can find that

$$\delta\omega \sum_\omega |\eta(\omega)B_j(\omega_0 - \omega)|^2 = \delta\omega \sum_\omega \frac{1}{2} |\eta(\omega)|^2 \left\{1 + (-1)^j \cos[(\omega_0 - \omega)\Delta t]\right\}$$

$$= \frac{1}{2} + (-1)^j \frac{1}{2} \underbrace{\int d\omega\, \eta(\omega) \cos[(\omega_0 - \omega)\Delta t]}_{\approx 0} \approx \frac{1}{2}. \qquad (13)$$

The probability to detect a photon at D_1 is the same as at D_2. The last approximation in Eq.(13) may be used because the function $|\eta(\omega)|^2$ varies much more slowly than the cosine term in virtue of the assumption that $\Delta t \gg t_{\text{coh}}$.

However, performing coincidence measurements with the signal from the detector D_a placed behind a narrowband filter, whose pass-band width is much less than the reciprocal transit time difference $(\Delta t)^{-1}$, one obtains something quite different. The rate of coincidence detection or the probability density that a photon will be detected by the detector D_a just behind the tunable frequency filter in the route a at time t, and a photon will be detected by the detector D_1 or D_2 in the route b behind the interferometer at time $t + \tau$, is proportional to the correlation function of the fourth order and is given by the formula

$$R_{aj}(t, t + \tau) = \alpha_a \alpha_j \langle\psi| E_a^{(-)}(t)E_j^{(-)}(t + \tau)E_j^{(+)}(t + \tau)E_a^{(+)}(t) |\psi\rangle$$

$$= \alpha_a \alpha_j \frac{(\delta\omega)^3}{(2\pi)^2} \left|\sum_\omega \exp[i\omega(\tau - t_a + t_b)]\, \eta(\omega)B_j(\omega_0 - \omega)T_f(\omega)\right|^2. \qquad (14)$$

Here again $j = 1$ or 2, corresponding to a count at D_1 or D_2.

As the frequency dependence of the transmissivity of the filter is assumed very narrow, we can formally put

$$T_f(\omega) = \begin{cases} 1 & \text{if } \omega = \omega_f, \\ \\ 0 & \text{otherwise,} \end{cases} \tag{15}$$

where ω_f is the central frequency of the pass band. Then, substituting into Eqs. (14), we obtain

$$R_{aj}(t, t + \tau) = \alpha_a \alpha_j \frac{(\delta\omega)^3}{(2\pi)^2} |\eta(\omega_f) B_j(\omega_0 - \omega_f)|^2, \tag{16}$$

Using Eq. (5), one finally obtains the following expressions for the quantity $|B_j(\omega_0 - \omega_f)|^2$ appearing in Eqs. (16)

$$\begin{aligned} |B_1(\omega_0 - \omega_f)|^2 &= \tfrac{1}{2}\{1 - \cos[(\omega_0 - \omega_f)\Delta t]\}, \\ |B_2(\omega_0 - \omega_f)|^2 &= \tfrac{1}{2}\{1 + \cos[(\omega_0 - \omega_f)\Delta t]\}. \end{aligned} \tag{17}$$

These formulas show that varying ω_f (i.e., tuning the filter), the values of $|B_j(\omega_0 - \omega_f)|^2$ range between 0 and 1 (and always $|B_1|^2 + |B_2|^2 = 1$). That means that the coincidence detection rates are modulated in dependence on ω_f and Δt, i.e., interference appears in the remote interferometer placed in the branch b, in the route of the other photon of the pair.

4. CONCLUSIONS

As expected, no interference appears in separate measurements on the Mach-Zehnder interferometer if $\Delta t \gg t_{\text{coh}}$ [see Eq. (13)]. If a frequency filter prolonging the coherence length sufficiently were placed in front of the interferometer, interference would appear. Placing a (scanning) filter in front of one detector at the output of the interferometer, one could observe a frequency modulation since individual frequency components of the field (even in case of a single photon) interfere independently and the filter selects just "one" of them. However, in the case described above, there is no filter in the part containing the interferometer (i.e., in the route b); the spectral selection is done in the route a. Nevertheless, when a photon of frequency ω_f is registered at D_a, interference effects (dependent on ω_f) appear at the outputs of the interferometer in the part b (*in the sense of coincidence measurement*), as is evident from Eqs. (17). This happens even if the apparatus is arranged in such a way that the spectra of both photons do not overlap!

One can consider the arrangement where the wave packet first reaches the interferometer in part b and only after this its twin comes to the filter in part a; then we can, at least in principle, choose the frequency (tune the filter) after the detection at D_j. There is no contradiction: The measurement in the route b affects the state of the field at the route a in such a way that the frequencies that would allow the opposite result of the measurement in part b are no longer present there. The measurement at b modulates the spectrum at a.

Let us emphasize that there is nothing acausal here and nothing actual propagates at superluminal velocity because the interference effects (at b) are observable only in coincidence with the event at the (distant) detector D_a and information on this event can be obtained only by conventional means. Until we compare the results from the parts a and b, we do not find any interference.

ACKNOWLEDGEMENT

The author acknowledges support from the Grant Agency of the Czech Republic (projects 202/94/0458 and 202/95/0002) and from the Ministry of Education of the Czech Republic (project VS 96028).

REFERENCES

[1] A review with a number of references can be found in J. Peřina, Z. Hradil, and B. Jurčo, *Quantum Optics and Fundamentals of Physics* (Kluwer, Dordrecht, 1994).

[2] A. Aspect, P. Grangier, and G. Roger, Phys. Rev. Lett. **47**, 460 (1981).

[3] J.D. Franson, Phys. Rev. Lett. **62**, 2205 (1989).

[4] J.S. Bell, Physics **1**, 195 (1964).

[5] A.K. Ekert and G.M. Palma, J. Mod. Opt. **41**, 2413 (1994).

[6] L. Mandel, J. Opt. Soc. Am. **52**, 1335 (1962).

[7] E. Wolf, in *Proc. Symp. Huygens's Principle 1690-1990: Theory and Applications*, edited by H. Blok, H.A. Ferwerda, and H.K. Kuiken (North Holland, Amsterdam, 1992), p. 113.

[8] X.Y. Zou, T.P. Grayson, and L. Mandel, Phys. Rev. Lett. **69**, 3041 (1992).

[9] H. Rauch, Phys. Lett. A **173**, 240 (1993).

[10] D.L. Jacobson, S.A. Werner, H. Rauch, Phys. Rev. A **49**, 3196 (1994).

[11] N.D. Mermin, Rev. Mod. Phys. **65**, 803 (1993).

[12] When it be technically convenient, we will assume $\delta\omega \to 0$ and employ the conversion $\delta\omega \sum_\omega \to \int d\omega$.

[13] We assume the following commutation relations between the annihilation and creation operators: $[\mathsf{a}(\omega), \mathsf{b}^\dagger(\omega')] = (\delta\omega)^{-1}$ if both operators correspond to the same mode and $\omega = \omega'$; otherwise the commutator is zero.

[14] As we can see, the counting rate has the form corresponding to statistical ensemble of individual monochromatic photons with probability distribution $|\eta(\omega)|^2$. Indeed, the density matrix describing the subsystem (b), which one obtains tracing of $|\psi\rangle\langle\psi|$ over the subsystem (a), has a diagonal form: $\hat{\rho}_b = (\delta\omega)^2 \sum_\omega |\eta(\omega)|^2 \mathsf{b}^\dagger(\omega_0 - \omega) |vac\rangle\langle vac| \mathsf{b}(\omega_0 - \omega)$. Such a form of the density matrix of the subsystem is a consequence of the perfect correlation between the idler and signal photons.

QUANTUM STOCHASTIC SYSTEMS IN TERMS OF NON-EQUILIBRIUM THERMO FIELD DYNAMICS

T. Arimitsu, T. Saito, and T. Imagire

Institute of Physics, University of Tsukuba
Ibaraki 305, Japan
Internet: arimitsu@cm.ph.tsukuba.ac.jp

With the help of Non-Equilibrium Thermo Field Dynamics, a unified framework of the *canonical operator formalism* for quantum stochastic differential equations is constructed where the stochastic Liouville equation and the Langevin equation are, respectively, equivalent to the Schrödinger equation and the Heisenberg equation in quantum mechanics. It was found that there exist at least two attractive formulations; one is based on a non-Hermitian martingale (a realization of the conservation of probability), and the other on a Hermitian martingale (a realization of the conservation of norm of a wave function). In this paper, the structures of two formulations are investigated in a systematic manner by means of the difference of martingale operators.

1. INTRODUCTION

Recently we succeeded to construct a unified framework of the *canonical operator formalism* for quantum stochastic differential equations with the help of Non-Equilibrium Thermo Field Dynamics (NETFD) [1]- [6]. NETFD is a *canonical formalism* of quantum systems in far-from-equilibrium state which enables us to treat dissipative quantum systems by a method similar to the usual quantum mechanics and quantum field theory that accommodate the concept of the dual structure in the interpretation of nature, i.e. in terms of the *operator algebra* and the *representation space*. To authors' knowledge, it was not realized, until the formalism of NETFD had been constructed, to put all the stochastic differential equations for quantum systems into a unified method of canonical operator formalism (see Fig. 1); the stochastic Liouville equation [7] and the Langevin equation within NETFD are, respectively, equivalent to a Schrödinger equation and a Heisenberg equation in quantum mechanics. These stochastic equations are consistent with a quantum master equation which can be derived by taking random average of the stochastic Liouville equation.

In the course of its construction, it was found that there exist at least two attractive formulations [6]; one is based on a non-Hermitian martingale, and the other on a Hermitian martingale. The former employed the characteristics of the classical stochastic Liouville equation where the stochastic distribution function satisfies the conservation of probability within the phase-space of a relevant system (see appendix A for the system of classical stochastic differential equations). Whereas the latter employed the characteristics of the Schrödinger equation where the norm of the stochastic wave function preserves itself. In this case, the consistency with the structure of classical system is destroyed.

In this paper, we will show the structures of two formulations in a systematic manner by means of martingale $\hat{M}_t$.

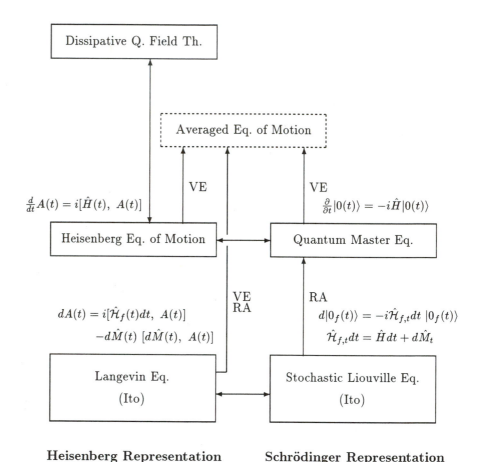

Heisenberg Representation   **Schrödinger Representation**

Figure 1. System of the stochastic differential equations within Non-Equilibrium Thermo Field Dynamics. RA stands for the random average. VE stands for the vacuum expectation.

2. STOCHASTIC LIOUVILLE EQUATION

2.1. SETTING

Let us start the consideration with the stochastic Liouville equation of the Ito type:

$$d|0_f(t)\rangle = -i\hat{\mathcal{H}}_{f,t}dt \, |0_f(t)\rangle. \tag{1}$$

The generator $\hat{V}_f(t)$, defined by

$$|0_f(t)\rangle = \hat{V}_f(t)|0\rangle, \tag{2}$$

satisfies

$$d\hat{V}_f(t) = -i\hat{\mathcal{H}}_{f,t}dt\ \hat{V}_f(t), \tag{3}$$

with the initial condition $\hat{V}_f(0) = 1$.

The hat-Hamiltonian is called a tildian operator satisfying

$$\left(i\hat{\mathcal{H}}_{f,t}dt\right)^\sim = i\hat{\mathcal{H}}_{f,t}dt. \tag{4}$$

Here, the tilde conjugation $\sim$ is defined by

$$(A_1 A_2)^\sim = \tilde{A}_1\tilde{A}_2, \tag{5}$$
$$(c_1 A_1 + c_2 A_2)^\sim = c_1^*\tilde{A}_1 + c_2^*\tilde{A}_2, \tag{6}$$
$$(\tilde{A})^\sim = A, \tag{7}$$
$$(A^\dagger)^\sim = \tilde{A}^\dagger, \tag{8}$$

with A's and c's being operators and c-numbers, respectively.

From the knowledge of the stochastic integral, we know that the required form of the hat-Hamiltonian should be

$$\hat{\mathcal{H}}_{f,t}dt = \hat{H}dt + d\hat{M}_t, \tag{9}$$

where the martingale $d\hat{M}_t$ is the term containing the operators representing the quantum Brownian motion $dB(t)$, $d\tilde{B}^\dagger(t)$ and their tilde conjugates (see appendix B for the quantum Brownian motion). $\hat{H}$ is given by

$$\hat{H} = \hat{H}_S + i\hat{\Pi}, \tag{10}$$

with

$$\hat{H}_S = H_S - \tilde{H}_S, \qquad \hat{\Pi} = \hat{\Pi}_R + \hat{\Pi}_D. \tag{11}$$

We divided the generator $\hat{\Pi}$ into two parts. The generators $\hat{\Pi}_R$ and $\hat{\Pi}_D$ are representing, respectively, a *relaxational* and a *diffusive* part.

Here, it is assumed that, at $t = 0$, the relevant system starts to contact with the irrelevant (random force) system representing the stochastic process consisting of the martingale $d\hat{M}_t$.[*]

2.2. SPECIFICATION OF THE MARTINGALE

Now, we need something which specifies the structure of the martingale. If we keep the characteristics satisfied by the system of classical stochastic differential equations (see appendix A), the something is the condition that the stochastic distribution function should conserve its probability just within the phase-space for relevant subsystem irrespective of irrelevant sub-system representing random forces (cf. (53)). The condition is given by

$$\langle 1|d\hat{M}_t = 0, \tag{12}$$

within the formalism of NETFD. It means that the martingale operator has zero eigenvalue for the ket-vacuum $\langle 1|$ of relevant system. We will refer to this case as (P) reminding us that it is based on the conservation of *probability*.

---

[*]Within the formalism, the random force operators $dB(t)$ and $dB^\dagger(t)$ are assumed to commute with any relevant system operator A in the Schrödinger representation: $[A,\ dB(t)] = [A,\ dB^\dagger(t)] = 0$ for $t \geq 0$.

On the other hand, if we demand that the martingale should be Hermitian, the something becomes

$$d\hat{M}_t^\dagger = d\hat{M}_t. \tag{13}$$

The Hermitian martingale is intimately related to the approach started with the stochastic Schrödinger equation where the norm of the wave function preserves itself in time [8–10]. In other words, the interaction between a relevant system and an irrelevant environment is given by an Hermitian Hamiltonian [6]. We will refer to this case as (N) reminding us that it is based on the conservation of *norm*.

In order to specify the martingale, we need another condition which gives us a relation between multiple of the martingale and the damping operator. For (P), we put

$$d\hat{M}_t \, d\hat{M}_t = -2\hat{\Pi}_D dt, \tag{14}$$

while for (N)

$$d\hat{M}_t \, d\hat{M}_t = -2\left(\hat{\Pi}_R + \hat{\Pi}_D\right) dt. \tag{15}$$

This operator relation for each case may be called a generalized fluctuation dissipation theorem of the second kind, which should be interpreted within the stochastic convergence.

2.3. QUANTUM MASTER EQUATION

Taking the random average by applying the bra-vacuum $\langle|$ of the irrelevant subsystem to the stochastic Liouville equation (1), we can obtain the quantum master equation as

$$\frac{\partial}{\partial t}|0(t)\rangle = -i\hat{H}|0(t)\rangle, \tag{16}$$

with

$$\hat{H}dt = \langle|\hat{\mathcal{H}}_{f,t}dt|\rangle. \tag{17}$$

The ket-vacuum

$$|0(t)\rangle = \langle|0_f(t)\rangle, \tag{18}$$

is a coarse-grained vacuum which, in terms of the classical system, corresponds to the distribution function $P(u, t)$ defined by (56).

3. QUANTUM LANGEVIN EQUATIONS

3.1. ITO'S FORMULA IN QUANTUM SYSTEMS

The dynamical variable of the relevant system is defined by

$$A(t) = \hat{V}_f^{-1}(t) \, A \, \hat{V}_f(t), \tag{19}$$

where A is an observable operator of the system constituted by only non-tilde operators. The equation for $\hat{V}_f^{-1}(t)$ is given by

$$d\hat{V}_f^{-1}(t) = \hat{V}_f^{-1}(t) \, i\hat{\mathcal{H}}_{f,t}^- dt, \tag{20}$$

with

$$\hat{\mathcal{H}}_{f,t}^- dt = \hat{\mathcal{H}}_{f,t} dt + id\hat{M}_t \, d\hat{M}_t. \tag{21}$$

For (P), the substitution of (14) into (21) leads us to

$$\hat{\mathcal{H}}_{f,t}^- dt = \hat{H}_S dt + i\left(\hat{\Pi}_R - \hat{\Pi}_D\right) dt + d\hat{M}_t. \tag{22}$$

Whereas, for (N), the substitution of (15) into (21) leads to

$$\hat{\mathcal{H}}_{f,t}^- dt = \hat{H}_S dt - i \left(\hat{\Pi}_R + \hat{\Pi}_D \right) dt + d\hat{M}_t. \tag{23}$$

In NETFD, the Heisenberg equation for $A(t)$ within the Ito calculus is the quantum Langevin equation in the form

$$
\begin{aligned}
dA(t) &= d\hat{V}_f^{-1}(t) \, A \, \hat{V}_f(t) + \hat{V}_f^{-1}(t) \, A \, d\hat{V}_f(t) + d\hat{V}_f^{-1}(t) \, A \, d\hat{V}_f(t) \\
&= i[\hat{\mathcal{H}}_f(t)dt, \, A(t)] - d\hat{M}(t) \, [d\hat{M}(t), \, A(t)].
\end{aligned} \tag{24}
$$

Here, we introduced the quantities in the Heisenberg representation:

$$\hat{\mathcal{H}}_f(t)dt = \hat{V}_f^{-1}(t) \, \hat{\mathcal{H}}_{f,t}dt \, \hat{V}_f(t), \qquad d\hat{M}(t) = \hat{V}_f^{-1}(t) \, d\hat{M}_t \, \hat{V}_f(t). \tag{25}$$

Since $A(t)$ is an arbitrary observable operator in the relevant system, (24) can be the Ito formula extended to quantum systems.

3.2. EQUATION OF MOTION FOR THE BRA-VECTOR

Applying the bra-vacuum $\langle\!\langle 1| = \langle 1|\langle 1|$ to (24) from its left-hand side:

$$d\langle\!\langle 1|A(t) = i\langle\!\langle 1|[H_S(t), \, A(t)]dt + \langle\!\langle 1|A(t)\hat{\Pi}(t)dt - i\langle\!\langle 1|A(t)d\hat{M}(t), \tag{26}$$

and making use of the thermal state conditions of the type

$$\langle 1|\tilde{A}^\dagger(t) = \langle 1|A(t), \qquad \langle 1|d\tilde{B}^\dagger(t) = \langle 1|dB(t), \tag{27}$$

in order to rewrite the tilde operators to the corresponding non-tilde operators, we can derive the quantum Langevin equation for the bra-vector state $\langle\!\langle 1|A(t)$ written by only non-tilde operators. In the derivation, use had been made of the property

$$\langle\!\langle 1|d\hat{M}(t) = 0, \tag{28}$$

valid both in (P) and (N) cases. For the case (P), it is apparent from (12). For the case (N), its physical meaning can be stated in terms of the classical stochastic Liouville equation; the stochastic distribution function conserves its probability in whole the phase-space consisting of two phase-spaces, one for the relevant and the other for the irrelevant sub-systems.

Applying further the fluctuation-dissipation theorem (14) and (15) to the respective equations (26) for the cases (P) and (N), we finally see that the derived Langevin equations coincide with each other; the quantum Langevin equation for the bra-vector state have the same structure in both cases (P) and (N).

3.3. AVERAGED EQUATION OF MOTION

Applying the ket-vacuum $|0\rangle\!\rangle = |0\rangle|\rangle$ to (26) from the right-hand side, we have the averaged equation of motion for the dynamical variable $A(t)$ in the form

$$\frac{d}{dt}\langle\!\langle 1|A(t)|0\rangle\!\rangle = i\langle\!\langle 1| [H_S(t), \, A(t)] |0\rangle\!\rangle + \langle\!\langle 1|A(t)\hat{\Pi}(t)|0\rangle\!\rangle, \tag{29}$$

which has the same structure both for (P) and (N) as is known from the derivation. It can be also derived by making use of the quantum master equation (16).

4.   AN EXAMPLE

We will study a harmonic oscillator embedded in an environment with temperature T, as an example. The Hamiltonian of the relevant system of the present model is

$$H_S = \omega a^\dagger a. \tag{30}$$

Here, a, $a^\dagger$ and their tilde conjugates are stochastic operators of the relevant system satisfying the canonical commutation relation

$$[a,\ a^\dagger] = 1, \qquad [\tilde{a},\ \tilde{a}^\dagger] = 1. \tag{31}$$

The tilde and non-tilde operators are related with each other by the relation

$$\langle 1|a^\dagger = \langle 1|\tilde{a}, \tag{32}$$

where $\langle 1|$ is the thermal bra-vacuum of the relevant system.

We will confine ourselves to the case where the stochastic hat-Hamiltonian $\hat{\mathcal{H}}_{f,t}dt$ is bi-linear in a, $a^\dagger$, $dB(t)$, $dB^\dagger(t)$ and their tilde conjugates, and is invariant under the phase transformation $a \to ae^{i\theta}$, and $dB(t) \to dB(t)\,e^{i\theta}$. Here, $dB(t)$, $dB^\dagger(t)$ and their conjugates are the operators representing the quantum Brownian motion given in appendix B.

Then, we have

$$\hat{\Pi}_R = -\kappa\left(\alpha^\ddagger\alpha + \text{t.c.}\right), \qquad \hat{\Pi}_D = 2\kappa\left[\bar{n} + \nu\right]\alpha^\ddagger\tilde{\alpha}^\ddagger, \tag{33}$$

with the Planck distribution function $\bar{n} = \left(e^{\omega/T} - 1\right)^{-1}$. Here, we introduced a set of canonical stochastic operators

$$\alpha = \mu a + \nu\tilde{a}^\dagger, \qquad \alpha^\ddagger = a^\dagger - \tilde{a}, \tag{34}$$

with $\mu + \nu = 1$, which satisfy the commutation relation $[\alpha,\ \alpha^\ddagger] = 1$.

The martingale operator for the case (P) is given by [4, 6]

$$d\hat{M}_t = i\left[\alpha^\ddagger dW(t) + \text{t.c.}\right], \tag{35}$$

and the one for the case (N) has the form [6, 10]

$$d\hat{M}_t = i\left[\alpha^\ddagger dW(t) + \text{t.c.}\right] - i\left[\alpha\ dW^\ddagger(t) + \text{t.c.}\right], \tag{36}$$

where the random force operators $dW(t)$ and $dW^\ddagger(t)$ are defined, respectively, by

$$dW(t) = \sqrt{2\kappa}\left(\mu dB(t) + \nu d\tilde{B}^\dagger(t)\right), \tag{37}$$
$$dW^\ddagger(t) = \sqrt{2\kappa}\left(dB^\dagger(t) - d\tilde{B}(t)\right). \tag{38}$$

The latter annihilates the bra-vacuum $\langle|$ of the irrelevant system:

$$\langle|dW^\ddagger(t) = 0, \qquad \langle|d\tilde{W}^\ddagger(t) = 0. \tag{39}$$

The martingale term (35) was also derived in [6] by generalizing the Theorem 5.3 in [11]. The martingale (36) is Hermitian.

The random force operators $dW(t)$, $d\tilde{W}^{\ddagger}(t)$ and their tilde conjugates are of the quantum Wiener process satisfying

$$\left\langle dW(t)\right\rangle = \left\langle d\tilde{W}(t)\right\rangle = \left\langle dW^{\ddagger}(t)\right\rangle = \left\langle d\tilde{W}^{\ddagger}(t)\right\rangle = 0, \tag{40}$$

$$\left\langle dW(t)dW(s)\right\rangle = \left\langle d\tilde{W}(t)d\tilde{W}(s)\right\rangle = \left\langle dW^{\ddagger}(t)dW(s)\right\rangle = \left\langle d\tilde{W}^{\ddagger}(t)d\tilde{W}(s)\right\rangle = 0, \tag{41}$$

and

$$\left\langle dW(t)d\tilde{W}(s)\right\rangle = \left\langle d\tilde{W}(s)dW(t)\right\rangle = 2\kappa\left(\bar{n}+\nu\right)\delta(t-s)dtds, \tag{42}$$

$$\left\langle dW(t)dW^{\ddagger}(s)\right\rangle = \left\langle d\tilde{W}(t)d\tilde{W}^{\ddagger}(s)\right\rangle = 2\kappa\delta(t-s)dt\,ds, \tag{43}$$

where $\left\langle\cdots\right\rangle = \left\langle|\cdots|\right\rangle$.

The quantum Langevin equation for the case (P) is given by [3]

$$\begin{aligned}
dA(t) = {} & i[\hat{H}_S(t),\ A(t)]dt \\
& + \kappa\left\{[\alpha^{\ddagger}(t)\alpha(t),\ A(t)] + [\tilde{\alpha}^{\ddagger}(t)\tilde{\alpha}(t),\ A(t)]\right\}dt \\
& + 2\kappa(\bar{n}+\nu)[\tilde{\alpha}^{\ddagger}(t),\ [\alpha^{\ddagger}(t),\ A(t)]]dt \\
& - \left\{[\alpha^{\ddagger}(t),\ A(t)]dW(t) + [\tilde{\alpha}^{\ddagger}(t),\ A(t)]d\tilde{W}(t)\right\},
\end{aligned} \tag{44}$$

and the one for (N) is given by [6,10]

$$\begin{aligned}
dA(t) = {} & i[\hat{H}_S(t),\ A(t)]dt \\
& + \kappa\left\{[\alpha^{\ddagger}(t),\ A(t)]\alpha(t) - \alpha^{\ddagger}(t)[\alpha(t),\ A(t)]\right. \\
& \left. + [\tilde{\alpha}^{\ddagger}(t),\ A(t)]\tilde{\alpha}^{\ddagger}(t) - \tilde{\alpha}^{\ddagger}(t)[\tilde{\alpha}(t),\ A(t)]\right\}dt \\
& + 2\kappa\left(\bar{n}+\nu\right)[\tilde{\alpha}^{\ddagger}(t),\ [\alpha^{\ddagger}(t),\ A(t)]]dt \\
& - \left\{[\alpha^{\ddagger}(t),\ A(t)]dW(t) + [\tilde{\alpha}^{\ddagger}(t),\ A(t)]d\tilde{W}(t)\right\} \\
& + \left\{dW^{\ddagger}(t)[\alpha(t),\ A(t)] + d\tilde{W}^{\ddagger}(t)[\tilde{\alpha}(t),\ A(t)]\right\},
\end{aligned} \tag{45}$$

with $\hat{H}_S(t) = \hat{V}_f^{-1}(t)\hat{H}_S\hat{V}_f(t)$.

The equation of motion for the bra-vector state [6], $\langle\!\langle 1|A(t)$, and the one for expectation value reduce, respectively, to

$$\begin{aligned}
d\langle\!\langle 1|A(t) = {} & i\langle\!\langle 1|[H_S(t),\ A(t)]dt + \kappa\left\{\langle\!\langle 1|[a^{\dagger}(t),\ A(t)]a(t) + \langle\!\langle 1|a^{\dagger}(t)[A(t),\ a(t)]\right\}dt \\
& + 2\kappa\bar{n}\langle\!\langle 1|[a(t),\ [A(t),\ a^{\dagger}(t)]]dt \\
& + \langle\!\langle 1|[A(t),\ a^{\dagger}(t)]\sqrt{2\kappa}\,dB(t) + \langle\!\langle 1|[a(t),\ A(t)]\sqrt{2\kappa}\,dB^{\dagger}(t),
\end{aligned} \tag{46}$$

and

$$\begin{aligned}
\frac{d}{dt}\langle\!\langle A(t)\rangle\!\rangle = {} & i\left\langle\!\left\langle[H_S(t),\ A(t)]\right\rangle\!\right\rangle + \kappa\left(\left\langle\!\left\langle[a^{\dagger}(t),\ A(t)]a(t)\right\rangle\!\right\rangle + \left\langle\!\left\langle a^{\dagger}(t)[A(t),\ a(t)]\right\rangle\!\right\rangle\right) \\
& + 2\kappa\bar{n}\left\langle\!\left\langle[a(t),\ [A(t),\ a(t)^{\dagger}]]\right\rangle\!\right\rangle,
\end{aligned} \tag{47}$$

both for the cases (P) and (N).

5.   COMMENTS

We showed that both of the two formulations, i.e., one based on the density operator formalism and the other based on the wave function formalism, give the same results in the *weak relation* (a relation between matrix elements in certain representation space) but with different equations in the *strong relation* (a relation between operators), while each formulation provides us with a consistent and unified system of quantum stochastic differential equations. Although we do not know yet if one can verify which of them nature is adopting, it can be said that a new point of view was provided for the understanding of nature. We hope that something will be extracted from this viewpoint in the near future by investigating nature including the field of quantum communication and measurement.

The derivation of stochastic differential equations from a microscopic stage is an old problem in statistical mechanics [12]- [18]. It may be necessary to think it over again after knowing the present unified formulations.

A. CLASSICAL STOCHASTIC DIFFERENTIAL EQUATIONS

We will show the structure of the system of classical stochastic differential equations [7] by making use of the stochastic Liouville equation of the type

$$\frac{\partial}{\partial t} f(u,t) = \Omega(u,t) f(u,t), \tag{48}$$

with

$$\Omega(u,t) = -\frac{\partial}{\partial u} \dot{u}, \tag{49}$$

where the flow $\dot{u}$ in the velocity space is defined by

$$\dot{u} = -\gamma u + \frac{1}{m} R(t). \tag{50}$$

Here, the random force $R(t)$ is a Gaussian white stochastic process defined by

$$\langle R(t) \rangle = 0, \qquad \langle R(t_1) R(t_2) \rangle = 2m\gamma T \delta(t_1 - t_2). \tag{51}$$

The initial condition for the stochastic distribution function $f(u,t)$ is given by

$$f(u,0) = P(u,0), \tag{52}$$

where $P(u,t)$ is the velocity distribution function defined below. Note that the stochastic distribution function conserves its probability within the velocity phase-space:

$$\int du \ f(u,t) = 1. \tag{53}$$

The system described by the stochastic Liouville equation (48) can be treated by the Langevin equation:

$$\dot{u}(t) = -\gamma u(t) + \frac{1}{m} R(t). \tag{54}$$

This should be interpreted as a Stratonovich type stochastic differential equation where one can proceed calculation as if the stochastic function $u(t)$ were an analytic one. Note that the Langevin equation does *not* contain the diffusion term.

Precisely, the stochastic distribution function is given by

$$f(u,t) = f(u,t; \Omega(u,t), P(u,0)). \tag{55}$$

Taking an average $\langle \cdots \rangle$ of $\Omega(u,t)$ over all the trajectories of the stochastic process $\{R(t)\}$, we have an ordinary velocity distribution function $P(u,t)$:

$$P(u,t) = \langle f(u,t; \Omega(u,t), P(u,0)) \rangle, \tag{56}$$

which satisfies the Fokker-Planck equation

$$\frac{\partial}{\partial t} P(u,t) = \frac{\partial}{\partial u} \gamma \left(u + \frac{T}{m} \frac{\partial}{\partial u} \right) P(u,t). \tag{57}$$

The fluctuation-dissipation theorem (51) of the second kind is introduced in order that the stochastic Liouville equation (48) and the Langevin equation (54) be consistent with the Fokker-Planck equation (57).

B.   QUANTUM BROWNIAN MOTION

Let us introduce the annihilation and creation operators $b(t)$, $b^\dagger(t)$ and their tilde conjugates satisfying the canonical commutation relation:

$$[b(t),\ b^\dagger(t')] = \delta(t - t'), \qquad [\tilde{b}(t),\ \tilde{b}^\dagger(t')] = \delta(t - t'). \tag{58}$$

The vacuums $(0|$ and $|0)$ are defined by

$$b(t)|0) = 0, \quad (0|b^\dagger(t) = 0, \quad \tilde{b}(t)|0) = 0, \quad (0|\tilde{b}^\dagger(t) = 0. \tag{59}$$

The argument t represents time.

Introducing the operators

$$B(t) = \int_0^t dt'\ b(t'), \qquad B^\dagger(t) = \int_0^t dt'\ b^\dagger(t'), \tag{60}$$

and their tilde conjugates for $t \geq 0$, we see that they satisfy $B(0) = 0$, $B^\dagger(0) = 0$,

$$[B(s),\ B^\dagger(t)] = \min(s, t), \tag{61}$$

and their tilde conjugates. These operators represent the quantum Brownian motion. These operators annihilate the vacuums $|0)$ and $(0|$:

$$dB(t)|0) = 0, \quad d\tilde{B}(t)|0) = 0, \quad (0|dB^\dagger(t) = 0, \quad (0|d\tilde{B}^\dagger(t) = 0, \tag{62}$$

where

$$dB(t) = b(t)dt, \quad dB^\dagger(t) = b^\dagger(t)dt, \quad d\tilde{B}(t) = \tilde{b}(t)dt, \quad d\tilde{B}^\dagger(t) = \tilde{b}^\dagger(t)dt. \tag{63}$$

Let us introduce a set of new operators by the relation

$$dC(t)^\mu = \mathcal{B}^{\mu\nu} dB(t)^\nu, \tag{64}$$

with the Bogoliubov transformation defined by

$$\mathcal{B}^{\mu\nu} = \begin{pmatrix} 1 + \bar{n} \ , & -\bar{n} \\ -1 \ , & 1 \end{pmatrix}, \tag{65}$$

where $\bar{n}$ is the Planck distribution function. We introduced the thermal doublet:

$$dB(t)^{\mu=1} = dB(t), \quad dB(t)^{\mu=2} = d\tilde{B}^\dagger(t), \quad d\bar{B}(t)^{\mu=1} = dB^\dagger(t), \quad d\bar{B}(t)^{\mu=2} = -d\tilde{B}(t), \tag{66}$$

and the similar doublet notations for $dC(t)^\mu$ and $d\bar{C}(t)^\mu$. The new operators annihilate the new vacuum $\langle|$ and $|\rangle$:

$$dC(t)|\rangle = 0, \quad d\tilde{C}(t)|\rangle = 0, \quad \langle|dC^\dagger(t) = 0, \quad \langle|d\tilde{C}^\dagger(t) = 0. \tag{67}$$

We will use the representation space constructed on the vacuums $\langle|$ and $|\rangle$. Then, we have, for example,

$$\langle|dB^\dagger(t)dB(t)|\rangle = \bar{n}dt, \qquad \langle|dB(t)dB^\dagger(t)|\rangle = (\bar{n} + 1)\,dt. \tag{68}$$

REFERENCES

[1] T. Arimitsu and H. Umezawa, Prog. Theor. Phys. **74** (1985) 429.

[2] T. Arimitsu, Phys. Lett. **A153** (1991) 163.

[3] T. Saito and T. Arimitsu, Mod. Phys. Lett. B **6** (1992) 1319.

[4] T. Saito and T. Arimitsu, Mod. Phys. Lett. B **7** (1993) 1951.

[5] T. Arimitsu and N. Arimitsu, Phys. Rev. E **50** (1994) 121.

[6] T. Arimitsu, Condensed Matter Physics (Lviv, Ukraine) **4** (1994) 26, and the references therein.

[7] R. Kubo, M. Toda and N. Hashitsume, *Statistical Physics II* (Springer, Berlin 1985).

[8] R. L. Hudson and J. M. Lindsay, J. Func. Analysis **61** (1985) 202.

[9] K. R. Parthasarathy, *An Introduction to Quantum Stochastic Calculus*, Monographs in Mathematics **85** (Birkhäuser Verlag, 1992).

[10] T. Saito, Ph.D. Thesis (Univ. of Tsukuba, 1995).

[11] L. Accardi, Rev. Math. Phys. **2** (1990) 127.

[12] R. Kubo, in *Lectures on Theoretical Physics*, vol. I, ed. W. E. Brittin and L. G. Dunham (1959) p. 120.

[13] S. Nakajima, Prog. Theor. Phys. **20** (1958) 948.

[14] R. Zwanzig, J. Chem. Phys. **33** (1960) 1338.

[15] H. Mori, Prog. Theor. Phys. **33** (1965) 423.

[16] F. Shibata and T. Arimitsu, J. Phys. Soc. Japan **49** (1980) 891.

[17] T. Arimitsu, J. Phys. Soc. Japan **51** (1982) 1720.

[18] T. Arimitsu and T. Imagire, in preparation.

CONSIDERATIONS IN THE TIME-ENERGY UNCERTAINTY RELATION FROM THE VIEWPOINT OF HYPOTHESIS TESTING

S. Osawa and K. Matsumoto

Department of Mathematical Engineering and Information Physics
University of Tokyo, Tokyo 113, Japan

1. INTRODUCTION

The purpose of this study is to investigate time-energy uncertainty relation from the viewpoint of hypothesis testing.

There are various derivations of time-energy uncertainty relation, and interpretation of Δt is also various. The most acceptable derivation is that the relation is derived from the condition that the state of a system can hardly be distinguished from the initial state. For example, it is derived in the explanation of the sudden approximation in Messiah [2]. The outline is as follows.

We suppose the Hamiltonian to change-over in a continuous way from a certain initial time t_0 to a certain final time t_1. We put

$$\Delta t = t_1 - t_0 \tag{1}$$

and denote by $H(t)$ the value taken by the Hamiltonian at time t.

Let $|0\rangle$ denote the state vector of the system at time t_0, Q_0 the projector onto the space of the vectors orthogonal to $|0\rangle$, and $U(t_1, t_0)$ the time evolution operator from t_0 to t_1. Supposing $|0\rangle$ to be of norm 1, we have

$$Q_0 = 1 - |0\rangle\langle 0|. \tag{2}$$

The sudden approximation consists in writing

$$U(t_1, t_0)|0\rangle \approx |0\rangle. \tag{3}$$

Messiah regarded a probability w as that of finding the system in a state other than the initial state and interpreted it to be a measure of the error involved in this approximation:

$$w = \langle 0|U^\dagger(t_1, t_0)Q_0 U(t_1, t_0)|0\rangle. \tag{4}$$

One obtains the expansion of w in powers of Δt by the perturbation method. Put

$$\overline{H} = \frac{1}{\Delta t}\int_{t_0}^{t_1} H(t)dt. \tag{5}$$

Quantum Communication, Computing, and Measurement
Edited by Hirota *et al.*, Plenum Press, New York, 1997

We then have

$$w = \frac{\Delta t^2}{\hbar^2} \langle 0|\overline{H}Q_0\overline{H}|0\rangle + O(T^3).$$ (6)

And since

$$\langle 0|\overline{H}Q_0\overline{H}|0\rangle = \langle 0|\overline{H}^2|0\rangle - \langle 0|\overline{H}|0\rangle^2 = (\Delta\overline{H})^2$$ (7)

where $\Delta\overline{H}$ is the root mean squre deviation of the ovservable $\overline{H}$ in the state $|0\rangle$, one has

$$w = \frac{\Delta t^2 (\Delta\overline{H})^2}{\hbar^2} + O(T^3).$$ (8)

Thus the condition for the validity of the sudden approximation, $w \ll 1$, requires that

$$\Delta t \ll \frac{\hbar}{\Delta\overline{H}}$$ (9)

We can point out some questions about the derivation of the relation. Messiah remarked that w is "the probability of finding the system in a state other than the initial state" and the condition that the state of a system can hardly be distinguished from the initial state is $w \ll 1$. The first question is that the physical meaning of "finding the system in a state other than the initial state" is so ambiguous that the above condition cannot have a firm basis. We can find the state of the system only through measurements. Therefore, the degree of discernibility between the two states is dependent on the way of detection of the system. The second question is that the detection scheme is not shown in Messiah's discussion and the indicator of discernibility is not shown from this point of view.

In this study, we investigate these questions from the viewpoint of hypothesis testing.

2. TIME-ENERGY UNCERTAINTY RELATION FROM THE VIEWPOINT OF HYPOTHESIS TESTING

2.1. APPROPRIATE INDICATOR OF DISCERNIBILITY

We investigate pure state in the following discussion. The scheme of detection of the system should be constructed from a viewpoint of measurement and the decision rule of measurement outcomes. Here, we propose an appropriate indicator of discernibility by constructing the best detection scheme. Put n copies of state ρ_t, where t is a time parameter. Consider the following hypothesis teting problem about a parameter t.

$$H_0: \quad \rho_t = \rho_{t_0} \quad \text{(null hypothesis)}$$
$$H_1: \quad \rho_t = \rho_{t_1} \quad \text{(alternative hypothesis)}$$

From hypothesis testing theory, the power of this test could represent discernibility between the states. Therefore, we define an indicator of discernibility between ρ_{t_0} and ρ_{t_1} as a maximum power of test. Then let us construct the test that maximizes the power of test γ. Since the probability distribution of measured value is determined by parameter t and measurement M, two steps is needed to maximize γ in the test. The first step is to select the most powerful test based on Neyman-Pearson's theorem subject to a fixed measurement. The second step is to select measurement in order to maximize γ of the most powerful test dependent on measurement. These processes are called optimization of the test. The selected test and measurement by optimization are called optimum test and optimum measurement respectively. Thus, the indicator of discernibility is the power of the optimum test.

2.2. ASYMPTOTIC BEHAVIOR OF THE MAXIMUM POWER OF TEST

Let us consider the power of test and the optimum measurement when $\Delta t = t_1 - t_0$ is very small and n is very large.

To begin with, consider the first step. From stein's lemma (see Appendix), the maximum power of test subject to a fixed measurement M is

$$\gamma_M \approx 1 - \exp[-nD(p_{t_0}\|p_{t_1})], \qquad (10)$$

where $D(p_{t_0}\|p_{t_1})$ is Kullback divergence defined by (25) in appendix, p_{t_0} and p_{t_1} probability distriibution of measured value at time t_0 and t_1. Because of (10) and (26), the power of test is written as

$$\gamma_M \approx 1 - \exp[-\frac{n}{2}J_M(t_0)(\Delta t)^2] + o((\Delta t)^2) \qquad (\Delta t \ll 1), \qquad (11)$$

where $J_M(t_0)$ is classical Fisher information for the classical model $p(x|t_0) = \mathrm{Tr}\rho_{t_0}M(x)$ with a measurement M defined as follows:

$$J_M(t_0) \overset{\text{def}}{=} \lim_{t \to t_0} \Sigma_x \frac{\dot{p}(x|t)^2}{p(x|t)}. \qquad (12)$$

Then consider the second step. We select the measurement which maximize γ_M. Because of (11), the optimum measurement maximizes classical Fisher information $J_M(t_0)$. From the relation between classical and quantum Fisher information (27) in appendix, the optimum measurement M_{opt} is one which satisfies

$$J_{M_{opt}}(t_0) = J^s(t_0), \qquad (13)$$

where $J^s(t_0)$ is quantum Fisher information defined as follows:

$$J^s(t_0) \overset{\text{def}}{=} 4\mathrm{Tr}\rho_{t_0}(\frac{d\rho_{t_0}}{dt})^2. \qquad (14)$$

According to the pure state quantum estimation theory [1], we have

$$J^s(t_0) = \frac{4}{\hbar^2}\Delta H^2. \qquad (15)$$

Thus we have

$$J_{M_{opt}}(t_0) = \frac{4}{\hbar^2}\Delta H^2. \qquad (16)$$

From (11) and (16), the power of the optimum test is

$$\gamma_{max} = 1 - \exp(-\frac{2n}{\hbar^2}\Delta t^2 \Delta H^2) + o(\Delta t^2) \qquad (\Delta t \ll 1). \qquad (17)$$

If $\frac{2n}{\hbar^2}\Delta t^2 \Delta H^2 \ll 1$ holds,

$$\gamma_{max} \approx \frac{2n}{\hbar^2}\Delta t^2 \Delta H^2. \qquad (18)$$

Now we can show the condition that ρ_{t_1} can hardly be distingished from ρ_{t_0} using n data when $\Delta t \ll 1$ and $n \gg 1$ are satisfied. As it means $\gamma_{max} \ll 1$, we have

$$1 - \exp(-\frac{2n}{\hbar^2}\Delta t^2 \Delta H^2) + o(\Delta t^2) \ll 1 \qquad (\Delta t \ll 1), \qquad (19)$$

or

$$\frac{2n\Delta t^2 \Delta H^2}{\hbar^2} \ll 1. \qquad (20)$$

2.3. THE OPTIMUM MEASUREMENT

Denoting by Π the measurement which is made up of operators Q_0 and $1 - Q_0$, we can easily prove that Π is one of the optimum measurements as follows.

By fixing a state ρ_t and a measurement Π, measured value follows the probability function $p_i(t)$ $(i = 1, 2)$:

$$p_1(t) = \mathrm{Tr}[\rho_t(1 - Q_0)],$$
$$p_2(t) = \mathrm{Tr}[\rho_t Q_0]$$
$$= 1 - p_1(t).$$

Therefore, classical Fisher information is

$$J_\Pi(t_0) = \lim_{t \to t_0} \left[\frac{\dot{p}_1(t)^2}{p_1(t)} + \frac{\dot{p}_2(t)^2}{p_2(t)} \right]. \tag{21}$$

This limit is intermediate form, but $p_1(t)$ is easily expanded as follows:

$$p_1(t) = 1 + \dot{p}_1(t_0)(t - t_0) + \frac{1}{2}\ddot{p}_1(t_0)(t - t_0)^2 + \cdots$$
$$= 1 - \frac{1}{\hbar^2}[\langle 0|H^2|0\rangle - (\langle 0|H|0\rangle)^2](t - t_0)^2 + \cdots.$$

Hence,

$$J_\Pi(t_0) = \lim_{t \to t_0} \frac{(-\dot{p}_1(t))^2}{1 - p_1(t)}$$
$$= -2\ddot{p}_1(t_0)$$
$$= \frac{4}{\hbar^2}\Delta H^2. \tag{22}$$

From (16) and (22), Π is one of the optimum measurements. A probability w is that of a measured value of this measurement which supports H_1.

3. CONCLUSION AND DISCUSSION

A maximum power of test in the hypothesis testing $H_0 : \rho_t = \rho_{t_0}$ $H_1 : \rho_t = \rho_{t_1}$ can be regarded as an indicator of discernibility between the states. The condition that ρ_{t_1} can hardly be distinguished from ρ_{t_0} using n data is

$$1 - \exp(-\frac{2n}{\hbar^2}\Delta t^2 \Delta H^2) + o(\Delta t^2) \ll 1 \qquad (\Delta t \ll 1),$$

or if $\frac{2n}{\hbar^2}\Delta t^2 \Delta H^2 \ll 1$,

$$\frac{2n\Delta t^2 \Delta H^2}{\hbar^2} \ll 1.$$

This condition represents time-energy uncertainty relation from the viewpoint of hypothesis testing. Measurement Π made up of opetators Q_0 and $1 - Q_0$ is one of the optimum measurements. A probability w is that of a measured value of this measurement which supports H_1. It is remarcable that the previous study has suggested the optimum measurement that maximizes the power of test.

4. APPENDIX

Here we give a brief summary of the conventional hypothesis teting theory and related fields.

Suppose that random variables X_i $(i = 1 \cdots, n)$ obey the probability distribution $p(x|\theta)$ with a given parameter $\theta \in \Theta \subset \mathbf{R}$. Simple hypothesis testing about parameter θ is as follows:

$$H_0 : \quad \theta = \theta_0 \quad (\text{ null hypothesis})$$
$$H_1 : \quad \theta = \theta_1 \quad (\text{alternative hypothesis})$$

We consider nonrandomized test based on n data. Random variables $X_1, X_2, \cdots, X_n$ are independent and obey identical probability distribution $p(x|\theta)$. $(X_1, X_2, \cdots, X_n)$ is denoted by X. A hypothesis testing rule is a partition of the measurement space into two disjoint sets U_0 and $U_1 = U_0^c$. If observation value x is an element of U_0, we decide that H_0 is true; if x is an element of U_1, we decide H_1 is true.

Accepting hypothesis H_1 when H_0 actually is true is called a type I error, and the probability of this event is denoted by α. Accepting hypothesis H_0 when H_1 actually is true is called a type II error, and the probability of this event is denoted by β.

The problem is to specify (U_0, U_1) so that α and β are as small as possible. This is not yet a well-defined problem because α generally can be made smaller by reducing U_1, although β thereby increases. The Neyman-Pearson point of view assumes that a maximum value of α given by α^* is specified and (U_0, U_1) must be determined so as to minimize β subject to the constraint that α is not larger than α^*. We call $\gamma = 1 - \beta$ power of test, and the test with the maximum power of test subject to the above constraint is called the most powerful test.

A method for finding the optimum decision regions is given by the following theorem.

Theorem (Neyman-Pearson theorem)

Denote joint density function of random variables $X = (X_1, X_2, \cdots, X_n)$ by

$$p_n(x|\theta) = \Pi_{i=1}^n p(x_i|\theta), \quad x = (x_1, x_2, \cdots x_n),$$

and put

$$\Lambda_n \equiv \frac{p_n(x|\theta_1)}{p_n(x|\theta_0)}. \tag{23}$$

When a constant k is set so that

$$\int_{-\infty}^{\infty} \cdots \int_{-\infty}^{\infty} \phi^*(x) p_n(x) dx = \alpha^*$$

holds, the regions of the most powerful test are determined as

$$U_0 = \{x : \quad \Lambda_n \leq k\}$$
$$U_1 = \{x : \quad \Lambda_n > k\},$$

where $\phi^*(x)$ is the function which is defined as

$$\phi^*(x) = \begin{cases} 1 & (\Lambda > k) \\ 0 & (\Lambda \leq k). \end{cases}$$

The asymptotic behavior can be described in the following lemma.

Theorem (Stein's lemma)

Let $\alpha^* \in (0,1)$ be given. Suppose that observaton consists of n independent measurements. Let β^* be the smallest probability of type II error over all decision rules such that the probability of type I does not exceed α^*. Then all $\alpha^* \in (0,1)$,

$$\lim_{n \to \infty} (\beta_n^*)^{\frac{1}{n}} = \exp[-D(p_{\theta_0} \| p_{\theta_1})]. \tag{24}$$

Here, $D(p\|q)$ is called Kullback divergence and defined as

$$D(p\|q) \overset{\text{def}}{=} E_p[\log \frac{q}{p}], \tag{25}$$

where p and q are probability distributions and E_p means expectation by p.

On the other hand, the following relation between Fisher information in classical information theory (we call it classical Fisher information) and Kullback divergence holds ([4])

$$D(p_{\theta+\Delta\theta}\|p_\theta) = \frac{1}{2}J(\theta)(\Delta\theta)^2 + o((\Delta\theta)^2), \tag{26}$$

where $J(\theta)$ is classical Fisher information for the classical model p_θ.

Generally, the maximum value of classical Fisher information of a given state ρ_θ equals quantum Fisher information [3]:

$$J^s(\theta) = \max_M J_M(\theta), \tag{27}$$

where $J^s(\theta)$ is quantum Fisher information and $J_M(\theta)$ is classical Fisher information for the classical model $p(x|\theta) = \text{Tr}[\rho_\theta M(x)]$ with a measurement M.

REFERENCES

[1] Fujiwara, A. and H. Nagaoka, "Quantum Fisher metric and estimation for pure state models," Phys. lett, 201A, 119-124(1995).

[2] Messiah, A., "MECANIQUE QUANTIQUE," Dunod, Paris 1959

[3] Nagaoka, H., " On Fisher information of quantum statistical models," SITA'87, 241-246,(1987).

[4] Nagaoka, H., " On the relation between Kullback divergence and Fisher information - from calssical systems to quantum systems - ,"(1991).

AN OPEN SYSTEM APPROACH TO QUANTUM COMPUTERS

Luigi Accardi

Graduate School of Polymathematics, Nagoya University
and Centro Vito Volterra, Università di Roma "Tor Vergata"

1. INTRODUCTION

Two of the basic characteristics of any computational procedure are:

i) iteration of a basic operation

ii) convergence to the result in a finite number of steps.

Denoting V the basic operation of item (i), item (ii) can be rephrased as follows: for every input state ψ_{in} there exists an output state ψ_{out} (possibly depending on ψ_{in}) and an integer N (also depending on ψ_{in} in general) such that for each $n \geq N$

$$V^n \psi_{in} = \psi_{out} \tag{1.1}$$

The relation (1.1) means that the final state is reached after a finite number of steps and that the final state is a fixed point for the basic iteration procedure, i.e.

$$V \psi_{out} = \psi_{out} \tag{1.2}$$

If V is invertible, then (1.2) holds also for V^{-1} and therefore (1.1) is possible if and only if $\psi_{in} = \psi_{out}$. From this several authors (cf. [Deut85] for example) have concluded that a quantum computer cannot produce exact, but only probabilistic results. This conclusion is correct as long as one limits one's considerations to *isolated* quantum systems, which evolve according to the (reversible) Schrödinger evolution.

But *open systems* exist in nature: they can be built and controlled. Therefore nothing prevents the possibility to *enlarge the definition of quantum computer* by allowing it to be an open quantum system. The developments of quantum probability in the past ten years have produced some powerful and easy to use tools very well suited for the description of open quantum systems. In particular the theory of quantum Markov chains is built on some basic principles which are very similar to those currently used in the theory of quantum computers, namely:

I.) discrete time

II.) nearest neighbours (or more generally, local) interaction

III.) possibility of combining parallel local operations with nearest–neighbour global operations (typically the one step shift).

In the present note, using ideas and techniques of quantum Markov chains, we shall prove that an *open system approach to quantum computers* is in principle realizable. Even if we shall not discuss this problem abstractly, but rather in a concrete, important example: *the operation of addition*, we shall however formulate the various steps of the algorithm so to suggest generalizations in various directions.

In the addition, by quantum computer, of two real numbers x, x' one has to associate to them a quantum (input) state $\psi_{x,x'}$ and the output state should be a state $\psi_{x+x'}$ associated to their sum.

In the usual approach to quantum computers the basic operation V is described by a *unitary* operator V (both V^*V and VV^* are equal to the identity). In the open system approach the basic operation V is only a *partial isometry* (both V^*V and VV^* are projections). There are known theorems [Hal67] according to which a partial isometry V can always be extended to a unitary operator acting on a space $\mathcal{H}$ which contains the initial one $\mathcal{H}_0$ on which V was acting. This is called a *dilation* of the partial isometry V. In this picture the orthogonal complement of $\mathcal{H}_0$ in $\mathcal{H}$ is interpreted as *environment*; the unitary operator extending V is interpreted as *Schrödinger evolution of the original system coupled to the environment*; and the original partial isometry V is interpreted as *reduced evolution* obtained by *projecting away* all the degrees of freedom of the environment. It is clear that, in many important cases, the influence of the environment shall be only of a *global, collective nature* and therefore a single partial isometry can have several quite different dilations. Thus, working with partial isometries we are still in the framework of basic quantum theory.

Now let us examine in more detail what is needed to solve the quantum addition problem. In the notations introduced above, we are looking for:

i) a Hilbert space $\mathcal{H}$

ii) a partial isometry V from $\mathcal{H}$ to $\mathcal{H}$

iii) a map which to a pair of real numbers x, x' associates a unit vector $\psi_{x,x'} \in \mathcal{H}$

iv) a map which to a simple real number y associates a unit vector ψ_y

v) for each pair of real numbers x, x', an integer $N(x, x')$ such that for any $n \geq N(x, x')$

$$V^n \psi_{x,x'} = \psi_{x+x'} \tag{1.3}$$

Notice that condition (1.3), or more generally (1.1), has a weak analogue, in statistical physics, in the relation

$$\lim_{n \to \infty} V^n \psi_{in} = \psi_{out} \tag{1.4}$$

which is called *tendence to equilibrium*. The relation (1.4) is weaker than (1.3) because it is only asymptotic. Moreover in the most commonly studied physical phenomena there is *only one equilibrium state*, while in (1.3) we must have at least as many different equilibrium states as there are real numbers and, for any such number y, its *domain of attraction* (i.e. the set of all pairs $\psi_{x,x'}$, such that $V^N \psi_{x,x'} = \psi_y$ for some integer N) is the line $x + x' = y$.

So the problem of quantum addition corresponds to a highly anomalous statistical mechanics model: one which not only there are infinitely many equilibrium points but is also such that infinitely many of them are reached *after a finite number of steps* (this is what we call *finite convergence to equilibrium*).

Another interesting anomaly with respect to statistical physics is the following: usually dissipation tends to destroy coherence, i.e. to transform a pure state into a mixture. But, if we code numbers by pure states, then the result of addition, being also a number, should also correspond to a pure state. This means that our *dynamics* not only must have infinitely many equilibrium points but it must also be such that these equilibrium points are *pure states*.

The question is now: *can quantum theory produce concrete and easily manageable examples of such systems?*

In the following we shall prove that the answer is affirmative and that the solution is related to the theory of quantum Markov chains (but this connection shall be discussed elsewhere).

A final remark: the idea of *finite convergence* to a (possibly infinite) set of equilibrium points with disjoint domains of attraction can also be useful in image recognition or in some models of cognitive sciences. From this point of view the open system approach to quantum computer might be a viable alternative to models of such systems based on neural networks. In fact, as it shall be clear from the following, ours is a space–time model discrete in time and in which space is idealized by the lattice $\{1, 2\} \times \mathbf{Z}$. To replace the 2–point lattice $\{1, 2\}$ by arbitrary an finite (or infinite) lattice is not a big problem, but the construction of concrete and explicitly tractable higher dimensional models, with preservation of the *finite convergence property* and of the purity of the equilibrium states, requires some ingenuity.

2. AN ALGORITHM FOR ADDITION

In this Section we recall some elementary and well known facts about addition.

Let us start with the remark that $\{0, 1\}$ has two group structures: one for addition (mod 2), with identity 0, and another for multiplication, with identity 1.

$$\varepsilon \dotplus \varepsilon' := \varepsilon + \varepsilon' \pmod{2} = \begin{cases} 0, & \text{if } \varepsilon = \varepsilon' \\ 1, & \text{if } \varepsilon \neq \varepsilon' \end{cases}$$

$$\varepsilon \varepsilon' = \begin{cases} 1, & \text{if } \varepsilon = \varepsilon' = 1 \\ 0, & \text{otherwise} \end{cases}$$

LEMMA (2.1). For any $\varepsilon, \varepsilon' \in \{0, 1\}$ and $n \in \mathbf{Z}$ one has

$$(\varepsilon + \varepsilon')2^n = (\varepsilon \dotplus \varepsilon')2^n + \varepsilon \varepsilon' 2^{n+1} \tag{2.1}$$

PROOF. Direct verification.

Denote

$$\mathbf{Q}^\circ = \{x \in [0, 1] : \exists n = n(x) ; \ x = \sum_{k=n}^{\infty} \varepsilon_k 2^k ; \quad \varepsilon_k \in \{0, 1\} \text{ and almost all } \varepsilon_k = 0\} \tag{2.2}$$

Notice that, given any pair of numbers $x, x' \in \mathbf{Q}^\circ$, one can always assume that

$$n(x) = n(y) \tag{2.3}$$

In the following this assumption shall always be done for any pair of numbers in $\mathbf{Q}^\circ$. Moreover, for an arbitrary number $x \in \mathbf{Q}^\circ$ we shall use the notation

$$x = \sum_{k \in \mathbf{Z}} \varepsilon_k(x) 2^k \tag{2.4}$$

and when no confusion can arise we simply write ε_k instead of $\varepsilon_k(x)$.

LEMMA (2.2). For $x = \sum_{k \geq m} \varepsilon_k 2^k$, $x' = \sum_{k \geq m} \varepsilon'_k 2^k$ in $\mathbf{Q}^\circ$ and under the assumption (2.3), one has

$$x + x' = (\varepsilon_m \dot{+} \varepsilon'_m)2^m + \sum_{k \geq m+1} (\varepsilon_k \dot{+} \varepsilon'_k + \varepsilon_{k-1} \varepsilon'_{k-1})2^k \qquad (2.5)$$

REMARK. Notice that the second $+$ in $\varepsilon_k \dot{+} \varepsilon'_k + \varepsilon_{k-1} \varepsilon'_{k-1}$ is without the dot. Therefore (2.5) is not the binary expansion of a number.

PROOF. Using (2.1) one finds

$$x + x' = \sum_{k \geq m} (\varepsilon_k + \varepsilon'_k)2^k = \sum_{k \geq m} (\varepsilon_k \dot{+} \varepsilon'_k)2^k + \sum_{k \geq m} (\varepsilon_k \varepsilon'_k)2^{k+1} \qquad (2.6)$$

denoting $h := k + 1$, in the second sum, the right hand side of (2.6) becomes equal to the right hand side of (2.5).

In the notations of Lemma (2.2) the standard algorithm to perform the addition $x + x'$ can be described as follows: define two new numbers x_1, x'_1 characterized by the following binary expansions:

$$\varepsilon_h(x_1) = \begin{cases} 0 & \text{for } h \leq n \\ \varepsilon_h(x) \dot{+} \varepsilon_h(x') & \text{for } h \geq n+1 \end{cases}$$

$$\varepsilon_h(x'_1) = \begin{cases} 0 & \text{for } h \leq n \\ \varepsilon_{h-1}(x)\varepsilon_{h-1}(x') & \text{for } h \geq n+1 \end{cases}$$

apply Lemma (2.2) to them and iterate. To prove that the algorithm converges in a finite number of steps, denote M the largest integer such that $\varepsilon_n(x) = \varepsilon_n(x') = 0$ for any $n \geq M$. Then clearly

$$\varepsilon_h(x_1) = \varepsilon_h(x'_1) = 0 \quad \text{for } h \geq M+1$$

Moreover in any case

$$\varepsilon_M(x_1) \cdot \varepsilon_M(x'_1) = 0$$

and this implies that, starting from the second step of the algorithm, all the digits of index k, with $k \geq M+1$ will be zero. Therefore the algorithm converges in $M - n + 1$ steps.

The algorithm gives $x + x'$ according to the following rule:
The 1–st possibly nonzero digit of $x + x'$ is

$$(\varepsilon_m(x) \dot{+} \varepsilon_m(x'))2^m$$

For $k = 1, \ldots, M - n + 1$, the $(m + k)$–th digit of $x + x'$ is

$$\varepsilon_{m+k}(x_k) \dot{+} \varepsilon_{m+k}(x'_k)$$

where x_k, x'_k are the two numbers defined by the k–th step of the algorithm.

In the following Section we shall discuss how to implement this algorithm by a quantum computer.

3. AN ALGORITHM FOR ADDITION

We want to associate a quantum state to each pair of numbers $x, x' \in \mathbf{Q}^\circ$ in such a way that the algorithm described in Section (1.) is implementable by a unitary transformation. One might be tempted to associate to the pair $\varepsilon, \varepsilon'$ the vector $\varepsilon \otimes \varepsilon'$, however the following Lemma shows that this cannot be done in a unitary way.

LEMMA (3.1). The map

$$\varepsilon \otimes \varepsilon' \mapsto (\varepsilon \dot{+} \varepsilon') \otimes \varepsilon \varepsilon' \tag{3.1}$$

cannot be implemented by a unitary transformation.

PROOF. If it were, for $\varepsilon, \delta, \varepsilon', \delta' \in \{0, 1\}$, one should have:

$$\langle \delta, \varepsilon \rangle \langle \delta', \varepsilon' \rangle = \langle \delta \otimes \delta', \varepsilon \otimes \varepsilon' \rangle = \langle (\delta \dot{+} \delta') \otimes \delta \delta', \quad (\varepsilon \dot{+} \varepsilon') \otimes \varepsilon \varepsilon' \rangle$$

But, for fixed $\varepsilon, \varepsilon'$, the right hand side of the above identity is symmetric in δ, δ', while the left hand side is not.

The reason why the naive choice is not the natural one is that, since addition is commutative, the state associated to a pair of digits $(\varepsilon, \varepsilon')$ should not distinguish the order of the factors. A possible choice is to associate, to the pair $(\varepsilon, \varepsilon')$, the vector:

$$\psi_{\varepsilon, \varepsilon'} := \begin{cases} 0 \otimes 0 \text{ if } \varepsilon = \varepsilon' = 0 \\ 1 \otimes 1 \text{ if } \varepsilon = \varepsilon' = 1 \\ \frac{1}{\sqrt{2}} (0 \otimes 1 + 1 \otimes 0) \text{ if } \varepsilon = 0, \ \varepsilon' = 1 \\ \frac{1}{\sqrt{2}} (1 \otimes 0 - 0 \otimes 1) \text{ if } \varepsilon = 1, \ \varepsilon' = 0 \end{cases} \tag{3.2}$$

LEMMA (3.2). There is a unique unitary map $U_+ : \mathbf{C}^2 \otimes \mathbf{C}^2 \to \mathbf{C}^2 \otimes \mathbf{C}^2$ characterized by:

$$U_+ \psi_{\varepsilon, \varepsilon'} = (\varepsilon \dot{+} \varepsilon') \otimes \varepsilon \varepsilon' \quad , \qquad if \ (\varepsilon, \varepsilon') \neq (1, 0) \tag{3.3}$$

$$U_+ \psi_{1,0} = U_+ \left[\frac{1}{\sqrt{2}} (1 \otimes 0 - 0 \otimes 1) \right] = 1 \otimes 1 \tag{3.4}$$

REMARK. More explicitly, U_+ in Lemma (3.2) is defined by

$$U_+ \psi_{00} = 0 \otimes 0 \ , \ U_+ \psi_{01} = 1 \otimes 0 \ , \ U_+ \psi_{10} = 1 \otimes 1 \ , \ U_+ \psi_{11} = 0 \otimes 1 \tag{3.5}$$

PROOF. The 3 vectors (3.5) plus the singlet vector form an orthonormal basis of $\mathbf{C}^2 \otimes \mathbf{C}^2$ whose image under U_+ is the orthonormal basis $\varepsilon \otimes \varepsilon'$.

REMARK. Nothing changes in the above discussion if we exchange the roles of the singlet and the symmetric states, i.e. if we associate, to the pair $(\varepsilon, \varepsilon')$, the vector:

$$\phi_{\varepsilon, \varepsilon'} := \begin{cases} 0 \otimes 0 \text{ if } \varepsilon = \varepsilon' = 0 \\ 1 \otimes 1 \text{ if } \varepsilon = \varepsilon' = 1 \\ \frac{1}{\sqrt{2}} (0 \otimes 1 - 1 \otimes 0) \text{ if } \varepsilon \neq \varepsilon' \end{cases}$$

and we define the unitary map

$$U_- : \mathbf{C}^2 \otimes \mathbf{C}^2 \to \mathbf{C}^2 \otimes \mathbf{C}^2$$

by:

$$U_-\phi_{\varepsilon,\varepsilon'} = (\varepsilon \dot{+} \varepsilon') \otimes \varepsilon\varepsilon'$$

$$U_- \left[\frac{1}{\sqrt{2}} (1 \otimes 0 + 0 \otimes 1) \right] = 1 \otimes 1$$

It might however change from the point of view of the facility of the physical implementation. We shall use the notation U_o to denote either of the maps $U_\pm$. But to fix the ideas, in the following we shall only discuss U_+.

In order to deal with inputs of arbitrary length it is convenient to introduce the Hilbert space

$$\mathcal{H} := \otimes_\mathbf{Z}(\mathbf{C}^2 \otimes \mathbf{C}^2) \tag{3.6}$$

where the tensor product is considered with respect to the *vacuum* sequence

$$\Phi := \otimes_\mathbf{Z}(0 \otimes 0) = \otimes_\mathbf{Z}\psi_{00} \tag{3.7}$$

This means that the set of *input states*

$$\mathcal{I} := \{\otimes_\mathbf{Z}\psi_{\varepsilon_k,\varepsilon'_k} \ : \ \varepsilon_k, \varepsilon'_k \in \{0,1\} \ , \ \varepsilon_k = \varepsilon'_k = 0 \text{ for almost all } k\} \tag{3.8}$$

(*almost all* means *all but a finite number*) is an orthonormal basis of $\mathcal{H}$. Notice that the infinite tensor product

$$\otimes_\mathbf{Z}U_+$$

where U_+ is the (local) operator defined given in Lemma (3.2), is well defined (because U_+ is unitary and $U_+\psi_{00} = \psi_{00}$). From this it follows that also the family

$$\{\otimes_\mathbf{Z}(\varepsilon_k \otimes \varepsilon'_k) \ : \ \varepsilon_k = \varepsilon'_k = 0 \text{ for almost all } k\} \tag{3.9}$$

is an orthonormal basis of $\mathcal{H}$. Therefore we can define the right (i.e. from left to right) shift on the second factor, denoted S_2, by

$$S_2\Big(\otimes_\mathbf{Z}(\varepsilon_k \otimes \varepsilon'_k)\Big) := \otimes_\mathbf{Z}(\varepsilon_k \otimes \varepsilon'_{k-1})$$

This is a unitary operator because it maps the orthonormal basis $\mathcal{I}$ into itself. Finally we denote by P the orthogonal projection onto the symmetric subspace of $\mathbf{C}^2 \otimes \mathbf{C}^2$, i.e. the subspace generated by the vectors

$$\psi_{00} \ , \ \psi_{01} \ , \ \psi_{11}$$

the action of P on the $\varepsilon \otimes \varepsilon'$ basis is

$$P\varepsilon \otimes \varepsilon' = \psi_{\varepsilon \dot{+} \varepsilon',\varepsilon\varepsilon'}$$

With these notations we can introduce the partial isometry V on $\mathcal{H}$ defined by:

$$V := (\otimes_\mathbf{Z}P)S_2(\otimes_\mathbf{Z}U_o) \tag{3.10}$$

If, to every input state $\otimes_\mathbf{Z}\psi_{\varepsilon_k,\varepsilon'_k}$ we associate the sum of the two numbers $x, x' \in \mathbf{Q}^o$:

$$x = \sum \varepsilon_k 2^k \ ; \quad x = \sum \varepsilon'_k 2^k \tag{3.11}$$

and conversely to the sum of any pair $x, x' \in Q$, of the form (3.11), we associate the input state $\otimes_\mathbf{Z}\psi_{\varepsilon_k,\varepsilon'_k}$, the action of V on $\mathcal{H}$ can be schematized in the three steps illustrated in the following table, in which the products $a \otimes b$ are written as vertical columns with two components:

$$\text{INPUT STATE}$$

$\cdots$	$\psi_{0,0}$	$\psi_{\varepsilon_{-n},\varepsilon'_{-n}}$	$\psi_{\varepsilon_{-n+1},\varepsilon'_{-n+1}}$	$\cdots$	

$$\text{APPLICATION OF } \otimes_{\mathbf{Z}} U_o$$

$\cdots$	0	$\varepsilon_{-n} \dotplus \varepsilon'_{-n}$	$\varepsilon_{-n+1} \dotplus \varepsilon'_{-n+1}$	$\cdots$	
$\cdots$	0	$\varepsilon_{-n}\varepsilon'_{-n}$	$\varepsilon_{-n+1}\varepsilon'_{-n+1}$	$\cdots$	

$$\text{APPLICATION OF } S_2$$

$\cdots$	0	$\varepsilon_{-n} \dotplus \varepsilon'_{-n}$	$\varepsilon_{-n+1} \dotplus \varepsilon'_{-n+1}$	$\varepsilon_{-n+2} \dotplus \varepsilon'_{-n+2}$	$\cdots$
$\cdots$	0	0	$\varepsilon_{-n}\varepsilon'_{-n}$	$\varepsilon_{-n+1}\varepsilon'_{-n+1}$	$\cdots$

$$\text{APPLICATION OF } \otimes_{\mathbf{Z}} P$$

$\cdots$	$\psi_{0,0}$	$\psi_{\varepsilon_{-n} \dotplus \varepsilon'_{-n},0}$	$\psi_{\varepsilon_{-n+1} \dotplus \varepsilon'_{-n+1},\varepsilon_{-n}\varepsilon'_{-n}}$	$\cdots$	

$$\text{ITERATION}$$

Notice that at each step the number of vectors of the form $\psi_{\delta,0}$ increases of one unit, so after a finite number of steps all the vectors shall have this form.

With these notations we can sum up our discussion in the following statement:

THEOREM. For any $\psi_{\varepsilon_k,\varepsilon'_k}$, x, x' as above the limit

$$\lim_{N\to\infty} V^N(\otimes_{\mathbf{Z}}\psi_{\varepsilon_{k'},\varepsilon'_k}) = \otimes_{\mathbf{Z}}\psi_{\delta_k,0}$$

exists finitely, in the sense that there exists $N(x,x') < +\infty$ such that, for any $N \geq N(x,x)$

$$V^N(\otimes_{\mathbf{Z}}\psi_{\varepsilon_k,\varepsilon'_k}) = \otimes_{\mathbf{Z}}\psi_{\delta_k,0}$$

where the $\delta_k \in \{0,1\}$ are the coefficients of the binary expansion of $x + x'$, i.e.

$$x + x' = \sum \delta_k 2^k$$

REMARK. The theorem above shows that an open quantum computer, not unlikely a usual computer, can add two numbers with a finite binary expansion. In order to include all rational, and even real, numbers we loose not only finite convergence but also the Hilbert space picture. In fact the states corresponding to these numbers cannot live in the Hilbert space defined by (3.8) or (3.9) (more generally: the only Hilbert space where all the states (3.8), without the restriction of having almost all factors equal to the vacuum, can live is a nonseparable one). In order to include these numbers, the vector states (3.8) should be replaced by the corresponding expectation values and finite convergence by the usual convergence to equilibrium, i.e. (1.4) where the limit is meant in the sense of weak convergence. However, as long as we remain in the usual framework of Turing machines, which requires only a virtual and not actual infinity, the algebraic setting of the present note is sufficient.

REFERENCES

[BeBr84] C. H. Bennett and G. Brassard, in Proc. of the IEEE Int. Conf. on Computers, Systems, and Signal Processing, Bangalore, India (IEEE, New York, 1984), pp.175-179.

[Deut85] Deutsch, D., "Quantum theory, the Church-Turing principle and the universal quantum computer," Proc. R. Soc. Lond. A 400, 97-117 (1985).

[Deut92] D. Deutsh and R. Jozsa, "Rapid solution of problems by quantum computation", Proc. R. Soc. Lond. A 439 (1992) 553-558.

[Hal67] Halmos Paul R.: A Hilbert space problem book. Van Nostrand (1967).

Part IV.
Quantum Optics

ATOM LASERS

C. M. Savage, G. M. Moy, and J. J. Hope

Department of Physics and Theoretical Physics
Australian National University
Canberra, ACT 0200, Australia
Email: Craig.Savage@anu.edu.au

1. INTRODUCTION

Optical lasers produce beams of photons with high coherence and spectral brightness. Consequently they are enormously important for quantum communications and measurements. Atom lasers are proposed devices that would emit similarly coherent and bright beams of bosonic atoms. These properties would make them useful atomic sources for atom optics experiments and applications.

The slow speed of atoms compared to photons makes it unlikely that they will be useful for communications. However in the broader of context of *quantum* communications they may be useful for quantum cryptography [1] and quantum computation [2]. The primary advantage of atoms over photons is that atoms have internal electronic structure. This structure can potentially be used for quantum coding or computation.

This article introduces the physics of atom lasers. Practical schemes for constructing them and possible applications are discussed. We then focus on the particular problem of coupling the atoms out of the device. An atom laser design based on hollow optical fibers and a Raman transition for output coupling is described [3].

2. THE PHYSICS OF ATOM LASERS

Central to the physics of lasers are stimulated transitions between quantum states. The rate of such transitions are increased by the presence of bosons in the final state. With N bosons in the final state the rate is increased by the factor $N + 1$ over the rate with no bosons in the final state. This enhancement is a purely quantum statistical effect. It is due to the fact that quantum mechanics allows truly identical particles and in particular to the invariance of bosonic quantum states under particle interchange. This is in contrast to the case of fermions whose quantum state changes sign under particle interchange.

Stimulation of transitions by final state *atoms* has been discussed in the context of amplification of atom fields [4], and in the context of stimulated atomic [5] and nuclear decay [6, 7].

However there is more to a laser than stimulated transitions. In the optical laser the bosons are photons. The initial quantum state is an excited atom with N photons

Quantum Communication, Computing, and Measurement
Edited by Hirota *et al.*, Plenum Press, New York, 1997

Table 1. Examples of generic laser properties in the optical and atom laser cases.

Generic laser	Optical laser	Atom laser
A source of bosons	the pump	a source of atoms, perhaps not in the same electronic state as the output
A discrete single particle state, called the "lasing mode"	a mode of an optical cavity	an energy eigenstate of an atom trap
A dissipative mechanism for concentrating many bosons into the lasing mode	spontaneous emission	inelastic collisions between atoms *or* spontaneous emission of a photon
A mechanism for coupling the atoms out of the lasing mode into an output beam	a partially transmitting mirror	tunneling through a trap wall *or* switching of the internal atomic state

in the mode and the final state is a de-excited atom with $N+1$ photons in the mode. Therefore the transition rate increases as the mode becomes populated with photons. For a high enough pumping rate, the laser threshold, a positive feedback process occurs. This runaway process is terminated by depletion of the excited atoms, thus stabilizing the laser intensity.

Analogous lasing processes in principle can be achieved with other bosons besides photons and atoms; phonons and excitons have been suggested as possibilities. The exciton laser has been analyzed by Imamoglu and Ram. It can produce a coherent beam of either excitons or photons [8]. Amplification of a an exciton beam by stimulated emission has been observed in Cu_2O [9].

The atom laser concept is based on an analogy with the optical laser. There are four major components of a generic laser system:

- a source of bosons;

- a discrete single particle state, called the "laser mode";

- a dissipative mechanism for concentrating many bosons into the laser mode;

- a mechanism for coupling the atoms out of the laser mode into an output beam.

Table 1 gives examples of how these generic components can be realized in both optical and atom laser systems. We next consider the case of the atom laser in detail.

The *source atoms* may be in external (trap) and/or internal (electronic) states which are different from the laser mode state. The transition into the laser mode may be mediated electromagnetically, by lasers or spontaneous emission, or mechanically, by collisions.

The *laser mode* is usually an energy eigenstate of an atom trap. Usually this is the ground state, although unlike the case for Bose-Einstein Condensates (BECs) it does not have to be the ground state. Atom traps can utilize magnetic or optical forces. The magnetic force, used in BEC experiments [10–12], is the force on an atomic magnetic dipole in a magnetic field gradient. The optical force is the far detuned dipole force [13]. This can either attract atoms to, or repel them from, high field intensity regions, depending on the detuning between the atom and field. Blue detuning, in which the field is tuned above an atomic resonance, is usually preferred since it repels from high intensity regions. This minimizes the excited state population and hence unwanted spontaneous emission. In order to emphasize the importance of a directed output beam some traps are described as "atom cavities" by analogy with optical Fabry-Perot cavities [14, 15].

The *dissipative mechanism* cools the atoms. This cooling produces a degenerate quantum gas of atoms in the laser mode. This quantum degeneracy makes possible a high spectral brightness in the output atomic beam. The degenerate quantum gas is similar to the BECs. The main difference is that the BECs are close to thermodynamic equilibrium while the atom laser is strongly coupled to both inputs and outputs.

A possible atom laser scheme is to add output coupling to a BEC. The simplest coupling is to *turn off the trap* and release the condensate. This process conserves momentum but not energy. This is because, according to the Schrödinger equation, a sudden change in the Hamiltonian only changes the time derivative of the wavefunction, not the wavefunction itself [16]. As a result the output atoms have the same wavefunction, in position or momentum space, as the ground state of the trap. However once in free space the momentum distribution is equivalent to a $p^2/2M$ kinetic energy distribution. Energy is conserved because it is exchanged between the atoms and the moving walls of the trap. Hence, although the BEC atoms in the trap have a well defined energy the released atoms have an energy spread. By analogy with the optical case this spread is referred to as the atom laser "linewidth". It is ultimately due to the momentum spread required in the trap by the uncertainty principle. So larger traps have more monochromatic outputs.

Another suggestion is to make a "hole" in the trap, perhaps by using a laser to switch the atoms to an untrapped state. Although this may improve the directivity of the output beam it does not necessarily solve the linewidth problem. This is because switching the atom to an untrapped state is equivalent to turning off the trap for that atom. The output coupling problem will be discussed further in the next section.

We now briefly describe some proposed atom laser schemes. We classify them into two groups according to how the dissipation is achieved. One group uses photon spontaneous emission and the other atom-atom collisions.

The spontaneous emission based schemes include: the generic proposal of Olshanii, Castin and Dalibard [17]; the dark state cooling scheme of Wiseman and Collett [18]; the dipole trap scheme of Spreeuw *et al.* [19]; and our Raman output coupling scheme [3], which is discussed further in section 4. In these schemes the kinetic energy change of the recoiling atom depends on the direction and energy of the spontaneously emitted photon. Since we assume that the emitted photon is not reabsorbed the process is dissipative and irreversible. The scheme of Pfau and Gauck [20] also relies on spontaneous emission. However the atoms are confined in one dimension only, so the output may not be coherent across the transverse dimensions.

The collisions based schemes achieve dissipation in various ways. In the scheme of Holland *et al.* [21], elastic binary collisions result in one atom gaining and the other losing energy. The higher energy atom is assumed to be irreversibly lost from the system. This model has been considered in more detail by Wiseman, Martin and Walls [22] who find that the collisions broaden the laser linewidth beyond that of the empty mode. This is in stark contrast with the optical laser whose linewidth narrows dramatically above threshold. Guzman, Moore and Meystre [23] obtain dissipation with light assisted inelastic collisions.

For any atom laser, collisions are likely to limit the population of the lasing mode [24]. In addition their effect on atom laser linewidth is yet to be fully considered. It is likely to be an important practical problem.

Conventional optical lasers require atomic population inversion. This is because the emission of photons into the laser mode is a reversible process. In particular the ratio of the rate of stimulated emission of photons to that of absorption of photons equals the ratio of the excited to the ground state atomic population. So for stimulated emission to dominate, the excited state population must exceed the ground state population.

The corresponding rates in atom lasers are the transition rates of atoms into and out of the laser mode. In many atom laser schemes the transition into the laser mode is irreversible, so that the rate back out of the laser mode is negligible. This is achieved, for example, by involving a spontaneously emitted photon. With such input irreversibility population inversion is not required.

3. OUTPUT COUPLING

In this section we consider the problem of getting the atoms out of the laser mode into the laboratory. Three types of output coupling have been suggested for atom lasers: dropping a wall; tunneling through a wall; and switching the atomic state so it no longer sees the wall.

We have already considered some problems associated with *dropping a wall*. This process cannot produce a linewidth less than that of the laser mode wavefunction in free space. It also produces a pulsed rather than a a continuous output beam.

Tunneling through a potential barrier solves this problem. The barrier is analogous to a partially transmitting optical mirror. It could be, for example, a sheet of blue detuned light forming a dipole potential barrier. There are also problems with such an output coupler. Firstly the tunneling rate depends exponentially on the width and height of the barrier [25]. For an atom of mass M and energy E the transmission coefficient through a high and broad barrier $V(x)$ is approximately [16]

$$T \approx \exp\left\{-2\int_a^b \sqrt{2M(V(x) - E)/\hbar^2}\, dx\right\},\tag{1}$$

where $E = V(a) = V(b)$ and $V(x) > E$ for $a < x < b$. Thus the tunneling rate is very sensitive to fluctuations in the barrier. A second problem is that the tunneling rate increases with the energy of the atoms. If the laser mode is the ground state it will have the lowest output rate. Hence the output may be dominated by atoms from the higher laser cavity states.

Output coupling by *switching the atomic state* is likely to offer the most control. Switching the atomic state of all the laser mode atoms at some rate is a continuous version of dropping the wall and suffers from the same linewidth problems. However it may be possible to control the linewidth by selectively outputting particular laser mode momentum groups.

One way to switch the atomic state is with a two-photon Raman transition. Raman transitions have the advantage of potentially very small linewidths and long lifetimes for the final state. Small linewidths allow momentum selectivity using the doppler effect. The ultimate linewidth attainable with the Raman scheme remains to be determined. One difficulty is the momentum spread inevitably associated with a laser beam tightly focussed into the laser cavity. The output atoms must be isolated from this momentum spread.

4. AN ATOM LASER BASED ON RAMAN TRANSITIONS

In this section we describe our atom laser scheme. More details can be found in reference [3]. The scheme uses three different electronic states of the atoms. The pump

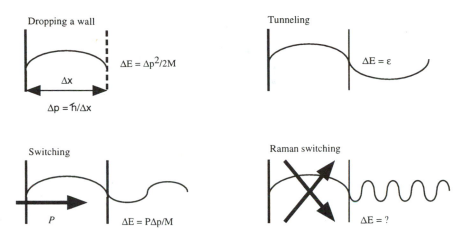

Figure 1. Schematic diagrams of four output coupling mechanisms. The vertical lines represent the laser cavity walls. The curves inside the cavity represent the laser mode wavefunction. The curves outside the cavity represent the output wavefunction. The arrows represent switching lasers. Δx is the cavity length and Δp the corresponding momentum uncertainty. ε is the time-energy uncertainty linewidth of the cavity mode, due to tunneling. P is the momentum transferred to an atom by the lasers.

atoms are in a metastable state $|1\rangle$. They spontaneously emit into state $|2\rangle$, which is the dissipative step, thus loading the laser mode. The output coupling is by a Raman transition into state $|3\rangle$.

A possible implementation of our atom laser scheme would use hollow optical fibres, see Figure 2. These have the advantage of providing confinement in two dimensions, so that the atom laser becomes quasi-one-dimensional like an optical laser. Longitudinal confinement, to form the laser cavity, is provided by blue detuned optical laser beams focussed into the fiber hole. Single mode hollow optical fibres, with holes of about

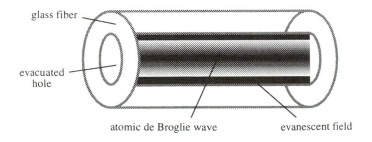

Figure 2. Schematic diagram of a hollow optical fiber atom waveguide.

1.6μm diameter have been proposed for guiding atoms [26] and multimode fibres have been demonstrated experimentally to guide atoms [27]. Other atom optics devices, such as interferometers, might also be made from hollow optical fiber. A hollow optical fiber atom laser would have the advantage of producing an atomic beam matched to such devices. Alternatively a donut mode laser beam, with a hole in the middle, might be used for transverse confinement.

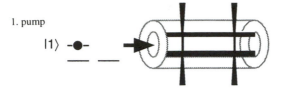

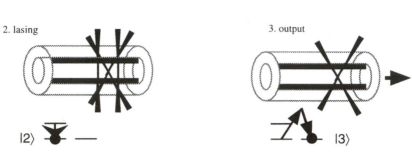

Figure 3. Schematic diagram of the three major steps in our atom laser scheme. In each step only the light interacting with the atoms in the *relevant* atomic state is shown (solid black shading). This state is indicated by a circle on the level diagram. Step 1 is the loading of the pump cavity. Step 2 is the transition to the laser mode of the laser cavity. Step 3 is the Raman transition to the output state.

For calculational convenience we assume that the pump atoms are accumulated in a pump cavity. The laser cavity is much shorter than, and inside of, the pump cavity, see Figure 3. We denote the number of atoms in the pump cavity by N_1, the number in the jth energy level of the laser cavity by N_{2j}, and the number of atoms in the output state $|3\rangle$ by N_3. Then we can derive the following rate equations

$$\frac{dN_1}{dt} = r - \gamma_{12} N_1 \sum_j g_j (N_{2j} + 1) - \gamma_{12} N_1 (1 - \sum_j g_j), \tag{2}$$

$$\frac{dN_{2j}}{dt} = \gamma_{12} N_1 g_j (N_{2j} + 1) - r_{23} N_{2j} + r_{23} G_j N_3 (N_{2j} + 1), \tag{3}$$

$$\frac{dN_3}{dt} = \sum_j r_{23} N_{2j} - \sum_j r_{23} G_j N_3 (N_{2j} + 1) - \Gamma N_3. \tag{4}$$

We now explain the meaning of each of the terms on the right hand sides of these equations. This also serves to fully define our model. The first term, r, in Eq.(2) is the rate of input of atoms into the pump cavity. The second term sums the transition rates from the pump cavity into each of the laser cavity modes. γ_{12} is the spontaneous emission rate from state $|1\rangle$ to state $|2\rangle$. g_j is the average wavefunction overlap between the populated pump cavity modes and the jth laser cavity mode, which has population N_{2j}. $(N_{2j} + 1)$ is the final state Bose stimulation factor. The last term in Eq.(2) is the transition rate out of the pump cavity into spatial modes *not* in the laser cavity.

The first term in Eq.(3) is the transition rate into the jth laser cavity mode from the pump cavity. The second term is the Raman transition rate into state $|3\rangle$, with r_{23} the single atom rate. The third term is the reverse Raman rate into the laser cavity. G_j is the proportion of the atoms N_3 that came via a Raman transition from the jth laser cavity mode, and hence that can make the reverse transition back to it.

The first term in Eq.(4) is the Raman transition rate from the laser cavity into state $|3\rangle$. The second term is the reverse Raman rate back into the laser cavity. The final term is the output coupling rate. It is the rate at which atoms leave the spatial interaction region occupied by the Raman laser beams. The single atom output rate is

$$\Gamma = \frac{P_R/M}{L}, \tag{5}$$

where M is the mass of the atom, L is the length of the Raman interaction region, approximately the laser beam waist, and P_R is the momentum given to an atom by the Raman transition. Note that once the atoms in the output beam have left the Raman interaction region they no longer interact with the atom laser system. Hence only atoms in the interaction region are counted in N_3. We have solved the rate equations (2,3,4) numerically for realistic values of the parameters. The results are shown in Figure 4. We assumed the atomic mass of lithium, a $2\mu m$ fiber hole diameter, a $100\mu m$ long pump cavity, and a $2\mu m$ long laser cavity. The Raman laser beams are assumed to occupy only the laser cavity, which is located at the output end of the pump cavity, see Figure 3. Other parameters can be found in reference [3].

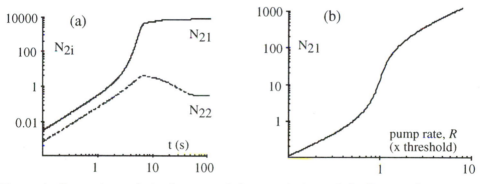

Figure 4. Dynamics and steady state of the populations of the laser cavity states as determined by the rate equations (2,3,4). (a) N_{21} (solid line) and N_{22} (dashed line) are plotted as a function of time in units of seconds. The pumping rate is approximately 50 times threshold. (b) N_{21} as a function of the dimensionless pumping rate R. Parameters: $r = 1000 \text{ s}^{-1}$, $g_1 = 0.00597$, $g_2 = 0.00134$, $r_{23} = 0.125 \text{ s}^{-1}$, $\Gamma = 5.9 \times 10^4 \text{ s}^{-1}$.

Figure 4(a) shows how the populations N_{21}, N_{22} of the lowest two laser cavity states evolve in time. The populations of all other laser cavity modes are smaller than $N_{22}(t)$. The most notable feature of Figure 4(a) is that the lowest laser cavity mode, the laser mode, dominates the population. The other modes never get more than a single atom or so. Under these conditions, and with a sufficiently large output coupling rate Γ, the steady state of the rate equations (2,3,4) can be approximated as

$$N_{21} = \frac{1}{2g_1}\left[(R-1) + \sqrt{(R-1)^2 + 4Rg_1}\right], \tag{6}$$

where $R = rg_1/r_{23}$ is a dimensionless pumping rate. This equation has a threshold at $R = 1$, see Figure 4(b), similar to those of standard optical laser models [28]. A similar result was found by Spreeuw et al. [19] for their atom laser model.

In the work discussed above the pump atoms are trapped in a thermal distribution in a pump cavity. However, the presence of a pump cavity is not necessary. The pumping could be achieved simply by sending cooled atoms down the fibre towards the laser cavity. We have evaluated the transition rate into the laser cavity from such a source. We model the input atoms as a mixture of gaussian wavepackets. Each wavepacket has a standard deviation in position of similar magnitude to the radius of the hollow fibre. These atoms are confined to a mixture of discrete energy states in the transverse direction by the fiber walls. However, the atoms are free to move with a continuous distribution of velocities in the longitudinal direction. If we choose a gaussian distribution of velocities with mean longitudinal velocity of the order $0.17 \mathrm{m}s^{-1}$, and a standard deviation of $\approx 0.02 \mathrm{m}s^{-1}$ we find populations of the laser cavity modes which are similar to the results presented in Figure 4. The preceding standard deviation corresponds to a temperature of ≈ 200nK.

5. CONCLUSION

An atom laser has yet to be constructed in the laboratory, although many groups have this as a long term goal. Obtaining high first order coherence, that is a narrow linewidth, will be difficult. In particular much more work must be done on output coupling mechanisms. A potentially more serious problem is atom-atom interaction, that is collisions, which are likely to place severe limits on atom laser design.

However the potential rewards for constructing an atom laser are great. Besides being the ideal source for many existing atom optics devices they may stimulate entirely new applications.

REFERENCES

[1] S. M. Barnett and S.J.D. Phoenix, Phil. Trans. Royal Soc. London Series A-Phys. Sci. and Eng., **354**, 793 (1996).

[2] A. Ekert and R. Jozsa, Rev. Mod. Phys., **68**, 733 (1996).

[3] G. Moy, J.J. Hope, and C.M. Savage, preprint, http://xxx.lanl.gov/abs/atom-ph/9604001 (1996).

[4] Ch.J. Bordé, Phys. Lett. A **204**, 217 (1995).

[5] J.J. Hope and C.M. Savage, Phys. Rev. A in press, http://xxx.lanl.gov/abs/atom-ph/9602002 (1996).

[6] V.A. Namiot and V.I. Goldanskii, Phys. Lett. A **213**, 56 (1996).

[7] J.J. Hope and C.M. Savage, Phys. Lett. A in press, http://xxx.lanl.gov/abs/atom-ph/9606007 (1996).

[8] A. Imamoglu and R.J. Ram, Phys. Lett. A **214**, 193 (1996); A. Imamoglu et al., Phys. Rev. A **53**, 4250 (1996).

[9] A. Mysyrowicz, E. Benson, and E. Fortin, Phys. Rev. Lett. **77**, 896 (1996).

[10] M. H. Anderson *et al.*, Science **269**, 198 (1995).

[11] C. C. Bradley, *et al.*, Phys. Rev. Lett. **75**, 1687 (1995).

[12] K. B. Davis, *et al.*, Phys. Rev. Lett. **75**, 3969 (1995).

[13] C.M. Savage, Aust. J. Phys. **49**, 745 (1996).

[14] M. Wilkens *et al.*, Phys. Rev. A **47**, 2366 (1993).

[15] H. Wallis, J. Dalibard, and C. Cohen-Tannoudji, Appl. Phys. B **54**, 407 (1992).

[16] E. Merzbacher, "Quantum Mechanics" (Wiley, NY, 1970).

[17] M. Olshanii, Y. Castin, and J. Dalibard, in "Laser Spectroscopy XII", ed. M. Inguscio *et al.* (World Scientific , Singapore, 1995).

[18] H. M. Wiseman and M. J. Collett, Phys. Lett. A **202**, 246 (1995).

[19] R. J. Spreeuw, *et al.*, Europhys. Lett. **32**, 469 (1995).

[20] T. Pfau and H. Gauck, Quantum Optics Konstanz Annual Report (1995).

[21] M. Holland, K. Burnett, and P. Zoller, Phys. Rev. A **54**, 1757 (1996).

[22] H. M. Wiseman, A. Martin and D. F. Walls, Quant. Semiclass. Opt. **8**, 737 (1996).

[23] A.M. Guzman, M. Moore, and P. Meystre, Phys. Rev. A **53**, 977 (1996).

[24] T.W. Hijmans, G.V. Shlyapnikov, and A.L. Burin, preprint, http://xxx.lanl.gov/abs/atom-ph/9606002 (1996).

[25] W.P. Zhang and B.C. Sanders, J. Phys. B **27**, 795 (1994).

[26] S. Marksteiner, *et al.*, Phys. Rev. A **50**, 2680 (1994).

[27] H. Ito, *et al.*, Optics Commun. **115**, 57 (1995).

[28] A. E. Siegman, *Lasers* (University Science Books, California 1986).

MEASUREMENT OF QUANTUM PHASE DISTRIBUTION BY PROJECTION SYNTHESIS

David T. Pegg[1] and Stephen M. Barnett[2]

[1] Faculty of Science and Technology
   Griffith University, Brisbane, Queensland 4111, Australia
[2] Department of Physics and Applied Physics
   University of Strathclyde, Glasgow G4 0NG, Scotland

It has been known for some time how to measure the quantum mechanical phase probability distribution for states of light with very narrow phase distributions, such as coherent states with mean photon numbers greater than unity. Here we show how it is possible to make a direct measurement of the phase distribution of weak fields well within the quantum domain, which have very broad distributions. The procedure involved, called projection synthesis, requires a particular type of reference state. We indicate how the reference states required for measuring the phase distribution of very weak fields may be generated.

1. INTRODUCTION

Before proposing a method for measuring some quantity, it is useful to know precisely what is to be measured. Although this may appear to be a trivial statement, it is necessary to keep it in mind when reading recent literature on phase and phase measurements. In 1986 we introduced a phase-dependent quantity which we called "measured phase" [1] as an operational definition pertaining to experiments commonly used to measure phase-dependent quantities at the time. The measured phase is a closer description of the quantity actually measured in those experiments than is Dirac's concept of phase [2]. More recently there have been other such operational definitions which, because they are based on different types of experiments, describe different quantities still. The best known of these is the operational phase defined by Noh *et al.* [3]. Because such an operational quantity is *defined* as the outcome of a particular experiment, the fact that the results of the experiment when actually performed agree with this definition in no way favours this particular description of phase over any others. One cannot experimentally prove or disprove a definition. This may also appear to be a trivial statement, but it is worth expressing in view of some minor confusion in some of the literature, (see for example [4]) where it is implied that such an experiment can serve as a test for all definitions of phase, although such confusion is by no means widespread. Recent reviews of phase are given in [5] and [6].

In this paper the quantity we wish to measure is the phase probability density, where phase is the complement of photon number in accord with Dirac's concept. Equivalently,

phase is the quantity which is shifted by a phase shifter and which obeys the fundamental correspondence relation between the energy-phase commutator of the quantum
field and the Poisson bracket of its classical counterpart. The action of a phase shifter
is represented by the unitary operator $\exp(-i\hat{N}\Delta\theta)$ where $\hat{N}$ is the photon number
operator and $\Delta\theta$ is the phase shift. The action of this operator on a number eigenstate
$|n\rangle$, including the vacuum, just multiplies the state by a factor $\exp(-in\Delta\theta)$ and does
not alter its physical properties, which will include its phase probability distribution.
However, as this is a phase shift operator, the phase distribution must be shifted by
$\Delta\theta$. The only distribution which is invariant under any shift is a uniform distribution.
Thus all number states, including the vacuum, must be states of random phase. This
is a manifestation of number-phase complementarity. It is possible to show [6] that the
phase probability density for a field in a physical state

$$|f\rangle = \sum_{n=0}^{\infty} c_n |n\rangle \tag{1}$$

is given by

$$P(\theta) = \frac{1}{2\pi} \left| \sum_{n=0}^{\infty} c_n \exp(-in\theta) \right|^2 . \tag{2}$$

The distribution given by (2) can be derived by a number of different approaches [6–8].
It is periodic with a period 2π, is normalised to unity over any 2π range, gives a uniform
distribution for number states and is shifted by $\Delta\theta$ when a phase shift of $\Delta\theta$ is applied to
the field. These considerations are what are required from a genuine phase distribution
but they do not indicate how to measure the distribution. We discuss a possible method
for measuring $P(\theta)$ in this paper.

2.   PROJECTION SYNTHESIS

It is useful for our purposes here to classify fields into two types, those with narrow
phase distributions and those with broad distributions. A narrow phase distribution
is one in which the phase probability density is effectively zero over a range of at
least π, that is, the non-zero part of the distribution can fit into half the available
range. This includes many common states but not, for example, the squeezed vacuum
or coherent states with mean photon numbers less than unity. We have discussed
elsewhere good approximation methods for measuring the phase distributions of states
with narrow distributions [9]. The simple balanced homodyne technique is sufficient for
coherent states, for example, with mean photon numbers down to about five [10] and a
modification to this technique described in Ref. [11] provides an approximate measure
of the phase distribution for coherent states with mean photon numbers down to about
unity. While these methods are adequate for most fields, recent experiments [12] have
been conducted with coherent state fields with mean photon numbers of 0.047 and
0.076, which places these fields very much in the quantum regime and out of the reach
of the above approximation methods. While it is still possible to determine the phase
probability distribution for such weak fields by measuring the whole state of the field
first by optical homodyne tomographic techniques [13] and then using this to calculate
the phase properties, it is desirable to have a direct measurement technique. There
are two strong reasons for this. The first involves a matter of fundamental principle,
to dispel doubts as to whether the phase distribution is directly measurable. Such
doubts are associated with the view of some that phase is not a respectable observable.
The second is of a more practical nature. It was shown recently that a knowledge of

the number state probability distribution and of its complement, the phase probability distribution, are sufficient to determine the state of the field [14]. Thus determining the phase probability distribution will be useful for this purpose, but only if we use a method which does not involve measuring the whole state of the field first.

Here we discuss a measurement procedure we have called projection synthesis [15]. The amplitude for a field in a pure state to be found with a particular photon number is the projection of the field state onto the corresponding number state. The probability is the square of the modulus of this amplitude. For a continuous variable such as phase we have a wavefunction instead of an amplitude such that the probability density is the square of the modulus of the wavefunction. As can be seen from (1) and (2), the phase probability density is proportional to a quantity which can be approximated to within any given non-zero error by square of the modulus of the projection of the physical state $|f\rangle$ onto the state

$$|\theta, N\rangle = \frac{1}{\sqrt{N+1}} \sum_{n=0}^{N} \exp(in\theta) |n\rangle \qquad (3)$$

by choosing N sufficiently large. That is we can replace (2) for N suitably large by

$$P_N(\theta) = \frac{1}{2\pi k_N} \left| \sum_{n=0}^{N} c_n \exp(-in\theta) \right|^2 \qquad (4)$$

where the normalisation constant $k_N = \sum_{n=0}^{N} |c_n|^2$ is inserted to ensure that $P_N(\theta)$ is normalised over a 2π range. This normalisation property allows us to find (4) by measuring a quantity which is proportional to it and later normalising the results for a large number of values of θ, provided, of course, that the proportionality constant is independent of θ. We should point out that (3) has the same mathematical form, with N in place of s, as the normalised and orthogonal phase states of the $(s+1)$-dimensional space which we used to derive the phase properties of light by means of a limiting procedure [7]. In the limit the exact expression (2) is obtained. Here, however, we are not taking the infinite N limit but are just ensuring that N is large enough for (4) to serve as a good approximation.

We thus seek an event whose amplitude is proportional to the projection of $|f\rangle$ onto $|\theta, N\rangle$. As we shall see, this amplitude can be equal to the projection of some other state $|M\rangle$ onto a state $|F\rangle$ where the former is an eigenstate of some measurement operator and $|F\rangle$ is the state of a system being measured which depends on $|f\rangle$, that is, we can synthesise the projection of $|f\rangle$ onto $|\theta, N\rangle$ by using the projection of $|M\rangle$ onto $|F\rangle$. Given that the standard measurement in quantum optics involves photon counting, a useful measurement state $|M\rangle$ might be expected to involve photon number states. We describe briefly a projection synthesis method below.

Consider a 50%:50% symmetric beam splitter with input modes a and b from the left and from the bottom respectively and output modes c and d to the right and to the top respectively. The photon annihilation operators for these four modes are $\hat{a}, \hat{b}, \hat{c}$ and $\hat{d}$. We measure the probability that N photons are detected in mode c while zero photons are detected in mode d. We can find the input state which would give this result with certainty by first writing the output state as

$$|N\rangle_c |0\rangle_d = \frac{\hat{c}^{\dagger N}}{\sqrt{N!}} |0\rangle_c |0\rangle_d . \qquad (5)$$

We then use the beam splitter relations (see, for example, [16]) to replace $\hat{c}^\dagger$ by $(\hat{a}^\dagger - i\hat{b}^\dagger)/\sqrt{2}$ and the output double vacuum by the input double vacuum to obtain the input state which yields $|N\rangle_c |0\rangle_d$ as

$$|M\rangle = \frac{2^{-N/2}}{\sqrt{N!}} \sum_{l=0}^{N} \left(^N C_l\right) \hat{a}^{\dagger(N-l)} (-i\hat{b}^{\dagger})^l |0\rangle_a |0\rangle_b$$

$$= 2^{-N/2} \sum_{l=0}^{N} \left(^N C_l\right)^{1/2} (-i)^l |N-l\rangle_a |l\rangle_b . \tag{6}$$

The amplitude for the output to be $|N\rangle_c |0\rangle_d$ is just the projection of the input state $|F\rangle = |f\rangle_a |B\rangle_b$ onto the state $|M\rangle$ given by (6), where $|B\rangle_b$ is a input reference state $\sum_n b_n |n\rangle_b$ in mode b. We easily find this amplitude to be

$$2^{-N/2} \sum_{l=0}^{N} (-i)^l \left(^N C_l\right)^{1/2} b_l^* c_{N-l}^* . \tag{7}$$

For the modulus of the amplitude (7) to be proportional to the modulus of the projection of $|f\rangle$ onto $|\theta, N\rangle$, we require

$$b_n^* \propto \left(^N C_n\right)^{-1/2} \exp[-in(\theta - \pi/2)] \tag{8}$$

for $0 \le n \le N$. The values of b_n for $n > N$ can be anything at all because, apart from the normalisation factor which is absorbed into the proportionality constant, they do not affect the projection of $|F\rangle$ onto $|M\rangle$ in (6).

3.   REFERENCE STATES

It is sufficient to generate a reference state with the first $N+1$ coefficients of the photon number state components proportional to the reciprocal square root of the binomial coefficients because the exponential factor in (8) can always be adjusted by phase shifting. The experimental procedure would involve measuring the probability of finding N photons in mode c and zero in mode d for a large number of values of θ covering a 2π range and then normalising the area under the probability histogram. (If we also measure the probability of finding N photons in mode d and zero in mode c, we can halve the number of phase shifts [15], but this need not concern us here.) If we assume access to efficient photodetectors, or make appropriate allowance for imperfect detectors, then the major problem to solve is how to generate the reciprocal binomial state $|B\rangle$. Before discussing this question, we estimate the value of N required for fields of interest, such as coherent states with mean photon number less than unity. For a partial phase state, that is one for which $c_n = |c_n| \exp(in\phi)$ which includes most common states [7], the maximum difference between (2) and (4) will be for $\theta = \phi$. At the limit of our region of interest, values for N of 4, 5 and 6 are sufficient to reproduce the phase probability distribution for a coherent state with a mean photon number of unity with maximum errors of about 8%, 3% and 1% respectively. For the weaker fields in which we are interested, specifically for coherent states with mean photon numbers of 0.047 and 0.076, it is not hard to show that a two-component reciprocal binomial state (that is, for which $N = 1$) gives maximum errors respectively of 5.8%, which is probably smaller than the experimental errors involved, and 9%. A three-component reciprocal binomial state will give maximum errors of 0.7% and 1.5% respectively. Thus even the simplest nontrivial reciprocal binomial states can be used to measure the phase distribution of very weak fields, well within the quantum regime, which are now being studied in experiments [12].

To use the two-component reciprocal binomial state we require that $|c_0| = |c_1|$ with any values for $c_2, c_3, \ldots$. The simplest such state satisfying this condition is a coherent state with a mean photon number of unity. Such a coherent state could thus be used in the projection synthesis method to measure the phase distribution of the weakest of the fields mentioned above. This state has the advantage of being relatively easy to prepare. The three-component reciprocal binomial state requires $|c_0|$ and $|c_2|$ to be $\sqrt{2}$ $|c_1|$. Such a state can be generated by displacing a sufficiently squeezed vacuum by an appropriate amount. The terms involving c_n with $n > 2$ dominate this state, however, so the probability of detecting $N = 2$ photons in mode c and zero in mode d is quite small and two orders of magnitude more readings must be collected than for the case where only the first three components are not zero. This situation can be markedly improved by using a beam splitter with a different transmissivity and reflectivity so that the reference state needed is no longer a reciprocal binomial state but is one for which $|c_2| < |c_0|$. For example, a reference state with the first three number state components appropriate for projection synthesis with a 60%:40% beam splitter can be a displaced squeezed vacuum with significantly less displacement and squeezing than required for a 50%:50% beam splitter reference state. In this case the first three number state components are relatively much larger and only a few times more readings are required than if the higher number state components were zero. The optimum case appears to be for approximately a 63%:37% beam splitter. It is also worth trying to find alternative ways to construct the three-component reciprocal binomial state. For fields with slightly narrower phase distributions four- and five-component reference states will be required. We shall show elsewhere how these might be generated by means of a series of beam splitters with fields in various superpositions of $|0\rangle$ and $|1\rangle$ as inputs, with detectors at all output ports except one to condition the output state. Other techniques which will be discussed in future work are the use of Schrödinger cat states as reference states.

4. CONCLUSION

In this paper we have described how the phase probability distribution can be measured by projection synthesis. The modulus of the amplitude for a state $|f\rangle$ to be found with a phase θ is proportional to the modulus of the projection of $|f\rangle$ onto the associated phase state which can be truncated by an amount dependent on the accuracy required. It is this projection which is synthesised in our approach. Normally we might regard the two photodetectors as the measuring apparatus and say that we are measuring the modulus of the amplitude for obtaining N photons in output mode c and zero photons in output mode d. This is the modulus of the projection of the output state of the beam splitter onto the state $|N\rangle_c |0\rangle_d$. This quantity, however, is also the modulus of the projection of the input state $|f\rangle_a |B\rangle_b$ onto the state $|M\rangle = \hat{U}^\dagger |N\rangle_c |0\rangle_d$ where $\hat{U}^\dagger$ is the unitary operator describing the action of the beam splitter. Thus we can also say that we are measuring the modulus of this projection and regard the system of the two photodetectors plus the beam splitter as the measuring apparatus. By choosing the reference state $|B\rangle$ appropriately we can ensure that the modulus of this projection is proportional to the modulus of the projection of $|f\rangle_a$ onto a phase state. In effect, this means choosing $|B\rangle$ so that $_b\langle B| M\rangle$ is proportional to a phase state. With this interpretation, we can regard the system of the input reference state $|B\rangle$, the beam splitter and the photodetectors as the measuring apparatus.

Although we have concentrated on pure states of light, the procedure described can also be used to measure the phase probability distribution of mixed states. The ability to make a direct measurement of the phase probability distribution is important for a number of reasons. The first is that it provides a means of measuring the state of the field when used with the complementary information provided by the photon number state distribution. The second is one of fundamental principle as described in the text. The third is that the projection synthesis method enables us to make an *operational* definition of the phase probability distribution which is consistent with (2) for N sufficiently large, that is, consistent with phase being the complement of photon number. No previous operational definition has this property (see Refs [1, 3, 11, 17]). This dispels the idea [4] that results of measurements by Noh *et al.* [3] might be used as experimental evidence against (2). There is now, at least in principle, a measurement process which enables experiments to be done which yield (2). Indeed, by using appropriate coherent and squeezed reference states it should be possible to distinguish experimentally between (2) and the operational definitions of Noh *et al.* for the fields studied in [12]. We might note in this regard that projection synthesis can be used to measure a phase difference probability distribution by measuring the individual phase distributions $P_1(\theta)$ and $P_2(\theta)$ and then finding the probability density for a phase difference of $\Delta\theta$ from $\int P_1(\theta)P_2(\theta + \Delta\theta)d\theta$, where the integral is over a 2π range. The phase difference defined by this method has the usual mathematical properties of a genuine difference. For example the property $a - b = (a - c) - (b - c)$, with suitable allowance made for numbers modulo 2π, is applicable if the distributions for the phase differences between the two fields and a third field with a very narrow phase distribution are found. The operational phase difference of Ref. [3] does not appear to be consistent with this property [12]. We might note that an operational definition based on projection synthesis is a precise definition only in the limit as $N \to \infty$. A finite value of N can always be found, however, so that the error is less than any given non-zero value for any physical state. This should not be too surprising in view of the fact that the distribution (2) itself is derivable from an Hermitian operator describing the phase observable only if an appropriate limiting procedure is used [7]. On the mathematical side, the usual infinite-dimensional Hilbert space would not accommodate the infinite limit of the reciprocal binomial state, and Vaccaro's space [18] would appear the more appropriate space to use.

There are still some questions to be considered. One is that allowance should be made for photodetectors which are not totally efficient. Another is how to generate the reference field in state $|B\rangle$. We have indicated how this can be done for small values of N which are sufficient for the very weak fields which are our present interest, but in order to extend the technique a method needs to be found for generating the reference field for higher values of N.

REFERENCES

[1] S. M. Barnett and D. T. Pegg, J. Phys. A: Math. Gen. **19**, 3849 (1986).

[2] P. A. M. Dirac, Proc. R. Soc. Lond. A **114**, 243 (1927).

[3] J. W. Noh, A. Fougères and L. Mandel, Phys. Rev. Lett. **71**, 2579 (1993).

[4] R. Lynch, Phys. Rep. **256**, 367 (1995).

[5] R. Tanaś, A. Miranowicz and Ts. Gantsog, in *Progress in Optics XXXV*, ed. E. Wolf (Elsevier, Amsterdam, 1996) p. 355.

[6] D. T. Pegg and S. M. Barnett, J. Mod. Opt. (in press).

[7] D. T. Pegg and S. M. Barnett, Europhys. Lett. **6**, 483 (1988); S. M. Barnett and D. T. Pegg. J. Mod. Opt. **36**, 7 (1989); D. T. Pegg and S. M. Barnett, Phys. Rev. A **39**, 1665 (1989).

[8] C. W. Helstrom, *Quantum Detection and Estimation Theory* (Academic, New York, 1976) pp. 53-57; J. H. Shapiro and S. R. Shepard, Phys. Rev. A **43**, 3795, (1991).

[9] D. T. Pegg, J. A. Vaccaro and S. M. Barnett, in *Quantum Optics VI*, eds. D. F. Walls and J. D. Harvey (Springer-Verlag, Berlin, 1994) p. 153.

[10] J. A. Vaccaro and D. T. Pegg, Opt. Commun. **105**, 335 (1994).

[11] W. Vogel and W. Schleich, Phys. Rev. A **44**, 7642 (1991).

[12] J. R. Torgerson and L. Mandel, Phys. Rev. Lett. **76**, 3939 (1996).

[13] D. T. Smithey, M. Beck, J. Cooper, M. G. Raymer and A. Faridani, Phys. Scr. **T48**, 35 (1993) and references therein.

[14] J. A. Vaccaro and S. M. Barnett, J. Mod. Opt. **42**, 2165 (1995); Z. Białynicka-Birula and I. Białynicki-Birula, J. Mod. Opt. **41**, 2203 (1994).

[15] S. M. Barnett and D. T. Pegg, Phys. Rev. Lett. **76**, 4148 (1996).

[16] G. Yeoman and S. M. Barnett, J. Mod. Opt. **40**, 1497 (1993).

[17] M. G. Raymer, J. Cooper and M. Beck, Phys. Rev. A **48**, 4617 (1993); V. Bužek and M. Hillery, J. Mod. Opt. **43**, 1633 (1996).

[18] J. A. Vaccaro, Phys. Rev. A **51**, 3309 (1995).

QUANTUM OPTICAL PHASE

Stephen M. Barnett[1] and David T. Pegg[2]

[1] Department of Physics and Applied Physics
University of Strathclyde, Glasgow G4 ONG, Scotland
[2] Faculty of Science and Technology, Griffith University
Nathan, Brisbane 4111, Australia

Simple physical ideas lead us to identify the phase of a single mode of the electromagnetic field as the quantity conjugate to the photon number. This in turn leads to the form of the phase probability distribution. The phase operator cannot be represented in the conventional infinite dimensional Hilbert space but can be expressed by means of a finite-dimensional state space together with a suitable limiting procedure. We introduce the Hermitian optical phase operator and describe its most important properties.

1. INTRODUCTION

The phase of a electromagnetic field was an important idea in the early development of quantum electrodynamics [1]. However, the problem of finding a suitable Hermitian optical phase operator led to the widely-held belief that no such operator exists [2,3]. A number of ingenious attempts have been made to resolve the problem and some of these are reviewed in [4]. In this brief article we will not attempt to review this early work, fascinating though it is. Our aim is rather to provide a logical derivation of the phase probability distribution and of the associated phase operator. A fuller analysis, filling in some of the inevitable gaps, can be found in our recent tutorial review [5].

The question we will address is: what is the correct quantum description of the phase of a single mode of the electromagnetic field? In answering this we are guided by the classical limit, but also require a criterion that we can apply in the quantum regime. There are compelling, even unanswerable reasons why this condition is that the phase should be the complement of the photon number. The first of these is that complementarity ensures that the number sates (including the vacuum) have random phase. This is natural for, if they are not states of random phase then what is it that provides their preferred phases? An even stronger requirement comes from the analysis of phase-shifting devices such as retarding plates. If we accept that these act to shift the phase in quantum optics in the same way as in classical optics, then we are led directly to the complementarity of photon number and phase. All phase-dependent experiments in quantum optics, such as homodyne detection, employ this idea of phase shifts.

Quantum Communication, Computing, and Measurement
Edited by Hirota *et al.*, Plenum Press, New York, 1997

2. FROM CLASSICAL TO QUANTUM PHASE

In classical physics we can define a phase for any periodic motion. We can relate the elapsed time t to a phase angle $\theta = 2\pi t/T$, where T is the period. Configurations of the system corresponding to phases differing by integer multiples of 2π are identical. It follows, therefore, that examining the state of the system will only allow us to determine θ modulo 2π. For example, the instantaneous position and momentum of a classical oscillator will provide $\cos\theta$ and $\sin\theta$, but this does not allow us to distinguish between values of θ that differ by 2π. It is conventional to choose a 2π range or window for the phase value. Common ranges are $-\pi$ to π and 0 to 2π. In order to maintain generality we allow this range to be θ_0 to $\theta_0 + 2\pi$. All distinct states of the system will correspond to a phase value in this chosen range of values. As time passes the phase takes values from $-\infty$ to ∞ but the values which correspond to *distinct states* will be in this 2π range.

Our classical definition was of a phase proportional to time so that if an oscillator of angular frequency ω evolves from time t_1 to time t_2 then its phase is shifted by $\Delta\theta = \omega(t_2 - t_1)$. Time plays a similar role as a parameter in quantum mechanics as it does in classical physics and so we would expect the proportionality between phase shift and time difference will also apply in the quantum domain. The additional feature in quantum theory is that we do not expect to be able to associate a single phase value with each state but rather a phase probability distribution. The phase probability distribution associated with the pure state $|f_1\rangle$ at time t_1 will be shifted by $\omega(t_2 - t_1)$ as $|f_1\rangle$ evolves into $|f_2\rangle$ at time t_2. These states are related by the unitary transformation:

$$|f_2\rangle = \exp[-i\hat{N}\omega(t_2 - t_1)]|f_1\rangle = \exp[-i\hat{N}\Delta\theta]|f_1\rangle, \tag{1}$$

where $\hat{N}$ is the photon number operator. It then follows that $\hat{N}$ is the phase-shift generator. This important result leads directly to phase-number complementarity and to the form of the phase probability distribution.

There are two important consequences of accepting the idea that $\hat{N}$ is the generator of phase shifts. The first is that the experimental practice of shifting the phase of a travelling field by changing the optical path length *still applies in the quantum domain*. The second is that the the photon number states, being eigenstates of $\hat{N}$ must have a uniform phase probability distribution and hence be states of random phase. This follows because the time evolution of these states merely multiplies the state by a factor of unit modulus and therefore does not change any of its physical properties, including its phase. The only distribution which is invariant under all phase shifts is the uniform distribution. It follows that the phase probability density for a number state will be $1/2\pi$.

Probabilities and probability densities in quantum mechanics are associated with the squared modulus of a complex amplitudes. We expect, therefore, to be able to write the phase probability distribution $P(\theta)$ for a pure state $|\psi\rangle$ in terms of a phase 'wavefunction' $\psi(\theta)$ so that

$$P(\theta) = |\psi(\theta)|^2. \tag{2}$$

In this phase representation [6] the phase is a simple multiplicative operator and the fundamental phase shift relation (1) becomes

$$\exp[-i\hat{N}\Delta\theta]\psi(\theta) = \psi(\theta + \Delta\theta). \tag{3}$$

Comparing this with Taylor's theorem

$$\exp\left(\Delta\theta\frac{\partial}{\partial\theta}\right)\psi(\theta) = \psi(\theta + \Delta\theta), \tag{4}$$

leads us to the phase representation of the number operator as

$$\hat{N} = i\frac{\partial}{\partial\theta}. \tag{5}$$

It then follows that the phase wavefunction for a number state $|n\rangle$ must have the form

$$\psi_n(\theta) = (2\pi)^{-1/2}\exp[i(\beta_n - n\theta)], \tag{6}$$

where β_n is real and can be chosen arbitrarily. The conventional number state basis corresponds to setting all the β_n equal to zero. It follows that the phase probability density for a field in a pure state of the form $\Sigma c_n|n\rangle$ is

$$P(\theta) = \frac{1}{2\pi}\left|\sum_{n=0}^{\infty} c_n \exp(-in\theta)\right|^2. \tag{7}$$

This expression is all that is required to find the phase properties of a state. In particular, the mean value of any function of the phase, $F(\theta)$ is simply

$$\langle F(\theta)\rangle = \int_{\theta_0}^{\theta_0+2\pi} F(\theta)P(\theta)d\theta. \tag{8}$$

The phase properties associated with any state can be found using these two expressions.

The representation of the phase operator will be a multiplicative operator but we should remember that physically distinguishable values of the phase will lie in the selected range θ_0 to $\theta_0 + 2\pi$. We represent the required multiplicative operator by ϕ_{θ_0} which denotes multiplication by θ modulo 2π. This leads to a sensible form for the photon number-phase commutation relation and a corresponding equation of motion for the expectation value of the phase of the form

$$\frac{d\langle\phi_{\theta_0}\rangle}{dt} = -\omega[1 - 2\pi P(\theta_0)]. \tag{9}$$

The 2π periodicity of the complex exponential function means that the operators represented by $\exp(-i\phi_{\theta_0})$ and $\exp(-i\theta)$ are equal. It follows from the the form of the number state wavefunctions (6) that this exponential acts to shift the photon number by unity:

$$\exp(-i\phi_{\theta_0})\psi_n(\theta) = \exp(-i\theta)\psi_n(\theta) = \psi_{n+1}(\theta). \tag{10}$$

Thus the phase operator generates shifts in the photon number much as the phase-shift relation (3) tells us that the number operator generates shifts in the phase. This mutual shifting property is a defining characteristic of canonically conjugate observables [7].

The above analysis seems straightforward. What therefore is the problem that has beset phase for so long? In order to expose the difficulty, let us try to construct the phase wavefunction $\psi_{\theta'}(\theta)$ for an eigenstate of ϕ_{θ_0} corresponding to the eigenvalue θ' lying somewhere between θ_0 and $\theta_0 + 2\pi$. In the phase representation the required eigenstate will simply be the delta function $\delta(\theta - \theta')$, in complete analogy with the coordinate representation of the eigenfunctions of position [8]. If we write the phase state as a superposition of number-state wavefunctions

$$\psi_{\theta'}(\theta) = \sum_{n=0}^{\infty} c_n\psi_n(\theta), \tag{11}$$

then we are led to the form

$$\psi_{\theta'}(\theta) = \frac{1}{2\pi}\sum_{n=0}^{\infty}\exp[in(\theta - \theta')]. \tag{12}$$

417

This is *not* a delta function or even a periodic string of delta functions. The corresponding Fourier series for the delta functions contains exponentials with negative values of n which are absent from (12) due to the non-existence of states with negative photon number. The problem is highlighted if we consider the action of $\exp(i\theta)$ on the number states:

$$\exp(i\theta)\psi_n(\theta) = \psi_{n-1}(\theta), \tag{13}$$

but for the vacuum we have

$$\exp(i\theta)\psi_0(\theta) = (2\pi)^{-1/2}\exp(i\theta), \tag{14}$$

which is orthogonal to all of the number states in the Hilbert space of the harmonic oscillator. The problem we have exposed is that the usual infinite-dimensional Hilbert space spanned by the photon number states *cannot accommodate the phase states* and that use of the multiplicative phase operator seems to require the introduction of *unphysical states* corresponding to negative photon numbers.

3.   THE HERMITIAN OPTICAL PHASE OPERATOR

The failure to obtain orthogonal phase eigenstates casts doubt on the interpretation of $P(\theta)$ as a genuine probability distribution. It is possible to show, however, by means of a suitable limiting procedure, that such an interpretation is indeed possible [5]. This idea of a limiting procedure also plays a crucial role in the formulation of the Hermitian optical phase operator [9–11]. In this section we present an outline of the phase operator formalism and refer the reader to these early papers and to our review [5] for a more comprehensive treatment.

We begin by considering the sub-space of the infinite-dimensional Hilbert space spanned by the first $s+1$ photon number states and within this construct the normalised states $|\theta_m\rangle$ given by

$$|\theta_m\rangle = (s+1)^{-1/2}\sum_{n=0}^{s}\exp(in\theta_m)|n\rangle. \tag{15}$$

If we choose the values of θ_m to be

$$\theta_m = \theta_0 + m\frac{2\pi}{s+1}, \tag{16}$$

with $m = 0, 1, 2, ...s$, then we find the states are orthormal. These states are also a *complete* set in the sense that they span the space Ψ_s of the first $s+1$ photon number states. In this space the identity can be resolved as

$$\sum_{m=0}^{s}|\theta_m\rangle\langle\theta_m| = 1 \tag{17}$$

and we can express the photon number states of Ψ_s, which also form a basis, as

$$|n\rangle = (s+1)^{-1/2}\sum_{m=0}^{s}\exp(-in\theta_m)|\theta_m\rangle. \tag{18}$$

We note that in the space Ψ_s the number states and the states $|\theta_m\rangle$ are equally weighted superpositions of each other and that this is a manifestation of complementarity. We must eventually include *all* of the number states in our formalism and so we will need to take the limit as $s \to \infty$. As an indication of what will happen, we can recover the phase probability distribution as follows. The squared modulus of the overlap between a state having number state coefficients c_n and the state $|\theta_m\rangle$ is

$$P_s(\theta_m) = (s+1)^{-1} \left| \sum_{n=0}^{s} c_n \exp(-in\theta_m) \right|^2, \tag{19}$$

which, on multiplication by $(s+1)/2\pi$, (the density of states in the 2π window), identifying θ_m with θ and taking the limit as $s \to \infty$ becomes the phase probability distribution (7).

Consider the operator

$$\hat{\phi}_\theta = \sum_{m=0}^{s} \theta_m |\theta_m\rangle\langle\theta_m|. \tag{20}$$

We have dropped the subscript zero to distinguish this operator, which is a function of s from the operator $\hat{\phi}_{\theta_0}$ which is not. The operator $\hat{\phi}_\theta$ clearly has the states $|\theta_m\rangle$ as eigenstates with corresponding eigenvalues θ_m. Because of the complementarity of its eigenstates with the number states in Ψ_s we call $\hat{\phi}_\theta$ the *phase operator* and the states $|\theta_m\rangle$ phase states. It is important to note that the phase operator acts on the space Ψ_s rather than the usual infinite Hilbert space and that it is both Hermitian and self-adjoint.

The orthonormality of the phase states means that we can express functions of the phase operator in the form

$$F(\hat{\phi}_\theta) = \sum_{m=0}^{s} F(\theta_m)|\theta_m\rangle\langle\theta_m|. \tag{21}$$

An important example is the complex exponential function which we expect, from (10) and (13), to shift the photon number up or down by unity. Using (21) for the exponential function together with the form of the number states as superpositions of phase states (18) gives

$$\exp\left(i\hat{\phi}_\theta\right)|n\rangle = (s+1)^{-1/2} \sum_{m=0}^{s} \exp[-i(n-1)\theta_m]|\theta_m\rangle = |n-1\rangle, \tag{22}$$

which verifies the action of the phase operator as the generator of shifts in the photon number. For $n = 0$ we find [9–11]

$$\exp\left(i\hat{\phi}_\theta\right)|0\rangle = \exp\left[i(s+1)\theta_0\right]|s\rangle, \tag{23}$$

for which the corresponding phase wavefunction is

$$\psi_s(\theta_m) = (2\pi)^{-1/2} \exp\left[i(s+1)\theta_0\right] \exp(-is\theta_m) = (2\pi)^{-1/2} \exp(i\theta_m). \tag{24}$$

The state generated by the action of $\exp\left(i\hat{\phi}_\theta\right)$ on the vacuum state is (apart from a phase factor) the state $|s\rangle$ which is a state in the space Ψ_s and in the limit as $s \to \infty$ becomes the 'infinite' photon number state.

The important question now arises as to how we are to take the limit as $s \to \infty$. There are two quite distinct ways by which we might obtain expectation values in the infinite s limit. The first is to calculate expectation values of the operators on Ψ_s as c-number functions of s and then evaluate the limit. That this leads to sensible results in accord with the complementarity of photon number and phase follows from the fact that the distribution (19) calculated using the phase states in Ψ_s tends to the required phase probability distribution (7) in this limit. We find that

$$\lim_{s\to\infty} \langle\psi|F\left(\hat{\phi}_\theta\right)|\psi\rangle = \int_{\theta_0}^{\theta_0+2\pi} F(\theta)P(\theta)d\theta, \tag{25}$$

where $|\psi\rangle$ is any state constructed in Ψ_s which tends to the required physical state in infinite Hilbert space as $s\to\infty$ and has the phase probability density $P(\theta)$ in this limit. This has the same form as (8) which was derived on the basis of the phase probability density (7). It follows that working with the state space Ψ_s and applying the $s\to\infty$ limit only once expectation values have been found leads to a fully consistent description of the phase of a single mode field. The second limiting procedure is to attempt to construct an operator as the infinite-s limit of $\hat{\phi}_\theta$ and use it in conjunction with states in the infinite Hilbert space. It turns out that this limiting procedure is not satisfactory in that it does not produce consistent results for phase.

4. OPERATORS OF INFINITE-DIMENSIONAL HILBERT SPACE

The phase operator $\hat{\phi}_\theta$ converges only *weakly* on the infinite-dimensional Hilbert space [12] so that only the weak limit exists. The problem with this is that weak limits of operators do not preserve the operator algebra. For example, the square of the weak limit of $\hat{\phi}_\theta$ is *not* the weak limit of the square of $\hat{\phi}_\theta$. Taking the weak limit leads to the operators studied by Popov and Yarunin [13] and by Garrison and Wong [14]. The weak limit $\hat{\phi}_{\theta w}$ of $\hat{\phi}_\theta$ does not yield results in accord with the phase probaility distribution (7). Moreover, it does not even give self-consistent results. In particular, $\langle\hat{\phi}_{\theta w}\rangle$ for the vacuum state is $\theta_0 + \pi$ for *any* choice of θ_0 and this means that the phase probability distribution must be uniform with an associated phase variance of $\pi^2/3$ [10]. However, the phase variance for the vacuum state calculated using the weak limit is [15, 16]

$$\langle 0|\hat{\phi}_{\theta w}^2|0\rangle - \langle 0|\hat{\phi}_{\theta w}|0\rangle^2 = \pi^2/6, \tag{26}$$

which is therefore not consistent with the random-phase value of $\langle\hat{\phi}_{\theta w}\rangle$ and therefore $\hat{\phi}_{\theta w}$ does not represent phase. A similar problem arises if we take the weak limit of the $\exp(i\hat{\phi}_\theta)$. In this limit we obtain the non-unitary operator which lowers the photon number by unity but annihilates the vacuum

$$\left[\exp(i\hat{\phi}_\theta)\right]_w |0\rangle = 0. \tag{27}$$

This weak limit is the operator introduced by Susskind and Glogower [2] and takes us back to the original problem with the infinite Hilbert space, namely that the action of $\exp(i\theta)$ on the vacuum does not produce a state in Hilbert space. The Susskind-Glogower operator is not unitary and, in particular $\left[\exp(i\hat{\phi}_\theta)\right]_w \neq \left[\exp(i\hat{\phi}_{\theta w})\right]$.

It is not possible to represent the phase operator within the usual Hilbert space. However, we can construct an arbitrarily good approximation to it [5]. This forms an important part of a possible measurement of the phase probability distribution [17, 18]

5. CONCLUSION

The most important idea in this brief article is that the phase of a single field mode is complementary to the excitation or photon number. This is a simple consequence of the facts that the Hamiltonian is the generator of time translations and that (with a suitable choice for the zero of energy) the Hamiltonian is proportional to the photon number.

The quantum phase problem is that we cannot represent phase states or the (exact) phase operator within the usual infinite Hilbert space. Our solution is to construct these quantities within the state space Ψ_s. We then recover the required phase properties by applying the limit $s \to \infty$ but only *after* c-number moments of the phase have been found as functions of s. If we were to apply the limit to the states and operators themselves we would be led to results that are neiter self-consistent nor consistent with the probability distribution (7) and are therefore not in accord with the requirements of number-phase complementarity.

The phase probability distribution (7) has been measured [19, 20]. It is important to emphasize, however, that not all phase-dependent measurements measure the phase itself. 'Phase' operators have been defined in order to interpret particular experimental arrangements and phase measurements [4, 21–25]. It is important to realise, however, that these operationally defined phases are not unique. Moreover, as the idea of a phase shifter shifting the phase of all fields which leads directly to the probability distribution (7), we may need to re-examine the use of phase shifts in these experiments. We can only conclude that the quantities obtained from such experiments are *phase dependent* rather than representing phase itself.

ACKNOWLEDGEMENTS

We wish to acknowledge the contributions made to our work by John Vaccaro during a long-standing and enjoyable collaboration.

REFERENCES

[1] P. A. M. Dirac, *Proc. R. Soc. A (Lond.)*, **114**, 243, (1927).

[2] L. Susskind and J. Glogower, *Physics*, **1**, 49, (1964).

[3] P. Carruthers and M. M. Nieto, *Rev. Mod. Phys.*, **40**, 411, (1968).

[4] S. M. Barnett and D. T. Pegg, *J. Phys. A*, **19**, 3849, (1986).

[5] D. T. Pegg and S. M. Barnett, *J. Mod. Opt.*, in press (1997).

[6] I. Bialynicki-Birula and C. L. Van, *Acta Phys. Polonica A*, **57**, 599, (1980).

[7] D. T. Pegg, J. A. Vaccaro and S. M. Barnett, *J. Mod. Opt.*, **37**, 1703, (1990).

[8] A. Messiah *Quantum Mechanics*, (North-Holand, Amsterdam) (1958) p. 179.

[9] D. T. Pegg and S. M. Barnett, *Europhys. Lett.*, **6**, 483 (1988).

[10] S. M. Barnett and D. T. Pegg, *J. Mod. Opt.*, **36**, 7 (1989).

[11] D. T. Pegg and S. M. Barnett, *Phys. Rev. A*, **39**, 1665 (1989).

[12] J. A. Vaccaro and D. T. Pegg, *Physica Scripta T*, **48**, 22 (1993).

[13] V. N. Popov and V. S. Yarunin, *J. Mod. Opt.*, **39**, 1525 (1992).

[14] J. C. Garrison and J. Wong, *J. Math. Phys.*, **11**, 2242 (1970).

[15] S. M. Barnett and D. T. Pegg, *J. Mod. Opt.*, **39**, 2121 (1992).

[16] T. Gantsog, A. Miranowicz and R. Tanas, *Phys. Rev. A*, **46**, 2870 (1992).

[17] S. M. Barnett and D. T. Pegg, *Phys. Rev. Lett.*, **76**, 4148 (1996).

[18] D. T. Pegg and S. M. Barnett, *Measurement of Quantum Phase Distribution by Projection Synthesis* Published in this volume, p.407.

[19] D. T. Smithey, M. Beck, J. Cooper, M. G. Raymer and A. Faridani, *Physica Scripta T*, **48**, 35 (1993).

[20] M. Beck, D. T. Smithey, J. Cooper and M. G. Raymer, *Opt. Lett.*, **18**, 1259 (1993).

[21] J. W. Noh, A. Fougeres and L. Mandel, *Phys. Rev. Lett.*, **67**, 1426 (1991).

[22] J. W. Noh, A. Fougeres and L. Mandel, *Phys. Rev. A*, **45**, 424 (1992).

[23] A. Fougeres, J. W. Noh, J. W. Grayson and L. Mandel, *Phys. Rev. A*, **49**, 530 (1994).

[24] J. W. Noh, A. Fougeres and L. Mandel, *Phys. Rev. Lett.*, **71**, 2579 (1993).

[25] M. G. Raymer, J. Cooper and M. Beck, *Phys. Rev. A*, **48**, 4617 (1993).

SINGLE-SHOT ADAPTIVE MEASUREMENTS
OF THE PHASE OF A SINGLE MODE FIELD

H. M. Wiseman[1,2] and R. B. Killip[3]

[1] Department of Physics, The University of Queensland
   St. Lucia 4072, Australia (wiseman@physics.uq.oz.au)
[2] Department of Physics
   The University of Auckland, Auckland, New Zealand
[3] Department of Mathematics
   The University of Auckland, Auckland, New Zealand

A standard single-shot measurement of the phase of single-mode field can be achieved by heterodyne detection (using a detuned local oscillator). This effects a joint measurement of both phase and amplitude quadratures, which introduces noise into both results. Such techniques are consequently less accurate than an ideal or *canonical* measurement of phase. If we assume that the phase of the field is already approximately known then homodyne detection (using a resonant local oscillator) could be used to accurately determine the phase, but this assumption is counter to the idea of a "phase measurement". Here we suggest a new sort of phase measurement using a resonant local oscillator with an adjustable phase. This scheme is adaptive, in that the local oscillator phase is continually adjusted to be shifted by $\pi/2$ from the *estimated* system phase. The estimate for the system phase is made from the results *so far* in the single-shot measurement. We show that for states with high photon number, the adaptive scheme has an accuracy intermediate between a canonical and a standard measurement.

1. INTRODUCTION

In textbooks of quantum mechanics one might find a statement such as

> Every physical quantity $\mathcal{Z}$ has associated with it an Hermitian operator Z. A measurement of $\mathcal{Z}$ will yield a result z which is an eigenvalue of Z. The probability of getting the result z is equal to $\langle z|\rho|z\rangle$ where $|z\rangle$ is the eigenstate of Z with eigenvalue z.

If only life were so simple! The number of physical quantities for which we have the scientific and technological knowledge to make a quantum-limited measurement of this form is very small. Nevertheless there are some. In the context of quantum optics, it is only detector inefficiencies (now quite small) which limit the measurement of photon number $a^\dagger a$ and quadrature operators such as $X = a + a^\dagger$ for single-mode optical fields. The former can be measured by direct photon counting and the latter by adding an essentially classical field of known phase (called the local oscillator) to the quantum field before counting photons (see [1] and references therein). However there is one obvious optical quantity of which we cannot make a quantum-limited measurement: the phase ϕ of the electromagnetic field.

There are practical reasons for wishing to measure phase, in addition to the challenge of being able to add to our meagre list of measurable physical quantities. For example, quantum-limited communication could be possible by encoding information in the phase of single-mode pulses of light. The first requirement for such a scheme would be to create states with very well-defined phase. This has been investigated by various authors (see Ref. [2] for some of these). The next step would be encoding the signal, which is easy to do using an electro-optic modulator. The third requirement is for the receiver measure the encoded phase as accurately as possible. Another application for accurate phase measurements could be in inferring the properties of other quantum systems which can cause a phase shift, such as the presence of an atom at a particular point in a single-mode standing wave. The problem of how to make a quantum-limited measurement of phase is one which has not received the attention it deserves, and is the topic of this paper.

1.1. CANONICAL PHASE MEASUREMENTS

It could be objected that phase is not a physical quantity because there does not exist an Hermitian phase operator in the harmonic oscillator Hilbert space. One can avoid such difficulties by considering phase to be the canonically conjugate variable to photon number. This leads to the definition of phase "eigenstates" as $|\phi\rangle = \sum_{n=0}^{\infty} e^{in\phi}|n\rangle$ [3,4]. The probability distribution function (PDF) for *canonical* phase measurements is then

$$P_{\text{can}}(\phi) = \text{Tr}[\rho F_{\text{can}}(\phi)], \quad \text{where} \quad F_{\text{can}}(\phi) = \frac{1}{2\pi}|\phi\rangle\langle\phi| \tag{1}$$

is a positive-operator-valued measure (POVM) [4–6] for ϕ. This PDF is guaranteed to be normalized from the requirement on all POVMs that $\int d\lambda F(\lambda) = 1$, where the integral is over all possible measurement results λ.

Considerable work has been done showing how the distribution (1) can be inferred from physically realizable homodyne measurements on an arbitrarily large ensemble of identical copies of the system [2]. However, this ability is not at all the same as the ability to make canonical phase measurements. To do the latter, one would have to make a measurement on a *single copy* of the system, the result of which would be a random variable drawn from the canonical PDF (1). There is no known way to achieve this in general, nor is there ever likely to be.

If one could make a canonical measurement of phase then the dispersion in one's measurement results would be due solely to the intrinsic phase uncertainty of the quantum system. This intrinsic uncertainty is limited by the number of photons in the system, because number and phase are conjugate variables. Because phase is a cyclic variable, the variance is not a good measure of its dispersion. In this work we will use instead the "chordal variance"

$$V(\phi) \equiv 2(1 - |\langle e^{i\phi}\rangle|). \tag{2}$$

We call it the chordal variance because if one considers the PDF $P(\phi)$ to be a PDF for the points $e^{i\phi}$ on the unit circle, then $V(\phi)$ is the mean of the square of the straight-line distance of these points from the point $\exp(i \arg\langle e^{i\phi}\rangle)$. It can be shown that if a state has at most N photons, then the chordal variance is bounded below by

$$V_{\text{can}}^{\min}(\phi) = 2 - 2\cos\left(\frac{\pi}{N+2}\right) \simeq \pi^2 N^{-2} + O(N^{-4}), \tag{3}$$

where this last result is an asymptotic for large N. It is easily understood because the variance in $a^\dagger a$ is limited above by N^2, so one would expect the variance in phase to be limited below by N^{-2}.

1.2. HETERODYNE MEASUREMENTS

At present, there are a number of practical (non-canonical) schemes for single-shot phase measurements, all of which give equivalent results [4]. One of these schemes (which here stands in place of any of them) is heterodyne detection, which uses a local oscillator highly detuned from the system. As the phase $\Phi(t)$ of the local oscillator changes, the photocurrent reflects the statistics of different field quadratures, $ae^{-i\Phi(t)} + a^\dagger e^{i\Phi(t)}$. The two Fourier components of the photocurrent record thus yield measurements of both quadratures of the field [7]. Setting $A = \frac{1}{2}(X + iY)$, where X and Y are the results of the measurements of the two quadratures, the POVM for the result A is

$$F_{\text{het}}(A) = \pi^{-1}|A\rangle\langle A|, \tag{4}$$

where $|A\rangle$ is a coherent state of complex amplitude A. From the result A the phase can be estimated to be $\phi = \arg A$. The POVM for this heterodyne phase estimate is obtained by integrating (4) over $r = |A|$:

$$F_{\text{het}}(\phi) = \pi^{-1} \int_0^\infty dr\, r\, |re^{i\phi}\rangle\langle re^{i\phi}|. \tag{5}$$

Being a joint measurement of both amplitude and phase quadratures (which do not commute), a heterodyne measurement necessarily introduces extra noise into both results. As a result, the heterodyne phase POVM (5) yields a much less accurate measurement of phase than the canonical POVM (1). Specifically, it can be shown that for a field with at most N photons the variance is bounded below by

$$V_{\text{het}}^{\min}(\phi) \simeq \tfrac{1}{4}N^{-1} + O(N^{-4/3}). \tag{6}$$

This asymptotic result is much worse than the canonical result (3). It is in fact equal to the phase variance of a coherent state of mean photon number N, which is easily understood from the POVM (4). This result shows that for communication purposes, nonclassical states (with an intrinsic phase uncertainty smaller than that of a coherent state of the same intensity) offer only a modest increase in efficiency if one is using standard detection techniques [5].

1.3. ADAPTIVE MEASUREMENTS

If one assumes that before starting the measurement one already knows the phase of the system to be φ within a small uncertainty $\delta\phi \ll 1$, then there is a simple way to obtain a very accurate estimate of it: homodyne detection. By choosing the local oscillator phase Φ to be equal $\varphi + \pi/2$, one would make a measurement of the phase quadrature $ae^{-i\Phi} + a^\dagger e^{i\Phi}$. Assuming that the amplitude r of the field is reasonably well defined (with $r \gg 1, \delta r$) and is also known prior to the measurement, then the phase of the field is very well approximated by the result $\varphi + (ae^{-i\Phi} + a^\dagger e^{i\Phi})/(2r)$. However by making these assumptions one is really removing the problem from the realms of phase measurements. A true phase measurement ideally should not rely on any prior knowledge of the amplitude of the field, and certainly should not rely upon any prior knowledge of that phase. The heterodyne measurements considered above are true phase measurements in this sense, although they are not perfectly accurate measurements.

While not being a true phase measurement, the phase quadrature measurement by homodyne detection suggests how it may be possible to construct a true phase measurement, which should be superior in accuracy to a heterodyne measurement. Rather than measuring a quadrature of predefined phase, the phase of the local oscillator could be adjusted during the course of the measurement to measure the *estimated* phase quadrature of the system by homodyne detection. Here the estimated phase of the system would have to be inferred from the photocurrent record *so far* from the *single* pulse. That is to say, the local oscillator phase is continuously adjusted by a feedback loop to be in quadrature with the estimated system phase over the course of a single measurement (see Fig. 1). This novel idea of *adaptive* single-shot measurements was proposed recently by one of us [8], but it turns out that it has been proposed, in a different context, at least once before [9]. It is a sort of quantum feedback which is quite different from that investigated previously (see Ref. [10] for a review) in that it has no effect on the evolution of the system.

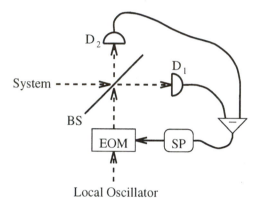

Figure 1. The adaptive phase measurement scheme. Light beams are indicated by dashed lines and electronics by solid lines. BS denotes a 50/50 beam splitter, D_1 and D_2 photodetectors, and SP a signal processor. The local oscillator phase is controlled by an electro-optic modulator (EOM).

To derive the results for an adaptive measurement, we require the general theory for detection using a local oscillator, the phase of which is an arbitrary function of time. This theory is presented in Sec. 2. In Sec. 3, the adaptive scheme is introduced. Some approximate analytical results are obtained in Sec. 4 and summarized in Sec. 5.

2. PHOTODETECTION WITH A LOCAL OSCILLATOR

The quantum measurement theory of photodetection with a strong local oscillator is derived in generality in Ref. [1], using the recently published theory of linear quantum trajectories of Goetsch and Graham [11]. Here we summarize it. For simplicity, let the single mode to be measured be prepared initially in a cavity in state ρ. Let the light leak out through an end mirror with an intensity decay rate of unity (in suitably scaled units). The emitted light is sent through a 50–50 beam splitter, with a strong local oscillator of complex amplitude $\beta(t) = |\beta|e^{i\Phi(t)}$ entering at the other port. The mean fields at detectors D_2, D_1 are thus proportional to $\beta \pm \langle a \rangle e^{-t/2}$ respectively, where $\langle a \rangle = \text{Tr}[a\rho]$ and a is the annihilation operator the cavity mode. The signal photocurrent $I(t)$ in the interval $[t, t + \delta t)$ is defined in terms of the difference between the photocounts $\delta N_2, \delta N_1$ at the two detectors: $I(t) = \lim_{|\beta| \to \infty} [\delta N_2(t) - \delta N_1(t)]/(|\beta| \delta t)$, as in Ref. [7]. It is easy to verify that the mean value of this current is

$$\langle I(t) \rangle = e^{-t/2} \langle ae^{-i\Phi(t)} + a^\dagger e^{i\Phi(t)} \rangle. \tag{7}$$

It is useful to introduce a new symbol $\mathbf{I}_{[0,t)}$ for the complete photocurrent record $\{I(s) : 0 \leq s < t\}$ from time 0 (the time of preparation) to just before time t. The quantum measurement theory we require to describe adaptive measurements is the POVM for the record $\mathbf{I}_{[0,t)}$, which would give the PDF for getting the result $\mathbf{I}_{[0,t)}$ given the initial state ρ. Note that $\mathbf{I}_{[0,t)}$ is a continuous infinity of a real numbers — a very complicated object. Fortunately, it turns out [1] that the POVM depends only on two complex functionals of $\mathbf{I}_{[0,t)}$. These two sufficient statistics are

$$\mathcal{F}_1[\mathbf{I}_{[0,t)}] = \int_0^t e^{i\Phi(s)} e^{-s/2} I(s) ds , \quad \mathcal{F}_2[\mathbf{I}_{[0,t)}] = -\int_0^t e^{2i\Phi(s)} e^{-s} ds. \tag{8}$$

Despite appearances, the second functional *does* depend on $\mathbf{I}_{[0,t)}$ in general, because the local oscillator phase $\Phi(t)$ depends upon $\mathbf{I}_{[0,t)}$ in adaptive measurements. Denoting the measured values of these functionals by A_t and B_t respectively, the POVM is [1]

$$F_t(A_t, B_t) = P_0(A_t, B_t) \exp(\tfrac{1}{2} B_t a^{\dagger 2} + A_t a^\dagger) \exp(-a^\dagger at) \exp(\tfrac{1}{2} B_t^* a^2 + A_t^* a), \tag{9}$$

where $P_0(A_t, B_t)$ is a positive function defined later.

The POVM (9) is normalized as usual so that $\int d^2 A_t \, d^2 B_t \, P(A_t, B_t) = 1$, where $P(A_t, B_t) = \text{Tr}[\rho F_t(A_t, B_t)]$ is the *actual* PDF for obtaining the results A_t, B_t given the initial state ρ. By contrast, the function $P_0(A_t, B_t)$ in Eq. (9) can be thought of as the *ostensible* PDF for A_t and B_t [1]. It is the PDF they would have if $I(t)dt$ were a Wiener increment $dW(t)$ [12] satisfying $dW(t)^2 = dt$. Explicitly,

$$P_0(A_t, B_t) = \int d\mathbf{I}_{[0,t)} P_0(\mathbf{I}_{[0,t)}) \delta^{(2)}(A_t - \mathcal{F}_1[\mathbf{I}_{[0,t)}]) \delta^{(2)}(B_t - \mathcal{F}_2[\mathbf{I}_{[0,t)}]). \tag{10}$$

Here $P_0(\mathbf{I}_{[0,t)})$ equals the continuously infinite product of the ostensible PDFs $P_0[I(s)] = \sqrt{ds/2\pi} \exp[-\tfrac{1}{2} ds I(s)^2]$ for each instantaneous current $I(s)$ over each interval $[s, s+ds)$.

This theory can be applied to all detection schemes using a local oscillator, including heterodyne detection. In this detection scheme the local oscillator is detuned from the system by an amount $\Delta \gg 1$. Thus $e^{2i\Phi(t)}$ rotates very rapidly and as a consequence the second functional B_t averages to zero. In this case the measurement result is just A_t, and at the end of the measurement we need consider only $A = A_\infty$. It can readily be shown [1] that the POVM $F_\infty(A, B)$ (9) is equal to $F_{\text{het}}(A)\delta^{(2)}(B)$, where $F_{\text{het}}(A)$ is as in Eq. (4). The final estimate for the phase of the system obtained by heterodyne detection is thus the argument of the functional $A = \mathcal{F}_1[\mathbf{I}_{[0,\infty)}]$ Some understanding of this result can be obtained as follows. Using the result (7) for the actual mean photocurrent we find

$$\langle A \rangle = \int_0^\infty e^{-t/2 + i\Phi(t)} \langle I(t) \rangle dt = \langle a \rangle \int_0^\infty e^{-t} dt + \langle a^\dagger \rangle \int_0^\infty e^{-t + 2i\Phi(t)} = \langle a \rangle - \langle a^\dagger \rangle B, \tag{11}$$

where we are considering $B = B_\infty$ as given. Since for heterodyne detection $B = 0$, we have simply $\langle A \rangle = \langle a \rangle$. Thus the phase estimate $\phi = \arg A$ arises naturally.

3. THE ADAPTIVE ALGORITHM

As explained in the introduction, the central idea of the scheme proposed here is to control the local oscillator to be in quadrature with the estimated system phase. That is, we set

$$\Phi(t) = \frac{\pi}{2} + \hat{\varphi}(t), \tag{12}$$

where $\hat{\varphi}(t)$ is the phase of the system estimated from $\mathbf{I}_{[0,t)}$. The next question is, what do we use for $\hat{\varphi}(t)$? From the theory presented above we know that the only relevant quantities are the two complex functionals (8). In this work we choose

$$\hat{\varphi}(t) = \arg \mathcal{F}_1[\mathbf{I}_{[0,t)}] = \arg A_t. \tag{13}$$

The motivations for choosing this estimate are as follows:

1. $\arg A_t$ is the best estimate for the case of heterodyne detection.

2. It gives the best possible result if the system has at most one photon [8].

3. As will be shown, it gives the feedback algorithm

$$d\Phi(t) = \frac{I(t)dt}{\sqrt{e^t - 1}} \tag{14}$$

which should be easy to implement experimentally because it is Markovian (does not require memory) and is linear in the photocurrent $I(t)$.

4. As will be shown, it can be approximately solved analytically.

The theoretical and experimental simplifications offered by this algorithm arise from the fact that the measurement result $A_t = \int_0^t e^{-s/2+i\Phi(s)} I(s)ds$ can be specified by the initial condition $A_0 = 0$ and the differential equation

$$dA_t = e^{-t/2+i\Phi(t)} I(t)dt. \tag{15}$$

Under the above algorithm, $e^{i\Phi(t)} = iA_t/|A_t|$, so that this equation becomes

$$dA_t = ie^{-t/2}\frac{A_t}{|A_t|}I(t)dt. \tag{16}$$

Now the *ostensible* statistics of A_t are those arising from the identification $I(t)dt = dW(t)$. With this replacement, the Ito stochastic differential equation (16) can be solved to yield

$$A_t = \sqrt{1 - e^{-t}}\exp(i\hat{\varphi}(t)), \quad \text{where} \quad \hat{\varphi}(t) = \int_0^t \frac{I(s)ds}{\sqrt{e^s - 1}}. \tag{17}$$

The phase estimate thus obeys $d\hat{\varphi}(t) = I(t)dt/\sqrt{e^t - 1}$, and since $d\Phi(t) = d\hat{\varphi}(t)$, the result (14) is now apparent. At $t = \infty$ we have simply $A = \exp(i\hat{\varphi})$, where $\hat{\varphi} = \hat{\varphi}(\infty)$. It turns out that $\hat{\varphi}$ is *ostensibly* a completely random phase due to the singularity in the integral (17) at $t = 0$. That is, $P_0(\hat{\varphi}) = (2\pi)^{-1}$.

Now although $\hat{\varphi}$ is ostensibly completely random, it is ostensibly correlated with the phase of the second measurement result B. However, if we define

$$C = B(A^*)^2 = e^{-2i\hat{\varphi}(\infty)}\int_0^\infty dt e^{-t+2i\hat{\varphi}(t)}, \tag{18}$$

we can prove that C is ostensibly independent of A. Thus the POVM for the results A, B is more simply expressed as

$$F(\hat{\varphi}, C) = \frac{1}{2\pi} P_0(C) \exp(\tfrac{1}{2} C(a^\dagger e^{i\hat{\varphi}})^2 + e^{i\hat{\varphi}} a^\dagger)|0\rangle\langle 0| \exp(\tfrac{1}{2} C(a e^{-i\hat{\varphi}})^2 + e^{-i\hat{\varphi}} a). \quad (19)$$

Unfortunately, it has proved impossible to obtain an expression for $P_0(C)$. It is possible to obtain a recursion relation for the moments of C, but these moments are of no use in evaluating $\mathrm{Tr}[\rho F(\hat{\varphi}, C)]$ for states ρ with very large photon number. Instead, we will adopt an approximate analytical approach based on the state $\rho = |r\rangle\langle r|$, where $|r\rangle$ is a coherent state with an amplitude $r \gg 1$ which can be assumed real without loss of generality. Noting that coherent states are eigenstates of a, and that $\langle r|0\rangle\langle 0|r\rangle = \exp(-r^2)$, the PDF to get the results $\hat{\varphi}, C$ is simply evaluated as

$$\langle r|F(\hat{\varphi}, C)|r\rangle = \frac{1}{2\pi} P_0(C) \exp(-r^2 + \mathrm{Re}[C e^{2i\hat{\varphi}}] r^2 + 2 \cos \hat{\varphi} r). \quad (20)$$

3.1. MARK I AND MARK II PHASE ESTIMATES

The above algorithm would suggest choosing as one's final $(t = \infty)$ estimate for the system phase

$$\phi_\mathrm{I} = \hat{\varphi} = \arg A. \quad (21)$$

Although this is the best estimate for a system with at most one photon [8], it actually gives a rather poor estimate of the system phase for large photon numbers N. This is the reason we subscript ϕ with a I: it is the phase estimate mark I. In fact, it can be shown that for states with a maximum photon number N, the measured variance of ϕ_I is bounded below by

$$V_\mathrm{I}^{\min}(\phi) = \tfrac{1}{4} N^{-1/2} + O(N^{-1}), \quad (22)$$

which is larger by a factor of $\sqrt{N}$ than that for heterodyne measurements (6).

The reason that A is not the best estimator of the phase in this case is that under this scheme $B = \mathcal{F}_2[\mathbf{I}_{[0,\infty)}]$ is not equal to zero, so from the general result (11), $\langle A \rangle$ is not simply proportional to $\langle a \rangle$. However, we find that for a given B the combination of $A + BA^*$ has a mean value

$$\langle A + BA^* \rangle = \langle a \rangle - \langle a^\dagger \rangle B + B \left(\langle a^\dagger \rangle - B^* \langle a \rangle \right) = \langle a \rangle \left(1 - |B|^2 \right). \quad (23)$$

Since $|B|^2 \leq 1$, this suggests an improved, mark II estimate for the final phase,

$$\phi_\mathrm{II} = \arg(A + BA^*) = \hat{\varphi} + \arg(1 + C), \quad (24)$$

where C is as defined above (18).

4. MEASURED PHASE VARIANCES FOR COHERENT STATES

4.1. CANONICAL MEASUREMENTS

The variance in a measured phase is a combination of the intrinsic phase variance of the input state and the variance due to the imperfections in the measurement scheme. To compare measurement schemes, we are interested in the latter contribution, but to do this we have to know the former. For this reason, we first evaluate the phase variance of a canonical measurement of a coherent state $|r\rangle$. We find from Eq. (1)

$$V_\mathrm{can}^\mathrm{coh}(\phi) = 2 \left(1 - \frac{\exp(-r^2)}{r} \sum_{n=0}^{\infty} \frac{\sqrt{n} r^{2n}}{n!} \right) \simeq \frac{1}{4r^2} + \frac{7}{64r^4} + O(r^{-6}). \quad (25)$$

We may regard this as the intrinsic phase variance of a coherent state.

4.2. MARK II ADAPTIVE MEASUREMENTS

For mark II adaptive measurements we choose $\phi = \hat{\varphi} + \arg(1+C)$. Thus the POVM for this measurement is

$$F_{\text{II}}(\phi) = \int d^2C \, d\hat{\varphi} \, F_\infty(\hat{\varphi}, C) \delta\left(\phi - \hat{\varphi} - \arg(1+C)\right) \qquad (26)$$

From the above expression (20), and using $\phi = \hat{\varphi} + \arg(1+C)$, we find

$$\langle r | F_{\text{II}}(\phi) | r \rangle = \int d^2C \exp\left(q(\phi, C, r)\right), \qquad (27)$$

where

$$q(\phi, C, r) = \log\left(P_0(C)\right) - r^2 + \text{Re}\left[Ce^{2i\phi}\frac{1+C^*}{1+C}\right]r^2 + 2\text{Re}\left[e^{i\phi}\sqrt{\frac{1+C^*}{1+C}}\right]r. \qquad (28)$$

Because the PDF (27) is normalized it follows that $\partial_r \int d\phi \langle r | F_{\text{II}}(\phi) | r \rangle = 0$. From this simple fact it can be shown that this PDF is sharply peaked about the point $\phi = 0$, $C = 1 - r^{-1}$ for $r \gg 1$. This enables us to use a method akin to that of steepest descents. Define $x_1 = \text{Re}[C - 1 + r^{-1}]$, $x_2 = \text{Im}[C]$, $x_3 = \phi$. Then $q(\mathbf{x})$ is maximized at $\mathbf{x} = \mathbf{0}$. Thus we can approximate (27) by

$$\langle r | F_{\text{II}}(\phi) | r \rangle = \int dx_1 \int dx_2 \exp\left(q_0 - \tfrac{1}{2}x_i \Lambda_{ij} x_j\right), \quad \text{where} \quad \Lambda_{ij} = -\left.\frac{\partial^2 q}{\partial x_i \partial x_j}\right|_{\mathbf{x}=\mathbf{0}} \qquad (29)$$

is the Hessian matrix. The following matrix elements are readily evaluated:

$$\Lambda_{13} = 0, \quad \Lambda_{23} = 0, \quad \Lambda_{33} = -4r^2 + 2r. \qquad (30)$$

Thus, near the maximum-likelihood point, ϕ is uncorrelated with C, which indicates that we have chosen the correct function of C in our phase estimate (24). This makes the integrations over x_1 and x_2 trivial, giving the following approximate PDF for $x_3 = \phi$:

$$\langle r | F_{\text{II}}(\phi) | r \rangle \propto \exp\left(-\tfrac{1}{2}\phi^2(4r^2 - 2r)\right). \qquad (31)$$

This has a chordal variance equal to

$$V_{\text{II}}^{\text{coh}}(\phi) = \frac{1}{4r^2} + \frac{1}{8r^3} + O(r^{-4}). \qquad (32)$$

Subtracting the intrinsic phase variance of a coherent state (25), we find the noise introduced by the measurement

$$V_{\text{II}}(\phi) = \frac{1}{8r^3} + O(r^{-4}). \qquad (33)$$

Although this result pertains to coherent states of mean photon number r^2, it can be used to find the minimum measured phase variance for a state with at most N photons. We have seen above that the intrinsic phase noise of a state with at most N photons can be as little as $\pi^2 N^{-2}$. This is far below the noise which would be introduced by this adaptive mark II measurement, which scales as $N^{-3/2}$ (33). To first order we can thus ignore the intrinsic phase uncertainty in the state, and look instead at the phase noise of the measurement. This will be minimized for a state with photon number as high as possible, given the upper bound N. This enables us to use the expression (33), replacing r^2 by N. Thus we have

$$V_{\text{II}}^{\text{min}}(\phi) = \tfrac{1}{8}N^{-3/2} + O(N^{-5/3}), \qquad (34)$$

where the error term is a second order correction due to the intrinsic phase uncertainty of the state. The exact magnitude of this term can be derived from a rigorous formulation of the above argument, and involves the first zero of the Airey function.

5. SUMMARY

The accuracy of any phase measurement scheme can be quantified by the minimum possible variance in the measured phase resulting from an input state with at most $N \gg 1$ photons. The first order asymptotic results for the four schemes discussed in this paper are summarized below:

Canonical	$\pi^2 N^{-2}$
Adaptive Mark II	$\frac{1}{8} N^{-3/2}$
Heterodyne	$\frac{1}{4} N^{-1}$
Adaptive Mark I	$\frac{1}{4} N^{-1/2}$

We see that the scaling for the results of the adaptive mark II scheme is intermediate between the best possible result allowed by quantum mechanics (canonical) and the previous best result for an experimentally feasible scheme (heterodyne). Since the feedback requires only electronics and an electro-optic modulator, it should also be experimentally feasible. It would be of great interest to verify these results by experiment, not only because of the possible applications in precision measurement and communication, but because single-shot adaptive measurements are a new type of measurement which have not yet been attempted.

REFERENCES

[1] H.M. Wiseman, Quantum Semiclass. Opt. **8**, 205 (1996).

[2] Physica Scripta **T48**, 13 (1993) *Quantum Phase and Phase Dependent Measurements* edited by W.P. Schleich and S.M. Barnett.

[3] F. London, Z. Phys. **40**, 193 (1927).

[4] U. Leonhardt, J.A. Vaccora, B. Böhmer, and H. Paul, Phys. Rev. A **51**, 84 (1995).

[5] M.J. Hall and I.G. Fuss, Quantum Opt. **3**, 147 (1991).

[6] C.W. Helstrom, *Quantum Detection and Estimation Theory* (Academic, New York, 1976).

[7] H.M. Wiseman and G.J. Milburn, Phys. Rev. A **47**, 1652 (1993).

[8] H.M. Wiseman, Phys. Rev. Lett. **75**, 4587 (1995).

[9] S.J. Dolinar, Research Laboratory of Electronics, MIT, Quarterly Progress Report **111**, p. 115 (1973). (unpublished).

[10] H.M. Wiseman, Modern Physics Lett. B **9**, 629 (1995).

[11] P. Goetsch and R. Graham, Phys. Rev. A **50**, 5242 (1994).

[12] C.W. Gardiner, *Handbook of Stochastic Methods* (Springer, Berlin, 1985).

AMPLITUDE SQUEEZING OF THE FUNDAMENTAL FIELD BY MEANS OF TRAVELING-WAVE QUASI-PHASEMATCHED SECOND-HARMONIC GENERATION IN A LiNbO$_3$ WAVEGUIDE

D. K. Serkland[1], Prem Kumar[1], M. A. Arbore[2], and M. M. Fejer[2]

[1] Department of Electrical and Computer Engineering
Northwestern University, Evanston, Illinois 60208-3118
[2] Ginzton Laboratory, Stanford University
Stanford, California 94305-4085

We have demonstrated amplitude squeezing of the fundamental field at 1.55 μm in single-pass second-harmonic generation using a 30-mm-long single-mode waveguide fabricated in periodically-poled lithium niobate. Squeezing of 0.7 ± 0.1 dB was observed with less than 1 mW of average input fundamental power.

Bulk $\chi^{(2)}$ materials have been employed to obtain substantial amounts of squeezing by means of second-harmonic generation [1] and frequency down-conversion [2]. However, waveguides fabricated in quasi-phasematched $\chi^{(2)}$ materials promise significant advantages over bulk devices for squeezing experiments. First, the tight confinement of light inside the waveguide yields a strong nonlinear coupling which reduces the laser power required for squeezing generation. Also, traveling-wave squeezing in single-mode waveguides should not suffer from the gain-induced diffraction phenomenon [3] that occurs in bulk-crystal experiments. Finally, the technique of quasi-phasematching allows one to fabricate devices to work at any desired wavelength in the transparency range of the nonlinear crystal. Specifically, quasi-phasematching has enabled us to produce squeezing at the 1.55 μm communications wavelength.

As in bulk-crystal squeezing experiments, the largest amounts of squeezing are expected to be obtained from the frequency down-conversion process. Hence, the initial waveguide experiments employed degenerate optical parametric amplifiers (DOPAs) to produce a squeezed-vacuum state [4,5]. The pump for the waveguide DOPA was generated by frequency doubling a mode-locked laser in an external nonlinear crystal. The traveling-wave DOPA in these experiments produced a squeezed-vacuum state that was measured by homodyne detection, using a portion of the mode-locked laser as the local oscillator. A 1 mm KTP waveguide and a Ti-sapphire laser were employed in the first experiment to obtain 12% squeezing at 830 nm [4]. In the second experiment, a 10 mm LiNbO$_3$ waveguide and a Nd:YAG laser yielded 14% squeezing at 1064 nm [5]. The limiting factors in these experiments were spatio-temporal mismatch between the local oscillator and squeezed vacuum modes and two-photon absorption of the pump radiation within the nonlinear crystal. In lithium niobate, two-photon absorption (TPA) occurs for wavelengths shorter than 570 nm. In order to avoid TPA, we have elected to

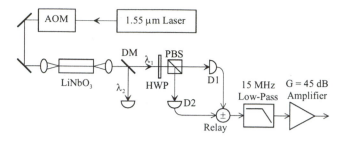

Figure 1. A schematic of the experimental setup to generate sub-Poissonian pulses of light by means of second-harmonic generation.

use a 1.55 µm laser, since the second-harmonic light at 775 nm remains below the TPA band edge.

Although extensions of the parametric amplifier experiments discussed above hold the greatest promise for producing highly-squeezed states of light, there are compelling reasons to investigate the second-harmonic generation (SHG) process as well. Theoretically, the equations that govern degenerate parametric amplification and SHG are identical, except that the input power is at different wavelengths [6]. As a practical matter, SHG experiments are easier to implement since there is no need to generate a "pump" beam with an additional nonlinear crystal. Furthermore, no local oscillator is required, since SHG produces (bright) amplitude-squeezed light for which the noise can be directly detected.

In spite of the simplicity of the experiments to generate squeezing by means of single-pass SHG, technical issues have impeded progress. In traveling-wave SHG, the high powers required to achieve significant conversion lead to saturation of the photodiodes and the subsequent amplifiers that are necessary to measure the squeezing. Nevertheless, a slight amount of squeezing was observed in a recent traveling-wave SHG experiment, using type-II phasematching [7]. In order to generate squeezing with low power, optical cavities have been employed to enhance the weak nonlinear interaction in bulk crystals [1]. Waveguides can also be used to generate squeezing with low power and hence overcome the detector saturation problem. In the case of optical waveguides, enhanced nonlinear coupling arises from the tight field confinement which is maintained over a long interaction length.

Theoretically, phasematched traveling-wave SHG is expected to create sub-Poissonian light in both the fundamental and second-harmonic fields [8]. As a function of conversion efficiency, the Fano factor for the second-harmonic field decreases gradually and approaches a −3 dB limit. However, the Fano factor for the transmitted fundamental field decreases without limit according to

$$S_{1x} = (1 - \zeta \tanh \zeta)^2 \operatorname{sech}^2 \zeta + 2 \tanh^2 \zeta \operatorname{sech}^2 \zeta, \tag{1}$$

where ζ is the input fundamental-field amplitude normalized such that the conversion efficiency obeys

$$\gamma = \tanh^2 \zeta. \tag{2}$$

Figure 1 shows our experimental setup for creating sub-Poissonian light by means of traveling-wave SHG. The 1.55 µm fundamental light was generated by a synchronously-pumped mode-locked KCl:Tl color-center laser that produced 20 ps FWHM $\operatorname{sech}^2(t/\tau_1)$ pulses at a 100 MHz repetition rate. An acousto-optic modulator (AOM) prevented

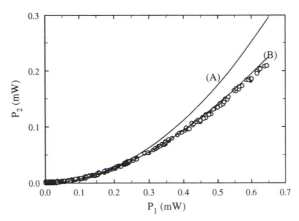

Figure 2. Measured second-harmonic power versus input fundamental power. CW theory curve (A) follows $P_2 = \eta_{ML}P_1^2$, while curve (B) accounts for fundamental depletion through $P_2 = P_1 \tanh^2(\sqrt{\eta_{ML}P_1})$. The data fits the CW theory curves with $\eta_{ML} = 0.7/\text{mW}$. The maximum conversion shown exceeds 30%, where clearly depletion must be considered.

feedback into the laser from destabilizing the output pulses. The pulses were coupled into and out of the waveguide with aspheric lenses that were anti-reflection (AR) coated at 1.55 μm. The 30-mm-long, 5-μm-wide waveguide was formed by annealed proton exchange [9] on a periodically-poled lithium niobate (PPLN) substrate, which was fabricated by electric-field poling [10] with a 14 μm period in order to achieve first-order quasi-phasematching of the 1550-to-775 nm interaction [11]. All fields were polarized parallel to the z-axis of the lithium niobate crystal to exploit the large d_{33} nonlinear coefficient.

Figure 2 shows that more than 30% conversion was achieved with only 0.6 mW of average input fundamental power. Throughout this paper, the coupling efficiency, the Fresnel reflections, and the waveguide losses are neglected by defining the input fundamental power to be equal to the sum of the transmitted powers at both wavelengths. The second-harmonic light experienced 50% linear loss before being detected because the output aspheric lens was not AR coated for 775 nm. Therefore, in Fig. 2 the measured second-harmonic power has been scaled by a factor of 2. Clearly, the square-law equation shown by curve (A) of Fig. 2 does not accurately follow the data taken in the medium-conversion regime, where fundamental depletion must be considered. The CW theory (including pump depletion) would also break down in the high-conversion regime since we used mode-locked pulses in our experiment. However, the lossless CW theory fits the data presented in this paper with reasonable accuracy. Characterization of the SHG with a CW laser indicated an internal small-signal normalized conversion of 1.5/W, which shows substantial improvement over the ∼0.01/W normalized conversion typical in bulk crystals. We note that the quasi-phasematching FWHM bandwidth was approximately 0.5 nm, as observed in Ref. [11].

Theory predicts a suppression of the amplitude noise of the transmitted fundamental light below the shot-noise level by the Fano factor given in Eq. (1). We measured the amplitude noise using a half-wave plate (HWP), a polarization beamsplitter (PBS), and two photodiodes (D1 and D2), as depicted in Fig. 1. A relay allowed us to switch between measuring the sum or the difference of the two photocurrents. In the sum position, the amplitude noise of the transmitted fundamental field was measured. In the difference position, the full shot-noise level appeared, due to the presence of the vacuum mode that was polarized perpendicular to the transmitted fundamental polarization. The sum or difference photocurrent was low-pass filtered to remove the coherent spikes at multiples of 100 MHz and then amplified by a low-noise RF amplifier (Miteq, model AU-1263) before the spectrum analyzer. The slight noise-amplitude variations below 15 MHz in Fig. 3 resulted from the (complex) bias impedances used in our detector circuit. Detuning the laser wavelength to suppress SHG resulted in equal noise levels for the sum and difference photocurrents to within 0.05 dB, indicating that the laser was shot-noise limited over the frequency range displayed in Fig. 3.

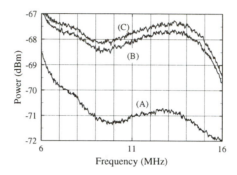

Figure 3. Noise power versus frequency. The electronic noise appears in trace (A), the sum photocurrent noise in trace (B), and the difference photocurrent noise in trace (C).

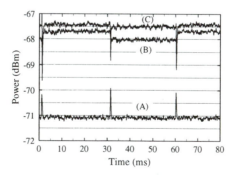

Figure 4. Noise power at 11 MHz versus time (photocurrents added from 32 to 60 ms). Trace (A) shows the electronic noise; traces (B) and (C) show squeezing with 30.3% and 4.2% conversion.

Although Fig. 3 clearly indicates squeezing of the amplitude noise, drift of the conversion efficiency between the acquisition of the sum and difference traces reduced the accuracy of such a squeezing measurement. A more accurate method involved continuously switching the relay between the sum and difference positions and recording the noise at a specific frequency versus time. Figure 4 shows the noise detected at 11 MHz, with a 1 MHz resolution bandwidth and 1 kHz video bandwidth, averaged

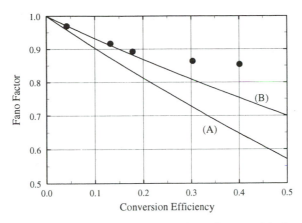

Figure 5. Measured Fano factor of the transmitted fundamental light plotted as a function of the second-harmonic conversion efficiency. Curves (A) and (B) show predictions of the CW theory for 100% and 70% detection efficiency, respectively.

over 20 consecutive traces where the measured photocurrent was quickly switched from difference to sum to difference. Trace (A) in Fig. 4 shows the electronic noise, trace (B) shows the photocurrent noise with 30.3% conversion, and trace (C) shows the noise with only 4.2% conversion. Trace (C) was obtained by increasing the mode-locked pulse width and reducing the power injected into the waveguide to obtain a mean transmitted power close to that of trace (B), where the depletion was 30.3%. The raw data in trace (B) of Fig. 4 show only 0.33 dB of noise reduction due to the presence of the relatively large electronic noise shown in trace (A).

The measured squeezing versus conversion efficiency appears in Fig. 5, where we have removed the electronic noise component. The five data points were obtained by recording scans like those of Fig. 4, taken at various conversion efficiencies. The CW prediction of Eq. (1) also appears in Fig. 5, where $F = \eta_{\mathrm{det}} S_{1x} + 1 - \eta_{\mathrm{det}}$ has been used to account for the overall detection efficiency η_{det}. The dominant factors which reduced the overall detection efficiency were the 85% quantum efficiency of the detectors (including losses at the aluminum mirrors ahead of the photodiodes) and the 14% Fresnel reflection at the exit face of the waveguide. The net transmission through the aspheric lens, dichroic mirror (DM), HWP and PBS, exceeded 96%. The detection efficiency was therefore roughly 70%. As seen in Fig. 5, up to 14.5% (0.7 dB) of noise reduction was measured, which was somewhat less than the theoretical expectation. We note that the waveguide losses, estimated to be $12 \pm 6\%/\mathrm{cm}$, have not been taken into account. The agreement between theory and measurements would improve if the waveguide losses were incorporated into the theoretical prediction.

In conclusion, we have observed 0.7 dB of amplitude squeezing of the transmitted fundamental in traveling-wave quasi-phasematched SHG using a 30-mm-long lithium niobate waveguide. Conversion efficiencies up to 40% were obtained at average fundamental powers below 1 mW, which permitted detection of the bright squeezed light without saturating the photodiodes or the subsequent electronics. Quasi-phasematching enabled the experiment to be implemented at 1.55 μm, and the single-mode waveguide avoided gain-induced diffraction effects. The observed amplitude noise reduction was slightly below the prediction of the lossless CW theory. In order to resolve the remaining discrepancy, the theory must be extended to include waveguide losses and to consider pulses rather than CW fields. Preliminary evidence suggests that photorefractive effects at the 775 nm second-harmonic wavelength may also limit the conversion efficiency and squeezing. We intend to reduce photorefractive effects and obtain higher conversion efficiencies by chopping the laser beam to lower the duty cycle and hence average power in the waveguides [5]. We anticipate that higher conversion will improve the fundamental squeezing and permit measurement of squeezing at the second-harmonic frequency as well.

REFERENCES

[1] S. F. Pereira, M. Xiao, H. J. Kimble, and J. L. Hall, Phys. Rev. A **38**, 4931 (1988); R. Paschotta, M. Collett, P. Kürz, K. Fiedler, H. A. Bachor, and J. Mlynek, Phys. Rev. Lett. **72**, 3807 (1994); T. C. Ralph, M. S. Taubman, A. G. White, D. E. McClelland, and H. A. Bachor, Opt. Lett. **20**, 1316 (1995); H. Tsuchida, Opt. Lett. **20**, 2240 (1995).

[2] L. A. Wu, M. Xiao, and H. J. Kimble, J. Opt. Soc. Am. B **4**, 1465 (1987); E. S. Polzik, J. Carri, and H. J. Kimble, Appl. Phys. B **55**, 279 (1992); C. Kim and P. Kumar, Phys. Rev. Lett. **73**, 1605 (1994); G. Breitenbach, T. Müller, S. F. Pereira, J.-Ph. Poizat, S. Schiller, and J. Mlynek, J. Opt. Soc. Am. B **12**, 2304 (1995).

[3] C. Kim, R.-D. Li, and P. Kumar, Opt. Lett. **19**, 132 (1994).

[4] M. E. Anderson, M. Beck, M. G. Raymer, and J. D. Bierlein, Opt. Lett. **20**, 620 (1995).

[5] D. K. Serkland, M. M. Fejer, R. L. Byer, and Y. Yamamoto Opt. Lett. **20**, 1649 (1995).

[6] R.-D. Li and P. Kumar, J. Opt. Soc. Am. B **12**, 2310 (1995).

[7] S. Youn, S.-K. Choi, P. Kumar, and R.-D. Li, Opt. Lett. **21**, 1597 (1996).

[8] R.-D. Li and P. Kumar, Opt. Lett. **18**, 1961 (1993); Z. Y. Ou, Phys. Rev. A **49**, 2106 (1994); R.-D. Li and P. Kumar, Phys. Rev. A **49**, 2157 (1994).

[9] M. L. Bortz and M. M. Fejer, Opt. Lett. **16**, 1844 (1991).

[10] L. E. Myers, R. C. Eckardt, M. M. Fejer, R. L. Byer, W. R. Bosenberg, and J. W. Pierce, J. Opt. Soc. Am. B **12**, 2102 (1995).

[11] M. A. Arbore and M. M. Fejer, in *Nonlinear Optics: Materials, Fundamentals, and Applications*, Vol. 11 of 1996 OSA Technical Digest Series, p. 112.

QUANTUM NOISE REDUCTION OF THE PUMP FIELD IN AN OPTICAL PARAMETRIC OSCILLATOR

Katsuyuki Kasai[1], Gao Jiangrui[2], Ling-An Wu[3], and Claude Fabre[4]

[1] Communications Research Laboratory
Ministry of Posts & Telecommunications
588-2 Iwaoka, Nishi-ku, Kobe 651-24 Japan
[2] Opto-Electronics Institute, Shanxi University
Taiyuan, Shanxi 030006, P R China
[3] Institute of Physics, Academia Sinica, Beijing 100080 P R China
[4] Laboratoire Kastler Brossel de l'Ecole Normale Supérieure
Université P.M.Curie
Case 74, 75252 Paris Cedex 05 France

Quantum noise properties of the pump field in an Optical Parametric Oscillator (OPO) are experimentally studied. We constructed a cw semimonolithic KTP triply resonant OPO, which had an extremely low oscillation threshold of 0.4 mW. The pump beam reflected back from this OPO is squeezed through strong parametric interactions. The observed intensity noise quickly changes in the bistable region of the OPO when the cavity length is scanned, and a quantum noise reduction of 24% is preliminarily demonstrated.

1. INTRODUCTION

Optical Parametric Oscillators (OPO's) have been very useful devices as tunable coherent light sources ever since they were invented. They are also useful in controlling quantum fluctuations of light. To date, the properties of quantum fluctuations affecting the output signal and idler fields have been studied in detail in experiments. Wu *et al.* demonstrated the generation of a squeezed vacuum state from a sub-threshold OPO [1]. Kasai also observed squeezing on the output field from a triply resonant OPO [2]. Heidmann *et al.* observed a significant noise reduction in the correlation between the twin-photon beams of an OPO working above threshold [3]. In this paper, we study the properties of quantum fluctuations of the pump field through experiments in an optical parametric oscillator. According to semi-classical calculation, the pump field reflected back from an OPO is squeezed [4]. To demonstrate this squeezing, we constructed a semimonolithic KTP triply resonant OPO pumped by a monolithic, frequency-doubled, YAG laser. The triple resonance ensures an extremely low oscillation threshold of 0.4 mW cw, and also interesting nonlinear behaviors such as optical bistability. Significant squeezing has been observed in the neighborhood of turning points for optical bistability [5]. This effect is due to very strong parametric interactions in the triply resonant OPO with cavity detuning.

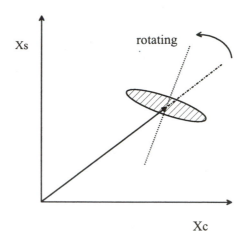

Figure 1. Rotation of squeezing direction in phase space.

2. QUANTUM NOISE PROPERTIES OF THE PUMP FIELD

We consider a triply resonant OPO which is simultaneously resonant for the pump, signal and idler fields. Taking into account the cavity detuning between the cavity modes and the three interacting light modes, one can obtain bistable or even unstable behaviors for the mean field. In this OPO, the parametric interaction process with the cavity detuning leads to an intensity dependent phase shift for the pump field, in a way similar to the situation encountered in a Kerr medium inserted in an optical cavity [6]. Quantum fluctuations undergo the phase shift as well, and therefore squeezing is expected to occur on the pump field reflected back from the OPO. Quantum noise reduction of this squeezing is obtained on a certain quadrature component which is usually neither phase nor amplitude, and the squeezing direction rotates in phase space as a function of cavity detuning, as shown in Fig. 1. Intensity squeezing, which is the projection of quantum fluctuations onto the mean field, is significant in the neighborhood of a turning point for optical bistability according to Ref. [4].

3. EXPERIMENTAL CONFIGURATION

Our experimental configuration is shown in Fig. 2. The semimonolithic OPO consists of a 15-mm KTP crystal (Type II) with flat ends and a spherical output mirror of 20-mm radius, and the cavity length is 21 mm. The input side of the crystal has a highly-reflective multidielectric coating for the signal and idler modes around 1.064 μm and a reflection coefficient of 85% for the pump mode at 0.532 μm. The other side of the crystal is anti-reflection coated. The spherical output mirror has highly-reflective coatings at 1.064 μm and at 0.532 μm, and is mounted on a piezoelectric transducer (PZT). The cavity finesses are 30 for the pump mode and roughly 1000 for the signal and idler modes. The signal, the idler, and the pump modes are simultaneously resonant, that is, triply resonant.

The OPO is pumped by a cw frequency-doubled (green) Nd:YAG laser (LIGHT-WAVE Model 140) which produces a narrow linewidth, stable frequency, single axial mode beam at a wavelength of 0.532 μm. The pump beam is carefully matched to the TEM$_{00}$ mode of the OPO cavity. The parametric oscillation is monitored by an infrared photodiode PD3.

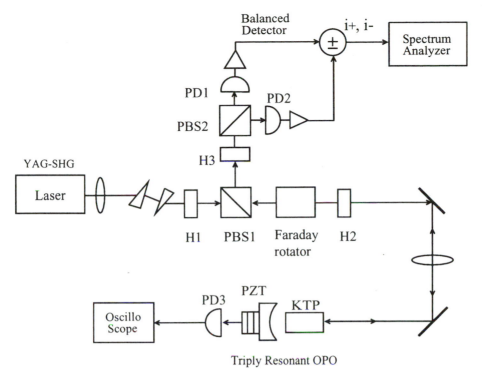

Figure 2. Sketch of the experimental setup (PD: photodiode, PBS: polarizing beam splitter, H: half-wave plate).

The pump beam reflected back from the OPO is halved by an effective 50% beam splitter (half-wave plate H3 and polarizing beam splitter PBS2) and directed to a balanced detector after passing through the optical circulator which consists of a Faraday rotator and a polarizing beam splitter (PBS1). The balanced detector is formed by two silicon photodiodes PD1 and PD2 (EG&G FND-100) with a quantum efficiency of $\eta = 0.80 \pm 0.05$. These high quantum efficiencies at a wavelength of 0.53 μm are obtained in this experiment when the beams reflected from the photodiodes (which are tilted) are sent back on themselves using highly-reflective mirrors.

The photocurrents of the two photodiodes are amplified, and are added or subtracted to produce photocurrents termed i_+ and i_-. The spectral densities of the photocurrent fluctuations $i_\pm$ are observed with a spectrum analyzer.

4. OBSERVATION OF BISTABILITY

The parametric oscillation of this semimonolithic OPO turned out to be very stable in spite of its triply resonant character, and we obtained an extremely low oscillation threshold of 0.4 mW cw. Continuous operation of the parametric oscillation was possible for several seconds even when free running. The signal and idler modes of the output had almost the same wavelength, close to 1.064 μm, and orthogonal polarization.

Figure 3 shows variations in the OPO output power measured with infrared photo-

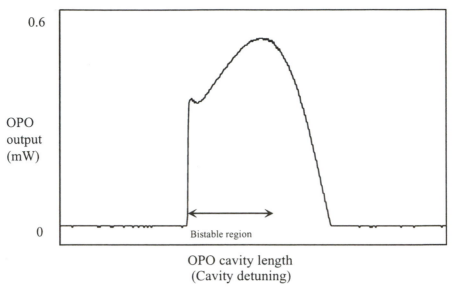

0.6

OPO
output
(mW)

0

Bistable region

OPO cavity length
(Cavity detuning)

Figure 3. Experimental variations in OPO output power as a function of cavity length.

diode PD3, as a function of the cavity length, when it is scanned through resonance of the pump field while the pump intensity is constant. This output power of parametric oscillation is the sum of the intensities of the infrared signal and idler beams. The output variation in Fig. 3 has a width to the order of 0.3 nm, corresponding to cavity resonance with signal and idler modes.

We should notice that there is a steep vertical part, that is a jump, on one side of the output variation. This jump is due to the bistable behavior of the triply resonant OPO [7], which depends on the cavity detuning conditions.

5.   OBSERVATION OF QUANTUM NOISE REDUCTION

The spectral densities of photocurrent fluctuations $i_{\pm}$ were observed on a spectrum analyzer with a balanced detector. The excess noise in the pump beam was suppressed by the balanced detector having a suppression factor greater than 20 dB, and the noise level of the photocurrent i_- gave us the shot-noise reference level. The noise of photocurrent i_+ gives us the intensity noise which is the projection of noise distribution onto the mean field. The spectral noise densities of i_- and i_+ coincide within 0.1 dB far from the cavity resonance in a frequency range of >20 MHz, which indicates that there is no excess noise in the pump beam in this frequency range.

We will focus our attention to the bistable region of Fig. 3, where significant squeezing is expected according to theory [4]. Figure 4 shows the intensity noise of i_- and i_+ at a fixed analysis frequency of 26 MHz, which was observed as a function of cavity length which corresponds to cavity detuning. The analysis bandwidth and the video filter of the spectrum analyzer were set at 1 MHz and 3 kHz. The incident pump power was 8 mW, and the electrical noise of the amplifier was 10 dB below the shot-noise level far from cavity resonance. The output mirror of the OPO was scanned by the PZT as slowly as possible, and the noise variations in the bistable region were observed in detail. The noise trace i_-, which showed the shot noise level, slowly changed due to pump depletion. A narrow dip of 1.2 dB in the bistable region of noise trace i_+ was observed as the arrow designates, whereas we could not observe such a dip in noise trace i_-. This dip corresponds to a quantum noise reduction of 24% below the shot noise level.

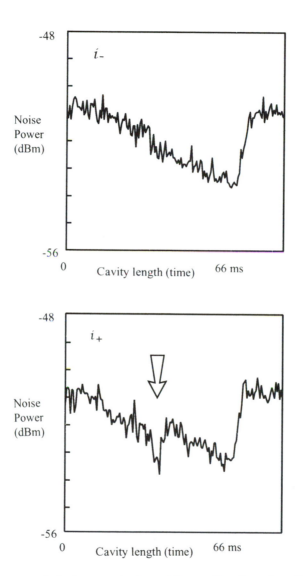

Figure 4. Noise power of photocurrents i_- and i_+ as a function of cavity length. (Arrow designates squeezing.)

6. CONCLUSION

The squeezing of the pump field, which was observed in the bistable region of the triply resonant OPO, appeared as a very narrow dip in noise reduction (see Fig. 4). This result was due to the rotation of the squeezing direction in phase space as discussed in Section 2. When the cavity length was scanned through the bistable region, the squeezing direction quickly rotated in phase space. It follows from this that intensity noise, which is the projection of noise distribution onto the mean field, quickly changes like the dip in noise reduction.

Taking into account a photodiode quantum efficiency of ~ 0.8, optical losses of ~ 0.1 and a mode-matching efficiency of ~ 0.99, inferred squeezing of 41% is expected to be generated immediately away from the OPO when we observe a noise reduction of 24% below the shot-noise level on the spectrum analyzer.

The squeezing obtained in this experiment was limited by the optical loss in the KTP crystal at the wavelength of the pump light. Use of a low-loss crystal in this experiment could improve squeezing, and this device may be expected to act as a 'Quantum Noise Eater' [8].

ACKNOWLEDGMENT

Thanks are due to E. Giacobino for assistance and discussions. This work was partly funded by the EC contract ESPRIT QUINTEC 6934.

REFERENCES

[1] Ling-An Wu, H. J. Kimble, J. L. Hall, and Huifa Wu, Phys. Rev. Lett. 57, 2520 (1986).

[2] K. Kasai, Quantum Communications and Measurement, edited by V. P. Belavkin et al., Plenum Press, New York, 479, (1995).

[3] A. Heidmann, R. J. Horowicz, S. Reynaud, E. Giacobino, C. Fabre, and G. Camy, Phys. Rev. Lett. 59, 2555 (1987).

[4] C. Fabre, E. Giacobino, A. Heidmann, L. Lugiato, S. Reynaud, M. Vadacchino, and W. Kaige, Quantum Opt. 2, 159-187 (1990).

[5] K. Kasai and C. Fabre, to be published in J. Nonl. Opt. Phys. Mater.

[6] S. Reynaud, C. Fabre, E. Giacobino, and A. Heidmann, Phys. Rev. A40, 1440 (1989).

[7] C. Richy, K. I. Petsas, E. Giacobino, and C. Fabre, J. Opt. Soc. Am. B 12, 456 (1995).

[8] C. Fabre, C. Richy, P. Kurz, A. Lambrecht, J. M. Courty, E. Giacobino, S. Reynaud, A. Heidmann, and M. Pinard, Quantum Communications and Measurement, edited by V. P. Belavkin et al., Plenum Press, New York, 455, (1995).

OPTICAL MEASUREMENTS OF WEAK ABSORPTION BEYOND SHOT-NOISE LIMIT [*]

Wang Hai, Xie Changde, Pan Qing, Xue Chenyang, Zhang Yun,
and Peng Kunchi

Institute of Opto-Electronics, Shanxi University
Taiyuan, Shanxi 030006, P.R.China
E-mail: pengkc@shanxi.ihep.ac.cn

The optical measurement of weak absorption beyond the shot-noise limit (SNL) has been achieved by employing quantum-correlated twin beams from a nondegenerate optical parametric oscillator operating above threshold. An improvement in signal-to-noise ratio of 2.5dB relative to SNL is obtained for the weak absorption measurements. Semiclassical theoretical analyses demonstrate that the minimum detectable absorptance is able to trend toward zero through the proposed regime if the intensity difference squeezing between the twin beams is perfect.

1. INTRODUCTION

Since a variety of schemes for the generation of squeezed states of the electromagnetic field have been implemented [1]-[5], investigations of application of nonclassical light states have excited intensive interest because of the potential for improving measurement sensitivity beyond the Shot-Noise-Limit (SNL). Quadrature-squeezed light has been used to demonstrate sub-shot-noise measurements in interferometry and spectroscopy [6]-[8]. In addition to quadrature squeezed light large squeezing of 86% in intensity difference between twin beams produced from a two-mode parametric optical oscillator was experimentally obtained by a research group in Paris [9].

Compared with quadrature-squeezing the intensity difference squeezing is relatively easier to realize [10]. "Robustness" and less restrictive experimental conditions are the most attractive features for applications. In 1990 C.D. Nabors and R.M.Shelby experimentally demonstrated sub-shot-noise signal recovery in a doubly resonant optical parametric oscillator [11]. Later the sub-shot-noise measurement of modulated absorption using spontaneous parametric down-conversion was realized by P.R.Tapster et.al [12]. J.J.Snyder et.al. proposed sub-shot-noise measurements employing the beat note between quantum-correlated photon beams [13].

Recently we have accomplished measurements of weak absorption with quantum-correlated twin beams emitted by a nondegenerate optical parametric oscillator operating above threshold. Semiclassical theoretical analyses demonstrate that the minimum

[*]SUPPORTED IN PART BY THE NATIONAL NATURAL SCIENCE FOUNDATION OF CHINA.

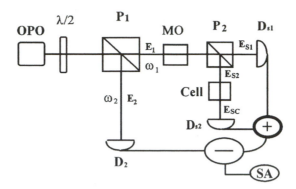

Figure 1. Schematic Diagram for sub-shot-noise measurement of weak absorption.

detectable absorptance can be below the SNL and can reach to zero through the proposed regime if the intensity difference squeezing between the twin beams is perfect. Improvements of sensitivity of about 2.5dB beyond the shot-noise-limit have been experimentally demonstrated.

2. THE PRINCIPLE OF MEASUREMENTS FOR WEAK ABSORPTION

A schematic diagram of the measurement system for weak absorption is shown in Fig.1. A non-degenerate optical parametric oscillator (OPO) operating above threshold generates quantum correlated twin beams ω_1 and ω_2 with perpendicular polarizations. The polarizing-beam-splitter P_1 separates the two cross-polarized beams. The idler field E_2 is directly monitored by the detector D_2, and the signal field E_1 passes through an optical modulator (OM). Then the second polarizing-beam-splitter (P_2) splits the signal field into two parts (Es_1 and Es_2) which are respectively detected by the photodiodes Ds_1 and Ds_2. The sample C for weak absorption measurement is placed in front of Ds_1. The photocurrents from Ds_1, Ds_2 and D_2 are amplified by low noise amplifiers. The photocurrents of Ds_1 and Ds_2 are added by a power combiner (+) and then subtracted from the photocurrent of D_2 by a 180° power combiner (−). The noise power spectrum of the intensity difference is analyzed by a spectrum analyzer (SA) connected to a storage oscilloscope.

The photons of the subharmonic fields E_1 and E_2 are emitted in pairs in the parametric process; therefore

$$2\omega_0 = \omega_1 + \omega_2 \qquad (1)$$

where $2\omega_0$ is the frequency of pump field.

If $p_i(t)$ and $q_i(t)$ express the quadrature amplitude and phase components of the light field E_i(i=1 or 2 respectively for E_1 or E_2 field), the positive frequency part of E_i can be written as

$$\epsilon_i(t) = \left(\frac{p_i(t) + iq_i(t)}{2}\right) e^{-i\psi_i} \qquad (i = 1, 2), \qquad (2)$$

where ψ_i is the phase at t=0. The average amplitude and intensity of E_i are equal to

$$< p_i(t) > = p_i$$

$$< q_i (t) >= 0$$

$$< |\epsilon_i (t)| >=< |\epsilon_i^* (t)| >= \frac{p_i}{2} \tag{3}$$

$$< I_i >= \frac{P_i^2}{4} \tag{4}$$

The fluctuations of intensity are

$$\delta I_i = \frac{p_i}{2} \delta p_i (t) \tag{5}$$

Since the ω_1 and ω_2 photons are always created simultaneously in the optical parametric frequency down-conversion, there is high intensity quantum correlation between E_1 and E_2. Neglecting systematic losses and assuming the frequency is nearly degenerate, we have approximately

$$< p_1 (t) > = < p_2 (t) >= p$$

$$< I_1 > = < I_2 >= \frac{P^2}{4} \tag{6}$$

The intensity difference noise of E_1 and E_2 is lower than shot noise limit [14].

The polarization of E_1 is modulated by OM. The modulation angle is

$$\theta = M \sin \omega_m t, \tag{7}$$

where M and ω_m stand for the modulation coefficient and the modulation frequency. When $\theta = 0$, the angle between the polarizations of P_1 and polarizer P_2 is 45°. The signal fields E_1 and E_2 are given by:

$$E_{s1} = E_1 \sin (45° - \sin \omega_m t)$$

$$E_{s2} = E_1 \cos (45° - \sin \omega_m t) \tag{8}$$

The average intensities of Es_1 and Es_2 can be calculated from Eqs. (2),(6) and (8):

$$< I_{s1} > = < \epsilon_{s1} (t) \epsilon_{s1}^* (t) >=< \epsilon_1 (t) \epsilon_1^* (t) > \sin^2 (45° - M \sin \omega_m t)$$

$$\approx \frac{p^2}{4} \frac{1}{2} (1 - M \sin \omega_m t) \tag{9}$$

$$< I_{s2} >=< \epsilon_{s2} (t) \epsilon_{s2}^* (t) >\approx \frac{p^2}{4} \frac{1}{2} (1 + M \sin \omega_m t) \tag{10}$$

After passing through the sample C the intensity I_{s1} attenuates to I_{sc}:

$$< I_{sc} >=< I_{s1} > e^{-\delta(\omega_1)l} \tag{11}$$

Here $\delta(\omega_1)$ is the absorption coefficient of the sample for the frequency ω_1, and l is the length of sample. Due to $\delta (\omega_1) l << 1$ Eq.(11) can be approximated as

$$< I_{sc} >\simeq< I_{s1} > [1 - \delta (\omega_1) l] \tag{12}$$

Substituting (9) for $< I_{s1} >$, we have

$$< I_{sc} >= \frac{p^2}{4} \frac{1}{2} [1 - \delta (\omega_1) l - 2M \sin \omega_m t + 2M\delta (\omega_1) l \sin \omega_m t] \tag{13}$$

To obtaining high precision of measurement the detection efficiencies should be as equal as possible. Supposing $\eta_1 = \eta_2 = \eta_3 = \eta$ the average signal photocurrent at the spectrum analyzer (SA) is

$$
\begin{aligned}
<i_{sig}> &= <i_{sc}> + <i'_{s2}> - <i_{s2}> \\
&= e\eta\left[<I_{sc}> + <I_{s2}> - <I_2>\right] = e\eta <I_{sig}>
\end{aligned}
\tag{14}
$$

Here

$$
I_{sig} = I_{sc} + I_{s2} - I_2
\tag{15}
$$

I_{sig} is the intensity of the analyzed light signal. Using (10),(13) and (6) we get

$$
<I_{sig}> = \frac{p^2}{4}\left[M\delta(\omega_1)l\sin\omega_m t - \frac{\delta(\omega_1)l}{2}\right]
\tag{16}
$$

$$
<i_{sig}> = e\eta\frac{p^2}{4}\left[M\delta(\omega_1)l\sin\omega_m t - \frac{\delta(\omega_1)l}{2}\right]
\tag{17}
$$

The first terms in Eqs. (16) and (17) are the pulsating signal with modulated frequency ω_m and with amplitude proportional to the absorption $\delta(\omega_1)l$.

Analyzing the photocurrent signal around the frequency ω_m one can measure the weak absorption $\delta(\omega_1)l$. The minimum detectable absorption is limited by the fluctuation of photocurrents. We shall demonstrate that if E_1 and E_2 are twin beams with the quantum correlation, the minimum detectable absorption is less than that using uncorrelated coherent state light.

3. NOISE POWER SPECTRUM AND MINIMUM DETECTABLE ABSORPTION

For determining the fluctuation of the light field the quantum noise of the vacuum field E_v entering the system from the "dark" port has to be included. The signal fields E_{s1} and E_{s2} depend on E_1 and E_v:

$$
\epsilon_{s1}(t) = \epsilon_1(t)\sin(45° - M\sin\omega_m t) + \epsilon_v(t)\cos(45° - M\sin\omega_m t)
\tag{18}
$$

$$
\epsilon_{s2}(t) = \epsilon_1(t)\cos(45° - M\sin\omega_m t) + \epsilon_v(t)\sin(45° - M\sin\omega_m t)
\tag{19}
$$

The positive frequency part of vacuum field E_v is

$$
\epsilon_v(t) = \left[\frac{x(t) + iy(t)}{2}\right]e^{-i\psi}
\tag{20}
$$

$$
<x(t)> = <y(t)> = 0
\tag{21}
$$

where $x(t)$ and $y(t)$ are the quadrature amplitude and phase components of E_v and ψ is the phase at t=0. The noise spectra of $x(t)$ and $y(t)$ are normalized:

$$
<|\delta x(\omega)|^2> = <|\delta y(\omega)|^2> = 1
\tag{22}
$$

For the calculation of fluctuations we approximately take $E_{sc} = E_{s1} = E_{s2}$ because only very weak absorption is considered . In this case the intensities of E_{sc} and E_{s2} are expressed as:

$$
\begin{aligned}
I_{sc} &= \epsilon_{s1}(t)\epsilon^*_{s1}(t) \\
&= \epsilon_1(t)\epsilon^*_1(t)\sin^2(45° - M\sin\omega_m t) + \epsilon_v(t)\epsilon^*_v(t)\cos^2(45° - M\sin\omega_m t) \\
&\quad + \epsilon_1(t)\epsilon^*_v(t)\sin(45° - M\sin\omega_m t)\cos(45° - M\sin\omega_m t) + c_\bullet c_\bullet
\end{aligned}
\tag{23}
$$

$$I_{s2} = \epsilon_{s2}(t)\, \epsilon_{s2}^*(t)$$
$$= \epsilon_1(t)\, \epsilon_1^*(t) \cos^2(45° - M\sin\omega_m t) + \epsilon_\nu(t)\, \epsilon_\nu^*(t) \sin^2(45° - M\sin\omega_m t) \quad (24)$$
$$+ \epsilon_1(t)\, \epsilon_\nu^*(t) \cos(45° - M\sin\omega_m t)\sin(45° - M\sin\omega_m t) + c.c.$$

The fluctuations of I_{sc} and I_{s2} are

$$\delta I_{sc} = \frac{p}{2}\sin^2(45° - M\sin\omega_m t)\,\delta p_1(t)$$
$$+ \frac{p}{2}\sin(45° - M\sin\omega_m t)\cos(45° - M\sin\omega_m t)\,\delta x(t)$$
$$\delta I_{s2} = \frac{p}{2}\cos^2(45° - M\sin\omega_m t)\,\delta p_2(t)$$
$$- \frac{p}{2}\cos(45° - M\sin\omega_m t)\sin(45° - M\sin\omega_m t)\,\delta x(t) \quad (25)$$

The sum of δI_{sc} and δI_{s2} is equal to the fluctuation of E_1 [Eq.(6)]:

$$\delta I_{sc} + \delta I_{s2} = \frac{p}{2}\delta P_1(t) = \delta I_1 \quad (26)$$

Therefore the intensity fluctuation of the final analyzed signal is the intensity difference fluctuation of the twin beams:

$$\delta I_{sig} = (\delta I_{sc} + \delta I_{s2}) - \delta I_2 = \delta I_1 - \delta I_2 = \frac{p\,[\delta p_1 - \delta p_2]}{2} \quad (27)$$

From ref. [14] the noise power spectrum of intensity difference fluctuation of δI_{sig} is

$$S_{sig}(\Omega) = S_{\triangle I}(\Omega) = S_0 S_{\triangle p}(\Omega) \quad (28)$$

Here $S_{\triangle p}(\Omega)$ is the noise power spectrum of the amplitude difference between E_1 and E_2

$$S_{\triangle p}(\Omega) = \langle \left| \frac{\delta p_1(\Omega) - \delta p_2(\Omega)}{2} \right|^2 \rangle \quad (29)$$

When E_1 and E_2 are uncorrelated coherent state light fields, $S_{\triangle p}(\Omega) = 1$ and thus $S_{sig}(\Omega) = S_0$. When E_1 and E_2 are the quantum correlated twin beams, the noise of intensity difference is squeezed[14]:

$$S_{\triangle p}(\Omega) = \frac{\Omega^2}{\Omega^2 + 4\lambda^2} \quad (30)$$

Here Ω is the analysis frequency and λ is the damping rate of the OPO. Therefore

$$S_{sig}(\Omega) = S_0 \frac{\Omega^2}{\Omega^2 + 4\lambda^2} \quad (31)$$

where S_0 is the shot noise of coherent state, which is equal to the total intensity of the twin beams [14]:

$$S_0 = <I_1> + <I_2> = \frac{p^2}{2} \quad (32)$$

Eq.(31) shows that using the twin beams the intensity noise of the analyzed signal is a factor of $(\frac{\Omega^2}{\Omega^2 + 4\lambda^2})$ lower than shot noise limit; i.e. the signal-to-noise ratio is correspondingly improved to the precision of the measurement beyond the vacuum noise level. Although at $\Omega = 0$ perfect quantum noise suppression is obtained in principle, the excess noise of the laser source and the OPO is quite high and not easy to cancel in the balanced homodyen detector. The measurement is usually performed from 1MHz to several megahertz.

For the imperfect detection system the correlation is destroyed by transmission losses and detector inefficiency. If the twin beams pass through a lossy medium with losses σ, then arrive the detector with quantum efficiency η, the fluctuation power spectrum of intensity difference is changed from $S_{\Delta p}$ to

$$S'_{\Delta I} = S_0 R \tag{33}$$

Here R is the correlation factor [13]

$$R = \eta (1 - \sigma) \left(\frac{\Omega^2}{\Omega^2 + 4\lambda^2} \right) + 1 - \eta + \eta\sigma \tag{34}$$

From Eq.(17)we get the average photocurrent of the signal with frequency ω_m

$$i_{sig}(\omega_m) = \frac{e\eta\delta(\omega_1) lMp^2}{4\sqrt{2}} \tag{35}$$

The root-mean-square of the photocurrent shot noise that would be detected in a bandwidth B with uncorrelated beams is equal to

$$(i_n)_{SNL} = \left[2e^2\eta B (< I_1 > + < I_2 >) \right]^{\frac{1}{2}} = \left(2e^2\eta B S_0 \right)^{\frac{1}{2}} \tag{36}$$

The signal-noise ratio (SNR) for the uncorrelated beams is

$$\Phi = \frac{[i_{sig}(\omega_m)]^2}{(i_n)^2} \tag{37}$$

Taking $\Phi = 1$ and $i_n = (i_n)_{SNL}$ we get the minimum detectable absorption for the uncorrelated beams:

$$[\delta(\omega_1)]_{SNL} = \frac{2}{Ml} \left(\frac{2B}{\eta < I_1 >} \right)^{\frac{1}{2}} \tag{38}$$

When the quantum correlated twin beams are used the minimum detectable absorption $[\delta(\omega_1)]_{sq}$ is reduced by a factor of $\sqrt{R}$ due to decrease of the signal noise,i.e.

$$[\delta(\omega_1)]_{sq} = [\delta(\omega_1)]_{SNL} \sqrt{R} \tag{39}$$

In the experiments the minimum intensity difference noise frequency should be chosen as the modulation frequency ω_m of the signal, and then the absorption for the signal light ω_1 should be measured at the noise frequency ω_m.

4. THE EXPERIMENT

A homemade CW frequency stabilized and intracavity frequency doubled ring Nd:YAP laser is used as the pump source. The OPO is a semimonolithic F-P cavity consisting of an a-cut KTP crystal. The front plane face of the crystal is a coated as the input coupler (transmission of 15% for the green light at $0.54\mu m$; high reflectivity for the infrared light at $1.08\mu m$), and the output coupler is a concave mirror with the curvature of 20mm (high reflectivity for the green light; transmission of 3% for the infrared light). The pump light at $0.54\mu m$ performs 90° non-critical phase matching parametric down conversion in the OPO to produce the infrared twin beams with cross polarizations and near degenerate wavelengths around $1.08\mu m$. The 90° non-critical phase matching confirms the collinear transmission of signal and idler beams without the walk-off effect. The threshold of the OPO is 50mW. At the output of the OPO, a filter blocks the green light and a polarizing beam-splitter separates the two cross-polarized twin beams,which are then monitored by a InGaAs photodiode (EXT300) with 88% quantum efficiency. We insert a rotatable half-wave plate of $1.08\mu m$ wavelength in the twin beams before the polarizing beamsplitter P_1 to change the polarizations of the twin beams. When the polarization of the twin beams is rotated by an angle of A=45°, the corresponding shot noise level is obtained and when A=0°, the noise of the intensity difference between the twin beams is analyzed [5].

At first, we directly measured the squeezing of the intensity difference with two photodiodes placed just behind the two output ports of P_1 [Fig.2]. The squeezing from 1MHz to 5MHz is 60%(4dB) below the shot noise level.

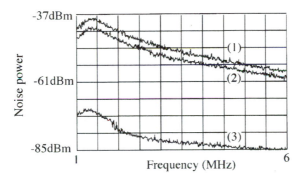

Figure 2. Intensity difference squeezing of twin beams.
      (1) Shot noise power spectrum.
      (2) The noise power spectrum of intensity difference
          between twin beams.
      (3) The electronic noise floor.

For the measurements of the weak absorption, we chose an aqueous solution of $Sm(CPFX)_2Cl_3(H_2O)_4$ as the absorption medium. The scheme of measurement is shown in Fig.3. After the modulator (MO) and the sample cell with the resolvent (pure water) are placed in the channel of E_1, we adjusted the intensities of signal in the channels of D_{s1} and D_{sc} to cancel the modulated signal by the power combination and then attenuated the light intensity in the channel E_2 to balance the dc photocurrents in the twin channels. Fig.3(a) is the noise power spectrum. A quantum noise reduction of 2.5 dB around 3.5 MHz on the intensity difference between the twin beams is obtained. Then we added a few drops of $Sm(CPFX)_2Cl_3(H_2O)_4$ solution into the resolvent. The absorbed signal around 3.6MHz was clearly observed with the correlated twin beams (Fig.3(b), lower trace). But with uncorrelated light (A=45°) the signal was submerged in the shot noise, so that it could not be recognized (Fig.3(b), upper trace). The signal-to-noise ratio of the measurement using the quantum correlated twin beam was improved 2.5 dB beyond the shot noise limit. Here the noise floors of the intensity

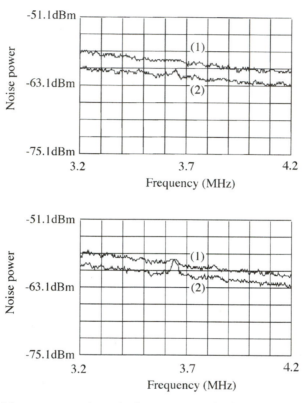

Figure 3. Measurements for sub-shot-noise weak absorption.
The rf bandwidth is 30kHz, and the video bandwidth is 30kHz.
(a) measured result without absorption medium:
   (1) Shot noise limit.
   (2) Noise power spectrum of intensity difference between
       twin beams.
(b) measured result with absorption medium:
   (1) Shot noise limit.
   (2) Noise power spectrum of intensity difference between
       twin beams with the absorbed information.

difference are higher by 1.5 dB (Fig.3) than that in Fig.2 due to the insertion losses of the modulator and absorption cell.

5. CONCLUSION

Precision measurements beyond the shot noise limit have been demonstrated by using quantum correlated twin beams. An accuracy 2.5 dB better than that predicted by the two-beam shot noise limit has been obtained for a weak absorption measurement at a frequency near 3.5MHz.

In principle the precision of the measurement can be higher if twin beams with better intensity correlation and a detection system with higher efficiency are employed.

REFERENCES

[1] R.E,Slusher st.al., Phys.Rev.Lett. 55,2409(1985)

[2] L.Wu et.al., Phs.Rev.Lett. 57,2520(1986)

[3] R.M.Shelby et.al., Phys.Rev.Lett. 57,691(1986)

[4] S,Machida et.al., Phys.Rev.Lett. 60,792(1988)

[5] A.Heidmann et.al., Phys.Rev.Lett. 59,2555(1987)

[6] Xiao M.et.al. Phys. Rev. Lett. 59,278(1987)

[7] Grangier P. et.al. Phys. Rev. Lett.59, 2153(1987)

[8] Polzik E.S. et.al. Appl. Phys.B 55,279(1992)

[9] J.Mertz et.al., Opt. Lett. 16,1234(1991)

[10] Zhang Tiancai, Xie Changde,Peng Kunchi,Scince in China (A),37,227(1994)

[11] C.D.Nabors and R..M. Shelby, Phys. Rev.A, 42,556(1990)

[12] P.R. Tapster et.al. Phys.Rev.A 44,3266(1991)

[13] J.J.Snyder et.al. J.Opt. Soc.Am.(B)7,2132(1990)

[14] S.Reynaud, C. Fabre and E.Gicobino, J.Opt. Soc.Am.(B)4,1520(1987)

[15] Z.Y.Ou et.al. Opt. Lett. 17,640(1992)

[16] Pan Qing et.al. Chinese J.of Laser, 23,6(1996)

DECOHERENCE AND RELAXATION OF
TWO STRONGLY COUPLED SPIN 1/2 ATOMS

Mio Murao

Department of Physics, Harvard University
Cambridge, MA 02138
Current address:
Blackett Laboratory, Imperial College, London SW7 2BZ, UK

Decoherence of two coupled spin 1/2 atoms caused by the surrounding environment is studied via phase and energy relaxation using a quantum statistical model toward thermal equilibrium. The model is formulated microscopically using a master equation. Raman-type dissipation mechanisms are introduced in addition to the usual bilinear coupling between the coupled system and the reservoir. The effects of various rotating wave approximations for deriving the master equation are investigated. The decoherence process is compared with another strongly coupled dissipative system, the dissipative Jaynes Cummings Model.

1. INTRODUCTION

Recent developments in technology allow the manipulation of real quantum mechanical systems. For example in quantum optics, cavity QED [1] and laser cooling [2] are candidates for use as quantum computing [3] devices. Decoherence [4], which destroys the quantum effects of the devices, is a serious problem. Decoherence is the decay of the quantum correlations, the decay of a pure quantum state into a mixed state.

We consider the decoherence due to dissipation from a quantum statistical viewpoint. Our aim is to formulate a quantum statistical model that describes relaxation toward thermal equilibrium and to study decoherence. Our interest is particularly focused on strongly coupled dissipative systems, which are important practically but have not been investigated extensively. The strongly coupled dissipative system exchanges energy between the subsystems and also dissipates energy to the surrounding environment. For strongly coupled systems, reversal of energy levels can occur when the levels are indexed by the quantum numbers of the uncoupled system.

Earlier papers [5] studied the dissipative Jaynes-Cummings model [6], which is a dissipative model for a spin 1/2 atom interacting with a light field. In this paper we apply the formulation to two strongly interacting spin 1/2 atoms. The study of the relaxation dynamics of coupled spin 1/2 atoms is not new. A phenomenological relaxation model was proposed in the 1950s [7] in connection with nuclear spin relaxation. But there has been no study of the relaxation to the correct thermal equilibrium with a fully quantum mechanical model.

Quantum Communication, Computing, and Measurement
Edited by Hirota *et al.*, Plenum Press, New York, 1997

In our formulation, we use a master equation method [8]. The master equation describes the time evolution of the reduced density matrix. This representation is convenient when we deal with the approach to thermal equilibrium: in the energy eigenstate basis at thermal equilibrium, the off-diagonal elements of the reduced density matrix vanish and the diagonal elements give the canonical distribution. Phase and energy relaxation are described by the off-diagonal and diagonal elements respectively.

The significance of treating this new prototype coupled system is that the eigenstates are exact whereas the Jaynes-Cummings model was solved within the rotating wave approximation. It is also a characteristic of this model that the density matrix is expanded in terms of a finite number of elements, whereas the Jaynes-Cummings model has an infinite number of elements originating from the character of the boson operator. This allow us to handle many kinds of dissipation mechanisms and to investigate the role of various rotating wave approximations (RWAs) for deriving the master equation.

2. FORMULATION

Our system consists of two spin $1/2$ atoms which are represented by spin operators $\boldsymbol{S}_1 = (S_1^x,\ S_1^y,\ S_1^z)$ and $\boldsymbol{S}_2 = (S_2^x,\ S_2^y,\ S_2^z)$. The Hamiltonian of the coupled system is given by

$$H = \hbar\omega_1 S_1^z + \hbar\omega_2 S_2^z + \hbar g \left(S_1^+ S_2^- + S_1^- S_2^+\right)/2 + \hbar g_z S_1^z S_2^z \tag{1}$$

where ω_1, ω_2 are Larmor frequencies, g, g_z are coupling constants and $S_\alpha^\pm \equiv S_\alpha^x \pm i S_\alpha^y$ for $\alpha = 1, 2$. This Hamiltonian includes the anisotropic case ($g \neq g_z$) and allows for two different kinds of atoms ($\omega_1 \neq \omega_2$), and hence can describe general interactions of two spin $1/2$ atoms.

The coupled system has four eigenstates which are expressed in terms of the product states of two atoms. The eigenstates are exact so we can freely vary the strength of the coupling constants (g, g_z) between the two atoms.

The coupled system is assumed to interact *weakly* with a reservoir consisting of many boson modes. The reservoir adds dissipative effects to the coupled system and leads to relaxation to thermal equilibrium. The Hamiltonian of the reservoir is given by

$$H_B = \hbar \sum_l \omega_l B_l^\dagger B_l \tag{2}$$

with $\omega_l > 0$ and where $B_l^\dagger$ and B_l represent the creation and annihilation operators of the reservoir bosons. We assume that the reservoir bosons are always in thermal equilibrium since the reservoir has many degrees of freedom. In short, the reservoir is in the canonical distribution at temperature T.

Next, we introduce the interaction Hamiltonian describing the coupling between the system and the reservoir. The usual bilinear interaction which causes energy exchange for each spin $1/2$ atoms, (i.e., absorption-emission type dissipation mechanisms) is given by

$$H_{\alpha B} = \hbar \left(S_\alpha^- + S_\alpha^+\right) \sum_l g_{\alpha l}\left(B_l^\dagger + B_l\right) \tag{3}$$

for $\alpha = 1, 2$. This is a first order interaction. We also introduce a second order interaction between the system and the reservoir which expresses a Raman-type dissipation process

$$H_{iB} = \hbar \left(S_1^+ S_2^\pm + S_1^- S_2^\mp\right) \sum_l g_{il}\left(B_l^\dagger + B_l\right) \tag{4}$$

where $i = +, -$ and the upper (lower) superscript corresponds to $+ (-)$.

Note that we keep the counter rotating wave (CRW) terms (for example, $S_\alpha^- B_l$ and $S_\alpha^+ B_l^\dagger$) in the interaction between the system and the reservoir. Conventionally, the rotating wave approximation (RWA) is used for the interaction Hamiltonian. Keeping the CRW terms in the Hamiltonian is necessary for the same reason they are necessary in the dissipative Jaynes-Cummings model [5]: the CRW terms are important when the coupling between the two atoms becomes strong ($g \gg \omega_1, \omega_2$), which happens when energy level reversal occurs as we will see in the next section.

Using a projection operator method (the "TCL" formalism of Ref. [9]), we reduce the Liouville-von Neumann equation of the total system including the reservoir operators to a generalised master equation for the density operator of the coupled system only (i.e., the reduced density operator, ρ). Because the coupling between the coupled system and the reservoir is weak, it is sufficient to take terms up to second order in the interaction between the coupled system and the reservoir expressed by Eqs. (3) and (4). The resulting master equation is

$$\frac{\partial}{\partial t}\rho(t) = \frac{1}{i\hbar}[H, \rho(t)] + \sum_{\alpha=1,2}\Gamma_\alpha\rho(t) + \sum_{i=\pm}\Gamma_i\rho(t).$$

For example, a damping term $\Gamma_\alpha\rho(t)$ is given as

$$\begin{aligned}
\Gamma_\alpha\rho(t) = \sum_l g_{\alpha l}^2 \int_0^t dt' &\Big\{ \Big(\langle B_l^\dagger(t') B_l\rangle_B + \langle B_l(t') B_l^\dagger\rangle_B\Big) \\
&\times \Big([S_\alpha^+(-t')\rho(t), S_\alpha^-] + [S_\alpha^-(-t')\rho(t), S_\alpha^+]\Big) \\
&+ \Big(\langle B_l^\dagger(-t') B_l\rangle_B + \langle B_l(-t') B_l^\dagger\rangle_B\Big) \\
&\times \Big([S_\alpha^+, \rho(t) S_\alpha^-(-t')] + [S_\alpha^-, \rho(t) S_\alpha^+(-t')]\Big)\Big\}.
\end{aligned} \quad (5)$$

The main improvement in our method is that the time evolution of the system operators in the damping terms are expressed in terms of the full Hamiltonian of the coupled system:

$$S_\alpha^\pm(t) = e^{iHt/\hbar} S_\alpha^\pm e^{-iHt/\hbar} \quad (6)$$

and

$$S_1^\pm S_2^\mp(t) = e^{iHt/\hbar} S_1^\pm S_2^\mp e^{-iHt/\hbar} = S_1^\pm(t) S_2^\mp(t). \quad (7)$$

This is one of the necessary conditions for the coupled system to evolve toward the correct thermal equilibrium.

In obtaining the master equation [Eq. (5)], we used the RWA on the original master equation [10], dropping the CRW terms because the coupling between the system and the reservoir is weak.

To avoid confusion between the two different RWAs we have mentioned, we emphasise the difference: Our damping term [Eq. (5)] was derived using the RWA *on the master equation* and including terms which are missing when the RWA is applied to *the interaction Hamiltonian* between the system and the reservoir. The missing terms, such as

$$\langle B_l^\dagger(t') B_l\rangle_B [S_\alpha^-(-t')\rho(t), S_\alpha^+] \quad (8)$$

which are present in Eq. (5), play an important role in energy level reversal as we will show later.

We expand all the operators in the master equation [Eq. (5)] in terms of the eigenstates and derive solvable equations for the time evolution of the expansion coefficients of the reduced density operator

$$\rho_{nm}(t) \equiv \langle n|\rho(t)|m\rangle. \quad (9)$$

We assume the narrowing limit condition: that the characteristic time scale of the reservoir motion is much shorter than that of the coupled system. Thus we take the upper bound of the integral in the damping terms Eqs. (5) to infinity. We also use the continuous limit for the reservoir modes $\omega_l \to \omega_B$ and take

$$\sum_l g_{xl}^2 \to \int_0^\infty d\omega_B \frac{\kappa_x(\omega_B)}{2\pi} \tag{10}$$

where

$$\kappa_x(\omega_B) = 2\pi D(\omega_B) \{g_x(\omega_B)\}^2, \tag{11}$$

$D(\omega_B)$ is the density of states of the reservoir frequency mode, $g_x(\omega_B)$ is the coupling between the system operator and the reservoir operator, and x represents α and i. Generally,

$$\kappa_x(\omega_B) \sim \omega_B{}^\delta \tag{12}$$

for $\delta > 0$ [11]. For ohmic dissipation ($\delta = 1$), we have

$$\kappa_x(\omega_B) = \frac{a_x}{2} \omega_B f_c(\omega_B/\omega_c) \tag{13}$$

where a_x is a constant related to the friction coefficient and $f_c(\omega_B/\omega_c)$ is a high frequency cut off function that satisfies the condition $f_c(0) = 1$ [11]. A three dimensional radiation field has $\delta = 3$ [12].

The further integral over ω_B provides the effective thermal photon number functions, $\hat{n}_x^1(\epsilon)$ and $\hat{n}_x^2(\epsilon)$, which are defined as

$$\hat{n}_x^1(\epsilon) = \kappa_x(\epsilon/\hbar) \bar{n}(\epsilon/\hbar), \tag{14}$$
$$\hat{n}_x^2(\epsilon) = \kappa_x(\epsilon/\hbar) \{\bar{n}(\epsilon/\hbar) + 1\}, \tag{15}$$

for $\epsilon > 0$, and

$$\hat{n}_x^1(\epsilon) = \kappa_x(-\epsilon/\hbar) \{\bar{n}(-\epsilon/\hbar) + 1\}, \tag{16}$$
$$\hat{n}_x^2(\epsilon) = \kappa_x(-\epsilon/\hbar) \bar{n}(-\epsilon/\hbar) \tag{17}$$

for $\epsilon < 0$ where

$$\bar{n}(\omega_B) = (\exp[\hbar\omega_B/k_B T] - 1)^{-1}. \tag{18}$$

When $\epsilon = 0$, the effective thermal photon number functions depend on the exponent δ, for example,

$$\hat{n}_x^1 = \hat{n}_x^2 = \frac{k_B a_x T}{2\hbar} \tag{19}$$

for $\delta = 1$ (ohmic dissipation) but

$$\hat{n}_x^1 = \hat{n}_x^2 = 0 \tag{20}$$

for $\delta > 1$. The imaginary part of the integral over t' gives the Lamb shift of the system frequencies which may generally be neglected [8].

The effective thermal photon number functions for $\epsilon < 0$ appear because of the extra terms in Eqs. (5). They lead the system to relax toward thermal equilibrium even when energy level reversal ($\epsilon < 0$) occurs. On the other hand, if we start with the RWA Hamiltonian, we have to put $\hat{n}_1(\epsilon) = \hat{n}_2(\epsilon) = 0$ for $\epsilon < 0$. Since all of the damping terms are linear in the effective thermal photon functions, they vanish for $\epsilon < 0$ and the relaxation of the system is interrupted at the reversed energy level

458

and the system does not reach to thermal equilibrium. This is why the CRW terms in the interaction Hamiltonian [Eqs. (3) and (4)] are important and we should not use the RWA Hamiltonian to derive the master equation, although we can use the RWA afterwards.

We have a solvable equation for the time evolution of each expansion coefficient ρ_{nm}. Introducing the vectors

$$\boldsymbol{\rho}_A(t) \equiv \begin{pmatrix} \rho_{11}(t) \\ \rho_{22}(t) \\ \rho_{23}(t) \\ \rho_{32}(t) \\ \rho_{33}(t) \\ \rho_{44}(t) \end{pmatrix}, \quad \boldsymbol{\rho}_B(t) \equiv \begin{pmatrix} \rho_{12}(t) \\ \rho_{13}(t) \\ \rho_{24}(t) \\ \rho_{34}(t) \end{pmatrix}, \quad \boldsymbol{\rho}_C(t) \equiv \begin{pmatrix} \rho_{14}(t) \end{pmatrix}, \tag{21}$$

and using the hermitian nature of the density matrix

$$\boldsymbol{\rho}_{B'}(t) \equiv \begin{pmatrix} \rho_{21}(t) \\ \rho_{31}(t) \\ \rho_{42}(t) \\ \rho_{43}(t) \end{pmatrix} = [\boldsymbol{\rho}_B(t)]^*, \quad \boldsymbol{\rho}_{C'}(t) \equiv \begin{pmatrix} \rho_{41}(t) \end{pmatrix} = [\boldsymbol{\rho}_C(t)]^*, \tag{22}$$

we have the time evolution in the form of first order vector simultaneous differential equations:

$$\frac{\partial}{\partial t}\boldsymbol{\rho}_X(t) = \left(\frac{1}{i\hbar}\boldsymbol{L}^X + \sum_{\alpha=1,2} \boldsymbol{Q}_\alpha^X + \sum_{i=\pm} \boldsymbol{Q}_i^X \right) \boldsymbol{\rho}_X(t) \tag{23}$$

for $X = A, B, B', C, C'$. The first term on the right hand side of Eq. (23) expresses the coherent motion due to the first term of the right hand side of Eq. (5). The second and third terms are damping terms originating from the absorption-emission and the Raman mechanisms, respectively.

The diagonal elements of the reduced density matrix are the probability distribution for each energy eigenstate and the off-diagonal elements express quantum coherence, or phase. We stress that the energy and phase refer to the coupled system, not to individual atoms. We also note that transitions between the diagonal elements are necessary for the system to relax to the canonical distribution. The absorption-emission type damping terms satisfy this condition, but the Raman type damping terms do not include transitions between some states. Thus, the Raman type damping terms alone can not describe the relaxation to the canonical distribution and thus need to be used together with the absorption-emission damping terms.

An important feature of the equations of time evolution is that they are divided into several sets, denoted A, B (B') and C (C'). The set A contains off-diagonal elements as well as diagonal elements, reflecting the fact that our system is non-trivially coupled. The dissipation mechanisms given by the damping terms of Eqs. (5) do not mix coefficients which belong to different sets. This is due to the representation of operators in terms of eigenstates. The expectation values of the system operators are related to the elements of the sets A, B and C.

Next, we consider the case with the CRW damping term included. The expansion coefficients are calculated in the same way and give solvable equations for time evolution of the same form as Eq. (23). But the CRW damping term leads to mixing of the coefficients which belong to different sets: The elements in sets A, C and C' form a new set A^* and those of B and B' form another new set B^*. However, even the CRW damping term does not mix the sets A^* and B^*. The time evolution of $\langle S_\alpha^z \rangle$, which belongs to set A^*, is still independent of the time evolution of $\langle S_\alpha^+ \rangle$, which belongs to set B^*.

3.   DECOHERENCE AND RELAXATION

We define new quantities to investigate decoherence via the phase and energy relaxation of the coupled dissipative system using the purity, $\mathrm{Tr}\rho^2$. The purity is often used to test whether the system is in a pure state ($\mathrm{Tr}\rho^2 = 1$) or in a mixed state ($\mathrm{Tr}\rho^2 < 1$) [8]. The purity characterises the quantum coherence of the system, so the decay of the purity shows decoherence.

In the eigenstate bases, the purity is

$$\mathrm{Tr}\left\{ \rho(t) \right\}^2 = \sum_{n,m=1}^{4} \rho_{nm}(t)\rho_{nm}^*(t), \tag{24}$$

which includes both diagonal elements and off-diagonal elements and contains both the phase relaxation and energy relaxation. In Fig. 1, we show the evolution of the purity of the strongly coupled two spin system at several different temperatures, $\tau = 0.01, 0.2, 0.5$ ($\tau = k_B T / \hbar g$) by the ohmic dissipation of the absorption-emission type. The initial conditions of the two spins are the product of certain Bloch states. It is very interesting that in each case the purity decreases once and then recovers. The equilibrium value of purity is much less than 1, except at low temperature where the equilibrium purity approaches one because the system relaxes close to the ground state. Relaxation from a pure state ($\mathrm{Tr}\rho^2 = 1$) to any mixed state ($\mathrm{Tr}\rho^2 < 1$) is decoherence. However, we stress that the purity does not decay monotonically.

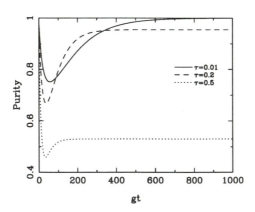

Figure 1. Time evolution of the purity at several different temperatures.

Next, we divide the purity into two parts ("partial purities"), $p_d(t)$ from diagonal elements and $p_o(t)$ from the off-diagonal elements of ρ:

$$p_d(t) = \sum_n \left\{ \rho_{nn}(t) \right\}^2, \tag{25}$$

$$p_o(t) = 2 \sum_{n>m} \rho_{nm}(t)\rho_{nm}^*(t). \tag{26}$$

Although purity is basis independent, the partial purities depend on the basis, so we will work exclusively in the basis of energy eigenstates. The decay of $p_o(t)$ clearly describes phase relaxation of the dissipative system. In contrast, the meaning of $p_d(t)$ is not trivial. It describes the unevenness of the probability distribution between the energy eigenstates. It takes values $1/4 \leq p_d \leq 1$ in our model: the minimum value when the distribution is equally divided between the four energy eigenstates and the maximum value when all of the weight is in one energy eigenstate. At thermal equilibrium $(t \to \infty)$, p_d coincides with the purity and is a monotonically decreasing function of temperature

$$p_d(t \to \infty) = \frac{\sum_n e^{-2E_n/k_B T}}{\left(\sum_n e^{-E_n/k_B T} \right)^2};$$
(27)

for example, $p_d(t \to \infty) = 1$ for $T = 0$ and $p_d(t \to \infty) = 1/4$ for $T = \infty$. In our model, the reduced density matrix of sets B (B') and C (C') contribute to p_o. The elements of set A contribute both to $p_d(t)$ and $p_o(t)$.

In Fig. 2, we see that the diagonal contribution (p_d) increases but the off-diagonal part (p_o), which expresses the phase relaxation of the coupled system, decays exponentially. The relaxation time of p_o is shorter than that of p_d. The long time behaviour of the purity is dominated by p_d.

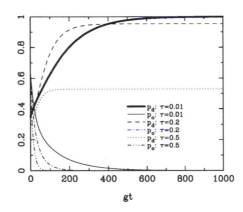

Figure 2. Time evolution of the partial purity p_d (from diagonal elements) and p_o (from off-diagonal elements) at several different temperatures.

To compare the relaxation of energy and phase more quantitatively, we define the following normalised relaxation functions from the partial purities, $\pi_d(t)$ and $\pi_o(t)$. Fig. 3 shows $\pi_d(t)$ and $\pi_o(t)$ at several different temperatures on a log scale. At long times both decay exponentially, but at short times, the phase relaxation is faster than exponential while the energy relaxation is slower.

In Fig. 4, we show the time evolution of the purity obtained using several different approximations. We compare results using the damping terms obtained from applying the RWA for the master equation (Γ_α), from the RWA Hamiltonian (Γ_α^H), from the conventional treatment, and without the RWA ($\Gamma_\alpha + \Gamma_\alpha^C$). The time evolution with Γ_α^C and with only Γ_α agrees very well (except for some small oscillation at small times with Γ_α^C for this situation with small damping). So the RWA on the master equation is a good approximation for smaller a. On the other hand, the results using Γ_α^H and

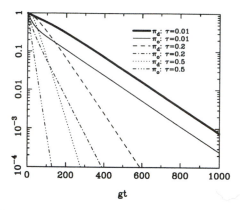

Figure 3. Log scale plot of the normalised relaxation function for the energy $[\pi_d(t)]$ and the phase $[\pi_o(t)]$ at several different temperatures.

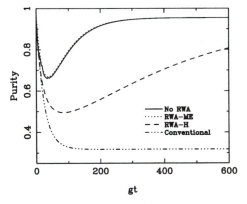

Figure 4. Comparing time evolution of the purity at $\tau = 0.2$ using different approximations. Solid line is without RWA $(\Gamma_\alpha + \Gamma_\alpha^C)$, dotted line is with RWA on the master equation (Γ_α), dashed line is with the RWA Hamiltonian (Γ_α^H), and dot-dashed line is with the conventional treatment.

the conventional treatment are very different — the system does *not* relax towards the correct thermal equilibrium.

4. CONCLUDING REMARKS

In this paper, we formulated a quantum statistical model for the relaxation of two strongly coupled atoms. We obtained a master equation which described relaxation dynamics towards the correct thermal equilibrium state of the coupled system. The master equation was solved by using the eigenstates of the coupled system. We studied decoherence, the decay of a pure quantum state into a mixed state, by observing the phase and energy relaxation of the coupled system by introducing new quantities, the partial purities. A new feature was the introduction of Raman-type dissipation mechanisms in addition to the normal first order (absorption-emission type) dissipation mechanisms. Extension of these methods from this prototype system to realistic models is left as future work.

Several important conditions were met in order to describe relaxation toward thermal equilibrium for the coupled system. First, the time evolution of the system operators in the damping terms were expressed by the full Hamiltonian of the coupled system including the mutual coupling of the atoms. Second, the interaction Hamiltonian for the coupling between the system and the reservoir included the CRW terms, although we used the RWA on the master equation afterwards. The CRW terms ensured relaxation to thermal equilibrium even when energy level reversal occurred. Third, the dissipation mechanism had to include transitions between diagonal elements of the reduced density matrix. The Raman type damping terms alone were not enough to lead the system to thermal equilibrium.

ACKNOWLEDGEMENTS

The author is grateful to F. Shibata, T. Arimitsu, A. Tameshtit and J. Watson for helpful discussions and would like to thank E. Heller for useful comments and for his hospitality at Harvard. This work was partially supported by the National Science Foundation via Grant Number CHE-932160.

REFERENCES

[1] See for instance, *Cavity Quantum Electrodynamics*, Advances in Atomic, Molecular, and Optical Physics, Supplement 2, ed. P. R. Berman, (Academic Press, Boston, 1994).

[2] J. I. Cirac, R. Blatt, A. S. Parkins and P. Zoller, Phys. Rev. A **49**, 1202 (1994).

[3] See for instance, D. P. DiVincenzo, Science **270** No.5234, 255 (1995), A. Ekert and R. Jozsa, Rev. Mod. Phys. (to appear) and references therein.

[4] See for instance, W. H. Zurek, Phys. Today **44**, 36 (1991).

[5] M. Murao and F. Shibata, Physica A **216**, 255 (1995), **217**, 348 (1995) and J. Phys. Soc. Jpn **64**, 2394 (1995).

[6] See for instance, E. T. Jaynes and F. W. Cummings, Proc. IEEE **51**, 89 (1963), B. W. Shore and P. L. Knight, J. Mod. Optics **40**, 1195 (1993), and references cited therein.

[7] I. Solomon and N. Bloembergen, J. Chem. Phys. **25**, 261 (1953), I. Solomon, Phys. Rev. **99**, 559 (1955), N. Bloembergen, Phys. Rev. **104** (1956) 1542.

[8] W. E. Louisell, *Quantum Statistical Properties of Radiation*, (John Wiley & Sons, Inc., New York, 1973).

[9] F. Shibata and T. Arimitsu, J. Phys. Soc. Jpn. **49**, 891 (1980), see also the appendices of [5].

[10] G. S. Agarwal, Springer Tracts in Modern Physics Vol. 70, 116, (Springer-Verlag, Berlin, 1974).

[11] A. J. Leggett, S. Chakaravarty, A. T. Dorsey, M. P. A. Fisher, A. Grag and W. Zwerger, Rev. Mod. Phys. **59**, 1 (1987), C. Aslangul, N. Potter and D. Saint-James, J. Physique **46**, 2031 (1985), A. Tameshtit and J. E. Sipe, Phys. Rev. A **49**, 89 (1994).

[12] C. H. Keitel, P. L. Knight, L. M. Marducci, M. O. Scully, Opt. Commun. **118**, 143 (1995).

SPATIAL CORRELATION EFFECTS IN MULTI–TRANSVERSE MODE LASERS

Ashish Agarwal and S. Chopra

Department of Physics, Indian Institute of Technology
New Delhi 110 016, India

1. INTRODUCTION

It has been shown by Wolf [1–3] that source correlations lead to Doppler–like frequency shifts in the spectrum of light in the far zone. Most of the theoretical and experimental activity in this regard has been confined to a restricted class of sources and mainly to the frequency domain. In contrast, changes in temporal coherence properties of the field on propagation were recently described by Chopra *et al.* [4, 5]. In the present paper, working in the time domain, we investigate the effects of spatial correlations in a laser oscillating in one or more transverse modes. The laser has been analyzed both theoretically and experimentally [6–9] in great detail but without paying any consideration to spatial coherence as the laser was assumed to be a perfectly spatially coherent source. Such an assumption is only valid when the laser is oscillating in one transverse mode. But spatial correlations become important in lasers oscillating in more than one transverse mode. Different transverse modes have different field distributions, they excite different spatial groups of active atoms, and therefore spatial correlations between spontaneously emitting atoms become important.

In Section 2, we incorporate the effects of spatial coherence in the semiclassical theory of a laser. The steady–state laser intensity and its fluctuations are calculated in Section 2.1. We find that the probability distribution of light intensity gets modified for the partially correlated field of a multi–transverse mode laser. In Section 2.2, we discuss how the partial coherence modifies the correlation function of intensity fluctuations. In Section 2.3, we show that the pump parameters of a two-mode ring laser are dependent on the field spatial coherence which arises due to the transverse–mode structure of the laser field. Finally, we summarize the results in Section 3.

2. SPATIAL COHERENCE IN A LASER

When the field is assumed to be spatially coherent, as in the case of a single transverse–mode laser, the evolution of the field is entirely determined by temporal fluctuations inside the laser medium. The complex amplitude E of the field inside the cavity need not be described in terms of space parameter [6]. However, when the field is not spatially coherent, as in the case of a laser oscillating with more than one transverse mode, its spatial structure affects the field evolution. Departing from the conventional treatments [6–8], we take the complex amplitude E of the field of a single-longitudinal mode laser to be dependent on the spatial parameter $\mathbf{r}$; it obeys a van–der Pol equation in the rotating–wave approximation with a noise term, viz.,

$$\dot{E}(\mathbf{r},t) = \beta(d - E^*E)E(\mathbf{r},t) + \Gamma(\mathbf{r},t), \tag{1}$$

where β and d are laser constants depending upon pumping intensity and the laser parameters. $\Gamma(\mathbf{r},t)$ describes the stochastic noise force (Langevin force) with zero time average

$$\langle \Gamma(\mathbf{r},t) \rangle = 0, \tag{2}$$

and δ-time correlation

$$\langle \Gamma(\mathbf{r},t)\,\Gamma^*(\mathbf{r}',t') \rangle = Q\Upsilon(\mathbf{r},\mathbf{r}')\delta(t - t'), \tag{3}$$

where Q is the strength of the Langevin forces and $\Upsilon(\mathbf{r},\mathbf{r}')$ is the spatial field correlation function expressible in terms of Fox–Li modes of the cavity [10]. The fluctuating force Γ gives finite linewidth or amplitude fluctuations to the laser and is dependent on the space parameter $\mathbf{r}$ for a multimode laser. In an active medium with many transverse modes, light quanta emitted spontaneously at two different space points at the same time are correlated in accordance with the transverse field distribution of modes. The expectation value of two Langevin forces with a different space argument but same time argument is dependent on the spatial field correlation function $\Upsilon(\mathbf{r},\mathbf{r}')$ which has a value of one for the perfectly correlated field of a single transverse mode laser, but falls below one when the field oscillates in more than one transverse mode.

The degree of spatial coherence for multimode lasers is not of similar form to one observed in thermal sources, viz., $J_1(k\rho)/k\rho$, or in Lambartian sources, viz., $\sin(k\rho)/k\rho$, where k is the wave vector of light and ρ is the spatial position coordinate on the source. Therefore the output light violates Wolf's scaling law [1], i.e., the form of degree of spatial coherence is in a particular functional form $h(k\rho)$.

In the case of a single transverse–mode laser, the pump parameter a_0 is given by [6]

$$a_0 = \left(\frac{4\beta}{Q}\right)^{1/2} d, \tag{4}$$

so that $a_0 < 0$ below, $a_0 = 0$ at, and $a_0 > 0$ above threshold. The partial spatial coherence changes the pump parameter for a multimode laser as [11]

$$a = \frac{a_0}{\sqrt{\Upsilon(\mathbf{r},\mathbf{r}')}}. \tag{5}$$

As the spatial correlation function $\Upsilon(\mathbf{r},\mathbf{r}')$ decreases for multi–mode lasers, the pump parameter a of the laser increases.

2.1. PROBABILITY DENSITY OF LIGHT INTENSITY

In Fig. 1, we plot the steady-state probability density $P(I)$ of light intensity I given by [8]

$$P(I) = \frac{\exp\left[-\frac{1}{4}\left(I - a\right)^2\right]}{\sqrt{\pi}\,\mathrm{erfc}\left(-\frac{a}{2}\right)}, \tag{6}$$

where erfc is the complimentary error function. As the spatial coherence decreases in a laser oscillating above threshold, the maximum light intensity as well as its fluctuation

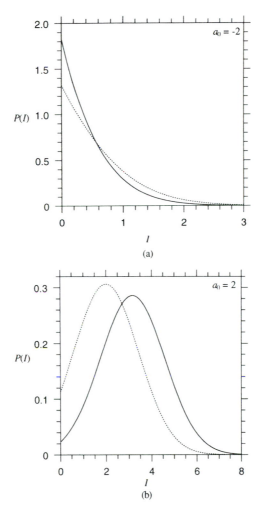

Figure 1. Probability distribution of the laser light intensity I in the steady state for spatial field correlation $\Upsilon = 0.4$ (solid curve), and $\Upsilon = 1.0$ (dashed curve) at pump parameter (a) $a_0 = -2$, and (b) $a_0 = 2$.

increases, while below threshold, the probability of getting zero output increases. At laser threshold, $P(I)$ has the form of a half–truncated Gaussian distribution which does not change for a partially correlated laser. In Fig. 2, we plot the mean light intensity [8]

$$\langle I(a) \rangle = a + \frac{2e^{-a^2/2}}{\sqrt{\pi} \operatorname{erfc}\left(-\frac{a}{2}\right)}, \tag{7}$$

for a single mode and a multimode laser with $\Upsilon(\mathbf{r}, \mathbf{r}') = 0.4$. This shows the increase in mean light intensity for a laser oscillating in more than one mode above threshold of oscillation. Below threshold, the intensity decreases as the spatial coherence of the field is reduced, which can be attributed to the fact that some spatial modes will now not be supported by the Fabry–Perot cavity. The variance of light intensity is given by [8]

$$\langle (\Delta I)^2 \rangle = 2 \left[1 - \frac{ae^{-a^2/4}}{\sqrt{\pi} \operatorname{erfc}\left(-\frac{a}{2}\right)} - \frac{2e^{-a^2/2}}{\pi \left[\operatorname{erfc}\left(-\frac{a}{2}\right)\right]^2} \right]. \tag{8}$$

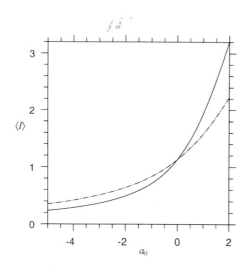

Figure 2: Variation of mean light intensity $\langle I \rangle$ with the pump parameter a_0 for spatial field correlation $\Upsilon = 0.4$ (solid curve), and $\Upsilon = 1.0$ (dashed curve).

Equations (7) and (8) allow us to plot the relative mean–squared fluctuations $\langle (\Delta I)^2 \rangle / \langle I \rangle^2$ against the pump parameter a_0. This is shown in Fig. 3 for the case of perfect spatial coherence $\Upsilon(\mathbf{r}, \mathbf{r}') = 1$ of a single mode laser and partial coherence $\Upsilon(\mathbf{r}, \mathbf{r}') = 0.4$ of a multimode laser. Above threshold, a reduction in spatial coherence leads to an increase in pump parameter, resulting in the decrease of intensity fluctuations.

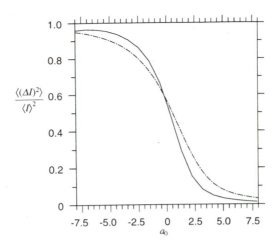

Figure 3. Variation of relative mean–squared light intensity fluctuations $\langle(\Delta I)^2\rangle/\langle I\rangle^2$ with the pump parameter a_0 for spatial field correlation $\Upsilon = 0.4$ (solid curve), and $\Upsilon = 1.0$ (dashed curve).

2.2. CORRELATION FUNCTION

We plot the correlation function of the intensity fluctuations $K(a, \tau)$ given by [11]

$$K(a, \overline{\tau}) = \left\langle \left(|E(\mathbf{r}, t + \overline{\tau})|^2 - \langle |E|^2 \rangle \right) \left(|E(\mathbf{r}, t)|^2 - \langle |E|^2 \rangle \right) \right\rangle, \tag{9}$$

in Fig. 4 for pump parameter $a_0 = -2.2$. We infer that as $\Upsilon(\mathbf{r}, \mathbf{r}')$ decreases from the peak value of 1, the shape of the correlation function is modified giving rise to slower decay of the fluctuations present.

2.3. IMPLICATIONS FOR A TWO–MODE LASER

The above treatment of single longitudinal mode laser can be extended to a two–mode ring laser, whose Langevin equations for the field amplitude E_i ($i = 1, 2$) become

$$\dot{E}_1(\mathbf{r}, t) = \left[a_1 - \left(|E_1|^2 + \xi|E_2|^2 \right) \right] E_1(\mathbf{r}, t) + q_1(\mathbf{r}, t), \tag{10}$$

$$\dot{E}_2(\mathbf{r}, t) = \left[a_2 - \left(|E_2|^2 + \xi|E_1|^2 \right) \right] E_2(\mathbf{r}, t) + q_2(\mathbf{r}, t), \tag{11}$$

where ξ is the dimensionless coupling constant, and q_1 and q_2 represent two normalized, independent, complex, Gaussian white noises of equal strength, with

$$\langle q_i(\mathbf{r}, t) \, q_i^*(\mathbf{r}', t') \rangle = 2\Upsilon(\mathbf{r}, \mathbf{r}')\delta(t - t'), \qquad i = 1, 2. \tag{12}$$

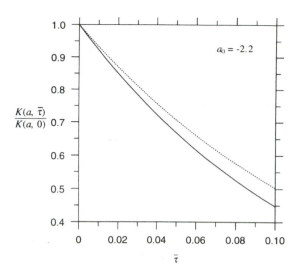

Figure 4. Normalised Correlation Function of Intensity Fluctuations $K(a,\bar{\tau})/K(a,0)$ as a function of Normalised time difference $\bar{\tau}$ for spatial field correlation $\Upsilon = 0.4$ (solid curve) and $\Upsilon = 0.1$ (dashed curve) at pump parameter $a_0 = -2.2$.

The parameters a_i are the modified pump parameters of the same form as the parameter a for the single–mode laser :

$$a_i = \frac{a_i^0}{\sqrt{\Upsilon(\mathbf{r},\mathbf{r}')}}. \tag{13}$$

Hence laser light properties will be modified by the partial coherence of the field.

An inhomogeneously broadened ring laser operating at line center exhibits an interesting behaviour in the case of unequal pump parameters for two modes. For large pump parameter, the electromagnetic waves propagating one way around the ring acquire the characteristics of coherent laser light, while those propagating in the opposite direction have the character of thermal or incoherent light [8]. This implies that by changing the pump parameters, we can control the laser fluctuations. Field correlation times for both the laser modes increase steadily with pump parameter above threshold [8]. Modification in spatial coherence will lead to changes in the field correlation function, thereby leading to changes in the laser spectrum. Hence a two–mode laser will show Wolf–like effects .

3. CONCLUSIONS

It has been shown by Wolf [3] that spatial coherence properties of a source affect the spectrum of emitted radiation. We have established that spatial coherence in a laser affects its output spectrum.

We find that the pump parameter of the laser depends on the spatial coherence which arises due to transverse mode structure of the laser field [11]. As the spatial correlation of the laser field decreases, the pump parameter is found to increase. This results in increase of mean light intensity and decrease of mean–squared intensity fluctuations with the reduction of spatial correlation in a laser oscillating above threshold. In the other extreme, when the laser is operating near and below threshold, the output intensity is non–zero and its probability distribution is nearly exponential in intensity. In this case, we find that the probability of getting zero output increases with the decrease in spatial coherence and hence the mean intensity of the output light decreases. The intensity decreases with the increase in transverse modes as some spatial modes will not be supported by the laser cavity. The correlation function of intensity fluctuations also gets modified showing slower decay of the fluctuations present. The Fourier transform of the correlation function shows that the laser linewidth decreases with the reduction in spatial coherence. Thus the laser spectrum depends on the transverse–mode structure of the field. Similar effects are found in a two–mode laser where the pump parameter is shown to depend on the spatial correlation of the laser field.

ACKNOWLEDGEMENT

This work is supported by the Department of Science and Technology, New Delhi, India.

REFERENCES

[1] E. Wolf, Phys. Rev. Lett. **56**, 1370 (1986).

[2] E. Wolf, Phys. Rev. Lett. **58**, 2646 (1987).

[3] E. Wolf, Phys. Rev. Lett. **63**, 2220 (1989).

[4] S. Chopra *et al.*, Opt. Commun. **109**, 205 (1994).

[5] J. Rai, S. Rai and S. Chopra, Phys. Rev. A **47**, 4400 (1993)

[6] H. Risken, in *Progress in Optics*, Vol. VIII, edited by E. Wolf (North–Holland, Amsterdam, 1970) p. 239.

[7] M. Sargent, M. O. Scully and W. E. Lamb, Jr., *Laser Physics* (Addison–Wesley Publishing, Reading, MA, 1977).

[8] L. Mandel and E. Wolf, *Optical Coherence and Quantum Optics* (Cambridge University Press, Cambridge, 1995).

[9] S. Chopra and L. Mandel, Phys. Rev. Lett. **30**, 60 (1973).

[10] E. Wolf and G. S. Agarwal, J. Opt. Soc. Am. A **1**, 541 (1984).

[11] Ashish Agarwal and S. Chopra, Phys. Rev. A **54**, 2503 (1996).

GENERATION OF NONCLASSICAL PHOTONS IN A JOSEPHSON-JUNCTION CAVITY

Takanori Maki[1], Tetsuo Ogawa[2], and Noriyuki Hatakenaka[3]

[1] Department of Applied Physics, Osaka City University
Sumiyoshi-ku, Osaka 558, Japan
[2] Department of Physics, Tohoku University
Aoba-ku, Sendai 980-77, Japan
[3] NTT Basic Research Laboratories
Atsugi-shi, Kanagawa 243-01, Japan

A novel scheme for generating nonclassical photon states is introduced, which makes the best use of an intrinsic nonlinear interaction between quantized photon fields and Cooper pairs. The relevant system of a single-mode photon field and a tunneling supercurrent in a Josephson junction is described with a two-component boson model, and the quantum dynamics is investigated numerically by using the normal-ordering method. We show that the photon field inside the junction resonator evolves temporally from the vacuum state into quadrature-phase amplitude squeezed states and/or sub-Poissonian states. Backaction to the supercurrent fluctuation is also examined.

1. INTRODUCTION

Squeezing of a quantum state means a reduced quantum fluctuation compared with zero-point fluctuations in one of the two noncommuting observables while preserving the minimum uncertainty product. Generation and control of quantum states of light have been extensively studied recently, and, in particular, the quadrature-phase amplitude squeezed states and/or the sub-Poissonian photon states have attracted the interest not only of fundamental researchers but also of engineers in application areas. So far, such states have been generated by using optical nonlinear media [1].

In a Josephson junction, tunneling Cooper pairs interact nonlinearly with electromagnetic (EM) fields, and the junction itself plays the role of a resonator of the EM fields. Thus we can expect a remarkable nonlinear optical effect [2] by using the Josephson junction. We here introduce a novel method for generation of squeezed states of photons in a microwave region with a Josephson system pumped internally [3]. The main aims of this paper are (i) to construct a quantum-mechanical model for the coupled photon-Cooper pair system in a Josephson junction and (ii) to clarify the quantum dynamics of the systems taking into account their quantum fluctuations.

This paper is organized as follows. In Section 2, the two-component boson model is introduced to describe a single-mode quantized photon field and the Cooper pairs in a mesoscopic junction. Temporal evolution of the system is studied with the method of normal ordering, as shown in Section 3. Numerical results are given in Section 4 to demonstrate the formation of squeezed photon states. Fluctuation characteristics of the supercurrent are also given there.

2. TWO-COMPONENT BOSON MODEL

We shall consider the Josephson junction at low temperature, which is driven by a constant dc current (the bias current J_{bias}). Quantum fluctuation of the Josephson phase is distributed around its classical value θ_0 (corresponding to the difference between macroscopic phases of the two superconductors). This phase fluctuation couples to the quantized photons. This coupling determines the quantum fluctuations of both the photon state and the supercurrent.

In a mesoscopic junction, the longitudinal modes of the EM field inside the junction resonator are well separated in energy compared to the thermal energy at low temperature. Then we can pay attention only to a single-mode quantized photon field with energy $\hbar\omega$. For simplicity we neglect the loss of radiation through leakage to the outside. Then the Hamiltonian of the relevant system is given by

$$\hat{\mathcal{H}} = \hat{\mathcal{H}}_{\text{T}}^{\text{J}-\text{P}} + \hat{\mathcal{H}}_{\text{P}} + \hat{\mathcal{H}}_{\text{C}}, \tag{1}$$

where $\hat{\mathcal{H}}_{\text{T}}^{\text{J}-\text{P}}$ describes the tunneling Hamiltonian for Cooper pairs interacting with the photon field, $\hat{\mathcal{H}}_{\text{P}} = \hbar\omega(\hat{a}^\dagger\hat{a} + \frac{1}{2})$ is the photon energy in the junction resonator ($\hat{a}^\dagger$ and $\hat{a}$ are the photon creation and annihilation operators, respectively), and $\hat{\mathcal{H}}_{\text{C}}$ is the electrostatic energy depending on the charge imbalance between the two superconductors: $\hat{\mathcal{H}}_{\text{C}} = E_{\text{C}}\hat{n}_{\text{J}}^2$. Here $E_{\text{C}} = (2e)^2/2C$ is the charging energy of a Cooper pair (with a capacitance C) and $\hat{n}_{\text{J}}$ is a number operator of tunneling Cooper pairs.

The tunneling Hamiltonian $\hat{\mathcal{H}}_{\text{T}}^{\text{J}-\text{P}}$ is given as

$$\hat{\mathcal{H}}_{\text{T}}^{\text{J}-\text{P}} = \sum_{k,p} \left(T_{k,p}\hat{c}_k^\dagger\hat{d}_p e^{i\hat{\phi}_{\text{EM}}} + \text{h.c.} \right) = \hat{\mathcal{H}}_{\text{T}}^{(0)} \cos\hat{\phi}_{\text{EM}} + \frac{\hbar}{2e}\hat{\mathcal{J}}_{\text{T}} \sin\hat{\phi}_{\text{EM}}, \tag{2}$$

where $T_{k,p}$ is the tunneling matrix element, $\hat{c}_k$ and $\hat{d}_p$ are annihilation operators of an electron with momentum k and p in the left and right superconductors, respectively. Here $\hat{\phi}_{\text{EM}}$ is an EM phase operator [4]:

$$\hat{\phi}_{\text{EM}} = \sqrt{\frac{E_{\text{C}}}{\hbar\omega}} \left(\hat{a}^\dagger + \hat{a} \right). \tag{3}$$

In Eq. (2), $\hat{H}_{\text{T}}^{(0)}$ is the *bare* tunneling Hamiltonian in the case where the interaction between the tunneling Cooper pairs and the photon field is absent. In the dc current-biased Josephson junction, $\hat{\mathcal{H}}_{\text{T}}^{(0)}$ and the current operator $\hat{\mathcal{J}}_{\text{T}}$ are effectively described with a constant phase $\theta_0 = \arcsin(J_{\text{bias}}/J_0)$ (which is a c number) and its quantum fluctuation $\delta\hat{\theta}$ (q number) around θ_0, which obeys the commutation relation, $[\delta\hat{\theta}, \hat{n}_{\text{J}}] = i$. We write them explicitly as

$$\hat{\mathcal{H}}_{\text{T}}^{(0)} = -E_{\text{J}}\cos\left(\theta_0 + \delta\hat{\theta}\right) - E_{\text{J}}\frac{J_{\text{bias}}}{J_0}\left(\theta_0 + \delta\hat{\theta}\right), \tag{4}$$

$$\hat{\mathcal{J}}_{\text{T}} = i\frac{2e}{\hbar}\sum_{k,p}\left(T_{k,p}\hat{c}_k^\dagger\hat{d}_p - \text{h.c.} \right) = J_0\sin\left(\theta_0 + \delta\hat{\theta}\right), \tag{5}$$

with the Josephson coupling energy E_{J} and the Josephson critical current $J_0 = 2eE_{\text{J}}/\hbar$. Here $-E_J(\theta_0 + \delta\hat{\theta})\sin\theta_0$ describes the "washboard potential," which characterizes the dc current bias, as shown in Fig. 1.

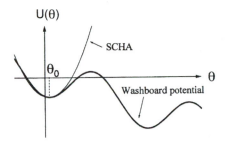

Figure 1. The washboard potential $U(\theta)$ is plotted as a function of the phase difference θ. A local minimum of $U(\theta)$ exists at $\theta = \theta_0$. Our model treats the quantum fluctuation of θ around the minimum point.

Here we shall consider a regime of small phase fluctuation, where the bias current is not so large. Then we can employ the self-consistent harmonic approximation (SCHA) for the washboard potential, that is,

$$\cos \delta\hat{\theta} \approx e^{-\langle \delta\hat{\theta}^2 \rangle_{\mathrm{J}}/2} \left[1 - \frac{1}{2} \left(\delta\hat{\theta}^2 - \langle \delta\hat{\theta}^2 \rangle_{\mathrm{J}} \right) \right], \tag{6}$$

$$\sin \delta\hat{\theta} \approx e^{-\langle \delta\hat{\theta}^2 \rangle_{\mathrm{J}}/2} \, \delta\hat{\theta}. \tag{7}$$

Here $\langle \delta\hat{\theta}^2 \rangle_{\mathrm{J}}$ is the mean square of the phase fluctuation averaged by the time-independent electronic ground state. This mean square $\langle \delta\hat{\theta}^2 \rangle_{\mathrm{J}}$ satisfies the self-consistency equation $F(z) = \tan^2 \theta_0$, where $z = \langle \delta\hat{\theta}^2 \rangle_{\mathrm{J}}$ and

$$F(z) = z - \left(\frac{E_{\mathrm{C}}}{2E_{\mathrm{J}} \cos \theta_0} \right)^{1/2} e^{z/4} + \left(2e^{z/2} - e^z \right) \tan^2 \theta_0. \tag{8}$$

The function $F(z)$ of $z \geq 0$ has an upper bound at $z = z^* > 0$. Hence the self-consistency equation has solutions only when $F(z^*) \leq \tan^2 \theta_0$.

Next we shall bosonize the Hamiltonian of the junction part. When the photon field is absent, the Hamiltonian for the junction system only is rewritten as

$$\hat{\mathcal{H}}_{\mathrm{J}} \equiv \hat{\mathcal{H}}_{\mathrm{T}}^{(0)} + \hat{\mathcal{H}}_{\mathrm{C}} = \hbar\Omega \left(\hat{b}^\dagger \hat{b} + \frac{1}{2} \right) + \text{const.}, \tag{9}$$

where the Josephson-plasma frequency Ω is defined as

$$\hbar\Omega \equiv \left[2E_{\mathrm{C}} E_{\mathrm{J}} \cos \theta_0 e^{-\langle \delta\hat{\theta}^2 \rangle_{\mathrm{J}}/2} \right]^{1/2}. \tag{10}$$

Here $\hat{b}$ and $\hat{b}^\dagger$ are boson operators (obeying $[\hat{b}, \hat{b}^\dagger] = 1$) acting only on the Josephson system, which are defined through

$$\delta\hat{\vartheta} \equiv \frac{1}{\sqrt{2}} \left(\frac{2E_{\mathrm{C}}}{E_{\mathrm{J}} \cos \theta_0 e^{-\langle \delta\hat{\theta}^2 \rangle_{\mathrm{J}}/2}} \right)^{1/4} \left(\hat{b} + \hat{b}^\dagger \right), \tag{11}$$

$$\hat{n}_{\mathrm{J}} \equiv \frac{1}{\sqrt{2}\, i} \left(\frac{E_{\mathrm{J}} \cos \theta_0 e^{-\langle \delta\hat{\theta}^2 \rangle_{\mathrm{J}}/2}}{2E_{\mathrm{C}}} \right)^{1/4} \left(\hat{b} - \hat{b}^\dagger \right), \tag{12}$$

where $\delta\hat{\vartheta} \equiv \delta\hat{\theta} - (e^{\langle\delta\hat{\theta}^2\rangle_J/2} - 1)\tan\theta_0$. We note again that the temperature of the Josephson junction should be lower than $\hbar\Omega/k_B$.

Equation (2) contains an arbitrary order of photon transition processes. Because we confine ourselves to the case of mesoscopic size of the junction with small E_C ($E_C \ll \hbar\omega$), we take into account only the one- and two-photon transition terms. In this procedure, the higher-order effects are considered by employing the SCHA for the photon part of the Hamiltonian, e.g.,

$$\cos\hat{\phi}_{EM} \approx e^{-\langle\hat{\phi}_{EM}^2\rangle_P/2}\left\{1 - \frac{1}{2}\left[\frac{E_C}{\hbar\omega}\left(\hat{a}^\dagger + \hat{a}\right)^2 - \langle\hat{\phi}_{EM}^2\rangle_P\right]\right\}. \tag{13}$$

Here $\langle\ \ \rangle_P$ means an average over the photon state at time t. As a result, our relevant system is described by two coupled boson subsystems ($\hat{a}, \hat{a}^\dagger$ and $\hat{b}, \hat{b}^\dagger$) with a complicated nonlinear interaction between them, which is not written down here explicitly.

3. METHOD OF NORMAL ORDERING

In this section, we mention how to solve the temporal evolution of the quantum state of photons and the Josephson systems with the aid of the method of normal ordering [5]. To this end, we make the rotating-wave approximation (RWA), which neglects counter-rotating terms (e.g., $\hat{a}\hat{a}\hat{b}\hat{b}$, $\hat{a}\hat{b}$) in the Hamiltonian. We here denote $|\psi(t)\rangle_P$ and $|\psi(t)\rangle_J$ as the state vectors of the photon (P) state and the Josephson junction (J), respectively. Thus the total system is described by $|\Psi(t)\rangle = |\psi(t)\rangle_P \otimes |\psi(t)\rangle_J$. We note here that the number states $|n\rangle_P \equiv (n!)^{-1/2}(\hat{a}^\dagger)^n|0\rangle_P$ ($|n\rangle_J \equiv (n!)^{-1/2}(\hat{b}^\dagger)^n|0\rangle_J$) for $n = 0, 1, 2, \cdots$ constructs an orthonormal basis set for the photon (junction) part of the Hamiltonian. Here $|0\rangle_P$ ($|0\rangle_J$) is the ground state of the photon (junction) subsystem, that is, $\hat{a}|0\rangle_P = 0$ ($\hat{b}|0\rangle_J = 0$).

Assuming that the initial state at $t = 0$ is the vacuum state $|\psi(t = 0)\rangle_P = |0\rangle_P$ for the photon part and the ground state $|\psi(t = 0)\rangle_J = |0\rangle_J$ for the junction part, $|\Psi(t)\rangle$ is written as

$$|\Psi(t)\rangle = \mathcal{N}e^{g_1(t)\hat{a}^\dagger}e^{g_2(t)(\hat{a}^\dagger)^2}e^{g_3(t)\hat{b}^\dagger}e^{g_4(t)(\hat{b}^\dagger)^2}e^{g_5(t)\hat{b}^\dagger\hat{a}^\dagger}|0\rangle_P \otimes |0\rangle_J, \tag{14}$$

where $\mathcal{N}$ is the normalization constant. The time development of $|\Psi(t)\rangle$ is now described by a set of c-number (complex) coefficients $g_i(t)$'s, which obey coupled ordinary differential equations [6].

Our model contains three control parameters: $0 < E_C/\hbar\omega \equiv \tilde{E}_C \ll 1$, $1 \ll E_J/\hbar\omega \equiv \tilde{E}_J$, and $0 < \theta_0 < \pi/2$. The SCHA becomes a good approximation when both E_C/E_J and $\theta_0 = \arcsin(J_{bias}/J_0)$ are much smaller than unity.

We here make a comment on characteristic time scales of the quantum dynamics in our system. The stability exponent of a set of stationary solutions of $g_i(t)$'s is calculated with the linear stability analysis in the semiclassical limit [7]. There are four pure imaginary exponents, $\pm i\eta$, and $\pm 2i\eta$, with $\eta \equiv (2\tilde{E}_C\tilde{E}_J\cos\theta_0 + 1)^{1/2}/\tilde{E}_J$, which means that the stationary solutions are marginally stable, and the time evolution of $|\Psi(t)\rangle$ has two characteristic periods, $2\pi/\eta$ and π/η. This corresponds to the Rabi flopping time in the Jaynes-Cummings model.

4. NUMERICAL RESULTS

The temporal evolution of $g_i(t)$'s is followed by numerical integration and the following physical quantities are evaluated: (i) the mean photon number, $\langle\hat{n}_P(t)\rangle \equiv {}_P\langle\psi(t)|\hat{a}^\dagger\hat{a}|\psi(t)\rangle_P$, (ii) the photon-number fluctuation, $\langle[\Delta\hat{n}_P(t)]^2\rangle \equiv \langle[\hat{n}_P(t)]^2\rangle - \langle\hat{n}_P(t)\rangle^2$, (iii) the Fano factor, a measure of the photon-number statistics (photon-number squeezing), $F(t) \equiv \langle [\Delta \hat{n}_{\mathrm{P}}(t)]^2 \rangle / \langle \hat{n}_{\mathrm{P}}(t) \rangle$, (iv) the variance of two quadrature-phase amplitudes, $\langle [\Delta \hat{q}_{\mathrm{P}}(t)]^2 \rangle$ and $\langle [\Delta \hat{p}_{\mathrm{P}}(t)]^2 \rangle$, where $\hat{q}_{\mathrm{P}} \equiv \hat{a}^\dagger + \hat{a}$ and $\hat{p}_{\mathrm{P}} \equiv (\hat{a}^\dagger - \hat{a})/i$, and (v) for the junction system, the mean supercurrent, which is defined as $\langle \hat{\mathcal{J}}_{\mathrm{T}} \rangle / J_{\mathrm{bias}}$.

Numerical computation is carried out by the Runge-Kutta-Gill routine. In this paper, we report only the resonance case: $\omega = \Omega$. Control parameters are chosen to be $\tilde{E}_{\mathrm{C}} = 0.1$, $\tilde{E}_{\mathrm{J}} = 6.07$, and $\theta_0 = \pi/6$, which satisfy the resonance condition $\omega = \Omega$. Here $\tilde{E}_{\mathrm{C}}$ represents the degree of the optical nonlinearity, and $E_{\mathrm{C}}/E_{\mathrm{J}}$ is a measure of the quantum nature of the junction.

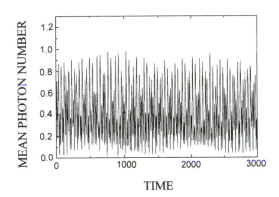

Figure 2. Time evolution of the mean photon number: $\langle \hat{n}_{\mathrm{P}}(t) \rangle$ is plotted as a function of a normalized time $t' = E_{\mathrm{J}} t / \hbar$. Control parameters are chosen to be $\tilde{E}_{\mathrm{C}} = 0.1$, $\tilde{E}_{\mathrm{J}} = 6.07$, and $\theta_0 = \pi/6$, which satisfy $\omega = \Omega$.

Figure 2 shows the temporal evolution of the mean photon number $\langle \hat{n}_{\mathrm{P}}(t) \rangle$. The amplitude of this oscillation becomes larger with decreasing $\tilde{E}_{\mathrm{C}}/\tilde{E}_{\mathrm{J}}$. The temporal evolution of the quantity seems to be quasiperiodic, which is in a striking contrast to the case of the semiclassical limit, where the time evolution is perfectly periodic. To see this, we carry out the Fourier transformation of the $\langle \hat{n}_{\mathrm{P}}(t) \rangle$ dynamics to get its power spectrum, as shown in Fig. 3. In the semiclassical limit, the spectrum has two distinct peaks, whose frequencies correspond to the characteristic frequencies, η and 2η, given by the linear stability analysis. In the fully quantum-mechanical model, on the other hand, the spectrum shows not only commensurate frequencies but also many incommensurate frequencies, which indicate the quasiperiodic motion. This results from an interplay between the photon fluctuation and the junction-phase fluctuation, which have different (incommensurate) characteristic frequencies. Thus we find that when the junction system is quantized as well as the photon field, periodic motion of the mean photon number is disturbed by the quantum fluctuation of the junction variables, leading to the quasiperiodic dynamics.

In order to clarify the photon-number statistics, the Fano factor $F(t)$ is plotted in Fig. 4, which shows oscillations across unity ($F = 1$) indicating that the sub- ($F < 1$) and super-Poissonian ($F > 1$) photon states are realized alternatively. The characteristic period is the same as of the mean photon number. We find that the sub-Poissonian feature of the photon-number statistics is enhanced for $\tilde{E}_{\mathrm{C}} > 0.1$.

The amplitude squeezing of the photon state is studied by plotting the variances of the two quadrature-phase amplitudes in Fig. 5. These variances are normalized to be

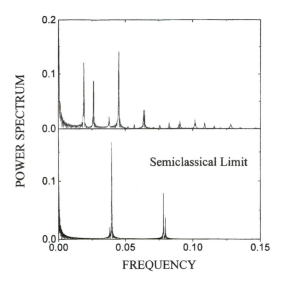

Figure 3. Top: The power spectrum of the evolution of the mean photon number shown in Fig. 2. There are many incommensurate frequencies, indicating the quasiperiodic motion. Bottom: The power spectrum of the mean photon number in the semiclassical limit. There are two commensurate peaks corresponding to the imaginary part of two stability exponents, η and 2η.

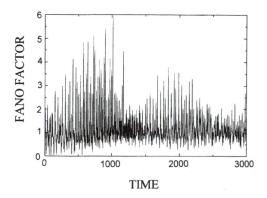

Figure 4. Time evolution of the Fano factor $F(t)$ for the photon state is plotted as a function of a normalized time. Control parameters are the same as in Fig. 2.

$\langle[\Delta\hat{q}_P(t)]^2\rangle = \langle[\Delta\hat{p}_P(t)]^2\rangle = 1$ when the photon is in the coherent state. The variance of one quadrature amplitude oscillates around unity and becomes less than unity. This indicates that the photon state evolves into a quadrature-phase amplitude squeezed state. However, the uncertainty product $\langle[\Delta\hat{q}_P(t)]^2\rangle\langle[\Delta\hat{p}_P(t)]^2\rangle$ deviates from unity, which means that the obtained photon state is *not* the minimum-uncertainty state.

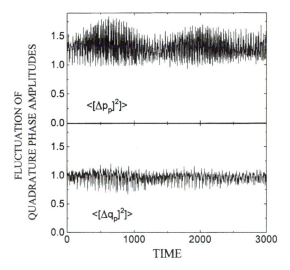

Figure 5. Top: Time evolution of the fluctuation of quadrature-phase amplitude for the photon state, $\langle[\Delta\hat{q}_P(t)]^2\rangle$, is plotted as a function of a normalized time. Bottom: Time evolution of $\langle[\Delta\hat{p}_P(t)]^2\rangle$ is plotted.

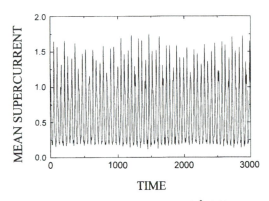

Figure 6. Time evolution of the mean supercurrent $\langle\hat{\mathcal{J}}_T(t)\rangle$ is plotted as a function of a normalized time.

Characteristic quantum fluctuations of the photon state affect those of the electronic state of the junction. We draw in Fig. 6 the temporal dynamics of the mean supercurrent normalized by J_{bias}. This oscillates around unity. In Fig. 7, the power spectrum of the mean supercurrent is drawn. The spectrum shows that the oscillation of the mean supercurrent is also quasiperiodic with frequencies the same as those of the mean photon number.

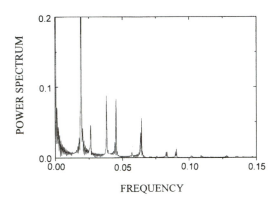

Figure 7. The power spectrum of the temporal behavior of the mean supercurrent. Frequency positions of all the peaks coincide with those in Fig. 3 (top).

5.   CONCLUDING REMARKS

In the present work, we have fixed the initial state of photon system to be the vacuum. However, when the photon state is initially a coherent state, the quantum dynamics may differ qualitatively from the present result. Therefore the dependence on initial photon states should be clarified. Moreover, effects of the RWA should also be crucially reexamined. Higher-order multiphoton transitions are also an interesting problem to be clarified. Lastly we note that the quantum nondemolition (QND) measurement for the photon number is possible by measuring the supercurrent fluctuation in this system. This is reported in detail elsewhere [8].

In summary, we have described the current-biased Josephson junction interacting with a single-mode quantized photon field by the two-component boson model. We have analyzed numerically their temporal dynamics to clarify characteristics of the quantum fluctuations of the photon state and the electronic states. For the photon state, sub-Poissonian statistics and quadrature-phase amplitude squeezed states are found to be generated from initial vacuum states. Thus our scheme offers a novel method for generation of nonclassical photon states without using the usual optical nonlinear materials.

ACKNOWLEDGMENTS

We would like to thank K. Nakamura and S. Kurihara for valuable discussions. This work is supported by a Grant-in Aid for Scientific Research on Priority Areas, "Mutual Quantum Manipulation of Radiation Field and Matter," from the Ministry of Education, Science and Culture of Japan.

REFERENCES

[1] L.-A. Wu, H. J. Kimbel, and H. Wu, Phys. Rev. Lett. **57**, 2520 (1980).

[2] B. Yurke, J. Opt. Soc. Am. **B4**, 1551 (1987).

[3] N. Hatakenaka, T. Ogawa, and S. Kurihara, Physica B **194–196**, 1701 (1994).

[4] M. H. Devoret, D. Esteve, H. Grabert, G.-L. Ingold, H. Pothier, and C. Urbina, Phys. Rev. Lett. **64**, 1824 (1990).

[5] H. Heffner and W. H. Louisell, J. Math. Phys. **6**, 474 (1965).

[6] Coupled ordinary equations for $g_i(t)$ are too complicated to be written explicitly in this paper.

[7] The "semiclassical limit" means the case where quantum fluctuations of the junction variables, $\delta\hat{\theta}$ and $\hat{n}_J$, are neglected, that is, the junction variables are treated as c numbers instead of q numbers. Even in this semiclassical limit, the quantum nature of the photon field is completely incorporated.

[8] N. Hatakenaka and T. Ogawa, J. Low Temp. Phys. (in print).

POLARIZATION-SQUEEZED LIGHT GENERATION IN A SECOND ORDER NONLINEAR MEDIUM

V. N. Beskrovnyi and A. S. Chirkin

Physics Department, Lomonosov Moscow State University
Moscow 119899, Russia
e-mail: chirkin@foton.ilc.msu.su
and chirkin@icono.phys.msu.su

We have considered forming light with a nonclassical state of polarization by nondegenerate second harmonic generation. This occurs due to photon anticorrelation of orthogonal polarization modes of the fundamental radiation. Photon statistics of polarization modes and quadrature component fluctuations are discussed. Calculations are carried out within an accuracy of the terms proportional to the fourth power of the nonlinear coupling coefficient.

1. INTRODUCTION

There exists the possibility of forming polarization-squeezed light in media with $\chi^{(3)}$ cubic nonlinearities: anisotropic [1], gyrotropic [2], and spatially inhomogeneous [3] ones. For the case of such light the fluctuation level of some of the Stokes parameters is below standard quantum level corresponding to those in a coherent state. Recently we have shown [4] that in a $\chi^{(2)}$ quadratic nonlinear medium polarization-squeezed light can be formed at the fundamental frequency in SHG by a mixing process (so called nondegenerate SHG process). From the point of view of suppressing fluctuations media with $\chi^{(2)}$ nonlinearities seem to be preferable to ones with $\chi^{(3)}$.

The quantum theory of second harmonic generation (SHG) has been developed for 20 years (see Refs. 5-6). The process of SHG has been used to obtain light with nonclassical properties at the fundamental [7] as well as doubled [8-10] frequencies. In experiments [7-10] the degenerate process of SHG was used, namely the fundamental ordinary wave excited a SH extraordinary wave (*ooe* type of interaction in negative nonlinear crystals). For this case the quantum theory of frequency doubling was developed in many references (e.g. see Refs. [5-6] and [10-11] as well as the references there).

Only Refs.11, 12 were devoted to the quantum theory of SH generation by mixing the ordinary and extraordinary fundamental waves. In Ref.12 the linear theory of quantum fluctuations of interacting waves based on a perturbation method was developed. In Ref. 4 we developed a nonlinear theory of quantum fluctuations at SHG. Quantum equations of SHG were solved with an accuracy to the square of the nonlinear wave coupling coefficient. We investigated statistical properties and quantum polarization structure of the fundamental radiation.

In contrast to Ref.4 in this paper we carried out calculations of SHG by mixing within an accuracy to the terms proportional to the fourth power of coupling coefficient. This allowed us to find the area of validity of the expressions obtained earlier as well as to get new results.

2. NONLINEAR OPERATOR EQUATIONS, THEIR APPROXIMATE SOLUTION

Let us consider SHG process of mixing orthogonally polarized fundamental waves in a $\chi^{(2)}$ nonlinear medium. It is described by the interaction Hamiltonian

$$H_{int} = \hbar\beta(a_1^+ a_2^+ b + a_1 a_2 b^+), \tag{1}$$

where a_j^+ (a_j), b^+ (b) are the creation (annihilation) operators for the fundamental and second harmonic waves accordingly. The indices $j = 1, 2$ refer to the fundamental waves with the ordinary and extraordinary polarizations, β is the nonlinear coupling coefficient, and $\hbar$ is Planck's constant.

The evolution of the operators a_1 and b in the nonlinear medium is given by the set of equations

$$
\begin{cases}
da_1/dz &= i\beta a_2^+ b, \\
da_2/dz &= i\beta a_1^+ b, \\
db/dz &= i\beta a_1 a_2,
\end{cases} \tag{2}
$$

where $z = vt$, and v is the phase velocity in the medium.

The initial conditions for Eqs. (2) are

$$a_1(z = 0) = a_{10}, \quad a_2(z = 0) = a_{20}, \quad b(z = 0) = b_0. \tag{3}$$

Here we will confine our consideration to the case that the initial fundamental waves at the input to the nonlinear medium are in a coherent state and the initial SH is in the vacuum state:

$$a_j|\alpha_j\rangle = \alpha_j|\alpha_j\rangle, \quad b_0|0\rangle = 0. \tag{4}$$

It is impossible to find the exact solution of the set of the operator equations (2). As we have noted above, the analysis of the equations (2) within an accuracy to the terms proportional to g^2, where $g = \beta z$, was carried out in Ref. 4.

In this paper we performed calculations within an accuracy to the terms proportional to g^4. To find the solution of this problem we developed an algorithm of solving nonlinear operator equations on a computer. Our algorithm allows us to solve the set of operator equations within an arbitrary accuracy. Within the considered accuracy we have

$$a_1 = a_{10} + ig a_{20}^+ b_0 + (g^2/2)(a_{10} b_0^+ b_0 - a_{10} a_{20}^+ a_{20})$$
$$+ (ig^3/6)(-a_{20}^+ b_0 + a_{20}^+ b_0^+ b_0^2 - a_{20}^{+2} a_{20} b_0 + 2a_{10}^2 a_{20} b_0^+ - 2a_{10}^+ a_{10} a_{20}^+ b_0)$$
$$+ (g^4/24)(-7a_{10} b_0^+ b_0 + a_{10} b_0^{+2} b_0^2 + a_{10} a_{20}^+ a_{20} - 10 a_{10} a_{20}^+ a_{20} b_0^+ b_0 +$$
$$a_{10} a_{20}^{+2} a_{20}^2 + 4 a_{10}^+ a_{20}^{+2} b_0^2 - 4 a_{10}^+ a_{10}^2 b_0^+ b_0 + 4 a_{10}^+ a_{10}^2 a_{20}^+ a_{20})$$

$$b = b_0 + ig a_{10} a_{20} + (g^2/2)(-b_0 - a_{20}^+ a_{20} b_0 - a_{10}^+ a_{10} b_0)$$
$$+ (ig^3/6)(-a_{10} a_{20} + 2 a_{10} a_{20} b_0^+ b_0 - a_{10} a_{20}^+ a_{20}^2 - 2 a_{10}^+ a_{20}^+ b_0^2 - a_{10}^+ a_{10}^2 a_{20})$$
$$+ (g^4/24)(b_0 - 4 b_0^+ b_0^2 + 3 a_{20}^+ a_{20} b_0 - 4 a_{20}^+ a_{20} b_0^+ b_0^2 + a_{20}^{+2} a_{20}^2 b_0 - 4 a_{10}^2 a_{20}^2 b_0^+$$
$$+ 3 a_{10}^+ a_{10} b_0 - 4 a_{10}^+ a_{10} b_0^+ b_0^2 + 10 a_{10}^+ a_{10} a_{20}^+ a_{20} b_0 + a_{10}^{+2} a_{20}^2 b_0) \tag{5}$$

where the label "0" refers to the input values. The expression for a_2 is obtained from the one for a_1 by replacing indices $1 \leftrightarrow 2$.

Within accuracy used the operators a_j and b obey the following commutation relations:

$$
\left[a_j, a_j^+\right] = [b, b^+] = 1, \quad [a_j, b] = [a_j, b^+] = 0, \quad j = 1, 2.
$$
$$
\left[a_1^+, a_2\right] = [a_1, a_2] = 0, \tag{6}
$$

These relations also follow from Eqs.2. Therefore a check whether our solution satisfies these relations can be considered as a way to ensure that our method gives correct results.

Using the expressions (5), quadrature-component and Stokes-parameter fluctuations and photon statistics of the fundamental radiation will be analyzed.

3. QUADRATURE COMPONENTS

Let us first analyze quadrature component fluctuations of both fundamental radiation polarizations. We define the quadrature operators as follows:

$$
\begin{aligned}
X_j &= (a_j e^{-i(\phi_j+\psi)} + a_j^+ e^{i(\phi_j+\psi)})/2, \\
Y_j &= (a_j e^{-i(\phi_j+\psi)} - a_j^+ e^{i(\phi_j+\psi)})/(2i), \tag{7}
\end{aligned}
$$

where ψ is the heterodyne phase, ϕ_1, ϕ_2 are the phase additions for the jth polarization.

According to the solutions (5) and the initial conditions (4), for mean quadrature values, for example, we obtain

$$
\langle X_1 \rangle = \langle X_{10} \rangle (1 - (g^2/2)\bar{n}_{20} + (g^4/24)(\bar{n}_{20}^2 + \bar{n}_{20} + 4\bar{n}_{10}\bar{n}_{20})),
$$

$$
\langle Y_1 \rangle = \langle Y_{10} \rangle (1 - (g^2/2)\bar{n}_{20} + (g^4/24)(\bar{n}_{20}^2 + \bar{n}_{20} + 4\bar{n}_{10}\bar{n}_{20})),
$$

where $\bar{n}_{j0} = |\alpha_j|^2$ is the mean photon number of the jth polarization at the input to the nonlinear medium.

For dispersions of the quadrature components we have simple formulas

$$
(\Delta X_1)^2 = 1/4 + (g^4/24)\bar{n}_{10}\bar{n}_{20}(3 + \cos 2(\phi_1 + \psi)),
$$

$$
(\Delta Y_1)^2 = 1/4 + (g^4/24)\bar{n}_{10}\bar{n}_{20}(3 - \cos 2(\phi_1 + \psi)), \tag{8}
$$

where $(\Delta X)^2 = \langle X^2 \rangle - \langle X \rangle^2$. One can see that the dispersions of the quadratures increase in the nonlinear medium and the product

$$
(\Delta X_j)^2 (\Delta Y_j)^2 = \frac{1}{16}(1 + g^4 \bar{n}_{10}\bar{n}_{20}).
$$

Therefore, the quadrature components became noisier as a result of back-action of the second harmonic on the fundamental radiation. Orthogonally polarized mode quadratures of the fundamental radiation get correlated in the SHG process. Their correlation is equal to

$$
\langle \Delta X_1 \Delta Y_1 + \Delta Y_1 \Delta X_1 \rangle = (g^4/12)\bar{n}_{10}\bar{n}_{20} \sin 2(\phi_1 + \psi) \tag{9}
$$

where $\Phi = \arg \alpha_1 + \arg \alpha_2 + \phi_1 - \phi_2 - 2\psi$. Correlation between orthogonally polarized quadratures does not allow us to obtain quadrature-squeezed light.

485

4. THE STOKES PARAMETERS OF FUNDAMENTAL RADIATION

To analyze the polarization structure of the fundamental radiation, we consider the Stokes operators

$$S_0 = a_1^+ a_1 + a_2^+ a_2, \qquad S_2 = a_1^+ a_2 e^{i(\phi_1 - \phi_2)} + a_2^+ a_1 e^{-i(\phi_1 - \phi_2)},$$
$$S_1 = a_1^+ a_1 - a_2^+ a_2, \qquad S_3 = i(a_2^+ a_1 e^{(-i\phi_1 - \phi_2)} - a_1^+ a_2 e^{i(\phi_1 - \phi_2)}). \tag{10}$$

The operator S_0 is the operator for the total photon number of both polarizations of the fundamental radiation.

It is well known that the operators (10) obey the commutation relations of the SU(2) algebra, for example

$$[S_1, S_2] = i2S_3. \tag{11}$$

According to Eq. (11) there exists an uncertainty relation

$$(\Delta S_1)^2 (\Delta S_2)^2 \geq |\langle S_3 \rangle|^2. \tag{12}$$

The other commutation and uncertainty relations can be obtained from Eqs. (11) and (12) by cyclic permutation of the indices. The operator S_0 commutes with any operator S_j $(j = 1, 2, 3)$.

The expressions for the Stokes operators turn out to be very lengthy. As an example we write down the expression for the operator S_0:

$$S_0 = a_{10}^+ a_{10} + a_{20}^+ a_{20} + 2ig(a_{10}^+ a_{20}^+ b_0 - a_{10} a_{20} b_0^+)$$

$$+ 2g^2(b_0^+ b_0 + a_{20}^+ a_{20} b_0^+ b_0 + a_{10}^+ a_{10} b_0^+ b_0 - a_{10}^+ a_{10} a_{20}^+ a_{20})$$

$$+ (4ig^3/3)(a_{10} a_{20} b_0^+ - a_{10} a_{20} b_0^{+2} b_0 + a_{10} a_{20}^+ a_{10}{}^2 b_0^+$$

$$- a_{10}^+ a_{20}^+ b_0 + a_{10}^+ a_{20}^+ b_0^+ b_0^2 - a_{10}^+ a_{20}^{+2} a_{20} b_0 + a_{10}^+ a_{10}{}^2 a_{20} b_0^+ - a_{10}^{+2} a_{10} a_{20}^+ b_0)$$

$$+ (g^4/3)(-2b_0^+ b_0 + 2b_0^{+2} b_0{}^2 -$$

$$6a_{20}^+ a_{20} b_0^+ b_0 + 2a_{20}^+ a_{20} b_0^{+2} b_0{}^2 - 2a_{20}^{+2} a_{10}{}^2 b_0^+ b_0 + 3a_{10}{}^2 a_{10}{}^2 b_0^{+2} -$$

$$6a_{10}^+ a_{10} b_0^+ b_0 + 2a_{10}^+ a_{10} b_0^{+2} b_0{}^2 + 2a_{10}^+ a_{10} a_{20}^+ a_{20} - 12a_{10}^+ a_{10} a_{20}^+ a_{20} b_0^+ b_0 +$$

$$2a_{10}^+ a_{10} a_{20}^{+2} a_{10}{}^2 + 3a_{10}^{+2} a_{20}^{+2} b_0{}^2 - 2a_{10}^{+2} a_{10}{}^2 b_0^+ b_0 + 2a_{10}^{+2} a_{10}{}^2 a_{20}^+ a_{20}).$$

The mean values of the Stokes parameters of the fundamental radiation vary according to the following expressions

$$\langle S_0 \rangle = \bar{n}_{10} + \bar{n}_{20} - 2g^2 \bar{n}_{10} \bar{n}_{20} + \frac{2}{3} g^4 \bar{n}_{10} \bar{n}_{20} (1 + \bar{n}_{10} + \bar{n}_{20}),$$

$$\langle S_1 \rangle = \bar{n}_{10} - \bar{n}_{20},$$

$$\langle S_2 \rangle = 2\sqrt{\bar{n}_{10} \bar{n}_{20}} \cos(\phi_2 - \phi_1)$$
$$\times \left[1 - \frac{g^2}{2}(\bar{n}_{10} + \bar{n}_{20}) + \frac{g^4}{24}(\bar{n}_{10}^2 + \bar{n}_{20}^2 + \bar{n}_{10} + \bar{n}_{20} + 14\bar{n}_{10}\bar{n}_{20}) \right],$$

$$\langle S_3 \rangle = 2\sqrt{\bar{n}_{10} \bar{n}_{20}} \sin(\phi_2 - \phi_1)$$
$$\times \left[1 + \frac{g^2}{2}(\bar{n}_{10} + \bar{n}_{20}) + \frac{g^4}{24}(\bar{n}_{10}^2 + \bar{n}_{20}^2 + \bar{n}_{10} + \bar{n}_{20} + 14\bar{n}_{10}\bar{n}_{20}) \right]. \tag{13}$$

It follows from Eqs.(13) that the mean photon number of the fundamental radiation decreases, whereas the difference in the photon numbers $\langle S_1 \rangle$ between orthogonally polarized modes does not change. The mean values $\langle S_2 \rangle$, $\langle S_3 \rangle$ decrease. The dispersions of the Stokes operators are

$$(\Delta S_0)^2 = \bar{n}_{10} + \bar{n}_{20} - 4g^2 \bar{n}_{10} \bar{n}_{20} + (4g^4/3)(\bar{n}_{10}\bar{n}_{20})(1 + 2\bar{n}_{10} + 2\bar{n}_{20}),$$

$$(\Delta S_1)^2 = \bar{n}_{10} + \bar{n}_{20},$$

$$(\Delta S_2)^2 = \bar{n}_{10} + \bar{n}_{20} - 4g^2\bar{n}_{10}\bar{n}_{20} + \frac{g^4}{6}\bar{n}_{10}\bar{n}_{20}(15 + cos(\phi_2 - \phi_1))(\bar{n}_{10} + \bar{n}_{20} + 8),$$

$$(\Delta S_3)^2 = \bar{n}_{10} + \bar{n}_{20} - 4g^2\bar{n}_{10}\bar{n}_{20} + \frac{g^4}{6}\bar{n}_{10}\bar{n}_{20}(15 + sin(\phi_2 - \phi_1))(\bar{n}_{10} + \bar{n}_{20} + 8). \quad (14)$$

We will describe the Stokes parameter fluctuations by the relative value

$$p_j = (\Delta S_j)^2/(\Delta S_j^{(coh)})^2, \quad j = 0, 1, 2, 3, \quad (15)$$

where $(\Delta S_j^{(coh)})^2$ is the dispersion of the Stokes parameter for the case of a coherent state of the same intensity. This dispersion is determined by the mean intensity [1]:

$$(\Delta S_j^{(coh)})^2 = \langle S_0 \rangle = \bar{n}_{10} + \bar{n}_{20} - 2g^2\bar{n}_{10}\bar{n}_{20} + \frac{2}{3}g^4\bar{n}_{10}\bar{n}_{20}(1 + \bar{n}_{10} + \bar{n}_{20}), \quad j = 0, 1, 2, 3. \quad (16)$$

It should be noted that all $p_j = 1$ for the case of coherent radiation.

It follows from the expressions (14) and (15) that the fluctuations of the Stokes parameters S_0, S_2, S_3 are suppressed in the nonlinear medium, while the ones of the parameter S_1 increase. Thus the polarization-squeezed light is formed. One can show that simultaneous suppression of fluctuations of the Stokes parameters S_2, S_3 does not contradict to the uncertainty relation.

Fig.1 and Figs.2 (a, b) show the dispersion behaviour of the Stokes parameters S_0, S_2, and S_3. It follows from Fig.1 that maximum fluctuation suppression in the S_0 parameter occurs when the mean photon numbers of the polarization modes at the input into a nonlinear medium are equal ($\xi = 1$). For this case Figs.2 are plotted. We can see that Stokes parameter fluctuation reduction does not exceed 20% and there exists an optimal value of $g^2\bar{n}_0$.

5. PHOTON STATISTICS

Above we have investigated the behavior of fluctuations of the total photon number. They are described by the parameter p_0, that is the Fano factor. According to Eqs. (14-16) $p_0 < 1$, i.e. the total field statistics is sub-Poissonian.

Let us now analyze fluctuations of the photon number of the output polarization components ($n_j = a_j^+ a_j$, $j = 1, 2$.) Mean photon numbers are equal

$$\hat{n}_1 = \bar{n}_{10} - g^2\bar{n}_{10}\bar{n}_{20} + (g^4/3)\bar{n}_{10}\bar{n}_{20}(\bar{n}_{10} + \bar{n}_{20} + 1)$$

$$\hat{n}_2 = \bar{n}_{20} - g^2\bar{n}_{10}\bar{n}_{20} + (g^4/3)\bar{n}_{10}\bar{n}_{20}(\bar{n}_{10} + \bar{n}_{20} + 1) \quad (17)$$

The dispersions of the photon numbers are given by

$$(\Delta n_1)^2 = \bar{n}_{10} - g^2\bar{n}_{10}\bar{n}_{20} + (g^4/3)\bar{n}_{10}\bar{n}_{20}(3\bar{n}_{10} + \bar{n}_{20} + 1)$$

$$(\Delta n_2)^2 = \bar{n}_{20} - g^2\bar{n}_{10}\bar{n}_{20} + (g^4/3)\bar{n}_{10}\bar{n}_{20}(\bar{n}_{10} + 3\bar{n}_{20} + 1) \quad (18)$$

Since $(\Delta n_1)^2 > \bar{n}_{10}$ and $(\Delta n_2)^2 > \bar{n}_{20}$ photon statistics of the polarization modes become super-Poissonian.

Photons of orthogonal polarization modes turn out to be anticorrelated:

$$\langle \Delta n_1 \Delta n_2 + \Delta n_2 \Delta n_1 \rangle = -g^2\bar{n}_{10}\bar{n}_{20} + (g^4/3)\bar{n}_{10}\bar{n}_{20}(2\bar{n}_{10} + 2\bar{n}_{20} + 1) \quad (19)$$

Formula (28) explains the fact that the total field possesses sub-Poissonian statistics.

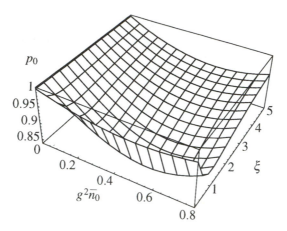

Figure 1. Relative dispersion p_0 of the Stokes parameter S_0 versus ratio $\xi = \bar{n}_{10}/\bar{n}_{20}$ and parameter $g^2\bar{n}_0$, where $\bar{n}_0 = \bar{n}_{10} + \bar{n}_{20}$ is the mean initial total photon number of fundamental radiation and $\bar{n}_{j0}$ is the jth mode photon number.

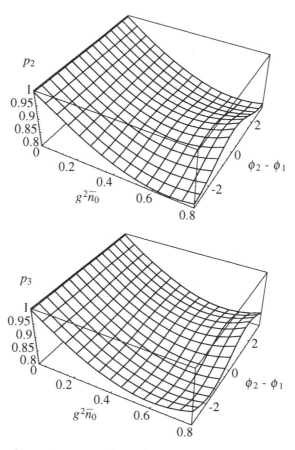

Figure 2. Relative dispersions p_2 and p_3 of the Stokes parameters S_2 S_3 versus phase difference $\phi_2 - \phi_1$ and parameter $g^2\bar{n}_0$, for the case $\bar{n}_0 = 2\bar{n}_{10} = 2\bar{n}_{20}$.

6. CONCLUSIONS

Thus in this paper we have presented results of a quantum analysis of SHG by mixing. Computer methods allow us to carried out the calculations within an accuracy to the terms proportional to the fourth power of coupling coefficient g. In other words, in the present paper a nonlinear theory of suppression of quantum fluctuations of interacting waves was developed.

It should also be noted that our results within an accuracy of the terms proportional the second power of g [4] coincide with the results in Ref. 4 and besides define the area of validity of conclusions of Ref.4. However, the results we obtained are very different from those in Ref. 12, where the calculations were carried out using a method of fluctuation perturbations. According to (8) no quantum fluctuation suppression occurs in quadrature components of polarization modes, while the calculations in Ref.12 show a possibility of complete fluctuation suppression in the quadrature.

ACKNOWLEDGEMENT

This work was supported in part by the Russian Foundation for Basic Research (Grant No.96-02-16714a).

REFERENCES

[1]   A.S.Chirkin, A.A.Orlov, D.Yu.Paraschuk, Quantum Electronics, **23**, 870 (1993).

[2]   A.S.Chirkin, V.V.Volokhovsky, J. Rus. Laser Research, **16**, 526 (1995).

[3]   A.P.Alodjants, S.M.Arakelyan, A.S.Chirkin, JETP, **81**, 34 (1995).

[4]   V.N.Beskrovnyi, A.S.Chirkin, Quantum Electronics, **26**, p.843 (1996).

[5]   J.Perina, Quantum Statistics of Linear and Nonlinear Optical Phenomena. D.Reidel Publishing Company. Dordrecht, 1984.

[6]   M.Kozerovsky, A.A.Mamedov, V.I.Manko, S.M.Chumakov, Squeezed and Correlated States in Quantum Optics, Proc. P.N. Lebedev Phys.Inst., **200**, 106 (1991) (in Russian).

[7]   S.F.Pereira, M.Xiao, H.G.Kimble, Phys.Rev. A, **38**, 4931 (1989).

[8]   A.Sizman, R.J.Horovicz, G.Wagner, G.Leuch, Opt.Comms, **80**, 138 (1990).

[9]   R.Pashota, M.Collet, Phys.Rev.Letters, **72**, 3807 (1994).

[10] H.-A.Bachor, M.Taubman, A.G.White, T.Ralph, D.E.McClelland, Fourth International Conference on Squeezed States and Uncertainty Relations, NASA Conf. Publication, **3322**, 381 (1996).

[11] A.S.Chirkin, N.V.Korolkova, Laser Physics, 4, 726 (1994).

[12] R.-D. Li, P.Kumar, 1994, Phys.Rev. A, **49**, 2157; 1995, J. Opt. Soc. Amer., **12**, 2310.

RECONSTRUCTION OF EXTERNAL FORCES IN QUANTUM NOISES OF PARAMETRIC MEASURING SYSTEM WITH DISSIPATION

A. V. Gusev and V. V. Kulagin

Sternberg Astronomical Institute, Moscow State University
Universitetsky prospect 13, 119899, Moscow, Russia
Tel: (095)939-5327, Fax (7-095)-932-8841
e-mail: gusev@sai.msu.su, kul@sai.msu.su

Reconstruction of external forces contaminated by the quantum noise of a dissipative parametric measuring system is considered. A quasioptimal filtration procedure is suggested and an error of force reconstruction is estimated. This filtration procedure becomes optimal for sufficiently small dissipation in the parametric measuring system. To realize such measurements one has to use a phase sensitive device and a dual homodyne detector with proper local oscillator phase.

Reconstruction of a small external force acting on a mechanical system is of great importance in experiments with test bodies. However there is a Standard Quantum Limit (SQL) on force resolution [1] in conventional measurement schemes: if one measures the coordinate of a mechanical oscillator then for an amplitude F_0 of gravitational force acting on it one has:

$$F_0 \geq F_Q = (2/\hat{\tau})(M\hbar\omega_\mu)^{1/2}, \tag{1}$$

where ω_μ and M are the resonant frequency and mass of the mechanical oscillator and the external signal is assumed to be in the following form ($\omega_\mu \approx \omega_f$):

$$F_s(t) = F_0 \sin\omega_f t, 0 \leq t \leq \hat{\tau},$$

On the other hand there are special measurement procedures which can achieve a sensitivity better than SQL [1-4]. For example in [4] an optimal processing of an output signal in periodically nonstationary noise of parametric measuring system is considered. The filtration procedure utilizes the fact that fluctuations on signal and idler frequencies are highly correlated. For realization of such measurements one has to use a phase sensitive device with appropriate dependence of amplification coefficient on frequency and dual homodyne detector with proper local oscillator phase. However all results were obtained in [4] for the case of vanishing dissipation in the mechanical system. Therefore an analysis of the measurement procedure for small but finite dissipation is very desirable.

The goals of this paper are to construct a quasioptimal filtration procedure for dissipative parametric measuring system which becomes optimal for zero dissipation and to estimate a force reconstruction error.

Quantum Communication, Computing, and Measurement
Edited by Hirota *et al.*, Plenum Press, New York, 1997

Let us consider a scheme of parametric measuring system and receiver that processes an output signal E_1

$$E_1(t) = Y_1(t) \cos \omega_p t - Y_2(t) \sin \omega_p t \qquad (2)$$

where quadrature components $Y_1(t)$ and $Y_2(t)$ consist of signals $S_i(t)$ (proportional to external force F_s and pump amplitude of parametric measuring system) and time stationary noises $n_i(t)$:

$$Y_i(t) = S_i(t) + n_i(t), \qquad i = 1, 2.$$
$$W_{ik}(\omega) = m_1\{Y_i(\omega)Y_k^+(\omega) \mid F_s = 0\} \qquad (3)$$

Here $W_{ik}(\omega)$ is the spectral correlation matrix of noises, and m_1 is the symmetrical operator of statistical averaging [5]. According to the optimal filtration theory of vector signals [6] the following statistics must be constructed for detection and parameter estimation of external force [4,7]

$$Z_{opt} = C_0 \int_{-\infty}^{\infty} [Y_1(t)\rho_1(t) + Y_2(t)\rho_2(t)]dt =$$
$$\{(C_0/\pi)Re \int_0^{\infty} [Y_1(\omega)\rho_1^*(\omega) + Y_2(\omega)\rho_2^*(\omega)]e^{j\omega(t-t_0)}d\omega\}_{|t=t_0} \qquad (4)$$

where C_0 is an arbitrary scale factor, and $\rho_1(t)$ and $\rho_2(t)$ are reference signals with spectra defined by the following system of equations

$$W_{11}(\omega)\rho_1(\omega) + W_{12}(\omega)\rho_2(\omega) = S_1(\omega),$$
$$W_{12}^*(\omega)\rho_1(\omega) + W_{22}(\omega)\rho_2(\omega) = S_2(\omega), \qquad (5)$$

In the case $S_1 = 0$ from (5) one can obtain

$$\rho_1(\omega) = -[W_{12}(\omega)/\Delta(\omega)]S_2(\omega),$$
$$\rho_2(\omega) = [W_{11}(\omega)/\Delta(w)]S_2(\omega), \qquad (6)$$
$$\Delta(\omega) = W_{11}(\omega)W_{22}(\omega) - \mid W_{12}(\omega) \mid^2 .$$

and

$$Z_{opt}(t) = (C_0/\pi) \, Re \int_0^{\infty} G_i(\omega)Y_{mi}(\omega)S_2^*(\omega) \exp(j\omega(t-t_0))d\omega \qquad (7)$$

where

$$Y_{mi}(\omega) = -Y_1(\omega)g_i(\omega) + Y_2(\omega)g_i^{-1}(\omega) \qquad (8)$$
$$g_i(\omega) = [W_{12}^*(\omega)/W_{11}(\omega)]^{1/2} \qquad (9)$$

and

$$G_i(\omega) = W_i(\omega)/\Delta(\omega)$$
$$W_i(\omega) = [W_{11}(\omega)W_{12}^*(\omega)]^{1/2}. \qquad (10)$$

In [4] it was suggested to construct the variable Z_{opt} with the help of a phase sensitive device which transforms the quadrature components according to (8). Then the receiver must measure only one quadrature component $Y_{mi}(t)$ (this can be done in a dual homodyne detection scheme [8]). However in spite of the fact that the product of amplification coefficients for quadrature components is equal to 1 this device must add noise to the output signal when an imaginary part of $g_i(\omega)$ is not zero [5] (cf. (8), (9)) and the added noise can be large for large phase of $g_i(\omega)$ (large dissipation in the system). Therefore a formal utilization of equations (8), (9) is not appropriate.

Let us suppose for simplicity that an external force is limited to the bandwidth $[\omega_1, \omega_2]$ and in this bandwidth the function $Re(W_{12}^*(\omega))$ does not change sign. Then in the limit of small dissipation one can obtain from (9), (10) the following equations

$$g_i(\omega) = g(\omega) = [|\ Re(W_{12}^*(\omega))\ |\ /W_{11}(\omega)]^{1/2} \tag{11}$$
$$W_i(\omega) = W(\omega) = [W_{11}(\omega)\ |\ Re(W_{12}^*(\omega))\ |]^{1/2}, \tag{12}$$

and in equation (8) the proper combination of quadrature components must be chosen according to the sign of $Re(W_{12}^*(\omega))$.

One can use equations (11) and (12) also with finite dissipation in the system but in this case the filtration procedure will be only quasioptimal. Actually according to equation (7) the receiver can be realized with two series filters: linear filter F_1 with transfer function

$$G(\omega) = W(\omega)/\Delta(\omega) \tag{13}$$

and concordant filter F_2 with transfer function

$$K(\omega) = S_2^*(\omega)\exp(-j\omega t_0) \tag{14}$$

A mixture of the signal and noise at the input of the linear filter F_1 has the following form

$$Y_m(\omega) = Y_1(\omega)g(\omega) + Y_2(\omega)g^{-1}(\omega) \tag{15}$$

where for definiteness we suppose that $Re(W_{12}^*(\omega)) < 0$. Linear transformation of the quadratures (15) can be made with the help of a phase sensitive device with appropriate dependence of amplification coefficient $g(\omega)$ on frequency. In this case this transformation can have zero additive (excess) noise because the function $g(\omega)$ is real [5].

Spectral characteristics of the signal S_{2f} and stationary gaussian noise n_2 at the output of the filter F_1 have the following form

$$S_{2f} = W_{11}S_2 \qquad W_n = W_{11}(\Delta + Im^2W_{12}) \tag{16}$$

Therefore the quasioptimal processing has an increased noise level with respect to the optimal procedure

$$W_n - (W_n)_{opt} = W_{11}Im^2W_{12} \tag{17}$$

Let us specialize the general expressions to an optical displacement sensor. In the simplest realization an optical sensor is a mirror attached to mechanical resonator and illuminated with coherent pump field.

Let the reflection coefficient of the mirror be $r \approx -1$. Then one can obtain [4,7]

$$W_{11}(\omega) = N_0, \qquad W_{22}(\omega) = N_0 + (2A_0k)^2 \mid G(\omega) \mid^2 (N_\mu + \lambda^2 N_0),$$
$$W_{12}(\omega) = -N_0(2A_0k)\lambda G^*(\omega), \qquad S_2(\omega) = 2A_0kG(\omega)F_{s\omega}(\omega) \tag{18}$$

where $A_0 = (2P_0z_0/S)^{1/2}$ is the amplitude of coherent pump with power P_0, $N_0 = \hbar\omega_p z_0/(2S)$, $z_0 = 120\pi$ [ohm] is the resistance of free space, S is the cross section of pump beam, $k = \omega_p/c$, $G(p) = \left[M(p^2 + 2\alpha p + \omega_\mu^2)\right]^{-1}$ is the mechanical oscillator transfer function, $p = d/dt$, $2\alpha = H/M$, $\omega_\mu^2 = K/M$; $\lambda = SA_0/(z_0c)$, M, K and H are dynamical parameters of the mechanical oscillator. The force $F(t)$ acting on the mechanical oscillator has the following form

$$F(t) = F_s(t) + F_\mu(t), \tag{19}$$

where $F_s(t)$ is the signal force and $F_\mu(t)$ is a zero mean white Gaussian process with covariance function (thermal noise of mechanical oscillator)

$$< F_\mu(t)F_\mu(t+\tau) >= N_\mu\delta(\tau), \tag{20}$$

and $F_{s\omega}(\omega)$ is the spectrum of the signal $F_s(t)$.

Then instead of equations (16) one has

$$S_{2f}(\omega) = 2N_0A_0kG(\omega)F_{s\omega}(\omega)$$
$$W_n(\omega) = N_0(N_0^2[1 + (2A_0k)^2 Im^2 G(\omega)\lambda^2] + N_0(2A_0k)^2 \mid G(\omega) \mid^2 N_\mu) \tag{21}$$

The signal $S_{2f} + n_2$ at the output of the filter F_1 can be used as input for force reconstruction. Let a transfer function for the inverse filter be the following

$$K_1 = [N_0 2A_0kG(\omega)]^{-1} \tag{22}$$

Then at the output of such filter one has an additive mixture of the signal F and gaussian noise f with spectral density

$$W_f = W_n \mid K_1 \mid^2 = N_\mu + N_0[1 + (2A_0k)^2 Im^2 G(\omega)\lambda^2]/((2A_0k)^2 \mid G(\omega) \mid^2) \tag{23}$$

The maximum likelihood estimate $\hat{F}$ of unknown signal F is defined by the following expression [6]

$$\hat{F} = \pi^{-1} Re \int_{\omega_1}^{\omega_2} (F + f)\exp(j\omega t)d\omega \tag{24}$$

If we suppose that $\omega_1 \gg \omega_\mu$ then for large A_0 one can obtain a dispersion of the estimate $\hat{F}$

$$\sigma_F^2 \approx \pi^{-1}N_\mu(\omega_2 - \omega_1) + 2\alpha^2\pi^{-1}N_0\lambda^2(\omega_1^{-1} - \omega_2^{-1}) \tag{25}$$

Therefore the quasioptimal algorithm of filtration has an additional (excessive) noise which increases in the limit of large pump power and the accuracy of force reconstruction depends not only on the thermal noise of mechanical oscillator N_μ (as in [4]) but also on the vacuum fluctuations N_0. However the second term in (25) is proportional to the second power of α and the first term only linearly proportional to α so for sufficiently small dissipation of mechanical oscillator α the result of [4] will be valid.

494

It is worth mentioning that the supposition that an external force is limited to the bandwidth $[\omega_1, \omega_2]$ and in this bandwidth the function $Re(W_{12}^*(\omega))$ does not change sign is not important for results (16), (17) and (25). When a point at which $Re(W_{12}^*(\omega))$ changes its sign is inside the frequency bandwidth of external force then one has to divide the entire frequency bandwidth into parts where the sign of $Re(W_{12}^*(\omega))$ is constant. Then for each of these parts the considered algorithm is valid. Such division can be made with the help of passive filters at frequencies about ω_p without excessive noise because all frequency intervals will be nonoverlaping.

ACKNOWLEDGMENTS

This work was supported by Fundamental Natural Science Competitive Center of Russian Federation State Committee of Higher Education.

REFERENCES

[1] C. M. Caves, K. S. Thorne, R. W. P. Drever, V. D. Sandberg, M. Zimmerman: Rev. Mod. Phys., **52**, 341 (1980).

[2] V. V. Kulagin, V. N. Rudenko: JETP, **94**, 54 (1988).

[3] V. V. Kulagin, V. N. Rudenko: Nuovo Cimento C, **10C** 601 (1987).

[4] A. V. Gusev, V. V. Kulagin, Appl. Phys. B, to be published.

[5] C. M. Caves: Phys. Rev. D, **26** 1817 (1982).

[6] H. Van Treece: Detection, estimation and modulation theory. Plenum Press, N.Y.-L., 1968.

[7] A. V. Gusev, V. V. Kulagin: In Proc. of the Fourt Int. Conf. on Squeezed States and Uncertainty Relations, Taiyuan, Shanxi, P. R. China, June 5-8, 1995, NASA Conference Publ. 3322, 427 (1996).

[8] J. H. Shapiro: IEEE J. Quantum Electronics, **QE-21** 237 (1985).

SQUEEZED STATE GENERATION IN THE PROCESS OF LIGHT INTERACTION WITH A SYSTEM OF FREE ELECTRONS

V. V. Kulagin[1] and V. A. Cherepenin[2]

[1] Sternberg Astronomical Institute, Moscow State University
Universitetsky prospect 13, 119899, Moscow, Russia
Telephone: (095)939-5327, e-mail: KUL@SAI.MSU.SU
[2] Institute of Radioengineering and Electronics RAS
Mohovaya 18, 103907, Moscow, Russia
e-mail: CHER@CPLIRE.RU

Production of squeezed states in the process of light interaction with a system of a large number of free electronic mirrors is considered. Coherent cooperative processes play an important role in this case. A squeezing coefficient is estimated; for a large number of electronic mirrors it can be considerably larger than 1. An effective bandwidth of squeezing is evaluated.

The possibility of generation of squeezed state light with large squeezing coefficient is of great importance for modern experimental physics [1-6]. Systems of free electrons have great promise for squeezed state generation because of small dissipation and high nonlinearity in the electron beam. In [7] the possibility of squeezed state generation during the process of light reflection from a system of successive free electronic mirrors was demonstrated. However the expression for the squeezing coefficient was obtained only for the case of a small number of electronic mirrors in the system. In this case the squeezing can not be large because of contamination of the output field by equilibrium vacuum fluctuations. The goal of this paper is to estimate the squeezing in the case of a large number of electronic mirrors when coherent cooperative effects can play an important role in the dynamics of the system.

Let us consider firstly the statistics of an electromagnetic wave reflected from an ordinary moving mirror with amplitude reflection coefficient r_m smaller than 1 and transmission coefficient t_m. One can take the incident field from left side and the reflected field in the following form [7]

$$
\begin{aligned}
E_i &= (A + a_1) \cdot \cos \omega_p (t - x/c) + a_2 \cdot \sin \omega_p (t - x/c) \\
E_r &= (B + b_1) \cdot \cos \omega_p (t + x/c) + b_2 \cdot \sin \omega_p (t + x/c)
\end{aligned}
\tag{1}
$$

where A and B are mean amplitude values of the incident and reflected pump waves, and a_1, a_2, b_1 and b_2 are operators of quadrature components. Then for b_1 and b_2 one has [7] (we suppose for simplicity that $r_m > 0$ and $t_m = -it_0, t_0 > 0$)

$$b_1(\omega) = r_m a_1(\omega) - \mid t_m \mid d_2(\omega)$$
$$b_2(\omega) = r_m(a_2(\omega) + 2\omega_p X(\omega)A/c) + \mid t_m \mid d_1(\omega) \tag{2}$$

where d_1 and d_2 are operators of quadrature components of the field in vacuum state which falls on the mirror from the back side (from the right), and X is a coordinate operator of the mirror. For correlation matrix of spectral densities of a_1 and a_2 one has [5,7] (we suppose this wave in coherent state)

$$< a_1^+(\omega)a_1(\omega') + a_1(\omega')a_1^+(\omega) > /2 = < a_2^+(\omega)a_2(\omega') + a_2(\omega')a_2^+(\omega) > /2 = N_0\delta(\omega - \omega')$$
$$< a_1(\omega')a_2(\omega) > = < a_1^+(\omega')a_2(\omega) > \approx 0 \tag{3}$$

where $N_0 = \pi\hbar\omega_p/(cS)$ is spectral density of vacuum fluctuations, S being the cross section of laser beam . The correlation matrix of spectral densities of quadratures d_1 and d_2 also satisfies eq.(3).

In the linear approximation a fluctuating component of radiation pressure force acting on the mirror due to the incident wave is the following

$$F_p = Sr_m^2 A a_1/(2\pi). \tag{4}$$

Then for the coordinate of the mirror $X(\omega)$ one can obtain

$$X(\omega) = SAr_m^2 a(\omega)/(2\pi L(\omega)) \tag{5}$$

where $L(\omega)$ is "force-displacement" transfer function for the mirror. For the quadratures of the reflected wave one has from (2) and (5)

$$b_1(\omega) = r_m a_1(\omega) - \mid t_m \mid d_2(\omega)$$
$$b_2(\omega) = r_m(a_2(\omega) + \rho(\omega)a_1(\omega)) + \mid t_m \mid d_1(\omega) \tag{6}$$

where the correlation coefficient $\rho(\omega)$ has the following form

$$\rho(\omega) = S\omega_p A^2 r_m^2/(\pi c L(\omega)) = 8\omega_p W r_m^2/(c^2 L(\omega)) \tag{7}$$

and W is the power of a laser emitting the incident wave.

The correlation matrix of quadratures spectral densities for reflected wave has the following form according to (6) (in usual notation [8] (cf. (3))

$$<\mid b_1(\omega) \mid^2> = N_0 \qquad <\mid b_2(\omega) \mid^2> = N_0(1 + r_m^2 \mid \rho(\omega) \mid^2)$$
$$< b_1(\omega)b_2^+(\omega) > = < b_1^+(\omega)b_2(\omega) >^* = N_0 r_m^2 \rho^*(\omega) \tag{8}$$

Introducing new quadrature components "rotated" by an angle ϕ with respect to the old quadratures

$$E_r = (B_1 + \tilde{b}_1) \cdot \cos(\omega_p(t + x/c) + \phi) + (B_2 + \tilde{b}_2) \cdot \sin(\omega_p(t + x/c) + \phi) \tag{9}$$

and choosing the phase ϕ so as to maximize the spectral density of $\tilde{b}_2$ and minimize of $\tilde{b}_1$, one can obtain from (6), (8) and (9) (we suppose for simplicity that correlation coefficient $\rho(\omega)$ is real, which corresponds to a mechanical system with extremely small dissipation)

$$<| \ \tilde{b}_1(\omega) \ |^2> = (1 - r_m^2 \rho^2 ((1 + 4/\rho^2)^{1/2} - 1)/2) \cdot N_0$$
$$<| \ \tilde{b}_2(\omega) \ |^2> = (1 + r_m^2 \rho^2 ((1 + 4/\rho^2)^{1/2} + 1)/2) \cdot N_0 \tag{10}$$

Therefore the spectral density of quadrature $\tilde{b}_1$ is smaller than the spectral density of a quadrature in the vacuum state N_0, and $\tilde{b}_2$ is larger, i.e. the reflected wave is in the squeezed state. The optimal phase is defined by an expression

$$tg2\phi = 2\rho(\omega) \tag{11}$$

As one can see from equations (10) that the product of the spectral densities of quadrature components $\tilde{b}_1$ and $\tilde{b}_2$ is larger that N_0^2 for $r_m < 1$; therefore the state of the reflected wave does not have "minimum uncertainties":

$$<| \ \tilde{b}_1(\omega) \ |^2><| \ \tilde{b}_2(\omega) \ |^2> = N_0^2(1 + r_m^2 \rho^2 (1 - r_m^2)) \tag{12}$$

If the value of correlation coefficient ρ is large enough (that is the condition of large squeezing) then the product (12) will be considerably larger than N_0^2.

For a squeezing coefficient (which one can define as the ratio of spectral densities of quadrature component in coherent and squeezed states) one has

$$g = (1 - r_m^2 \rho^2 ((1 + 4/\rho^2)^{1/2} - 1)/2)^{-1} \tag{13}$$

In the limit of large pump power W the value $\rho \gg 1$ and for squeezing coefficient one can obtain

$$g_{\max} = (1 - r_m^2 + r_m^2/\rho^2)^{-1} \tag{14}$$

Therefore the maximum squeezing is limited by the equilibrium vacuum fluctuations d_1 and d_2 from the back (right-hand) side of the mirror. These fluctuations admix in the reflected wave and degrade the squeezing. The lower the reflection coefficient, the more the vacuum fluctuations pass through the mirror and the weaker the squeezing of the reflected wave. This is also the explanation of equality (12).

Let us specialize the general expressions to the case of the mirror consisting of the large number of consecutive electronic mirrors arranged one after another. Let each electronic mirror have a thickness l_m and a constant density of electrons N. Then for effective index of refraction one has [9]

$$n = 1 - \alpha = 1 - \omega_c^2/(2\omega_p^2), \tag{15}$$

where the critical frequency is $\omega_c^2 = 4\pi N e^2/m_e$ (e and m_e are the charge and the mass of an electron), and ω_p is the frequency of incident beam. Choosing the mirror thickness l_m so as to maximize the amplitude reflection coefficient r_1 for the mirror

$$l_m = \lambda_p/4 + l\lambda_p/2 \qquad l = 0, 1, 2 \ldots \tag{16}$$

one can obtain [9]

$$r_1 = (1 - n^2)/(1 + n^2) \qquad t_1 = 2ni/(1 + n^2) \tag{17}$$

where t_1 is the amplitude transmission coefficient for electron mirror. Let us consider a Fabry-Perot interferometer consisting of two such electronic mirrors. Then for reflection r_2 and transmission t_2 coefficients of the Fabry-Perot interferometer one can obtain

$$r_2 = (1 - n^4)/(1 + n^4) \qquad t_2 = -2n^2i/(1 + n^4) \tag{18}$$

where the distance between the mirrors of Fabry-Perot interferometer is chosen according to equation (16) so as to maximize the reflection coefficient r_2.

Let us suppose that another Fabry-Perot interferometer has mirrors with coefficients r_2 and t_2 (each mirror consists of two electronic mirrors). Then for reflection r_4 and transmission t_4 coefficients of that interferometer one has

$$r_4 = (1 - n^8)/(1 + n^8) \qquad t_4 = -2n^4i/(1 + n^8) \tag{19}$$

where the length is also optimized according to (16). One can continue to increase the number of electronic mirrors in the mirror of the overall Fabry-Perot interferometer. Then for a mirror of interferometer consisting of 2^{k-1} electronic mirrors (the whole number of electronic mirrors in the interferometer is equal to $m = 2^k$) one has

$$r_m = (1 - n^{2m})/(1 + n^{2m}) \qquad t_m = -2n^m i/(1 + n^{2m}) \tag{20}$$

where the distances between all electronic mirrors are equal and defined according to equation (16). Therefore even for $n \approx 1$ one can take so large a number of electronic mirrors m that the reflection coefficient of the system will be $r_m \approx 1$. It is worth mentioning that in this case the total reflection coefficient r_m is not simply the sum of reflection coefficients of all electronic mirrors as was in [7] and therefore coherent cooperative effects are important in the dynamics of the system.

Let us consider the radiation pressure force acting on the mirrors in the system. In strict calculations one has to take into consideration decrease of the amplitude of pump wave when it propagates from one electronic mirror to another inside the system (existence of some kind of skin effect). In this case the radiation pressure force is smaller for inner mirrors and larger for outer and the corresponding displacements are also larger for outer mirrors. This effect causes the decoherence of the waves reflecting from different electronic mirrors. However if the real displacements of the mirrors are smaller than the length of the pump lightwave (that is a good approximation for not very large amplitude A of the pump wave) then for order-of-magnitude estimates this effect can be neglected and one can consider that the displacements of all electronic mirrors in the skin layer are the same. Therefore for estimation of the radiation pressure force acting on the system of electronic mirrors one can use the expression (4).

A mass M of the moving mirror is the mass of the skin layer. The number of electronic mirrors in the skin layer is about (cf. (15), (17)) α^{-1} [7]; therefore the mass M of the skin layer is the following (we suppose that the thickness of one electronic mirror is minimal and equal to $\lambda/4$ according to (16))

$$M \approx M_1/\alpha = SNm_e\lambda/(4\alpha) \tag{21}$$

where M_1 is the mass of one electronic mirror. As one can see from (15) and (21) the mass M of the moving electronic mirror is independent of the density of electrons N because if N is decreasing then the thickness of skin layer is increasing. It is worth mentioning that for order-of-magnitude estimates one can take $M = mM_1$ because the dependence of required number of electronic mirrors m on r_m is logarithmic (cf. (20))

$$m \approx (2\alpha)^{-1} \cdot \ln((1 + r_m)/(1 - r_m)) \tag{22}$$

The correlation coefficient from (7) is the following

$$\rho(\omega) = 8\omega_p W r_m^2/(c^2 M(\omega_\mu^2 - \omega^2)) \tag{23}$$

where we assume that the "force-displacement" transfer function $L(\omega)$ for the electronic mirror can be taken in the following form

$$L(\omega) = M(\omega_\mu^2 - \omega^2) \tag{24}$$

Here ω_μ is the equivalent frequency of mechanical oscillations of electronic mirror in a direction perpendicular to its surface. The value of ω_μ is defined by the real confining fields in the system. Let us make some numerical estimates. For electron density N it is useful to take two different values: the value $N_p = 10^{13}\mathrm{cm}^{-3}$ that is realistic at present time and the value $N_f = 10^{17}\mathrm{cm}^{-3}$ that can be achieved in future. Then for an effective index of refraction one can obtain: $n_p = 1 - 1.1 \cdot 10^{-9}$ and $n_f = 1 - 1.1 \cdot 10^{-5}$. From equation (22) one can estimate a required number of electronic mirrors: $m_p = 2.7 \cdot 10^9$ and $m_f = 2.7 \cdot 10^5$ where we assume that the reflection coefficient r_m must be about 0.995, which gives for the maximum squeezing $g_{\max}$ according to equation (14) the value about 100. Then for the whole thickness $L = m\lambda/2$ of electronic mirror one can obtain the values $L_p = 700\mathrm{m}$ and $L_f = 7\mathrm{cm}$. The first value is rather unrealistic at present for technical realization but for future generations of electron accelerators the value L_f seems appropriate.

The situation is more promising for the pump wave in microwave band. Then the coefficient α in (15) increases by 5-7 orders of magnitude and correspondingly the required number of electronic mirrors m drastically decreases. However the problem of excessive noise in the microwave band requires a special investigation. Let us estimate in conclusion the effective bandwidth of squeezing. For correlation coefficient ρ one can obtain from equation (23)

$$\mid \rho \mid = 3 \cdot 10^{15}/\mid \omega^2 - \omega_\mu^2 \mid \tag{25}$$

where the frequency is in $s^{-1}, r_m^2 = 0.99, S = 1\mathrm{mm}^2, \lambda_p = 5 \cdot 10^{-5}\mathrm{cm}$ and $W = 10\mathrm{Wt}$. If we assume that ω_μ is not very large then a bandwidth of squeezing (the frequency bandwidth in which $1 - r_m^2 > r_m^2/\rho^2$) from (14) and (23) is the following: $\omega < 1.7 \cdot 10^7\mathrm{s}^{-1}$ (2.7 MHz), which is large enough for different applications [5,6].

It is worth mentioning that the required number of electronic mirrors can be decreased also with the help of optical resonators. In this case the required length L_p can be decreased to a reasonable value of several meters.

Practical realization of the considered scheme of squeezed state generation depends on the ability of creation of the electron beams with required configuration: a long sequence of bunches with high electron density in a bunch and small dispersion of electron velocities. These requirements are rather different from that for free electron lasers where the quality of the bunches does not play a significant role. Therefore the present installations of free electron lasers are not appropriate without modifications for the considered scheme of squeezed state generation.

ACKNOWLEDGMENT

This work was supported by the Russian Fund for Fundamental research (grant No. $95 - 02 - 04476a$).

REFERENCES

[1] Yuen, H. P., 1976, *Phys. Rev.* **A13**, 2226.

[2] Walls, D. F., 1983, *Nature (L)*, **306**, 141.

[3] Braginsky, V. B., Vorontsov, Yu. I., Thorne, K. S., (1980) *Science*, **209**, 547.

[4] Caves, C. M., Thorne, K. S., Drever, R. W. P. et. al., 1980, *Rev. Mod. Phys.*, **52**, 341.

[5] Kulagin, V. V., Rudenko, V. N., 1988, *Sov. Phys. JETP*, **67**, 677.

[6] Shapiro, J. H., 1980, *Opt. Lett.*, **8**, 351.

[7] Kulagin, V. V., Cherepenin, V. A., *Pis'ma Zh. Eksp. Teor. Fiz.*, **63**, 160 (1996).

[8] Rytov, S. M., 1976, Introduction to Statistical Radio Physics [in Russian] (Nauka, Moscow).

[9] Born, M., Wolf, E., 1968, Principles of Optics (Pergamon Press, N.Y.-L.).

DIODE STRUCTURE FOR GENERATION OF SUB-POISSONIAN PHOTON FLUXES BY STARK-EFFECT BLOCKADE OF EMISSIONS

Masahide Kobayashi, Hiroyuki Sumitomo, Yutaka Kadoya,
Masamichi Yamanishi, and Masahito Ueda

Department of Physical Electronics, Faculty of Engineering
Hiroshima University
Kagamiyama 1-chome, Higashihiroshima 739 Japan

By a new scheme for the generation of sub-Poissonian photon fluxes named quantum-confined Stark effect (QCSE) blockade, it is predicted that sub-Poissonian photons at 10-photon levels can be generated with a small size semiconductor light emitter driven even by a constant voltage source. We demonstrate how to design a semiconductor diode for the proposed scheme. As a result, it is shown that a strict adjustment of the doping concentration in the p- and n-doped widegap regions is not always required. Both stray capacitance and leakage conductance are unavoidable in such a small size device, but are pointed out not to affect the sub-Poissonian photon generation because of the constant voltage operation.

1. INTRODUCTION

At present day, the performance of light communication systems and the sensitivity of various measurements have been limited by the standard quantum limit (SQL) determined by Heisenberg's uncertain principle. Hence, the generation of nonclassical light, such as photon-number squeezed states and quadrature-phase squeezed states, has been recently attracting much attention. Among a variety of the schemes for nonclassical light generation, the generation of sub-Poissonian photon-states using semiconductor devices is especially attractive because of the simplicity of experimental arrangement, low energy consumption and the possibility of a large degree of noise suppression. Sub-Poissonian photon states have been generated using semiconductor lasers [1] or light-emitting diodes (LEDs) [2] [3] driven by high-impedance constant current sources. Specifically, the LED-mode operation is crucially important for the realization of small photon numbers (≤ 10) for photon communication. This is because the pump current ~ 16 nA required to generate for instance ten photons in 100 psec pulse width is below the fundamental lowest threshold current for the onset of lasing [4]. Thus, the generation of sub-Poissonian photons in LEDs has an engineering significance from the standpoint of their application to extremely low energy consumption and errorless communication.

However, in such low-current (≤ 16nA), high frequency (≥ 1GHz) regimes, a high impedance (≥ 1MΩ) required for the constant current operation would be unfortunately

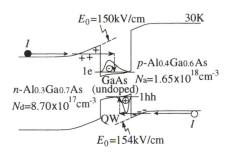

Figure 1. Energy-band diagram of a semiconductor heterojunction diode designed for generation of sub-Poissonian photon states even under the constant voltage operation[6].

shunted by a (even small) stray capacitance or the vacuum impedance. Hence the generation of sub-Poissonian photons by pump control in such extreme regimes is very hard to realize unless individual pump events could be regulated by using, for example, Coulomb blockade and the effects of quantum confinement [5]. The schemes proposed in ref. [5], however, are not easy to implement in practice because of the very low device temperature (<1K) and the extremely small device size inherent to single-electron devices. In this view, any new idea by which sub-Poissonian photon states can be generated without recourse to pump-control would be urgently required.

A novel scheme for the generation of sub-Poissonian photon fluxes named quantum-confined Stark effect (QCSE) blockade of photon emissions in a tailor-made semiconductor diode driven by a constant voltage source has been recently proposed to overcome the problems mentioned above, accompanied by the constant current operation [6]. The scheme relies on emission control based on automodulation of the bimolecule-recombination lifetime due to QCSE and recharging effects characteristic of the constant-voltage operation of a semiconductor p-i-n junction diode. In fact, both photon and pump noise can be drastically suppressed to below SQL level by the QCSE blockade. Further, this scheme allows us to generate sub-Poissonian photons whose number $\sim$10 is smaller than that of electron-hole pairs $\sim$100 in the diode.

In this paper, we shall be primarily concerned with realistic design of diode structure by which feasibility of the QCSE blockade becomes significant. The influences of stray capacitance and leakage conductance on the sub-Poissonian photon generation will be discussed.

2. DIODE STRUCTURE

In order to make the emission control (QCSE blockade) scheme realistic, we design the p-i-n junction diode with a quantum well (QW) structure. The band diagram of our diode is shown in Fig. 1. Henceforth, the subscript 0 denotes the average values of physical quantities. The diode is designed in such a way that by a forward bias junction voltage at T$\leq$30K, an injection current density of 160 A/cm^2 due primarily to tunneling process through the potential barriers is supplied to maintain high density stationary electron-hole pairs of 10^{12} cm^{-2} in the QW, whose thickness is L_z (typically $\sim$180Å), with a small area $S = N_0/10^{12} = 10^{-10}$ cm^2 and with an assumed recombination lifetime of $\tau_{r0} = 1$ nsec. It should be noted that the forward bias voltage, 1.73V, is chosen to be substantially below the flat-band voltage, 1.98V, allowing the presence of the high electric fields. The high density polarized pairs in the QW partially screen

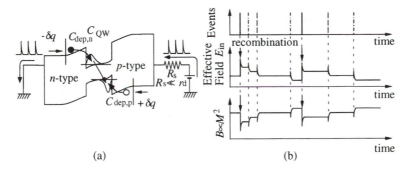

(a)   (b)

Figure 2. (a) Diode connected to a voltage source through a very small resistance R_s; (b) schematic drawings of time evolution of recombination (solid lines) and electron-pump (dashed lines) and hole-pump (dash-dotted lines) events, where E_{in} is the effective electric field in the QW, and B the recombination coefficient ($\propto M^2$) under the constant-voltage operation[6].

the external electric field $E_0 \sim 150$ kV/cm with a depolarization field $E_{d0} \sim 80$ kV/cm. In this particular case, the doping concentration in the n- and p-type regions are determined to make the average electron and hole populations equal, $N_0 = P_0 \sim 100$. The radiative recombination rate R is assumed to be bimolecular, $R = BPN$ where B, P and N denote the recombination coefficient, hole and electron populations in the QW, respectively. The assumption of the free electron-hole pair recombination would be justified since two dimensional excitonic states cease to exist because of complete screening of the excitonic Coulomb potential within the QW plane by the high density electron-hole plasma [7].

3.   QCSE BLOCKADE

Suppose that the tailor-made diode shown in Fig. 1 is driven by a voltage source V_0 through a series resistance R_s, which is much smaller than the differential input resistance of the diode r_d, as shown in Fig. 2(a). We are concerned with the relatively large number of electron-hole pairs, for instance, $P_0 = N_0 \sim 100$. Hence, we can easily ignore the quantum charge fluctuations on the junctions for almost any values of R_s and R_t as $R_s, R_t \gg (h/2\pi e^2)/(N_0 + 1/2) \sim 40\Omega$, where R_t ($\sim 1 M\Omega$ in the present case) is the tunneling resistance at the potential barrier.

In the constant voltage operation, the regulation mechanism consists of three stochastic processes as follows [6]: (i) The pump event of one electron produces a positive excess charge $+e$ in the n-side depletion layer and negative one $-e$ in the QW. This pump induced charge dipole increases the electric field in the n-side depletion layer and the electron localized region of the QW, pushing the electron wave function toward the n-side potential barrier. The pump-induced increase of the charging energy of the n-side junction slightly suppresses subsequent electron pump events (Coulomb blockade of pump events) [8]. Similarly, dynamics induced by hole pump events take place around the p-side potential barrier. (ii) One electron-hole pair in the QW disappears when a spontaneous photon emission event occurs as shown in Fig. 2(b), as a result of decrease of the depolarization field leading to a step-wise increase of the electric field E_{in} around the center of the QW, and in turn decreasing the recombination rate because of reduction of the overlap integral between the electron and hole wave function in the QW. Hence, subsequent photon emissions are suppressed (QCSE blockade of emission events). (iii) The electron- and hole-pump and recombination events induce current spikes in the external circuit, which quickly recover the voltage drop across the diode. And, the charges due to ionized dopants in the depletion layers are diminished by the external current. The charging processes consequently decrease the electric field E_{in} and recover the recombination rate as shown in Fig. 2(b).

One of the most important points involved in the present scheme is that both the *QCSE blockade of emission events and Coulomb blockade of pump events can survive even under a constant voltage operation*. This is because the diode can be viewed as consisting of three series-connected capacitors: the capacitance $C_{dep,n}$ in the n-side depletion layer, the capacitance $C_{dep,p}$ in the p-side depletion layer, and the effective capacitance C_{QW} due to the polarized electron-hole pairs in the QW, as illustrated in Fig. 2(a) so that the electric charge carried by each current spike is a *fraction of the elementary charge*, i.e., $\delta q_e = (C_t/C_{dep,n})e, \delta q_r = (C_t/C_{QW})e$, or $\delta q_h = (C_t/C_{dep,p})e < e$ where, $1/C_t = 1/C_{dep,n} + 1/C_{QW} + 1/C_{dep,p}$. The effective capacitance C_{QW} is given by

$$C_{QW} = e/\int_0^{L_z} \delta E(z)dz, \tag{1}$$

where $\delta E(z)$ is the increment of the internal field induced by the annihilation of one electron-hole pair in the QW. The fractional charge transfer precisely induced at each stochastic event is caused by extremely small displacement of large number of carriers as a whole (collective motion of carriers in the external circuit). Note that the fractional charges may not be masked by thermal noise due to the series resistance R_s if $(4k_BT/r_d)(R_s/r_d) \ll 2eI_0$ as in the present case, $R_s \ll r_d$. Thus, the reduction of the bimolecule recombination rate (the coefficient $B \propto M^2 = | < \phi_{1e}|\phi_{1hh} > |^2$) induced by an emission event is expected to suppress the subsequent emission events until the recombination rate B is recovered by pump event-induced charge transfers. Similarly, the reduction of the electron- or hole-pump rate by an electron- or hole-pump event is also not completely recovered by the pump induced fractional charge transfer δq_e or δq_h.

4. MONTE CARLO SIMULATION

Before the demonstration of numerical result of noise spectra, let us summarize generalized expressions for recombination- and pump-rate. The radiative recombination rate is given by

$$R(t) = B(t)P(t)N(t), \tag{2}$$

where

$$P(t) = P_0 + \sum_j \Delta P_{pj}(t) - \sum_k \Delta N_{rk}(t), \tag{3}$$

$$N(t) = N_0 + \sum_i \Delta N_{pi}(t) - \sum_k \Delta N_{rk}(t), \tag{4}$$

$$B(t) = B_0 \left(1 - c_e K_B \frac{\sum_i \Delta N_{pi}(t)}{N_0} - c_h K_B \frac{\sum_j \Delta P_{pj}(t)}{P_0} \right.$$
$$\left. -c_r K_B \frac{\frac{1}{N_0} + \frac{1}{P_0}}{2} \sum_k \Delta N_{rk}(t) + K_B \frac{\frac{1}{N_0} + \frac{1}{P_0}}{2} \frac{\int^t(i_e + i_h + i_r)dt'}{e} \right). \tag{5}$$

In the expression for $B(t)$, K_B represents the linearized response of the B-coefficient to external fields in the n- and p-side barriers, $E_{\text{ext},n}$ and $E_{\text{ext},p}$ for the fixed carrier populations, $P_0 \neq N_0$ in general and is given by

$$K_B = -\frac{2N_0 P_0}{B_0(N_0 + P_0)} \frac{e}{\epsilon S} \left(\frac{\partial B}{\partial E_{\text{ext},n}} + \frac{\partial B}{\partial E_{\text{ext},p}} \right) \tag{6}$$

The coefficients c_e, c_h and c_r are all positive and given by

$$c_e = -\frac{N_0}{B_0} \left(\frac{\partial B}{\partial N} + \frac{e}{\epsilon S} \frac{\partial B}{\partial E_{\text{ext},n}} \right) / K_B, \tag{7}$$

$$c_h = -\frac{P_0}{B_0} \left(\frac{\partial B}{\partial P} + \frac{e}{\epsilon S} \frac{\partial B}{\partial E_{\text{ext},p}} \right) / K_B, \tag{8}$$

$$c_r = \frac{2P_0 N_0}{B_0(P_0 + N_0)} \left(\frac{\partial B}{\partial N} + \frac{\partial B}{\partial P} \right) / K_B. \tag{9}$$

Obviously, they satisfy the following relation to guarantee the stability of the device operation,

$$\frac{c_e}{N_0} + \frac{c_h}{P_0} + \frac{\frac{1}{N_0} + \frac{1}{P_0}}{2} c_r = \frac{\frac{1}{N_0} + \frac{1}{P_0}}{2}. \tag{10}$$

The electron pump rate is described by [8]

$$R_{\text{pump},e} = R_{p0} \exp \left(-r_e \sum_i \Delta N_{\text{pi}}(t) + r_e \int^t [I(t')/e] dt' \right). \tag{11}$$

The pump rate is characterized by the relaxation time constant of the n-side junction τ_{te} or the inverse cut-off frequency for Coulomb blockade Ω_{ce}^{-1}, i.e., $\tau_{\text{te}} = 1/\Omega_{\text{ce}} = e/r_e I_0 = \tau_{r0}(N_0 + P_0)/2r_e N_0 P_0$ where τ_{r0} is the average recombination lifetime, $\tau_{r0} = 2/B_0(N_0 + P_0)$. Also, the parameter r_e represents the strength of the Coulomb blockade for electron pump events, given by

$$r_e = \frac{8}{3} \frac{e\sqrt{m_e^* \epsilon / N_d}}{\hbar C_{\text{dep},n}}, \tag{12}$$

for a triangular potential barrier at low temperature (i.e., $k_B T \ll$ Fermi energy of electrons in the n-type region) [9], where m_e^* and N_d denote the electron effective mass and doping density in the n-type barrier layer. The hole pump rate is described by a similar expression characterized by r_h, namely, Ω_{ch}^{-1}.

4.1. GENERATION OF SUB-POISSONIAN PHOTON FLUXES UNDER CONSTANT VOLTAGE OPERATION

Electrons (holes) injected into the QW are thermally equilibrated within a short time ~ 1 psec in the conduction (valence) bands [7]. Hence, we can confirm the reality of generation of sub-Poissonian photon states based on the QCSE blockade of photon emissions by applying a Monte Carlo method which stochastically simulates pump and radiative recombination processes.

Figure 3 shows the results of Monte Carlo simulations for noise power spectra of photon fluxes and single (electron or hole) and total (sum of electron and hole) pump events in a diode with the simplest combination of physical parameters (see the caption of Fig. 3) driven by a constant voltage source ($R_s = R_t/100$).

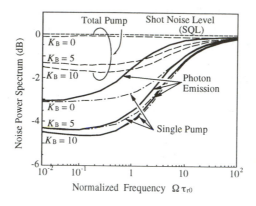

Figure 3. Noise power spectra of photon fluxes and total (sum of electron and hole) and single (electron or hole) pump events in diodes driven by constant-voltage sources ($R_s = R_t/100$) for values of the parameter which characterizes the QCSE blockade, $K_B = 0, 5$, and 10. For $K_B = 0$, the capacitors are assumed to be $C_{dep,n} = C_{dep,p}$ and $C_{QW} = \infty$, which means the absence of polarization of electron and hole wave functions in the QW. For $K_B = 5$ and 10, the three capacitors are reasonably assumed to be equal, $C_{dep,n} = C_{dep,p} = C_{QW}$. The remaining parameters are commonly taken to be $P_0 = N_0 = 100$, $\Omega_{ce}\tau_{r0} = \Omega_{ch}\tau_{r0} \equiv \Omega_c\tau_{r0}$ ($= r_e N_0 = r_h N_0$) $= 10, c_r = 2/3$, and $c_e = c_h = 1/6$ for all values of K_B[6].

In the case of no QCSE blockade $K_B=0$, both single pump events and photon emission events show 3 dB noise reduction at low frequencies because the diode forms the double barrier structure. Here, the capacitors are assumed to be $C_{dep,n} = C_{dep,p}$ and $C_{QW} = \infty$, which means the absence of the polarization of electron- and hole-wave functions in the QW. This noise reduction occurs as a result of the macroscopic Coulomb blockade for the pump events. However, the noise reduction is effective only at the low frequency regime $\Omega\tau_{r0} < 1$ (then, a large number of photons >100 are involved), and at the higher frequency regime, photon emission events show noise greater than that of single pump events. This is because each photon emission has the stochastic nature. The noise spectra of photons and electrons (or holes) coincide at the limit of low frequency regime because of the conservation of the particle number. Furthermore, the fact that the total pump noise is at SQL level indicates that an almost perfect correlation exists between electron- and hole-pump events.

On the other hand, when the QCSE blockade is switched on, $K_B = 5$ or 10, the noise power of single pump and photon emission events decrease with increasing values of K_B because the electrons and holes polarized in the QW form an effective capacitor. And, further noise reduction takes place compared with the case of no QCSE blockade ($K_B = 0$). Besides, the noise power spectra of photon emission and single pump events almost coincide over a wider spectral range. From this fact, we can conclude that the QCSE blockade makes both electrons and photons quiet. For $K_B = 10$, the noise of photon emission events is suppressed to 1.2 dB below SQL level even for only ten photons in a time interval 100 psec, despite the existence of a much greater number of electrons and holes ~ 100 in the QW.

4.2. THE INFLUENCE OF CHANGE IN DOPING CONCENTRATION ON NOISE SUPPRESSION

When we actually try to make a semiconductor diode for the present purpose, it is questionable whether we can control very precisely values for the doping concentration for instance to be $N_d = 8.70 \times 10^{17} \text{cm}^{-3}$ and $N_a = 1.65 \times 10^{18} \text{cm}^{-3}$ (see Fig. 1). Furthermore, the physical parameters relevant to the QCSE- and Coulomb-blockade are uniquely determined once the doping concentration N_d and N_a and the bias current density I_0/S are given. Hence, the combination of the physical parameters used in the computation shown in Fig. 3 may not be allowed. In this view, it is important to examine how the noise suppression of photon emission events is influenced by changes of the doping concentration in a diode characterized by realistic parameters.

Figure 4 shows computed noise power spectra of photon emission events for realistic diode parameters actually estimated with eqs. (1), (6)–(9) and (12) for three kinds of doping concentration N_d ($4.35 \times 10^{17} \text{cm}^{-3}, 1.13 \times 10^{18} \text{cm}^{-3}$ and $1.48 \times 10^{18} \text{cm}^{-3}$) in the n-type region and a fixed doping concentration N_a ($1.65 \times 10^{18} \text{cm}^{-3}$) in the p-type region. The values of the physical parameters used in the Monte-Carlo simulations are listed in Table 1.

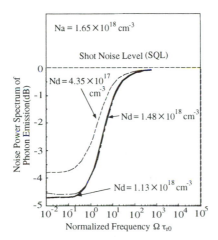

Figure 4. Noise power spectra of output photon fluxes in diodes with three kinds of doping concentration ($N_d = 4.35 \times 10^{17} \text{cm}^{-3}, 1.13 \times 10^{18} \text{cm}^{-3}$ and $1.48 \times 10^{18} \text{cm}^{-3}$) in the n-type region and a fixed doping concentration N_a ($= 1.65 \times 10^{18} \text{cm}^{-3}$) in the p-type region. The diodes are assumed to be driven by a constant voltage source ($R_s = R_t/100$). $N_d = 8.70 \times 10^{17} \text{cm}^{-3}$ and $N_a = 1.65 \times 10^{18} \text{cm}^{-3}$ is the doping concentration in the n- and p-type region resulting in $P_0 = N_0$. K_B estimated with eq. (6) ranges from 3.49 to 6.66 with increasing N_d from $4.35 \times 10^{17} \text{cm}^{-3}$ to $1.65 \times 10^{18} \text{cm}^{-3}$.

The electron population in the QW, N_0 and the electric field in the n-side depletion layer $E_{ext,n}$ increase with increasing doping concentration N_d in the n-type region. Obviously, the noise suppression of photon emission events is optimized at the specific value of the doping concentration, $N_d \sim 1.3 \times 10^{18} \text{cm}^{-3}$. It has been confirmed that the noise suppression is relatively insensitive to the change of the N_d. In fact, 30%-deviation of the doping concentration N_d from the optimum value is allowable. From this fact, we can conclude that a strict adjustment of N_d relative to N_a is not always required for the substantial noise suppression. This may allow us to in practice make the tailor-made diode for the present purpose, namely noise-suppression relying on the QCSE blockade.

Table 1. The values of the physical parameters used in the Monte-Carlo simulation

$N_a[\text{cm}^{-3}]$	1.65×10^{18}		
$N_d[\text{cm}^{-3}]$	4.35×10^{17}	1.13×10^{18}	1.48×10^{18}
N_0	58	123	155
P_0	100	96	96
$E_{\text{ext},n}[\text{kV/cm}]$	83.8	187	233
$E_{\text{ext},p}[\text{kV/cm}]$	150	151	149
$C_{\text{dep},n} : C_{\text{QW}} : C_{\text{dep},p}$	1 : 3.14 : 2.10	1 : 2.82 : 1.80	1 : 2.78 : 1.72
K_B	3.49	5.72	6.43
c_e	0.18	0.13	0.16
c_h	0.16	0.10	0.10
c_r	0.63	0.76	0.74
$r_e N_0$	4.55	21.5	33.8
$r_h P_0$	13.6	13.1	13.1

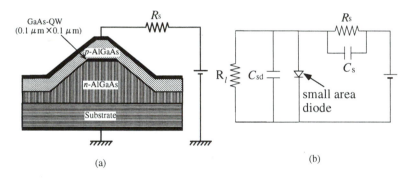

Figure 5. (a) A cross section of the diode with the QW (area $S = 10^{-10}\text{cm}^2$) designed for avoiding the nonradiative surface recombination. (b) The equivalent circuit of the diode connected to the large series-resistance R_s. C_s is the stray capacitance for R_s. C_{sd} and R_l are the parasitic elements which is parallel-connected to the diode.

4.3. DISCUSSION

To make the QCSE blockade significant (large K_B-value realized by a high carrier density, $\sim 10^{12}\text{cm}^{-2}$) at such low current regime, $I = 16\text{nA}$, the area of the QW should be very small, $S = 10^{-10}\text{cm}^2$. A possible diode structure is shown in Fig. 5(a). The QW structure on the top of n-AlGaAs mesa, would be fabricated by growth technique on patterned substrates [10]. However, the capacitance of the AlGaAs p-n junction C_{sd} outside the active junction involving the GaAs QW may be much larger than that of the active junction because of the large areal ratio of those junctions. A substantial leakage current flowing in the AlGaAs p-n junction may also be unavoidable. However, both the stray capacitance C_{sd} and leakage conductance $1/R_l$ may not seriously degrade the nose-suppression since the diode is driven by the constant voltage source. This is in marked contrast to the cases of high impedance noise suppression in which such parasitic elements result in, in general, degradation of the noise-suppression [1]- [3].

Another problem is thermal run-away of current flow in a diode directly driven by a constant voltage source. This can be easily solved by incorporating a large series resistance between the diode and voltage source, $R_s \gg (1/r_d + 1/R_l)^{-1} \sim 1\text{M}\Omega$. Such a large series resistance is shunted by stray capacitances C_s and C_{sd} as shown in Fig. 5(b) in the frequency range, $\Omega > 1/R_s(C_s + C_{sd}) = 100\text{kHz}$ for instance for $R_s = 10\text{M}\Omega$ and $C_s + C_{sd} = 1\text{pF}$. Hence, in the frequency range, the diode can be viewed as being driven by the constant voltage source.

5. CONCLUSION

By the new regulation mechanism named QCSE blockade of photon emission events, the generation of sub-Poissonian photons is possible even under the constant voltage operation. For realistic diode parameters, the noise suppression of photon emission events is relatively insensitive to change of the doping concentration. If the doping concentration can be set within $\pm 30\%$ centered at the optimized one ($N_d = 1.3 \times 10^{18}\text{cm}^{-3}$), the noise power of photon emission events is suppressed sufficiently ($\sim 4.5\text{dB}$ below SQL level) over a wide band ($>1\text{GHz}$). Also, the parasitic elements may not seriously degrade the noise suppression since the diode is driven by the constant voltage source. These facts may allow us in practice to make the tailor-made diode for the present purpose.

ACKNOWLEDGEMENTS

The work has been in part supported by Scientific Research Grant-in-Aids for the priority area of Mutual Quantum Manipulation of Radiation Field and Matter from the Ministry of Education, Science and Culture of Japan and by JST-CREST.

REFERENCES

[1] W. H. Richardson, S. Machida and Y. Yamamoto, Phys. Rev. Lett. **66**, 2867 (1991) and references therein.

[2] P. R. Tapster, J. G. Rarity and J. S. Satchell, Europhys. Lett. 4, 293 (1987).

[3] The 3 dB noise suppression over a wide bandwidth ($\sim 10\text{MHz}$) with LEDs has recently been observed by G. Shinozaki, T. Hirano, T. Kuga, and M. Yamanishi, contribution to the Conference at CLEO/Pacific Rim'95, Chiba, Japan, 1995, Abstract No. WG3.

[4] M. Yamanishi and Y. Lee, Phys. Rev. A **48**, 2534 (1993).

[5] A. Imamoglu, Y. Yamamoto, and P. Solomon, Phys. Rev. B **46**, 9555 (1992); A. Imamoglu and Y. Yamamoto, *ibid.* **46**, 15 982 (1992); Phys. Rev. Lett. **72** , 210 (1994).

[6] M. Yamanishi, K. Watanabe, N. Jikutani and M. Ueda, Phys. Rev. Lett. **76**, 3432 (1996).

[7] For instance, D. S. Chemla, D. A. B. Miller, and S. Schmitt-Rink, in *Optical Non-linearities and Instabilities in Semiconductors*, edited by H. Haug (Academic Press, San Diego, 1988), Chap. 4.

[8] A. Imamoglu and Y. Yamamoto, Phys. Rev. Lett. **70**, 3327 (1993).

[9] For instance, S. M. Sze, *Physics of Semiconductor Devices* (Wiley Interscience, New York, 1969), Chap. 4.

[10] S. Koshiba, Y. Nakamura, M.Tsuchiya, H. Noge, H.Kano, Y. Nagamune, T. Noda, and H. Sakaki, J. Appl. Phys. **76**, 4138 (1994).

CONTROL OF QUANTUM STATES IN NONSTATIONARY CAVITY QED SYSTEMS

S. V. Prants

Pacific Institute of the Russian Academy of Sciences, Vladivostok, Russia

Interaction of atoms, moving through a lossless cavity, with a cavity field having a spatial structure, is treated with the aim of controlling quantum evolution of the field and atomic states. General fully-quantum analysis of the atom-field dynamics is applied for solving the finite-control problem for a micromaser device consisting of two-level atoms moving through a single-mode cavity. The semiclassical treatment of the same system shows that out of resonance between atoms and the field it may be fully uncontrollable in the sense of exponential sensitivity to initial conditions. By calculating maximal Lyapunov exponents we demonstrate dynamical chaos for a wide range of magnitudes of the detuning, the atom-field strength and the velocity of atoms which may be considered as control parameters for the micromaser.

1. INTRODUCTION

Fundamental quantum properties of both matter and radiation, such as vacuum Rabi oscillations and collapse and revival of atomic populations, have been clearly demonstrated in experiments with cavity quantum electrodynamical systems (CQED) (for review see [1]). Micromasers, microlasers and other purely quantum devices have been used successfully for creating and monitoring nonclassical states of electromagnetic radiation and of atoms. With the perspectives of quantum computing with the CQED systems [2] the task of controlling the quantum evolution is becoming more and more attractive. In its general formulation the problem of finite control of the atom-field interaction was considered in [3] using the ideas of quantum control [4]. Here we will concentrate on the control of nonstationary versions of the CQED system, consisting of two-level atoms moving through a single-mode lossless cavity, which is known as a prototype for a micromaser. Another problem we will deal with is limits of control under such a system. Whether it can undergo a transition to the regime of dynamical chaos in which any predictions and control, even in the quantum-mechanical sense, become impossible.

2. THE ATOM-FIELD DYNAMICS: GENERAL DESCRIPTION

The model we will deal with in this section is atoms moving through a single-mode cavity. Taking into account a spatial structure of the cavity field and neglecting all the dissipation processes one can write the fully-quantum Hamiltonian of the model with N-level atoms in the following rotating-wave approximation (RWA) form [5]

$$H(t) = \hbar\omega_f a^\dagger a + \hbar \sum_{m=1}^{N-1} \omega_m R_m + \hbar \sum_{j \neq k} \Omega_{jk}(t)[a^{k-j} R_{jk} + (a^\dagger)^{k-j} R_{kj}] , \quad k > j . \quad (1)$$

The field mode with the frequency ω_f is described by the creation and annihilation operators a and $a^\dagger$. A bare N-level atom is described in terms of the commuting operators

$$R_m \equiv R_{mm} - R_{m+1,m+1} , \quad m = 1, 2, \cdots, N-1 , \quad (2)$$

of the Cartan subalgebra of the $SU(N)$ algebra, where R_{ij} denote generators acting in the N-dimensional space of an unitary irreducible representation (UIR) of the $SU(N)$ group. In the Weyl basis they are given by the $N \times N$-matrices

$$(R_{ij})_{kl} = \delta_{ik}\delta_{jl}, \quad i,,j,k,l = 1, 2, \cdots, N , \quad (3)$$

with the following commutation relations

$$[R_{ij} , R_{kl}] = \delta_{jk}\delta_{il} - \delta_{il}\delta_{kj} . \quad (4)$$

The hierarchy of the energy levels of a bare N-level atom is described in the following way

$$\begin{aligned}
E_0 = -\hbar\omega_{N-1} < E_1 = \hbar\omega_{N-1} - \hbar\omega_{N-2} < \cdots \\
\cdots < E_{N-i} = \hbar\omega_i - \hbar\omega_{i-1} < \cdots < E_{N-1} = \hbar\omega_1, \\
i = 1, 2, \cdots, N , \quad (\omega_0 = \omega_N = 0),
\end{aligned} \quad (5)$$

where E_0 and E_{N-1} are the energies of the lower and upper states, respectively, and $\omega_0 = \omega_N = 0$.

In the generalized version (1) of the standard model (see, for example, [1]) all possible atomic transitions are allowed in the first-order perturbation theory with emission or absorption of n photons with $n = 1, 2, \cdots, N-1$. The generalized Rabi frequencies, $\Omega_{jk}(t) = \Omega_{kj}^*(t) , \; j \neq k$, are assumed to be arbitrary differentiable c-number functions of time. For moving atoms their time dependence corresponds, in fact, to the type of spatial structure of the cavity mode.

In the RWA the atom-field system possesses the well-known integral of motion reflecting conservation of the interaction energy in the process of the energy exchange between atoms and the field. The respective operator

$$Q = \frac{1}{2} \sum_{m=1}^{N-1} m(N-m)R_m + a^\dagger a \quad (6)$$

commutes with the Hamiltonian (1). The eigenvectors of the charge operator Q generate the basis

$$\begin{aligned}
Q|q, m\rangle &= (q - \tfrac{N-1}{2})|q, m\rangle , \\
|q, m\rangle &\equiv |q - N + m\rangle_f |m\rangle_a , \quad \max(1, N-q) \leq m \leq N ,
\end{aligned} \quad (7)$$

in the subspace Γ_q which is labeled by a fixed value of the charge q. By the definition (7) the state of the coupled atom-field system $|q, m\rangle$ describes a cavity mode containing $q - N + m$ quanta and an atom being on the $(N-m)$th level.

Due to the integral of motion (6) the whole Hilbert space of the RWA atom-field system is decomposed into an infinite direct sum of N-dimensional subspaces corresponding to different fixed values of the charge operator. The operators R_m , $a^{k-j}R_{jk}$ and $(a^\dagger)^{k-j}R_{kj}$ act in the subspaces as the generators of an N-dimensional UIR of the $SU(N)$ group. The total Hamiltonian matrix (1) can be written in a block-diagonal form with N-dimensional blocks. As a result the system evolves in such a way that transitions between states belonging to different subspaces are forbidden.

In the subspace with a fixed value of the charge q the time-evolution equation reduces to the $N \times N$-matrix equation

$$i\hbar\frac{d}{dt}U_q(t,0) = H_q(t)U_q(t,0) ,\tag{8}$$

where the elements of the matrix $H_q(t)$ are given by

$$(H_q)_{kk} = \omega_k - \omega_{k-1} - \frac{N - 2k + 1}{2} ,\tag{9}$$

$$(H_q)_{ij} = \Omega_{ij}(t) \prod_{n=i+1}^{j} \sqrt{q - N + n} , \qquad i < j.\tag{10}$$

For solving the matrix evolution equation of the type (8) with a time-dependent Hamiltonian matrix one can use the group-theoretical method [6] based on a decomposition of such a matrix into a finite sum of generators of the respective group of dynamical symmetry ($SU(N)$, in general) in an appropriate representation. Thus we can reduce the initial infinite-dimensional evolution problem with the Hamiltonian (1), which generates an infinite-dimensional dynamical Lie algebra, to an infinite set of N-dimensional evolution subproblems (8).

3. QUANTUM CONTROL WITH MOVING TWO-LEVEL ATOMS

The results of the preceding section will be applied here for solving the problem of finite quantum control of field and atomic states in a micromaser device in which a monoenergetic beam of Rydberd atoms is injected into a single-mode high-Q microwave resonator at such a low rate that only one atom at a time is present inside the cavity. The problem of constructing the cavity field in a desired state, say, in a Fock state, after interacting with atoms has been considered in a number of papers [1]. Usualy, one deals with the standard Jaynes-Cummings model (JCM) trying to find such a perturbation of an initial state of the cavity mode by injecting two-level atoms that enables to access a desired final state of the field at the moments when atoms leave the cavity. However, when flying through the cavity atoms "see" not the constant field amplitude as it is assumed in the standard JCM, but a variable amplitude. This effect is important especially in a microwave range where only a few wave lengths fit along the resonator axis. It can be described by simply incorporating a mode-shape function $f(vt)$ in the standard JCM

$$H_{JCM}(t) = \hbar\omega_f a^\dagger a + \hbar\omega_a R_0 + \hbar\Omega_0 f(vt)(aR_+ + a^\dagger R_-) ,\tag{11}$$

where v is the velocity of atoms and Ω_0 is the vacuum Rabi frequency, and the generators $R_{0,\pm}$ satisfy the following commutation relations: $[R_+ , R_-] = 2R_0 , [R_0 , R_\pm] = \pm R_\pm$.

The space of states of the model (11) splits up into an infinite set of two-dimensional noncommunicating subspaces each of which is labeled by a fixed value of the charge q. In the RWA the atom-field system evolves in such a way that transitions between subspaces with different values of q are forbidden. The operator acting in the subspace Γ_q has the matrix form

$$H_q = \begin{pmatrix} \omega_f(q-1) + \frac{1}{2}\omega_a & \Omega_0 f(t)\sqrt{q} \\ \Omega_0 f(t)\sqrt{q} & \omega_f q - \frac{1}{2}\omega_a \end{pmatrix} , \tag{12}$$

which is a two-dimensional UIR of the $U(2)$ group. Parametrizing the group in a special way [3] we can write the $U(2)$ element in the following form

$$U_q = \begin{pmatrix} \exp i[\omega_f(q-1) + \frac{1}{2}\omega_a]t & 0 \\ 0 & \exp[-i(\omega_f q - \frac{1}{2}\omega_a)t] \end{pmatrix} \begin{pmatrix} g_q & -\tilde{g}_q^* \\ \tilde{g}_q & g_q^* \end{pmatrix} , \tag{13}$$

which is the solution of the time-evolution equation (8) in the subspace Γ_q. The parameters of the $U(2)$ group satisfy the conservation law

$$|g|^2 + |\tilde{g}|^2 = 1 . \tag{14}$$

In fact, the evolution problem of the generalized JCM (11) can be resolved after solving the single governing equation for the $U(2)$ group parameter

$$\frac{d^2 g_q}{dt^2} - \left(\frac{df/dt}{f} + i(\omega_a - \omega_f) \right) \frac{dg_q}{dt} + (\Omega_0 f)^2 q g_q = 0 , \; g_q(0) = 1 , \; \dot{g}_q(0) = 0 . \tag{15}$$

The general problem of finite quantum control for a single-mode micromaser device can be formulated as follows. Let the cavity mode be described by the density operator ρ_f at the initial moment when the first atom enters the cavity with the velocity v being in a state given by the density operator ρ_a. After the interaction time $\Delta t = L/v$ the atom leaves the cavity in a state which may be described by the reduced density matrix

$$\rho_a(\Delta t) = Tr_f[U(\Delta t)\rho_a \otimes \rho_f(0)U^+(\Delta t)] , \tag{16}$$

while the field is left in the state

$$\rho_f(\Delta t) = Tr_a[U(\Delta t)\rho_a \otimes \rho_f(0)U^+(\Delta t)] , \tag{17}$$

where L is the cavity length and Tr_f and Tr_a are the traces over the field and atomic states, respectively. After l atoms, the field density matrix is given by

$$\begin{aligned} &\rho_f(l\Delta t) \\ &= Tr_a[U(\Delta t)\rho_a \cdots Tr_a[U(\Delta t)\rho_a Tr_a[U(\Delta t)\rho_a \otimes \rho_f(0)U^\dagger(\Delta t)]U^\dagger(\Delta t)] \cdots U^\dagger(\Delta t)] , \end{aligned} \tag{18}$$

where we assumed for simplicity equal interaction times Δt for all the atoms and identical density matrices ρ_a at the instants when they enter the cavity.

The physical objectives we wish to achieve at the target time T may involve the following points.

1. A desired state of an atom leaving the cavity.

2. A desired state of the field in the cavity after interaction with atoms.

3. Desired expectation values of certain variables

516

$$\langle A(T)\rangle = Tr\rho(0)U^\dagger(T,0)A(0)U(T,0) , \tag{19}$$

refering to the atomic or field subsystems. If we desire to control, for example, higher field moments we must calculate the following expectation value

$$\left\langle a^{\dagger p}(T)a^s(T)\right\rangle = \left(\frac{\partial}{\partial\eta}\right)^p \left(-\frac{\partial}{\partial\eta^*}\right)^s Tr_f\left[\rho(0)U^\dagger(T,0)e^{\eta a^\dagger(0)}e^{-\eta^* a(0)}U(T,0)\right] . \tag{20}$$

Let us conclude this section by a few examples of controlling the quantum evolution. The task is especially simple if the field is initially in a Fock state. Let an atom, when entering the cavity, occupy $(2-m)$th level, and the field mode contain $q-2+m$ quanta, where $m=1,2$. Then the probability of finding the field and the atom at the time T in their initial states $\mid q,m>$ is simply $\mid g_q(T)\mid^2$. The transition probabilities $\mid q,1>\rightarrow\mid q-1,2>$ and $\mid q,2>\rightarrow\mid q+1,1>$ are equal and given by the squared modulus of another $U(2)$ group parameter $\left|\tilde{g}_q(T)\right|^2$. If the initial state of the field is a coherent state $\mid\alpha>_f$, then the transition probabilities to the Fock states are given by

$$\begin{aligned}
\left|\langle\alpha,1\left|U_q(T,0)\right|q,1\rangle\right|^2 &= \frac{|\alpha|^{2(q-1)}}{(q-1)!}\left|g_q(T)\right|^2 , \\[2mm]
\left|\langle\alpha,2\left|U_q(T,0)\right|q,2\rangle\right|^2 &= \frac{|\alpha|^{2q}}{q!}\left|g_q(T)\right|^2 , \\[2mm]
\left|\langle\alpha,1\left|U_q(T,0)\right|q,2\rangle\right|^2 &= \frac{|\alpha|^{2(q-1)}}{(q-1)!}\left|\tilde{g}_q(T)\right|^2 , \\[2mm]
\left|\langle\alpha,2\left|U_q(T,0)\right|q,1\rangle\right|^2 &= \frac{|\alpha|^{2q}}{q!}\left|\tilde{g}_q(T)\right|^2 .
\end{aligned} \tag{21}$$

4. SEMICLASSICAL CHAOS WITH MOVING TWO-LEVEL ATOMS

We have found in the preceding section the ordinary differential equation of the second order (15) governing the temporal evolution of the fully quantum system "moving two-level atoms + single-mode quantized field + cavity" in the invariant subspace Γ_q. In general one has an infinite set of such independent equations which are labeled by the values of the charge $q=0,1,2,\cdots,\infty$. In rectangular cavities TE modes are defined by the functions

$$f(vt) = \sin(p\pi vt/L) , \tag{22}$$

where p is the number of half-wavelengths of a chosen mode. In the case of a single mode (15) for the fixed value q has the form

$$\frac{d^2 g_q}{dt^2} - [\omega_c\cot\omega_c t + i(\omega_a-\omega_f)]\frac{dg_q}{dt} + (\Omega_0\sin\omega_c t)^2 q g_q = 0. \tag{23}$$

where $\omega_c = p\pi v/L$ is the driving frequency.

One of the main questions in control theory and the theory of dynamical systems is how complicated can be the behavior of a dynamical system. The answer depends, in particular, on the relations between the systems characteristic frequencies. Numerical calculations of the trajectories of (23) in the pseudophase plane $Re\,g - Im\,g$ have shown [7] that the motion is quasiperiodic even in the case of incommensurability of the characteristic frequencies ω_c, ω_a, ω_f and Ω_0. For numerical integration we must truncate the set of these equations to a finite number. As a result we will deal with a finite-dimensional set of linear differential equations whose solutions are regular and insensitive (in a sense of exponential divergency) to initial conditions. Because of an infinite number of governing equations of the type (23) we can not definitely say whether the total motion of the atom-field system will be regular or not.

There is another way for treating the dynamics of atoms interacting with a field in a self-consistent manner [7-10]. Starting with a fully quantum Hamiltonian for an atom-field system one can derive the Heisenberg equations for the atomic and field operators. Averaging them with an arbitrary quantum state an infinite hierarchy of equations for expectation values can be obtained. A finite-dimensional dynamical system, suitable for numerical integration, can be then derived from this infinite set with the help of a factorization procedure.

Let us consider a spatially confined, monoenergetic bunch of n two-level atoms, not interacting with each other and moving through a single-mode lossless cavity with the same velocity v. It should be emphasized that we deal now with many atoms interacting simultaneously with a cavity mode. The Hamiltonian of such a generalized Dicke model (DM) has the following RWA form

$$H_{DM} = \frac{1}{2}\hbar\omega_a \sum_{j=1}^{n} \sigma_z^j + \hbar\omega_f(a^\dagger a + \frac{1}{2}) + \hbar\Omega_0 f(vt) \sum_{j=1}^{n}(\sigma_+^j a + \sigma_-^j a^\dagger) , \qquad (24)$$

that is written for convenience in terms of the usual Pauli matrices σ_z and $\sigma_\pm = \sigma_x \pm i\sigma_y$ which are simply connected with the $SU(2)$ generators $R_0 = \frac{1}{2}\sum \sigma_z^j$, $R_\pm = \sum \sigma_\pm^j$. Let us take expectation values of the Heisenberg operators supplemented by the factorization assumption of the type $< a\sigma > = < a >< \sigma >$, $< a^\dagger\sigma > = < a^\dagger >< \sigma >$. Transforming to the dimensionless time $\tau = \omega_a t$ we get the following semiclassical dynamical system

$$\dot{x} = -y + 2\Omega z P f ,$$

$$\dot{y} = x - 2\Omega z E f ,$$

$$\dot{z} = 2\Omega(yE - xP)f ,$$

$$\dot{E} = -\omega P - 2\omega y f , \qquad (25)$$

$$\dot{P} = \omega E + 2\Omega x f ,$$

$$\ddot{f} = -(b\omega)^2 f , \quad f(0) = 0 , \dot{f}(0) = 1 ,$$

for the following classical quantities

$$x = \frac{1}{n} < \sum \sigma_x > , \; y = \frac{1}{n} < \sum \sigma_y > , \; z = \frac{1}{n} < \sum \sigma_z > ,$$

$$E = \frac{1}{\sqrt{n}} < a + a^\dagger > , \; P = \frac{i}{\sqrt{n}} < a - a^\dagger > , \qquad (26)$$

where dots denote derivatives with respect to τ. To make our dynamical system an autonomous one we have added the equation for the mode shape function f which is given by (22). The control parameters of the system (25) have the following sense: $\Omega = \Omega_0\sqrt{n}/2\omega_a$ is the dimensionless cooperative Rabi frequency, $\omega = \omega_f/\omega_a$ the ratio of the field and atomic frequencies, $b = v/c$ the ratio of the velocity of atoms to the velocity of light in vacuum.

For $f(vt) \neq const$ the system (25), generally speaking, possesses two integrals of motion

$$x^2 + y^2 + z^2 = 1 ,$$

$$E^2 + P^2 + 2z = const , \qquad (27)$$

resulting from unitarity and total energy conservation, respectively. In the case of exact atomic-field resonance, $\omega_a = \omega_f$, the system admits an additional integral of motion

$$xE + yP = const .\qquad(28)$$

It is well-known that the standard DM within the RWA has three integrals of motion even for a nonzero detuning. Therefore, any transition to deterministic chaos is impossible in this model since it possesses in the RWA only two independent variables: five equations for the expectation values x, y, z, E and P minus three integrals of motion. Without the RWA one of the integrals of motion, connected with the conservation of the interaction energy, breaks down, and the DM with the counter-rotating terms may become chaotic when the cooperative Rabi frequency exceeds some critical value [7-9]. Lacking the third integral (28) in our generalized DM with the mode structure included allows to suppose that out of resonance it may undergo deterministic dynamical chaos *even in the RWA without any threshold conditions*.

For searching transitions to the dynamical chaos in the system (25) we have calculated the maximal Lyapunov exponents in the ranges of magnitudes of the parameters that are typical for the usual micromaser devices with Rydberg atoms [1]: $\Omega_0 = (10^3 \div 10^4)rad/s$ and $\omega_a \simeq (10^{10} \div 10^{11})rad/s$. With such the magnitudes we have the following estimations for the control parameters: $\Omega \simeq \sqrt{n/\omega_a 10^3}$ and $\omega \simeq (0.3 \div 3)p$. To illustrate transitions to chaos in dependence on both the control parameters Ω and ω we have calculated the charts of chaos [10] for the following initial conditions

$$x(0) = y(0) = 0 , \quad z(0) = 1 , \quad E(0) = 1 , \quad P(0) = -1 ,\qquad(29)$$

which mean that all the atoms enter the cavity in excited states, and the cavity field is supposed to be in the coherent state.

Our previous numerical results show that dynamical chaos appears in the atom-field system (25) without any threshold conditions becoming stronger and stronger with increasing control parameters Ω, ω and b. We have calculated the maximal Lyapunov exponents of the dynamical system (25) in a wide range of the dimensionless collective Rabi frequency $\Omega = (0.1 \div 10)$ and the detuning $\omega = (0.1 \div 2)$ for two fixed values of the atomic velocities, $v = 0.01c$, and, $v = 0.1c$. For example, the chaos appears for $\omega = 0.9$ and $v = 0.1c$ when the collective Rabi frequency reaches the value of the order of $\Omega \simeq 0.05$ which corresponds approximately to $n \simeq 10^{10} \div 10^{11}$ atoms in a bunch for the typical microwave frequencies. All the calculations show that the motion is regular for all the values of v and Ω if atoms are in resonance with the field, i.e. $\omega = 1$. As it was shown above our system has the third integral of motion (28) in the case of resonance even for $f(vt) \neq const$. The model with the three integrals of motion is integrable and hence nonchaotic. We have also calculated the respective power spectra which have confirmed the results of calculating the maximal Lyapunov exponents and the conclusions mentioned above.

5. CONCLUSION

Our present work was motivated by the desire to control the quantum evolution of the nonstationary cavity quantum electrodynamical systems consisting of atoms moving through a single-mode electromagnetic cavity and interacting with a spatially structured cavity field. After treating the general model (1) of such an interaction in Sec.2 we have considered in detail in Sec.3 the problem of finite control of the atomic and field states in the nonstationary Jaynes-Cummings model (11) which is known as a prototype for a micromaser device. We have shown that the problem of controlling quantum evolution in micromasers can be, in fact, reduced to the solution of a single $c-$number differential equation of the second order (15). We have found it is interesting to investigate the dynamical complexity of the strongly coupled atom-field system described by the generalized Dicke Hamiltonian (24). It was surprisingly found that the semiclassical version of this model may demonstrate chaotic behavior even in the rotating-wave approximation. More comprehensive numerical elaboration on this topic will be done in a future publication.

ACKNOWLEDGMENTS

I would like to thank L.Kon'kov for numerical work. The work was supported by the Grants No. 96-02-19827 and No. 96-02-18746 from the Russian Foundation for Basic Research. I am also grateful to the Organizing Committee for support.

REFERENCES

[1] B.L.Berman (ed), *Cavity Quantum Electrodynamics* (Academic Press, Boston, 1994); B.W.Shore and P.L.Knight, J.Mod.Opt. **40** (1993) 1195.

[2] C.H.Bennett, Physics Today, No10 (1995) 24; L.Davidovich, N.Zagury, M.Brune, J.M.Raimond and S.Haroche, Phys.Rev.A **50** (1994) 895.

[3] S.V.Prants, J.Rus.Laser Res. **16** (1995) 83: Automatika i Telemekhanika [in Russian] No2 (1996) 66.

[4] A.G.Butkovsky and Yu.I.Samoilenko, *Control of Quantum Mechanical Processes* [in Russian] (Nauka, Moscow, 1984).

[5] V.V.Dodonov, V.I.Man'ko and S.M.Chumakov, *Proc. Lebedev Physical Institute* [in Russian] (Nauka, Moscow, 1982), vol.176, p.57.

[6] S.V.Prants, Phys.Lett.A **144** (1990) 225.

[7] L.E.Kon'kov and S.V.Prants, J.Math.Phys. **37** (1996) 1204.

[8] S.V.Prants and E.V.Dmitrievsa, Phys.Rev.B (submitted).

[9] R.Graham and M.Höhnerbach, Z.Phys.B **57** (1984) 233; R.F.Fox and J.C.Eidson, Phys.Rev.A **36** (1987) 4321; R.Roncaglia, L.Bonci, P.Grigolini and B.J.West, J.Stat.Phys. **68** (1992) 321.

[10] S.V.Prants and L.E.Kon'kov, Phys.Lett.A (submitted).

A SIMULATION OF PULSED SQUEEZING IN SHORT OPTICAL FIBER LOOP MIRROR

Norihiko Nishizawa[1], Masakazu Mori[1], Toshio Goto[1], and Akira Miyauchi[2]

[1] Department of Quantum Engineering, Nagoya University
Nagoya 464-01, Japan
[2] Lightwave Transmission Engineering Department, Fujitsu Ltd.
Kawasaki 211, Japan
E-mail : nishizawa@nuee.nagoya-u.ac.jp

Quadrature squeezed light generation with picosecond optical pulses in a fiber loop mirror whose length is as short as 2 m is analyzed through the computer simulation. When the pulse width is 10 ps, the evolution of the squeezing parameter is almost independent of the second order dispersion β_2 in the region of $|\beta_2| < 15$ ps^2/km. When the pulse width is 1 ps, enhancement of the squeezing in the normal dispersion regime occurs. On the other hand, the squeezing in the anomalous dispersion regime is obviously degraded. These results are due to the pulse broadening or narrowing effects. When the pulse width is 1 ps and the peak power is 1 kW, the maximum squeezing at 2.2 m is 8.2 dB for $\beta_2 = 15$ ps^2/km.

1. INTRODUCTION

An optical fiber is one of the most effective devices to get the nonlinear optical effects. The quadrature squeezed vacuum has been generated with a fiber loop mirror in a few laboratories [1–3]. In those experiments, the guided acoustic wave Brillouin scattering (GAWBS), which is a very weak forward scattering in optical fibers, acts as an excess noise and degrades the detected squeezing value [4,5]. The characteristics of the GAWBS have been studied by a few groups [6–9]. The magnitude of the GAWBS noise increases in proportion to the fiber length, and the shorter the fiber length is, the smaller the GAWBS noise is. So far the optical fiber used for squeezing was as long as 50 m. Thus, if we can use a short fiber whose length is 2 m, the magnitude of the GAWBS noise may be reduced by $\sim$14 dB.

In this study, the possibilities of the squeezing with optical pulses in a fiber loop mirror whose length is as short as 2 m is examined through the computer simulation. Recently, the simulation method for pulsed squeezing in optical fibers with chromatic dispersion was established by Doerr *et al.* [10] However they calculated the squeezing for femtosecond pulses, and the squeezing for picosecond pulses has never been analyzed. In the experiments of the squeezed light generation, the picosecond pulses are mainly used for the pump beam. In this paper, the optimum conditions for the pulsed squeezing in short optical fibers are investigated in terms of the pulse width and the magnitude of the second-order dispersion.

2. THEORY

To calculate the squeezing of optical pulses, we start with the simplified quantized nonlinear Schrödinger equation, [10,11]

$$\frac{\partial \hat{A}}{\partial z} = i\gamma \hat{A}^\dagger \hat{A} \hat{A} - \frac{1}{2} i\beta_2 \frac{\partial^2 \hat{A}}{\partial t^2},\tag{1}$$

where $\hat{A}$, the complex envelope of the pulse, is a function of z and t, γ is the Kerr nonlinear coefficient, t is the time variable, and z is the propagation distance. In this study, because the squeezing of the picosecond pulses in short optical fibers is investigated, all the dispersion can be neglected except for the second-order dispersion β_2. The effects of the fiber loss and the Raman scattering can be also neglected [12].

To calculate the squeezing of the quantum noise approximately, $\hat{A}$ is assumed linear as

$$\hat{A} = A + \hat{b},\tag{2}$$

where A is a c number representing the classical amplitude of the pulse envelope and $\hat{b}$ is the quantum-mechanical part(quantum noise). This linearization approximation is valid for the quadrature squeezed light generation in optical fibers [10]. Ignoring higher-order terms in $\hat{b}$ and canceling the classical terms, we obtain the evolution equation for $\hat{b}$ as

$$\frac{\partial \hat{b}}{\partial z} = 2i\gamma |A|^2 \hat{b} + i\gamma A^2 \hat{b}^\dagger - \frac{1}{2} i\beta_2 \frac{\partial^2 \hat{b}}{\partial t^2}.\tag{3}$$

Next, in order to calculate the pulse propagation, the continuous functions are transformed into the discrete functions in terms of z and t. Thus $A(z,t)$ and $\hat{b}(z,t)$ are transformed as $A_j(n)$ and $\hat{b}_j(n)$, respectively, where the pulse is broken into time intervals of width Δt labeled by integer j and distance intervals of width Δz labeled by integer n. Transforming Eq. (3) into the discrete form and solving for $\hat{b}_j(n+1)$ gives

$$\hat{b}_j(n+1) = [1 + 2j\gamma \Delta z |A_j(n)|^2]\hat{b}_j(n) + i\gamma \Delta z [A_j(n)]^2 \hat{b}_j^\dagger(n)$$
$$- \frac{1}{2} i\beta_2 \Delta z \frac{\hat{b}_{j-1}(n) - 2\hat{b}_j(n) + \hat{b}_{j+1}(n)}{(\Delta t)^2}.\tag{4}$$

From Eq. (4), we can see that the dispersion causes coupling between the operators at different time slots. Thus the operator $\hat{b}_j(n)$ is a linear combination of the operators at the input port $\hat{b}_k(0)$. Because the quantum mechanical part of the initial field corresponds to the vacuum state, $\hat{b}_k(0)$ can be represented by the annihilation operators, $\hat{a}_k$. Thus we can write

$$\hat{b}_j(n) = \sum_k [\mu_{jk}(n)\hat{a}_k + \nu_{jk}(n)\hat{a}_k^\dagger],\tag{5}$$

where $\mu_{jk}(n)$ and $\nu_{jk}(n)$ are the matrix coefficients relating the operators at distance n to the initial operators. Substituting Eq. (5) into Eq. (4), and using the commutation relations for $\hat{a}$ and $\hat{a}^\dagger$, we find the discrete evolution equations for μ and ν as

$$\mu_{jk}(n+1) = \left[1 + 2i\gamma \Delta z |A_j|^2 + \frac{i\beta_2 \Delta z}{(\Delta t)^2}\right]\mu_{jk}(n)$$
$$+ i\gamma \Delta z [A_j(n)]^2 \nu_{jk}^*(n) - \frac{i\beta_2 \Delta z}{2(\Delta t)^2}[\mu_{j-1,k}(n) + \mu_{j+1,k}(n)],\tag{6}$$

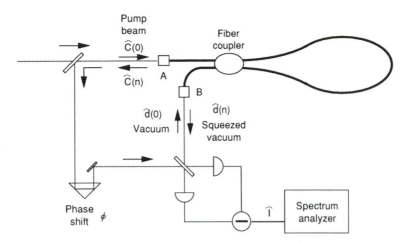

Figure 1. Scheme of fiber loop mirror for quadrature squeezed vacuum generation.

and

$$\nu_{jk}(n+1) = \left[1 + 2i\gamma\Delta z|A_j|^2 + \frac{i\beta_2\Delta z}{(\Delta t)^2}\right]\nu_{jk}(n)$$

$$+ i\gamma\Delta z[A_j(n)]^2\mu_{jk}^*(n) - \frac{i\beta_2\Delta z}{2(\Delta t)^2}[\nu_{j-1,k}(n) + \nu_{j+1,k}(n)]. \tag{7}$$

The scheme of quadrature squeezed light generation and detection is shown in Fig. 1. The fiber loop mirror is used for quadrature squeezed vacuum generation. In this scheme, the pump beam $\hat{C}(0) = C(0) + \hat{c}(0)$ enters from the port A and the vacuum state $\hat{d}(0)$ enters from the port B. The two beams are overlapped at the fiber coupler and divided into two beams. Thus C, $\hat{c}$, and $\hat{d}$ are overlapped and copropagate along the optical fiber. In the fiber loop, the two beams suffer self-phase modulation and group-velocity dispersion, and then come back to the fiber coupler. In this case, owing to the linearization approximation, the evolutions of $\hat{c}$ and $\hat{d}$ can be considered independently [10]. Thus the output from the port A is the pump beam $\hat{C}(n) = C(n) + \hat{c}(n)$ and the one from the port B is the squeezed vacuum $\hat{d}(n)$. In the detection process, $\hat{d}(n)$ and $\hat{C}(n)$ are overlapped again at the beam splitter and enter into the balanced homodyne detector. The differential current of the detector output is

$$\hat{I}_j = C_j^*(n)\exp(-i\phi)\hat{d}_j(n) + C_j(n)\exp(i\phi)\hat{d}_j^\dagger(n), \tag{8}$$

where ϕ is the phase difference between $\hat{C}(n)$ and $\hat{d}(n)$.

The detector output is observed with the spectrum analyzer. The power spectrum of the current at low frequency, Φ, is given by

$$\Phi \equiv \frac{1}{2M^2}\sum_{j,l}\langle\hat{I}_l\hat{I}_{l-j} + \hat{I}_{l-j}\hat{I}_l\rangle, \tag{9}$$

where M is the total number of the discrete points. The squeezing ratio R, which is defined as the detected noise normalized to the shot noise, is written as

$$R = \frac{\Phi(\mu,\nu)}{\Phi(\mu_{jk} = \delta_{jk}, \nu_{jk} = 0)}. \tag{10}$$

Substituting Eqs. (6) ∼ (9) into Eq. (10), we find that

$$R = \frac{\sum_{j,k,l} Re[C_l^* C_j^* \exp(-2i\phi)(\mu_{lk}\nu_{jk} + \mu_{jk}\nu_{lk}) + C_l C_j^* (\mu_{lk}^* \mu_{jk} + \nu_{lk}^* \nu_{jk})]}{\sum_l |C_l|^2}. \tag{11}$$

By adjusting the phase difference ϕ, the minimum squeezing ratio (squeezing parameter) and the maximum squeezing ratio (anti-squeezing parameter) are written as

$$R_{\min(\max)} = \frac{\sum_{j,k,l} Re[C_l C_j^* (\mu_{lk}^* \mu_{jk} + \nu_{lk}^* \nu_{jk})] \mp |\sum_{j,k,l} [C_l^* C_j^* (\mu_{lk}\nu_{jk} + \mu_{jk}\nu_{lk})]|}{\sum_l |C_l|^2}. \tag{12}$$

To get the squeezing parameter, we first calculate the evolution of the classical amplitude of the pulse at one step with the split-step Fourier method [11]. Then μ and ν parameters are calculated with the resulting amplitude components using Eqs. (6) and (7). After propagation of the unit length, the squeezing parameters are obtained with Eq. (12).

3. SIMULATION RESULTS AND DISCUSSION

In optical fibers squeezing occurs owing to the optical Kerr effect [2]. The Kerr nonlinear coefficient γ is written as

$$\gamma = \frac{n_2 \omega}{c A_{\text{eff}}}, \tag{13}$$

where n_2 is the nonlinear-index coefficient, ω is the frequency of the propagation beam, c is the optical velocity, and A_{eff} is the effective core area of the fiber [11]. Equation (13) shows that γ depends on the wavelength of the pump beam and the characteristics of the optical fiber. For example, when the wavelength is 1.5 μm and the optical fiber is 1.5 μm single-mode fiber, γ is estimated to be 1.5×10^{-3} W^{-1}m^{-1}. On the other hand, when the wavelength is 1 μm and the optical fiber is 0.85 μm single-mode fiber, γ is about 7.5×10^{-3} W^{-1}m^{-1}. In this study, the nonlinearity γ and the peak intensity are set to be 2×10^{-3} W^{-1}m^{-1} and 1 kW, respectively, and the squeezing of the optical pulse along a few meter of optical fibers is investigated in terms of the pulse width and the magnitude of the second order dispersion β_2.

First, the squeezing for the pulse width of 10 ps at FWHM is examined in the dispersion region from -15 to 15 ps^2/km. The pulse shape is assumed to be an unchirped sech-shaped amplitude pulse. Figures 2(a) and (b) show the simulation results of the squeezing and anti-squeezing parameters. In Fig. 2(a), the squeezing parameters monotonically increase along the fiber and are gradually saturated. The saturation of the squeezing parameter is due to the nonlinear phase difference along the pulse envelope. At the propagation length of 2.2 m, the squeezing of 7.4 dB is obtained. This value is as large as those obtained in the experiment with a 50 m fiber. In Fig. 2(b), the anti-squeezing parameters monotonically increase to infinity with the propagation length. At the propagation length of 2.2 m, the anti-squeezing parameter is about 16 dB.

In Fig. 2, the evolutions of the squeezing and anti-squeezing parameters are almost independent of β_2 for 10 ps pulses in the region of $|\beta_2| \leq 15$ ps^2/km. The reason is that when the pulse width is 10 ps, the pulse shapes are almost unchanged along the fiber length in this dispersion region.

Next, the squeezing for the pulse width of 1 ps at FWHM is also examined. The other parameters used for this simulation are the same as those above. Figure 3 shows the evolution of the pulse shapes propagating along the optical fiber when $\beta_2 = \pm15$ ps^2/km.

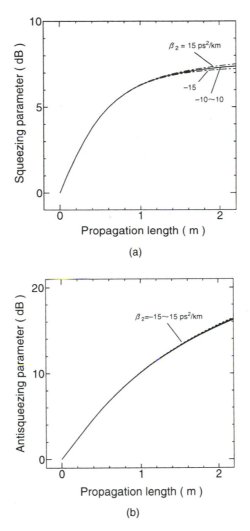

Figure 2. Squeezing and anti-squeezing evolution when pulse width is 10 ps.

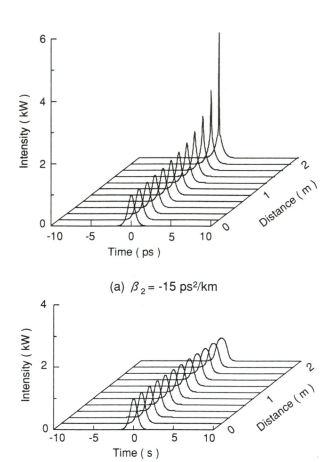

(a) $\beta_2 = -15$ ps²/km

(b) $\beta_2 = 15$ ps²/km

Figure 3. Evolution of the pulse shape along the optical fiber when the input pulse width is 1 ps. (a) $\beta_2 = -15$ ps²/km, (b) $\beta_2 = 15$ ps²/km.

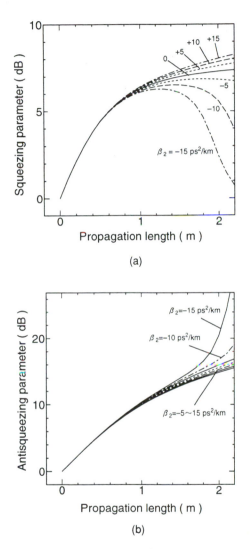

(a)

(b)

Figure 4. Squeezing and anti-squeezing evolution when the pulse width is 1 ps.

When $\beta_2 = -15$ ps^2/km, pulse compression occurs in an optical fiber of only a few meters. After propagation of about 1.5 m, the top of the pulse begins to be sharp and narrow. On the other hand, when $\beta_2 = 15$ ps^2/km, we can see the pulse broadening. In this case, the pulse shape becomes dull and wide, and the top of the pulse is flattened along the fiber length.

The evolutions of the squeezing and anti-squeezing parameters for 1 ps pulses are shown in Fig. 4(a) and (b). In Fig. 4(a), the evolution of the squeezing is obviously dependent on the magnitude of the second-order dispersion β_2. When $\beta_2 = 0$ ps^2/km, the squeezing parameter monotonically increases along the fiber, and is gradually saturated, as in the case of 10 ps pulses. When β_2 is negative, the squeezing parameter attains a maximum at the propagation distance shorter than 2 m, and then begins to be degraded. When $\beta_2 = -15$ ps^2/km, the maximum squeezing is 6.3 dB at 1.3 m. This degradation of squeezing in anomalous dispersion regime is due to the pulse narrowing effect as shown in Fig. 3(a). On the other hand, when β_2 is positive, the larger the dispersion is, the larger the squeezing parameter is. The maximum squeezing at 2.2 m is 8.2 dB when $\beta_2 = 15$ ps^2/km. This enhancement of squeezing is due to the fact that the pulse is broadened by the dispersion, and as a result, the pulse peak is flattened as shown in Fig. 3(b).

For the anti-squeezing parameters, they are also dependent on β_2. When β_2 is negative, the anti-squeezing parameters become larger than those of $\beta_2 = 0$. The remarkable increase occurs when $\beta_2 = -15$ ps^2/km. When β_2 is positive, the anti-squeezing parameters are a little smaller than those of $\beta_2 = 0$.

4. CONCLUSION

In conclusion, the squeezing for picosecond optical pulses in a fiber loop mirror whose length is as short as 2 m is analyzed through computer simulation. When the pulse width is larger than 10 ps, the evolution of the squeezing parameter is almost independent of β_2 for $|\beta_2| < 15$ ps^2/km. The squeezing parameter at 2.2 m is about 7.4 dB for the peak power of 1 kW. This value is as large as that for the 50 m fiber loop mirror. When the pulse width is 1 ps, enhancement of the squeezing in the normal dispersion regime occurs. On the other hand, the squeezing in the anomalous dispersion regime is obviously degraded. These results are due to the pulse broadening or narrowing effects. The maximum squeezing at 2.2 m is 8.2 dB for $\beta_2 = 15$ ps^2/km.

REFERENCES

[1] M. Rosenbluh and R. M. Shelby, Phys. Rev. Lett. **66** (1991) 153.

[2] K. Bergman and H. A. Haus, Opt. Lett. **16** (1991) 663; H. A. Haus, J. Opt. Soc. Am B **12** (1995) 2019.

[3] N. Nishizawa, S. Kume, M. Mori, T. Goto, and A. Miyauchi, Jpn. J. Appl. Phys. **33** (1994) 138.

[4] R. M. Shelby, P. D. Drummond, and S. J. Carter, Phys. Rev. A **42** (1990) 2966.

[5] K. Bergman, H. A. Haus, and M. Shirasaki, Appl. Phys. B **55** (1992) 242.

[6] R. M. Shelby, M. D. Levenson, and P. W. Bayer, Phys. Rev. B **31** (1985) 5244.

[7] A. J. Poustie, J. Opt. Soc. Am. B **10** (1993) 691.

[8] N. Nishizawa, S. Kume, M. Mori, T. Goto, and A. Miyauchi, J. Opt. Soc. Am. B **12** (1995) 1651.

[9] N. Nishizawa, S. Kume, M. Mori, T. Goto, and A. Miyauchi, Opt. Rev. **3** (1996) 29.

[10] C. R. Doerr, M. Shirasaki, and F. I. Khatri, J. Opt. Soc. Am. B **11** (1994) 143.

[11] G. P. Agrawal, *Nonlinear Fiber Optics* (Academic, New York, 1989)

[12] F. X. Kärtner, D. J. Dougherty, H. A. Haus, and E. P. Ippen, J. Opt. Soc. Am. B **11** (1994) 1267.

QUANTUM PROPERTIES OF THE TRAVELING-WAVE $\chi^{(2)}$ PROCESS: THEORY, EXPERIMENTS, AND APPLICATIONS

Prem Kumar, Michael L. Marable, and Sang-Kyung Choi

Department of Electrical and Computer Engineering
Northwestern University, Evanston, Illinois 60208-3118
Phone: (847)491-4128; Fax: (847)491-4455;
E-mail: kumarp@nwu.edu

Novel quantum states of light can be obtained through the interaction of intense light pulses in a $\chi^{(2)}$ nonlinear medium. Over the past several years we have investigated the processes of parametric amplification, sum-frequency, and second-harmonic generation (SHG) to produce highly squeezed pulses of light. In this paper we give an overview of the various generation schemes including results from our recent SHG experiments. Progress in the application of squeezed light in imaging is also described.

1. Q-SWITCHED PULSES IN QUANTUM OPTICS

Large pump intensities are generally required for the efficient observation of nonlinear optical phenomenon. One possible way to reduce the large pump-intensity requirement is to operate near a resonance of the nonlinear medium. In quantum optics, where one is concerned with the generation and detection of novel quantum states of light, this approach has not proven very successful. The reason is that near resonance a large number of spontaneously-emitted photons are produced which drastically degrade the quantum state generated by the ideal nonlinear interaction. Many researchers have made use of optical cavities to reduce the large pump-intensity requirement while maintaining the ideal nature of the nonlinear interaction [1]. Optical cavities, however, place an undue restriction on the bandwidth over which quantum-optic phenomenon can be observed.

At Northwestern University, we have followed a different approach to quantum-optic experiments by using a mode-locked and Q-switched laser which is capable of generating high pump powers. Since no cavities are employed and a traveling-wave (TW) type of interaction is used [2], the above-mentioned bandwidth restriction does not apply. We have demonstrated the generation of squeezed states of light [3–5], twin-beam states of light [6,7], and sub-Poissonian states of light [8]. In the first two cases a high degree of quantum-noise reduction is observed over a broad bandwidth. In one recent experiment, which employed a setup that self-generates a matched local oscillator (LO) for the detection of squeezing, we observed $5.8 \pm 0.2\,\mathrm{dB}$ of quadrature squeezing—*highest to date for a single-pass traveling-wave experiment* [5].

Quantum Communication, Computing, and Measurement
Edited by Hirota *et al.*, Plenum Press, New York, 1997

In the sub-Poissonian light generation experiment [8], the observed reduction of the Fano factor below unity is relatively small. We have discovered the phenomenon of *gain-induced diffraction* (GID) [10], which limits the noise reduction in such experiments. In the quadrature squeezing experiment [5], on the other hand, even though the squeezing at the output of the parametric amplifier is in a mode that is spatially distorted due to GID, the matched LO is able to extract the high degree of squeezing. In the sub-Poissonian experiment, however, direct detection is employed and no such spatial selection is possible. Nevertheless, we have theoretically modeled GID in the quantum description of a parametric amplifier [11]. The experimentally observed Fano factor is in excellent agreement with the predictions of this model [8].

Although the experiments cited above have employed the frequency downconversion (or optical parametric amplification) process, the reverse process, namely, second-harmonic generation (SHG), has also attracted considerable attention [12–16]. There are many reasons that make SHG attractive for squeezing creation. Foremost is the simplicity of the experimental setup; one avoids having to frequency double a laser first, a necessary step in the downconversion squeezing experiments due to the need for a pump beam at twice the frequency of the squeezed beam. In addition, SHG can be used to create nonclassical light for both the fundamental and the harmonic fields, and to produce the so-called bright squeezed light—squeezing with a non-zero mean field. Furthermore, SHG is widely used commercially and high conversion efficiencies can be routinely obtained.

Many demonstrations of squeezing by means of SHG have been reported [12, 13]. However, in almost all these experiments, the nonlinear medium was enclosed in an optical cavity to enhance the interaction by multiple passes through the medium. To the best of our knowledge, our recent observations of squeezing by means of single-pass TW SHG in bulk [17] and waveguide media [18] are the first of their respective kinds.

With use of the mode-locked and Q-switched pump source, we have also recently demonstrated the process of *quantum frequency conversion* (QFC) for the first time [19]. QFC is a process by which an input beam of light can be converted into an output beam of a different frequency while preserving the quantum state. We theoretically showed that in the up-conversion process, a complete depletion of one of the pump beams leads to QFC [20]. In our experiment, nonclassical intensity correlations ($\simeq 3\,\mathrm{dB}$) between a pair of beams at 1064 nm, the twin beams, were used as the input quantum property. When the frequency of one of the twin beams was converted from 1064 nm to 532 nm, nonclassical intensity correlations ($\simeq 1.5\,\mathrm{dB}$) appeared between the up-converted beam and the remaining twin beam, thus demonstrating the QFC process. Furthermore, our measurements were in excellent agreement with the quantum theory of frequency conversion [20].

2. PULSED SQUEEZING EXPERIMENTS BY MEANS OF PARAMETRIC DOWNCONVERSION

Initially in our incoherent squeezed-state generation experiments [3], the degree of observable squeezing ($\simeq 1\,\mathrm{dB}$) was limited by two factors: First, due to intensity fluctuations underneath the Q-switched pulse envelopes, that result from beating of the various longitudinal modes, large parametric gain could not be obtained without damaging the down-converting $KTiOPO_4$ (KTP) crystal. Second, a spatio-temporal mismatch existed between the squeezed mode generated by the down-converter and the LO mode that was employed in the homodyne detector. In recent years, we have performed experiments in which attempts were made to overcome the above two limitations [4]. The first limitation was removed by pumping the down-converter with a mode-locked and Q-switched laser. Mode locking eliminates the intensity fluctuations underneath the Q-switched pulse envelopes and large parametric gains can be easily obtained [6]. To overcome the second limitation, a matched LO was generated by means of an optical parametric amplifier (OPA) that is pumped by the same laser as the down-converter.

2.1. SQUEEZING DETECTION WITH A MATCHED LO

In our first version of the experiment a matched LO was generated with the use of an independent optical parametric amplifier that was pumped by the same laser as the down-converter [4]. Using the fundamental beam of the laser as an LO, we observed 2 dB of squeezing for a parametric gain of 2.0. However, when the matched LO was employed, we observed 2 dB squeezing for a parametric gain of only 1.5. Thus, although the observed squeezing was not significantly larger than that observed when using a Q-switched multimode pump (2 dB vs. 1 dB), the importance of a matched LO was clearly demonstrated by the fact that the same amount of squeezing could be obtained at a lower OPA gain when using the matched LO.

In this experiment [4], however, uncontrollable phase fluctuations prohibited us from making squeezing measurements at OPA gains larger than 2. We could not increase the quantum-noise reduction beyond 2 dB and observe the limitation predicted by LaPorta and Slusher [21]. The quantum-noise reduction observable with our setup actually decreased as the parametric gain was increased.

2.2. SELF-GENERATED MATCHED LO

The phase fluctuations arise from acoustic perturbations of the different beam paths that the squeezed mode and the matched LO follow. We then re-designed our experiment in such a way that the two beams followed more or less the same path [5]. The modified setup, in addition to being insensitive to phase perturbations, was far less complicated because the matched LO and squeezing were generated in the same OPA. Unlike many other squeezing experiments, the LO in this experiment was not in a coherent state but rather in a squeezed-coherent state. Nevertheless, because of our use of the dual-detector homodyne detection scheme [22], when the squeezed-input port to the homodyne detector was blocked, the observed noise agreed with the vacuum-state noise level for the incident LO power.

Figure 1(left) shows squeezing data taken by means of an OPA that consisted of a 3 mm-long KTP crystal. The vacuum-state noise level was recorded by simply blocking the squeezed input to the homodyne detector. To observe the squeezed-state noise, first the LO phase was scanned and the noise recorded for each phase setting [triangles plotted in Fig. 1(left)]. After the scan, the LO phase was fixed and a time trace [labeled "Fixed LO Phase" in Fig. 1(left)] of the squeezed-quadrature noise recorded. Because of some uncontrollable residual LO phase drift the squeezed-quadrature noise varied to within ±0.4 dB of the average noise minimum. As seen from the fixed LO-phase time trace in Fig. 1(left) the maximum measured squeezing was 5.8 ± 0.2 dB. This much squeezing is the *highest observed in any traveling-wave experiment to date.* The squeezing limitation predicted in Ref. [21], which is based on the Gaussian-LO assumption, was clearly circumvented.

Following the above procedure, squeezing was measured for various values of the measured OPA gain as plotted in Fig. 1(right). The solid curve is a theoretical fit for a measured detection efficiency of 0.785. The theory assumes single-mode fields for both the squeezed and the LO beams. Good agreement of the theory with the experiment

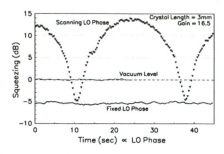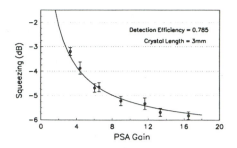

Figure 1. Left—Time trace of the squeezed-vacuum noise at 27 MHz as the matched-LO phase was scanned. Right—Dependence of the measured quadrature squeezing on the OPA gain.

then verifies that the LO was matched to the spatio-temporally distorted squeezed-vacuum state produced in the experiment, as if both the squeezed-vacuum state and the LO were single-mode plane waves [5].

3. SUB-POISSONIAN LIGHT GENERATION BY PARAMETRIC DEAMPLIFICATION

A nondegenerate optical parametric amplifier (NOPA) is equivalent to two independent degenerate optical parametric amplifiers (DOPA's). Using this property and with a proper choice for the NOPA input state, one can produce squeezed-vacuum at the output of one DOPA and a spatio-temporally matched local oscillator (LO) at the output of the other. Employing such a matched LO for detecting the squeezing generated by the first DOPA, we measured up to 5.8 dB of quadrature squeezing as described in Sec. 2.2. The above equivalence can also be utilized to generate sub-Poissonian (amplitude squeezed) light. The NOPA input state can be chosen in such a way that when the output of one DOPA, say DOPA2, is maximally amplified, which occurs for a given pump-phase setting, that of the other (DOPA1) is maximally deamplified. If the amplified output of DOPA2 is direct detected and used to lock the pump phase, then the deamplified output of DOPA1 should lock into an amplitude squeezed state.

We recently conducted an experiment to demonstrate the generation of sub-Poissonian light by means of such parametric deamplification [8]. In our experiment the output of DOPA1 was direct detected by using two InGaAs p-i-n photodiodes, each receiving 50% of the DOPA1 output. The photocurrents of the two detectors were either subtracted or added and fed into the detection electronics, which picked up noise power at 27 MHz with a 3 MHz resolution bandwidth. A pulsed-noise measurement scheme [9] was implemented to record the noise power. The sum-photocurrent noise power thus measured the photon-number fluctuations whereas the subtracted noise power calibrated the shot-noise limit corresponding to the DOPA1 output.

Figure 2(left) shows an example of the sum (solid trace) and difference (dashed trace) photocurrent noise pulses measured for a DOPA2 gain of 1.5. As shown, at the peak of the noise pulses the sum-photocurrent noise fell below the difference-photocurrent noise by 0.6 dB, corresponding to a Fano factor (ratio of the sum noise to the difference noise) of 0.87. In Fig. 2(right) we plot the measured Fano factor, F, as a function of the DOPA2 gain, g_m, which was controlled by varying the pump power to the KTP crystal of length ℓ. As shown, the minimum observed Fano factor was limited to around -0.5 dB. At high gain values the Fano factor increased in contrast to the prediction of the quantum

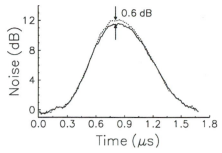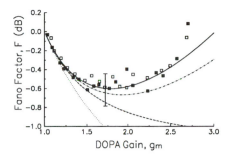

Figure 2. Left—Sum (solid trace) and difference (dashed trace) photocurrent noise pulses at 27 MHz that were measured for $g_m = 1.5$. Right—Measured Fano factor plotted as a function of the DOPA2 gain (filled and unfilled squares represent data sets taken on two different days). See text for a description of the various curves.

theory of a DOPA [dotted curve in Fig. 2(right)], which holds for a parametric amplifier in which the interacting beams are plane waves. In our experiment, however, the various beams were Gaussian, so GID played a crucial role [10].

We have developed a quantum theory of a DOPA that includes the GID effect [11]. To compare our data with the Gaussian-beam theory, we measured the various parameters that enter the theory, viz, ℓ/z_0, $\langle \delta\theta^2 \rangle$, and η. The measured confocal distance z_0 was 18 ± 2 mm which yields $\ell/z_0 = 0.17 \pm 0.02$ for the 3 mm crystal. To estimate the phase fluctuations, $\langle \delta\theta^2 \rangle$, we measured standard deviations of the intensity noises on the input signal, pump, and amplified DOPA2 output beams for a given gain setting. From these data, we then calculated the phase fluctuations using a classical noise analysis. Consistently we obtained $\langle \delta\theta^2 \rangle^{1/2} = 0.16 \pm 0.03$ for various settings of the DOPA2 gain. The quantum efficiency η had three contributions, i.e., $\eta = \eta_m \eta_l \eta_d$, where η_m is the mode-matching efficiency between the signal and idler beams, $1 - \eta_l$ is the optical loss, and η_d is the quantum efficiency of the photodetectors. We measured the mode-matching efficiency η_m to be 0.65 ± 0.07 by varying the pump phase and monitoring the extinction ratio between the signal and idler beam paths. The photon-detection efficiency $\eta_l \eta_d$ was measured to be 0.77 ± 0.02 by monitoring the direct-differenced detection noise reduction of the NOPA twin beams [6]. These values gave an overall detection efficiency $\eta = 0.50 \pm 0.07$.

The solid curve in Fig. 2(right) is a theoretical plot for the above measured parameters. The agreement between the data and the theory is remarkably good. Using the same η we have also plotted the predictions of the plane-wave theory (dotted curve) and the Gaussian-beam theory without the GID correction (dashed curve). They both fit well with the data in the low-gain region. In the high-gain region, in addition to GID, the phase fluctuations also degrade the observable squeezing. One can clearly see the effect of phase fluctuations by comparing the solid curve with the dot-dash curve for which we have set $\langle \delta\theta^2 \rangle = 0$.

4. QUANTUM-NOISE REDUCTION BY MEANS OF SECOND-HARMONIC GENERATION

Recently, we have studied the possibility of squeezing generation by means of the TW SHG process [15]. Type-II phase-matched SHG, such as that used to frequency

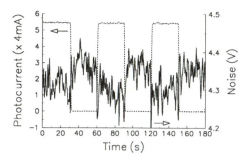
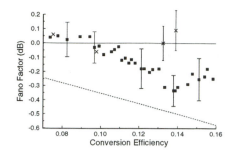

Figure 3. Left—Time trace of the average photocurrent (dashed trace, left ordinate) and the associated noise (solid trace, right ordinate) as the photocurrents from the two detectors are alternately summed and differenced. On the right-ordinate scale, 0.1 V corresponds to a change in noise power of 0.5 dB. Right—Dependence of the observed Fano factor on the SHG efficiency. The 0.0 dB line indicates the coherent-state noise level with crosses as the measured values.

double the output of a Nd:YAG laser with use of a KTP crystal, was shown to generate squeezed vacuum in the mode that is polarized orthogonally to the strong fundamental beam. In the phase-matched case, the generated squeezing was found to be given by $S = 1 - \gamma$, where γ is the SHG efficiency. By means of a more general analysis [16], we also showed that if at the input the orthogonally-polarized mode is in a coherent state, then amplitude-squeezed light is produced in this mode at the output of the nonlinear medium. In this case S is the observable Fano factor. Of course, in an experiment, the output beam suffers unavoidable losses in propagation from the nonlinear medium to the detectors and, in addition, the latter have less-than-unity quantum efficiencies. If the overall detection efficiency is η, then the measurable Fano factor is given by $F = \eta S + 1 - \eta = 1 - \eta\gamma$. We have recently carried out an experiment that verifies the creation of squeezed light in the type-II phase-matched TW SHG process.

In our experiment, a type-II non-critically phase-matched sodium-doped KTP crystal was pumped by the 1064 nm pulses from a Q-switched and mode-locked Nd:YAG laser to generate the second-harmonic field at 532 nm. At the output of the Na:KTP crystal, after dispersing the harmonic beam away, the birefringence of the Na:KTP crystal was compensated and the output fundamental field A_1 was blocked with use of a high-extinction ratio ($1{:}10^5$) polarizer. The orthogonally polarized field A_2 that passed the polarizer was direct detected by using two InGaAs p-i-n photodiodes. To measure the intensity noise levels, the photocurrents from the two detectors were either subtracted or added and the resultant current noise (at 29 MHz) was analyzed in the same way as for the parametric deamplification experiment in Sec. 3.

Figure 3(left) shows a representative time trace of the average photocurrent (dashed trace) and the associated noise (solid trace) at the peak of the Q-switch envelope as the outputs of the two detectors were alternately summed and differenced. As shown, the sum-photocurrent noise (regions of high average photocurrent) fell below the difference photocurrent noise (regions of low average photocurrent) by $\simeq 0.3$ dB, corresponding to a Fano factor of 0.94. In Fig. 3(right) we plot the measured Fano factor as a function of the SHG efficiency, which was controlled by varying the fundamental-field power to the Na:KTP crystal. As shown, the observed Fano factor decreased as the SHG efficiency increased. By removing the Na:KTP crystal from the beam path, we measured the coherent-state noise (shot noise) level for various average powers incident on the photodetectors as marked by the crosses in Fig. 3(right). In this case, summing or differencing the output photocurrents gave the same noise level within the measurement accuracy of ± 0.1 dB.

The main difficulty in the experiment was to separate the strong fundamental field A_1 from the orthogonally-polarized weak squeezed field A_2 at the output of the Na:KTP crystal. Despite our best efforts, there was significant leakage of A_1 into the orthogonal polarization (i.e., along A_2). In addition, Linear response from the photodetectors (and the associated electronics) could be obtained only for incident average powers of up to $\simeq 10\,\mu$W, corresponding to Q-switch-envelope peak powers of $\simeq 25$ mW for the parameters of our laser. The leakage average power approached this limit for $\gamma \simeq 0.15$, even though γ values > 0.3 were achievable. For the data shown in Fig. 3(right), saturation of the detectors and/or the associated electronics had begun to take place for $\gamma > 0.14$. This saturation effect added extra noise to the measurement, thus preventing the noise reduction to improve beyond the value at $\gamma = 0.14$; a maximum noise reduction of 0.3 ± 0.2 dB was measured in our experiments.

The dotted line in Fig. 3(right) is a plot of $1 - \eta\gamma$ with $\eta = 0.78$, a value which was independently measured. The major contributors to loss were the photodetector quantum efficiencies ($\simeq 0.9$) and Fresnel reflection at the uncoated output surface of the Na:KTP crystal. As shown, the measured noise reduction, although in qualitative agreement, was less than that predicted by the theory. There could be several reasons for this discrepancy. Firstly, the theory in Ref. [15] was developed for CW plane-wave fields, whereas the fundamental field A_1 in our experiment is spatio-temporally Gaussian. Secondly, the leakage-field phase, which was fixed and could not be varied in the experiment, may not be optimum for the measurement of squeezing in A_2.

5. APPLICATION OF SQUEEZED LIGHT IN SUB-SHOT NOISE IMAGING

Experiments in interferometry [23,24], detection of directly-encoded amplitude modulation [25], high-resolution spectroscopy [26], and quantum frequency conversion [19] have shown that enhancement in the precision of optical measurements beyond the shot-noise limit is possible. In all these demonstrations the signal and noise of the measurement scheme were in the time domain. Little attention has been paid to the applications of squeezed light in physical phenomena which involve modulation in space—such as optical imaging, diffraction, holography, etc.

We have recently proposed a scheme with which spatially-multimode squeezed light can be used to detect faint objects with sensitivity better than the shot-noise limit [27]. Such light can be generated by means of a TW OPA [28], of the kind discussed in Sec. 2. Conceptually, our scheme parallels in the spatial domain what has been experimentally demonstrated in the time domain [23]. We calculated the sensitivity to the LO phase and enhancement of the minimum detectable spatially-varying phase change of an object, that is inserted into a Mach-Zehnder interferometer, when using squeezed light. We showed that at the properly chosen operating point, illumination of the normally unused port of the interferometer by spatially-multimode squeezed vacuum with maximum squeezing in a region of spatial frequencies $q \sim q_s$, reduces the minimum detectable phase change of the object at these spatial frequencies by a factor of e^{-2r_s}. Here r_s is the squeezing parameter at the spatial frequency q_s. This result is the spatial analog of the time domain result first derived by Caves [29].

6. QUANTUM-NOISE CORRELATIONS IN PARAMETRIC IMAGE AMPLIFICATION

In this section, we describe our recent progress in the application of squeezed light to phenomena in the spatial domain. In particular, we demonstrate quantum-noise correlations between spatial frequencies of a parametrically amplified image and its generated conjugate (idler) image. Classically, such spatially-resolved parametric amplification has been shown to have practical applications in time-gated image recovery [30, 31]. The object is imaged into the OPA, where the real image is amplified in a twin beams configuration. For a signal photon at a spatial frequency of q, a conjugate idler photon is generated at $-q$. In order to observe quantum-noise correlations between the signal and idler photons, we place photodetectors in the Fourier (spatial frequency) plane, where the spatial frequencies are well resolved. With a pair of two-dimensional photodetector arrays sampling all relevant spatial frequencies, this technique can be applied to the sub-shot–noise imaging of faint objects.

6.1. THEORY

A simple theoretical model for quantum-noise reduction as a function of spatial frequency can be derived from the standard equations for optical parametric amplification. The equations governing a traveling-wave OPA are [6]

$$\hat{b}_s = \mu \hat{a}_s + \nu \hat{a}_i^\dagger, \qquad \hat{b}_i = \mu \hat{a}_i + \nu \hat{a}_s^\dagger, \tag{1}$$

where $\hat{a}_s$ and $\hat{a}_i$ are the input and $\hat{b}_s$ and $\hat{b}_i$ are the output annihilation operators for the signal and idler modes, respectively. In our experiment, the idler input is in the vacuum state. If the quantum efficiency is η, then the quantum-noise reduction observable in a spatially broadband twin beams type of experiment [6] is given by

$$R = 1 - \eta + \eta / \left(|\mu|^2 + |\nu|^2 \right), \tag{2}$$

Where the coupling coefficients are

$$\mu(q) = [\cosh(h\ell) + i(\Delta k_{\mathrm{eff}}/2h) \sinh(h\ell)] \exp(-i\Delta k_{\mathrm{eff}}\ell/2), \tag{3}$$
$$\nu(q) = [(\kappa/2h) \sinh(h\ell)] \exp(i\Delta k_{\mathrm{eff}}\ell/2). \tag{4}$$

Here $h \equiv [\kappa^2 - (\Delta k_{\mathrm{eff}})^2]^{1/2}$, Δk_{eff} is the effective phase mismatch, κ is proportional to the pump intensity, and $\ell = 5.25\,\mathrm{mm}$ is the crystal length. Optimum amplification occurs when $\Delta k_{\mathrm{eff}} = 0$. For a spatial frequency of $q = 0$, this phase matching condition is fulfilled for $\Delta k = (\vec{k}_p - \vec{k}_s - \vec{k}_i) \cdot \vec{i}_z = 0$, where $\vec{k}_p$, $\vec{k}_s$, and $\vec{k}_i$ are the wavevectors for the pump, signal, and idler waves, respectively. However, for higher spatial frequencies, phase matching occurs only when $\Delta k \neq 0$. Using the paraxial approximation [31], it can be shown that the effective phase mismatch is a function of q:

$$\Delta k_{\mathrm{eff}}(q) = \Delta k + q^2 \left(k_s^{-1} + k_i^{-1} \right) /2. \tag{5}$$

Hence for negative values of Δk, phase matching occurs for nonzero spatial frequencies.

Since μ and ν depend on q through Δk_{eff}, we can calculate the signal and idler outputs, and the resulting quantum-noise reduction, as a function of spatial frequency for any given signal input. The simplest case is for an input that has a small spread centered at $q = 0$, as shown in Fig. 4(a). Note that $\xi = q/2\pi$, so that spatial frequency is in units of mm^{-1}. Here the phase matching condition is satisfied for $\Delta k = 0$, and

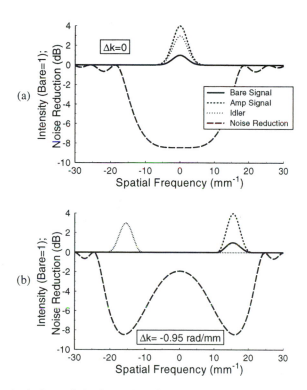

Figure 4. Theoretical plots of the bare signal, amplified signal, idler, and quantum-noise reduction as a function of spatial frequency. (a) Low-pass amplifier with $\Delta k = 0$. (b) Band-pass amplifier with $\Delta k = -0.95\,\mathrm{rad/mm}$.

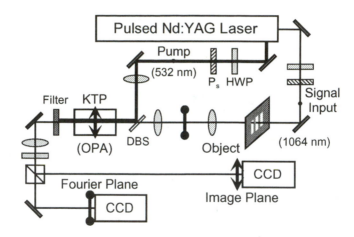

Figure 5. Experimental layout for parametric image amplification.

we have chosen a gain of $g \equiv |\mu(0)|^2 = 4$. As expected, the signal and idler outputs and the noise reduction are maximized when $\xi = 0$. From the noise-reduction curve, we estimate that the spatial bandwidth of the OPA is $\simeq 15 \, \text{mm}^{-1}$ (HWHM). In this configuration, the OPA functions as a low-pass amplifier.

In order to investigate the noise reduction at a nonzero spatial frequency, we must place an object in the signal beam in front of the OPA. For the experiments described below, we have chosen three vertical lines with a horizontal line spacing of 16 lines/mm from a 1951 USAF test pattern. The Fourier transform of this image is proportional to

$$\left[\frac{\sin(\pi a \xi)}{(\pi a \xi)} \right]^2 \left[\frac{\sin(3\pi d \xi)}{(\pi d \xi)} \right]^2, \tag{6}$$

where the slit spacing is $d = 62.5 \, \mu\text{m}$, and the slit width is $a = d/2$. The Fourier image is essentially one large peak centered at $\xi = 0$ and two smaller peaks centered at $\xi = \pm 16 \, \text{mm}^{-1}$. By blocking the peaks at $\xi = 0$ and $-16 \, \text{mm}^{-1}$ in front of the OPA, we can construct a signal input at $+16 \, \text{mm}^{-1}$.

From Fig. 4(a), it is evident that a spatial frequency of $+16 \, \text{mm}^{-1}$ will be amplified very little when $\Delta k = 0$. For this spatial frequency, the phase matching condition is fulfilled for $\Delta k = -0.95 \, \text{rad/mm}$. In practice, we adjust Δk by tilting the angle of the KTP crystal in the OPA. As shown in Fig. 4(b), the signal at $+16 \, \text{mm}^{-1}$ is amplified with a gain of $g = 4$, and the conjugate idler is generated at $-16 \, \text{mm}^{-1}$. A gain of four is obtained for the same value of κ as in the low-pass configuration ($\Delta k = 0$). The noise reduction at $\xi = \pm 16 \, \text{mm}^{-1}$ is not diminished from that at $\xi = 0$ in the low-pass case, although the spatial-frequency bandwidth is reduced.

For values of $\Delta k < 0$, the OPA acts like a band-pass amplifier, allowing us to amplify higher spatial frequencies more effectively. This feature of the OPA makes it possible to obtain significant quantum-noise reduction at higher spatial frequencies. There are also many applications of this technique to edge and contrast enhancement in parametric image amplification [30, 31].

6.2. EXPERIMENT

The layout of the parametric-image amplification experiment is depicted in Fig. 5. The 5.25 mm-long KTP crystal (the OPA) is pumped by a Q-switched, mode-locked, and frequency-doubled Nd:YAG laser. The infrared signal input (1064 nm) and the

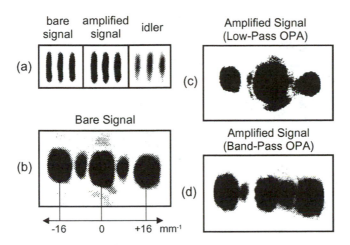

Figure 6. (a) Bare signal, amplified signal, and idler images in the output image plane. The object consists of three vertical lines with 62.5 μm center-to-center spacing. (b) Bare signal in the output Fourier plane. (c) Amplified signal in the output Fourier plane with low-pass amplification. (d) Amplified signal in the output Fourier plane with band-pass amplification.

green pump (532 nm) are each p-polarized for type-II phase-matching in the crystal. The object (three vertical lines at 16 lines/mm) is placed in the signal beam in front of the OPA. A real image of this object is formed in the center of the KTP crystal by a ×1 telescope consisting of two 10-cm focal-length lenses. The spatial frequencies of this image are amplified by the pump beam, which is made coincident with the signal beam using a dichroic beamsplitter. The green pump is blocked after the crystal using a filter which passes only the infrared. Separate CCD cameras are placed at the output image and Fourier planes, which are formed using a 20-cm focal-length lens and a polarization beamsplitter. Since the amplified signal and idler are orthogonally polarized, we can place the image of either at the Fourier or the image plane, by rotating a half-wave plate in front of the beamsplitter.

As recorded in the output image plane, real images of the bare signal, amplified signal, and idler are shown in Fig. 6(a), for an OPA gain of $\simeq 1.2$. The output Fourier image of the bare signal is shown in Fig. 6(b). Figure 6(c) shows the Fourier image of the amplified signal in the low-pass configuration of the OPA ($\Delta k = 0$) with the central peak strongly amplified at a gain of $\simeq 4$. Band-pass amplification at the same gain with $\Delta k = -0.95$ rad/mm is shown in Fig. 6(d). Here, the amplification has been maximized for the two side peaks at ± 16 mm^{-1}. These results compare favorably with the theoretical predictions in Fig. 4 above.

The OPA is optimized for maximum gain and quantum correlations by aligning the signal and idler images to be coincident in both the output real-image and Fourier planes simultaneously. In the input Fourier plane, using an iris we block all spatial-frequency components of the signal input except the single peak centered at $+16$ mm^{-1}. This beam is band-pass amplified in the OPA when $\Delta k \simeq -0.95$ rad/mm, corresponding to a rotation of the KTP crystal by about 3.4°. At the same time, a conjugate idler beam at -16 mm^{-1} is generated. Since the amplified signal and idler beams at ± 16 mm^{-1} exit the OPA at a difference angle of $2 \times 17 = 34$ mrad, it is easy to separate them using mirrors only. The mirror that sends the beams to the CCDs is removed, and each beam is directed into a photodetector located in the far-field (Fourier plane), where the

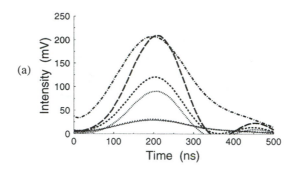

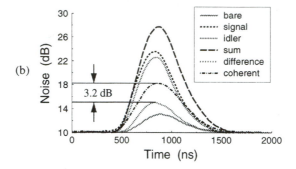

Figure 7. (a) Temporal profiles of the Q-switch envelopes for the bare signal, amplified signal, idler, difference, sum, and reference coherent-state levels. (b) Corresponding temporal profiles of the noise power.

spatial frequencies are well resolved. Twin-beam type noise measurements are made using direct difference detection as in the twin-beam experiments described in Ref. [6].

The Q-switch envelope profiles for the bare signal, amplified signal, idler, difference, sum, and the reference coherent-state levels are plotted in Fig. 7(a), for an OPA gain of ≃4. The vertical axis is voltage (mV) corresponding to the recorded photocurrent into a 50-Ω load. We have arranged for the coherent-state mean and the mean sum of the amplified signal and idler photocurrents to have nearly the same value. Figure 7(b) shows the corresponding temporal profiles of the noise powers. The difference noise clearly falls below the coherent-state noise level by ≃3 dB; once the background electronic noise is subtracted, the observed noise reduction is > 4 dB. These experimental results are in good agreement with the predictions of Eq. (2) for an OPA gain of 4, when the overall detection efficiency of $\eta = 0.76$ is taken into account.

REFERENCES

[1] L.-A. Wu, H. J. Kimble, J. L. Hall, and H. Wu, Phys. Rev. Lett. **57**, 2520 (1986); A. Heidmann, R. J. Horowicz, S. Reynaud, E. Giacobino, C. Fabre, and G. Camy, Phys. Rev. Lett. **59**, 2555 (1987); E. S. Polzik, J. Carri, and H. J. Kimble, Appl. Phys. B **55**, 279 (1992); G. Breitenbach, T. Müller, S. F. Pereira, J.-Ph. Poizat, S. Schiller, and J. Mlynek, J. Opt. Soc. Am. B **12**, 2304 (1995).

[2] R. E. Slusher, P. Grangier, A. LaPorta, B. Yurke, and M. J. Potasek, Phys. Rev. Lett. **59**, 2566 (1987).

[3] P. Kumar, O. Aytür, and J. Huang, Phys. Rev. Lett. **64**, 1015 (1990).

[4] O. Aytür and P. Kumar, Opt. Lett. **17**, 529 (1992).

[5] C. Kim and P. Kumar, Phys. Rev. Lett. **73** 1605 (1994).

[6] O. Aytür and P. Kumar, Phys. Rev. Lett. **65**, 1551 (1990).

[7] O. Aytür and P. Kumar, J. Mod. Opt. **38**, 815–819 (1991).

[8] R.-D. Li, S.-K. Choi, C. Kim, and P. Kumar, Phys. Rev. A (Rapid Communications) **51**, R3429 (1995).

[9] O. Aytür and P. Kumar, Opt. Lett. **15**, 390 (1990).

[10] C. Kim, R.-D. Li, and P. Kumar, Opt. Lett. **19**, 132-134 (1994).

[11] R.-D. Li, S.-K. Choi, and P. Kumar, Quant. Semiclass. Opt. (J. Euro. Opt. Soc. B), Vol. 7, No. 4, 1995, pp. 705–713.

[12] S. F. Pereira, M. Xiao, H. J. Kimble, and J. L. Hall, Phys. Rev. A **38**, 4931 (1988).

[13] A. Sizmann, R. J. Horowicz, G. Wagner, and G. Leuchs, Opt. Commun. **80**, 138 (1990); P. Kürz, R. Paschotta, K. Fiedler, A. Sizmann, G. Leuchs, and J. Mlynek, Appl. Phys. B **55**, 216 (1992); R. Paschotta, M. Collett, P. Kürz, K. Fiedler, H. A. Bachor, and J. Mlynek, Phys. Rev. Lett. **72**, 3807 (1994); T. C. Ralph, M. S. Taubman, A. G. White, D. E. McClelland, and H.-A. Bachor, Opt. Lett. **20**, 1316 (1995); H. Tsuchida, Opt. Lett. **20**, 2240 (1995).

[14] Z. Y. Ou, Phys. Rev. A **49**, 2106 (1994).

[15] R.-D. Li and P. Kumar, Opt. Lett. **18**, 1961 (1993); R.-D. Li and P. Kumar, Phys. Rev. A **49**, 2157 (1994).

[16] R.-D. Li and P. Kumar, J. Opt. Soc. Am. B **12**, 2310 (1995).

[17] S. Youn, S.-K. Choi, P. Kumar, and R.-D. Li, Opt. Lett. **21**, 1597 (1996).

[18] D. K. Serkland, P. Kumar, M. A. Arbore, and M. M. Fejer, in *Quantum Communication, Computing, and Measurement*, edited by O. Hirota, A. S. Holevo, and C. M. Caves (Plenum, 1997), to be published.

[19] J. Huang and P. Kumar, Phys. Rev. Lett. **68**, 2153 (1992).

[20] P. Kumar, Opt. Lett. **15**, 1476 (1990).

[21] A. LaPorta and R. E. Slusher, Phys. Rev. A **44**, 2013 (1991).

[22] H. P. Yuen and V. W. S. Chan, Opt. Lett. **8**, 177, 345(E) (1983).

[23] M. Xiao, L.-A. Wu and H. J. Kimble, Phys. Rev. Lett. **59**, 278 (1987).

[24] P. Grangier, R. E. Slusher, B. Yurke and A. La Porta, Phys. Rev. Lett. **59**, 2153 (1987).

[25] M. Xiao, L.-A. Wu and H. J. Kimble, Opt. Lett. **13**, 476 (1988); P. Kumar, J. Huang, and O. Aytür, in *Laser Noise*, R. Roy, Ed., Proc. SPIE **1376**, 192–197 (1991); K. Bergman and H. A. Haus, Opt. Lett. **18**, 643 (1993).

[26] E. S. Polzik, J. Carri and H. J. Kimble, Phys. Rev. Lett. **68**, 3020 (1992).

[27] M. I. Kolobov and P. Kumar, Opt. Lett. **18**, 849-851 (1993).

[28] M. I. Kolobov and I. V. Sokolov, Sov. Phys. JETP **69**, 1097 (1989).

[29] C. M. Caves, Phys. Rev. D **23**, 1693 (1981).

[30] F. Devaux and E. Lantz, Opt. Commun. **118**, 25 (1995); F. Devaux and E. Lantz, Opt. Commun. **114**, 295 (1995).

[31] A. Gavrielides, P. Peterson, and D. Cardimona, J. Appl. Phys. **62**, 2640 (1987); P. A. Laferriere, C. J. Wetterer, L. P. Schelonka, and M. A. Kramer, J. Appl. Phys. **65**, 3347 (1989).

INDEX